International Human Resource Management

The third edition of the outstanding *International Human Resource Management* book, by the leading HR gurus in the UK, is both timely and extremely important given the dramatic workplace changes during and since the 'great recession' of 2008. The chapters highlight issues of major importance in the changing landscape of people management going forward. This is a 'must read' for all HR professionals in Europe and beyond.'

–Sir Cary Cooper,
University of Manchester, President of the CIPD, UK

International Human Resource Management: Contemporary Human Resource Issues in Europe provides a concise overview of the rich HR landscape in Europe to help students develop cutting-edge people management skills.

The innovative, multi-disciplinary approach of the book provides a holistic picture of key issues on the individual, organizational and societal levels. The book is divided into three parts:

- Part I explores the institutional and economic contexts that organizations face in different European countries. This section goes beyond exploring issues of diversity to include a discussion of the impact of the recent financial crisis.
- Part II concentrates on the key challenges and trends facing HR, including an aging population, migration, and sustainability, and analyzes the unique and inventive ways these are addressed in different countries across Europe.
- Part III focuses on the fundamental HR areas – recruitment and selection, performance management and rewards, employment relations, global careers, and so forth – and the ways in which these policies and practices are shaped by the European Union.

With broader coverage, the latest thinking in the field, and cutting-edge cases, examples and insights, this edition will prove a highly valuable resource for students, researchers, and practitioners working in human resource management and international business.

Michael Dickmann is Professor of International Human Resource Management and Director of the MSc in Management at Cranfield University, UK. His research interests are predominantly in international HRM and global careers. He is editor of *The International Journal of Human Resource Management*.

Chris Brewster is Professor of International Human Resource Management at Henley Business School, UK, Vaasa University, Finland, and Radboud University, the Netherlands. He researches international and comparative HRM, and has published more than 25 books, and almost 200 journal articles.

Paul Sparrow is Director of the Centre for Performance-led HR and Professor of International Human Resource Management at Lancaster University, UK. He is lead editor of the *Journal of Organizational Effectiveness* and is included in the Top 10 Most Influential HR Thinkers for *Human Resources Magazine* 2014–2015.

Routledge Global Human Resource Management Series
Edited by Randall S. Schuler, Susan E. Jackson, and Paul Sparrow

Routledge Global Human Resource Management is an important series that examines human resources in its global context. The series is organized into three strands: Content and issues in global human resource management (HRM); Specific HR functions in a global context; and comparative HRM. Authored by some of the world's leading authorities on HRM, each book in the series aims to give readers comprehensive, in-depth and accessible texts that combine essential theory and best practice. Topics covered include cross-border alliances, global leadership, global legal systems, HRM in Asia, Africa and the Americas, industrial relations, and global staffing.

Dedication: The late Professor Michael Poole was one of the founding series editors, and Professors Schuler, Jackson, and Sparrow wish to dedicate the series to his memory.

Manager-Subordinate Trust
A global perspective
Edited by *Pablo Cardona and Michael J. Morley*

Managing Human Resources in Asia-Pacific (second edition)
Edited by *Arup Varma and Pawan S. Budhwar*

Human Resource Management and the Institutional Perspective
Edited by *Geoffrey Wood, Chris Brewster, and Michael Brookes*

International Human Resource Management (fifth edition)
Policies and practices for multinational enterprises
Ibraiz Tarique, Dennis Briscoe, and Randall S . Schuler

International Human Resource Management: Contemporary Human Resource Issues in Europe (third edition)
Michael Dickmann, Chris Brewster, & Paul Sparrow

Globalizing Human Resource Management (second edition)
Paul Sparrow, Chris Brewster & Chul Chung

International Human Resource Management

Contemporary HR Issues in Europe

Third Edition

Edited by Michael Dickmann, Chris Brewster and Paul Sparrow

Routledge
Taylor & Francis Group

NEW YORK AND LONDON

First published 2016
by Routledge
711 Third Avenue, New York, NY 10017

and by Routledge
2 Park Square, Milton Park, Abingdon, Oxon OX14 4RN

Routledge is an imprint of the Taylor & Francis Group, an informa business

© 2016 Taylor & Francis

Library of Congress Cataloging in Publication Data
A catalog record for this book has been requested

ISBN: 978-1-138-77602-9 (hbk)
ISBN: 978-1-138-77603-6 (pbk)
ISBN: 978-1-315-77348-3 (ebk)

Typeset in Bembo
by Swales & Willis Ltd, Exeter, Devon, UK

Dedications

To my parents for their limitless optimism and love and
to Onkel Peter and Tante Elke for their inspiration and gentle
guidance.
(Michael Dickmann)

To our readers: thank you and good luck.
(Chris Brewster)

To those IHRM academics and practitioners future and present who
can make a difference.
(Paul Sparrow)

Contents

List of Illustrations   xvi
Author Biographies   xix

1 Introduction and Overview of IHRM: Contemporary
   HR Issues in Europe   1
   MICHAEL DICKMANN, CHRIS BREWSTER AND
   PAUL SPARROW

   A European Perspective on HRM   1
   HRM in an International Context   4
   References   13

Part I
Macro-Views: IHRM and Its Response to Crisis in Europe   15

2 Macro-Views: Shaping HRM in Crises and Beyond –
   Overview of Part I   17
   MICHAEL DICKMANN, CHRIS BREWSTER
   AND PAUL SPARROW

   References   20

3 How Does European Integration Influence
   Employment Relations?   21
   DENISE CURRIE AND PAUL TEAGUE

   Introduction   21
   EU Market Influences on Employment Relations   23
   EU Institutional Influences on Employment Relations   28
   The European Social Dialogue   34
   EU Employment Policy   38

Social Europe in the Crisis 42
Conclusions 44
Key Learning Points 45
Note 46
References 46

4 Mediterranean HRM: Key Trends and Challenges 49
ELENI T. STAVROU AND NANCY PAPALEXANDRIS

HRM Institutional Challenges 49
HRM Organizational Challenges 56
Integration of Institutional and Organizational
HRM Challenges 67
Key Learning Points 70
References 70

5 Developments in Human Resource Management in
Central and Eastern Europe in Comparative Perspective 73
MICHAEL MORLEY, JÓZSEF POÓR, NOREEN
HERATY, RUTH ALAS AND ALEKSY POCZTOWSKI

Introduction 73
The Context for Developments in HRM in CEE 76
Analysing Organizational-Level Developments in
HRM in CEE: A Comparative Perspective 82
Unionization 91
Conclusion 93
Key Learning Points 94
Acknowledgement 95
References 95

6 Nordic HRM: Distinctiveness and Resilience 100
TORBEN ANDERSEN AND FREDDY HÄLLSTÉN

Introduction 100
Economic Development and Crisis in Nordic Countries 101
HR Institutions 104
Work Relations in the Nordic Countries 105
Conclusions 110
Key Learning Points 111
References 112

7 Western European HRM: Reactions and Adjustment
to Crises 115
ALEXANDROS PSYCHOGIOS, CHRIS BREWSTER
AND EMMA PARRY

Introduction 115
The Western European Context of Crisis 116
HRM Challenges in Crisis Context 119
HRM's Role in Dealing with Crisis: A European View 123

Conclusions   127
Key Learning Points   129
References   129

Part II
Mezzo-Views: Cross-National HRM Strategies, Structures,
Policies and Practices   135

8   Mezzo-Views: Cross-National and Organizational Level
HRM Strategies, Structures, Policies and
Practices – Overview of Part II   137
PAUL SPARROW, MICHAEL DICKMANN AND
CHRIS BREWSTER

Reference   144

9   Beyond the Private Sector: International HRM in the
Not for Profit Sectors   145
CHRIS BREWSTER, PAUL BOSELIE, PETER LEISINK AND
KERSTIN ALFES

The Importance of the Not for Profit Sector   145
HRM in Public Sector Organizations   149
HRM in Intergovernmental Organizations   154
HRM in International Non-Governmental Organizations   159
Conclusions   163
Key Learning Points   164
References   165

10   The HRM of Foreign MNCs Operating in Europe   169
CHUL CHUNG AND MASAYUKI FURUSAWA

Introduction   169
Managing Human Resources in MNCs   169
The HRM of US MNCs   171
The HRM of Japanese MNCs   175
The HRM of South Korean MNCs   181
Conclusion   184
Key Learning Points   185
Notes   185
References   185

11   Human Resources and Corporate Responsibility   190
TODD CARDARELLI, DAVID GRAYSON AND MICHAEL
DICKMANN

Introduction   190
Corporate Responsibility: A Journey   191
The Business Case for Corporate Responsibility   192
CR on the Agenda of Global Companies   194

Role of the HRM Function in Supporting CR Efforts 195
Embedding Strategic CR: The Role of the
HRM Professional 198
Achieving HRM Outcomes through Strategic
CR: Creating a Sustainability Culture 203
CR/HRM Initiative in Focus: International
Corporate Volunteering 204
The European Perspective 206
HRM and CR in Europe: The Desso Example 208
Opportunities for Further Research 212
Conclusions 213
Key Learning Points 214
References 215

12 Age and Diversity in Europe 219
EMMA PARRY, HEIKE SCHRÖDER, MATT FLYNN
AND DEIRDRE ANDERSON

Introduction 219
National Reactions to Demographic Change and Old
Age Employment: The Examples of the UK
and Germany 221
Managing an Ageing Workforce: The Case
of Employers 226
Summary 230
Key Learning Points 231
References 231

13 International Migration and International Human
Resource Management 237
AKRAM AL ARISS, JEAN-LUC CERDIN
AND CHRIS BREWSTER

Understanding the Importance of Migration 237
Defining Who Is a Migrant 239
Key Figures and Facts about Migration 241
Typology of Migration and Its Consequences in
Terms of IHRM 242
Understanding the Micro-Individual Level
of Migration 244
Understanding the Meso-Organizational Level
of Migration 246
Understanding the Macro-Social Level of Migration 248
Relevance of this Typology to HRM
Policies/Practices 250
Specific HRM Practices for Migrants 251
Conclusion 253
Key Learning Points 254
References 255

Part III
Micro-Views: Organizational Approaches and Individual
(Re-)Actions in Europe   257

14 Micro-Views: Organizational Approaches and Individual
    (Re)Actions in Europe – Overview of Part III   259
    CHRIS BREWSTER, MICHAEL DICKMANN AND
    PAUL SPARROW

        References   261

15 Employment Relations in Europe   262
    RICHARD CROUCHER

        Introduction   262
        European Employment Relations in 1995   264
        National Laws and Institutions   266
        National-Level Collective Bargaining and Social Pacts   269
        The European Level: Institutionalizing 'Social Dialogue'?   271
        Employment Relations at Workplace Level   274
        Conclusion   275
        Key Learning Points   276
        References   277

16 Recruitment and Selection: Debates,
    Controversies and Variations in Europe   282
    GEOFFREY WOOD AND LESLIE T. SZAMOSI

        The Foundations of Recruitment and Selection (R&S)   282
        Recruitment   285
        Selection   286
        European Context and R&S   288
        Conclusions   292
        Key Learning Points   293
        References   293

17 Global Careers in European MNEs: Different
    Career Patterns in Europe?   297
    MICHAEL DICKMANN, JEAN-LUC CERDIN AND
    WOLFGANG MAYRHOFER

        Global Careers: An Exploration   297
        Europe: Its Quest for Higher Integration and
        International Mobility   299
        MNEs and Global Careers: 'Organizational Perspective'   300
        The Motivations of Global Careerists and
        Some European Specifics   301
        MNEs and Global Career Management   303
        Pre-assignment Considerations   303
        During an Assignment   309

Global Career Management during the
Transition Phase to the Next Position 317
Global Careers in European MNEs 323
Key Learning Points 323
Notes 324
References 324

18 Talent Management in Europe 329
AGNIESZKA SKUZA, HUGH SCULLION
AND DAVID G. COLLINGS

Introduction 329
Talent Management: Overview 330
The European Context of Talent Management 335
Talent Management in Europe 338
Conclusion 346
Key Learning Points 348
Note 348
References 348

19 Pay-for-Performance in Europe 354
IHAR SAHAKIANTS, MARION FESTING
AND STEPHEN PERKINS

Introduction 354
National Pay Distinctiveness 355
Diffusion of Pay-for-Performance in Europe 366
The Case of Pay-for-Performance in MNEs 368
Conclusion 370
Key Learning Points 370
Notes 371
References 371

20 Employee Financial Participation 375
ERIK POUTSMA, ERIC KAARSEMAKER
AND PAUL LIGTHART

Learning Objectives 375
Introduction 375
What Is Employee Financial Participation? 377
Theoretical Approaches 379
Employee Financial Participation in an
International Context 384
MNCs and Employee Financial Participation 385
Incidence 387
Consequences for IHRM 394
Key Learning Points 395
References 396

21 Flexible Working in Europe 401
CLARE KELLIHER

    Introduction 401
    Defining Flexibility, Why and When Is It Used? 402
    Changes in the Environment Resulting in
    Increased Need for Flexibility 404
    Employer-Driven Flexibility across Europe 406
    Employee-Driven Flexibility across Europe 411
    Discussion 415
    Key Learning Points 417
    References 417

22 Conclusions: The Evolving HRM Landscape in Europe 420
PAUL SPARROW, CHRIS BREWSTER AND
MICHAEL DICKMANN

    Introduction 420
    Macro-Level Trends 422
    Mezzo-Level Trends 425
    Micro-Level Questions 427
    Conclusions 428
    References 431

    Index 432

Illustrations

Figures

4.1	Percentage of people receiving training in Europe	63
5.1	Proportion of the organizational respondents in the four sub-samples	84
9.1	Influences on the shaping of HRM	155
10.1	The influences on subsidiary HRM practices of MNCs	170
10.2	J-style organization and F-style organization	176
11.1	UNGC/Accenture CEOs' Sustainability Survey 2013	195
11.2	BSR/Globescan Survey	196
11.3	From Cradle to Cradle: The Desso approach	212
13.1	Typology of QIs mobility according to their motivation to migrate	245
16.1	Recruitment process	284
19.1	Companies implementing variable pay schemes, in percentage terms	356
19.2	European companies implementing variable pay schemes based on team performance, in percentage terms	357
19.3	European companies implementing variable pay schemes based on individual performance, in percentage terms	358
19.4	European companies implementing profit-sharing schemes, in percentage terms	359
20.1	Incidence rate of narrow-based and broad-based Employee Share Ownership (ESO) per country (proportion of companies; companies with >100 employees)	388
20.2	Incidence rate of narrow-based and broad-based Profit Sharing Schemes (PS) per country (proportion of companies; companies with >100 employees)	390

20.3 Incidence rate of narrow-based and broad-based Stock
Options (SO) per country (proportion of companies;
companies with >100 employees)   391
21.1 Employees with a contract of limited duration
(annual average) – 2014. Percentage of total number
of employees   408
21.2 Persons employed part-time – total – 2014. Percentage
of total employment   410
21.3 Flexible working time arrangements, by country and
flexibility scope (%)   414

Tables

3.1 EU employment Directives   30
4.1 Proportion of organizations with various types of
financial participation and performance related
pay per country   58
4.2 Proportion of organizations with various types of
staffing adjustments   61
4.3 Training in Europe   64
4.4 Trade union influence in Europe   67
5.1 Key economic indicators of CEE countries   78
5.2 Foreign Direct Investment inflows into the CEE
Region (2004–2012) (in $ million)   83
5.3 Sectorial distribution of respondents in the
sub-samples (%)   85
5.4 Size distribution of respondents in the sub-samples (%) 85
5.5 The position and role of the HR function and the
HR department   86
5.6 Method of workforce reduction (%)   87
5.7 Assessment applied via formal appraisal systems (%)   88
5.8 The usage of appraisal results   89
5.9 Proportion of annual payroll costs spent on training   89
5.10 Number of training days/year   90
5.11 Levels of unionization (%)   92
6.1 Real GDP growth rate – volume, Nordic
countries, 2005–2013   103
6.2 Unemployment rate (25–74 years), Nordic
countries, 2005–2013   103
6.3 Average trade union density in the Nordic
countries (latest figures)   106
7.1 HRM-specific practices in times of crises   126
9.1 Categorization of not for profit organizations   148
9.2 Illustrations of IGOs   156
9.3 Examples of INGOs   161

11.1	Seven steps for CR implementation	199
13.1	International migrant populations by major area of origin and destination, 2013 (millions)	238
13.2	A typology of migration	243
13.3	Type of migrants and HRM policies	254
17.1	Global career management: strategic and operational pre-assignment considerations	305
17.2	Global career management during international work	310
17.3	Global career management at the point of the next move	318
19.1	Index values for cultural dimensions	361
19.2	Proposed link between national cultural dimensions and pay-for-performance	362

Box

11.1	Broadening and Focusing Corporate Social Responsibility	191

Case

10.1	Reform of International HRM in Panasonic	179

Appendix

15.1	Continued key differences in employment relations. Western Continental Europe and USA compared	281

Author Biographies

Akram Al Ariss is Professor of Human Resource Management (HRM) at Université de Toulouse, Toulouse Business School, France. He has a PhD from Norwich Business School, University of East Anglia (UK) and a Habilitation à Diriger des Recherches from Université Paris-Dauphine, France. Akram's research interests include expatriation and career and global talent management. He has published work in journals such as the *Journal of World Business*, *Thunderbird International Business Review*, the *British Journal of Management* and the *International Journal of Human Resource Management*, among others. Akram is Associate Editor for Career Development International and Editorial Board member for a number of top journals.

Ruth Alas is Professor and Head of the Department of Management at the Estonian Business School, where she teaches Change Management, Crisis Management, and Human Resource Management. She received the CEEMAN (International Association for Management Development in Dynamic Societies) Champions' Award 2011 for for her research on 'How to Prevent Crisis by Means of Organisational Change Management'. She has authored or co-authored 27 books and more than 150 articles on human resource management, change management, employee attitudes, learning abilities, organizational culture, leadership, crisis management, business ethics and corporate social responsibility. Her work has been published in the *Journal of Business Ethics*, *Employee Relations*, *Chinese Management Studies*, the *Journal of Change Management*, etc. She has organized several international conferences, serving as conference Chair of IHRM 2007 and EURAM 2011,which were held in Tallinn. She is Chair of the EIASM Academic Workshop Series on 'Organizational Development and Change', which have been held annually since 2006.

Kerstin Alfes joined ESCP Europe (Berlin Campus) as Professor of Organization and Human Resource Management in September 2015. Previously, she held several roles at Kingston University London and Tilburg University (Netherlands). Her research interests include employee engagement, strategic human resource management, over qualification, and volunteering. Together with colleagues in the UK, she recently completed an evidence synthesis on employee engagement funded by the National Institute for Health Research.

Torben Andersen is Head of Campus and Department and PhD at the Department of Leadership and Corporate Strategy, University of Southern Denmark, Campus Slagelse. He is the editor of the Danish HRM handbook and the regional editor of Northern Europe, in the *European Journal of International Management*. Torben Andersen's research concentrated on structural and strategic aspects of HRM and International HRM. He has a long history of teaching experience, from undergraduate studies to executive MBA programs, and has, as Associate Professor, been affiliated to Danish universities with two periods as a visiting professor: one at San Francisco State University, Autumn 2000 when the dot.com bubble burst and one at The University of Auckland, New Zealand, studying deregulation and liberalization.

Deirdre Anderson is Senior Lecturer in Organizational Behavior at Cranfield University, School of Management. Her research interests include flexibility, work and family, gendered careers and the challenges faced by senior professionals in meeting demands from both the work and non-work domains. In all her work she seeks to increase awareness of diversity and inclusion, challenging the often unconscious processes that can limit individual actions and organizational practices. Deirdre is an academic fellow of the Chartered Institute of Personnel and Development and a member of the British Psychological Society, the British Academy of Management, and the Work and Families Researchers Network. Before taking up academic research and teaching, Deirdre spent over 15 years as an independent business psychology consultant with an emphasis on assessment and personal development.

Paul Boselie is Professor of Strategic HRM at the Utrecht University School of Governance (Utrecht University, the Netherlands), Research Director and Chair of the Dutch HRM Network and Associate Editor for the *International Journal of HRM*. Paul is the author of three books, including *Strategic HRM: A Balanced Approach* (McGraw-Hill Education, 2014). His research is focused on the added value of HRM in different institutional and multi-stakeholder contexts.

Chris Brewster is Professor of International Human Resource Management at Henley Business School, University of Reading, UK; Nijmegen University, the Netherlands; the University Vaasa, Finland; and ISCTE, Lisbon, Portugal. He had substantial experience as a practitioner and gained his doctorate from the LSE before becoming an academic. He researches in the field of international and comparative HRM. Chris has consulted with major international companies and international organisations such as the UN and the EU, and taught on management programmes throughout the world. He is a frequent international conference speaker. He has written or edited around 30 books on a variety of HR topics. He has also written almost 100 book chapters and over 200 articles. In 2002, Chris was awarded the Georges Petitpas Memorial Award by the practitioner body, the World Federation of Personnel Management Associations, in recognition of his outstanding contribution to international human resource management; and in 2006 Chris was awarded an honorary doctorate by the University of Vaasa, Finland.

Todd Cardarelli is currently a PhD student at Cranfield University and a Global Learning and Development Director at EY, a global professional services firm. Before starting his PhD, Todd completed graduate degrees in International Development at American University, International Human Resource Management at Cranfield University, Global Human Resource Development at the University of Illinois at Urbana Champaign, and International Management at Thunderbird, the American Graduate School of International Management. Todd's professional and academic interests focus on corporate responsibility, adult learning, cross-cultural management, organizational change, and how learning and development can help promote sustainable development.

Jean-Luc Cerdin is Professor of Human Resource Management at ESSEC Business School, France. He has served as a visiting professor at Rutgers University and University of Missouri St. Louis, and a visiting scholar at Wharton. His research interests include expatriate management, career management and international human resource management. Most recently, he has been working on global talent management.

Chul Chung (PhD) is an assistant professor (UK Lecturer) in International Business and Strategy at Henley Business School, specializing in International Human Resource Management. His broad research interests encompass the areas of intersections between international business, human resource management, strategic management and organization studies. His research focuses on managing people and knowledge in multinational enterprises, executive staffing and strategic outcomes and the role of corporate governance and business models in employment practices and outcomes. Chul has substantial experience as a management consultant specializing in organization design and human resource management with multinational consultancies. He earned a PhD in Management, an MA in Human Resource/Knowledge Management from Lancaster University Management School and a MBA and BBA from Yonsei University in South Korea.

David G. Collings (PhD) is Professor of HRM at Dublin City University Business School, where he leads the HR Directors' Roundtable and is Joint Director of the Leadership and Talent Institute. He is also principal academic advisor to the Maturity Institute – a global network striving to create vibrant, healthy, and successful organizations through maximizing the value of people. He previously held academic appointments at the University of Sheffield and the National University of Ireland, Galway and visiting appointments at King's College London and Strathclyde University. His research and consulting interests focus on talent management and global mobility. A key focus of his recent work is on understanding how employees add value in organizations and how organizations can support key employee groups, including international assignees, in generating sustainable performance. In 2014 he was named as one of the most influential international thinkers in the field of HR by *HR Magazine* and in 2015 he was awarded the President's award for research by Dublin City University. He has published seven books and is currently editing *The Oxford Handbook of Talent Management* with Wayne Cascio and Kamel Mellahi. He is Senior Editor at the *Journal of World Business*, former Editor in Chief of the *Human Resource Management Journal* and the *Irish Journal of Management* and sits on the editorial board of the *British Journal of Management*, the *International Journal of Human Resource Management*, the *Journal of Management Studies* and a number of other journals.

Richard Croucher is Professor of Comparative Employment Relations and Director of Research at Middlesex University Business School, London. His main research interests are in labour management and employee voice at the global and international level. He earned his PhD from the University of Warwick in 1977. He was formerly Senior Research Fellow at Cranfield School of Management, where he is currently Visiting Professor. Richard has carried out research funded by the ESRC, the Leverhulme and

Nuffield Foundations, the International Labour Organization, the Department of Trade and Industry, the Low Pay Commission, and others. His work has been published in *Human Relations, Work, Employment and Society, Industrial Relations: A Journal of Economy and Society,* and elsewhere.

Denise Currie is a lecturer in Management at Queen's University Management School. She is a graduate of Queen's University Management School, where she completed her PhD. Her research interests include HRM and innovative workplace conflict management, governing the employment relationship in non-profit and voluntary sector organizations, and comparative industrial relations.

Michael Dickmann is Professor of International Human Resource Management at Cranfield University School of Management. He lectures in the areas of international and strategic HRM. After being the Global Head of Human Resources in a multinational corporation based in Munich, Germany, he joined Cranfield to lead in the areas of global mobility and IHRM. His research focuses on human resource strategies, structures and processes of multinational organizations, international mobility, global careers, and change management. In October 2015 he became the Director of the Cranfield MSc in Management, a highly innovative, practice-centered masters that incorporates an internship with leading-edge organizations. Michael has published more than 100 academic and professional papers and reports. He is Editor of *The International Journal of Human Resource Management.* Michael has several years of work experience with major consultancies and in industry. He has conducted a variety of consulting and research assignments with cutting-edge multinational organizations, mostly from the financial, automotive, telecommunications, chemical, electrical engineering, and electronics industries. He has also consulted for humanitarian agencies, the government and the United Nations.

Marion Festing is Professor of Human Resource Management and Intercultural Leadership and the Rector of ESCP Europe's Berlin Campus. She gained her PhD at the University of Paderborn, Germany. She has gained educational, research and work experience in France, Australia, Tunisia, Taiwan and the USA. She served as an associate editor of the *International Journal of Human Resource Management* and is a co-editor of *the German Journal of Research in HRM.* Her current research and teaching interests are concerned with International Human Resource Management, with a special emphasis on strategies, careers, compensation, performance, and talent management in differing institutional and cultural contexts.

Matt Flynn is a senior lecturer at Newcastle University and director of the Centre for Research into the Older Workforce. He has conducted research for the ESRC on age diversity from a cross-national comparative stance in the UK, Hong Kong and Germany as well as for the British Council (on the UK and Japan) and the EU. He has conducted research which has had high public policy impact for the UK government and United Nations Secretariat. He has worked with employers and unions, including the National Health Service, Trades Union Congress and the CIPD, which represents British HR professionals to disseminate good practice on age diversity to businesses and others. He has published in high quality journals such as *Human Relations*, *Work, Employment and Society*, and the *Human Resource Management Journal* on the subjects of HRM policies on work and retirement, older workers' expectations from and experiences in work and trade union representation of older workers. Info on all his work can be found at: www.agediversity.org. His publication list as, well as the projects which he has led or been involved with, can be found at: http://www.ncl.ac.uk/nubs/staff/profile/matt.flynn#tab_profile.

Masayuki Furusawa (PhD) is Professor of International Human Resource Management at Osaka University of Commerce in Japan and a member of the John H. Dunning Centre for International Business at Henley Business School of the University of Reading in the UK. He serves as a member of the board of directors at the Academy of Multinational Enterprises in Japan and a steering committee member at the Japan Academy of International Business Studies. He obtained a MBA from Kwansei Gakuin University and a PhD from University of Hyogo. He also acts as a management consultant certified by the Japan Productivity Centre and an advisor to DAIHEN Corporation, one of the largest welding equipment manufacturers in Japan. Before joining academia, he had 16 years of professional experience in a non-profit think tank. He has conducted extensive research in the field of international HRM and engaged in numerous training and consultancy projects for management executives and HR specialists as well as trade union leaders from all over the world. He has published more than 50 books and articles and was awarded four academic prizes for his publications on international HRM.

David Grayson (CBE) is Professor of Corporate Responsibility and founder director of the Doughty Centre for Corporate Responsibility at Cranfield University, School of Management. David did his first degree in Law at Cambridge University, followed by a Masters in the Politics and Economics of the European Communities (now Union) at the ULB in Brussels.

He did a part-time MBA in 1983–1985, whilst running Project North East, an innovative social enterprise and local development agency he co-founded in 1980, after a spell in marketing management with Procter and Gamble. He was subsequently Joint Managing Director of the Prince's Youth Business Trust and then of Business in the Community. He has also led a third HRH the Prince of Wales charity: The Prince of Wales Innovation Trust. He has chaired several UK government agencies and taskforces including the National Disability Council, and amongst his third sector chairmanships was a five-year term at the social enterprise Housing 21, providing sheltered and extra-care housing, domiciliary care, and dementia services for older Britons. He now chairs Carers UK, which champions the role of the UK's 6.5 million voluntary carers. David has an Honorary Doctorate of Laws, from London South Bank University and was a visiting senior fellow at the CSR Initiative of the Kennedy School of Government, Harvard University (2005–2010). David received an OBE for his services to industry (1994) and a CBE for his services to disability (1999). *The Guardian* has named David as one of the top ten tweeters on sustainable leadership alongside Al Gore and Tim Cook.

Freddy Hällstén is a senior lecturer in Business Administration, especially HRM, at the School of Business, Economics and Law, University of Gothenburg, Sweden. His current research is focused on the organizing of HRM functions. He has published articles and books about HR transformation and shared service organizations. His experience also includes research in leadership and co-workership/employeeship.

Noreen Heraty is Senior Lecturer in Human Resource Management and Organizational Behaviour in the Kemmy Business School at the University of Limerick, Ireland, where she has also served as Assistant Dean for Academic Affairs. She has published widely on aspects of age and ageism in the workplace, international human resource management, organizational learning, and the work–family interface in sources such as the *Human Resource Management Journal*, the *Human Resource Management Review*, *Advances in International Management*, *International Studies of Management and Organization*, and the *Journal of Managerial Psychology*. Her current research interests include generational issues in employment, attitudes towards age in the workplace, and the creation and development of learning environments at the organizational level.

Eric Kaarsemaker is Accurate Equity Fellow at Rutgers University in the USA. He studies employee share ownership from an HR viewpoint and from a business strategy perspective. He has a PhD in management science from Radboud University, Nijmegen, the Netherlands and was a Lecturer in HRM at the University of York in the United Kingdom from 2006 until 2009. He is currently based in the Netherlands as a consultant and independent researcher.

Clare Kelliher (BSc, MA, PhD) is Professor of Work and Organization at Cranfield University, School of Management. Clare holds a PhD in Organizational Behavior from London Business School, an MA in Industrial Relations from the University of Warwick, and a first degree in Management from the University of Surrey. Her research interests center on the organization of work and the management of the employment relationship. She has a long-standing interest in flexible working and has directed a major project concerned with examining the impact of flexible working on performance, sponsored by seven companies. She recently completed a project looking at employee engagement in multinational organizations, funded by the US Society for HRM Foundation. Clare is a member of the UK Engage for Success Guru Group Steering Committee, which supports the Engage for Success Taskforce set up by the government. Clare is the author of many published papers and book chapters and regularly speaks at national and international conferences. Her recent book, *New Ways of Organising Work: Developments, Perspectives and Experiences*, co-edited with Julia Richardson, was published by Routledge in 2012. She has also written a text book on Strategic HRM together with Katie Truss and David Mankin. She has considerable experience running management programs and advising organizations both in the UK and overseas. She frequently acts as an external examiner for doctoral and masters degrees at universities in the UK and overseas.

Peter Leisink is Professor of Public Administration and Organizational Science at the Utrecht University School of Governance, the Netherlands. His research interests are in the areas of strategic human resource management, public service employment relations, public service motivation, the creation of public value and the quality of public service performance, and the study of public issues from a governance perspective. Recent articles were published in the *Human Resource Management Journal*, *Review of Public Personnel Administration*, *Public Money & Management*, the *Journal of Public Administration Research and Theory*, the *International Journal of Human Resource Management*, the *International Review of Administrative Sciences* and the *European Journal of Industrial Relations*. Peter Leisink is a co-chair of the study Public Personnel Policies of the European Group for Public Administration.

Paul Ligthart (1959) is Assistant Professor of Strategic Management in the Department of Business Administration of Nijmegen School of Management, Radboud University of Nijmegen. He studied (experimental) social and organizational psychology (MSc) and received his PhD in Theoretical Sociology at Interuniversity Center of Social Science Theory and Methodology (ICS), both at the Rijksuniversiteit Groningen. His main research interest is the study of effective configurations of strategy practices in organizations. Specifically, he studies the coherency effects of HRM policies and practices (e.g. financial participation), and innovation practices in the manufacturing industry. Dr. Paul Ligthart is a partner of the international research networks of Human Resource Management (http://www.cranet.org) and the European Manufacturing Survey (EMS) on effective business innovation.

Wolfgang Mayrhofer is Full Professor and Head of the Interdisciplinary Institute of Management and Organizational Behavior, Department of Management, WU Vienna (Vienna University of Economics and Business), Austria. He previously held full-time research and teaching positions at the University of Paderborn, Germany, and at Dresden University of Technology, Germany, after receiving his diploma and doctoral degrees in Business Administration from WU. He conducts research in comparative international human resource management, careers, and systems theory and management, and has received several national and international rewards for outstanding research and service to the academic community. He has authored, co-authored, and co-edited 27 books, more than 110 book chapters, and 70 peer-reviewed articles. Wolfgang Mayrhofer is a member of the editorial board of several international journals and an associate at the Centre for Research into the Management of Expatriation (Cranfield, UK), a research fellow at the Simon Fraser University Centre for Global Workforce Strategy (Vancouver, Canada), and a member of the academic advisory board of AHRMIO, the Association of Human Resource Management in International Organizations. His teaching assignments, both at the graduate and executive level, and his role as Visiting Scholar have led him to many universities around the globe.

Michael Morley is Professor of Management at the Kemmy Business School, University of Limerick, Ireland, where he has also served as Head of the Department of Management and Marketing, Head of the Department of Personnel and Employment Relations, and Assistant Dean of Research. He has published some 20 books, 24 guest-edited journal special issues and over 100 journal articles and book chapters. Among his recent edited volumes are: *Manager-Subordinate Trust: A Global Perspective*, with P. Cardona (Routledge, 2013) and *Managing Human Resources in Central and Eastern Europe*, with N. Heraty and S. Michailova (Routledge, 2009). He served as Associate Editor of the *Journal of Managerial Psychology* from 2007 to 2012 and is a member of the editorial board of several other international journals, including the *International Journal of Cross Cultural Management*, *Human Resource Management Review*, the *International Journal of Human Resource Management*, the *British Journal of Management* and the *International Journal of Emerging Markets*. He was the 2007–2010 Chair of the Irish Academy of Management and the 2012–2014 President of the International Federation of Scholarly Associations of Management.

Nancy Papalexandris is Professor of Human Resource Management and Academic Coordinator of the MSc Programme in Human Resource Management of the Athens University of Economics and Business. She has served as Vice-Rector for Academic Affairs and Personnel of her University for the period 2001–2007 and has represented the Greek Rectors' Conference at the European University Association. She has studied Business Administration and obtained a Master's Degree from New York University and a PhD from the University of Bath in the UK. She teaches various subjects such as Human Resource Management, Management for Public Organizations, Comparative Management, Public Relations, Organizational Behavior, Women in Management, Business Ethics, and Corporate Social Responsibility and Entrepreneurship. She has also taught in various EU Universities and in post-training and management development seminars in Greece and abroad. She has served as University evaluator and PhD examiner in various Universities outside Greece. She represents Greece in the CRANET Network and has done extensive research in comparative human resource management since 1992. She has published books and articles in international journals and has organized and participated in a number of international conferences. She is a member of the editorial board of various academic journals. She is President of the Greek Association of Women University Professors.

Emma Parry is Professor of Human Resource Management at Cranfield University, School of Management. Her research focuses on the impact of the changing context on talent management and HRM, specifically the impact of national and sector contexts and the impact of changing demographics, and technological advancements in managing people. Emma leads a number of global

research projects. She manages CRANET, a worldwide network
of over 40 business schools that conducts comparative research
into HRM. She is also a director of 5C, a global research project
conducted with academics from around 30 institutions around the
world, examining cultural differences in attitudes towards careers.
Emma is a UK representative on the global team for the Center
of Aging and Work at Boston College, USA. She has conducted
a wide range of research for a number of clients, including the
Ministry of Defence, the Department of Work and Pensions, the
National Health Service, the Chartered Institute of Personnel and
Development and several private-sector organizations. Emma is
the co-author or editor of five books and publishes regularly in
high quality academic journals. She regularly speaks at academic
conferences and maintains an extensive network of leading UK
and international scholars. She is a visiting research fellow at
Westminster Business School and an academic fellow of the
Chartered Institute of Personnel and Development.

Stephen Perkins is Dean at the Guildhall Faculty of Business and
Law and Professor of Corporate Governance and Leadership,
London Metropolitan University. He obtained his DPhil from the
University of Oxford, UK. Drawing on experience in leadership
and the governance of organizations over more than three
decades—as a large business manager, small business entrepreneur,
and researcher, consultant and educator—he strives to enable
academic, business, and professional worlds to align in ways that
benefit all stakeholders.

Aleksy Pocztowski is Professor and Chair of the Human Capital
Management Department at the Cracow University of Economics
(CUE), Poland. He served as Dean of the Economic and
International Relations Faculty at the CUE from 2002 to 2008,
and is currently serving as Vice-Rector for Research at the
University. Among his main fields of interest are the transformation
of HR function, strategic and international HRM, performance
management, leadership, talent management and diversity issues.
He is a Member of the Management and Organization Committee
and the Labour Studies and Social Policy Committee of the Polish
Academy of Science in Warsaw. A former DAAD and Volkswagen
Foundation scholarship holder in Germany, he was awarded the title
'Man of the Year in HR in Poland' in 2008.

József Poór is Professor of Management at the Faculty of Economics
and Social Sciences, Szent István University, Hungary. He earned
his PhD from the Hungarian Academy of Sciences, Budapest. He

is also Professor of Management at J. Selye University, Komarno, Slovakia. He has served as a guest professor at five different US universities (PAMI, Honolulu: Bellermine, Louisville: EKU, Richmond; Saginaw, Michigan; and CSU, Cleveland) and has delivered 14 short summer semester courses. He has also lectured at Catholic University, Lyon, France on three occasions. He has been an Erasmus Guest Lecturer at many other European universities (Cranfield, UK; University of Applied Sciences in Frankfurt am Main, Germany; University Arnhem, Holland; Bergen School of Economics, Norway) and Visiting Professor at University Bucharest and University Cluj, Romania, as well. He was Senior Manager (Managing Director, Country Manager and Senior Consultant) at different professional service firms (Mercer, HayGroup, Diebold) and at a private business school (International Management Center, Budapest). His scholarly publications have appeared in more than 10 internationally refereed journals. In addition he has authored or co-authored 34 books and book chapters in Hungarian, English, and Romanian.

Erik Poutsma is Associate Professor in International Labour Studies at the Institute of Management Research, Radboud University of Nijmegen. He studied sociology (MA) at Rijksuniversiteit Groningen and received his PhD in Business Administration at Radboud University. He was an honorary research fellow at Manchester Metropolitan University (UK) and is Visiting Professor at the University of Greenwich (UK). He is a fellow and mentor at the School of Management and Labor Relations, Rutgers University, New Jersey (USA), and partner of the CRANET network. His research interests are in the study of entrepreneurship, international human resource management, and employee participation, including financial participation, profit sharing, and employee share ownership. Findings from his research have been published in *Industrial Relations, Human Resource Management, Economic and Industrial Democracy*, the *International Journal of Human Resource Management,* and the *Journal of Industrial Relations* among others.

Alexandros Psychogios holds a BSc in Political Science and Public Administration (University of Athens), an MSc in Public Policy and Public Finance (University of Athens), an MA in Public Services Management (University of York) and a PhD in Industrial and Business Studies (University of Warwick). He is currently a senior lecturer on Organizational Behavior (OB) and HRM at Hull University Business School. He is also a research visitor at the South Eastern European Research Centre (SEERC) and Associate

Researcher in the GNOSIS Research Group of the Management School at the University of Liverpool. His specialization and research interests are on Organizational Change, Leadership and Complexity, and International Human Resource Management. His publication record focuses on a variety of OB/HR issues in different, but rather challenging contexts like economies in transition, Small–Medium-sized Enterprises (SMEs) in crisis, the public sector, etc. He has published several articles in journals like the *International Journal of Human Resource Management* and the *Journal of Human Resource Management, Emergence: Complexity & Organisation, Total Quality Management & Business Excellence, Employee Relations, The International Journal of Quality & Reliability Management*, etc. Dr Psychogios has wide-ranging experience of participating in various consultancy and research projects on issues like leadership, human resource management, total quality management, performance management, and reward systems. He has participated in many professional training courses offered at both private and public organizations. Moreover, he has been invited to many professional and academic conferences as an expert speaker on issues like leadership, complexity, and performance management.

Ihar Sahakiants received his PhD from the ESCP Europe in Berlin, Germany, where he acted as a research associate and gave lectures in Human Resource Management. Currently he holds the Professorship in International Human Resource Management at the Cologne Business School (CBS), Germany. His research interests include topics such as international compensation, socially responsible human resource practices, corporate governance and executive rewards, as well as path dependence and institutional isomorphism of organizational practices.

Heike Schröder is a lecturer of Management at Queen's University, Belfast, Northern Ireland (UK). She received a PhD in Human Resource Management from Middlesex University, London (UK) in 2011 and was a postdoctoral researcher at the University of St. Gallen (Switzerland), Vienna University of Economics and Business (Austria), and the Korea Labor Institute (Republic of Korea). Her research centers on demographic change and workforce ageing in Germany, the UK, Austria, Japan, and the Republic of Korea. Using comparative HRM, institutional theory, institutional entrepreneurship, and life course theory lenses as well as qualitative case study data, she explores how workforce ageing affects and is managed by stakeholders such as the state, trade unions, firms, and individuals workers. She has published her research in the *International Journal of Human Resources Development and Management*, *Human Relations*, the *Journal of Social Policy*, and the *Human Resource Management Journal*.

Hugh Scullion is Established Professor in International Management in the School of Business and Management at NUI Galway, Ireland and previously worked at Strathclyde, Nottingham, Warwick and Newcastle Universities. Hugh is a specialist in International HRM and has published in leading journals such as the *Academy of Management Journal*, the *Journal of World Business*, the *Human Resource Management Journal*, and the *International Journal of Human Resource Management*. He has established an international reputation as a leading researcher in the niche areas of global staffing and global talent management and with colleagues he has published several books in this area, including *Global Staffing* (Routledge, 2008), *Global Talent Management* (Routledge, 2011), and *Strategic Talent Management: Contemporary Issues in International Context* (Cambridge University Press, 2014).

Agnieszka Skuza is Assistant Professor of Management at Poznan University of Economics, Poland. She is also a visiting professor of Management at the University of Texas, Dallas, USA. Her research focuses on international management with particular focus on talent management. Agnieszka has acted as advisor and consultant to leading MNCs in Poland and the USA. Her teaching focuses on human resource management, international human resource management and cultural differences. She has taught and delivered executive education in the USA, France, Spain, Portugal, Finland, and Mexico.

Paul Sparrow is the Director of the Centre for Performance-led HR and Professor of International Human Resource Management at Lancaster University Management School. He has worked as a research fellow at Aston University, Senior Research Fellow at Warwick University, Consultant and Principal Consultant at PA Consulting Group, Reader and Professor at Sheffield University and, whilst, at Manchester Business School he took up the Ford Chair from 2002–2004 and was the Director for Executive Education 2002–2005. He has consulted with major multinationals, public-sector organizations, and inter-governmental agencies, and was an Expert Advisory Panel member to the UK government's Sector Skills Development Agency. He is regularly voted amongst the Most Influential HR Thinkers by *Human Resources* magazine, listed from 2008–2012, and in the Top 10 Most Influential HR Thinkers 2014–2015. His research interests include cross-cultural and international HRM, HR strategy, and the employment relationship. His latest books include *Do We Need HR? Repositioning People Management for Success*, published by Palgrave in 2015 and *Strategic Talent Management*, published by Cambridge University Press in 2014. He is Co-editor of the *Journal of Organizational Effectiveness: People and Performance* and Editorial Board Member for *Human Resource Management*, the *International Journal of Human Resource Management*, the *British Journal of Management*, *Cross-Cultural Management: An International Journal*, the *International Journal of Cross-Cultural Management*, the *European Management Review*, and *Career Development International*.

Eleni T. Stavrou is Associate Professor of Management at the University of Cyprus. She received her PhD at the George Washington University, USA, where she was Co-founder and Director of Programs and Operations of the Center for Family Enterprise. She has published widely, including articles in various academic journals such as the *Journal of Organizational Behavior*, the *Journal of International Business Studies*, *Human Resource Management*, the *Journal of Business Ethics*, the *International Journal of Human Resource Management*, the *British Journal of Management*, and *Entrepreneurship Theory and Practice*. Her research interests include: work–life issues; strategic and comparative human resource management; and intergenerational transitions in family firms. Largely as a result of her initiative, the University of Cyprus is one of the few institutions in Southern Europe and the Middle East to promote and publish research in the emerging field of family enterprise. Finally, she is involved in helping businesses with various human resource management issues, especially intergenerational transitions in family firms.

Leslie T. Szamosi is Senior Lecturer in Organizational Behavior and Human Resource Management and MBA Academic Director at the International Faculty of the University of Sheffield, CITY College. He has authored and co-authored in book chapters and peer-reviewed journal articles in leading publications and is a highly sought after seminar and workshop leader in this subject area. Leslie's current research interests centre on organizational change and its impact on HRM as well as in the areas of Human Resource Policies and Practices during crisis situations.

Paul Teague is a professor of Management at the Queen's University, Belfast. He holds a PhD from the London School of Economics and has been a Fulbright Scholar at the University of Massachusetts. He has written widely on the theme of the employment relations consequences of deeper European integration, social partnership and employment performance, workplace conflict management, and human resources in the recession.

Geoffrey Wood is Professor of International Business and Dean of the Essex Business School, University of Essex, UK. Previously he was Professor of International Business at Warwick Business School, UK. He has authored, co-authored, and edited 12 books and over 120 articles in peer-reviewed journals. Geoff's research interests centre on the relationship between institutional settings, corporate governance, firm finance, firm-level work, and employment relations.

Introduction and Overview of IHRM: Contemporary HR Issues in Europe

MICHAEL DICKMANN, CHRIS BREWSTER AND
PAUL SPARROW

A European Perspective on HRM

This edition of the book continues the tradition of exploring
international human resource management (IHRM) using a European
perspective. It explores the underlying commonalities with people
management elsewhere and investigates the fascinating variations of the
HRM mosaic in Europe. Given the increasingly volatile, ambiguous
and uncertain context in a region that has experienced massive change
in the time following the various financial and other crises post-2008,
this book synthesizes some of the key business and HRM reactions,
ideas and challenges that Europe is faced with.

The first edition – edited by Chris Brewster and Hilary Harris – was
published in 1999 and at that time deemed groundbreaking in that
it drew on some eminent human resource management thinkers in
Europe to debate ideas that were distinct, yet linked to the dominant
US-led HRM discourse. In the 1990s it had increasingly become clear
that North American and Asian multinational corporations (MNCs)
managed their international staff in often highly distinct ways from their
European counterparts. This led to European researchers investigating
a range of different issues that were integrated in the book. However,
the first edition covered the European perspective on IHRM,
predominantly by exploring the issues from a firm's orientation and
also intended to identify practitioner concerns and to present insights
in relation to these. This led, at times, to a descriptive view and some
manifestly prescriptive recommendations.

The second edition covered the area in a more analytical and critical
way. The second edition was published in 2008 but written, of course,

just prior to the subsequent economic convulsions that were to come. Edited by Michael Dickmann, Chris Brewster and Paul Sparrow, it built on the previous distinctive contribution and broadened the perspective and approach to IHRM in Europe. It charted global work and careers within European MNCs in more detail and presented new ways to manage expatriates and other international workers. Incorporating the thoughts of leading European academics, it treated IHRM more strategically and explored international structures, strategies, policies and practices in relation to corporate configurations. In the second edition we observed that IHRM, and its more recent terminology of strategic IHRM, was still mostly conceptualized and examined from a North American – predominantly US – perspective. However, the variety of institutional environments, such as the more coordinated market economies that can be found in several of the European Union (EU) states, organizational strategies and structures, the broader economic context, employment relation systems as well as general decision patterns and preferences (to name but a few), were leading to distinct HRM landscapes in Europe. The original motives behind the series were still relevant. As we extended the coverage of the volume, it was evident that providing a European perspective was important because the predominance of North American thoughts in the sphere of management and in the diffusion through universities, consultancies and US MNCs meant that the North American paradigm still tended to dominate our thinking. DeFidelto and Slater (2001) noted that there exists a 'Gulf Stream' in management ideas, with them originating in the USA and reaching the UK first and then spreading over the European continent to finally reach the Southern European states. While some of this certainly takes place and is picked up by some of our contributors to this third edition, such as Stavrou and Papalexandris when they write about Greece and Cyprus, it is important to present competing ideas and distinct approaches. Various countries have developed diverse 'solutions' to their specific HRM challenges and will continue to display divergence. Moving beyond the predominant HRM paradigm to explore variations allows researchers and scholars to further develop and broaden their HRM concepts and insights.

Since the second edition of this book, many scholars have presented national or regional perspectives of HRM. Amongst those making a case for European distinctiveness are Brewster et al. (2004), Scholz and Böhm (2008), Brewster et al. (2008), Gooderham et al. (2008) and Morley et al. (2009). In addition, other continents have also had scholarly attention, with academics arguing for diversity in relation to Asia (Varma and Budhwar, 2013), Africa (Kamoche et al., 2004) or South America (Elvira and Davila, 2007). A recent handbook also looks at HRM in emerging markets (Horwitz and Budhwar, 2015).

This third edition is building on this earlier work. The starting point remains the same. We argue that there are a multitude of institutional, cultural and organizational factors that create a European distinctiveness of (international) HRM, albeit we outline a picture of diverse national approaches that lead to a European mosaic and admit that there are various degrees of convergence of HRM with other nations inside and outside the continent. But, in this edition, we are more ambitious and have radically reconceptualized and reintegrated the most pertinent discourse on European HRM. Since 2008 many countries in the world – and especially several states within Europe – have experienced some of the most challenging times for many decades due to the financial and sovereign debt crises that influenced the economies of nations, their GDP growth, unemployment and many other people-related issues.

Using predominantly institutional, organizational and individual perspectives the book sets out to illuminate the European HRM landscape in its present form, providing insights into its developments in relation to the key challenges and crises experienced. Given the intellectual history of this volume, our selection of contributions has been driven by two considerations: what are the contemporary issues; and can we discern and give voice to a specifically European perspective? This presents us potentially with a very wide-ranging set of issues and topics at the macro-, mezzo- and micro-level; we could cover a huge choice of subjects. Drawing on contemporary institutional theory, we identify those areas where the HRM activities of an organization in Europe are relatively constrained by institutional requirements (such as legislation, trade unions and so forth) and those where organizations have more autonomy. In the latter instance, where there is the opportunity for more autonomy, organizational policies and practices might not actually be specific to Europe and other mezzo-level factors might be at play; whilst in the former instance, where institutional pressures are strong, they likely will. Building on this, the third edition is characterized by:

Institutional, Organizational and Individual Perspectives. Discussions of HRM in European MNCs and/or in Europe are highly 'critical' and they go beyond the interest of organizations (Brewster, 2007). The discourse on institutional contexts and the interplay of stakeholders is very vibrant in Europe. In particular, Part I presents comprehensive data on GDP in different countries, unemployment rates, training and development investments and employment relations systems, and allows us to distinguish the different actors and their interests in Eastern, Western, Northern and Southern Europe.

Broad Foundations. The distinguished authors who contributed to this edition use a large number of theoretical foundations and a range of empirical data. Using the variety of perspectives outlined above allows the authors to access a large number of data sources, including economic, sociological, organizational and psychological data. Thereby, the book presents a nuanced picture of the variety of HRM approaches across Europe.

Long-Term Relationships and Developments. The book traces HRM developments in Europe over time. The authors were encouraged to adopt a long-term focus in order to be able to identify underlying determining forces and influencing factors. Obviously, the time perspective varies depending on the subject discussed. For instance, exploring HRM in Central and Eastern Europe (CEE) contrasts the current status quo with the situation found when the 'iron curtain' collapsed in 1989 and develops an impression of partial convergence to more established HRM systems in the Anglo-Saxon world. Several chapters use the massive financial crisis starting from 2008 as a point of departure to trace HRM reactions and the ability of employment systems and organizational, as well as individual, actors to react to these and to shape their context and linkages. It is interesting to see the variety of these reactions and coping mechanisms within Europe. For instance, Chapter 6 on Nordic HRM depicts the resilience of the Swedish, Norwegian, Danish, Finnish and Icelandic HRM systems. By contrast, Chapter 4, on Mediterranean HRM outlines the massive changes that Spain, Italy, Portugal and especially Greece and Cyprus have undergone and the enduring challenges they face. It recommends a more proactive management and strategic positioning of HRM in a move that would be likely to increase convergence to a more Western European HRM approach.

Interactions and Boundaries. A perspective that includes multiple stakeholders also needs to look at the interactions between them. Throughout the book we trace these, albeit that the level of analysis and the boundaries to the discussion vary. In Part I we look at regions and countries within Europe so that the reader will find a macro-analysis of HRM. Part II looks at sectors, industries and key challenges within organizations and presents a mezzo-analysis of HRM (see below). Part III concentrates on the micro-view of HRM and analyses; in particular, the interactions of global careerists and organizations. The boundaries of Parts II and III tend to be narrower and the recommendations more specific.

HRM in an International Context

More than half a century has passed since MacLuhan (1960) first described the world as a 'global village'. However, international working is not a recent phenomenon. Four millennia ago, Assyrian 'commercial organizations' had expatriates, activities in several geographical regions and a strategy to search for new markets and resources (Moore and Lewis, 1999). In addition, they had head offices and foreign affiliates as well as management and operational structures. Today's MNCs are not too dissimilar in that they also have organizational structures that stretch across borders and have the challenge of managing diverse national contexts and an international workforce.

In the last decades we have witnessed massive technological, sociocultural, political, legal and economic changes. The higher integration that has been a feature of economic liberalization and increased cross-national flows of services, goods and people has had enormous beneficial effects but has also created a very high degree of national interdependency and also some dysfunctional outcomes. The last years have shown all too clearly the potential downsides of increased international interdependence, with the sub-prime mortgage crisis emerging from the USA and spreading to other parts of the world. The massive impact on sovereign debts (and the ensuring crisis for several countries such as Ireland, Portugal, Italy, Spain, Greece and Cyprus), unemployment levels, GDP of countries and average wages have been felt by millions of people.

The associated challenges are at the heart of Part I of the book, which explores 'Macro-Views: IHRM and Its Response to Crises in Europe'. While this part reinforces the argument that there is rich diversity of HRM in Europe, we go beyond earlier editions by focusing on distinct reactions to the financial and other crises of the early twenty-first century. This section uses mostly institutional, sociological and HRM management perspectives to trace the status quo of HRM policy and regulations, people management approaches and employment relations in Europe and to develop a nuanced landscape of country-level HRM.

In Chapter 3, Denise Currie and Paul Teague outline the history and impact of HRM regulation in Europe and on European firms. They depict a situation in which many EU governments have started to weaken employment protection, have curtailed the position of trade unions and have reduced social benefits. Similar changes are evident in the European institutions, such as courts, as well. This overall view develops an excellent basis for the in-depth investigations of HRM in specific regions of Europe that follow it.

In Chapter 4, Eleni T. Stavrou and Nancy Papalexandris discuss the evolving challenges to HRM in Mediterranean countries. Using a range of economic and social data sources they depict how austerity policies have led to a substantial decrease in GDP, a rise in unemployment and cuts in social security and real wages. They chart the reactions of workers and employment relation systems and recommend that HRM professionals undertake a range of change activities in order to raise productivity while reaping efficiency effects. In short, the authors suggest that Southern European HRM, especially that of Greece and Cyprus, needs to counter the severe crisis by becoming more strategic and moving to a stronger change management role. As events continue to unfold around Greece and its relationship with the EU, not surprisingly, the regional picture that is presented here is one of significant change.

In Chapter 5, Michael Morley, József Poór, Noreen Heraty, Ruth Alas and Aleksy Pocztowski analyse HRM developments in Central and Eastern Europe (CEE). The CEE region consists of Bulgaria, Croatia, the Czech Republic, Estonia, Hungary, Latvia, Lithuania, Poland, Romania, Serbia, Slovakia and Slovenia. The chapter argues that the CEE countries had undergone massive employment relations and HRM changes in the 1990s, with a shift towards more pluralism, an increase in HRM function legitimacy and a move of human resource activities towards a more strategic and value adding orientation. These developments then facilitated a relative robustness of HRM in these countries when hit by the financial crises of the early twenty-first century. The picture is one of change which then established a new normality and continuity.

Chapter 6 also develops a picture of relatively robust HRM systems and significant continuity. Torben Andersen and Freddy Hällstén discuss the distinctiveness and resilience of Nordic HRM. While the CEE countries were seen to have moved towards a more strategic HRM and the Mediterranean countries were urged to adopt a stronger business and change focus in the preceding chapters, the authors depict a highly distinct approach to HRM in Sweden, Denmark, Finland, Iceland and Norway. At the core of the Nordic HRM model they identify co-workership with highly committed and engaged workers who are co-leaders of their organizations. The functioning of Nordic HRM relies on mutual trust, collaboration and accountability, with employers investing in people and meaningful jobs. The authors make a strong case for the enduring resilience of Nordic HRM which is supported by data, such as all these countries have unemployment levels lower than the EU average.

Given these themes of change and continuity, in Chapter 7 Alexandros Psychogios, Chris Brewster and Emma Parry draw up a crisis model that distinguishes crises of management, operations and legitimacy. They outline how countries in Western Europe have reacted to the financial crises. They depict a context in which workers are getting older (and fewer) within a rapidly changing technological and social environment. The authors observe that many organizations are less able to increase pay, offer new job opportunities or invest in talent. This leads to lower engagement and morale just at a time when this is crucial to create agile organizations that enable rapid learning and innovation. In addition, they urge HRM to be more strategic and to create a scalable workforce, flexible and adaptable infrastructures and networks that can absorb external and internal shocks more easily.

Part II of the book presents 'Mezzo-Views: Cross-national HRM Strategies, Structures, Policies and Practices' in diverse sectors or for key challenges of European HRM. By concentrating on the mezzo issues, our intention is to provide insight into some of the key challenges and trends of this and coming decades. While these developments are often generic, for example, an aging population, migration, sustainability, etc., we have encouraged the authors to analyse the inventive and often unique ways that they are dealt with in different European countries, or by a range of sophisticated European multinational corporations (MNCs). The chapters develop an in-depth understanding of the variety of choices that organizations can take to address some of the most important HRM issues of our times.

In Chapter 8 we introduce the agenda and purpose of the second section of this book, explaining our selection of topics. The discussion begins in Chapter 9, where Chris Brewster, Paul Boselie, Peter Liesink, and Kerstin Alfes remind us that whilst most discussions of IHRM are either explicitly or implicitly about the private sector and are often dominated by the concerns of MNCs, there are many other forms of multinational enterprise that operate and employ people internationally. It is often assumed that the not for profit (NfP) sector, involving organizations such as national and local governments, hospitals and utilities, is driven by local operations and therefore can teach us little about international HRM. They argue that this is wrong. They provide an overview of HRM in public sector organizations from an international perspective and then focus on HRM in three different kinds of NfP organizations: the national public sector, intergovernmental organizations and international non-governmental organizations, to show the connections to IHRM. In so doing, they develop three lines of argument. First, they remind us that whilst the not for profit (NfP) sector covers a broad category of organizations, a common feature is that they all operate in highly institutionalized contexts and therefore tend to have unique governance structures, with activities shaped by multiple actors and stakeholders. Second, politics and the political dimension have a powerful effect on the governance of these organizations, their missions and their goals. Consequently there are models and frameworks from other areas of academic research, such as on new public management, that can help inform our understanding.

Third, the sector brings with it complex questions about the nature of performance and performance management, what it is and how it should be measured. These questions bring to the fore considerations about accountability and social legitimacy, that can not only help broaden IHRM research, but that also have direct relevance to the management of MNCs where they too face the challenges of corporate social responsibility. The solutions that the NfP sector is developing, whilst initially unique to its context, can also serve as a source of learning for all organizations.

Another key mezzo-level issue in the management of MNC human resources is the adaptation of headquarters-based ways of managing to different national contexts. However, the uniqueness of European traditions and the high levels of diversity that MNCs can experience across their European operations present them with some specific challenges. In Chapter 10, Chul Chung and Masayuki Furusawa discuss the impact of foreign MNCs operating in Europe on HRM. They examine how MNCs from three different countries, the USA and Japan as triad economies and South Korea as a home base of emerging MNCs, deal with the challenges of managing human resources in their European operations. Overseas investment from US MNCs formed a first wave of foreign direct investment in Europe, followed by a second wave from Japanese MNCs and the latest third wave, from MNCs from emerging economies. They argue that understanding this context brings with it the promise of contributing to two core debates within the IHRM literature: the degree of global standardization versus localization of subsidiary HRM practices and the best ways to manage and utilize either parent country nationals (PCNs) or host country nationals (HCNs) within subsidiaries. They first present the findings from studies of HRM practices in the European subsidiaries of US MNCs. In so doing, they highlight those areas that are less receptive to global standardization, such as diversity management, employee voice and involvement. They remind us of the stereotypical stance of Japanese MNCs to their overseas operations – a high context culture leading to low levels of localization and persistent glass ceilings – and the debates about the need for internal internationalization, i.e. a high degree of internationalization within the headquarters of MNCs. In addition to examining the reform of IHRM activities within the European operations of Panasonic, they report on the maturing investment behaviour of Japanese MNCs in Europe and their progress of localization. The experience of Korean MNCs in Europe is then contrasted with this development. The authors conclude that when MNCs come to Europe, they show distinctive approaches to subsidiary HRM, largely originated from their home country. Moreover, different challenges emerge for each of the US, Japanese and Korean MNCs.

In Chapter 11, Todd Cardarelli, David Grayson and Michael Dickmann pick up on some of the issues raised in Chapter 9. They focus on the HRM challenges faced by European MNCs around corporate responsibility and sustainability and argue that the role of business in society is a priority concern for many of the world's largest MNCs. However, they believe that if we are to support this need, we should use the concept of corporate responsibility (CR) rather than the more commonly used corporate social responsibility (CSR). A range of phrases are used interchangeably by researchers and practitioners alike, such as corporate (social) responsibility, corporate citizenship and corporate sustainability. It would be easier to advance research by adopting the broader concept of corporate responsibility, which they define as the responsibility a business takes for social, economic and environmental impacts. They note the intensive activities of non-profit organizations, think-tanks, consultancies and governments to lay out the business arguments for its importance. This has led to much rhetoric about the need for a more strategic approach to leverage the core competencies of MNCs for the benefit of society as well as for themselves. They go on to explore the evolution in thinking and practice in corporate responsibility and show how HRM functions can play both a more active role and embed CR into their organizations. The chapter organizes the CR business case literature in various ways in order to understand why organizations engage with CR and draws attention to arguments about cost and risk reduction, competitive advantage, reputation, legitimacy and value creation. They note the evidence about the financial benefits of CR strategies and connect this to the IHRM agenda by highlighting the role of the intangible assets of a firm, such as employee skills, employee engagement, community goodwill and the perception of trustworthiness. Finally, they develop a European perspective through the example of a Dutch-headquartered company, Desso. Their review of the HRM dimensions of CR shows that this literature continues to point out that the HRM function is often absent from the design and implementation of CR strategy. To address this, they surface the generic, culture-free things that HRM professionals can do to support various stages of CR strategy development and implementation in an organization, alongside the need to focus on European approaches. The chapter highlights the importance played by institutional factors – such as components of national business systems and national culture – in influencing how CR is perceived and implemented at the local level.

Emma Parry, Heike Schröder, Matt Flynn and Deirdre Anderson examine another mezzo-level issue in Chapter 12, when they discuss the challenges created by age and diversity issues in Europe. They portray the EU as a project in diversity management and analyse the reactions of European policy makers and employers to the ageing workforce and increased age diversity. They examine the nature and implications of ageing workforce demographics across Europe, analyse the national-level reactions to these trends and capture the organizational responses to the ageing workforce. In so doing, they take a multi-level perspective, noting that the trend has implications for governments and institutions because of the impact on the sustainability of social security and health systems and for employers through changes in the availability of labour and skills and loss of organizational memory, which in turn will shape their talent and human capital strategies. They lay out the range of employer practices across Europe, but also remind us that the recent recession and increasing youth unemployment have moved the emphasis from older workers back onto the younger end of the workforce. In general, there will be a need to encourage older workers to be economically active and remain in the workforce for longer. However, there will also be tension arising from the need to deal with an ageing workforce, whilst simultaneously addressing high youth unemployment and questions about the quality of work across generations.

In Chapter 13 Akram Al Ariss, Jean-Luc Cerdin and Chris Brewster address another important mezzo-level trend, that of migration. This has become a key issue in many political debates around the world and has led to complex and unresolved discussions about its costs and benefits across multiple layers of analysis: pan-national institutions, labour markets, nations, organizations, occupations and individuals. However, the EU creates a unique issue whereby citizens from any member country are free to move to, work in, buy property in and enjoy the social benefits and healthcare system of every other country in the EU. They bring together two academic fields, migration and IHRM, to analyse the trends behind recent developments and propose a typology of the types and parameters of migration. Reflecting the various debates within the field of IHRM around different forms of international working, definitions of different types of migrant have not been widely adopted by academics and are difficult to apply. For example, even with the sub-category of skilled migrants, typologies suggest there are four types: felicitous, dream, chance and desperate migrants. Their particularities need to be addressed by HRM policies. They analyse the implications of various types of migration for HRM in general and IHRM in particular. As with the previous mezzo-trend of ageing, they find that the complexity of migration leads to linkages to HRM at several levels: individual, organizational, the macro level (through legislation) and the role of professional bodies. They also discuss what companies can do through their IHRM policies and practices to better integrate migrants.

Part III of the book, which we preview in Chapter 14, develops 'Micro-Views: Organizational Approaches and Individual (Re-)Actions in Europe'. The section covers a number of core HRM functions – such as recruitment and selection, global careers, performance management, rewards, employment relations – which are often shaped by uniquely European (or EU) forces and, therefore, display idiosyncratic policies and practices. By adopting a micro-view of organizational HRM approaches and individual (re-)actions in Europe, this section builds strongly on the second edition of the book, in that it focuses on important subsections of the HRM domain.

In Chapter 15, Richard Croucher addresses employment relations in Europe. Across the world, Europe has the largest number of people who are members of independent free trade unions. So the careful examination of developments in employment relations since 1995 offered in this chapter is crucial to HRM in Europe. The chapter notes the wide range of systems of employment relations and the significant differences in union membership in the various European countries. The position of the Central and Eastern European (CEE) countries and the way they have adapted their employment relations following the collapse of communism is emphasized. The chapter shows that whilst there has been a reduction in collective employee representation in Europe that has been adopted enthusiastically by employers in some of the CEE states, it remains a significant feature of HRM.

Chapter 16, by Geoffrey Wood and Leslie T. Szamosi examines recruitment and selection in Europe. As compared to employment relations, recruitment and selection in Europe may not differ significantly from the rest of the world but there are some distinguishing features. The authors note in particular the costs of making wrong decisions (legislation means that it may be expensive to correct wrong recruitment decisions), the influences of the differing comparative capitalisms at play in Europe and the fact that small companies obtain their employees differently from medium-sized and large ones. They also point to the effects of the economic crisis that began in 2008 (see Chapters 1 and 7) and the substantial increase in employment that is 'only just' employment: systems such as zero-hours contracts and unpaid and lowly paid internships. Like Denise Currie and Paul Teague in Chapter 3, they conclude that things are changing and that the benefits previously enjoyed by employees may now be in the process of being eroded.

In Chapter 17, Michael Dickmann, Jean-Luc Cerdin and Wolfgang Mayrhofer focus on global careers in European MNCs. Global careers are now in the forefront for many European employers. The European Union allows citizens of any country the unqualified right to live and work in any other EU state. Indeed, the EU offers education opportunities and other programmes to encourage its citizens to be mobile. Building on this, the authors summarize the field, focusing on issues and benefits from the perspective of both the careerists themselves and their employers.

Chapter 18 examines the related issue of talent management, a subject with a rapidly growing literature. Agnieszka Skuza, Hugh Scullion and David G. Collings provide a general overview of the topic and then focus on the European context. Calling Europe the most internationalized continent, they identify characteristics that mark it out as different from other regions and examine the empirical research that has been conducted there. The key features they identify are a growing use of psychological contracts as an analytical lens, and the attention to context, including different cultural approaches and the way that different strategies lead to different outcomes. They argue that the European research has brought the context and the individual into sharper focus in talent management research.

Chapter 19, by Ihar Sahakiants, Marion Festing and Stephen Perkins considers pay-for-performance. This team of experts takes a broad approach to the topic, encompassing almost all contingent pay systems. They argue that the banking crisis that began in 2008 raised the significance of pay-for-performance to the point where the EU is creating Directives limiting bankers' bonuses. They show the extensive use of pay-for-performance schemes in the CEE countries. They argue, with Mayrhofer *et al.* (2011), that this may be one area where there are signs of convergence of practice, but, like Vaiman and Brewster (2015), they are wary of assigning these variations to cultural differences and instead explore the institutional differences between European countries. They conclude that the difference in practice between European states is likely to diminish, but is only likely to do so slowly.

In Chapter 20, the topic of financial participation is addressed by some of the leading authorities in this field: Erik Poutsma, Eric Kaarsemaker and Paul Ligthart. These authors explore the issues of profit-sharing and stock option schemes as a means of sharing out both the success of the organization and of tying employees into the corporate strategy. They deploy extensive data to show the differences between countries and offer brief country profiles to explain them. They particularly note the contrasting impacts of national institutions and MNC policies on the uptake of financial participation.

Chapter 21, by Clare Kelliher, examines what has happened to a topic that has been gathering a lot of attention recently: flexible working in Europe. Arguably this has been one of the continents that has developed the most constraints on managerial autonomy, creating fairly rigid patterns of employment. Recently, therefore, Europeans have worked hardest to find new ways of being flexible. The chapter reviews the different types of flexible working that are available and the different reasons for flexible working, including industry differences. It also notes the different implications it has for both employers and employees. The spread of flexible working and the varying incidence of preferred forms of flexible working in the different countries are noted. Again, the CEE countries stand out, seeming to prefer more traditional ways of working.

In Chapter 22 we attempt to draw together some of the common threads of the book and to use the aforementioned chapters to ask what it is that makes HRM in Europe distinctive.

HRM exists in a volatile, uncertain, complex and ambiguous world. The globalization discussion has made a strong case that our world is on a journey to stronger international integration and interdependencies. It has become clear that the direction of travel leads to stronger volatility due to its inherent dynamism and higher degrees of complexity through increased operational sophistication, more dynamic and interrelated supply chains or higher organizational interaction across borders and firms. In addition, the diverse strategic international configurations of MNCs have become more complex and dynamic, which is reflected in the IHRM strategies, structures, policies and practices of worldwide operating organizations (Farndale *et al.*, 2010; Dickmann and Müller-Camen, 2006). Since the 2008 crisis, levels of uncertainty and ambiguity have increased. Assessing the context of organizations has become more challenging and the potential for surprises in an environment that has such multiple shades and levers has grown substantially.

This book has a strong focus on the crises that have hit Europe in the past years. However, it also depicts other major trends: corporate responsibility, age and diversity, the impact of non-European MNCs on HRM, flexible organizational structures, etc., that have major HRM effects in a dynamic world. In addition, it presents a large array of critical insights and individual, organizational and societal options on HRM in Europe. We will return to these developments and insights in the last integrating chapter. For now, we hope that the reader will thoroughly enjoy and benefit from the authors' ideas.

References

Brewster, C. (2007) 'A European perspective on HRM', *European Journal of International Management*, 1(3), 239–259.

Brewster, C., Mayrhofer, W. and Morley, M. (2004) *Human Resource Management in Europe: Evidence of Convergence?* London: Routledge.

Brewster, C., Wood, G. and Brookes, M. (2008) 'Similarity, isomorphism or duality? Recent survey evidence on the human resource management policies of multinational corporations', *British Journal of Management*, 19(4), 320–342.

Dickmann, M. and Müller-Camen, M. (2006) 'A typology of international human resource management strategies and processes', *The International Journal of Human Resource Management*, 17(4), 580–601.

DeFidelto, C. and Slater, I. (2001) 'Web-based HR in an international setting', in Walker, A.J. (ed.), *Web-Based Human Resources: The Technologies that Are Transforming HR*. London: McGraw-Hill.

Elvira, M. and Dávila, A. (eds) (2007) *Managing Human Resources in Latin America: An Agenda for International Leaders*. London: Routledge.

Farndale, E., Paauwe, J., Morris, S.S., Stahl, G.K., Stiles, P., Trevor, J. and Wright, P.M. (2010) 'Context-bound configurations of corporate HR functions in multinational corporations', *Human Resource Management*, 49(1), 45–66.

Gooderham, P., Parry, E. and Ringdal, K. (2008) 'The impact of bundles of strategic human resource management practices on the performance of European firms', *The International Journal of Human Resource Management*, 19(11), 2041–2056.

Horwitz, F. and Budhwar, P. (eds) (2015) *Handbook of Human Resource Management in Emerging Markets*. Cheltenham: Edward Elgar Publishing.

Kamoche, K., Debrah, Y., Horwitz, F. and Muuka, G.N. (eds) (2004) *Managing Human Resources in Africa*. London: Routledge.

MacLuhan, M. (1960) *Explorations in Communication*. Boston, MA: Beacon Press.

Mayrhofer, W., Brewster, C., Morley, M. and Ledolter, J. (2011) 'Hearing a different drummer? Evidence of convergence in European HRM', *Human Resource Management Review*, 21(1), 50–67.

Moore, K. and Lewis, D. (1999) *Birth of the Multinational*. Copenhagen: Copenhagen Business Press.

Morley, M., Heraty, N. and Michailova, S. (eds) (2009) *Managing Human Resources in Central and Eastern Europe*. London: Routledge.

Scholz, C. and Böhm, H. (eds) (2008) *Human Resource Management in Europe*. London: Routledge.

Vaiman, V. and Brewster, C. (2015) 'How far do cultural differences explain the differences between nations? Implications for HRM', *International Journal of Human Resource Management*, 26(2), 151–164.

Varma, A. and Budhwar, P.S. (2013) *Managing Human Resources in Asia-Pacific* (Vol. 20). London: Routledge.

Part I

Macro-Views: IHRM and Its Response to Crisis in Europe

Macro-Views: Shaping HRM in Crises and Beyond – Overview of Part I

MICHAEL DICKMANN, CHRIS BREWSTER AND PAUL SPARROW

The collapse of the sub-prime mortgage market in the USA in 2007 quickly spread to Europe, with governments having to bail out a range of financial institutions (Northern Rock, Royal Bank of Scotland, IKB Deutsche Industriebank, etc.). In the European Union (EU) one of the effects was a reduction of 4 per cent of gross domestic product (GDP) in 2009 alone (Hodson and Quaglia, 2009). Throughout most of Europe, restriction of credit, rising unemployment levels and lower central bank interest rates were experienced in the following years. A sovereign debt crisis unfolded, with Ireland, Portugal, Italy, Spain and Greece especially affected. This section looks at the impact on HRM in Europe in times of crises and beyond. It uses a variety of perspectives, including a general analysis of labour markets, the investigation of governmental responses and firm reactions. Overall, it presents a detailed view of how HRM evolved in terms of reacting or responding to the challenges of major financial crises in Northern, Eastern, Southern and Western Europe.

In Chapter 3, Denise Currie and Paul Teague explore how European integration has influenced employment relations over the long term and in these challenging times. They outline EU market and institutional influences on employment relations and depict the EU employment policy, setting a scene for the understanding of the manifold developments and pressures on labour in Europe. The authors outline how the economic crisis has led to an increased diffusion of HRM practices in national public sectors and how it has challenged collective industrial relations processes. In addition, many EU governments have weakened employment protection, reduced social benefits and diminished the role and special status of trade unions, weakening their legitimacy at a time when they experience membership losses. The authors conclude that the social dimension of the European integration project has experienced additional strain in the recession of the early twenty-first century and, partly as a result of this, has changed direction.

Chapter 4 broadens the discussion to explore a variety of trends and challenges in relation to Mediterranean HRM. Eleni T. Stavrou and Nancy Papalexandris also observe a weakening of labour within an extremely challenging economic, governmental and institutional environment triggered by the financial crisis. Especially for the Southern EU context (as we write the Greek economy continues to be mired in a dramatic crisis), the anti-crisis austerity policies triggered a loss of employment, a reduction of real wages, social security cuts and a push to privatize public assets (Busch *et al.*, 2013). Stavrou and Papalexandris discuss the sharp contractions of GDP, especially with respect to Greece and Cyprus, the rise in unemployment levels, the impact of migration and institutional changes before focusing on HRM and organizational challenges. Using CRANET data (2006; 2011), they trace developments in pay, staffing, training and development and employment relations for the whole of Europe and explore implications for Mediterranean countries. They argue that direct pressures from the EU and other institutions have resulted in an effort to diminish unemployment through job creation activities, the promotion of atypical employment forms, the stabilization of employment through wage subsidies and initiatives to improve labour migration. For HRM professionals they observe activities to reform pay, benefits and performance management systems. The authors conclude that HRM needs to achieve more with less; it needs to raise productivity while cutting costs. They outline a number of activities that HRM professionals can undertake to work with human assets more effectively and draw up a list of activities and recommendations that would see HRM in Greece and Cyprus, as well as in other Mediterranean countries, move to a much more strategic role which would incorporate professionally planned and executed change management and communication activities.

Chapter 5 charts the development of HRM in Central and Eastern Europe (CEE) from comparative perspectives. The authors, Michael Morley, József Poór, Noreen Heraty, Ruth Alas and Aleksy Pocztowski, use the personnel management role, organization and activities in 1989 (the fall of the Berlin Wall/Iron Curtain) as a starting point and explore the developments that have taken place since. The chapter outlines some broad socio-economic changes, labour market data and foreign direct investment flows within the various contexts of the CEE countries. As in some other chapters, CRANET data are used to investigate HRM status, policies and practices in relation to the HRM function, organizational staffing, performance management, development and remuneration approaches as well as unionization levels. Clearly, the CEE countries had a substantially different HRM landscape thirty years ago compared to liberal or even coordinated market economies such as Germany. Since then the CEE countries have undertaken substantive reforms of their labour markets and organizational HRM approaches and the authors argue that they have been able to display a relative 'robustness' when faced with the financial crisis of the early twenty-first century. Taking a general perspective, the CEE countries have shifted towards more pluralist systems, their HRM has moved beyond administration to be able to add more value to organizations and their HRM function has increased its legitimacy and power. HRM functions now have more strategic roles and the authors suggest that in the last decades, the differences in HRM between CEE nations and other countries have narrowed substantially.

Chapter 6, by Torben Andersen and Freddy Hällstén, explores the distinctiveness and resilience of Nordic HRM. The authors look at Denmark, Finland, Sweden, Iceland and Norway and argue that the impact of the economic crisis meant that the unemployment figures in Nordic countries went up after 2008 and GDP growth suffered. However, unemployment has been, and continues to be, substantially below the EU average. The authors argue that one of the strengths of the Nordic system is its distinct employment relations and stress the concept of co-workership, which they characterize as a type of co-leadership of joint organizational operations. Co-workership, it is argued, needs four key parts that support and reinforce each other: trust and open-mindedness, commitment and meaningfulness, fellowship and collaboration, and employee accountability and agency. This special Nordic approach embodies a stronger role for a wider range of stakeholders and active creativity that have supported resilience in the face of crises.

Chapter 7, the last chapter in this section, looks at the reactions and adjustment to the crises in Western Europe. Alexandros Psychogios, Chris Brewster and Emma Parry suggest that the context of Western Europe is distinct from most (emerging) markets outside Europe, as there are fewer and older workers in a highly dynamic environment characterized by strong technological and societal changes. In generic terms, HRM is encouraged to build resilience within organizations through incorporating resource and coordination flexibility, intensive training and communication activities, knowledge networking, informal coordination and flat hierarchies. They suggest a variety of HRM approaches to three types of crises: crises of management, operational crises and crises of legitimacy. Reflecting on the financial crisis in Western Europe, the authors argue that it was akin to a shock wave that has affected the parameters within which HRM acts. On the one hand, the crisis has led to a restriction in the ability of organizations to offer improved pay, intensive training and development or new job opportunities and this is leading to lower commitment, engagement and morale of workers. On the other hand, the need for organizations to become more resilient, agile and able to develop dynamic capabilities has become ever clearer. Thus, the journey to use strategic and operational HRM to enable rapid learning and innovation, to create a scalable workforce and adaptable organizational infrastructures and networks, is proving to be highly important in the new context of volatility, uncertainty, complexity and ambiguity.

References

Busch, K., Hermann, C., Hinrichs, K. and Schulten, T. (2013) 'Euro Crisis, Austerity Policy and the European Social Model How Crisis Policies in Southern Europe Threaten the EU's Social Dimension', *Friedrich-Ebert-Stiftung International Policy Analysis*, Berlin, Germany.

CRANET (2006) Comparative Human Resource Management: International Executive Report 2005. Available at: http://www.ef.uns.ac.rs/cranet/download/internationalreport2005-1.pdf (accessed 1 November 2015).

CRANET (2011) Comparative Human Resource Management: International Executive Report 2011. Available at: http://www.ef.uns.ac.rs/cranet/download/cranet_report_2012_280212.pdf (accessed 1 November 2015).

Hodson, D. and Quaglia, L. (2009) 'European Perspectives on the Global Financial Crisis: An Introduction', *Journal of Common Market Studies*, 47(5), 939–953.

How Does European Integration Influence Employment Relations?

DENISE CURRIE AND PAUL TEAGUE

Introduction

The institutional character of the EU is not easily understood. As a result, it is common for the character of EU policies to be misinterpreted, sometimes wildly so. Over the years, the frequent misrepresentation of how the EU influences employment relations and related matters – normally referred to as EU social policy – is symptomatic of this deeper failure to understand accurately the institutional capabilities and authority of the EU. Sometimes EU social policy is portrayed as consisting of a body of employment regulations, thought up by a Brussels command-and-control centre, creating labour market rigidities in the economies of the member states (Alesina and Giavazzi, 2006). At other times, EU social policy is depicted in the opposite manner: on this account, EU social policy plays second fiddle to aggressive market-led European economic integration processes that have resulted in not only timid employment policies being adopted by the member states, but also huge constraints being placed on national social models (Scharpf, 2011). The purpose of this chapter is to avoid these potholes of misrepresentation and present a comprehensive overview of the various ways the field of employment relations is influenced by the EU and the wider European integration process.

Probably the best starting point for this analysis is to recognize that the EU can impinge on employment-relations matters in three related ways: through market influences, institutional influences and macro-economic influences. Market influences relate to the pressures released by deeper trade and business integration in Europe that oblige firms to change corporate strategies, including how they manage people. It also relates to how market integration opens up national business systems to each other, which results amongst other things in greater labour mobility across the member states.

Institutional influences mostly refer to the creation of rules that impact on the governance of the employment relationship within and across member states. For the most part, these rules arise from two overlapping processes. One is the effort to develop forms of pan-European collective bargaining either through the conclusion of social dialogue agreements at the EU centre or through the creation of some form of cross-border dialogue with multinational companies, mostly to create pan-European forms of information and consultation with employees. The other relates to the development of regulatory rules to govern the employment relationship. EU employment regulation can arise either through the member states adopting pieces of legislation, usually known as Directives, or by the European Court of Justice, the judicial arm of the EU, setting case law when ruling on particular employment-related test cases.

Macro-economic influences are of recent origin and relate to the new rules and procedures that Eurozone countries have adopted to govern the conduct of fiscal policy at member state level. Potentially, these procedures give the EU greater capacity to shape national wage-setting institutions, pensions systems and even more broadly the size of respective national public sectors.

Some of these influences will have a more direct impact on the management of the employment relationship than others. The adoption of a specific piece of employment legislation is likely to have a greater direct influence on how people are managed in organizations than some form of market integration where the influence is likely to be more indirect. This chapter examines EU market, institutional and macro-economic influences in detail in an effort to understand their nature and magnitude. The discussion is organized as follows. The first section examines the various ways in which market integration can influence the management of the employment relationship in the EU. The next section explores the strength of EU institutional influences and assesses the degree to which they have affected organizational-level people management policies. Then an assessment is made of how macro-economic influences embodied in the new European Semester will impact not only people management policies, but the wider employment relations systems prevailing in particular member states.

EU Market Influences on Employment Relations

The Internal Market and Employment Relations Systems

Deepening trade and market relations inside the EU are widely seen as triggering a range of dynamic effects (for a classical representation of this view, see Smith and Venables, 1988). Perhaps the main one is intensifying competitive pressures on firms, which encourages them to rethink core aspects of their corporate strategies – logistical plans, marketing strategies, supplier relations and even where they are located. In other words, creating the EU internal market triggers continuous and far-reaching corporate restructuring, which in turn has an impact on the manner in which people are managed in particular member states. Eastern enlargement of the EU during the 1990s, the process through which former communist countries in Eastern Europe were admitted to the EU, is a standout example of how market integration can impinge on people management policies and practices (Meardi, 2011). Allowing them entry into the EU not only enhanced the political credibility of these democratizing countries, but crucially brought a swathe of low-wage locations inside the internal market. As a result, unsurprisingly, an FDI (Foreign Direct Investment) boom followed Eastern enlargement, largely fuelled by large German firms relocating or partially relocating to some countries in Central and Eastern Europe – specifically the Czech Republic, Hungary, Poland, the Slovak Republic and Slovenia.

This wave of corporate relocation had an important impact on the renowned German employment relations system, the engine room of the country's highly coordinated economic system. At the centre of the so-called 'German model' is a specific constellation of institutions of collective bargaining (industrial trade unions, collective bargaining at the sector level); corporate governance (co-determination, cross-ownership between firms and banks); coordination through intermediary organizations (business associations); and supporting employment policies. These institutions interlocked with each other to encourage and sustain industrial specialization in medium-range technology sectors (motor cars, most famously), promote long-term investments in skills and create the corporate space for the enactment of stakeholder, rather than shareholder, corporate strategies (Hassel, 2014a). After EU enlargement, these coordinated employment relations institutions came under immense pressure as huge segments of German industry started to vertically disintegrate by creating production facilities in the countries of Central and Eastern Europe (Krzywdzinski, 2014).

Some of this FDI by German firms involved the creation of low-cost production sites, dedicated to manufacturing specialized, but unsophisticated, component parts. Effectively, it amounted to the transfer of low-skilled, low-value-added production activity from Germany to Eastern Europe. Carlin and Soskice (2009) argue that some of the core institutions of the German employment relations systems actually facilitated this transfer process by discarding their traditional functions and performing new roles. In particular, they suggest that in many organizations works councils stopped being the forum through which employee representatives ensured employer compliance with collective bargaining agreements and other legally mandated employment rights. Instead, they became the forum through which skilled employees colluded with management in the design and delivery of corporate strategies that involved keeping high-skilled 'insider' jobs in Germany and at the same time outsourcing low-skilled production activity to places like the Czech or Slovak Republics. In other words, works councils were captured by insider employees to protect their interests.

Other parts of the FDI made by German industry in Eastern Europe aimed to create parallel production in the two locations. The explicit purpose of this corporate strategy, commonly referred to in the employment relations literature as 'whipsawing', was to accelerate the reform of particular institutional features of the German model by opening up the possibility of outsourcing production activity from Germany to low-cost sites in Eastern Europe. Whipsawing strategies of this kind impacted most on the system of sector or industry-wide collective bargaining (Doellgast and Greer, 2007). Traditionally, sector-wide collective bargaining was used to establish industry-wide levels of wages and working conditions so that firms could not poach each other's workers by offering higher rates of pay. During the bad economic times that followed German reunification, employers were able to get 'opening clauses' inserted into industry-wide collective bargaining agreements that allowed firms experiencing commercial hardship to suspend their implementation. Originally, these opening clauses were intended to relieve the pressure on former East German companies that found themselves in a precarious competitive position after reunification (Dustmann *et al.*, 2014). But companies used the spectre of outsourcing production to Eastern Europe to massively increase the number of firms using opening clauses to secure deviations from sector-level bargaining agreement. The use of these agreements has become so prevalent that Hassel (2014b) argues it has led to collective bargaining being decentralized to firm level.

Thus, processes associated with deepening market integration in the EU have helped to erode further the coordinating capacities of employment relations institutions in Germany. Hassel goes as far as to suggest that the German model has fragmented (2014b). The industrial restructuring triggered by the Eastern enlargement of the EU has had a particular impact on the German labour market. More generally, deeper market integration has also accelerated the institutional erosion of other North European employment relations systems. A common argument is that neo-liberalism has now triumphed in the once coordinated or corporatist economies in Northern Europe. A more persuasive argument is presented by Thelen (2014), who suggests that in response to market pressures coordinated market economies are not following the deregulation/neo-liberal model prevalent in the Anglo-American countries. Instead, they are pursuing what she calls 'socially embedding flexiblization' strategies. Thus, Sweden is liberalizing largely through decentralizing collective bargaining structures that were previously heavily centralized. Denmark is adjusting through the pioneering 'flexicurity model', which combines weak employment security rules with generous income and training provision for the unemployed. The Netherlands has sought greater labour market flexibility through permitting the extension of part-time and temporary work at the same time as introducing a raft of family-friendly employment policies.

Thus, coordinated economies are reforming, but in a manner that is consistent with their employment relations history and traditions. This is an important insight. Market integration may be releasing, or at least adding to the common competitive pressures being experienced by EU member states. But in response to these pressures, member states are travelling distinctive national reform pathways. In other words, even in the context of intensive market integration, national employment relations systems continue to matter. There has been no systematic convergence towards the neo-liberal model of governing the employment relationship – or towards any other common model for that matter. The institutional organization of labour markets inside the EU continues to be largely national in character: there is no European (or perhaps more precisely EU) model of employment relations.

EU Labour Mobility and National Labour Markets

Alongside the release of more intense market competition, European integration has also (belatedly) increased labour mobility across the member states. The free movement of workers is a legal cornerstone of the EU – the others are free movement for goods, capital and services. Removing barriers to people moving across the member states was seen as important for both economic and social reasons. On the economic side, labour mobility is considered important to allow economies to respond effectively to economic shocks. In the USA, for example, when economic conditions deteriorate in a particular region causing unemployment to rise, a fairly immediate response is for people to move to more prosperous areas in search of better job opportunities.

In other words, labour mobility is seen as an economic adjustment mechanism that allows an economy to return to equilibrium when bad economic times arrive (Blanchard and Katz, 1992). Thus, promoting the free movement of workers inside the EU was seen as a key way of building shock absorbers into the European economy. On the social side, the free movement of workers was seen as playing an important role in the creating of what Karl Deutsch called in the 1950s 'a social-psychological' community across the member states (Deutsch, 1953). If people started working in member states that were not their country of origin, then, it was envisaged, old national animosities would start to wither away. Free movement of workers was seen as creating the social foundations to economic integration in Europe.

Up until the end of the 1990s, the free movement of workers largely remained a promise: only meagre numbers of people moved across the member states to work. A range of entrenched barriers were seen as preventing labour mobility. Top of most people's list were language barriers; workers, it was argued, would be most reluctant to take a job in another country if they did not know the language. High levels of social benefits were seen as acting as a huge disincentive against labour mobility – people who lose jobs would be more prepared to receive unemployment benefits and wait for alternative job opportunities in their home country rather than move to another member state, even if more immediate job openings were available. Other barriers to free movement were identified. The non-recognition of diplomas and qualifications across member states was seen as tying people to national labour markets. Transactions costs associated with searching for work opportunities in different countries were deemed high as the institutional mechanisms to advertise job vacancies was next to non-existent. Over the years a battery of initiatives was introduced to address these barriers – member states started recognizing each other's qualifications, coordination was improved between national employment and careers services, and so on. The effectiveness of these initiatives is open to debate, but there is little doubt that they did little to increase labour mobility across the EU (Teague, 2001).

From 2004, the situation radically changed, the scale of cross-border labour flows increased significantly. The decisive factor precipitating this change was the accession of what was known at the time as the A10 countries to the EU.[1] Eastern enlargement hugely changed the economic, political and social dynamics of European integration. In the four years after 2004, the number of citizens from the former communist countries of Eastern Europe living in other EU member states increased from 1.7 to 5.6 million. The two most popular destinations have proven to be Germany and the UK. These countries offered greater employment opportunities at wage rates three times higher than those prevailing in their home countries. Workers from Eastern Europe have proven to be comparatively more mobile than citizens from other parts of the EU periphery (apart from Ireland). Migration from countries like Greece and Portugal has consistently been relatively small – a trend that has continued during the current deep recession. Thus, some member states are more 'stay-at-home' countries than others.

All in all, the latest Eurostat data suggest that about 2.3 per cent of EU citizens (11.3 million people) reside in a member state other than the state of which they are a citizen, an increase of more than 40 per cent since 2001. Mobile EU workers have the following characteristics: they are on average younger than the population of the host country; they increasingly possess higher qualifications – 41 per cent of recent intra-EU movers had tertiary education in 2013 compared to 27 per cent in 2008; they have a significantly higher employment rate of 68 per cent than host countries' nationals (65 per cent) or non-EU nationals (53 per cent); and they are often over-qualified for the jobs they perform in the host countries (European Commission, 2014). Although the rate at which workers moved across member states slowed during the recent recession, the past decade has seen this aspect of European integration radically transformed. So much so that a deep, not-easy-to-resolve, paradox reigns with regard to labour mobility inside the EU. On the one hand, labour mobility is still too low to act as an effective economic adjustment mechanism in the face of economic shocks. The EU has an annual flow of no more than 0.3 per cent of its population – one-tenth of the corresponding USA figure (European Commission, 2013). On the other hand, it has been large enough to trigger a social backlash against European integration. In many member states, the popular press cultivate the image of hordes of migrants arriving from Eastern Europe either 'stealing' jobs or scrounging on benefits. As a result, the free movement of workers has become a deeply unpopular feature of the EU in many member states. Thus although the EU needs even more labour mobility to operate as a genuinely open internal market, to push ahead with this policy may rupture the social foundations of European integration (Rowthorn, 2014).

How to solve this conundrum is outside the scope of this chapter. Of more interest is the impact of free movement of workers on employment relations systems inside the EU. Two matters tend to dominate this discussion. One is the extent to which migration inside the EU has accelerated the expansion of low-wage labour markets. A substantial literature has emerged on this topic. It would be misleading to say that a consensus has emerged from this literature, but the conclusions most commonly reached are the following. Technological change and growing international trade interdependence rather than labour mobility are considered the main drivers of low wage labour markets. Generally, EU migrants are found not to have any impact on the job opportunities of 'native' workers. With regard to wages, most studies suggest that the free movement of workers has had a small, though significant, negative impact on average wages, with the biggest impact occurring in semi/unskilled service jobs (Collier, 2014). The other theme that has dominated the literature is the ineffectiveness of the traditional sources of labour market regulation to provide effective protection to EU migrants – and other workers – in precarious employment. Low-wage labour markets have proved to be beyond the organizing reach of trade unions, while weak enforcement and the drive towards employment flexibility have rendered statutory employment rules ineffectual in many member states (Migration Advisory Committee, 2014). Overall, the employment relations implications of greater EU labour mobility have been significant. It has thrown into sharp relief some of the institutional inadequacies of traditional national employment relations systems, whilst at the same time altering the cultural, ethnic and racial character of national labour markets.

EU Institutional Influences on Employment Relations

Legal Influences on Employment Relations

The EU is not simply an open trade arena. It is a hard-to-define political structure standing above the member states that influences European economic and social life in various ways and to varying degrees. A number of EU institutional influences emanate from this political structure that impact on the governance of the employment relationship. Over the years, the EU has built up a body of employment legislation – Directives – which ensures that it legally influences employment relations in member states. It was not envisaged that the EU would acquire this influence when it was first established in 1957. The Treaty of Rome, which established the EU, was not particularly coherent on employment-related matters. The opening section of the Treaty contained some broad declaratory statements hinting that economic and social integration should evolve in tandem. Yet the body of the Treaty contained only a few explicit clauses on social policy, in areas such as holiday entitlements, health and safety and equal treatment in employment (Teague, 1989).

In terms of employment legislation, the EU did next to nothing until the publication of the 1974 Social Action Programme, which proclaimed that equal importance should be attached to social and economic matters in European construction. It set out a menu of 30 measures that needed to be adopted in three broad areas:

(1) the attainment of full and better employment in the EU; (2) the improvement of living and working conditions; and (3) the increased involvement of workers in company-level decisions. At the time, the Social Action Programme, which set out the 30 measures, was commonly viewed as an attempt to give the EU a human face (Brewster and Teague, 1989). Since the adoption of the Social Action Programme, the EU has passed a considerable body of employment Directives. Apart from the area of health and safety, Table 3.1 sets out the EU employment Directives that have been adopted. A wide range of employment-relations matters are covered by these Directives, including health and safety (on which the EU has a wealth of Directives that will not be discussed here), equality, employment protection, information and consultation and working time arrangements.

Despite a large number of employment Directives being placed on the EU statute book, it would be misleading to say that the EU has adopted an integrated body of supranational employment legislation that places major regulatory constraints on national labour markets. A more accurate assessment is that the Directives amount to a patchwork quilt of legal initiatives, with some legislation having greater impact on the member states than others (Barnard, 2014). Political opportunity rather than a well-developed plan to enact a coherent body of EU employment law lay behind the adopting of much EU employment legislation. In the 1970s the focus was heavily on Directives in the areas of equality and health and safety, as these areas were seen as very much helping the EU to develop a human face. At the time, the EU Commission also actively promoted Directives on employment protection, as it detected a willingness on the part of richer member states, particularly Germany, to discourage competition from other member states simply on the basis of lower social and employment standards. The Commission displayed similar policy entrepreneurship in the late 1980s when the member states (apart from the UK) agreed to the Social Charter. At the time, it used a perceived window of opportunity to push through Directives on health and safety, working time, young workers and pregnant workers (Teague, 2001).

In adopting Europe-wide employment legislation, the EU has never sought to harmonize employment relations institutions or rules across the member states. From the very start, there was recognition that the institutional diversity of national employment relations systems placed enormous constraints on the adoption of EU legislation that sanctioned a single or common employment relations procedure or practice for the EU. A characteristic of many of the employment Directives is that they only laid down minimum standards, which in most instances only paralleled existing national legislation. Moreover, most EU employment legislation takes the form of framework Directives, which only set

Table 3.1 EU employment Directives

Directive	Summary of Directive
Information on Individual Employment Conditions Directive (Directive 91/533)	Employers must notify new employees of essential aspects of employment contract within two months of starting
Collective Redundancies Directive (Directive 98/59). Repealed Directives 75/129 and 92/56	Employers making 20+ redundancies must inform and consult employee representatives, and notify government authorities
Transfer of Undertakings or Acquired Rights (Directive 2001/23: Repealed Directives 77/187 and 98/50)	Protects employees where their employer changes as a result of a transfer of the undertaking or business in which they work. Employees automatically transfer to the new employer; terms and conditions of employment must be maintained; employees may not be dismissed on the grounds of the transfer itself; employee reps must be informed and consulted
European Works Council (Directive 2009/38)	Employers with 1000+ employees in the European Economic Area to set up a European Works Council on request, to inform and consult employee representatives about 'transnational issues'
Information and Consultation of Employees (Directive 2002/14)	Employers with 50+ employees to set up arrangements for informing and consulting employees or their representatives about the business
Equal Opportunities and Treatment of Men and Women Directive ('recast') (Directive 2006/54)	Prohibits discrimination on grounds of sex with regard to pay, social security schemes, recruitment, employment and working conditions, promotion, dismissal and training. Also gives the right to return to the same or an equivalent job after maternity leave.
Equal Treatment Irrespective of Racial or Ethnic Origin Council (Directive 2000/43)	Prohibits discrimination on grounds of race or ethnic origin with regard to recruitment, employment and working conditions, promotion, training, pay, dismissal, social protection and more

Framework for Equal Treatment in Employment and Occupation (Directive 2000/78)	Prohibits discrimination on grounds of religion or belief, disability, age or sexual orientation with regard to recruitment, employment and working conditions, promotion, training, pay and dismissal. Also requires employers to make reasonable accommodation for disabled employees unless it would impose a disproportionate burden on the employer
Parental Leave (Directive 2010/18)	A right to four months' unpaid time off for each parent of a child aged up to 8 (actual age to be determined by each Member States – UK says 5, to be extended to 18). A right to unpaid time off for urgent family reasons in cases of sickness or accident. A right to return to the same or an equivalent job, and to request changes to working hours or patterns
Part-Time Work (Directive 97/81)	Prohibits less favourable treatment of part-time workers compared to full-time workers. Requires employers to consider requests to transfer from part-time to full-time work and vice versa, to give all workers information on part- and full-time job opportunities, and to facilitate part-time workers' access to training
Fixed-Term Work (Directive 99/70)	Prohibits less favourable treatment of fixed-term workers compared to permanent workers. Restricts the use of successive fixed-term contracts. Requires employers to give fixed-term workers information on permanent job opportunities and access to training
Temporary Agency Workers (Directive 2008/104)	Requires equal treatment of agency workers in respect of pay, working time and annual leave, plus access to collective facilities and permanent job opportunities at the hirer

(continued)

Table 3.1 (continued)

Posting of Workers (Directive 96/71)	Minimum terms and conditions laid down by law must apply to employees temporarily posted from another member state. Applies legislation on relevant employment rights (for example working time, paid annual leave, minimum pay, health and safety)
Pregnant Workers (Directive 92/85)	Protects women who are pregnant, have recently given birth or are breastfeeding – at least 14 weeks' maternity leave (paid at least at sick pay rates), a right to paid time off to attend ante-natal examinations, a prohibition on night work, protection against discriminatory dismissal, and protection against health and safety risks
Working Time (Directive 2003/88)	Regulates working hours, night work, rest breaks and annual leave

down general principles and rules so that the member states are able to implement the law in line with national employment relations custom and practice. The Directives on parental leave, information and consultation, and fixed-term work are examples of this type of legislation. In an interesting paper, Deakin and Ragowski (2011) label as 'reflexive law' EU employment Directives that do not mandate prescriptive institutional models and encourage member states to virtually self-regulate on the matter at hand, subject to various default penalties and derogations.

EU legal influences on employment relations have been greatly shaped by the European Court of Justice (ECJ), the judicial arm of the EU. Although not a legislative body in itself, the ECJ's rulings have played an important role in shaping the economic and social architecture of the EU. Weiler (1991) suggests that a process of what he calls 'judicial activism' has allowed the ECJ to perform this role. For the most part, this process involves the European Court of Justice making rulings that significantly extend the reach of existing employment Directives or add to EU employment law by interpreting Treaty clauses in a particular way. Until recently, judicial activism on the part of the ECJ was seen as strengthening EU employment standard setting. For example, in the landmark *Barber* case in the 1970s, the ECJ ruled that pension rights were covered by Article 119 of the Treaty of Rome, thus bringing this area within the legal competence of the EU. The effect of this ruling was to mobilize trade unions and equal opportunity groups in various member states to strengthen existing domestic equality legislation by taking test cases to the ECJ in the anticipation of a favourable ruling. Thus, during the 1980s and 1990s, the legal dimension to EU social policy was extended as much by national interest groups using the ECJ as an opportunity structure to extend EU legal competence on particular employment matters as by the member states adopting EU employment Directives through the formal decision-making process. The ECJ was considered an institutional locomotive to push forward the idea of an EU plinth of employment rights (Brewster and Teague, 1989).

This view has been seriously called into question as a result of a number of recent rulings made by the ECJ, most notably in the *Viking* and *Laval* cases. The first case started when a ferry company, Viking, which operates a service across the Baltic Sea between Estonia and Finland, decided to re-flag one of its ships under the Estonian flag so as to circumvent Finnish collective agreements. Finnish trade unions, outraged by the decision, accused the company of social dumping and threatened industrial action. In addition, the International Transport Workers' Federation, which had long protested about the use of 'flags of convenience', urged its national member associations to boycott Viking. In response, Viking started legal proceedings against the trade unions, which eventually ended up at the ECJ. The company argued that the trade union action was illegal as it contravened Article 49 of the *Treaty on the Functioning of the European Union* (TFEU) on freedom of establishment. The *Laval* case also concerned social dumping. A construction company that operates under Latvian law, Laval decided to 'post' workers to Vaxholm in Sweden to build a school for a Swedish subsidiary of the company. In other words, the workers would receive Latvian rates of pay and working conditions rather than the much higher Swedish employment terms and conditions. The Swedish construction workers' union reacted strongly to this decision, immediately initiating industrial action in an attempt to force the company to negotiate and to apply the conditions laid down by the Swedish collective agreement for the construction industry. Like Viking, Laval responded with legal action, which again arrived at the ECJ. In this case, the company claimed that the collective action by the Swedish trade union was illegal as it contravened Article 56 of the TFEU on the right to provide services with the EU (Davies, 2008).

The ECJ made long complex rulings in both cases in favour of the companies. The Court upheld that that the right to strike is a basic right within the legal framework of the European Union. However, it then went on to rule that the exercise of the right to strike may not unreasonably restrict the 'four freedoms' laid down in the Treaties – the rights to free movement of capital, goods, persons and services. The import of these rulings is pretty far reaching, as it appears to make national employment relations systems, including employment legislation, subservient to the EU's four freedoms. These rulings came as a huge shock not only because the Court had in the past tried to maintain a careful balance between the preservation of national employment law and free movement rules, but also because it had long been seen as an institutional advocate for a stronger social dimension to the EU. In the *Viking* and *Laval* cases, the ECJ used judicial activism to weaken employment rights in the context of integrating the European market. In particular, they appeared to open the legal door for the aggressive use of posted workers by cross-border service providers inside the EU (Barnard, 2013). Trade unions continue to be deeply unhappy with these rulings, saying they are a license for widespread social dumping. Once seen as a key institution for advancing Social Europe, the ECJ is now seen as its nemesis.

The European Social Dialogue

Alongside efforts to develop a body of EU employment legislation, there have been ongoing attempts at building some form of European social dialogue between trade unions and employers organizations. Attempts to create a European social dialogue have proceeded along vertical and horizontal dimensions. Whereas the vertical dimension relates to efforts at getting greater policy coordination and joint action by unions and employers inside the institutional framework of the EU in Brussels, the horizontal dimension has been mostly concerned with promoting trade union/employer agreements and cooperation at the enterprise and market levels. Almost immediately after the EU was established in 1957, both employer and trade union organizations established 'vertical' representative bodies in Brussels: the Union of Industrial and Employers' Confederations of Europe (UNICE) was set up by the employers, whilst the non-communist trade unions established the European Trade Union Secretariat (SSE). The organizational structure of EU trade union and employers was substantially revamped in the 1970s. On the trade union side, years of bitter rivalry between communist, social democratic and Christian democratic international trade union bodies was left behind with the creation of the ETUC in 1977. In addition, industry- or sector-wide trade union federations such as the European Metal Workers Federations were either revamped or created anew. Similarly, a plethora of industry-wide EU employers industrial groups were formed, whilst the internal organization of UNICE was radically upgraded (Teague, 1989).

Thus by the beginning of the 1980s, quite an elaborate institutional structure existed at the EU level to represent the interests of employers and workers. A distinct EU language emerged around how to talk about this institutional structure. In particular, trade union and employer organizations were given the name of social partners, while their interactions were referred to as a social dialogue. Just what the core purpose of this dialogue should be has been the source of ongoing, deep dispute (Keller and Weber, 2011). For the trade unions, the structure should be mainly focused on creating collective agreements that would commit employers and trade unions at national or even company level to particular employment policies and practices. In other words, they wanted a form of 'vertical' European collective bargaining to occur in Brussels that would stand above, yet be connected to, national systems of collective bargaining. Employers have consistently opposed the emergence of any form of European collective bargaining. They envisaged EU-level employer organizations performing mostly a lobbying role, ensuring that the interests of employers were incorporated within any policy proposals produced by the European Commission. For its part, the Commission has consistently adopted an open definition of social dialogue: in 2000 it said that the social dialogue was a 'process of continuous interaction between the social partners with the aim of reaching agreements on the control of certain economic and social variables, at both macro and micro levels' (European Commission, 2000, p. 8).

In the 1980s, a big push was made under the Jacques Delors Presidency of the Commission to implement a form of social dialogue that was nearer the trade union rather than the employers' vision of the process. Known as the Val Duchesse talks, the Commission, supported by the trade unions, sought to get employers to enter a process that would lead to 'agreement-based outcomes'. Employer organizations stood firm against this pressure, arguing that they would not countenance signing a European level collective agreement. Instead what emerged from the process was a series of informal 'Joint Opinions' on such things as information and consultation, employment strategies, and education and training. While the Val Duchesse talks may not have led to European collective agreements, they did lay the groundwork for social dialogue to be incorporated into the formal EU decision-making process in the Maastricht Treaty (Welz, 2008).

This Treaty provided the social dialogue with a formal legal base, which has been revised and upgraded by subsequent Treaties. The result is that the Commission is now formally required to consult European social partners prior to presenting any legislative proposal in the social field. The social partners can issue a Joint Opinion on the proposal, which will be formally considered in the EU decision-making process.

However, the social partners can bring a halt to the Commission's proposal by signalling that they are prepared to negotiate a collective agreement on the topic, which could subsequently be introduced as EU legislation. Additionally, the social partners have the option to implement any EU employment legislation through national collective bargaining structures rather than through national law. Incorporating the social dialogue into the formal EU decision-making process has resulted in the social partners concluding four collective agreements that have been made legally binding through EU Directives on Parental Leave (1995, revised in 2009), Part-time Work (1997), and Fixed-term Work (1999).

Side-by-side with these attempts to incorporate social dialogue into the formal EU institutional machinery, efforts have continued at developing an autonomous social dialogue process between EU-level employer and trade union organizations – known formally as the bilateral social dialogue process. No meaningful collective bargaining agreement has emerged from these deliberations, but a number of EU framework agreements, which informally commit national trade unions and employers to do something on the relevant topic, have been concluded on telework (2002), work-related stress (2004), harassment and violence at the workplace (2007) and inclusive labour markets (2010). In addition, a range of other looser joint agreements and action plans have been adopted. Supporting the bilateral social dialogue is the sector-level dialogue (Pochet *et al.*, 2009). Currently, there are 63 European-level sectoral employers' bodies and 15 sectoral trade union organizations involved in 41 different EU Sectoral Social Dialogue Committees. These committees are formally recognized by the European Commission, which sometimes consults them on policy proposals that may impinge on their particular sector. But for the most part, these committees are engaged in producing guidelines on identified good practice and codes of conduct on voluntary standards. Crucially, the impact of these EU sector agreements is entirely dependent on the commitment and effort of national social partner organizations, as they have no binding status. All in all, there is a significant amount of social dialogue activity at the 'vertical' EU level, but a big question mark exists about the impact of these deliberations on national employment relations systems (Keller and Weber, 2011).

In addition to these vertical social dialogue initiatives, efforts have been made to develop some form of 'horizontal' social dialogue/collective bargaining, particularly with multinational companies. The origins of these efforts date back to the 1970s, when international collective bargaining between trade unions and multinationals emerged as an important employment relations theme. Charles Levinson, at the time the Secretary General of the International Chemical Federation, wrote an influential book in 1972 called *International Trade Unionism* (Levinson, 1972). He argued that multinationals should be obliged to conclude international collective bargaining agreements with international trade secretariats (international trade union sector-level federations) to close the gap between national collective bargaining systems and global-level, corporate decision-making. This thinking was hugely influential as it contributed to the view that any type of European trade union activity should not be confined to some type of corporatist engagement inside the Brussels bureaucracy. Instead, it should involve some form of cross-border collective bargaining, mostly with multinationals within the context of the EU.

One strong trade union demand was for EU-level legislative action to oblige multinational companies to engage in 'horizontal' collective bargaining. Legislation of this type was deemed necessary as multinationals were refusing point blank to engage in any form of international collective bargaining and no serious institutional pressure could be brought to bear at the international level to encourage them to change their stance. The European trade union position got a shot-in-the-arm when the European Commission produced the draft Vredeling Directive in 1980, a proposal for harmonized information and consultation rights in what was termed 'complex organizations' operating in the EU, but which mostly related to multinationals and their subsidiaries. The Draft Directive was quite prescriptive, as it set out in great detail the financial, economic and employment information that multinationals should provide to their employees on a regular basis. The publication of the draft Directive was greeted with a storm of protest from European employers and some member states, led by the new UK Prime Minister at the time, Mrs Thatcher. As a result, the adoption of the draft as EU law was blocked (Brewster and Teague, 1989).

Over the next 15 years, the original draft went through several revisions and consultation procedures until it proved acceptable to the member states in 1994. Renamed the European Works Council Directive, this piece of legislation applies to all companies with 1,000 or more workers and with at least 150 employees in each of two or more EU member states. The Directive is a pale shadow of the original draft, as the main intent is to promote voluntary agreements on information and consultation in multinational companies; individual MNCs companies were permitted to determine the shape and content of their European works council provided they secured an agreement with their employee representatives. Nevertheless, the Directive was widely seen as a significant development, as it obliges multinationals to establish European Works Councils to bring together employee representatives (usually trade unionists) from all the EU member states in which the company operates to meet with management to receive information and give their views on current strategies and decisions affecting the enterprise and its workforce.

The ETUC maintains a database on the incidence of European Works Councils (EWCs) and it estimates that of the 2,264 companies covered by the legislation, some 828 (34 per cent) have EWCs in operation. A number of studies have been completed on how EWCs have operated in practice (Müller *et al.*, 2013). The consensus view seems to be that most EWCs are only 'symbolic' in nature (Eurofound, 2013). The trend is for management and employee representatives to meet once a year, with management providing a comprehensive overview of the current state of play in the multinational. A common complaint of employee representatives is that consultation rarely occurs in time to affect business decisions and, at best, only the implementation of transnational business decisions can be influenced. Only a select minority of EWCs are considered to be launching pro-active or meaningful initiatives. Normally these take the form of some type of protocol or agreement or a particular working condition, with equality and health and safety being the areas covered most commonly by agreements. No EWC has been recorded as concluding a collective agreement on pay. Thus, the activities of EWCs have not given rise to international forms of collective bargaining as envisaged originally by Levinson and others. Perhaps the most optimistic assessment that can be made of EWCs is that they have facilitated the development of new transnational trade unions networks that may not have existed otherwise and have provided institutional opportunities for management and employees to share information and concerns about the business model being followed by the company. Any assessments that convey a more positive view of EWCs need to be treated with caution, as the supporting evidence is threadbare.

EU Employment Policy

Before the late 1990s, the EU centre was only minimally concerned with employment policy, mostly producing action programmes that encouraged member states to introduce new policies on topics such as disability, equality, the free movement of workers and so on (Teague, 2001). However, after this date the situation changed significantly as greater emphasis started to be placed on active employment measures at EU level. This change occurred for two reasons. First of all, the European Commission calculated that the traditional EU social policy agenda of developing employment regulation and social dialogue initiatives had reached its political limits: member states were now more interested in labour market flexibility than in strengthening workers' rights and employer resistance to deepening the EU social dialogue had effectively put shackles on this policy area. Second, a process of what the French call *engrenage* – the deepening of national administrative structures and EU institutions – had started to embed itself in the EU social policy area. At the centre of this *engrenage* process was the use of technical committees and expert policy networks to build consensus among national policy-makers for EU employment initiatives. Eichner (1997) gives an authoritative account of how this process worked in the health and safety area. These two developments that emerged more or less at the same time nudged the European Commission to focus more on employment policy rather than on employment rights and interactions between trade unions and employers as the basis of EU social policy.

Thus, the European employment strategy (EES) was born – first in what was known as the Luxembourg process in 1998 and then as the Lisbon strategy in 2001 – which emphasized coordinated policy mobilization across the member states on four key themes, employability, entrepreneurship, adaptability and equality. At the centre of this policy coordination effort was the open method of coordination (OMC). Under this process, each member state was required to submit a national action plan (NAP) setting out the domestic policies that would be followed to advance the four policy priorities of the EES and explaining how these initiatives would be evaluated. The Commission then reviewed the NAPs to benchmark performance across the member states and to identify best practice. The intention of the OMC was to establish cycles of information exchange and forums for policy debate in the hope that convergence on effective policies could be achieved even where decision-making remained with the member states. Supporters of this process enthused that it promoted employment policy convergence across the member states in the context of institutional diversity: Europe was beginning to learn from Europe (Zeitlin and Sabel, 2010).

Overall, the literature on the OMC process is less sanguine. One view is that it has led to little meaningful policy coordination or innovation, as most member states assigned little priority to the development of their national action plans. As a result, the OMC was seen as lacking focus and giving rise to a multiplicity of targets that were never properly implemented (Keune and Serrano, 2014). Other assessments are more critical (Grahl and Teague, 2013). In the early 2000s, when the European Commission upgraded its new employment strategy in what was called the Lisbon strategy, member states were encouraged to learn from each other on the theme of flexicurity – an employment policy invented in Denmark and the Netherlands that combined the flexible use of labour with economic security for workers. However, the European Commission adopted an *á la carte* definition of the concept, which opened the way for member states to adopt the flexibility aspects of the policy and discard the security components. Thus, the EU flexicurity agenda threatened to mimic the straightforward labour market flexibility programmes of some member states, thereby weakening standard employment contracts so that these would confer fewer social rights and offer less employment protection (Keune and Jepsen, 2006).

In what was tacit acceptance of these criticisms, the Lisbon strategy was revised and re-launched in 2005. The main changes introduced were a sharper focus on job creation, poverty reduction and social exclusion and the introduction of a new 'bilateral in-depth dialogue between the Commission and member states on a national-based national action programme' to complement the iterative benchmarking OMC process (European Commission, 2005). This new strategy was getting into full swing when the economic crisis started. Although the impact of the crisis varied significantly across the member states, it had far-reaching implications for EU economic and social policy-making. In Brussels, one of the lessons taken from the crisis was that there needed to be greater EU-level surveillance of macro-economic policies of the member states to ensure the survival of the euro and to create a stable European economy in the future.

As a result, a drastic tightening occurred to the Growth and Stability Pact through two intergovernmental agreements – the 'Pact for the Euro' in 2011 and the 'Stability Treaty' in 2012 – and through the 'Six Pack' of Directives passed by the European Parliament in late 2011. These had the effect of setting more restrictive fiscal targets, controlling the process of budget setting, making litigation against delinquent governments more automatic and less open to political intervention and introducing new targets on macro-economic 'imbalances' to go along with the previous ones on public-sector debt and public-sector deficits. These changes were embedded in the introduction of a new 'European Semester' that introduced a strengthened cycle of EU economic policy coordination (Grahl and Teague, 2013).

In the first half of each year, member states are required to submit both a stability programme and a national reform programme, the first dealing with macro policy in the short to medium run, the second with 'structural' reforms – essentially deregulations, privatizations and so on. The viability of these plans would be assessed by the European Commission to assess if they were consistent with their designated fiscal stability pathway; if any member state were to be deemed not to be in line with projected trends then they would be obliged to take corrective measures otherwise they would face legal sanctions and financial penalties. The primary focus of the surveillance drive is on fiscal policy, but fiscal targets set by the EU are accompanied by detailed prescriptions of the measures to be taken to achieve them. Habermas (2011) spells out the implications of this approach: governments will be inspected every year to see whether 'the level of debt, labour market deregulation, the system of social security, the health care system, wages in the public sector, the wage share, the rate of corporation tax and much more correspond to the reckoning of the Council'. As a result of what can be called the rise of surveillance Europe, member state policy autonomy is severely compromised on pension systems, trade union rights, minimum wage levels and structures, public service provision and much more.

Not everyone shares this bleak analysis. Some argue that as attempts to strengthen EU employment policy coordination have been integrated into the European Semester so an opportunity has opened up to counterbalance restrictive macro-economic policies with EU flagship initiatives to alleviate poverty or to reduce youth unemployment (Zeitlin and Vanhercke, 2014). In other words, it is still possible to socialize the European Semester. This assessment appears to be an extremely optimistic view of current developments. Since no resources were committed by the EU to achieve its employment policy targets, since there are no effective levers to influence policy in the stronger states and since the weaker ones have to subordinate social objectives to deficit reduction, EU employment policy targets and guidelines seem empty aspirations. In the strategy laid down as *Europe 2020*, the key socio-economic objective is 'inclusive growth' (European Commission, 2010) yet everywhere economic growth is meagre and social exclusion is on the rise. Leschke *et al.* (2012) point out that planned retrenchment in social spending is most severe in just those member states where indicators of poverty and social exclusion are highest.

Thus, the European Semester, far from inaugurating a coherent social regime at European level, signals both a general deterioration and a dangerous divergence of weaker from stronger member states. On current trends it is hard to avoid the conclusion that EU employment policy coordination is subordinate to the economic objectives of fiscal discipline and budgetary austerity. The implications of this situation are immense: the character of the social dimension to European integration could be radically changing. Up until now, the EU social dimension was discussed in terms of how it could strengthen or at least complement national employment relations and welfare systems. Under the new EU macro-economic regime the real danger is that European integration will accelerate the dismantling of national social systems. European integration may be starting to drive through Social Europe backwards.

Social Europe in the Crisis

The social dimension to European integration has come under further strain as a result of the so-called global recession, which started in 2008. Although the economic crisis adversely affected some member states more than others, there are a number of discernible patterns across the EU. First of all, none of the member states have adopted a Keynesian demand-led economic strategy to stave off the worst effects of the crisis. In fact, the opposite has been the case, with all member states following austerity economic programmes to some degree or another. At the centre of these programmes almost everywhere are large-scale public expenditure cutbacks that are reducing the scope and nature of social protection in all member states. As a result, public-sector employment is shrinking in most member states, which is yet a further blow to collective industrial relations in Europe as the sector has been traditionally a receptive ground for trade union organizing and recruitment. Moreover, those who have retained their jobs are being asked to accept far-reaching organizational change as governments search for more cost-effective ways to delivery public services. HRM innovations such as new forms of team working, performance pay and management, and conflict management practices such as mediation and arbitration, are being diffused to both facilitate and deal with the consequences of more rapid organizational change. Thus, the economic crisis is simultaneously weakening collective industrial relations processes and intensifying the diffusion of new HRM practices in national public sectors across the EU.

Another common pattern that has emerged across industrial relations in the EU as a result of the economic crisis has been the virtual disappearance of social pacts. During the 1990s, social pacts, which normally took the form of centralized wage agreements, emerged in many non-corporatist EU member states to help countries gain membership of the then proposed new European single currency by helping to address competiveness and budgetary retrenchment challenges. However, no government has sought to adjust to the current economic crisis through the use of these arrangements. Across member states, governments have clearly calculated that they do not need to incorporate trade unions into the public policy decision-making process either to stave off potential industrial unrest or to assist the implementation of austerity measures. As a result, social pacts have more or less disappeared from the industrial relations scene in Europe. This development is significant as it signals that governments no longer regard it as important to provide trade unions with a special public status. Instead, trade unions are being treated as just another narrow interest group, which is further evidence of their loss of legitimacy.

A third pattern has been the acute political pressure encountered by the member states in the European periphery to reform their industrial relations systems. For most of these countries, the initial financial crisis of 2008 metamorphosed into a sovereign debt crisis, which obliged them to seek bail out finance from a specially formed body known as the Troika, consisting of the European Commission, the European Central Bank (ECB) and the International Monetary Fund. In return for large amounts of financial assistance, these member states were obliged to implement far-reaching fiscal retrenchment and labour market flexibility programmes. Policies that have been implemented due to these programmes include weakening employment protection rules, reducing social benefits and minimum wage levels and re-organizing and weakening collective bargaining systems. In some countries, most notably Spain, Greece and Portugal, these programmes amount to a significant recasting of established industrial relations systems. Importantly, these reforms are being introduced reluctantly and they are widely perceived as being imposed from the outside. As a result, an unhealthy dualism may be emerging between debtor countries in the European periphery, which now consider themselves under the tutelage of creditor countries in Northern Europe. Political and economic dualism inside the EU could have a devastating effect on the *acquis communautaire*, the collective identity and shared understanding necessary to develop common EU policies on employment and industrial relations matters.

All in all, the global recession has had two significant impacts on employment systems inside the EU. First of all, it has accelerated the pace of decline of collective industrial relations processes almost everywhere. In non-corporatist member states, social pacts have disappeared and in the corporatist countries of Northern Europe the decentralization and weakening of collective bargaining have continued unabated. Trade unions across member states have been losing members at an uncomfortably high rate. Moreover, they have been unable to amount an effective challenge, anywhere, to austerity programmes. Second, the economic crisis has decisively weakened the credibly of the established trade union/social democratic agenda for Social Europe. Traditionally, as we have seen, a key part of this agenda has been the building of a robust system of European social dialogue, even collective bargaining. But with national level forms of collective bargaining fragmenting in a good many member states, how realistic or credible is this demand? In other words, the economic crisis has brought into sharper focus the need to rethink the nature and purpose of Social Europe. These developments suggest that we are coming to the end of the period of organized industrial relations that has been such a dominant feature of economic life in Europe since the Second World

War. As a result, the manner in which the employment relationship is governed is not only likely to increasingly diverge across member states, but also within them.

Conclusions

Over the years, European integration has influenced employment relations in many different ways – through deepening market integration, by enacting EU employment legislation, by promoting some form of institutionalized dialogue at EU level between employers and trade unions, and so on. The relative importance of these various different influences has changed over time, but at no point did EU social policy amount to an integrated governance structure for the European labour market. At the same time, it needs to be recognized that considerable creativity has been displayed in the development of EU social policies. A fair amount of policy ingenuity was shown, for example, in developing the open method of coordination that seeks to promote policy convergence in the context of institutional diversity of national employment relations systems. Moreover, employers and trade unions appear to have been persuaded to interact with each other at EU level on the basis of democratic deliberation rather than adversarial bargaining. Both sides seem committed to using reasoned arguments to develop the European social dialogue in the absence of a shared view about the core purpose of the entire process.

These are positive features of EU social policy, but they pale into relative insignificance when set against how European integration mostly influences employment relations matters. At the moment, European integration is putting national social systems, including employment relations institutions, under massive strain. On the one hand, the stability and order of national labour market regulations has been seriously disturbed by a combination of the competitive pressures released by deeper market integration and a big increase in labour mobility across the member states. On the other hand, the new macro-economic regime that has been installed at EU level threatens to place a straitjacket on the autonomy of the member states to go their own way on employment policy. This pincer movement has thus drastically weakened national sovereignty over employment and welfare policies. As a result, the EU is functioning in the absence of any legitimating social foundations. With popular support for European integration at an all-time low in the member states, the EU has entered a highly precarious phase of its development. Just how events will turn out cannot be predicted in advance, but, for sure, the EU has entered turbulent waters.

Key Learning Points

- European integration influences employment relations practices in different EU member states in both direct and indirect ways.
- Deepening and widening the European internal market has intensified the competitive pressures experienced by European industry. As a result, firms have been obliged to revise established human resource management policies.
- A legal cornerstone of the EU is the free movement of workers across member states. Before the 1990s, little labour mobility occurred within the EU. But as a result of the Eastern enlargement of the EU, large numbers of workers have moved from former communist countries to richer parts of the EU, most notably Germany and the UK. An ongoing controversy is the impact these workers are having on the wages and employment opportunities of 'domestic' workers.
- Over the years, the EU has adopted a wide number of legally-based labour market regulations in the form of employment Directives. In combination, these Directives have created an EU-wide plinth of employment rights, most notably in the area of equality and health and safety.
- The European Court of Justice, the judicial arm of the EU, has made legal rulings that have sometimes strengthened workers' rights and sometimes weakened them.
- For more than 50 years, efforts have been made to develop some form of European collective bargaining. For the most part, these efforts have not been fully successful. A European social dialogue does occur, but this only weakly impinges on collective bargaining in the member states.
- European works councils have been successful in developing information and consultation on a pan-European basis. But virtually no meaningful multinational collective bargaining agreement has emerged from the workings of any European works council.
- The EU has sought to improve policy coordination in the area of employment and industrial relations. But these initiatives have not been hugely significant.
- The new macro-economic rules and procedures introduced by the member states in the wake of the Eurozone crisis has resulted in increased EU-level surveillance of the public expenditure plans of member states inside the Eurozone. This development has been widely interpreted as placing heavy restrictions on national social systems – the type of pension schemes, child benefit arrangements, etc., that member states can follow.

Note

1 The A10 countries included Cyprus, the Czech Republic, Estonia, Hungary, Latvia, Lithuania, Malta, Poland, Slovakia and Slovenia.

References

Alesina, A. and Giavazzi, F. (2006) *The Future of Europe: Reform or Decline*. Cambridge, Mass: MIT Press.

Barnard, C. (2013) *Free Movement and Labour Rights: Squaring the Circle?* University of Cambridge, Faculty of Law, Research Paper No. 23/2013.

Barnard, C. (2014) *EU Employment Law and the European Social Model: The Past, the Present and the Future*. University of Cambridge, Faculty of Law, Research Paper No. 43/2014.

Brewster, C. and Teague, P. (1989) *European Community Social Policy and the UK*. London: IPM Books.

Blanchard, O. and Katz, L. (1992) *Regional Evolutions*. Brookings Papers on Economic Activity: 1, 1–75.

Carlin, W. and Soskice, D. (2009) 'German economic performance: disentangling the role of supply-side reforms, macroeconomic policy and coordinated economy institutions', *Socio-Economic Review*, 7(1), 67–99.

Collier, P. (2014) *Exodus: How Migration Is Changing Our World*. London: Penguin Books.

Davies, A. (2008) 'One step forward, two steps back? The *Viking* and *Laval* cases in the ECJ', *Industrial Law Journal*, 37(2), 126–148.

Deakin, S. and Ragowski, R. (2011) 'Reflexive law, capabilities and the future of social Europe', in Ragowski, R., Salais, R. and Whiteside, N. (eds) *Transforming European Employment Policy: Labour Market Transitions and the Promotion of Capability*. Cheltenham: Edward Elgar.

Deutsch, K. (1953) *Nationalism and Social Communication: An Inquiry into the Foundations of Nationality*. New York: John Wiley & Sons.

Doellgast, V. and Greer, I. (2007) 'Vertical disintegration and the disorganisation of German employment relations', *British Journal of Employment Relations*, 45(1), 55–76.

Dustmann, C., Fitzenberger, B., Schönberg, U. and Spitz-Oener, A. (2014) 'From sick man of Europe to economic superstar: Germany's resurgent economy', *Journal of Economic Perspectives*, 28(1), 167–188.

Eichner, V. (1997) 'Effective European problem solving: lessons from the regulation of occupational safety and environmental protection', *Journal of European Public Policy*, 4(4), 591–608.

Eurofound (2013) *National Practices of Information and Consultation in Europe*. Dublin: European Foundation for the Improvement of Living and Working Conditions.

European Commission (2000) *Employment Relations in Europe 2000*. Brussels: European Commission.

European Commission (2005) *Working Together for Growth and Jobs: A New Start for the Lisbon Strategy*, COM (2005) 24. Brussels: European Commission.

European Commission (2010) *Europe 2020: A Strategy for Smart, Sustainable and Inclusive Growth*, COM (2010) 2020 final. Brussels: European Commission.

European Commission (2013) *Free Movement of EU Citizens and Their Families: Five Actions to Make a Difference*, COM(2013) 837 final. Brussels: European Commission.

European Commission (2014) *Labour Mobility within the EU*, MEMO Brussels, 25 September 2014. Available at: http://europa.eu/rapid/press-release_MEMO-14-541_en.htm (accessed 1 November 2015).

Grahl, J. and Teague, P. (2013) 'Reconstructing the Eurozone: the role of EU social policy', *Cambridge Journal of Economics*, 37(3), 677–692.

Habermas, J. (2011) 'Europe and the "new German question"', in Calliess, C., Enderlein, H., Fischer, J., Guérot, U. and Habermas, J. (eds) *Eurozine* [Online] 26/08/2011. Available at: http://www.eurozine.com/articles/2011-08-26-habermas-en.html (accessed 1 November 2015).

Hassel, A. (2014a) 'The German model in transition', in Padgett, S., Paterson, W. and Zohlnhöfer, R. (eds) *Developments in German Politics*, 4th edn. London: Palgrave.

Hassel, A. (2014b) 'The paradox of liberalization – understanding dualism and the recovery of the German political economy', *British Journal of Employment Relations*, 52(1), 57–71.

Keller, B. and Weber, S. (2011) 'Sectoral social dialogue at EU level: problems and prospects of implementation', *European Journal of Employment Relations*, 17(3), 227–243.

Keune, M. and Jepsen, M. (2006) 'The rise of flexicurity in Europe: why the Commission adopted flexicurity and how it understands the concept', Working document presented at the *CARMA Conference 'Flexicurity and Beyond'*, Aalborg, October 11–14 2006.

Keune, M.J. and Serrano, A. (2014) 'The power to name and struggles over meaning: the concept of flexicurity', in Keune, M. and Serrano, A. (eds) *Deconstructing Flexicurity and Developing Alternative Approaches: Towards New Concepts and Approaches for Employment and Social Policy*. New York, London: Routledge.

Krzywdzinski, M. (2014) 'How the EU's eastern enlargement changed the German productive model: The case of the automotive industry', *Revue de la Régulation*, 15(1), 1–61.

Leschke, J., Theodoropoulou, S. and Watt, A. (2012) 'How do economic governance reforms and austerity measures affect inclusive growth as formulated in the Europe 2020 strategy?', in Lehndorf, S. (ed.) *A Triumph of Failed Ideas: European Models of Capitalism in the Crisis*. Brussels: ETUI.

Levinson, C. (1972) *International Trade Unionism*, London: Allen & Unwin.

Meardi, G. (2011) *Social Failures of EU Enlargement: A Case of Workers Voting with Their Feet*. London: Routledge.

Migration Advisory Committee (2014) Migrants in low-skilled work – the growth of EU and non-EU labour in low-skilled jobs and its impact on the UK, [online] Available at: https://www.gov.uk/government/organisations/migration-advisory-committee (accessed 1 November 2015).

Müller, T., Platzer, H.P. and Rüb, S. (2013) *Transnational Company Agreements and the Role of European Works Councils in Negotiations: A Quantitative Analysis in the Metalworking Sector*. Report 127, Brussels: European Trade Union Institute.

Pochet, P., Léonard, E., Perin, E., and Peeters, A. (2009) *Dynamics of the European Sectoral Social Dialogue*. Luxembourg: Office for Official Publications of the European Communities.

Rowthorn, R. (2014) *Large-scale Immigration: Its Economic and Demographic Consequences for the UK*. London: Civitas.

Scharpf, F.W. (2011) 'Monetary union, fiscal crisis and the pre-emption of democracy', *Zeitschrift für Staats- und Europawissenschaften*, 2, 163–198.

Smith, M. and Venables, A. (1988) 'Completing the internal market in the European Community: some industry simulations', *European Economic Review*, 32, 1501–1525.

Teague, P. (1989) *The European Community: The Social Dimension*. London: Kogan Page.

Teague, P. (2001) 'Deliberative governance and EU social policy', *European Journal of Employment Relations*, 7(1), 7–26.

Thelen, K. (2014) *Varieties of Liberalization: The New Politics of Social Solidarity*. New York: Cambridge University Press.

Weiler, J.H.H. (1991) 'The transformation of Europe', *The Yale Law Journal*, 100, 2403–2483.

Welz, C. (2008) *The European Social Dialogue under Articles 138 and 139 of the EC Treaty: Actors, Processes, Outcomes*. Alphen aan den Rijn: Kluwer Law International.

Zeitlin, J. and Sabel, C. (2010) 'Learning from difference: the new architecture of experimentalist governance in the EU', in Sabel, C. and Zeitlin, J. (eds) *Experimentalist Governance in the European Union: Towards a New Architecture*. Oxford: Oxford University Press.

Zeitlin, J. and Vanhercke, B. (2014) *Socializing the European Semester? Economic Governance and Social Policy Coordination in Europe 2020*, Watson Institute for International Studies Research Paper No. 2014–2017.

4 Mediterranean HRM: Key Trends and Challenges

ELENI T. STAVROU AND NANCY PAPALEXANDRIS

Much of the industrialized world entered a deep recession that began in 2008 as the financial crisis in the USA evolved to a global recession with multiple economic, employment and social implications. Despite measures taken by governments worldwide, unemployment, poverty, inflation and national debts rose in an unprecedented manner (Eurostat, 2009; World Bank, 2009). Southern European countries, such as Greece, Cyprus, Italy, Spain and Portugal, have been affected the most. As a result, the European Union (EU) reacted with harsh anti-crisis austerity policies, creating growing unemployment, falling real wages, cuts in the social security system, erosion of the collective agreement system and privatization of public property (Busch et al., 2013).

In this context, we explore which major HRM-related institutional and organizational challenges are prevalent in Southern Europe and identify possible HRM practices and efforts that may help mitigate or overcome the most negative outcomes or even act as protecting shields for people and organizations. We offer a special account of the situation in two of the countries emerging from a severe economic crisis: Greece and Cyprus, with emphasis on HRM issues. Finally the role of HRM in fighting crisis and HRM challenges for Southern European countries will be discussed.

HRM Institutional Challenges

Institutional theories have received considerable attention by academics as useful frameworks to explore and explain how organizations are influenced by their external environments (Barringer and Milkovich,

1998; Meyer and Rowan, 1977; Wood *et al.*, 2014). Specifically, DiMaggio and Powell (1983) argued that organizations adopt various practices to conform to their institutional environment and to gain resources, such as legitimacy, reputation and talented employees. Further, Baron (1995) and Kassinis and Stavrou (2013) suggested that a high degree of interdependence exists between a firm's competitive environment and national context. To illustrate, according to the OECD (2001), firms in countries with the highest levels of national support tend to rely almost entirely on that support, adding relatively little of their own resources to it. And Griffin and Dunn (2004) reported that organizations tend to develop similar structures and procedures in response to similar institutional pressures: for example, those subject to the same laws, policies and regulations adopt similar ways.

In this respect, Aysan (2009) considers it appropriate to classify the South European countries as a separate institutional welfare cluster. In a similar fashion, Amable (2003) refers to the 'Mediterranean' countries of Italy, Greece, Spain and Portugal, as a separate form of capitalism from the other forms in Europe. He explains that in this cluster employment protection is high but social protection moderate. Indeed, Southern European countries share certain characteristics, including their welfare and political systems as well as their bureaucracies (Kickert, 2011).

Specifically, in Southern Europe, welfare largely consists of social insurance for old age and special provisions for particular occupational groups such as civil servants. In addition, national health systems are the norm in the South. The state has low administrative capacities (Ferrera, 2011); public spending as a percentage of GDP is relatively low; and half of this spending is for pensions – which are now being privatized due to high budget deficits (Aysan, 2009). An irregular and underground economy is dominant (Ferrera, 2011). The family was the most important 'pillar' in managing social risks in the Southern European countries, by taking care of child care, unemployment assistance, care for the elderly and disabled, and housing. But it is slowly losing its power. Specifically, unpaid family labour is very common for women, providing childcare, elderly care, health care and other services (Aysan, 2009). On top of these, a significant decline in fertility rates presents new social and economic challenges.

In a nutshell, the South lacks a social assistance system against poverty, with little social safety net for the long-term unemployed, for newcomers to the labour market, for workers in the black economy or for new immigrants (Ferrera, 2011). According to the Third European Quality of Life Survey (Eurofound, 2012a), perceived social exclusion is highest in Europe among people in Cyprus and Greece. Further, trust in public institutions is lowest in Greece and optimism about the future is expressed by less than 30 per cent of people in Greece and Portugal. Finally, it seems that the South has very much suffered over the years through large-scale corruption, misuse of public funds and haphazard, high-level decisions servicing only the few in society.

To illustrate, in Portugal, according to local reports (Diário de Notícias, 2011, 2012), the crisis was worse because state funds were mismanaged, generating debt creation and head officer compensation was inflated for a very long period of time leading up to the 2010 crisis. Furthermore, recruitment policies consistently boosted the number of public servants beyond the requisite.

The main exacerbating cause of Spain's crisis seems to have been its enormous housing bubble, along with an artificial and unsustainably high GDP growth rate (Hidalgo, 2012). Furthermore, Spain has a very high secondary labour market of fixed-term contracts, implying negative spill overs of human capital investment and labour mobility. The country basically has a two-tiered employment system, where privileged employees are permanent and receive wage increases and where unprivileged ones are easily replaceable (*The Economist*, 2009).

In Greece, the financial crisis seems to be the result of a combination of structural weaknesses in the system, along with very high long-term structural deficits and debt versus GDP levels on the public accounts. The Greek economy deteriorated, with sharp contractions of GDP reaching 20 per cent between the end of 2007 and 2009. Since the start of the crisis, poverty rates have increased to record levels. By the end of 2009, the Greek economy faced its most severe debt crisis. This was due to the fact that Greece, like many other European countries, was borrowing money beyond its means. In 2010 Greece's ability to repay its sovereign debt was questioned and high borrowing rates effectively prohibited access to the financial markets. In May 2010, the International Monetary Fund, the European Commission and the European Central Bank ('The Troika') agreed to a rescue package. To secure this funding Greece was required to adopt harsh austerity measures and reforms to bring its deficit under control. In 2014 a small GDP growth was evident due to the austerity measures and the growth in the tourist sector. The current Greek government, elected in January 2015, came to power after declaring that it would stop austerity measures and negotiate new terms with 'The Troika', placing the economy at a standstill and awaiting reforms and further agreements with lenders.

In a similar fashion, the Cypriot economy entered a recession in late 2009, as the economy shrank by 1.67 per cent. By 2012, the public debt rose to 80 per cent of GDP and in June of that year, Cyprus became the fifth country of the Eurozone (after Greece, Ireland, Portugal and Spain) to request financial aid from 'The Troika' in an effort to recapitalize its largest banks as well as its public sector. In order for Cyprus to get financial assistance, harsh measures were imposed by the lenders: uninsured deposits over 100,000 euros at the second largest Cypriot bank (Laiki), which practically closed down, were lost while those at the largest Cypriot bank (BoC) were cut by 47.5 per cent. Since then, hardship has become part of the landscape where approximately 5.7 per cent of the adult population on the island is dependent on municipal food banks or other charities for food.

Unemployment

Several countries across Europe have experienced persistent problems with unemployment since the start of the financial crisis. However, the grimmest situation lies in the South. According to the Third European Quality of Life Survey (Eurofound, 2012a) an increasing sense of pessimism about jobs is seen in the South, especially in Cyprus and Greece.

Furthermore, while Southern EU countries have very high unemployment rates for the general population, their youth unemployment rates are unprecedentedly high. These levels are partly attributed to their being considered as 'rigid' labour markets, where employers are reluctant to hire because of high hiring costs or difficulty in dismissal stemming from high rates of unionization or universal statutory severance payments. Especially for the young, this rigidity is detrimental as, even though they may be more qualified than the older generations of workers, those who entered the labour market during the period of growth between the 1960s and 1990s are protected as 'insiders', making it harder for new entrants to get in. As an example, Spain's youth is considered the most educated ever in the country, yet it faces among the greatest rates of unemployment in Europe.

To combat the general unemployment problem, one approach suggested by Afonso (2013) is for governments to increase employment while keeping a cap on public expenditure – namely, mass deregulation to hire workers at the bottom of the labour market. A second approach involves a substantial enlargement of the public sector to provide a wide variety of social services funded by higher levels of taxes. And a third approach is the extensive use of part-time employment and robust systems of job-related skills, stimulating wages in the bottom of the labour market.

In the case of Greece, the unemployment rate was 26.8 per cent in 2014, reaching 55.3 per cent for people below the age of 24. The main challenge for the Greek economy at present is to increase job creation and protect the most vulnerable part of its population. Some of the following are needed (Karantinos, 2014): a reform in unemployment benefits, which have been reduced; control of undeclared work, which is estimated at 24 per cent of GDP in 2012 and which deprives employees of their legal social security benefits; and active labour market measures such as job-search assistance, counselling, employment, subsidies, aid for self-employment and re-training.

In Cyprus, the overall unemployment rate rose from 3.9 per cent in 2007 to 16.4 per cent in 2014, while that for youth reached 42.3 per cent. As in Greece, among the major challenges in Cyprus is to increase employment through measures taken by the government and the Cyprus Human Resource Development Authority. At the same time, the government must try to reduce emigration among the highly educated Cypriots, who are leaving the country for better job opportunities and salaries abroad.

In Spain, the unemployment rate reached 24.4 per cent by March 2012, a rate twice the Eurozone average (House and Roman, 2012), while unemployment for those under 25 is nominally 50 per cent. Furthermore, over 65 per cent of youth are willing to leave the country in order to find employment. At least, given Spain's reliance on international family ties, as in the rest of Southern Europe, family businesses can provide some employment support to their family members (Galloni, 2012).

Work–Life Balance

The financial crisis and its aftermath have also exacerbated the earlier gendered and sectoral patterns of work–life conflict in Southern Europe. This happened because the participation of women in the labour market in Southern Europe, particularly in the paid service sector, has increased over the last decades, bringing changes to family structures (Aysan, 2009). Poor childcare, combined with a strong 'male breadwinner' model and the loosening of family structures, made work–life balance for parents, especially women, in Southern Europe even more difficult during the crisis.

The Third European Quality of Life Survey (Eurofound, 2012a) ranks Cyprus first in having more than 10 per cent of workers report finding it 'difficult to concentrate at work because of my family responsibilities'. Disruptions at home and doing household jobs are relatively common and reported most frequently in Cyprus, Malta and Spain. Problems fulfilling family responsibilities 'because of the amount of time I spend on the job' were reported 'several times a week' by more than 20 per cent of workers in Cyprus and Greece.

According to the same survey (Eurofound, 2012a), workers were most likely to report job insecurity and negative effects of work on family and home life in Cyprus and Greece than anywhere else, reflecting the economic crisis and their perceptions of the likelihood of them holding onto their jobs. Interestingly, these were also the two countries in which the proportion seeing high tension between men and women exceeds the European average of 10 per cent (Cyprus, 30 per cent; Greece, 18 per cent). Furthermore, these were also countries in which work–life balance was particularly poor diachronically.

Migration

People have always emigrated for better job or career opportunities. With the financial crisis, this behaviour is even more common and measures are being taken to curtail it, especially in Southern Europe where migration from within but also from outside Europe has always been a problem (Kasimis, 2012).

To illustrate, the two largest labour importers in Southern Europe, namely Italy and Spain, have both reacted to the crisis with temporary decisions to severely decrease employment from abroad for non-seasonal, low- and medium-skilled occupations (Pastore, 2010). As a result, a substantial amount of illegal immigration to the European Union flows through the Greek borders, which are hard to control due to the extensive sea front in the east and the long mountainous frontiers in the north. Specifically, 90 per cent of all arrests for unauthorized entry into the European Union took place in Greece in 2010, compared to 75 per cent in 2009 and 50 per cent in 2008. Unfortunately, Greece has not managed to design satisfactory and operational policies for both the regularization of unauthorized immigrants already in the country and legal ways of entry for skilled immigrants that the country needs to attract (Kasimis, 2012).

At the same time, the number of migrants from Southern Europe moving to other EU states, such as Germany and the UK, rose by approximately 45 per cent (Hamel, 2013). Quite often these migrants are educated and highly qualified. Therefore, given that the German labour market faces skill shortages, it accommodates migrant workers with jobs that could not otherwise be filled. Furthermore, many universities, as well as the financial services industry in the UK, rely heavily on EU migrant employees (Chase and Seeleib-Kaiser, 2014).

Matching Skills with Jobs

One of Europe's main challenges today and in the years to come is not just to improve skills, but to match the people with the right skills to the jobs available. One out of three European employees today is either over- or under-qualified, with the mismatch especially high in Southern Europe. Specifically, in these countries the high-mismatch group exhibiting over-qualification rates is more than 20 per cent. Reasons involve lower than EU average levels of public investment in education and training, lower expenditure on labour market programmes and more rigid and segmented labour markets. The qualification mismatch affects mainly younger male workers on non-standard contracts. Generally, young people and immigrants suffer more from over-qualification, while ageing workers are more susceptible to skills obsolescence (European Commission, 2013).

Crisis Induced Institutional Changes

According to the Third European Quality of Life Survey (Eurofound, 2012a), the crisis brought about a variety of tensions among various societal groups. Among those affected, the most dramatic general increase was found in Cyprus, where the rate of those reporting high tension between rich and poor increased by 29 per cent from previous surveys, between management and workers by 27 per cent, and by 24 per cent between racial and ethnic groups. In addition to the case of Cyprus, the perception of racial and ethnic tensions rose significantly in Greece (by 11 per cent) as well. Furthermore, perceived tensions between the young and the old are highest in Cyprus among 24 per cent of the population.

Ageing and Delayed Retirements

Studies show that after the crisis began, an emerging trend towards delayed retirements not only continued but accelerated (Burtless and Bosworth, 2013). Furthermore, these trends toward later retirement and higher participation rates in old age, which are much slower in Southern Europe compared with the rest of Europe, are most prevalent among men.

According to Aysan (2009), Southern Europe will become, by the year 2040, the oldest population in Europe. Nevertheless, these countries have particularly low labour force participation rates for men and especially women aged 55–64, reflecting not only policies for early retirement, but broader labour market and social policies. The pension eligibility age in this group is among the lowest in

OECD countries. These rates also reflect the importance placed on families for social security, and thus on women having caring rather than labour force roles.

The first reform undertaken in Southern Europe, to improve financial sustainability and cost containment and to rationalize the pension system in which life expectancy has been increased over time, was raising pension eligibility ages. Hence, raising the age at eligibility became the most common feature of pension reform packages in Southern European countries.

HRM Organizational Challenges

The aforementioned institutional challenges affect organizations and their wellbeing. In turn, organizations are called to address them in many different ways in order to survive. One way is through their human resource management (HRM) policies and practices. According to Zagelmeyer and Gollan (2012), the global financial crisis is an external shock wave which has modified the parameters within which HRM professionals need to operate at all levels. On the one hand the crisis has affected the way employees are managed within organizations and on the other, the way employees are managed can have an important impact on how the issues related to the crisis are addressed.

In this chapter we review a number of such HRM policies and practices that, on the one hand, are affected by the current financial crisis and, on the other, could help organizations alleviate their negative effects. Economic and financial crises reduce labour demand significantly and place pressures on organizations to reduce labour costs (Gunnigle et al., 2013: 216). These include reductions in pay (freezes/cuts; reduced bonuses/variable pay allocations), reductions or controls on headcount (redundancies; recruitment freezes; use of atypical labour), changes in performance management systems, more targeted training (i.e. greater focus on multi-skilling; shift from external to in-house and on-the-job training) and the undermining of trade unions.

Pay

It is well documented that, given the global financial crisis, organizations of all sorts are making changes to both pay – where the bulk of firms have frozen or cut pay – and benefit structures, particularly pension plans and profit-sharing schemes (Gunnigle et al., 2013). To illustrate, a Hay Group (2009) study stated that companies are changing their compensation and benefit schemes, while also reviewing their performance management system. Furthermore, Busch *et al.* (2013) report that Southern European countries have introduced reforms that significantly confine spending growth in pension systems, resulting in a dramatic fall of relative pension levels in these countries by the year 2040, measured in terms of the wage replacement rate.

According to Eurofound (2012b), during the financial crisis and particularly among vulnerable groups (low-skilled, young, migrants), wages have been reduced in most of the EU countries along with wage deceleration and pay freezes. These reductions and freezes were particularly felt in Southern Europe, starting in the public sector and subsequently spilling over to the private sector. According to Busch *et al.* (2013) the severest cuts totalling around 30 per cent were implemented in the Greek public sector and the most radical consecutive minimum wage cut in the Greek private sector. Overall, the wage decrease in Southern Europe during the period of 2010–2012 has been 2.5 per cent in Italy, 6 per cent in Spain, 8 per cent in Cyprus, 4.5 per cent in Malta, 10 per cent in Portugal and 20 per cent in Greece (Busch *et al.*, 2013).

Wage subsidies have been proposed to boost employment and avoid the devaluation of skills connected to both unemployment and informal work. For example, wage subsidies that are employer-based can cost less and have a larger social impact if targeted to lower paid employees. Governmental employee-based subsidies can also be targeted to vulnerable groups and connected with other active labour market programs.

In addition to basic wages, a number of changes have been reported in terms of variable pay where the higher compensation seen in higher-ranking jobs was reduced through cuts in bonuses and other rewards. This, however, has not always been the case. As shown in Table 4.1, data from the international CRANET reports (2006, 2011) show that organizations in various European countries have reacted in different ways to the crisis in respect to different forms of variable pay. Even in Southern European countries, such as Greece, Cyprus and Italy for example, the situation is not uniform or the trend between 2006 and 2011 one-directional.

Staffing

Given the dire economic conditions of the crisis, Southern European countries saw a dramatic decline in the level of recruitment and selection and a concurrent growth in initiatives to adjust staffing levels

Table 4.1 Proportion of organizations with various types of financial participation and performance related pay per country

| | Financial Participation (Only Private Sector), (%) | | | | | | Performance Related Pay (Private and (Semi-)Public Sectors), (%) | | | |
| | Share Plan | | Options | | Profit Sharing | | Bonus Based on Individual Goals | | Bonus Based on Team Goals | |
	2011	2006	2011	2006	2011	2006	2011	2006	2011	2006
Southern EU										
Greece	26	27	30	32	19	18	81	72	49	52
Cyprus	10	15	2	13	22	15	25	25	19	13
Italy	25	24	34	38	14	15	87	84	78	58
Central–Western EU										
Austria	13	13	13	19	65	65	67	54	37	34
Germany	17	18	25	16	71	83	76	66	45	34
Belgium	37	29	46	25	36	24	73	61	59	32
France	22	33	10	29	79	93	44	77	22	46
United Kingdom	32	34	23	29	19	29	30	37	35	21

Nordic EU

Netherlands	27	21	24	26	59	54	72	45	55	21
Finland	23	12	16	28	80	88	71	38	55	31
Denmark	25	56	18	24	13	16	62	55	58	36
Sweden	16	15	11	19	22	37	79	30	44	30
Central–Eastern EU										
Estonia	10	21	10	10	17	34	61	64	48	56
Bulgaria	17	28	13	28	23	38	59	67	50	45
Hungary	30	23	26	26	4	29	73	59	60	41
Slovakia	31	19	10	10	20	49	62	72	41	58
Slovenia	16	22	9	10	35	38	64	85	55	54

downwards in line with the economic situation of organizations. These adjustments often involved, among others, voluntary or mandatory redundancies, recruitment freezes, early retirement options, outsourcing and non-renewal of contracts. Table 4.2 shows information from the international CRANET report (2011) showing the most common types of staffing adjustments. In Cyprus, the most common types are voluntary redundancies and internal transfers (redeployment), while in Greece and Italy it is recruitment freezes.

Furthermore, other forms of staffing such as temporary and part-time employment have been increasing (Eurofound, 2012b). This change has often been promoted by changes in national legislation. For example, as part of the First Memorandum policies in Greece the maximum period for temporary employment contracts was extended from 18 to 36 months while the renewal period was extended from two to three years. Specifically in the south of the EU, during the period 2011–12, temporary employment grew in Malta, Cyprus and Italy, while it decreased in Greece and Spain after having increased in previous years. In contrast, during the same period, part-time employment grew in Cyprus, Greece, Spain and Malta while it decreased in Italy (Eurofound, 2013). To illustrate, the share of full-time contracts in the labour market in Greece fell from 66.9 per cent in 2010 to 55 per cent in 2012 (Stamati, 2013). Nevertheless, since 2008 the increase in involuntary part-time employment has been particularly high in all these countries, with the exception of Malta.

Training and Development

According to Hart and Sundelius (2013), training is pivotal during times of crisis: as major crises are rare but far-reaching, everyone within organizations needs to be educated, tested and challenged on a regular and frequent basis. Yet, during crises, training budgets often shrink in size in order for organizations to cope with diminished resources (Gunnigle et al., 2013). Eurofound (2013) reports the lowest levels of participation in training to be found in Southern and Eastern Europe.

Data from the international CRANET reports (2006, 2011) show mixed results (Table 4.3). While training days per year, per employee generally show a decrease, we also see cases where an increase is noted, particularly among managerial and professional/technical personnel. Greece in particular shows this increase in training for higher rank employees. This might be due to the efforts towards reorganization that companies are undertaking in order to meet competition as well as to the reduction in the number of employees, which requires multi-tasking and extra skills among the remaining ones.

Table 4.2 Proportion of organizations with various types of staffing adjustments

	Recruitment Freeze (%)	Early Retirement (%)	Voluntary Redundancy (%)	Compulsory Redundancy (%)	Internal Transfer (%)	No Renewal of Contracts (%)	Outsourcing (%)
Southern EU							
Greece	76.3	46.9	41.3	43.2	65.0	67.5	38.3
Cyprus	66.7	50.0	77.8	62.5	77.8	42.9	50.0
Italy	93.2	71.6	90.3	50.0	85.5	88.7	39.1
Central–Western EU							
Austria	90.0	56.8	51.3	41.0	71.1	76.3	51.4
Germany	86.0	83.9	87.7	51.0	78.7	94.9	46.5
Belgium	89.5	83.7	79.1	73.2	81.4	80.5	64.3
France	93.3	80.0	73.3	26.7	100	100	40.0
United Kingdom	50.0	61.5	75.0	53.8	60.0	75.0	53.8
Nordic EU							
Netherlands	71.8	53.8	69.2	59.0	46.2	76.9	33.3
Denmark	72.5	45.1	61.8	76.5	80.4	58.8	30.4
Finland	81.3	63.8	63.8	34.0	97.8	93.6	86.0
Sweden	66.7	33.3	100.0	77.8	60.0	66.7	50.0

(continued)

Table 4.2 (continued)

	Recruitment Freeze (%)	Early Retirement (%)	Voluntary Redundancy (%)	Compulsory Redundancy (%)	Internal Transfer (%)	No Renewal of Contracts (%)	Outsourcing (%)
			Central–Eastern EU				
Estonia	70.2	70.6	14.3	84.6	30.8	63.0	63.5
Bulgaria	56.8	89.2	80.5	44.7	73.7	48.8	34.2
Czech Republic	88.2	81.3	100.0	100.0	93.8	87.5	13.3
Hungary	85.0	60.0	65.0	90.5	73.9	63.6	50.0
Slovenia							
Slovakia	89.6	40.4	75.0	92.0	92.2	86.7	30.8

The situation as painted in Table 4.3 is similar in the Eurostat database for persons aged 25 to 64 who stated that they received education or training. In Figure 4.1 below, comparison information for years 2006 and 2013 is provided among the percentage of people who received training.

Given these data, one may conclude that, at least in Southern Europe, training is not necessarily reduced as a result of the financial crisis even if budgets are indeed reduced. Training may be people's ticket to self-enhancement during bad financial conditions or possibly their way out of unfortunate situations (via prospective unemployment, for example) when opportunity knocks.

Employment Relations

In this environment of terrible financial conditions, the bargaining power of unions and employees decreases. Gunnigle *et al.* (2013) report

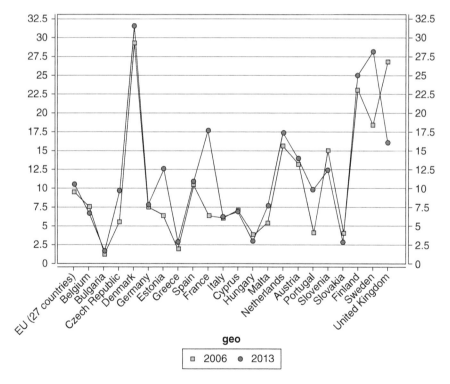

Figure 4.1 Percentage of people receiving training in Europe

Table 4.3 Training in Europe

| Country | Training Days Per Year Per Employee | | | | | | | | Training Cost (%) | |
| | Manual | | Clerical | | Professional/Technical | | Management | | | |
	2011	2006	2011	2006	2011	2006	2011	2006	2011	2006
European Union (EU) Average	4.14	3.67	4.71	4.14	7.88	6.22	7.20	6.24	3.72	2.99
					Southern EU					
Greece	4.32	6.46	5.24	6.10	11.74	9.47	8.00	7.74	3.75	4.02
Cyprus	3.39	3.12	5.20	4.29	9.98	7.04	6.98	7.29	4.26	1.46
Italy	2.56	3.42	4.50	4.86	4.82	6.39	4.58	5.23	2.89	3.48
					Central–Western EU					
United Kingdom	2.80	4.05	3.07	3.68	5.23	5.54	4.44	5.13	3.02	3.45
Austria	2.69	2.91	4.32	3.70	5.03	5.05	6.24	5.88	2.42	2.60
Belgium	3.21	2.96	3.40	3.07	5.89	5.17	5.44	5.90	3.65	2.85
France	3.81	3.54	4.73	3.45	4.34	4.17	4.32	4.44	2.83	3.32
Germany	2.21	2.33	3.88	2.92	6.76	3.86	7.74	4.85	3.56	2.26

				Nordic EU						
Netherlands	4.58	4.58	3.38	3.48	5.62	5.75	6.10	5.02	4.11	3.09
Finland	4.03	3.23	5.20	4.55	6.51	6.37	6.76	6.93	3.85	2.96
Denmark	4.26	4.06	4.56	4.04	5.77	6.11	6.44	6.47	2.83	3.13
Sweden	3.52	3.91	4.23	4.86	5.35	6.84	5.65	6.62	4.56	4.04
				Central–Eastern EU						
Bulgaria	7.90	9.66	5.75	6.39	10.90	9.93	7.62	10.65	3.92	6.32
Czech Republic	3.56	3.21	5.35	3.67	8.00	8.00	8.15	7.98	2.04	2.58
Estonia	5.11	4.39	6.78	5.88	13.10	7.65	12.66	8.11	5.51	3.55
Hungary	1.98	3.62	3.53	3.80	6.63	5.86	6.81	5.75	4.12	3.65
Slovakia	5.50	1.75	7.10	4.21	10.45	4.94	10.11	6.10	4.83	2.19
Slovenia	6.25	2.75	3.89	2.71	10.45	6.50	7.97	6.72	3.55	2.82

that firms that may have wished for some time to terminate or alter the employment relationship or conditions are now better able to do so under the excuse of recession, even though their motives are not necessarily always recession grounded.

Furthermore, Busch *et al.* (2013) explain that the EU's new policies attempt to transform national collective agreement systems towards much more strongly enterprise-oriented negotiating structures. This attempt will have particularly adverse effects in various HRM-related matters such as the wage structures in Southern Europe, where the majority of firms are small or medium in size. To illustrate, in Greece and Portugal initiatives to change national collective agreement systems are an integral part of the joint memoranda with 'The Troika'. Specifically, in Greece laws were passed in 2010 and 2011 that made radical changes to employment relationships and aimed at increasing labour market flexibility and minimizing labour costs (Karantinos, 2011). Similarly, in Italy and Spain the European Central Bank has pushed strongly for reforms of collective agreement systems, using the purchase of government bonds as political collateral.

According to Eurofound (2013), a decline in union density is reported in a number of European countries including Cyprus, Greece and Spain, while an increase is reported in membership of employer's associations, including in Cyprus and Greece. The same source reports a high increase in labour disputes in countries such as Cyprus, Spain, Italy, Greece and Portugal. To illustrate (Eurofound 2013: 50–51), a total of 56 strikes were reported in Cyprus resulting in 48,294 working days lost in 2012, compared with 42 strikes and 25,305 working days lost in 2011. And in Spain, 608 out of a total of 641 strikes were recorded up to October 2012 as due to labour disputes. Moreover, 495 of these strikes were called for reasons not related to collective bargaining but other reasons such as dismissals or cut-backs. During November 2012, workers in the telecommunications company Telefónica (Barcelona) held a hunger strike, protesting against unfair dismissals. On 31 December 2012, workers at Roca, a ceramic sanitary-ware manufacturer, carried out a sit-in demonstration in the cathedral in Alcalá de Guadaría, Seville, where the enterprise is located. Finally, Psychogios *et al.* (2014) note that, partly due to the crisis, substantial deregulation has been taking place in the Industrial Relations (IR) systems as well as a rapid deconstruction of the IR systems in both Greece and Cyprus.

Data from the international CRANET survey report (2011) in Table 4.4 support the overall decrease in trade union influence at least in Southern Europe, but also in other parts of the European Union (for example, see the change in trade union influence in France).

Table 4.4 Trade union influence in Europe

Country	Change in Trade Union Influence during Past Three Years (2011), (%)		
	Decreased	Same	Increased
Southern Europe EU			
Greece	19.9	66.7	13.5
Cyprus	17.6	63.5	18.9
Italy	20.5	62.9	16.6
Central-Western EU			
Austria	15.7	74.1	10.3
Belgium	7.8	72.6	19.6
France	79.4	17.5	3.2
Germany	11.7	74.5	13.8
United Kingdom	23.6	70.0	6.4
Nordic EU			
Netherlands	21.1	72.2	6.7
Finalnd	9.7	74.2	16.1
Sweden	16.3	76.8	6.9
Denmark	22.2	69.2	8.6
Central-Eastern EU			
Bulgaria	20.8	71.7	7.5
Czech Republic	13.0	73.9	13.0
Estonia	13.5	75.7	10.8
Hungary	7.4	90.5	2.1
Slovakia	17.4	76.8	5.8
Slovenia	13.8	71.8	14.4

Integration of Institutional and Organizational HRM Challenges

Research has shown that when the appropriate human resource management (HRM) strategies have been formulated and implemented successfully, then sustainable competitive advantage can be achieved even in the most dynamic and complex environments. Nordic Europe has proved that. The appropriate HRM strategies will probably differ from environment to environment, but the desired result can be reached. And of course, the word 'environments' entails many important parameters such as financial, cultural, institutional, economic and policy among others, at both the organizational and the larger national or supra-national levels.

As became evident from the crisis, the appropriate human resource management strategies at these different levels of context have not been formulated or implemented in Southern Europe over the past decades. Otherwise, these economies, their cultures and their institutions – organizational and others – would not suffer such dire negative consequences. Examining the various HRM-related issues discussed in this chapter, some actions have been taken recently while many more remain be taken.

At the supra-organizational level, and to a large extent due to direct pressures from the EU, HRM-related efforts have intensified to: curb unemployment through the creation of jobs; improve people's living conditions and keep them employed through wage subsidies and the promotion of atypical forms of employment; improve migration policies; match skills with jobs; and introduce reforms in performance management systems, pay and benefits.

At the organizational level, the current crisis has highlighted once again the importance of integrated strategic planning in which HRM should actively participate by knowing the capacities of its organization so that it can propose realistic HRM-related strategies. Given the crisis, HRM professionals in the organizations surviving the crisis so far have had the dual task of increasing productivity while cutting costs. Instead of hiring, retaining and promoting, many HRM professionals have been forced to change structures, cut benefits, dismiss employees and reduce days of work. The overall workload and burden to HRM departments/functions has been very heavy.

In Greece at present the general impressions are that, at least among larger companies, HRM professionals have taken the necessary steps and have introduced ways to increase performance and sustain employee morale. In this context, the notion of sustainability has been widely discussed and the role of HRM in contributing to business sustainability through employees has been promoted. Furthermore, employee morale can be kept strong with better team work, concern for those in need and involvement in company matters. Some examples showing efforts for facing the situation are the following:

- Out-placement and in-placement programmes to help redundant employees.
- Interventions to assist employees in facing the 'survivors' syndrome' following firing of their colleagues.

- Career development or counselling programmes for young employees and trainee schemes for young graduates who wish to acquire some business experience or start their own small business.
- Employee assistance programmes offering advice on family, social and legal matters.
- Corporate social responsibility programmes aiming at underprivileged members of the company and their families.
- Opportunities for employees to act as volunteers in projects of their choice, during company time, in order to help the local community or the environment.
- Finally, better employee communication and opportunities for employees to get involved in company problems, offer their suggestions and propose innovative ways for handling the existing crisis.

In Cyprus, the practice of requisite HRM is a bit more challenging. Besides the very large public sector, the majority of private firms are very small in size and hardly practice HRM formally other than to the extent that is absolutely essential. Organizations with at least 100 employees, including the wider public sector, are fewer than 300 in number. In this respect, according to a recent forum of the Cyprus Human Resource Management Association (2013), HRM professionals or those practicing HRM within organizations have been generally excluded from strategic decisions related to the crisis within their respective organizations. Nevertheless, they expressed the need for HRM to attempt the following steps in helping to combat the negative effects of the crisis on both employees and organizations alike:

- Get to know the company they work for very well, as well as its workforce and operations.
- Focus on alternative ways of employment, organization and personnel management, such as: part-time jobs, reduction of working hours, job sharing, or work from home.
- Redesign the payroll system and various benefits and make the necessary adjustments before implementing salary reductions.
- Redesign employee performance evaluation in order to boost productivity and performance. This is especially important for the wider public sector where performance evaluations have minimal value due to the way the system works.
- Implement a comprehensive policy to deal with low performers.
- Invest in, rather than cut, training.
- Maintain closer collaboration with other internal departments such as the Risk Management Department, which could assist in forecasting possible dangers considered to be a threat for the company. HRM can then use this information to prepare the organization for future challenges.

- Make coherent proposals at all levels, aimed at identifying necessary skills and capacities, placing the right people with the right skills to the right place and thus reducing expenses.
- Encourage and build a corporate culture that will enable employees to innovate every day across the organization.

Key Learning Points

If any lessons are to be learned for organizations from the crisis so far, then we highlight the following three. First, effective performance management of employees must have a central role in the change process across functions and titles. Second, boosting productivity without increasing costs could be made possible with a combination of employee training and development programmes as well as improvements in the ways in which HRM is conducted. Finally, it is paramount that the HRM function within any type of organization practices effective communication, both internally with employees and externally with union representatives and other stakeholders. For maximum efficiency, the HRM function has to communicate before, during and after any changes take place. By understanding how best to communicate, organizations during a crisis can learn how to increase motivation and commitment, which will help them survive and prosper in the long run.

For governments and related institutions such as unions or employers organizations in the south of Europe, the most important lesson to be learned should be requisite HRM for all stakeholders, formulated and implemented with justice, fairness and transparency. Otherwise, the 'lion' that roamed around before 'The Troika' set foot in the South will re-surface from its cave stronger and mightier once 'The Troika' leaves.

References

Afonso, A. (2013) *Southern Europe Should Consider an Economic 'Third Way' to Tackle Unemployment and Inequality*. London School of Economics and Political Science. Available at: http://blogs.lse.ac.uk/europpblog/2013/12/12/southern-europe-should-consider-an-economic-third-way-to-tackle-unemployment-and-inequality (accessed 1 November 2015).

Amable, B. (2003) *The Diversity of Modern Capitalism*. Oxford: Oxford University Press.

Aysan, M.F. (2009) 'Welfare Regimes for Ageing Populations: Divergence or Convergence?' *The 26th International Population Conference IUSSP*. Marrakech, Morocco, 2 October 2009.

Baron, D.P. (1995) 'Integrated Strategy: Market and Non-market Components', *California Management Review*, 37, 47–65.

Barringer, M.W. and Milkovich, G.T. (1998) 'A Theoretical Exploration of the Adoption and Design of Flexible Benefit Plans: A Case of Human Resource Innovation', *Academy of Management Review*, 23, 305–324.

Burtless, G. and Bosworth, B.P. (2013) *Impact of the Great Recession on Retirement Trends in Industrialized Countries.* Center for Retirement Research at Boston College, Boston, USA.

Busch, K., Hermann, C., Hinrichs, K. and Schulten, T. (2013) *Euro Crisis, Austerity Policy and the European Social Model: How Crisis Policies in Southern Europe Threaten the EU's Social Dimension.* Friedrich-Ebert-Stiftung International Policy Analysis, Berlin, Germany.

Chase, E. and Seeleib-Kaiser, M. (2014) 'Migration, EU Citizenship, and Social Europe', *Social Europe Journal.* Available at: http://www.social-europe. eu/2014/01/eu-citizenship-social-europe/ (accessed 1 November 2015).

CRANET (2006) *Comparative Human Resource Management: International Executive Report 2005.*

CRANET (2011) *Comparative Human Resource Management: International Executive Report 2011.*

CyHRMA (2013) RTD: *Cyprus in Crisis: HR Coping Mechanisms.* Nicosia, Cyprus.

Diário de Notícias (2 March 2011, 2012) 'O estado a que o Estado chegou' no 2.° lugar do top. Available at: http://en.wikipedia.org/wiki/European_debt_crisis (accessed 1 November 2015).

DiMaggio, P.J. and Powell, W.W. (1983) 'The Iron Cage Revisited: Institutional Isomorphism and Collective Rationality in Organizational Fields', *American Sociological Review*, 48, 147–160.

Eurofound (2012a) *Third European Quality of Life Survey – Quality of Life in Europe: Impacts of the Crisis.* Publications Office of the European Union, Luxembourg.

Eurofound. (2012b) *Industrial Relations and Working Conditions Developments in Europe 2012.* Publications Office of the European Union, Luxembourg.

Eurofound (2013) *Women, Men and Working Conditions in Europe.* Publications Office of the European Union, Luxembourg.

European Commision (2013) *Employment and Social Developments in Europe 2012.* Commission Staff Working Document. VIII/IX. Brussels.

Eurostat (2009) *Europe in Figures: Eurostat Yearbook 2009.* doi:10.2785/29733

Ferrera, M. (2011) *The Boundaries of Welfare: European Integration and the New Spatial Politics of Social Protection.* New York: Oxford University Press.

Galloni, A. (2012) 'The Nonna State', *Wall Street Journal,* 15 June. Available at: http://en.wikipedia.org/wiki/European_debt_crisis (accessed 1 November 2015).

Griffin, J.J. and Dunn, P. (2004) 'Corporate Public Affairs: Commitment, Resources, and Structure', *Business & Society*, 43(2), 196–220.

Gunnigle, P., Lavelle, J. and Monaghan, S. (2013) 'Weathering the Storm? Multinational Companies and Human Resource Management through the Global Financial Crisis', *International Journal of Manpower*, 34, 214–231.

Hamel, M. (2013) 'Europe's Economic Crisis Prompting Huge South-to-North Migration Within EU', *International Business Times*, 2 July. Available at: http://www.ibtimes.com/europes-economic-crisis-prompting-huge-south-north-migration-within-eu-1330257 (accessed 1 November 2015).

Hart, P. and Sundelius, B. (2013) 'Crisis Management Revisited: A New Agenda for Research, Training and Capacity Building within Europe', *Cooperation and Conflict*, 48(3), 444–461.

Hay Group (2009) *Reward in a Downturn*. Available at: http://www.haygroup.com/ Downloads/au/misc/Reward_in_a_downturn_-_global_report.pdf (accessed 1 November 2015).

Hidalgo, J.C. (31 May 2012) *Looking at Austerity in Spain*. Cato Institute. Available at: http://en.wikipedia.org/wiki/European_debt_crisis (accessed 18 November 2015).

House, J. and Roman, D. (2012) 'Spain Jobless Crisis Deepens', *Wall Street Journal*, 28 April. Available at: http://en.wikipedia.org/wiki/European_debt_crisis (accessed 18 November 2015).

Karantinos, D. (2011) *Wages and Labour Costs: Recent Developments and Prospects*, Social Cohesion Bulletin Vol.2/2011, EKKE. Athens.

Karantinos, D. (2014). *Policy Note: An Evaluation of the Social and Employment Aspects and Challenges in Greece*. EKKE. Athens. Available at: http://www.europarl. europa.eu/document/activities/cont/201402/20140204ATT78729/20140204 ATT78729EN.pdf (accessed 1 November 2015).

Kasimis, C. (2012) *Greece: Illegal Immigration in the Midst of Crisis*. Migration Policy Institute.

Kassinis, G. and Stavrou, E. (2013) 'Non-standard Work Arrangements and National Context', *European Management Journal*, 31, 464–477. Available at: http://www.migrationpolicy.org/article/greece-illegal-immigration-midst-crisis (accessed 1 November 2015).

Kickert, W. (2011) 'Distinctiveness of Administrative Reform in Greece, Italy, Portugal and Spain: Common Characteristics of Context, Administrations and Reforms', *Public Administration*, 89, 801–818.

Meyer, J.W. and Rowan, B. (1977) 'Institutionalized Organizations: Formal Structure as Myth and Ceremony', *American Journal of Sociology*, 83, 440–463.

OECD (2001) *The Well-being of Nations: The Role of Human and Social Capital. Education and Skills*. Paris: Centre for Educational Research and Innovation, Organization for Economic Co-operation and Development.

Pastore, F. (2010) 'Managing Migration through the Crisis: Evolving Patterns in European Policies on Labour Migration and Mobility', *FieriWorking Papers*.

Psychogios, A. Brewster, C., Missopoulos, F., Kohont, A., Vatchkova, E. and Slavic, A. (2014) 'Industrial Relations in South-eastern Europe: Disaggregating the Contexts', *The International Journal of Human Resource Management*, 25, 1592–1612.

Stamati, A. (2013) 'The Impact of the Crisis on Industrial Relations', *European Industrial Relations Observatory*, 8 July.

The Economist (2009) 'Two-tier Flexibility', 9 July. Available at: http:// en.wikipedia.org/wiki/European_debt_crisis (accessed 18 November 2015).

Wood, G.T., Brewster, C. and Brookes, M. (eds) (2014) *Human Resource Management and the Institutional Perspective*. London: Routledge.

World Bank (2009) *Global Development Finance 2009: Outlook Summary*.

Zagelmeyer, S. and Gollan, P.J. (2012) 'Exploring Terra Incognita: Preliminary Reflections on the Impact of the Global Financial Crisis upon Human Resource Management', *The International Journal of Human Resource Management*, 23(16), 3287–3294.

5 Developments in Human Resource Management in Central and Eastern Europe in Comparative Perspective

MICHAEL MORLEY, JÓZSEF POÓR, NOREEN HERATY, RUTH ALAS AND ALEKSY POCZTOWSKI

Introduction

Our purpose in this chapter is to chart aspects of the contemporary landscape of Human Resource Management (HRM) in Central and Eastern Europe (CEE). The chapter is structured as follows. First, we place developments against the backdrop of the historical context of social and political changes in CEE, noting that the developmental trajectory is not homogeneous. Then in an effort to contextualize developments, broader socio-economic changes, labour market characteristics and patterns of FDI are set down in order to underscore the commonalities and differences that shape developments. We then present data on organizational-level developments in HRM in CEE. Developments are set in comparative context allowing for both a comparison between CEE and other regions and an exposition of the extent to which the CEE transition countries are characterized by idiosyncratic elements relative to their counterparts elsewhere. Our organizational-level trends focus on the importance of the HR function, staffing, performance management and development, compensation and benefits and unionization as major configurational and practice elements of HRM.

Prior to the fall of the Berlin Wall in 1989 and the subsequent wave of political, social, cultural and administrative transitions that this

major development heralded, the chief domain aspects of HRM
policy and practice in most of CEE operated under strict state control.
Characterized in the literature as "a politically oriented decision-
making system" (Garavan *et al.*, 1998: 210), the human resource
(HR) function and all its associated activities were closely supervised
by the Communist Party and government officials (Karoliny *et al.*,
2010). This historical approach has resulted in an underlying
ideational legacy which is important in the context of landscaping and
interpreting contemporary developments in CEE and the spread of
HRM practices (Piper, 1992; Turnock, 2000; Hetrik, 2002; Dalton
and Druker, 2012). In Pocztowski's account of the period preceding
the transition process when the Western term 'HR' was not yet in use
in CEE,

> the personnel function lacked a comprehensive systematic perspective
> and was characterized by the following features: the haphazard and
> temporary nature of the actions undertaken, politicization and the
> impact of third parties on personnel-related decisions, a high level
> of centralization within organizations, the low competence of the
> people taking care of HR issues, insufficient tools used to solve
> personnel related problems and finally insufficient institutionalization
> or even its complete absence.
>
> (Pocztowski, 2011: 14)

The result, he notes, was a low-ranking function, characterized by
over-staffing, high fluctuation and limited effectiveness. It served not
just as a function performing administrative tasks, but also particular
ideological and social purposes in the socialist era (Morley *et al.*,
2012). The system and the architecture governing this in CEE was
not conducive to the growth of more sophisticated value-adding
activities, with the result that there was always going to be significant
ground to be made up if the transition economies were going to be
able to support, sustain and expand a developmental trajectory based
on free market principles. Generally speaking, HRM activity in most
East European countries, prior to the changes that took place at the
end of the 1980s, was very tightly controlled by the state. Personnel
related issues were under the close control of the Party and heads
of state. The key positions in companies were closely monitored by
the Party and by state bureaucracy. Management was not considered
to be a profession (Cakrt, 1993) and decisions regarding promotion
were not based on performance criteria (Pearce, 1991). In several
cases the selection of specialists and personnel-related decisions were
greatly influenced by Communist Party and government politics
and objectives, and the Party instructed company directors to blend
together the aspects of individual and collective leadership. The

traditional personnel department consisted of two separate sections. One dealt with office staff and management and the other with blue-collar workers. The group dealing with office staff reported to the Personnel Manager, whilst the one dealing with blue-collar staff reported to the Finance Director.

That said, it would certainly be an over simplification to simply suggest that all countries in the region operated precisely the same model and approach. Importantly, the CEE region was never, nor is it today, homogenous (Kornai, 1994). In reality there were significant variations in preferred approaches among the countries in the region, arising as they did from distinct developmental trajectories and with the result that the transition point of departure from socialism towards market-oriented systems differed for different CEE countries. Morley, Minbaeva and Michailova (2012) argue that because the developmental trajectory that they had experienced was not uniform, the notion of a single model of HRM explaining unifying aspects of people management practices in the countries of CEE is a stretch too far, especially since, as noted by Dirani *et al.* (2015: 358), this region is characterized by "vast differences in cultural, religious, ethnic and socio-political backgrounds among, and in some cases, within countries". By way of example, they highlight two specific country-derived idiosyncratic legacies that hold particular explanatory power in accounting for variations across the region:

- Some countries in CEE, such as Hungary and the Czech Republic for example, were historically far more integrated into the Western economic and political system than others.
- Importantly, in the context of the contemporary developmental trajectory secured by some CEE countries, countries such as Poland and Hungary were able to retain elements of private enterprise during Soviet occupation, which in turn resulted in a different point of departure for their transition journey, relative to some of their neighbours.

Thus it was that, as early as 1982 and long before the collapse of communism in CEE, Kozinski and Listwan (1982) were able to call attention to the beginnings of a managerial transition in Poland where, under conditions of a deep social and economic crisis, new concepts of economic management emerged that provided an entirely new look at the whole national economy and its basic unit – the enterprise. For these and a variety of other reasons, the countries in the CEE region have experienced distinctive developmental trajectories and embarked on transitions towards a variety of capitalist models encompassing liberal and coordinated approaches (Lane, 2007; Frane *et al.*, 2009) and, some would argue, an ex-communist-specific variety of capitalism (Brewster and Viegas Bennett, 2010).

Contextually CEE is, in relative terms, under-documented in the HRM literature and several contributors have noted the lack of detailed knowledge, or particular types of knowledge such as organizational-level insights relative, for example, to Western Europe (Jankowicz, 1998; Morley, 2004; Zupan and Kase, 2005; McCann and Schwartz, 2006; Soulsby and Clark, 2006). In their characterization of the literature to date on aspects of HRM in CEE, Michailova *et al.* (2009) note that a great deal of the evidence has extensively utilized case studies and drawn conclusions from relatively small samples and many of the studies have been at a conceptual and macro level of analysis, emphasizing the firm-external perspective rather than a firm-internal perspective and rarely touching on the core tasks and basic functions of HRM. A common approach has been to present country-specific general descriptions, or to engage in, for example, two-country comparisons, which are considered appropriate when seeking to observe phenomena in significantly understudied contexts. Moreover, some countries of the region, most notably Hungary, Poland, Slovenia and Russia, have been the focus of considerably more attention than others in CEE.

The Context for Developments in HRM in CEE

Recent Socio-economic Trends

While the socialist system stretches back to 1917 in Russia, the other countries of CEE – whose HR practices we explore in this chapter – broadly met with this system after the Second World War and, as mentioned above, while the outside world was of the opinion that the whole region was rather homogenous in the shadow of socialism, there were significant variations. After the collapse of the system, democracy began to build in rather similar, though separate, ways in these countries. Differences arose primarily for reasons of their distinct developmental trajectories heretofore and the specific endowments of each country (Berend, 1996). Pertinent examples of how distinct transition events unfolded include the Czech–Slovak peaceful split, the secession of the Baltic States from the former Soviet Union and last but not least, the disintegration of the former Yugoslavia after the Balkan civil wars.

In accounting for underlying heterogeneity, cultural analyses of CEE countries have also proven instructive in identifying variations in

HRM and the extent to which they arise as a result of differences in basic cultural tenets (Jarjabka, 2010). Such analyses point to similarities between the Bulgarian and Russian cultures which are, in part at least, accounted for by the cultural ties of these countries, their geographic proximity and their Orthodox religious roots. In a similar vein, the underlying connections between Estonian and Finnish cultures and the differences between the Estonian and Russian cultures can be observed. The Czech and Slovak cultural differences are sometimes considered surprising due to state ties and language similarities, yet Hofstede's (2001) data demonstrate that the Czech culture is more similar to German or Austrian culture than it is to Slovak.

An important shared trajectory of relatively recent vintage has been their encounter with and experience of "Europeanization" branded by Ladrech (1994: 69) as "a process reorienting the direction and shape of politics to the degree that the EC political and economic dynamics become part of the organizational logic of national politics and policy making" and eventual membership of the European Union (EU). Their membership of the EU, which has been characterized as a boon for Europe at large "because they have been the engine of dynamism . . . often blatantly absent from the EU-15" (Ederer et al., 2007: 2) occurred for an initial cohort of eight CEE transition countries (the Czech Republic, Estonia, Hungary, Latvia, Lithuania, Poland, Slovakia and Slovenia) in 2004 and subsequently for Bulgaria and Romania in 2007, with Croatia becoming the newest Member State in 2013.

Table 5.1 presents economic indicator headline data on the nine CEE countries discussed in this chapter. The unemployment rate has oscillated between 7.1 and 12.4 per cent during the period 2008–2013, while the average rate of inflation for the nine CEE countries decreased from 8.2 to 1.6 per cent. The GDP of these countries ranges from 60 to 67 per cent of the combined EU-28 average.

Labour Market Approaches and Developments

Underneath the veneer of full employment among the labour markets of the former socialist system, it is possible to distinguish between at least three separate traditions in the management of labour market dynamics. First, there is what some classify as an "ex-Yugoslav tradition", which pertained in Slovenia and Serbia, for example, and which was characterized by the operation of a self-management system and a relatively high incidence of open unemployment, something of an inimitable feature among the broader swathe of socialist countries (Arandarenko, 2004). Svetlik et al. (2010) note that by way of design and operation, this approach allowed important decisions, including

Table 5.1 Key economic indicators of CEE countries

Country	Indicator	Years					
		2008	2009	2010	2011	2012	2013
Bulgaria	GDP (%)	6.7	−5.0	1.1	4.4	1.2	1.4
	Unemployment (%)	5.6	6.8	10.3	11.3	12.3	13.0
	Inflation (%)	12.0	2.5	3.0	3.4	2.4	0.4
	GDP per capita in PPS EU-28=100%	44.0	44.0	44.0	47.0	47.0	
Czech Republic	GDP (%)	2.0	−5.1	2.2	2.0	−1.1	−1.0
	Unemployment (%)	4.4	6.7	7.3	6.7	7.0	7.0
	Inflation (%)	6.3	0.6	1.2	2.1	3.5	1.4
	GDP per capita in PPS EU-28=100%	81.0	83.0	81.0	81.0	81.0	
Estonia	GDP (%)	−4.0	−14.10	2.6	9.5	4.0	0.8
	Unemployment (%)	5.5	13.5	16.7	12.3	10.0	8.6
	Inflation (%)	10.6	0.2	2.7	5.1	4.2	3.2
	GDP per capita in PPS EU-28=100%	69.0	64.0	64.0	69.0	71.0	
Hungary	GDP (%)	1.1	−6.6	1.3	1.9	−1.2	1.4
	Unemployment (%)	7.8	10.0	11.2	10.9	10.9	10.2
	Inflation (%)	6.0	4.0	4.7	3.9	5.7	1.7
	GDP per capita in PPS EU-28=100%	64.0	65.0	66.0	67.0	67.0	
Lithuania	GDP (%)	4.0	−13.9	3.7	8.5	5.1	4.4
	Unemployment (%)	5.8	13.8	17.8	15.4	13.4	11.8
	Inflation (%)	11.1	4.2	1.2	4.1	3.2	1.2
	GDP per capita in PPS EU-28=100%	64.0	58.0	62.0	68.0	72.0	

Russia	GDP (%)	5.2	-7.8	4.0	2.4	-1.0	
	Unemployment (%)	7.2	8.4	7.6			
	Inflation (%)	10.0	11.7	6.7			
	GDP per capita in PPS EU–28=100%	50.0	49.0	49.0	36.0	36.0	
Serbia	GDP (%)	4.3	-3.1	1.4			
	Unemployment (%)	13.6	16.1	19.2			
	Inflation (%)	10.8	3.6	8.6			
	GDP per capita in PPS EU–28=100%	36.0	36.0	35.0			
Slovakia	GDP (%)	5.6	-5.1	4.2	3.6	1.6	0.8
	Unemployment (%)	9.6	12.1	14.5	13.7	14.0	14.2
	Inflation (%)	3.9	0.9	0.7	4.1	3.7	1.5
	GDP per capita in PPS EU–28=100%	73.0	73.0	74.0	75.0	76.0	
Slovenia	GDP (%)	3.2	-8.8	0.9	0.5	-2.7	-1.2
	Unemployment (%)	4.4	5.9	7.3	8.2	8.9	10.1
	Inflation (%)	5.5	0.9	2.1	2.1	2.8	1.9
	GDP per capita in PPS EU–28=100%	91.0	86.0	84.0	84.0	84.0	
Average of the 9 CEE countries	GDP (%)	3.1	-7.7	2.4	4.1	0.7	0.9
	Unemployment (%)	7.1	10.4	12.4	11.2	10.9	10.7
	Inflation (%)	8.5	3.2	3.4	3.5	3.6	1.6
	GDP per capita in PPS EU–28=100%	63.6	62.0	62.1	65.9	66.8	
Average of the EU–28	GDP (%)	0.4	-4.5	2.0	1.6	-0.4	0.1
	Unemployment (%)	7.0	8.9	9.6	9.6	10.4	10.8
	Inflation (%)	3.7	1.0	2.1	3.1	2.6	1.5
	GDP per capita in PPS EU–28=100%	100.0	100.0	100.0	100.0	100.0	100.0
	GDP per capita in PPS EU–28 in Euro	25000.0	23500.0	24400.0	25100.0	25600.0	

Source: Eurostat (2014)

those relating to personnel matters, to be exercised by workers' councils. A second model may be referred to as the more "orthodox Soviet system", which operated in Bulgaria, Estonia, Lithuania and Russia. In this system strong centralization was the order of the day, with the Central Planning Office having significant oversight of, and an interventionist role in, the management of the labour market (Ericson, 1991; Kornai, 1994). The third model, and one favoured in the Czech Republic, Slovakia, Poland and Hungary, is characterized as a "moderate interventionist model" along the continuum of approaches that operated under socialism, whereby a degree of local economic freedom provides greater flexibility (Brada and Dobozi, 1989; Kolodko, 1989).

On the question of representation, the European Trade Union Institute estimates union density among the 11 CEE countries that joined the EU, to range from lows of 10 per cent in Estonia and Lithuania to highs of 27 per cent in Slovenia, 33 per cent in Romania and 35 per cent in Croatia. Figures for the remainder are estimated to be at 12 per cent (Hungary), 13 per cent (Latvia), 15 per cent (Poland), 17 per cent (the Czech Republic and Slovakia) and 20 per cent (Bulgaria). A confluence of circumstances may account for this trend. First, albeit with some exceptions (most notably Solidarnosc in Poland), the political role and the over-centralized structures operated by the trade unions during socialism, together with the overall poor regard for unions, resulted in a diminution of their status and scepticism concerning their role post transition (Dimitrova and Petkov, 2005). The net effect of this was a credibility issue. Second, several empirical studies confirm that in CEE countries, FDI from multinational companies and privatization served to weaken the union movement as it struggled to find its place and role in the emerging business landscape (Toth, 1997). Third, and rather separately, the transition process witnessed the emergence of a new management authority at the firm level, which was not sympathetic towards the unions (Dabu and Aguilera, 2005).

Overall therefore, the unions were ill-prepared for the new political and economic realities that emerged as part of the transition process. The majority of workers were minded to escape from the constraints of union membership and the payment of union membership fees and with the exception of traditional industries and the public sector, the level of unionization dropped. In addition the new institutional provisions and changing employment relations framework that accompanied the transition meant that trade union representatives themselves lacked many of the competences required for this new situation (Zupan and Kase, 2005). Changes in labour laws have brought new flexibility for both workers and employers.

Foreign Direct Investment and the Influence of MNCs in Shaping Developments

Multinational companies emerged as key players in this new situation. There is little doubt that the role of these companies in reshaping the characteristics of the labour market and HR practice in the former socialist countries has been significant. In this respect both the entry of foreign capital in terms of FDI and the arrival of foreign managers in leadership positions in CEE organizations signalled the openness of the institutional regimes to new practices and became a wellspring for changes related to HRM practices and approaches as a result of introducing new management ideas (Berber *et al.*, 2015; Poutsma *et al.*, 2015). Significant growth in the region has been achieved through the securing of FDI and empirical research on the subsidiaries of multinational companies operating in the CEE region points to this FDI playing a role in the emergence of a more strategic approach to HRM, and for the first time in the history of HRM and its predecessor, Personal Management, in the CEE region there is evidence of HR managers becoming members of the boards of foreign-owned multinational subsidiaries operating there (Farkas *et al.*, 2008). In his book on the role of international companies in Eastern Europe, Lewis (2005) argues that multinational companies have redrawn the labour market map of the former socialist countries in many respects. Among other things, they have removed the historical principle of egalitarianism and introduced basic salary systems which give expression to and reward the nature and the importance of the type of job actually being performed. High performers are rewarded with higher compensation to reflect the effort–reward relationship. Festing and Sahakiants (2010: 211) also call attention to the fact that "the main mimetic pressures in CEE countries with respect to rewards can be attributed to MNCs". In this way FDI in CEE serves as both a conduit for economic development, employment and economic growth, as well as a bulwark for institutionalizing new HR approaches and systems and occupies an important place in the narrative on developments in the region since the transition process began. International companies were able to exploit their so-called human resource-based advantage in the face of local institutional systems that were relatively weak and undeveloped (or in transition). The attraction of a significant amount of FDI into several of the CEE economies is proving significant and a parallel developing internationalization among many historically domestic CEE companies is also proving important (Berber *et al.*, 2015).

It must also be remembered however that FDI alone could not solve the employment problems of the CEE countries. A good example is the case of Slovakia, where despite the relatively high level of FDI inflows, unemployment also remained stubbornly high at between 12 and

15 per cent. In addition, there is the burning issue of income disparities between the CEE labour market and Western Europe (Fawell, 2008) and the migration of young and well-trained people from CEE to the West.

Table 5.2 presents data on FDI inflows into the CEE region. As will be noted, Slovakia has recorded rapid economic growth in recent years as a result of economic reform and relatively high levels of FDI inflow. In Hungary and Poland, foreign investors have been part of the business landscape since the early 1990s, these countries clearly having been ahead of the curve on FDI relative to other CEE countries. In Hungary between 1990 and 1991, FDI increased from $569 million to $2.1 billion, while in 1992 the growth rate declined, but it did manage to reach $3.4 billion. By 1993, FDI to Hungary exceeded $6 billion. In the same year the FDI flow to Poland and the Czech Republic, in total, amounted to $2.6 and $2.2 billion respectively (Szakács, 2013).

Of note on the FDI front, the Western Balkan countries have received significantly less than the other countries of CEE. The political and economic instabilities in these countries have resulted in them proving less attractive to international investors. The FDI inflow was especially low until 2000 in the Balkan countries, with the exception of Croatia which began to attract a significant amount of FDI in relative terms from 1997 onwards (Poór *et al.*, 2011).

Analysing Organizational-Level Developments in HRM in CEE: A Comparative Perspective

Data and Analytical Approach

We now turn to our organizational-level survey data on HRM. Our data are drawn from the CRANET Survey. The survey is the largest and most representative independent survey of HRM policies and practices in the world. Surveys were translated and mailed to the highest ranking manager with responsibility for HRM in representative national samples of organizations. For further details of the survey rounds of data collection and methodology, see Parry *et al.* (2011); Steinmetz *et al.* (2011), and Brewster *et al.* (2004).

Our dataset for the analysis presented here comprises the responses from a total of 6,039 organizations across 30 countries. From this total sample, we created four sub-samples (see Figure 5.1) in order to set developments in HRM in CEE in comparative context with developments in other European and non-European contexts.

Table 5.2 Foreign Direct Investment inflows into the CEE Region (2004–2012) (in $ million)

Countries	FDI Inflows								
	2004	2005	2006	2007	2008	2009	2010	2011	2012
Croatia	1 262	1 695	3 468	4 997	6 180	3 355	394	1 494	1 251
Bulgaria	3 443	2 223	7 805	12 389	9 855	3 385	1 601	1 864	1 899
Czech Republic	4 974	10 991	5 463	10 444	6 451	2 927	6 141	5 405	10 592
Estonia	1 049	2 853	1 797	2 716	1 729	1 839	1 540	257	1 470
Hungary	4 654	6 699	6 818	3 951	6 325	2 048	2 274	4 698	13 469
Latvia	699	632	1 663	2 322	1 261	94	379	1 562	988
Lithuania	773	1 009	1 817	2 015	1 965	66	753	1 217	835
Poland	12 873	7 724	19 603	23 561	14 839	12 932	8 858	15 139	3 356
Romania	6 517	6 388	11 367	9 921	13 909	4 844	2 940	2 670	2 242
Serbia	966	1 481	4 256	3 439	2 955	1 959	1 329	2 709	352
Slovakia	1 261	1 908	4 693	3 581	4 687	6	526	2 143	2 826
Slovenia	827	496	644	1 514	1 947	653	359	999	145
CEE region	39 298	44 099	69 394	80 850	72 103	32 790	27 094	40 157	

Source: UNCTAD (2013)

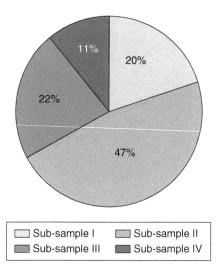

Figure 5.1 Proportion of the organizational respondents in the four sub–samples
Source: Karoliny *et al.* (2011)

- *Sub-sample I (Central and Eastern European)* comprisees the nine CEE countries of Bulgaria, the Czech Republic, Estonia, Hungary, Lithuania, Russia, Serbia, Slovakia and Slovenia that are the central focus of analysis in this chapter. They represent some 20 per cent of the total sample.
- *Sub-sample II (European non-CEE)* comprises Austria, Belgium, Cyprus, Denmark, Finland, France, Germany, Greece, Iceland, Norway, Sweden and the United Kingdom, representing 47 per cent of the total sample.
- *Sub-sample III (Non-European Anglo-Saxon)* comprises Australia, South Africa and the USA, which represents 22 per cent of the total sample.
- *Sub-sample IV (South-east Asian)* is made up of Japan, the Philippines and Taiwan, which together constitute 11 per cent of the respondents.

Table 5.3 provides a sectoral distribution of respondents in each of our four sub–samples and Table 5.4 provides a breakdown by organization size.

The remainder of the chapter focuses on configurational and practice aspects of HRM, including the findings on the importance of the HR function, staffing, employee development, compensation and benefits, and unionization.

Table 5.3 Sectorial distribution of respondents in the sub-samples (%)

Sectors	Sub-Samples				
	I. Central and Eastern European	II. European Non–CEE	III Non–European Anglo-Saxon	IV. South-east Asian	V. All Surveyed
Agriculture	4	2	2	0	2
Manufacturing	49	40	28	60	42
Services	38	47	52	17	44
Other	9	11	19	23	12
Total	100	100	100	100	100

Source: Karoliny *et al.* (2011)

Table 5.4 Size distribution of respondents in the sub-samples (%)

Size Category (Number of Employees)	Sub-samples				
	I. Central and Eastern European	II. European Non–CEE	III. Non–European Anglo-Saxon	IV. South-east Asian	V. All Surveyed
1–250	60	33	25	34	35
251–1000	27	39	54	36	41
1001–5000	10	19	12	22	17
5001+	3	9	9	7	8
Total	100	100	100	100	100

Source: Karoliny *et al.* (2011)

Importance of the HR Function

Writing about developments in the mid-1990s based on interview data gathered in 25 Polish companies, Garavan *et al.* (1998: 206) noted that the evidence clearly indicated that the formal HR function was best characterized as having a personnel, rather than an HRM orientation. They concluded that:

there is limited evidence of any involvement in strategy, policy or operational decision making or major HR issues. Few departments engaged in long-term human resource planning and there was a significant administrative burden associated with the maintenance of personnel files and records.

In our current analysis, we present data on the leadership of the function, along with data on two indicators of the importance of the HR function, namely, whether the HR Director is a member of the Board of Directors or the top management team and whether and at what stage they are involved in development of business strategy. From a leadership perspective, it is apparent that the function is predominantly female-led across all clusters analysed and most particularly, in CEE, a trend previously signalled in the work of Zupan and Kase (2005), Poór *et al.* (2007) and Reichel *et al.* (2009). In addition, the increasing strategic orientation of the function is also apparent. Approximately two-thirds of respondents in each of the clusters analysed report the inclusion of the Functional Head as a member of the Board. Strategic planning appears commonplace, with the HR Functional Head playing an active role in the development of strategy. While extant literature from the 1990s and early 2000s based on studies in the Czech Republic, Poland and Slovenia (Koubek and Brewster, 1995; Tung and Havlovic, 1996; Garavan *et al.*, 1998; Zupan and Kase, 2005) reported a squarely operational and administrative orientation within the function, the data here point to a more involved role for the Functional Head and the range of activities they engage in (see Table 5.5).

Table 5.5 The position and role of the HR function and the HR department

Sub-Samples	Leadership of the HR Function Male/ Female (%)	Head of HR on Board of Directors (%)	Involvement of Head of HR in Strategy Development (%)	Existence of Strategies (%)	
				Business	HR
I. CEE	13:87	62	88	91	77
II. European Non-CEE	28:72	69	91	94	84
III. Non-European Anglo-Saxon	25:75	66	87	83	83
IV. South-east Asian	28:72	67	94	95	86
V. All surveyed	28:72	67	90	91	81

Source: Karoliny *et al.* (2011)

Staffing Practices

Turning to preferred approaches to selection, our survey data reveal the continuing popularity of face-to-face interviews across all clusters analysed and across the full range of job categories from managerial, professional/technical, administrative/clerical and manual. Reference checks are commonly relied on, most especially in CEE when selecting managerial and professional staff. The use of technical testing for the selection of professional staff is common in the South-east Asian sub-sample.

In addition to workforce entry, we also explored workforce reduction strategies. In all sub-samples recruitment freezes were a common approach, though significantly less so in CEE (in 56 per cent of cases, but between 74 per cent and 82 per cent in the comparative clusters). Approximately two-thirds of responding organizations use a combination of voluntary and compulsory redundancies, which appears broadly in line with practices elsewhere, as is the non-renewal of existing contracts at 63 per cent. Outsourcing also features as a common approach to workforce reduction across the clusters analysed (see Table 5.6).

Table 5.6 Method of workforce reduction (%)

Methods	Sub-Samples				
	I. Central and Eastern European	II. European Non-CEE	III. Non-European Anglo-Saxon	IV. South-east Asian	V. All Surveyed
Recruitment freeze	56	81	81	82	74
Early retirement	50	61	49	51	56
Voluntary redundancies	68	71	45	81	65
Compulsory redundancies	66	62	66	60	61
Internal transfer	65	79	72	85	73
No renewal of contracts	63	79	65	74	71
Outsourcing	42	44	39	48	42
Other	17	29	62	3	24

Source: Karoliny *et al.* (2011)

Performance Management and Development

While in general performance management systems were not commonplace during the socialist era or at the beginning of the transition process (Pearce, 1991), there is some evidence to suggest their earlier existence in some CEE countries characterized by the more moderate interventionist socialist model referred to earlier. In this respect, Czubasiewicz (2005) notes that designing, implementing and conducting employee appraisals was performed during the 1950s in Poland, while Nadolski (1972) highlights that one of the first technical manuals on employee appraisal was published in Poland. While our data in this analysis show that formalized performance appraisal is less common in CEE than in the other clusters examined, it emerges as a significant practice in all four employee categories in the region, a development in part driven by performance management as a preferred approach in the growing multinational sector in the region. Takei and Ito (2007) call attention to the enabling nature of context as a determinant of the likelihood of performance management gaining legitimacy. Their research, for example, points to the potential for capacity building in Slovakia, where a focus on growing competitiveness through a strong emphasis on individual competition and performance-based systems is systemically accommodated (see Table 5.7).

Beyond the question of who is subject to performance appraisal lies the purpose for which it is actually employed. Our analysis explored whether it is utilized in a variety of situations. The evidence suggests a CEE pattern of usage that is not dissimilar to that pertaining in the broader European cluster. For example, performance appraisal is

Table 5.7 Assessment applied via formal appraisal systems (%)

Sub-Samples	Percentage Use of Formal Appraisal Systems			
	Management	Professional Staff	Clerical Staff	Manual Staff
I. CEE	57	61	55	48
II. European Non-CEE	67	63	61	45
III. Non-European Anglo-Saxon	90	90	88	68
IV. South-east Asian	91	92	91	24
V. All surveyed	71	70	68	54

Source: Karoliny *et al.* (2011)

used primarily to inform reward decisions, to identify training and development needs and, to a slightly lesser extent, in career planning. Its utilization for workforce planning is less marked (see Table 5.8).

On the developmental side, two key aspects were explored, namely, the annual expenditure on developmental interventions as a percentage of payroll costs and the actual number of days training provided to different categories of employees (see Table 5.9).

Table 5.8 The usage of appraisal results

Use of Appraisals	Sub-Samples				
	I. Central and Eastern European	II. European Non-CEE	III. Non-European Anglo-Saxon	IV. South-east Asian	V. All Surveyed
Inform pay determination	77	78	70	85	92
Training and development needs	77	68	82	85	82
Career	74	66	77	79	57
Workforce planning	56	53	51	64	69

Source: Karoliny *et al.* (2011)

Table 5.9 Proportion of annual payroll costs spent on training

Training Cost Ratio (%)	Sub-Samples				
	I. Central and Eastern European	II. European Non-CEE	III. Non-European Anglo-Saxon	IV. South-east Asian	V. All Surveyed
0–2	58	55	52	55	54
2.01–4	11	18	11	14	15
4.01–6	12	14	17	9	13
6.01–10	11	8	9	12	10
10.01+	8	5	10	8	8

Source: Karoliny *et al.* (2011)

The pattern of expenditure is remarkably similar across the four clusters analysed where the majority spend up to 2 per cent annually on development interventions. When this is translated into the number of days training provided to each category of employee, we see some variation. For example, managerial employees in CEE receive more days training than do their counterparts in other clusters, while professional categories receive a similar number of days to their counterparts in Europe more broadly. Clerical and manual staff receive slightly fewer days proportionally. The results here lend support to Sheehan's (2014) argument that in the CEE context sustained investment in training and development can no longer be viewed as a non-essential expenditure and must be retained and even increased to ensure sustained competitiveness, despite a volatile and uncertain macroeconomic environment pertaining (see Table 5.10).

Compensation and Benefits

As a result of the ongoing transition process in CEE, it has been argued that reward systems have also undergone a radical transformation in the region (Festing and Sahakiants, 2013), though research on compensation in the region is scarce and a comprehensive analysis of factors influencing the adoption and transformation of compensation practices in CEE countries is lacking (Festing and Sahakiants, 2010). Our analysis explored three particular aspects of compensation, namely, the level at which basic pay is determined, to what extent and on what basis variable pay is offered and, finally, the extent of financial participation schemes in operation.

Table 5.10 Number of training days/year

Sub-Samples	Number of Training Days/Year			
	Management	Professional Staff	Clerical Staff	Manual Staff
I. CEE	8.9	9.3	5.6	5.6
II. European non-CEE	6.4	9.4	4.2	3.3
III. Non-European Anglo-Saxon	7.9	8.8	7.0	8.4
IV. South-east Asian	7.7	8.9	6.5	5.7
V. All surveyed	7.7	9.1	5.9	5.8

Source: Karoliny *et al.* (2011)

The basic pay offered to managers is determined primarily at the individual level, with only negligible differences in evidence across the clusters analysed. Conversely, the basic pay of manual workers is predominantly determined at national level or via industry-wide collective bargaining mechanisms, though less so for CEE. This in part may be accounted for by the more limited coverage of industry-wide/national bargaining. In the European Non-CEE sample, as in the total sample for manual workers, national/industry-wide collective bargaining is important. Clerical pay is determined by a combination of individual, company and national levels. Overall however, it can be concluded that basic pay determination at the level of local establishments is the predominant mechanism.

Turning now to the issue of variable pay, our data suggests that variable pay and alternate forms of financial participation are more likely to be utilized for managerial categories of employees than for other categories, across all countries. The calculation of variable pay tends to be primarily based on individual performance across employee categories, with the exception of professional employees who are assessed at team/departmental level. Festing and Sahakiants (2010) contend that, while variable pay in the form of a cash bonus existed in the former socialist countries, it was by no means consistent with the efficiency-based philosophy of pay-for-performance, but was person-based, rather than performance-based.

Performance related pay is the most commonly offered form of financial participation across every staff category. This is followed by flexible benefits (except in the case of the South-east Asian sample, where profit sharing is more important than flexible benefits in all employee categories). As might be expected, across the countries, managers are most likely to receive profit-sharing payment forms than are clerical and manual employees.

Unionization

Referring to the nature of the employment relationship in CEE, Festing and Sahakiants (2010: 214) suggest that the

> lack of a strong institutional environment on the national level, the weak position of trade unions and the absence of strong institutional pressures on the part of the EU have led to a situation where the main features of socialist employment relations still retain a certain relevance.

The result is that organizations have a certain latitude around the pursuit of preferred practices. During the socialist regime, there were quasi 100 per cent unionization rates whereby the trade unions in respective countries played an active role in the accomplishments of the communist parties and the implementation of state performance goals at national, sectoral and company levels (Alas, 2004). Among the main activities performed by the trade unions were the distribution of welfare benefits, overseeing employee housing, social event organization and the provision of catering services (Kazlauskaite and Buciuniene, 2010) (see Table 5.11).

In the total sample of organizations surveyed, we can see a clear division in terms of levels of unionization. For example, the tradition of unionization remains most robust among the European Non-CEE cluster and so only a small percentage of organizations are non-unionized (14 per cent). This is in sharp contrast with CEE countries, where non-unionized firms account for 50 per cent of the total CEE sample, which may be partly explained by Trif's (2007) observation that trade unions in these countries have only been engaged in collective bargaining since the early 1990s. The transformation process in CEE proved to be an enormous challenge for trade unions. Kohl (2008) highlights that their earlier function as mass organizations operating in the socialist system with a clearly defined mandate from the state suddenly disappeared after 1989 and since the beginning of the transition in CEE, trade unions have faced a challenging climate that has impacted rates of trade union membership.

Table 5.11 Levels of unionization (%)

| Proportion of Trade Union Members | Sub-Samples | | | | |
	I. Central and Eastern European	II. European Non-CEE	III. Non-European Anglo-Saxon	IV. South-east Asian	V. All Surveyed
0	50	14	49	75	32
1–10	10	21	14	3	16
11–25	7	9	7	2	7
26–50	13	11	10	2	11
51–75	11	16	9	5	13
76–100	9	29	11	13	21
Total	100	100	100	100	100

Source: Karoliny *et al.* (2011)

Conclusion

The events of 1989 in CEE bringing about the ultimate collapse of socialism and subsequent institutional atrophy and the commencement of a long-term transition process have been characterized as among the most significant economic and social processes of recent times (McCann and Schwartz, 2006) and as a unique re-modernization (Stojanov, 1992). Through extensive reforms, many of the CEE economies have demonstrated a robustness in the face of the recent global financial crisis (Åslund, 2012). Against this backdrop, our aim in this chapter has been to landscape some of the developments in HRM in the CEE region as part of an effort to a more unified analysis of domain aspects of the field across a broad swathe of countries. We set the CEE countries in comparative perspective in order that our empirically derived organizational-level developments in HRM in CEE can be interpreted in light of developments elsewhere. It will be obvious to the reader that an understanding of HRM systems in CEE requires an appreciation of a complex blend of both external and internal contextual factors with the result that charting the landscape of HRM in the region is challenging from a research perspective (Horwitz, 2011; Brewster et al., 2010). HRM across the CEE has had to re-invent itself and, in the process, become newly defined according to market economy criteria and operating principles whereby old methods and techniques, particularly those of an HR nature, collapsed in the face of new requirements (Domsch and Lidokhover, 2007; Pocztowski, 2011). The shift has variously been characterized as essentially that from a unitarist towards a more pluralist system, from an administrative towards a more value-adding model and from a low-legitimacy function to one marked by more power and acceptability (Morley et al., 2009; Festing and Sahakiants, 2010). Writing on the period of transition over the past 20 years and the consequences for HRM, Pocztowski (2011: 9) notes that it has been:

> particularly significant for the discipline. During that time, traditions have frequently clashed, challenges have arisen, scientific research and the consulting services market have developed, and many businesses have undergone a dramatic change in thinking and action in relation to their HR functions. Most importantly, however, a certain professional environment has come to exist.

Despite the development of the field in CEE, both as an area of academic enquiry and as a field of professional practice, Kazlauskaité and Buciuniene's (2010) contextual analysis points to the existence of an ongoing competency deficit in HR practice. Thus, in interpreting developments, it is important to recognize that the CEE countries are heterogeneous and their HRM patterns must not be taken as a uniform management model (Kazlauskaite *et al.*, 2013).

While it was only after the fall of the socialist regimes throughout CEE that HRM, as we have come to understand it, started taking hold in the discourse of management thinking and in emerging practice, our analysis here suggests that in the intervening 25 years, differences in HRM between CEE and other countries have narrowed. Of particular note, females now occupy a larger portion of HR specialist roles in organizations in the CEE region in comparison to other countries, something previously attested to by Reichel *et al.* (2009) in their treatise on the status of the specialist HR function and the increase of female HR professionals. Core indicators of the emergence of a more strategic role for the HRM function in the CEE region presented in our analysis, including board-level participation and involvement in strategy formulation and implementation, are suggestive of a narrowing of the gap between CEE countries and their surveyed counterparts elsewhere. CEE respondents report investing more in training and development than in other countries, especially at the managerial and professional level. Taking into consideration that the modern methods of performance appraisal did not exist in the old "cadre" system at all, though as indicated by Buchelt (2015) there were some exceptions to that, their current levels of application more broadly throughout CEE also demonstrate growth. The level of unionization remains relatively low overall, with nine of the eleven CEE countries that joined the EU recording union density levels lower than the EU average. While their future will be determined by many developments, the nature of the variety of capitalism that becomes institutionalized in the region will be a critical determinant of any renewed legitimacy that may be secured.

Key Learning Points

- Contextually CEE is under-documented in the HRM literature, with several contributors noting the dearth of detailed knowledge.
- Prior to the fall of the Berlin Wall, HRM policy and practice in most of CEE operated under strict state control.
- The developmental trajectory experienced is not uniform with the result that the CEE countries and their HRM patterns are heterogeneous.
- EU Membership has been an important shaping, shared influence for Bulgaria, Croatia, the Czech Republic, Estonia, Hungary, Latvia, Lithuania, Poland, Romania Slovakia and Slovenia.
- The role and influence of multinational companies on the labour market and HR practice over the past two decades is significant.

- Recent years have witnessed a narrowing of the gap between CEE countries and their Western counterparts in terms of HRM configuration, policy and practice.

Acknowledgement

The authors wish to acknowledge the contributions of Professor Zsuzsanna Karoliny and Profesor Ferenc Farkas of the University Pécs, Hungary, in preparing this chapter.

References

Alas, R. (2004) "The Reasons for the Low Popularity of Trade Unions in Estonia", *Journal of Human Resource Management*, 1(2), 14–28.

Arandenko, M. (2004) "International Advice and Labour Market Institutions in South-east Europe", *Global Social Policy*, 4(1), 27–53.

Åslund, A. (2012) *Lessons from Reforms in Central and Eastern Europe in the Wake of the Global Financial Crisis.* Working Paper, Peterson Institute for International Economics, Washington, DC.

Berber, N., Morley, M.J., Slavic, A. and Poór, J. (2015) *Management Compensation Systems in Central and Eastern Europe: A Comparative Analysis.* Working Paper, Faculty of Economics Subotica University of Novi Sad.

Berend, T. (1996) *Central and Eastern Europe, 1944–1993: Detour from the Periphery to the Periphery.* Cambridge: Cambridge University Press.

Brada, J.C. and Dobozi, I. (1989) "Economic Reform in Hungary: An Overview and Assessment", *Eastern European Economics*, 28(1), 3–13.

Brewster, C., Mayrhofer, W. and Morley, M. (2004) *Human Resource Management in Europe: Evidence of Convergence?* London: Butterworth.

Brewster, C., Morley, M.J. and Buciuniene, I. (2010) "The Reality of Human Resource Management in Central and Eastern Europe: A Special Issue to Mark the 20th Anniversary of CRANET (the Cranfield Network on Comparative Human Resource Management)", *Baltic Journal of Management*, 5(2), 145–155.

Brewster, C. and Viegas Bennet, C. (2010) "Perceptions of Business Cultures in Eastern Europe and Their Implications for International HRM", *International Journal of Human Resource Management*, 21(14), 2568–2588.

Buchelt, B. (2015) "Performance Management in Polish Companies Internationalising Their Market Activities", *The International Journal of Human Resource Management*, 26(15), 1965–1982.

Cakrt, M. (1993) "Management Education in Eastern Europe: Toward Mutual Understanding", *Academy of Management Executive*, 7(4), 63–68.

Czubasiewicz, H. (2005) *Periodic Evaluations of Employees: Configuration and System Design.* Gdansk: University of Gdansk.

Dabu, A. and Aguilera, R.V. (2005) "The Transformation of Employment Relations Systems in Central and Eastern Europe", *Journal of Industrial Relations*, 47(1), 16–42.

Dalton, K. and Druker, J. (2012) "Transferring HR Concepts and Practices within Multinational Corporations in Romania: The Management Experience", *European Management Journal*, 30(6), 588–602.

Dimitrova, D. and Petkov, K. (2005) "Comparative Overview: Changing Profiles, Action and Outcomes for Organized Labour in Central and Eastern Europe", in Dimitrova, D. and Vilrokx, J. (eds) *Trade Union Strategies in Central and Eastern Europe: Towards Decent Work*. Budapest: International Labour Office.

Dirani, K.M., Ardichvili, A., Cseh, M. and Zavyalova, E. (2015) 'Human Resource Management in Russia, Central and Eastern Europe', in Horwitz, F. and Budhwar, F. (eds) *Handbook of Human Resource Management in Emerging Markets*. Cheltenham: Edward Elgar, pp. 357–371.

Domsch, M. and Lidokhover, T. (eds.) (2007) *Human Resource Management in Russia*. Aldershot: Ashgate.

Ederer, P., Schuler, P. and Wilms, S. (2007) *The European Human Capital Index: The Challenge of Central and Eastern Europe*. Brussels: The Lisbon Council.

Ericson, R.E. (1991) "The Classical Soviet-type Economy: Nature of the System and Implications for Reform", *The Journal of Economic Perspectives*, 5(4), 11–27.

Eurostat. (2014) *The Yearbook*. Brussels: European Commission.

Farkas, F., Karoliny, M.-né and Poór, J. (2008) *In Focus: Hungarian and Eastern European Characteristics of Human Resource Management – an International Comparative Survey*. (Research study) Pécs, University of Pécs.

Fawell, A. (2008) "The New Face of East–West Migration in Europe", *Journal of Ethnic and Migration Studies*, 34(5), 701–716.

Festing, M. and Sahakiants, I. (2010) "Compensation Practices in Central and Eastern European EU Member States – An Analytical Framework Based on Institutional Perspectives, Path Dependencies, and Efficiency Considerations", *Thunderbird International Business Review*, 52(3), 203–216.

Festing, M., and Sahakiants, I. (2013) "Path-dependent Evolution of Compensation Systems in Central and Eastern Europe: A Case Study of Multinational Corporation Subsidiaries in the Czech Republic, Poland and Hungary", *European Management Journal*, 31(4), 373–389.

Frane, A., Primož, K. and Matevž, T. (2009) 'Varieties of Capitalism in Eastern Europe (with Special Emphasis on Estonia and Slovenia)', *Communist and Post-Communist Studies*, 42(1), 65–81.

Garavan, T.N., Morley, M.J., Heraty, N., Lucewicz, J. and Schudolski, A. (1998) "Managing Human Resources in a Post Command Economy: Personnel Administration or Strategic Human Resource Management?", *Personnel Review*, 27(3), 200–213.

Hetrick, S. (2002) "Transferring HR Ideas and Practices: Globalization and Convergence in Poland", *Human Resource Development International*, 5(3), 333–351.

Hofstede, G. (2001. *Culture's Consequences: Comparing Values, Behaviours, Institutions and Organisations across Nations*. 2nd edn. Thousand Oaks, CA: Sage.

Horwitz, F. (2011) "Future of HRM Challenges for Multinational Firms in Eastern and Central Europe", *Human Resource Management Journal*, 21(4), 432–443.

Jankowicz, A.D. (1998) "Issues in Human Resource Management in Central Europe", *Personnel Review*, 27(3), 169.

Jarjabka, A. (2010) "Similarities and Differences in Company Cultures of Eastern-Europeans" (in Hungarian) in Poór, J., Boday, P. and Kispalne, V, Zs. *Trends and Tendencies in Human Resources Management in Eastern-Europe*. Budapest: Gondolat Publishing House.

Karoliny, Z., Farkas, F. and Poór, J. (2010) "Sharpening Profile of HRM in Central-Eastern Europe in Reflection of Its Developments in Hungary", *Review of International Comparative Management*, 11(4), 733–747.

Karoliny, Zs., Farkas, F. and Poór, J. (2011) "Varying Importance of HR and Its Outcomes in Different Management Cultures with CEE Focus", *EURAM Conference*. Tallinn. (Conference CD and proceedings).

Kazlauskaite, R. and Buciuniene I. (2010) "HR Function Developments in Lithuania", *Baltic Journal of Management*, 5(2), 218–241.

Kazlauskaite R., Buciuniene I., Poor J., Karoliny Z., Alas R., Kohont A. and Szlavicz A. (2013) "Human Resource Management in the Central and Eastern European Region", in Parry, E., Stavrou, E. and Lazarova, M. (eds) *Global Trends in Human Resource Management*. Houndmills: Palgrave Macmillan, pp. 103–121.

Kohl, H. (2008) *Where Do Trade Unions Stand Today in Eastern Europe? Stock-taking after EU Enlargement*. Briefing Paper No. 5: Bonn, Friedrich-Ebert-Stiftung.

Kolodko, G.W. (1989) "Eastern European Economics, Economic Reform in Socialism and Inflation Determinants and Interrelations", *Eastern European Economics*, 28(3), 36–49.

Kornai, J. (1994) *Overcentralization in Economic Administration*. Oxford: Oxford University Press.

Koubek, J. and Brewster, C. (1995) "Human Resource Management in Turbulent Times: HRM in the Czech Republic", *International Journal of Human Resource Management*, 6(2), 223–247.

Kozinski, J. and Listwan, T. (1982) *Selection of Top Management Executives by Open Competition in Poland*. MIMEO, Academy of Economics, Wroclaw.

Ladrech, R. (1994) "Europeanization of Domestic Politics and Institutions: The Case of France", *Journal of Common Market Studies*, 32(1), 69–88.

Lane, D. (2007) "Post-Communist States and the European Union", *Journal of Communist Studies and Transition Politics*, 23(4), 461–477.

Lewis, P.C. (2005) *How the East Was Won*. New York: Palgrave Macmillan.

McCann, L. and Schwartz, G. (2006) "Terms and Conditions Apply: Management Restructuring and the Global Integration of Post-socialist Societies", *The International Journal of Human Resource Management*, 17(8), 1339–1352.

Michailova, S., Heraty, N. and Morley, M.J. (2009) "Studying Human Resource Management in the International Context: The Case of Central and Eastern Europe", in Morley, M.J., Heraty, N. and Michailova, S. (eds) *Managing Human Resource Management in Central and Eastern Europe*. London: Routledge, pp. 1–24.

Morley, M.J. (2004) "Contemporary Debates in European Human Resource Management: Context and Content", *Human Resource Management Review*, 14(4), 353–364.

Morley, M.J., Heraty, N. and Michailova, S. (2009) *Managing Human Resource Management in Central and Eastern Europe*. London: Routledge.

Morley, M.J., Minbaeva, D. and Michailova, S. (2012) "The Transition States of Central and Eastern Europe and the Former Soviet Union", in Brewster, C.

and Mayrhofer, W. (eds) *Handbook of Research on Comparative Human Resource Management*. Cheltenham: Edward Elgar, pp. 550–575.

Nadolski, J. (1972) *How to Appraise Employees*. Warsaw: Publishing Institute.

Parry, E., Stavrou-Costea, E. and Morley, M.J. (2011) "CRANET: An International Network of Research", *Theory and Practice Human Resource Management Review* 21(1), 1–4.

Pearce, J. (1991) "From Socialism to Capitalism: The Effects of Hungarian Human Resource Practices", *Academy of Management Executive*, 5(4), 75–88.

Piper, R. (1992) "Socialist HRM: An Analysis of HRM Theory and Practice in the Former Socialist Countries of Eastern Europe", *The International Executive*, 34(6), 499–516.

Pocztowski, A. (2011) "Transformation of the HR Function", in Pocztowski, A. (ed.) *Human Resource Management in Transition: The Polish Case*. Warszawa: Wolters Kluwer.

Poór, J., Karoliny, Zs. Farkas, F. (2007) "Human Resource Management in Hungary in Light of Eastern European and Global Comparison", *Estonian Business School Review*, 2, 19–36.

Poór, J., Karoliny, Zs., Alas, R. and Vatchkova, E.K. (2011) "Comparative International Human Resource Management (CIHRM) in the Light of the CRANET Regional Research Survey in Transitional Economies", *Employee Relations*, 33(4), 428–443.

Poutsma, E., Moerel, H. and Ligthart, P.E. (2015) "Multinational Enterprises: Comparing Performance-related Pay between Companies in Eastern and Western Europe", *Journal of Industrial Relations*, 57(2), 291–316.

Redman, T. and Keithley, D. (1998) "Downsizing Goes to East? Employment Re-structuring in Post-socialist Poland", *The International Journal of Human Resource Management*, April: 274–295.

Reichel, A., Brandl, J. and Mayrhofer, W. (2009) "Departmental Status in Light of a Growing Proportion of Female Staff: The Case of Human Resource Management", *European Journal International Management*, 3(4), 457–477.

Sheehan, M. (2014). "Investment in Training and Development in Times of Uncertainty", *Advances in Developing Human Resources*, 16(1), 13–33.

Soulsby, A. and Clark, E. (2006) "Changing Patterns of Employment in Post-socialist Organizations in Central and Eastern Europe: Management Action in a Transitional Context", *The International Journal of Human Resource Management*, 17(8), 1396–1410.

Steinmetz, H., Schwens, C., Wehner, M. and Kabst, R. (2011) "Conceptual and Methodological Issues in Comparative HRM Research: The CRANET Project as an Example", *Human Resource Management Review*, 21(1), 16–26.

Stojanov, C. (1992) "The Post-Socialist Transformation: A Unique (Re)-modernization", *Conflicts and Change*, 14, 211–235.

Svetlik, I., Barisic, A.F., Kohont, A., Petkovič, M., Mirič, A.A., Slavić, A., Vaupot, Z. and Poór, J. (2010) "Human Resource Management in the Countries of the Former Yugoslavia", *Review of International Comparative Management*, 11, 807–833.

Szakacs, N. (2013) *Similarities and Differences of HR Practices in Foreign Owned Subsidiaries: Focus CEE Region and Slovakia* (in Hungarian) (PhD Dissertation). Komárno: J.Selye University.

Takei, H. and Ito, Y. (2007) *Human Resource Management and Governance in Central and Eastern Europe: Case Studies in Bulgaria and Slovak Republic*. The 21st Century Center of Excellence Program – Policy Innovation Initiative: Human Security Research in Japan. Policy and Governance Working Paper Series (119).

Toth, A. (1997) "The Invention of Work Councils in Hungary", *European Journal of Industrial Relations*, 3(2), 161–181.

Trif, A. (2007) "Collective Bargaining Eastern Europe: Case Study Evidence from Romania", *European Journal of Industrial Relations*, 13, 237–246.

Tung, R.L. and Havlovic, S.J. (1996) "Human Resource Management in Transitional Economies: The Case of Poland and the Czech Republic", *The International Journal of Human Resource Management*, 7(1), 1–19.

Turnock, D. (2000) "The Human Resources of Eastern Europe: A Preliminary Discussion", *GeoJournal*, 50, 75–90.

UNCTAD (2013) *World Investment Report 2013*. New York and Geneva: United Nations Conference on Trade and Investment (UNCTAD).

Zupan, N. and Kase, R. (2005) "Strategic Human Resource Management in European Transition Economies: Building a Conceptual Model on the Case of Slovenia", *The International Journal of Human Resource Management*, 16(6), 882–906.

6 Nordic HRM: Distinctiveness and Resilience

TORBEN ANDERSEN AND FREDDY HÄLLSTÉN

Introduction

The Nordic countries – Finland, Sweden, Denmark, Norway and Iceland – are often described as a distinct regional area and emphasis has been placed on similarities, rather than differences, in institutions and culture in the description of the HRM model characterizing these societies (see, for example, Brewster and Larsen, 2000; Rogaczewska *et al.*, 2004; Lindeberg *et al.*, 2013). This way, the distinctiveness of this region is not a new phenomenon (for older and more profound contributions, see Esping-Andersen, 1990 and Andersen, 2008). The new aspect is the level of resilience characterizing the countries and even though the concept seems to be open for discussion, it has its *raison d'être* in the present case. Our perspective is that resilience has often been initiated at the individual level (see, for example, Bardoel *et al.*, 2014), aggregated to an organizational context (Lengnick-Hall *et al.*, 2011) and could be further elevated to an institutional level, here in the Nordic region. The different levels of analysis do not exclude each other. Employees' level of resilience is something which indeed can be developed and maintained through various HR principles and policies at company level (see Bardoel *et al.*, 2014, p. 283 and Lengnick-Hall *et al.*, 2011, p. 247) and the national institutional context does provide the overall framework for these HR policy decisions and practices. In this chapter we argue that there is a Nordic resilience tradition which is anchored in the institutional contexts and reinforced by HRM practices focused on individual development. This tradition contributes to a capability to recover from economic crises.

Definitions of employee resilience often include elements like the individual's ability to successfully adapt to change and use this capacity to overcome challenging situations (Lengnick-Hall *et al.*, 2011, p. 244, first type of resilience). With respect to workplaces, authors have argued that it is important to increase the awareness of how resilience functions in order to improve it. In so doing employers can augment organizational benefits including increased productivity, output and potential financial gains (see Lengnick-Hall, Beck and Lengnick-Hall's second type of resilience, Walker and Nilakant, 2014). A higher level of resilience means that employees are better equipped to deal with challenges both inside and outside the work environment, including restructuring, workload and changes in personal circumstances, and this provides a basis for the development of new capabilities and expanded abilities. Walker and Nilakant (2014) state that New Zealand studies have shown that workplaces with a learning orientated culture, where mistakes were seen as an opportunity for development and workers were encouraged to ask questions, had a higher level of employee resilience than those where these situations were perceived negatively. This focus on capabilities and expanded abilities to adapt and learn is, in our view, the basis for the Nordic model of resilience. In this light, our contribution will, to a lesser extent, be an account of national cultural and institutional developments, but with a more selective approach, where we will focus on HRM institution development and the more profound and older work relations between management and employees. These institutions will include a combination of collective industrial relations aspects of Nordic work life, together with individual and group-related HRM practices. In the next section, we present a background including the economic development, followed by some facts about the Nordic HRM institutions. Thereafter, we unfold the work-life tradition, including collaboration, co-determination and co-workership. Finally, we conclude with a section on how collective aspects of working life can cooperate with individual HRM measures and thereby support resilience.

Economic Development and Crisis in Nordic Countries

Fluctuations in the world economy during the last two decades have presented the Nordic countries with several challenges. Very few commentators, as well as people in research communities, were in doubt about the seriousness of the economic downturn taking place in the autumn of 2008. Earlier studies have shown that the average fall in GDP during a banking crisis is about 9 per cent, while unemployment rises by more than 7 percentage points over a shorter period of years (Reinhart and Rogoff, 2009). The fall in real GDP, for example in Denmark, was not this high (+5 per cent) and unemployment rose

+6 per cent from 2009 (see Tables 6.1 and 6.2 below). Still, perhaps because of the breakdown of some of the central financial institutions like some of the major banks and building societies, the public debate categorized it as 'an economic crisis'. Recession has, for a while, got a foothold in some countries following a long period of extreme growth (with a short, but deep crisis for about one to two years). This way one could claim that stability and predictability are relatively high once again, but with a rather negative outcome. Economic cycles exist no matter if a country or region has strong resilient institutions or not, and financial crisis is not a new phenomenon in the Nordic countries. Finland and (partly) Sweden were in severe trouble back in 1991–1993, when some of the financial institutions collapsed and implications for HR practices were profound (see Lähteenmäki and Viljanen, 2009). The Finnish GDP fell by 9.3 per cent, while unemployment went from 6.6 per cent to 16.3 per cent and many companies had to move from a classical (but unrealistic) patriarchal employer role towards a much more flexible, modern approach to managing employees, with a major transition of the Finnish economy. Here, two decades later, a recent OECD survey on adult skills showed that temporary employees tended to be relatively well educated and highly skilled, and temporary agency employees in Finland (and Denmark) were the best in Europe at problem solving (see the PIIAC-study in OECD, 2014).

These two measures, real GDP and unemployment rate, can both be seen as indicators of pressures on companies and organizations in general and thereby placing demands on changes in HR practices and tasks and pressures exerted on HR functions themselves towards better use of (fewer) resources – in public as well as private organizations. This is also because the public sector in the Nordic countries covers a rather large proportion of the labour market, estimated at one-third of the total workforce. Denmark, Finland and Sweden are some of the EU countries where labour costs comprise the largest share of total operating costs, between 50 per cent and 60 per cent (CRANET, 2011, p. 13).

As can be seen from Table 6.1, the downturn, measured in the national level of activity, varies somewhat among the neighbouring Nordic countries. A country like Norway is only experiencing a minor decrease in GDP (in 2009), whereas Denmark and Finland are still struggling with no, or very limited, growth. Surprisingly enough, Iceland is doing quite well (better than Finland in the worst year, 2009) and is recovering rather quickly. Denmark has, over the years, been close to the EU average and has thereby been characterized by some of the problems experienced in many of the other member states with limited growth and relatively high unemployment. From autumn 2008, companies were very hesitant in their spending and investments and public-sector income dropped drastically. Cost cutting was experienced

Table 6.1 Real GDP growth rate – volume, Nordic countries, 2005–2013

	2005	2006	2007	2008	2009	2010	2011	2012	2013
Denmark	2.4	3.8	0.8	−0.7	−5.1	1.6	1.2	−0.7	−0.5
Finland	2.8	4.1	5.2	0.7	−8.3	3.0	2.6	−1.5	−1.2
Sweden	2.8	4.7	3.4	−0.6	−5.2	6.0	2.7	−0.3	1.3
Iceland	6.0	4.2	9.7	1.1	−5.1	−2.9	2.1	1.1	3.5
Norway	2.6	2.4	2.9	0.4	−1.6	0.6	1.0	2.7	0.7
EU	2.0	3.4	3.1	0.5	−4.4	2.1	1.7	−0.4	0.0

Source: Eurostat (2015a)

Table 6.2 Unemployment rate (25–74 years), Nordic countries, 2005–2013

	2005	2006	2007	2008	2009	2010	2011	2012	2013
Denmark	4.2	3.2	3.2	2.6	4.9	6.3	6.3	6.3	5.9
Finland	6.8	6.2	5.4	4.9	6.4	6.6	6.1	6.1	6.5
Sweden	5.7	5.0	4.3	4.1	5.9	6.2	5.5	5.7	5.7
Iceland	1.6	1.8	1.3	1.9	5.5	5.8	5.5	4.5	4.3
Norway	3.4	2.6	1.8	1.7	2.2	2.7	2.4	2.3	2.6
EU	7.7	7.0	6.1	5.9	7.6	8.2	8.3	9.0	9.5

Source: Eurostat (2015b)

in the public as well as the private sector, where recruitment had been at a very high level since the mid-1990s.

Looking at the unemployment figures above, all the Nordic countries are placed at a relatively modest level, well below the EU average, even in times of crisis. It is, however, possible to detect a minor rise in all countries (except Norway) after 2008. Sweden and Finland move to around 6 per cent, while Iceland has quickly reduced its unemployment level to be the second highest Nordic country in terms of employment. Iceland is the most extreme case in the Nordic region and – surprisingly enough – the major crisis had a much smaller and shorter-term effect on the labour market than would have been expected (considering the the magnitude of its financial difficulties). The Icelandic labour market proved to be highly flexible and it 'acted' in a way that minimized the rise in the unemployment rate while spreading the effects of the shock across the labour market (Olafsdottir, 2010). Alternative downsizing methods were used, together with wage cuts. Many organizations were decreasing overtime, cutting management pay and transferring employees within the organization instead of using mass layoffs (Olafsdottir and Einarsdottir, 2013). In this way, the Icelandic example shows how varied flexibility can lead to a fast recovery from the economic crisis (Guðlaugsdóttir and Raddon, 2013; see also Chapter 21 in this book).

HR Institutions

The Nordic countries have traditionally been characterized by a high level of institutionalization and robustness of these institutions. Strong and flexible institutions have been seen as the basis for long-term stability and effectiveness of good, trust-based, HR practices (Brewster and Larsen, 2000; Ferner and Hyman, 1992, p. xxxiii). During the last two to three decades, more recent HR associations and professional bodies have developed steadily and their potential and strength seem to be closely linked to the national industrial relations (pay bargaining) systems within the individual countries. The emergence of specific HRM interest associations and the inclusion of HRM themes in management association are also supported by a steady production of graduates from universities and business schools who become members of these associations. This provides a strong level of input to the public debate on good management practices in the transition from industrial to knowledge societies (Larsen, 2009). Another important input has been provided by the CRANET studies and the continuous production of data on (strategic) HRM. In particular, the focus on HR being part of the top management group where product market strategies and HR strategies are formulated and aligned as a consequence of organizational changes is continuously taking place. This formal representation and presence has been taken as an indicator of HR strength. Compared to the other participating countries in the CRANET studies, the Nordic participants are doing well (CRANET, 2011, p. 15):

- HR on the board of the organization/Executive Committee: Sweden +90 per cent; Finland +80 per cent; Norway +75 per cent and Denmark +60 per cent.
- HR strategies (written down): Norway +80 per cent; Sweden and Finland +75 per cent and Denmark +65 per cent.
- HR involvement right from the outset on changes: Norway +65 per cent; Sweden and Finland +65 per cent and Denmark +45 per cent.

Even though the reply rate varies substantially from country to country and from year to year, from 7 per cent to 41 per cent (CRANET, 2011, p. 9), the high level scored on the three dimensions mentioned above do not go down during or after the economic crisis in many of the countries.

According to the CRANET studies, another characteristic aspect of the Nordic perspective is the line managers' responsibility for HR issues.

The devolution of HR has been going on for many years in the Nordic countries, which makes it obvious that it is not just HR functions that handle HR issues. Thus, line managers contribute to the HRM as an institution (see also Brewster and Larsen, 2000, p. 195).

Besides the global CRANET project, HR work models (mainly Anglo-Saxon) have contributed to the further development of the institutional landscape. The 'Great Place to Work' and 'Ulrich HR' role models of the division of labour within the HR domain (and the line organization) have, to a large degree, influenced management and work–life discussions in the Nordic countries. 'Great Place to Work' tries to further develop the relatively long tradition for focus on high commitment and good working conditions, with the use of quantitative measures providing benchmarking opportunities. There are a great number of companies participating in the annual celebration of the best workplace in the four countries (Iceland not included) and in Europe, arranged by 'Great Place to Work'.

The Dave Ulrich model of HR roles is implemented via organizations like the Confederation of Danish Industry and the Centre for Leadership. These have, for a while, provided courses for member organizations in this area, mainly as a way of transforming HR functions to be more output oriented and to deliver value to the line organization, i.e. restructuring the HR organization. It is not easy to find empirical documentation for the dispersion of these ideas, but the translation of the books by Dave Ulrich and colleagues indicates a certain level of influence. However, in Sweden there have been national CRANET studies about Ulrich's ideas (focused on the Shared Service Model), which show that 57 per cent of employers with more than 500 employees have completely or partially implemented the model (Boglind et al., 2013). The latest CRANET study from 2014 (not yet published) shows a further increase of the use of the Shared Service Model. Another result of this model is that line managers' responsibility for HR issues have been strengthened (Boglind et al., 2013). Altogether, we argue that an HRM perspective, focused on performance and value, has complemented the previously strong industrial relations tradition, focused on work relations, in the Nordic countries.

Work Relations in the Nordic Countries

Looking at the work relations level, the primary reason for the fast recovery from the financial crisis is, according to Bjørn Gustavsen (2012), Emeritus Professor at the Work Research Institute in Oslo, the fact that the labour markets are characterized by collaboration between employers and trade unions. In Norway, Denmark and Sweden, there has been a long and voluntaristic tradition for partnerships between trade and industry organizations and unions (Brewster and Larsen, 2000; Lindeberg *et al.*, 2013). This close collaboration is bound up with a high degree of unionization and political decisions, which guarantee employees a say through their unions. Co-determination has become a well-established phenomenon in the Nordic model, historically mostly within a country like Sweden, to some extent Norway and Denmark and with Finland and Iceland being the laggards, even though we do see major changes in the density of trade unions in the individual countries (see Table 6.3 below).

As can be seen from Table 6.3, average union density is still relatively high (compared to the rest of Europe). Between three-quarters and four-fifths of the employees in Nordic organizations and companies are members of trade unions – the 2012 figures being very similar to Scheuer's 2011 survey (Scheuer, 2011). In our view, this continuous high union density, during and after the crisis, is also an indicator of the resilience of the system.

The legal framework established at the end of the 1970s is based on the fact that it is still the employer who makes the decisions, but there is an obligation to provide information or to negotiate prior to decisions being made. Employees on their side are expected to be competent, reliable and able to act independently: 'When the trust that this reflects is confirmed, it becomes natural to involve the employees to a greater extent' (Lindeberg *et al.*, 2013, p. 153). Co-determination provides both parties with opportunities for influence and the advantages of a limited risk of industrial conflicts. By means of this, the parties feel that 'they can control their own destiny, primarily because of the limited intervention from the state', according to Bergström and

Table 6.3 Average trade union density in the Nordic countries (latest figures)

	Year	**%**
Finland	2012	75
Sweden	2012	81
Denmark	2012	84
Norway	2012	72
Iceland	2002★	92

Source: ILO (2015)

Note: ★ Data from Iceland is ten years older than data from the other countries. In Denmark, Finland and Norway, the decrease since 2002 has been about 3.5 percentage points. Sweden has experienced a decrease of 16.8 percentage points.

Diedrich (2008, p. 162). Through a healthy climate of collaboration, opportunities to change and restructure companies and organizations also increase (see also Lengnick-Hall *et al.*, 2011, p. 247), and these can be made relatively quickly (Bergström, 2014). Thus, cost cutting is seldom an acute problem for employees in many Swedish companies (in the sense that they become unemployed), since measures are taken at an early stage, e.g. transfer programmes to new jobs or training while simultaneously receiving a wage, to prevent this. In Denmark, on the other hand, there has been a long tradition for greater mobility between jobs (Sweden and Denmark are, in this respect, the two opposites). The Danish combination of growth-enhancing flexibility for employers and income security for employees, i.e. the flexicurity model, has supported continuous development and stabilization of the economy on a regular basis (Wilthagen and Tros, 2004; Jørgensen and Madsen, 2007; see also Chapter 21 of this volume). The question is, however, whether this basis for resilience will continue due to the more recent developments towards increasingly high demands for flexibility, but decreasing security levels (Madsen, 2015).

The Nordic use of a high level of co-determination is also based on a tradition and culture that encourages flat organizations with few hierarchical levels. As described by Lengnick-Hall *et al.* (2011, p. 247), these contextual elements are important for the development and continuous reinforcement of organizational resilience. Besides low hierarchy, psychological safety, broad resource networks and, not least, respectful interaction, are other important elements. Gustavsen (2012) touches upon this by stressing self-governing groups and continuous learning at work. Something which in particular has been tested in Norway, Sweden and Denmark:

> This indicates that the idea of autonomy and workplace learning has reached relatively far, while the Nordic countries score highly also in other areas – which again indicates that treating all people in the workplace as active and creative actors will pay off, not least because it makes cooperation possible.
>
> (Gustavsen, 2012)

Many of the changes (and attempted changes) in the work organization made in Nordic organizations and companies between the 1960s and 1980s were based on the continuous need for labour, i.e. industry was finding it difficult to find employees who were prepared to do jobs considered monotonous and boring (Tengblad and Andersson, 2014). For instance, in the Volvo factories in Kalmar and Uddevalla work was designed to be more interesting through replacing limited conveyor-belt work with the opportunity to build entire cars. Even though this production philosophy did not last, longer-term effects included an increased focus on collaboration within organizations and the encouragement of learning and creativity in order to promote efficiency and competitiveness.

The spirit of collaboration between the labour market parties and self-governing groups at many workplaces continues to play a major part in Nordic working life. This is due to the existence of an aspiration to unite various interests, both on a more overarching level within the respective country, and on a local level among line managers, co-workers and HR people. Managers, too, expect employees to be able to act without someone having to micro-manage them (Lindeberg *et al.*, 2013). This way resilience is an indirect outcome of a management approach that is, in the Nordic context, based on what could be called co-workership or employeeship (see Hällstén and Tengblad, 2006). The concept could be described as the opposite of leadership and more than the passive followership. Co-workers, in this sense, are active co-leaders of joint operations. Among managers as well as employees in the Nordic countries, co-workership is considered to be a complement to leadership, meaning that workers are responsible for their own work and for their relations with their colleagues and their employers, according to Hällstén and Tengblad (2006). These authors concluded that co-workership is a long-term philosophy that is characterized by four pairs of connected concepts, a 'co-workership wheel' which has different parts that support and reinforce each other:

- employee accountability and agency
- commitment and meaningfulness
- fellowship and collaboration
- trust and open-mindedness.

Co-workership, or *medarbetarskap* (in Swedish), is a well-established concept that has been in use for many years by some of the largest companies and organizations in Sweden and Norway (Hällstén and Tengblad, 2006; Velten *et al.*, 2008; Velten, 2014). For instance, the Swedish word *medarbetarskap* has been used by Volvo Cars all over the world to explain the way in which employees are expected to work. Although there is no guarantee that workers at Volvo, or other companies, really accept the idea of co-workership, there are several examples of employees at Volvo in Sweden thinking that co-workership is something important that should be retained. Co-workership then becomes a philosophy, either for operative development or as a key part of organizational culture (Andersson, 2014, p. 97).

We use the concept of co-workership, or *medarbetarskap* here, but the original concept in the Nordic countries was presented by the Danish entrepreneur Claues Møller in a book entitled *Employeeship: Mobilizing*

Everyone's Energy to Win (1986, 1992). Møller had worked as a consultant for SAS and had been influenced by Jan Carlzon, a former CEO of SAS, who was of the opinion that 'every employee should be regarded as a manager' (Andersson *et al.*, 2011, p. 272). Jan Carlzon wrote a famous book, *Moments of Truth* (1987), initially published in Sweden under the title *Riv pyramiderna* [*Tear Down the Pyramids*] (1985), which confirms his interest in the flat organization. The flat organization was one of the dominant values characterizing the SAS headquarters in Copenhagen in that period and it resonated well with the many Danish small and medium-sized companies that were trying to stay flexible.

Employers in Sweden started to use the word *medarbetarskap*, or co-workership, in the 1980s with the purpose of creating responsible co-workers (Kilhammar, 2011). Many empirical research projects have been carried out since then, both in companies and public organizations. One of the best-known examples is Volvo Cars, explaining the way in which employees are expected to work. Volvo's Floby factory (sold in 2015 to AMTEK Group) is an excellent example, although the word co-workership is seldom used (Andersson, 2014). Here, there is a strong assumption of responsibility down on the shop floor, e.g. among the machine operators, who can and are allowed to take their own initiatives, even though this can go wrong at times. Employees are given responsibility and, in doing so, are shown trust with regard to doing their duties in the best way. Trust is based on openness, which is also advanced by collaboration. Here, according to Andersson, there is good kinship, a feeling of togetherness that indicates a low power distance. The level of commitment to work and to the entire unit is great, something which, in this case, is also connected with the fact that it is a small locality. Social kinship can compensate for the fact that the duties are not always terribly interesting.

Another example of constructive co-workership is the Nordic bank *Handelsbanken* – Sweden's most profitable bank, which today has branches in Denmark, Norway, Finland and other European countries. Since the start of the 1970s, this bank has had a clear, decentralized philosophy, while simultaneously employing frameworks and guidelines with regard to how operations are to be governed (Tengblad *et al.*, 2007). The individual responsible for these thoughts is previous MD and Chairman of the Board, Jan Wallander, who made it clear from the start that it is more important to be cost-focused than budget-controlled and that 'it is more important to be able to parry than to be able to plan' (Tengblad, 2014, p. 143). Thus, closeness to the customer requires local branches and individual bank employees to be given a high level of autonomy and the opportunity to make their own decisions. The manager of the local branch, as one of their most significant duties, has to contribute towards the development of their co-workers, simultaneous to management being ultimately responsible for the co-workers' actions. However, co-workers are required to activate and participate in their own development and this is achieved through agency and influence, especially vis-à-vis the customer. This in turn leads to the advancement of commitment and meaningfulness for co-workers.

Obviously the degree of co-workership in Nordic countries varies across sectors, organizations and companies. The reasons for this can be many, but the most commonly known factor is managers not being 'mature enough' to delegate responsibility to co-workers and thus not having shown them the necessary trust. Accomplishing co-workership cannot be achieved overnight; it does require long-term and insightful headship – and, not least, leadership, which provides employees with the scope to develop knowledge, skills and abilities. Early experiences have shown that this cannot be accomplished by sending co-workers on courses about co-workership, when it is, in actual fact, the managers who should attend these courses first in order to understand the preconditions (Tengblad *et al.*, 2007). Finally, one course is not enough; continual change is required over a long period of time, which can build up the culture that is a pre-requirement of constructive co-workership.

Conclusions

Since autumn 2008, the Nordic economies – like all other European economies – have gone through an economic crisis. They have been characterized by a much faster recovery than some of the other Western economies (Katz, 2008). One very important reason is resilience. The 2008 crisis has of course changed the context influencing, but not determining, the evolution of HRM in individual countries. Nordic HR functions do actively contribute to this systems-level resilience, through classical HR practices of planning and training and varied and broadly distributed flexibility. HR functions are not working on their own, but together with line managers at different levels and in collaboration with trade unions. The strategic choices made by HR happen within the framework of national level institutions, which provides a good basis for HRM reinforced resilience. One of the most important factors in this process is co-workership, or employeeship. This is based on a long tradition of collaboration between parties in the labour market and between local managers and co-workers in workplaces within the Nordic region. The outcome is greater flexibility and a faster ability to adapt at aggregate level. Co-workership, like other Nordic phenomena focusing on working life, could be seen as an example of HRM-focused or organizational resilience. 'Co-workership is a potentially important social resource that generates organizational resilience . . . ' explains Andersson (2014, p. 110). But, as mentioned above, co-workership did not originate from HRM theories, though it has been still influenced by HRM. Co-workership could not be constructed just by using HRM theories or industrial relations-based traditions of collaboration. It is the combination of theories and perspectives that creates the specific spirit of co-workership, focusing, for instance, on influence, accountability and trust, but from different perspectives: from a collective and an individual perspective. By balancing employers' and employees' interests, organizational resilience is built up and reinforced. Summing up, the learning and reflection points taken from this distinct regional perspective on HRM in five countries are as follows.

Key Learning Points

- In this chapter we have focused on a region of geographical and historical proximity, with similarities in institutional set-up and developments. In our analysis the resilience concept works on many levels at the same time and it enables explanation (besides description) in cross-national and regional studies like this. Its simultaneous presence at different levels (individual, organizational and institutional) provides a good basis for a continuing resilience phenomenon: resilience as a shared responsibility, where all have a role in contributing to and benefiting from it.
- One could ask whether fast recovery and thereby incremental changes at national level are a sign of a whole systems' resilience? How many of the role models' characteristics we have presented can be found across the region? This is indeed highly dependent on which level of accuracy and detail one chooses – i.e. what is the appropriate perspective (Brewster and Mayerhofer, 2009, p. 278)?
- Finally, if Nordic institutions are so flexible and individual countries are under pressure to move in the same direction as the rest of the European countries (Brewster and Mayerhofer, 2009), what happens then to 'the Nordic model' in the long run? Looking at the EU affiliation: Denmark became a member state in 1973, while Sweden and Finland joined in 1995. In contrast, Iceland right now is hesitating (withdrawing its application) and Norway is still opting out of the EU. Norway (and to some extent Denmark) has, according to some studies, developed in a separate direction

(Gooderham *et al.*, 2015), a sort of hybridization of the Nordic model (CRANET, 2011). Still, we do see similarities in HR practices and work organization across countries, both Nordic EU members and non-members, leading to the conclusion that Nordic institutions, at the moment, seem to be stronger than the EU pressure for convergence. Brewster *et al.* (2004, p. 415) have emphasized the difficulties in proving evidence for (European) convergence at the empirical level.

References

Andersen, T. (2008). 'The Scandinavian Model – Prospects and Challenges', *International Tax and Public Finance*, 15, 45–66.

Andersson, T. (2014) 'Sociala resurser avgörande för organisatorisk resiliens – även i teknikorienterade organisationer', in Tengblad, S. and M. Oudhuis. *Organisatorisk resiliens – vad är det som gör företag och organisationer livskraftiga*. Lund: Studentlitteratur.

Andersson, T., Kazemi, A., Tengblad, S. and Wickelgren, M. (2011) 'Not the Inevitable Bleak House? The Positive Experiences of Workers and Managers in Retail Employment in Sweden', in Grugulis, I. and Bozkurt, Ö. (eds) *Retail Work*. Basingstoke: Palgrave Macmillan.

Bardoel, E.A., Pettit, T.M., De Cieri, H. and MacMillan, L. (2014) 'Employee Resilience: An Emerging Challenge for HRM', *Asia Pacific Journal of Human Resource Management*, 52, 279–297.

Bergström, O. (2014) *Managing Restructuring in Sweden: Innovation and Learning after the Financial Crisis*. IRENE Policy Paper N° 12/2014.

Bergström, O. and Diedrich, A. (2008) 'The Swedish Model of Restructuring', in Gazier, B. and Bruggeman, F. (eds) *Restructuring Work and Employment in Europe: Managing Change in an Era of Globalisation*. Cheltenham, UK: Edward Elgar.

Boglind, A., Hällstén, F. and Thilander, P. (2011) *HR transformation på svenska: om organisering av HR-funktioner*. Lund: Studentlitteratur.

Brewster, C. and Larsen, H.H. (eds) (2000) *Human Resource Management in Northern Europe*. Oxford: Basil Blackwell.

Brewster, C. and Mayerhofer, W. (2009) 'Comparative HRM', in Collings, D.G. and Wood, G. (eds) *Human Resource Management: A Critical Approach*. Abingdon: Routledge.

Brewster, C., Mayrhofer, W. and Morley, M. (eds) (2004) *Human Resource Management in Europe: Evidence of Convergence?* Oxford: Elsevier Butterworth-Heineman.

Carlzon, J. (1985) *Riv pyramiderna!: en bok om den nya människan, chefen och ledaren*. Stockholm: Bonniers.

Carlzon, J. (1987) *Moments of Truth*. Cambridge, Mass.: Ballinger Publishers.

CRANET. (2011) *CRANET Survey on Comparative Human Resource Management, International Executive Report 2011*. Cranfield University.

Esping-Andersen, G. (1990) *The Three Worlds of Welfare Capitalism*. London: Polity Press.

Eurostat (2015a) Available at: http://ec.europa.eu/eurostat/tgm/table.do?tab=tabl e&init=1&language=en&pcode=tec00115&plugin=1 (accessed 23 November 2015).

Eurostat (2015b) Available at: http://ec.europa.eu/eurostat/tgm/printTable.do? tab=table&plugin=1&language=en&pcode=tsdec460&printPreview=true (accessed 23 November 2015).

Ferner, A. and Hyman, R. (eds) (1992) *Industrial Relations in the New Europe.* Oxford: Oxford University Press.

Gooderham, P.N., Navrbjerg, S.E., Olsen, K.M. and Steen, C.R. (2015) 'The Labour Regimes of Denmark and Norway – One Nordic Model?', *Journal of Industrial Relations,* 57, 166–186.

Guðlaugsdóttir, S.E. and Raddon, A. (2013) *After the Economic Collapse: What Happened to Human Resources in Iceland?.* Reykjavik: Félagsvísindastofnun Háskóla Íslands.

Gustavsen, B. (2012) 'Workplace Cooperation Key to Nordic Model's Success', *Nordic Labour Journal.* Available at: http://www.nordiclabourjournal.org/ artikler/forskning/research-2012/article.2012-12-06.2375033159/?searchterm= Gustavsen. (Accessed 1 April 2015). Arbeidsforskningsinstituttet i Oslo.

Hällstén, F. and Tengblad, S. (eds) (2006) *Medarbetarskap i praktiken.* Lund, Sweden: Studentlitteratur.

ILO (2015) International Labour Office, Industrial Relations Indicators. Trade Union Membership Statistics. Geneva.

Jørgensen, H. and Madsen, P.K. (eds) (2007) *Flexicurity and Beyond: Finding a New Agenda for the European Social Model.* Copenhagen: Djøf Publishing.

Katz, R. (2008) *A Nordic Mirror: Why Structural Reform Has Proceeded Faster in Scandinavia Than Japan,* New York: Columbia Business School, Center on Japanese Economy and Business, Working Paper Series, October, No. 265.

Kilhammar, K. (2011) *Idén om medarbetarskap: En studie av en idés resa in i och genom två organisationer.* Linköping Studies in Arts and Science, No. 539. Linköping University, Sweden.

Lähteenmäki, S. and Viljanen, M. (2009) *Business and People – Three Finnish Companies' HRM Response to the Global Financial Crisis,* Turku School of Economics, Working Paper.

Larsen, H.H. (2009) 'HRM: ledelse af virksomhedens menneskelige ressourcer', *Ledelse & Erhvervsøkonomi,* 4, 7–18.

Lengnick-Hall, C.A., Beck, T.E. and Lengnick-Hall, M.L. (2011) 'Developing a Capacity for Organizational Resilience through Strategic Human Resource Management', *Human Resource Management Review,* 21, 243–255.

Lindeberg, T., Månson, B. and Larsen, H.H. (2013) 'HRM in Scandinavia – Embedded in the Scandinavian Model?', in Parry, E., Stavrou, E. and Lazarova, M. (eds) *Global Trends in Human Resource Management.* Basingstoke: Palgrave Macmillan.

Madsen, P.K. (2015) 'Dansk flexicurity under pres – både indefra og udefra', *Samfundsøkonomen,* 1, 5–10.

Møller, C. (1986) *Mobilizing Everyone's Energy to Win.* TMI Publishing.

Møller, C. (1992) *Employeeship: Mobilizing Everyone's Energy to Win.* Copenhagen: Hillerod.

OECD (2014) *Employment Outlook.* Paris: OECD.

Olafsdottir, K. (2010) *The Icelandic Labour Market – Is It Really Flexible?* Cornell University: PhD dissertation.

Olafsdottir, K. and Einarsdottir, A. (2013) *From Recession to Growth – Recovery in the Labour Market*, Reykjavik: University, Working Paper, July.

Reinhart, C.M. and Rogoff, K.S. (2009) *This Time Is Different – Eight Centuries of Financial Folly*. N.J.: Princeton University Press.

Rogaczewska, P.A., Larsen, H.H., Nordhaug, O., Dølvik, E. and Gjersvik, M. (2004) 'Denmark and Norway: Sibling or Cousins?', in Brewster, C., Mayrhofer, W. and Morley, M. (eds) *Human Resource Management in Europe: Evidence of Convergence?* Oxford: Elsevier Butterworth-Heineman.

Scheuer, S. (2011) 'Union Membership Variation in Europe: A Ten-Country Comparative Analysis', *European Journal of Industrial Relations*, 17(1), 57–73.

Tengblad, S. (2014) 'Resilient företagsledning – lärdomar från tre legendariska företagsledare', in Tengblad, S. and Oudhuis, M. (eds) *Organisatorisk resiliens – vad är det som gör företag och organisationer livskraftiga*. Lund, Sweden: Studentlitteratur.

Tengblad, S. and Andersson, T. (2014) 'From Industrial Democracy to "Coworkership": Development Trends in Work Organization Practices in Sweden', *International Labour Process Conference (ILPC)*, London, 7–9 April, 2014.

Tengblad, S., Hällstén, F., Ackerman, C. and Velten, J. (2007) *Medarbetarskap: från ord till handling*. Malmö, Sweden: Liber.

Velten, J. (2014) *Medarbeiderskap*. Teamwork OU AS. Available at: http://www.teamwork.no/medarbeiderskap.asp (Accessed 8 April, 2015).

Velten, J., Tengblad, S., Ackerman, C. and Hällstén, F. (2008) *Medarbeiderskap – fra ord till handling*. Oslo, Norway: Universitetsforlaget AS.

Walker, B. and Nilakant, V. (2014) 'Organizational Resilience. Resorgs: High Performing Today, Agile for Tomorrow, Thriving in the Future', *Human Resources,* August/September, 8–9.

Wilthagen, T. and Tros, F. (2004) 'The Concept of "Flexicurity": A New Approach to Regulating Employment and Labour Markets, in Transfer', *European Review of Labour and Research*, 10, 166–186.

Western European HRM: Reactions and Adjustment to Crises

ALEXANDROS PSYCHOGIOS, CHRIS BREWSTER AND EMMA PARRY

Introduction

The recent global financial crisis not only affected the economic, political and social environments in many countries, it also represented 'an external shock wave that changes the parameters in which HR professionals at all levels operate' (Zagelmeyer and Gollan, 2012: p. 3287). Arguably, HRM practices – such as the remarkable bonuses available for successful gambles in the financial services sector – contributed to the latest crisis, but in this chapter we examine the resultant effects of the crisis – the impact on organizations, on the workforce and on both the nature of human resource management (HRM) and the roles of HRM practitioners, in order to identify the implications for HRM practice and the need for further research.

The phenomenon of crisis has attracted extensive attention from many business scholars in different fields. Some of the early definitions describe a crisis as an event (wider or local) that threatens the survival and profitability of companies and causes extensive damage and social disruptions involving a variety of stakeholders (Shrivastava and Mitroff, 1987; Smith, 1999). More recent definitions have addressed the issue of crisis from the perspective of stakeholders' perception of concepts like threat, uncertainty and urgency (Kouzmin, 2008). In a similar vein, the term crisis is attributable to and encompasses all types of negative events and is applied to situations that are considered to be unexpected, undesirable, unpredictable and unthinkable – which most of the time produce uncertainty and disbelief (Heath *et al.*, 2009; Milasinovic *et al.*, 2010).

The definition of crisis and the attribution of its causes is much diversified, as well as biased, by the particular context in which it is studied. A central problem in trying to define crisis is the ambiguities that surround the concept itself. In the present chapter, the concept of a general (economic-societal) crisis (Jaques, 2010) is developed where the organizations are affected only as part of a broader context beyond any specific organizational crisis. Even though there is no generic acceptance regarding the precise meaning of social or/and economic crisis, there is a general acceptance of the fact that crises are situations that affect industrial and organizational systems as a whole. Such crises challenge previously held assumptions, offer urgent and novel decisions/actions, potentially lead to restructuring and affect the system and basic assumptions of the system's members (Herbane *et al.*, 1997; Smith, 2002; Elliott and Herbane, 2003; Elliott *et al.*, 2010). The arguments above support the view that crisis is a complex phenomenon that is best seen in its wider context of organization (in)effectiveness, with there being conditions in place that might create 'latent conditions' or 'error traps' or that enable the 'incubation' of a crisis (Smith, 2014). In other words, a crisis pushes organizations moving from an ordered, through complex, to chaotic systems state.

This seems to be the case with the 2008 global financial crisis, which took the form of a severe credit, banking, currency and trade crisis. The causes were mainly linked to the financial situation that emerged through US and European investment banks, insurance firms and mortgage banks (Torbat, 2008). The crisis first affected the financial institutions (Glassner and Galgóczi, 2009) worldwide and subsequently this was followed by the impact on a variety of different industries (Bardos and Varga, 2010). These events quickly became a crisis for national governments and then for multi-government organizations like the European Union. The impact had become obvious mainly through a global credit crisis, deflation, unemployment and reductions in production (Watt, 2008).

The Western European Context of Crisis

Recently, European economies faced (and some of them still face) a crisis with a wide impact. The crisis of the European economies was triggered by the wider global financial crisis of 2008, but occurred slightly later than this crisis in 2010, having a substantial impact within the Eurozone. The impact on EU economies was not the same, but since economies are interconnected the 2010 Euro-crisis negatively influenced the operation of a lot of different companies and organizations within Europe. In the spring of 2008, the EU

Commission forecast GDP growth rates of 2 per cent. In January 2009, the prediction was downgraded to 1 per cent (European Commission 2008a, 2008b and 2009). In fact, Italy, France and the UK showed decreases of between 6 per cent and 7 per cent between 2008 and 2009, while Eastern European countries suffered even more. For example, the Czech Republic showed a decrease of 17.4 per cent. The situation was even more serious in the Southern European countries (see Chapter 4). All this resulted in a reduction in industrial production. Initially, the banking and motor car industries were most affected, with other industries following (Gennard, 2009). This, in turn, led to mass redundancies in countries such as the UK, Belgium, the Netherlands, France, Germany and Denmark (Gennard, 2009; Glassner and Galgóczi, 2009). In particular, the global financial problems resulted in a number of European bank failures and declines in various stock indices, as well as reductions in the market value of equities and commodities. The cost of the banking bailout has been estimated at approximately one-sixth of world GDP (Torres, 2010).

It is usual for such a crisis to have an impact on labour markets (Gennard, 2009). In the crisis of 2008, this impact was widespread and came almost instantly. The steep economic depression resulted in great cuts in industrial output, whilst the jobs of many people were lost or were suddenly under risk in many European countries (Gennard, 2009). There was a substantial negative impact on both services (banking, ICT) and manufacturing (motor cars, chemicals and pharmaceuticals) (Glassner and Galgóczi, 2009). The retail industry did not escape, with temporary outlet closures and redundancies (Gennard, 2009). This resulted in numerous job loses, especially among fixed-term contract workers (Glassner and Galgóczi, 2009).

However, this high level of job losses seems not to be as much the case in continental Europe, where countries like Germany, France, Belgium and others have well-established employee protection policies in comparison to the UK, reflecting the difference between the Anglo-Saxon liberal markets and the coordinated market economies (Hall and Soskice, 2001). In the latter economies, characterized by wider rights of stake-holders, longer time horizons and a greater integration of employees and organizations (Whitley, 1999) there are specific measures to protect jobs from economic recession. For example, in France and Germany there are specific labour market policies that compensated employees working fewer hours during the economic crisis (Gennard, 2009). The reduction in working hours was followed by reductions of overtime as well as prolongation of holidays (Glassner and Galgóczi, 2009). Moreover, short-time working was used extensively by German manufacturing, especially in automotive production (including suppliers), metal and chemicals (Glassner and Galgóczi, 2009). In many cases, Federal or Länder government subsidies supported such approaches. The *Kurzarbeit* schemes provided government support for employees whose working hours were reduced due to lack of demand – thus maintaining capacity in the companies for future upturn, keeping people in employment through the crisis and reducing social security demands on the state (Crimmann *et al.*, 2010). French companies suffering from severe declines in demand introduced a group of measures including partial unemployment, reduction of working time, flexitime and voluntary redundancies. Also, some of them adopted occupational transition contracts that provided 80 per cent compensation of the annual income for those that were leaving the company as well as vocational training in order to help them find another job. In Belgium and Holland, the preferred policy was working time reductions (Glassner and Galgóczi, 2009 and see also OECD Economic Outlook, various dates; Eurostat, 2014).

The financial crisis also influenced Norwegian industry, resulting in significant increases in unemployment. The countermeasures involved the adoption of measures targeted to provide support and guarantees to the financial institutions (Gennard, 2009). Furthermore, Norwegian companies avoided collective redundancies and tried to introduce structural changes in order to reduce overall costs.

The situation was not the same in a lot of Eastern European countries (see also Chapter 5). For example, in countries such as Hungary, the Czech Republic, Slovakia and Poland there were radical employment cuts, with governments struggling to take measures against them (Glassner and Galgóczi, 2009). The situation was equally critical in the South-eastern European corner. Countries like Romania and Bulgaria, although under transition, were affected badly (Eurostat, 2014). However, the most dramatic impact was felt in Southern Europe, where Italy and particularly Greece and Portugal, followed by Spain and Cyprus suffered near-catastrophic collapses in their economies, leading to restructuring, huge increases in unemployment and social unrest.

Longer-term, but also crucial, was the impact of the crisis on wages (Stockhammer and Onaran, 2012). Even those who kept their jobs found that living standards were reduced for most of the years following the crisis (Denis and Shome, 2005). In some cases this was the result of explicit cuts in wages, in others the result of reduced overtime or straightforward reductions in hours and for most, living standards experienced a drop as stagnant or barely increasing wages failed to keep up with inflation (Farrell and Mavondo, 2004; Babecký *et al.*, 2010; Iverson and Zatzick, 2011).

The main conclusion of this initial analysis is that the economic crisis led the majority of European countries to change their labour market policies in order to tackle its impact. For instance, the austerity measures adopted (or imposed) by many of the South European economies had a critical impact on the labour force and especially on younger workers. Sometimes, social unrest ensued which initiated a series of political, economic and managerial changes. This resulted in the adoption of public policies that varied from country to country, reflecting substantial differences among European economies and the different level of implications for HRM.

HRM Challenges in Crisis Context

The relationship between HRM and crisis is important, since traditional economic crises have had a substantial impact on every aspect of organizational solidarity and more particularly on their people and their human resources (Cooper, 2008). According to Ramlall (2009) effective HRM can help organizations to adjust to changes that occur as a result of the economic downturn and help to maintain their competitiveness during and after the crisis. However, the same author claims that traditional HRM practices and policies became obsolete and inadequate for today's unprecedented crisis. In the recent global financial crisis, organizations faced various demands and challenges that required effective management handling with challenges, for example, in job redesign, structural changes, flexibility, etc. (Naudé *et al.*, 2012; Price and Chahal, 2006). For this reason some organizations seek to adopt softer HRM management practices and techniques during economic slowdowns in order to survive and be sustainable. However, the survival instincts of the leaders of each organization can also lead to ferocious and harsh measures, such as severe downsizing, which lead to significant numbers of people having to leave the organization and cost reductions that harm the working conditions and the well-being of the employees remaining inside it (Guthrie and Datta, 2008; Vandekerckhove *et al.*, 2012).

According to Roche *et al.* (2011) the most commonly used HRM practices during crisis are wage adjustment (cutting basic salaries, bonuses, fringe benefits and other rewards); workforce adjustment (organizational downsizing, layoffs, early retirement and staff sabbaticals); and re-organization of working methods and working time (short-time work, part-time and/or temporary work, and telework). The truth is that a lot of companies attempted to deal with the crisis through layoffs, salary freezes and cuts (Matz-Costa *et al.*, 2009; Zatzick and Iverson, 2006). This is supported by research in Ireland from Gunnigle *et al.* (2013), who found that the financial downturn had resulted in pay cuts in most organizations (with the exception of some MNCs in less affected sectors) and also significant training and development cuts. Given that salaries usually represent the largest single fixed cost, it is not surprising that organizations react in this way (Iverson and Zatzick, 2011). This approach is highly likely to have a negative effect on working conditions and on the welfare and behaviour of employees who 'survive' such actions (Gandolfi, 2008; Kammeyer-Mueller and Liao, 2006; Waraich and Bhardwaj, 2010) and in turn, this jeopardizes employee morale and performance.

It is true that the economic crisis of 2008 minimized the pivotal role of people within the majority of European organizations. Many enterprises diminished their human capital in order to cut their expenses and reduce operating costs (Roche *et al.*, 2011). For instance, companies tended to make redundancies and to increase both employees' responsibilities and working hours (Vosa, 2010). During crises, employees' trust, loyalty and performance can be influenced negatively (Maki *et al.*, 2005). In a report by the Institute of Economic and Social Research (WSI) (Bispinck *et al.*, 2010), 38 per cent of responders stated that the global economic recession negatively affected their working conditions, 44 per cent noted no change, while only 18 per cent expressed a positive opinion. In the heavy industries (manufacturing, metalworking), 65 per cent of respondents stated that their working conditions had been significantly intensified due to the economic crisis. More specifically, they stated that they were under greater pressure to perform, had suffered income losses and reduced promotion prospects as *de facto* life-time employment declined (Bispinck *et al.*, 2010). In addition, a study conducted in the UK with over 2,000 participants (employees) showed more specific changes in the working environment. For instance, 50 per cent of respondents reported feeling more anxious than before the crisis, 38 per cent felt increased job insecurity and 20 per cent reported being sick due to increased stress at work (Mulholland, 2009).

Furthermore, there is evidence from previous crises events that economic downturns have substantial impact on working conditions, making them harder (Hewlett and Luce, 2006). Hewlett and Luce found that 71 per cent of employees already working under extreme working conditions had seen cuts in their administrative support, while 37 per cent of them had no administrative assistants at all. This means that their workload and range of duties had increased. Similarly, other early working conditions surveys in France (Cartron and Gollac, 2002) and Europe (Boisard *et al.*, 2003) supported these results, showing that workload and pressure in the workplace in general had significantly increased. Similar results seem to be extracted from the later economic crises periods. In particular, and in response to the unfavourable business conditions, organizations make critical decisions concerning job redesign, discontinuance of training and development, suppression or elimination of functions and retrenchment of employees (Gomes *et al.*, 2013), increase of work-time flexibility, decreasing hours, reductions in remuneration, or freezing of remuneration and cutting or even eliminating additional payments (McDonnell and Burgess, 2013). Such courses of action are often considered by companies as required for the short-term sustainability of organizational viability in a business environment where the 'survival rule' is very apparent.

Since sustainability is widely recognized as a strategic goal of competitive companies, it is important for managers not only to emphasize such reactive practices to the economic crisis, but also to pay attention to the way employees respond to such changes. Naudé *et al.* (2012) claim that employees experience such organizational practices mainly in a negative way. Employee reactions may vary from frustration, discomfort, rage, fear, stress and uncertainty, to complete resistance (Brenner, 2008; Smollan *et al.*, 2010). In addition, in the context of adverse economic conditions, the sustainability of the motivational levels of employees may be seriously challenged. In uncertain times, employees are afraid that their jobs are under threat (Stefanescu and Darabaneanu, 2011) and that there is an increased likelihood of becoming unemployed. Highly concerned about their job security, most employees have lower engagement with their organizations (Blinov *et al.*, 2012). Their lower commitment levels result in decreased willingness to contribute additional effort for the achievement of organizational objectives. The crisis affects motivation, changing the importance of intrinsic and extrinsic motivating factors. For example, during a crisis situation people tend to focus on their earnings rather than on the importance of the job that they do (Blinov *et al.*, 2012).

Novick (2010) argues that in crisis, employees' morale rather than motivation is low. The distinction between the two is critical. Whilst morale is related to feelings, experienced emotions and psychological state, motivation is an activity, directly focused to achieve the defined aim. If we use the emotion hierarchy according to Hunter (2012), low morale is a consequence of an unpleasant deep subconscious state. In relation to crisis, the dominant emotion is hopelessness due to the perils of job loss, which can decrease self-esteem. Job insecurity can cause also high stress, fear, depression and feelings of social isolation (Gandolfi, 2008). Such emotions decrease the level of self-efficacy and can have an even more dramatic effect in worsening productivity and performance. Specifically amongst a group of employees, managers can also feel insecure and stressed as a result of the impact of economic crisis on their organizations. Managers usually take more responsibility in attempting to find survival strategies for their companies. They are also responsible for the 'hard' decisions related to downsizing. A lot of them face an ethical conflict, dealing with the contradiction between feelings like closeness to their immediate employees as well as unwillingness to harm them and their formal obligations for the company that is struggling for survival (Lämsä and Takala, 2000).

So, there are various effects of the recent economic crisis on HRM in organizations. Since the start of the financial crisis in 2008, companies in the majority of Western European countries, like many in other countries elsewhere in the world, faced incremental pressures to control costs by adopting a series of practices such as restructuring, downsizing, recruitment freezes and replacement ratios. In a similar vein, Pollitt and Bouckaert (2011) argue that the same tension is observed in the public sector in most European countries. According to the OECD (2011), countries such as the UK, the Netherlands and France have decreased the operational costs of their public sectors by approximately 10 per cent per year on average. The main target was to reduce public services personnel and therefore to decrease the cost. For example, the UK and the Netherlands planned (further) reductions of 490,000 and 150,000 jobs, while other countries (Italy, Spain, Greece, Austria and France, etc.) have taken similar measures (OECD, 2011). It seems that the trend in public staff reduction will continue in the near future as a main public policy among European countries. The effects of this on public service quality are becoming clear and are manifestly negative.

If to these trends we add the critical demographic changes that are occurring in Europe, then we can have a clearer picture of the potential employment future for the continent. For example, it seems that the average age of the workforce in the EU 27 will be increased by approximately 8.3 per cent by 2020 and by 14.8 per cent by 2060, having a substantial impact on workforces and on pension schemes and health provision (European Commission, 2012).

Together these trends could lead to the conclusion that there is a new financial, social and economic context that is complex and dynamic and will influence many aspects of social, economic and organizational life for at least a decade (Sheehan and Sparrow, 2012). In particular, the authors argue in favour of a long economic uncertainty with a variety of scenarios that could occur; from break-up with disorderly debt restructurings and the possible exit of weaker members, or greater integration implying some form of fiscal union. Whilst long uncertainty may be more likely than any of the more dramatic outcomes, labour markets will be influenced drastically in any case, since a new economic topography is emerging that will enhance even more the mobility of professionals and workers within Europe, changing labour demography and conditions and pushing organizations to apply complex productivity and arbitrage practices (Sheehan and Sparrow, 2012). This will have a serious impact on HRM. Thus, we need to understand how HRM in Europe can be organized under these circumstances.

HRM's Role in Dealing with Crisis: A European View

Bossaert (2014, p. 9) argues that, in a crisis context 'characterized by fewer and older staff, more moderate budgets and continuing technological and societal change, HRM should focus much more on tools and instruments which promote a more strategic, forward-looking and competency-based approach'. In other words, the role of HRM specialists needs to have a higher profile in order to contribute to efficient and effective HRM results in this more dynamic context. It is important to explore, therefore, the role of HRM and HR managers in the new reality being formulated from the financial crisis of 2008 and the 2010 Eurozone crisis.

The role of HRM in crisis is not a new concept. Kovoor-Misar and Nathan (2000) found that crisis uncovered organizational weaknesses that had been ignored before and hence specific outcomes could be developed that would help the organization to be better prepared in the future. In addition, Seeger *et al.* (2005) explored crisis as a motivating situation for an organization to learn how to become more flexible and adaptable, arguing that the role of HRM in crisis should be significant in the recovery of the company. Similarly, Premeaux and Breaux (2007) argued that HR managers should develop a plan for the organization's human capital in times of crisis. With their connecting function between management and employees, HR managers develop the human side of the company by helping employees to deal with all types of resultant issues, such as work, personal and even health problems. However, the research of Fegley and Victor (2005) showed that around 20 per cent of HRM experts consider that they do not have a role in developing organizational survival plans.

Another body of literature emphasizes the importance of both the resilience of organizations and, perhaps more importantly, their agility, during the global financial crisis. For the purposes of this chapter we adopt a wider definition of resilience, according to which organizational resilience is associated with all structural, group and individual level actions that ensure the continuation of business operations that remain capable in order to achieve organizational strategies during a period of drastic change (Wieland and Wallenburg, 2013) such as a crisis. Resilience is related to HRM, since effective human resource management is the 'golden key' for enterprises to overcome extreme conditions, build resilience and assistance them to compete in turbulent times (Ramlall, 2009). Resilient organizations need to develop dynamic capabilities (Ray *et al.*, 2004) and an agile workforce. Agility means the capacity to keep the workforce aligned to business needs by transitioning from one HRM configuration to another (Dyer and Ericksen, 2006). Agile organizations need the ability to learn quickly (Dyer and Shafer, 2003), which is important in order to create the organizational knowledge necessary to survive in a rapidly changing environment. Finally, organizations need an infrastructure that is highly adaptable (Dyer and Ericksen, 2006) in order to allow them to scale their workforce, coordinate and integrate new activities and deploy resources.

The literature above emphasizes the HRM role in crisis in general. It is important to explore the role of HRM in crisis in relation to the financial crisis of 2008 and the 2010 Eurozone crisis. For example, Nijssen and Paauwe (2012) explain that HRM practitioners need to develop bundles of HRM practices that support organizations during crisis. Specifically, they emphasize the importance of practices such as resource and coordination flexibility to allow easy workforce transitions, constant dialogue with employees about business planning; training to develop a broad skill set; knowledge sharing and monitoring of the outside world; and a flat hierarchy and informal coordination.

Some authors focused on the need to maintain employees' well-being and levels of motivation and engagement during difficult periods. It has been suggested that organizations have to show real concern for their employees' well-being in order to boost employee productivity and improve the overall organizational performance (Ramlall, 2009). The 'soft' HRM practices – counselling, coaching and mentoring for example – have to be implemented so as to address issues of instability and the fear of losing one's job that appear in turbulent times in order to maintain or even improve employee performance. Ironically, this is one of the primary HRM and organizational responsibilities that has not been fulfilled. In crisis, HRM specialists face the paradox of having to reduce costs, while retaining and motivating good employees. The research evidence indicates that in fraught periods, HRM should be in a central position (Vosa, 2010), using appropriate HRM practices and tools to motivate and influence employees, to boost their morale and enhance their productivity, such as effective communication, training programmes, etc.

There is evidence to suggest significant effects from building and maintaining a positive working environment during a crisis period. The concept of 'best places to work' that is related to positive organizational climate through the contribution of HRM (Carvalho and Areal, 2015) can help organizations face difficulties in uncertain times (Lyman, 2003), even if organizations that are recognized as great workplaces cannot avoid the negative effects of crisis, like downsizing

(Iverson and Zatzick, 2011). However, there is a growing literature supporting the fact that these organizations have a better chance of overcoming the negative effects of crisis and showing resilience (Carvalho and Areal, 2015). Iverson and Zatzick (2011) show that 'best places to work' organizations invest more in people commitment and thus deal better with downsizing. Training and communication seem to be the key HRM practices in this direction. Included in the requirements for being best workplaces, HRM practices that attempt to promote employee satisfaction, motivation and involvement may be particularly valuable to help organizations overcome difficult aspects of crisis (Meyer and Smith, 2009; Takeuchi et al., 2009). These practices can create the appropriate positive climate that will lead to positive emotions among employees. Avey et al. (2008) support the view that positive emotions can help employees cope with crisis situations that are new for employees and, therefore, stressful.

Similar messages may apply to Corporate Social Responsibility (CSR) practices. They can build and maintain a specific reputation of the company not only towards its external environment, but also towards its employees and stakeholders. Companies with well-recognized CSR practices seem to receive more positive evaluations from financial analysts (Ioannou and Serafeim, 2010). The same applies when companies have good records of employee well-being. They have a greater chance of avoiding bankruptcy and tend to receive better credit regardless of their debt (Verwijmeren and Derwall, 2010).

From the discussion above, we can conclude that there is only some limited evidence of HRM-specific practices that were enhanced during the period of the last international crisis incidents (global financial crisis of 2008 and Eurozone crisis of 2010). These HRM-specific practices seem to respond to the framework suggested by Smith (2014) of three interconnected stages of a crisis. In particular, the first stage is related to a crisis of management that allows the potential crisis conditions to develop. In this stage, sharing information coming from both the internal and external environment, as well as supporting employees by specific soft HRM practices like mentoring or coaching, may be useful. The second stage is the operational one, where the organization is seeking to contain the high energy situation that is causing harm. Some practices that may be well linked with this stage could be the open communication with employees, the emphasis on flat hierarchies and informal feedback and coordination that can facilitate change coming from crisis. Also, the application of staff flexibility practices may help in maintaining a positive working climate. The final stage is the crisis of legitimation, which is associated with the period after the event where the organization seeks to recover its reputation and to learn lessons from the experience. During this stage an emphasis can be given to maintaining employee morale and loyalty though training and development programmes and various CSR practices. Table 7.1 outlines the most substantial HRM-specific practices in a crisis in connection with the framework suggested by Smith (2014).

The Role of HR Managers in Crises Contexts

The effectiveness of any of these practices is strongly related to communication with employees and their union representatives in order to reach a consensus that will help the organization to at least avoid worsening any conflict that arises from the measures taken to handle the crisis (James and Wooten, 2005, 2006). A key role in this communication process is that of the HR manager (Erburu *et al.*, 2013). Traditionally, a crisis affects all personnel and leadership teams including HR managers. The latter seem to be unable to minimize the effects of crisis such as conflict, decreased reputation and reduced employee satisfaction (Garcia, 2006). It should be remembered that members of the HRM department may themselves be suffering from the same effects (insecurity, stress, etc.) as other

Table 7.1 HRM-specific practices in times of crises

Smith's (2014) Three-fold framework of crisis	HRM practices in crisis context
Stage 1: Crisis of management	• Sharing of knowledge coming from both internal and external environment • Enhancing 'soft' HRM practices (counselling, coaching and mentoring)
Stage 2: Operational crisis	• Enhancing open communication with employees • Emphasizing flat hierarchy and informal coordination • Investing and maintaining a positive working environment by promoting working flexibility of staff
Stage 3: Crisis of legitimation	• Emphasizing training and development • Investing in Corporate Social Responsibility

employees. It takes a substantial effort by HRM professionals to apply appropriate management concepts at such times and HR managers are more effective in such circumstances when they continually build relationships with employees and, by emphasizing continued investment in people and the organization, seek to enhance employee loyalty, trust and commitment. In other words, it seems that during crisis, the role of HR managers needs to be even more strategic (Erburu *et al.*, 2013). This role requires creativity and leadership ability in order to generate trust and facilitate communication. Leadership ability among senior HRM specialists was emphasized by a European study (Spencer Stuart, 2010) investigating the key challenges faced by HRM in financial services in European countries as a result of the economic crisis that began in 2008. According to this study, HR managers should take key responsibility for talent management and reward of employees. It is a common view among HRM directors who participated in the study that this leadership role needs to have a strong influential aspect so that HR managers can build the confidence and trust necessary to deal effectively with the negative effects of crisis (Spencer Stuart, 2010).

Conclusions

This chapter has examined the impact of the global financial crisis on both organizations and the workforce in general and on HRM and HRM practitioners in particular. Initial discussions in the literature about the effect of the financial crisis on HRM suggest that Zagelmeyer and Gollan's (2012) description of a 'shock wave' that has affected the parameters within which HRM operates might have some validity. These effects can be divided into two broad areas. First, the impact of the crisis on the labour market and the ability of organizations to provide job opportunities, pay increases and training and development are certainly bound to have altered the landscape in which HRM is operating. These changes also affect the emotions and motivations of employees, potentially leading to lower morale, lower engagement and lower commitment. This means that HRM practitioners need to find ways to improve and sustain employee motivation within these greater constraints on pay and other more intrinsic rewards such as training and development. Second, the need for organizations to be more agile in order to react to external uncertainty and to ensure survival, requires more dynamic capabilities and a more agile workforce. This means that, in line with Nijssen and Paauwe (2012), HRM needs to create competencies including having a scalable workforce, an adaptable organizational infrastructure and fast organizational learning and knowledge transfer. Both of these areas potentially imply different priorities for HRM in relation to bundles of HRM practices.

It should be noted that these conclusions are based on a currently limited amount of literature examining the impact of the 2008–1012 crisis on HRM; much of which is lacking in empirical evidence (though see new work in Sparrow, Hird and Cooper, 2014). Therefore, the role that HRM has played during and after the global financial crisis needs to be further explored. In particular, empirical research is needed that examines the approaches that organizations took to managing and motivating their workforce during this time. Given the emphasis on strategic HRM over the past ten years, it would be interesting to investigate whether, in practice, HRM and especially HRM departments, reverted to being more transactional or operational during this time or whether, in fact, the importance of HRM in strategic business planning increased. It is also not clear yet whether there have been any enduring employment or labour market consequences of the global economic downturn in Europe or whether the way that people think about HRM and HRM practitioners has changed. In addition, as countries (hopefully) begin to recover from the downturn, it is important to monitor how HRM's role develops during this time.

Finally, we suggest some specific areas in which we need further research:

- To what extent were ethical considerations taken into account in decisions related to HRM policies and practices in response to the crisis?
- Are there any enduring employment and labour market consequences of the global financial crisis in Europe?
- What is the leadership role in managing people during crisis?
- What impact has it had on employee morale, job and employee satisfaction or work–life balance?
- Did working conditions in Europe become extreme (or more extreme) because of the crisis?
- Did employers/managers change behaviour towards employees because of the crises?
- Have trust relationships among main organizational stakeholders (employers, employees, providers and customers) been influenced by the crisis?
- What has happened to the HRM departments themselves in response to the crisis? Have they been reduced in size? In importance? Has their role changed and if so how did it change?
- How have HRM departments been able to balance the need for short-term savings with the need to develop agility and to maintain motivation in the workforce?

Key Learning Points

- Understanding crises and the HRM adaptation to them requires a clear understanding of the meaning of terms. HRM responses to all crises may be similar but with specific adaptations to each form and each event of crisis.
- Western Europe has spent several years suffering from the effects of the global economic crisis that began in 2008. The impact on Europe and in particular on the Eurozone countries and the poorer ones of that group was dramatic.
- The impact of that crisis on core HRM policies and practices varied considerably and is still unclear. Most responses were short-term and reactive, but there were examples at different levels of more positive and long-term-oriented policies.
- Crises forces organizations to recognize even more clearly than usual the complexity of the dual-facing role of personnel specialists – on the one hand working to reduce labour costs and save money in a significant way, whilst at the same time trying to maintain morale and trust amongst the workforce.

References

Avey, J.B., Wernsing, T.S. and Luthans, F. (2008) 'Can Positive Employees Help Positive Organizational Change? Impact of Psychological Capital and Emotions on Relevant Attitudes and Behaviours', *Journal of Applied Behavioral Science*, 44(1), 48–70.

Babecký, J., Du Caju, P., Kosma, T., Lawless, M., Messina, J. and Rõõm, T. (2010) 'Downward Nominal and Real Wage Rigidity: Survey Evidence from European Firms', *Scandinavian Journal of Economics*, 112(4), 643–910.

Bardos, K.I. and Varga, E. (2010) 'The Reaction of Corporate Human Resources Management to the Economic Crisis: Finding the Ways-Out in HR', *Periodica Oeconomica*, October 2010, 101–109.

Bispinck, R., Dribbusch, H. and Öz, F. (2010) *Impact of the Economic Crisis on Employees: Results of an Online-Survey by the 'LohnSpiegel' Project*, The Institute of Economic and Social Research (WSI) Report, N. 2, March 2010.

Blinov, A., Zakharov, V. and Zakharov, I. (2012) 'Distinctive Characteristics of Personnel Motivation in a Crisis Situation', *Problems of Economic Transition*, 54(10), 3–12.

Boisard, P., Cartron, D., Gollac, M. and Valeyre, A. (2003) *Time and Work: Work Intensity*. Available from: http://edz.bib.uni-mannheim.de/www-edz/pdf/ef/02/ef0211en.pdf (accessed 1 November 2015).

Bossaert, D. (2014) 'Modernising Human Resource Management in Times of Financial Crisis: What Priorities to Maintain Capacity with Limited Resources', *Journal of Human Resource Management*, 2(1), 9–15.

Brenner, M. (2008) 'It's All About People: Change Management's Greatest Lever', *Business Strategy Series*, 9(3), 132–137.

Cartron, D. and Gollac, M. (2002) 'Fast-work et mal travail', Conference Paper for Organization, Intesification du Travail, Qualité du Travail, Centre d'Etudes de l'Emploi-CEPREMAP-LATTS, Paris, 21–22 November 2002.

Carvalho, A. and Areal, N. (2015) 'Great Places to Work: Resilience in Times of Crises', *Human Resource Management*. Available at: http://onlinelibrary.wiley.com/doi/10.1002/hrm.21676/full (accsessed 3 November 2015).

Cooper, R. (2008) 'Economic Crisis Is a Golden Opportunity for OH and HR', *Occupational Health*, 60(11), 10.

Crimman, A., Wiessner, F. and Bellmann, L. (2010) *The German Work-sharing Scheme: An Instrument for the Crisis*, Geneva, ILO.

Denis, D. and Shome, D. (2005) 'An Empirical Investigation of Corporate Asset Downsizing', *Journal of Corporate Finance*, 11(1), 427–448.

Dyer, L. and Ericksen, J. (2006) *'Dynamic Organizations: Achieving Marketplace Agility through Workforce Scalability'*, CAHRS Working Paper, 6–12.

Dyer, L. and Shafer, R. (2003) 'Dynamic Organizations: Achieving Marketplace and Organizational Agility with people', in Peterson, R.S. and Mannix, E.A. (eds) *Leading and Managing People in the Dynamic Organization*. Mahwah, NJ: Lawrence Erlbaum, 7–40.

Elliott, E.D. and Herbane, B. (2003) 'Greater Than the Sum of Its Parts: Business Continuity Management in the UK Finance Sector', *Risk Management: An International Journal*, 5(1), 65–80.

Elliott, D., Swartz, E. and Herbane, B. (2010) *Business Continuity Management: A Crisis Management Approach*. 2nd edn. New York: Routledge

Erburu, L.S., Ruz, E.S. and Arboledas, J.R.P. (2013) 'Economic Crisis and Communication: The Role of the HR Manager', *Business Systems Review*, 2(2), 278–296.

European Commission (2008a) *Economic Forecast Spring 2008, European Economy: 1*, Luxembourg, Office for Official Publications of the EC.

European Commission (2008b) *Economic Forecast Autumn 2008, European Economy. No. 6*, Luxembourg: Office for Official Publications of the EC.

European Commission (2009) *Interim Forecast*, January, Brussels.

European Commission (2012) *The 2012 Ageing Report, Economic and Budgetary Projections for the 27 EU Member States (2012–2060)*, Brussels 2012.

Eurostat (2014) *Unemployment Statistics*, Luxembourg: Office for Official Publications of the EC.

Farrell, M. and Mavondo, F. (2004) 'The Effect of Downsizing Strategy and Reorientation Strategy on a Learning Orientation', *Personnel Review*, 33(4), 383–402.

Fegley, S. and Victor, J. (2005) *2005 Disaster Preparedness: Survey Report (Oct.)*, Alexandria, VA: Society for Human Resource Management.

Gandolfi, F. (2008) 'Learning from the Past – Downsizing Lessons for Managers', *Journal of Management Research*, 8(1), 3–17.

Garcia, H. (2006) 'Effective Leadership Response to Crisis', *Strategy and Leadership*, 34(1), 4–10.

Gennard, J. (2009) 'The Financial Crisis and Employee Relations', *Employee Relations*, 31(5), 451–454.

Glassner, V. and Galgóczi, B. (2009) *Plant-level Responses to the Economic Crisis in Europe*, European Trade Union Institute for Research, Education and Health and Safety (ETUI-REHS) *WP 2009.01*.

Gomes, D.R., Asseiro, V. and Ribeiro, N. (2013) 'Triggering Employee Motivation in Adverse Organizational Contexts: "Going the Extra Mile" While Holding Hands with Uncertainty?', *Business and Management Research*, 2(1), 41–54.

Gunnigle, P., Lavelle, J. and Monaghan, S. (2013) 'Weathering the Storm? Multinational Companies and Human Resource Management through the Global Financial Crisis', *International Journal of Manpower*, 34(3), 214–231.

Guthrie, J.P. and Datta, D.K. (2008) 'Dumb and Dumber: The Impact of Downsizing on Firm Performance as Moderated by Industry Conditions', *Organization Science*, 19(1), 108–123.

Hall, P.A. and Soskice, D. (2001) 'An Introduction to Varieties of Capitalism', in Hall, P.A. and Soskice, D. (eds) *Varieties of Capitalism: The Institutional Foundations of Comparative Advantage*. Oxford: Oxford University Press.

Heath, R.L., Lee, J. and Ni, L. (2009) 'Crises and Risk Approach to Emergency Planning and Communication: The Role of Similarity and Sensitivity', *Journal of Public Relationship Research*, 21(2), 123–141.

Herbane, B., Elliott, D. and Swartz, E. (1997) 'Contingency and Continua: Achieving Excellence through Business Continuity Planning', *Business Horizons*, 40(6), 19–25.

Hewlett, S.A. and Luce, C.B. (2006) 'Extreme Jobs – The Dangerous Allure of the 70-hour Work Week', *Harvard Business Review*, 84(12), 49–59.

Hunter, M. (2012) 'How Motivation Really Works: Towards an Emoto-motivation Paradigm', *Economics, Management and Financial Markets*, 7(4), 138–196.

Ioannou, I. and Serafeim, G. (2010) *The Impact of Corporate Social Responsibility on Investment Recommendations*. Working Paper 11/017, Cambridge, MA: Harvard Business School.

Iverson, R. and Zatzick, C. (2011) 'The Effects of Downsizing on Labor Productivity: The Value of Showing Consideration for Employees Morale and Welfare in High-Performance Work Systems', *Human Resource Management*, 50(1), 29–44.

James, E.H. and Wooten, L.P. (2005) 'Leadership as (Un)usual: How to Display Competence in Times of Crisis', *Organizational Dynamics,* 34(2), 141–152.

James, E.H. and Wooten, L.P. (2006) 'Diversity Crises: How Firms Manage Discrimination Lawsuits', *Academy of Management Journal,* 49(6), 1103–1118.

Jaques, T. (2010) 'Reshaping Crisis Management: The Challenge for Organizational Design', *Organization Development Journal*, 28(1), 9–17.

Kammeyer-Mueller, J. and Liao, H. (2006) 'Workforce Reduction and Job-seeker Attraction: Examining Job Seekers' Reactions to Firm Workforce-Reduction Policies', *Human Resource Management,* 45(4), 585–603.

Kouzmin, A. (2008) 'Crises Management in Crises?', *Administrative Theory & Praxis*, 30(2), 155–183.

Kovoor-Misar, S. and Nathan, M. (2000) 'Timing Is Everything: The Optimal Time to Learn from Crises', *Review of Business*, 21(3/4), 31–36.

Lämsä, A-M. and Takala, T. (2000) 'Downsizing and Ethics of Personnel Dismissals: The Case of Finnish Managers', *Journal of Business Ethics*, 23(4), 389–399.

Lyman, A. (2003) 'Building Trust in the Workplace', *Strategic HR Review*, 3(1), 24–27.

McDonnell, A. and Burgess, J. (2013) 'The Impact of the Global Financial Crisis on Managing Employees', *International Journal of Manpower*, 34(3), 184–197.

Maki, N., Moore, S., Grunberg, L. and Greenberg, E. (2005) 'The Responses of Male and Female Managers to Workplace Stress and Downsizing', *North American Journal of Psychology*, 11(2), 295–312.

Matz-Costa, C., Catsouphes, M., Besen, E. and Lynch, K. (2009) 'The Difference a Downturn Can Make: Assessing the Early Effects of the Economic Crisis on the Employment Experiences of Workers', *Aging and Work*, 22(1), 1–22.

Meyer, J. and Smith, C. (2009) 'HRM Practices and Organizational Commitment: Test of a Mediation Model', *Canadian Journal of Administrative Sciences*, 17(4), 319–331.

Milasinovic, S., Kesetovic, Z. and Nadic, D. (2010) 'The Power and Importance of Crisis Management in Facing Modern Crises', *Megatrend Review*, 7(2), 273–290.

Mulholland, T. (2009) 'Preventing and Managing Stress: The Survivor Effect in Global Recession', *Journal of Human Resource*, 3(1), 8–11.

Naudé, M., Dickie, C. and Butler, B. (2012) 'Global Economic Crisis: Employee Responses and Practical Implications for Organizations', *Organizational Development Journal*, 30(4), 9–24.

Nijssen, M. and Paauwe J. (2012) 'HRM in Turbulent Times: How to Achieve Organizational Agility', *International Journal of Human Resource Management*, 23(16), 3315–3335.

Novick, D. (2010) 'Understanding Morale and Motivation Helps Managers Cope with Tough Times', *Printweek*, 16–16.

OECD (2011), *Public Servants as Partners for Growth*. Paris: OECD.

Pollitt, C. and Bouckaert, G. (2011) *Public Management Reform: A Comparative Analysis – New Public Management, Governance, and the Neo-Weberian State*. Oxford: Oxford University Press.

Premeaux, S.F. and Breaux, D. (2007) 'Crisis Management of Human Resources: Lessons from Hurricanes Katrina and Rita', *Human Resource Planning*, 30(3), 39–47.

Price, A.D.F. and Chahal, K. (2006) 'A Strategic Framework for Change Management', *Construction Management and Economics*, 24(3), 237–251.

Ramlall, S.J. (2009) 'Continuing the HR Evolution: Building Resilience in Turbulent Economic Times', *International Journal of Global Management Studies*, 1(3), 19–28.

Ray, G., Barney, J.B. and Muhanna W.A. (2004) 'Capabilities, Business Processes and Competitive Advantage: Choosing the Dependent Variable in Empirical Test of the Resource-based View', *Strategic Management Journal*, 25(1), 23–37.

Roche, K.W., Teague, P. and Coughlan, A. (2011) *Human Resources in the Recession: Managing and Representing People at Work in Ireland*, Final Report, Labour Relations Commission.

Seeger, M.W., Ulmer, R.R., Novak, J.M. and Sellnow, T. (2005) 'Post-Crisis Discourse and Organizational Change, Failure and Renewal', *Journal of Organizational Change Management*, 18(1), 78–95.

Sheehan, M. and Sparrow, P. (2012) 'Global Human Resource Management and Economic Change: A Multiple Level of Analysis Research Agenda', *The International Journal of Human Resource Management*, 23(12), 2393–2403.

Shrivastava, P. and Mitroff, I.I. (1987) 'Strategic Management of Corporate Crises', *Columbia Journal of World Business*, 23(1), 5–12.

Smith, D. (1999) 'Vicious Circles: Incubating the Potential for Organizational Failure', *Risk Management*, 46(10), 7–11.

Smith, D. (2002) 'Not by Error, but by Design – Harold Shipman and the Regulatory Crises for Health Care', *Public Policy and Administration*, 17(4), 55–74.

Smith, D. (2014) 'Organizational Ineffectiveness: Environmental Shifts and the Transition to Crisis', *Journal of Organizational Effectiveness: People and Performance*, 1(4), 423–446.

Smollan, R.K., Sayers, J.G. and Matheny, J.A. (2010) 'Emotional Responses to the Speed, Frequency and Timing of Organizational Change', *Time & Society*, 19(1), 28–53.

Sparrow, P.R., Hird, M. and Cooper, C.L. (2014) *Do We Need HR? Repositioning People Management for Success*. London: Palgrave.

Spencer Stuart (2010) *HR Leadership Challenges in European Financial Services Companies*. Amsterdam: SpencerStuart.

Stefanescu, F. and Darabaneanu, D. (2011) 'The Human Resources Management in the Context of the Economic Crisis', *Romanian Economic and Business Review*, 6(1), 104–117.

Stockhammer, E. and Onaran, Ö. (2012) 'Rethinking Wage Policy in the Face of the Euro Crisis. Implications of the Wage-Led Demand Regime', *International Review of Applied Economics*, 26(2), 191–203.

Takeuchi, R., Chen, G. and Lepak, D.P. (2009) 'Through the Looking Glass of a Social System: Cross-level Effects of High-performance Work Systems on Employees' Attitudes', *Personnel Psychology*, 62(1), 1–29.

Torbat, A.E. (2008) *Global Financial Meltdown and the Demise of Neoliberalism*. Global Research (Center for Research on Globalization).

Torres, R. (2010) 'Incomplete Crisis Responses: Socio-economic Costs and Policy Implications', *International Labour Review*, 149(2), 227–237.

Vandekerckhove, S.J., Van Peteghem, and Van Gyes, G. (2012) *Wages and Working Conditions in the Crisis,* Eurofound: Dublin. Available at: https://lirias. kuleuven.be/bitstream/123456789/355016/2/tn1203015s.pdf (accessed 3 November 2015).

Verwijmeren, P. and Derwall, J. (2010) 'Employee Well-being, Firm Leverage, and Bankruptcy Risk', *Journal of Banking & Finance*, 34(5), 956–964.

Vosa, H. (2010) *The Impact of Economic Crisis on HRM Practices in Estonia*. Unpublished M.Ed., Dissertation, Aalto University.

Waraich, S.B. and Bhardwaj, G. (2010) 'Workforce Reduction and HR Competencies: An Exploratory Study', *The Indian Journal of Industrial Relations*, 46(1), 100–110.

Watt, A. (2008) *The Economic and Financial Crisis in Europe: Addressing the Causes and the Repercussions European Economic and Employment Policy Brief, 3*. Brussels: ETUIREHS.

Whitley, R. (1999) *Divergent Capitalisms: The Social Structuring and Change of Business Systems*. Oxford: Oxford University Press.

Wieland, A. and Wallenburg, C.M. (2013) 'The Influence of Relational Competencies on Supply Chain Resilience: A Relational View', *International Journal of Physical Distribution & Logistics Management*, 43(4), 300–320.

Zagelmeyer, S. and Gollan, P.J. (2012) 'Exploring Terra Incognita: Preliminary Reflections on the Impact of the Global Financial Crisis upon Human Resource Management', *International Journal of Human Resource Management*, 23(16), 3287–3294.

Zatzick, C.D. and Iverson, R.D. (2006) 'High-involvement Management and Workforce Reduction: Competitive Advantage or Disadvantage?', *Academy of Management Journal*, 49(5), 999–1015.

Part II

Mezzo-Views: Cross-National HRM Strategies, Structures, Policies and Practices

8 Mezzo-Views: Cross-National and Organizational Level HRM Strategies, Structures, Policies and Practices – Overview of Part II

PAUL SPARROW, MICHAEL DICKMANN AND CHRIS BREWSTER

Part I shows us that there are many pressures on European MNCs to design their HRM configurations in ways that facilitate both the globalization of their people management function, whilst simultaneously being effective across multiple regions, each of which may be characterized by different patterns of continuity and change.

In Part II we adopt a mezzo-level perspective, with mezzo being defined as the middle level. We therefore identify a series of cross-national trends and developments that are also intimately linked to organizational level responses. In selecting the topics that we see as leading to important changes in HRM strategies, structures, policies and practices, we have been cognizant of the need to capture major trends that apply to most or all of Europe, but which are also potentially being dealt with in diverse and unique ways either across Europe as a whole, or across different countries within Europe. The various contributions to Part II first explain the pressures on European MNCs and other international organizations and then lay out the resulting changes that are under way.

We could of course examine many trends at this mezzo-level, but we have been guided by a series of challenges that are very contemporary and that are clearly also now beginning to shape academic work. In this chapter, we set up the various contributions that are to come and signal why and in what ways the discussions that they raise are important for the field. We include chapters on five IHRM issues: developments in the not for profit (NfP) sector; the impact of HRM in overseas MNCs operating within Europe; the pursuit of corporate responsibility strategies; demographic trends in relation to age and diversity; and international migration.

What is fascinating about these developments is that they are bringing a new impetus to academic research and are serving to enrich the field of IHRM by incorporating new models, theories, frameworks and levels of analysis.

In Chapter 9, Chris Brewster, Paul Boselie, Peter Liesink and Kerstin Alfes provide an overview of HRM in NfP organizations from an international perspective by focusing on HRM in the national public sector, intergovernmental organizations and international non-governmental organizations, the management of which has arguably been picked up more by European academics than other international colleagues. The public sector tends to be larger in European countries than in most other capitalist countries around the world. In a European context, activities such as health care, education, military defence, foreign affairs, infrastructure, transportation and social policies are nationally required and organizations involved in these activities can be major national employers. Many international inter-governmental organizations (IGOs), such as the European Union (EU), also feature intensively in policy debates that surround HRM. The chapter shows that the study of these sorts of organizations brings some important insights to IHRM. Their highly institutionalized contexts, unique governance structures involving multiple actors and stakeholders, politicized context, along with the complex questions associated with the nature of their performance and performance management, can help to broaden IHRM research. Learning about their IHRM has direct relevance to the management of MNCs, who too now find that they face challenges of social legitimacy, relevance and corporate social responsibility. It also, they argue, broadens the scope of analysis beyond the impact of international economic developments to include mezzo-level factors such as the effects of population ageing and environmental risks. The public management reform movement in Europe also carries potential messages for MNCs concerning the management of customer voice and new participation platforms. This is also relevant in the context of corporate social responsibility (CSR). Understanding how to manage international issues whilst dealing with the consequences of austerity policies is not just a concern for public sector, but will be important for MNCs too, as they attempt to address deep questions about productivity. The collaborative culture and constitutional context international non-governmental organizations (INGOs), with their need for high levels of dialogue, confidence, trust and conflict management, is now becoming a characteristic of much IHRM in MNCs as they operate through strategic alliances, risk-sharing joint ventures and collaborative business models. As MNCs become, themselves, increasingly embedded in a networked economy in which the boundaries between public and private sector blur, their own learning agenda is beginning to capture developments beyond their traditional competitors.

The chapter concludes that the study of NfP organizations brings with it a range of important research questions. For example, NfP organizations have significantly better outcomes when it comes to diversity management and, given the need to operate in countries with different values, it relies more on value-based recruitment (the right person-organization fit in combination with the right person-job fit). Having generally lower levels of resources, more has to be done with training and development, given that spending tends to be lower and their talent management and expatriate management strategies, whilst driven by the same overall goals stressed by the IHRM literature, must meet much more nuanced employee value propositions, stress far more collective goals and aims and leave behind strong local legacies and capabilities. The public service orientation of employees means that their motivations often relate more to affective commitment than to career drives and there are also particular challenges to employee engagement and employee health (such as job stress, safety and burnout risks). Compared to traditional MNCs, there can be a different balance between internal and external or horizontal and vertical staff mobility within and between the different parts of the NfP sector and between the NfP sector and the private sector. Finally, performance management is conceived in relationship to higher levels of accountability and social legitimacy. Whilst these research interests need to be addressed to a specific agenda that helps NfP organizations deal with their unique IHRM challenges, they also present potentially fruitful insights for the broader IHRM field. There is the potential for considerable transfer of learning both across sectors and across countries as a result.

In Chapter 10, Chul Chung and Masayuki Furusawa examine the impact on IHRM of foreign MNCs operating in Europe. In a book like this, it is useful to understand the unique agendas or policies that can be seen in European MNCs, but of course Europe has also been a major destination for foreign direct investment from other parts of the world, from the other triad economies, such as the USA and Japan, as well more recently from emerging economies. Foreign MNCs operating in Europe face some unique cross-national challenges. These mainly stem from the uniqueness of European traditions and high levels of diversity across their European operations. The European context brings with it dispersed workforces and more complex coordination of HRM operations, potentially making it more difficult for MNCs to exploit the benefits of scale. At the simplest practical level, the diverse employment relations frameworks can make regional coordination more complex. More intriguingly, by understanding how overseas MNCs learn how to transfer some of their own arrangements into Europe, we might, as researchers, learn more about the process of transfer and adaptation of HRM practices. They help us understand this context in order to contribute to a number of core debates within the IHRM literature. Their analysis provides insight into the degree of global standardization versus localization within subsidiary HRM practices, the utilization of parent country nationals (PCNs) and host country nationals (HCNs) within subsidiaries, specific country of origin effects, host country or local influences and transnational influences – the dominance effect.

In US MNCs, the trajectory towards globalization has evolved through a strongly ethnocentric approach until the 1980s, to a decentralized approach with more autonomy for national subsidiaries in the late 1980s, to the current regionalized approach since the 1990s. This has allowed European headquarters more influence over subsidiaries in the region, within a policy context driven by a strong tendency towards global standardization in HRM practices and a preference for the limited utilization of expatriates in order to promote the greater use of local employees in key positions in subsidiaries. The working assumption has been that MNCs need to bring about a high degree of codification of HRM practices in order to be able to transfer their practices across borders successfully. Does such an assumption hold if we examine the behaviour of Japanese MNCs through European eyes? Not necessarily. The progress of localization in European subsidiaries is driven by factors including the relative market size and power of the operations compared to the home market and higher levels of internal internationalization.

The HRM solutions that Korean MNCs have been putting in place in their European operations, in contrast, do not stem from an accepted and comfortable home market regime. Rather, Korean firms have been questioning and reforming the home market regime in parallel with adapting their overseas operations. Their approach to subsidiary HRM practices is characterized as part of a new route to globalization, called hybridization, which entails a blending of global HRM standards and local practices. The new insights that this chapter creates is into the IHRM processes that this hybridization entails. It reveals a more informed selection of the components of practices for global standardization, carefully based on relevant logics of action, mixed with the use of US best practices as a starting template for global standardization of the selected components in subsidiary HRM practices. The curious outcome is a perceived weaker legitimacy in managerial authority and pronounced 'liabilities of origin'. There is a noticeable 'dominance effect' (an influence of US thinking) in the subsidiary HRM practices of Korean MNCs. Not only does the chapter lead us towards thinking more openly about the different paths of globalization of HRM, it reminds us that each path likely brings its own inconsistencies and mixed messages, caused by the discrepancies between formal and informal practices. Each path becomes dependent on its own moderating mechanisms. Chul Chung and Masayuki Furusawa conclude that the pattern of IHRM approaches adopted by an MNC involves different combinations of multiple institutional influences, such as country of origin, local and dominance effects. Studying the behaviour of triad MNCs through a European lens makes this more evident. Moreover, it draws attention to a series of important intra-organizational factors, such as the capabilities of HRM-related actors and the relationships among them in the actual design and implementation of policies and practices in an international context.

Chapter 11 also highlights the importance of a number of intra-organizational factors in IHRM, this time in the context of corporate responsibility strategies. Todd Cardarelli, David Grayson and Michael Dickmann discuss the HRM challenges faced by European MNCs around corporate responsibility (CR) and sustainability. They argue that the role of business in society is a priority concern for many of the world's largest MNCs. Despite significant programmes, such as General Electric's *Ecomagination* and Unilever's *Sustainable Living Plan* there remains a performance gap between what CEOs believe their businesses should do and what their own companies are actually doing. They believe that if we are to support this need, we should use the concept of CR rather than the more commonly used corporate social responsibility (CSR).

The first contribution that the chapter makes is to broaden our definitions into the concept of corporate responsibility (CR), in order to integrate sustainability into everything that an organization does. This is necessary, they argue, because currently research is too focused on single initiatives associated with corporate social responsibility, corporate citizenship and corporate sustainability. It would be better served by focusing on the mindsets and behaviours required to take responsibility for social, economic and environmental impacts.

The second contribution is to question the assumption made by much of the literature that organizations should engage in CR activities purely because they will be rewarded in economic and financial terms.

This assumption has (dangerously) shifted the research agenda away from an ethics orientation towards a more performance-orientated one and has seen the level of analysis move from a macro-social level to the organizational level. Many of these activities, at heart, involve the creating of a global sustainability culture, which in turn entails common HRM outcomes such as the attraction and retention of employees, organizational commitment, skill development and employee engagement. Employees and managers must have the knowledge, skills and abilities to work effectively across borders, suggesting the need for a more developmental frame for the management of international assignments and the need to implement global management development programmes. In short, CR must act as a globally integrated initiative. Progress is also dependent on much greater collaboration at a corporate level and this has implications for the structural positioning of CR activity within corporate headquarters and within subsidiary activity. Unfortunately, the collaboration between the CR specialists and other parts of the business, especially HRM, is often very limited. This is the case despite the fact that many aspects of CR are concerned with how a business behaves towards its employees, the workplace impacts that it has and leadership competencies. The role of HRM professionals is to help the rest of the business embed responsible business practices and to create an authentic employer brand of choice to engage and motivate employees. However, the local responsiveness debate must also be incorporated into this. In reviewing the HRM dimensions of CR, they conclude that this literature continues to show that the HRM function is often absent from the design and implementation of CR strategy. To address this, whilst there are generic, culture-free things that HRM professionals can do to support various stages of CR strategy development and implementation in an organization (which the chapter lays out), we still need to focus on European approaches. The chapter stresses the importance played by institutional factors, such as components of national business systems and national culture in influencing how CR is perceived and implemented at the local level.

The third contribution the chapter makes is to introduce the notion of 'implicit' and 'explicit' aspects of the global strategy in order to manage this need to balance both global integration and local responsiveness. Whilst explicit elements might articulate societal interests, implicit elements might describe the actions that comply when institutional expectations align the actions of the MNC with the values, norms and rules that result in either mandatory or customary requirements to address specific stakeholders, such as unions or specific national concerns. The chapter also takes us into questions about the relative weight that can be given to the actions and initiatives of the players involved. In some instances, institutions above the level of the MNC (such as the EU in Europe) can have a powerful shaping effect. In other instances where there might be weaker institutional influences, MNCs might, by their integrated efforts, produce their own system-changing effects.

In Chapter 12, Emma Parry, Heike Schröder, Matt Flynn and Deirdre Anderson examine another mezzo-level issue, which is the challenge created in Europe by age and diversity issues. Their analysis shows that the HRM strategies of firms are deeply embedded in the national demographic and institutional context and actors need to work in an increasingly collaborative way to support age diversity through more innovative work practices around flexible working hours, lifelong learning, job rotation, healthy working, age inclusivity and career planning. They also compare and contrast the national reactions between Germany and the UK, giving particular attention to early retirement and linking different push and pull strategies to the different models of capitalism. The UK, as a liberal market economy, is seen as following a path of light touch intervention that encourages firms to maintain either older workers' productivity or else externalize (unproductive) older workers and promote redundancy-induced early retirement in order to create employment opportunities for younger individuals. In contrast, Germany, as a coordinated market economy, adopted a more proactive role with regard to early retirement, but as with the UK, also has to accommodate national pressures and EU legal pressures that call for the promotion of longer working lives, the discouragement of early retirement and the growth of socio-economic problem groups that do not have the occupational qualifications to match the required flexibility.

Finally, in Chapter 13, Akram Al Ariss, Jean-Luc Cerdin, and Chris Brewster address the issue of migration. They first point out there is a unique European context, with the phenomenon of intra-EU mobility, but also discuss the generic consequences of migration. The lesson for the field of IHRM is that their discussion of migration shows that the IHRM (and domestic) practices of organizations can be viewed against the broader socio-economic backdrop, which is one where freedom to move capital has been linked with freedom of movement of labour, but these two freedoms then have spin-off effects on the roles, responsibilities and accountabilities of a wide range of actors for the total system costs of the resultant behaviour of organizations and individuals. At a policy level, migration has impacts beyond its immediate role in resourcing, with debates ranging across issues such as boosts to productivity and entrepreneurship, the movement of highly-skilled migrants and knowledge workers and the development of a more globalized labour markets for craft-skilled employees, through to impacts on national skills systems, under-utilization of skills, wage impacts and unacceptable labour practices. They lay out what is a very wide range of HRM issues that are triggered by migration at the individual level, organizational level and macro level of policy context. They conclude that migrants can be a cost-effective option for internationalization, with knowledge and skills that can aid this internationalization. Migrants are a significant element of the international workforce. However, academic distinctions are problematic, in reality people can move from being a migrant to being an expatriate (Andresen *et al.*, 2014). This is an important issue to resolve, because different kinds of migrants have different motivations and need different forms of management to be of most value to the organization.

In summary, although Part II addresses issues that sit at the interface between cross-national trends and developments at the organizational level, they show that IHRM research, when seen through a contemporary and a European lens, is increasingly adopting a multi-level frame of analysis.

Reference

Andresen, M., Bergdolt, F., Margenfeld, J. and Dickmann, M. (2014) 'Addressing international mobility confusion: Developing definitions and differentiations for self-initiated and assigned expatriates as well as migrants', *The International Journal of Human Resource Management*, 25(16), 2295–2318.

9 Beyond the Private Sector: International HRM in the Not for Profit Sectors

CHRIS BREWSTER, PAUL BOSELIE, PETER LEISINK AND KERSTIN ALFES

The Importance of the Not for Profit Sector

Most discussions of HRM are explicitly, or more often implicitly, about the private sector. That is particularly the case in international HRM, where the discussion is dominated by analyses of the HRM of multinational corporations (MNCs). But the private sector is just one of many kinds of multinational enterprise operating internationally, employing people internationally and needing to think about how to manage them.

The not for profit (NfP) sector covers a broad category of organizations that are not primarily aimed at profit maximization. Not for profit organizations have a different ownership structure than private organizations. In contrast to the private organizations' shareholders and/or owners, not for profit organizations have members in the case of, for example, cooperatives and (voting) citizens in the case of, for example, governments. This has implications for governance structures amongst the non-governmental organizations. NfP organizations can have a wide set of organizational goals beyond economic returns aimed at contributing to some kind of public value (Leisink *et al.*, 2013). Given the unique constellation of NfP organizations, they often operate in highly institutionalized contexts and with unique governance structures (Vandenabeele *et al.*, 2013). This also includes multiple actors and stakeholders involved in the shaping of the organization. The distinction between not for profit and private organizations is fuzzy in practice, for example, as a result of privatization where governments often retain an interest or a 'golden share' and frequently arrange specific regulatory regimes. NfP organizations can be linked to governments (in areas such as schools, local governments and military services), semi-linked to governments (health care organizations) or be entirely non-governmental (for example, national charities and international non-governmental organizations such as the Red Cross).

In this chapter, three leading themes that characterize not for profit organizations will be used as guidelines:

1 multiple stakeholders and their influence on the shaping of (international) HRM in these organizations;
2 politics and the political dimension, for example, affecting the governance of these organizations, their missions and their goals; and
3 performance and performance management, for example, in terms of what is performance in these organizations and how is it measured/ managed?

This chapter starts with an overview of HRM in public sector organizations from an international perspective. The second part of the chapter is focused on HRM in international governmental organizations, in particular those located in and related to the European context. The third part is aimed at HRM in international non-governmental organizations, again focused on Europe.

But first, why is the topic important? Most HRM research in general has been concentrated on large multinational companies (Keegan and Boselie, 2006), and this is particularly true in international human resource management. There has been a long (if much smaller) tradition of research into HRM in the not for profit sector and there is now increasing HRM research in, for example, public sector organizations and in particular the health care sector (see, for example, the work of Bach and Kessler, 2007 and Gould-Williams, 2003). It is usually assumed, however, that such organizations (national and local governments, hospitals, utilities) are local operations and have little relationship with international HRM. In this chapter we argue that this is wrong, that there are many NfP organizations where international HRM is significant and that there is considerable scope for further research into such organizations and international HRM.

Not for profit organizations employ a significant number of employees. For most organizations the single largest element of operating costs is the cost of labour, but for many of these NfP organizations it is by far the outstanding element of costs. (Although there are exceptions: CERN, located in Geneva, for example, employs 2,400 people but their main costs are related to high technology and the particle accelerator.) Otherwise, human resources, or people as we used to call them, are almost the only major resource that these organizations have for achieving their mission. It's the people that make the difference in the end.

We consider three different kinds of not for profit organizations that have a direct relationship with international HRM:

- the national public sector;
- the intergovernmental organizations; and
- the international non-governmental organizations.

The range of organizations in each of these categories is immense, so we are forced into generalization but, given the paucity of attention that these organizations have received in the IHRM literature to date, we believe that the examination is nonetheless worthwhile.

The *public sector* comprises all those bodies owned and operated by national or local governments (Boyne *et al.*, 1999). In most cases this is a clear distinction – national civil services, local government administrations and the armed services are always in the public sector. But the boundaries are blurred and may be becoming more so. Increasingly, organizations may be owned by government but operated by private companies, or jointly owned by public and private sector organizations. The public sector mainly operates within national boundaries, but diplomatic services, armed services, trade missions and others operate across national borders and are largely un-studied. In addition there is an increasing international influence on national administrations.

The *intergovernmental organizations* are intrinsically and fundamentally international – indeed the most international of all organizations. Most of them operate in a separate 'space', where national laws are not applied and where governance, employees, objectives and operations are all independent and separate from any national authority. Such organizations range from those whose objective is nothing less than world peace (United Nations) to those whose objective is to foster trade in a particular region (the Organization of Black Sea Economic Co-operation), with some bringing together leading technical specialists (the International Atomic Energy Agency, the European Centre of Medium Range Weather Forecasting) and others mobilizing generalists concerned with resolving particular problems (the World Food Programme).

The *international non-governmental organizations* are international organizations which are independent from the direct influence of any government. They are founded to achieve a specific mission and are not about achieving political power or making money. INGOs

Table 9.1 Categorization of not for profit organizations

	National	**International**
Governmental	Public-sector organizations	Inter-governmental organizations
	For example health care organizations, schools, military defences, local governments, and ministries	For example UN-related and EU-related organizations
Non-governmental	National non-governmental organizations (not included in our analysis)	International non-governmental organizations
	National charities, religious bodies, clubs, etc.	International charities, religious bodies, clubs, etc. (for example Red Cross and Medicine Sans Frontiers)

most commonly focus on human rights (Amnesty International), environmental concerns (Greenpeace) or reducing poverty (CARE) (see Table 9.1). While there has been research into HRM in these sectors, there has been little attention to IHRM.

What distinguishes these organizations generally from the much more studied private sector is that they have a mission that is unrelated to making profits, with different norms and values related to public good; that they operate in a different legislative framework; and that their relationships with their multiple stakeholders and clients take a different form. Vandenabeele *et al.* (2013) state that,

> the principal value delivered by the government sector is 'the achievement of the politically mandated mission of the organization and the fulfilment of the citizen aspirations that were more or less reflected in that mandate' (Moore, 2000, p. 186). The difference between non-profit and governmental organizations stems from the fact that supporters and leaders of non-profit organizations such as the Salvation Army are free to claim that their particular purposes are public purposes as long as they stay within some fairly broad, legislatively established criteria; that is, these purposes do not have to be debated collectively or enacted in legislation. In contrast, the purposes of public bureaucracies can only be established through collective political processes.
>
> (Quoting Moore, 2000, p. 188)

HRM in Public Sector Organizations

The inclusion of public sector organizations in this overview of International HRM requires some explanation. In fact, the reasons for paying attention to public sector organizations have increased over the past decade or so. First, the public sector tends to be larger in European countries than in most other capitalist countries around the world. Public-sector organizations are the most common type of NfP organizations, given the link to nationally required activities such as health care, education, military defence, foreign affairs, infrastructure, transportation and social policies on, for example, unemployment, disability and retirement, policing and justice. These are all significant sectors in terms of employment. In Europe the health care sector is one of the largest employers in most countries and often has a strong public sector involvement. National governments international (diplomatic) staff and international intergovernmental organizations (IGOs) such as the European Union (EU) and the United Nations (UN), are visible in the media (for example, in the case of an emergency or crisis in the world), but less on the 'HRM radar' as an organizational focus. Finally, International non-governmental organizations (INGOs) are faced with a specific HRM challenge in that they need to manage two different groups in the workforce: paid staff and volunteers.

Second, since 2008 the global financial crisis that grew into a fiscal and economic crisis has confronted governments throughout Europe with pressures to cut back public spending. EU member states were constrained by the European Union's Maastricht criteria that prescribe maximum deficit levels of 3 per cent of gross domestic product (GDP) and a debt level of 60 per cent of GDP. As a consequence most governments have decided to cut public sector jobs and wages (Vaughan-Whitehead, 2013). Obviously, international economic developments and the European Union's institutional framework have had a homogenizing effect on public sector personnel policies. However, there are clear variations between countries in the severity of measures and their speed of implementation related to the differences in financial vulnerability of respective countries (Bach and Bordogna, 2013; Leisink and Bach, 2014; Lodge and Hood, 2012).

There are more external developments that are interesting from an IHRM perspective because they affect public sector organizations. Lodge and Hood (2012) broaden the scope of analysis beyond the impact of international economic developments by including the effects of population ageing and environmental risks. They argue that these external developments are likely to interact. Thus, countries where high ecological vulnerability coincides with a dramatically ageing population and a high financial vulnerability in government financing face much sharper pressures and demands than countries with younger populations and lower ecological vulnerability. Therefore, Lodge and Hood (2012) conclude that there will be homogenizing pressures but also that diversity is likely to continue in the way in which governments change what they call 'public service bargains' over matters of reward, competency and loyalty.

Homogenizing pressures on the strategic choices of governments do not affect public sector organizations evenly. Central government organizations in many European countries were similarly affected by austerity policies involving cuts in jobs and wages, as central governments are legislator and employer at the same time. However, local government organizations' personnel policies differed much more between countries (Leisink and Bach, 2014). Such differences also hold for public sector organizations in education and health care, which in some countries come under direct central government authority but have greater autonomy in other countries.

These differences between public sector organizations demonstrate that the term 'public sector' is rather ambiguous. Attempts to characterize the public sector have generally drawn on formal characteristics. Rainey (2009), for example, discusses the characteristics of ownership, funding and authority. He shows that these characteristics help to clarify the varying degrees of 'publicness' of public sector organizations, but still do not capture the full complexity of the public–private distinction. This complexity is related to the blurring of sectors because of social, political and administrative changes related first to the growth of the welfare state and later New Public Management (NPM) inspired reforms (Goldfinch and Wallis, 2009; Pollitt and Bouckaert, 2004). As a result there are core public sector organizations: central and local government, defence, police and justice organizations, next to education, health care and social welfare and public housing organizations. There are differences between these latter sectors and between countries as regards the extent to which the introduction of market-like mechanisms has turned organizations in these latter segments into hybrid organizations (Pestoff and Brandsen, 2008; Osborne, 2008). However, there is still a difference between these hybrid organizations, which can be characterized as 'public' by their organizational task, purpose or mission (Dahl and Lindblom, 1953) and private organizations, the primary goal of which consists of maximizing shareholder value (Grant, 2002). Although some public sector organizations have gained more autonomy from central government than others, all these organizations typically have to deal with three key issues impacting their human resource management policies:

1 multiple stakeholders;
2 politics and the political dimensions; and
3 performance and performance management.

Multiple Stakeholders

All public organizations have to deal with multiple stakeholders, including government, managers, employees, clients, trade unions, citizens, media (Rainey, 2009). Some public organizations, typically those which have more autonomy such as hospitals, have governing boards in which several stakeholders may be represented. All public organizations have society at large as a stakeholder, because as public organizations they have a mission such as serving public safety or public health, or providing good education. Typical of governmental organizations is that they have a politically mandated mission, whereas hybrid organizations governed by their board have some freedom to define their mission within some fairly broad legislatively mandated criteria (Moore, 1995).

The multiplicity of stakeholders and the shifts in their salience over time impacts on HRM in public sector organizations. Union density in the public sector was and still is relatively high. In the latter part of the twentieth century unions had a strong influence on employment conditions. Public sector HRM reflected their influence through a standardized, collectivized and paternalistic style of HRM, which is less prevalent in private organizations (Boyne *et al.*, 1999; Farnham and Horton, 1996; Martinez Lucio, 2007; Steijn and Leisink, 2007). Public sector HRM traditionally included activities such as staff training, the promotion of equal opportunities, and staff participation and consultation, which public sector organizations promoted because this represented what they regarded at the time as a model employer role (Farnham and Horton, 1996). However, from the 1980s the NPM movement took hold in Europe (Hood, 1991). Public sector organizations attempted to modernize their personnel policies and to replace the collectivized HRM model featuring unions by a more individualized, flexible business-oriented approach of private organizations (Bach and Bordogna, 2013; Pollitt and Bouckaert, 2004).

The public management reform movement also centred on the citizen/customer and led to attempts to improve the quality of public service. Subsequent government policies had a strong impact on public service provision and on related HRM policies. Public sector organizations, particularly in education, health care and social welfare, provided opportunities for client participation and introduced various horizontal accountability procedures (Schillemans, 2011). Clients' voices through participation platforms have various implications for HRM related to service provision and employee competences in communication and client friendly interaction.

Politics and the Political Dimension

One of the distinctive characteristics of public sector organizations is the way that direct political intervention restrains management's discretionary scope (Rainey, 2009). This holds particularly in relation to the scope for managing human resources, which is constrained by government directives and detailed personnel policy regulations (Boyne *et al.*, 1999; Rainey, 2009; Truss, 2008). The degree of political intervention varies however. Antonsen and Jorgensen (1997) found that those public organizations that have a higher degree of publicness – understood as the degree to which they serve various public values and are publicly funded for that purpose – are confronted with more determined efforts by ministries to control them. A case in point would be, for instance, schools as compared to postal services, where the latter have indeed been privatized in most European countries since Antonsen and Jorgensen's study.

The NPM reform trend claimed to correct the inefficiencies of the traditional bureaucratic model of public sector organizations by emancipating public sector managers from rigid adherence to civil service rules and giving them freedom to manage (Goldfinch and Wallis, 2009). However, the extent to which managers have gained more freedom to manage their human resources remains a moot point. Politics today does not restrict its role to deciding the mission, the public value to be created and allocating the requisite budget, leaving it to public managers to harness the operational resources, including human resources, which are necessary to achieve the desired public value outcomes (Moore, 1995). Increasingly, politics responds to media attention on public service incidents, such as the bullying of children at school or the negligence of elderly clients in elderly care homes, by intervening in operational day-to-day public service provision and demanding that public employees do better (Schillemans, 2012).

Performance and Performance Management

The NPM reform attempted to shift the focus from emphasizing procedural correctness characteristic of traditional public services towards performance by such policies as introducing purchaser/ provider separation so as to allow multiple forms of service provision and to create competition among providers, and by attempting to introduce financial performance incentives (Dunleavy *et al.*, 2006). Results of these reforms can be seen in the increasing prevalence of league tables, ranking schools, hospitals, elderly homes and other public sector organizations in terms of their quality of service. The twin aim of this form of transparency is to empower the citizen as customer, who can use this information to choose the best quality of service and simultaneously, to incentivize public sector organizations to improve service provision.

As a result, HRM in public sector organizations has faced the challenge of devising forms of performance management while at the same time struggling with the consequences of austerity policies by 'doing more with less staff'. A fundamental problem of performance management is that public sector organizations report specific performance indicators as required by government inspectorates, but this performance information falls short of providing a valid measure of the mission of the organization. For instance, secondary schools report performance information, such as the percentage of unqualified school leavers, but what does this information say about the mission of schools to contribute to preparing pupils for higher education, for the labour market, for society and to contribute to their personal development? Similarly, the police report the numbers of burglaries and vehicle crimes solved, but what does this information say about their mission to protect the constitutional state and public safety? More importantly, the requirement of providing performance information such as school exam results may cause all sorts of perverse performance effects such as teaching to the test and refusing to enrol less-talented pupils who may have a negative effect on exam results, which in turn may keep parents from enrolling better prepared children. A fundamental issue for performance management in public sector organizations, therefore, is to recognize that public sector organizations have multiple goals that are frequently ambiguous or even contradictory (Rainey, 2009) and that management and employees must consult on viable ways to achieve balanced outcomes. Public service performance researchers have made some progress in developing multidimensional public service performance constructs (e.g. Boyne, 2002; Boyne *et al.*, 2006) but the generic performance dimensions suggested, such as outputs, outcomes, responsiveness and efficiency, need to be complemented by context and/or organization-specific indicators for meaningful performance management.

Apart from the problem of setting meaningful objectives, the NPM approach to performance management through financial incentives has not been very successful. Public sector trade unions have opposed the introduction of forms of performance-related pay and where they could not block its introduction have succeeded in limiting its extent, as for instance, in German municipalities (Müller and Schmidt, 2013). More generally public sector employees tend to feel that performance-related pay does not fit. In a survey of civil servants in the Netherlands, a majority indicated that financial incentives would not increase their motivation to perform; if anything, immaterial rewards such as gaining extra training opportunities would motivate public servants more (Steijn et al., 2006). Recent examples, such as the financial bonus that British general practitioners can earn by diagnosing dementia among elderly people, cause astonishment and professional resistance.

Parallel to the NPM reform, research into public service motivation (PSM) has grown since the seminal article by Perry and Wise (1990). This concept refers to the motivation to help others and society and this kind of motivation is particularly prevalent among public sector employees. Research has shown that PSM can be fostered by HRM (Paarlberg et al., 2008) and by transformational leadership (Wright et al., 2012; Vandenabeele, 2014). Importantly, because of its relevance for performance management, PSM has a positive relationship with individual performance (Leisink and Steijn, 2009; Vandenabeele, 2009) and with organizational performance (Brewer and Selden, 2000; Kim, 2005). However, recent studies indicate that the contribution of PSM to performance is dependent on the institutional context (Vandenabeele et al., 2013; Van Loon et al., 2013), which means that designated HRM policies are needed to support public service motivated employees in delivering public service performance. See Figure 9.1 for an overview of the influence of multiple stakeholders, politics and contextual performance on the shaping of HRM in public sector organizations.

HRM in Intergovernmental Organizations

Human resource management in the IGOs is highly complex and complicated to administer. In IGOs, the typical human resource management (HRM) requirements of cost-effectiveness and future planning are carried out in an intensely political environment. For most IGOs, national laws and regulations do not apply because of diplomatic immunity: by international agreement, they operate in extra-jurisdictional territory and their laws and regulations are defended by the Tribunal of Administrative Justice and the International Labour Law Tribunal. Accountability and 'paper-trails' impose a high degree of bureaucracy. Employees are multi-lingual and come from a variety of nations, with no one pre-dominant and almost every manager is managed by and in turn manages someone from a different culture than themselves.

Generalizing about these organizations risks conflating important differences. Each IGO is unique in its internal and external organizational context: their age (year of foundation), their size

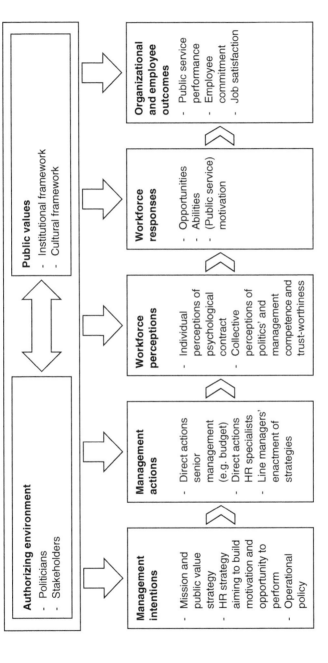

Authorizing environment
- Politicians
- Stakeholders

Public values
- Institutional framework
- Cultural framework

Management intentions
- Mission and public value strategy
- HR strategy aiming to build motivation and opportunity to perform
- Operational policy

Management actions
- Direct actions senior management (e.g. budget)
- Direct actions HR specialists
- Line managers' enactment of strategies

Workforce perceptions
- Individual perceptions of psychological contract
- Collective perceptions of politics' and management competence and trust-worthiness

Workforce responses
- Opportunities
- Abilities
- (Public service) motivation

Organizational and employee outcomes
- Public service performance
- Employee commitment
- Job satisfaction

Figure 9.1 Influences on the shaping of HRM

(number of employees), their headquarters location and annual budget (see Table 9.2 for some illustrations). Some are nominally or practically part of a parent organization (the UN or the EU for example) and each has its own governance structure. Some are specialist organizations, some normative, with resultant differences in the background of their professionals. For a variety of reasons (Brewster *et al.*, 2013) it seems that since the 2008 economic crisis many of these organizations are facing a reality of zero growth or ever-declining budgets. The new public management pressures noted for the national public sectors are having an impact on these internal organizations and their legitimacy has increasingly to be justified.

Multiple Stakeholders

Arguably, all organizations can be analysed in terms of their multiple stakeholders – the owners, the managers, the employees, the customers or clients, the local community, etc. (Beer *et al.*, 2015). Obviously, where the interests of these multiple stakeholders are relatively closely aligned, all aspects of management, including human resource management, become easier. Where the interests of the multiple stakeholders are more conflicting and where, therefore, satisfying one inevitably involves upsetting others, then management becomes more difficult. IGOs are quintessential examples of organizations with highly visible multiple stakeholders. By definition these organizations are governed by a combination of representatives of national governments, a point we explore further below. But the interests of their 'owners',

Table 9.2 Illustrations of IGOs

Organization	Focus	Headquarters	Employees
CERN	Science	Geneva	2,400
ICC	Criminal court	The Hague	600
NATO (IS)	Military services	Brussels	1,200
UN (plus)	World peace	New York	43,000
-UNICEF	Children	New York	8,000
-WHO	Health	Geneva	5,500
-WFP	Humanitarian aid	Rome	4,200
-FAO	Food production	Rome	3,300
-ILO	Labour standards	Rome	2,300
World Bank	Financial services	Washington DC	12,000

Source: http://www.unsceb.org/content/hr-statistics-staff-by-organization (accessed 3 November 2015)

the national governments who pay the costs of the IGO, may be quite distinct from the interests of its beneficiaries. Equally, the interests of the employees who provide the services to the beneficiaries and want to devote themselves to, for example, specific groups that they see as highly deserving of help, may be distinct from the interests of their managers who want to see carefully crafted reports on what has been done to show the overall success of the section.

Politics and the Political Dimension

IGOs are inherently political. Their missions, their management, their resourcing, their results and their very existence are determined by national governments. National governments consist of political parties and politicians with often very different agendas and objectives. Some will be left wing and some right wing; some will see the operations of the IGO as a global benefit, others will see it as a cost to be controlled. Some governments will use the notion of 'making the IGO as successful as possible' to mean that they support its agenda more or less uncritically, others will use that mantra to mean a tight focus on costs and spending; yet others will use it to justify interfering in the day-to-day operations of the organization. Furthermore, individual state representatives will have their own idiosyncratic approaches.

Some IGOs, such as UNESCO for example, have a set of 'permanent representatives' (including some of the diplomats mentioned above) co-located in their buildings in Paris. It is hard for the managers of such an organization to encourage the governing body representatives to focus on big-picture strategy, resources and outcomes. The representatives have to do something during their working days and the strategic role can be fulfilled in less time than they have available. A few perhaps use this time to enjoy Paris, but most use it to try to 'improve' the management of UNESCO. Given that there is not much they can do about operational issues, they tend to focus on HRM issues. They do this by having frequent meetings with senior HRM specialists, pushing the interests of their nationals in UNESCO employment and getting closely involved in day-to-day HRM matters. Other IGOs have government's permanent representatives covering a number of organizations represented in one city or varying with the type of organization (Ministries of Transport for international organizations specializing in transport, Finance Ministries for the international financial organizations, etc.) and they will tend to be less involved in such a hands-on way.

Within the political dimension there are divisions within the governing bodies. In the United Nations there is a sharp and often visible distinction between the Geneva Group nations and the others. The Geneva Group members are, in broad terms, those developed countries that pay the bills. For them, the cost-effectiveness and the efficiency of the organization (and hence, as we have seen, its HRM) are of paramount importance. For the other states, saving money is much less salient than ensuring that money is spent, meaning that resources – mainly HRM – are directed towards pet projects or projects in their countries. Cost or cost-effectiveness is very much a secondary issue.

Performance and Performance Management

By definition therefore, when multiple stakeholders, with often conflicting objectives, are assessing performance, their criteria will differ. Multiple stakeholders lead to multiple objectives and multiple ways of measuring performance. This has a significant impact both at the organizational level and also at the individual level. Organizationally, given ever-tightening budgets in most cases, the temptation to 'mission-creep' is high. Mission-creep occurs when individual organizations take on tasks that governments or other funders (charities and private funds) are willing to support, even if not directly within their mission. This leads to some governments giving high ratings to activities that they have funded, while other governments point to the overlapping targets and duplication of resources that apply as IGOs' missions begin to become competitive. There are probably a dozen different parts of the UN system looking at AIDS issues for example, where funding was easily available, in addition to the nominated UNAIDS agency.

The pressure on budgets, as a result of the global financial crisis and government cuts, will have important consequences for IGOs, as these organizations depend heavily on the member states' contributions. General budgets are expected to be reduced and staffing budgets especially will come under pressure. However, the financial pressures are not the only challenge intergovernmental organizations are currently facing. Together with the changes in material support (the declining aid budget), the ingredients for legitimacy support seem to be changing as well. A vivid example of this development is the report entitled *Taking Forward the Findings of the UK Multilateral Aid Review*, published by the UK Department for International Development (DfID, 2011). It summarizes the current principles for UK aid funding. The unambiguous starting point is 'that all multilateral organizations should be seeking to achieve the best possible results at the lowest possible cost in support of their mandated development or humanitarian objectives'. This evaluation highlights the performance focus in IGOs on both (a) organizational effectiveness and (b) social legitimacy of organizational activities. This applies to both IGOs and INGOs.

Individually, most intergovernmental organizations have a formal performance management approach. In most, it is no more than a formalized performance evaluation system. The problems are that there are rarely any outcomes from the system. Training and development budgets are low compared to other types of organization (Croucher *et al.*, 2004) and in effect, employees cannot be sanctioned. This becomes more of a problem because of the lack of turnover: most people are recruited into the IGOs at around the age of 40, when they have proven their merit in national governments or other relevant organizations. Salaries and terms and conditions are competitive with the US public sector – and therefore wildly above the contractual terms that many Third World recruits could ever expect in their home countries. The HRM system (steady increases, generous benefits and pension provisions) means that people rarely leave before they retire. Since the IGOs are not bound by national legislation, their terms and conditions are policed by a very old-fashioned, lengthy and bureaucratic independent legal process and there are many hurdles to be overcome before action can be taken against an employee as a result of a poor appraisal. As a result of this combination of factors, most managers do not bother to try and there are a small but significant number of disengaged employees simply waiting to reach retirement age in many of the IGOs. Any wider view of performance management is rare.

HRM in International Non-Governmental Organizations

International non-governmental organizations (INGOs) have played an increasingly important role in recent years, as austerity measures enacted by governments around the world have led to gaps in public services which are increasingly filled by the so-called 'Third Sector'. In providing their services, INGOs face the challenge of balancing two (often conflicting) objectives. First, INGOs need to advance and implement their values and missions. This includes activities such as reducing poverty, increasing women's rights, protecting and enforcing human rights, protecting the environment, democratization, or undertaking community development (see Table 9.3). Second, INGOs need to operate in a financially efficient way to be attractive to donors and applicable for receiving governmental funding. INGOs are often a combination of national NGOs, which coordinate the activities within a specific country.

In achieving their objectives, INGOs need to manage a workforce which consists of two different groups. In addition to paid staff, employed by INGOs under employment regulations, INGOs also rely on the support of unpaid workers, i.e. volunteers. Volunteering relates to activities 'in which time is given freely to benefit another person, group, or organization' (Wilson, 2000: 15). According to United Nations Volunteers (2011), in developed countries volunteer work amounts to 2.7 per cent of GDP. In the USA, it is estimated that 64.5 million Americans volunteered 7.9 billion hours in 2012, which was worth $175 billion (The Independent Sector, 2014). In the European Union, between 92 and 94 million adults engage in volunteering every year (United Nations Volunteers, 2011). While not all of these activities occur within INGOs, the data nevertheless demonstrates the importance of volunteering and the need for INGOs to manage their volunteers effectively.

Multiple Stakeholders

Similar to IGOs, INGOs are influenced by a range of powerful stakeholders. Some INGOs, such as the Institute of Internal Auditors, provide services to their members, be it individuals or organizations, in return for a fee. These members are important stakeholders, as they have certain expectations about the benefits they receive from being a member of that INGO. The majority of INGOs, however, provide a service or product to beneficiaries, without getting any resources in return. For these INGOs, financial support is typically received from philanthropic individuals or organizations or through government funding. For example, Amnesty International campaigns against the abuse of human rights by researching and publishing facts on individual as well as systematic patterns of human rights violations in different countries. In this case, the beneficiaries who receive Amnesty International's support are different from the individuals or organizations who actually donate the money to support these activities. Both groups, however, are important stakeholders influencing how INGOs carry out their work. They need to ensure that they are able to provide the services to their beneficiaries, while complying with requirements set up by their donors as they have to maintain their ability to attract and secure funding (Schmidtke and Cummings, 2013). Finally, volunteers and paid staff are important stakeholders for INGOs with potentially competing interests. While both groups are likely to share some common interests and attitudes, when working for the same INGO, there are also some fundamental differences between volunteers and paid staff (Liao-Troth, 2001). For example, paid staff are rewarded for their work in monetary terms, whereas volunteers are rewarded in non-material ways. Moreover, paid staff work within the structure and formal guidelines of their INGO, whereas volunteers benefit from a greater sense of autonomy in how their work is carried out. This can result in conflicting priorities and ways of working between both stakeholder groups.

Table 9.3 Examples of INGOs

Organization	Focus
Médecins Sans Frontières	Health
SOS Children's Villages	Children
CARE	Poverty
International Committee of the Red Cross	Humanitarian
Amnesty International	Human rights
International Federation for Human Rights	Human rights
Greenpeace	Environment
The Institute of Internal Auditors	Professional body

Source: Organizational information

Politics and the Political Dimension

INGOs are usually led by executive directors and their teams who are responsible for executing policies and strategies which determine the future direction of the organization. They are governed by a board of directors who ensure that the INGO fulfils its mission and manages its finances in a responsible way. Board members mainly work on a voluntary basis and in contrast to for-profit organizations, are not rewarded for the time they spend on the board. Instead, they dedicate their time because they are committed to the mission of the INGO. Board members often feel a strong connection to the cause the INGO is serving, which can be based on their own personal experiences or because they have been a member of the INGO for a long time before being elected to the board. For these reasons, board members often display a high level of involvement and passion for their voluntary work. Naturally, the executive team and the board of directors might have different perspectives or interests in running the INGO. Whereas the executive team is involved in the day-to-day management of the organization, which involves dealing with the different stakeholders mentioned above, the directors are mainly focused on ensuring that the values and mission are taken forward. Hence, conflicts or dissatisfaction on both parts are likely to occur.

In order to minimize the negative outcomes resulting from disagreement, Jacobs and Johnson (2013) outline a number of guidelines which INGOs can follow to facilitate a positive collaborative atmosphere. For example, it is important that both parties establish a regular dialogue to increase confidence and trust and have a procedure for handling conflicts. INGOs are also advised to develop and implement clear regulations outlining the responsibilities of both the executive team and the board of directors. Enduring dissatisfaction can negatively impact morale and satisfaction within the INGO, but also its reputation towards outside stakeholders.

Performance and Performance Management

Performance management is an important task for INGOs, at the organizational as well as the individual level. At the organizational level, Sawhill and Williamson (2001) suggest that performance evaluations in INGOs should focus on three areas. Measuring impact focuses on how much progress the INGO makes in achieving its mission. Measuring activity relates to assessing the extent to which the INGO's programmes and activities help to achieve its objectives. Indicators for humanitarian organizations are, for example, response time to natural catastrophes, or number of victims helped. Measuring capacity is about the degree to which the INGO has the resources to fulfil its objectives. Carrying out performance evaluations is critical as INGOs are accountable to their stakeholders, specifically their donors and supporters.

On an individual level, most INGOs have similar performance management programmes to international private sector companies. This means that the performance of paid staff is evaluated on a regular, often yearly, basis using formal evaluation procedures. However, as INGOs are expected to keep administrative costs down in order to increase spending of their funds on activities related to improving the welfare of their beneficiaries, other HRM practices which are usually related to the performance appraisal are available to a reduced extent only. INGOs do not pay any large end-of-year bonus and training budgets also tend to be smaller compared to private sector counterparts (Alfes, 2016 forthcoming; Brewster and Lee, 2006).

With regards to their volunteers, INGOs are increasingly turning towards a more professional and active management of their volunteering workforce. From an HRM perspective this poses an interesting challenge, as INGOs lack the formal reward and power structures to influence volunteers' behaviour. Performance management is important in the volunteering context, as the high level of autonomy in volunteer roles allows volunteers to carry out their role in a way that is not always linked to the overall objective of the INGO or impacts on the work of other volunteers or staff members. Hence, ensuring that volunteers have clarity about what is expected from them is a key HRM issue in INGOs. Performance management for volunteers is often carried out on an informal basis and focuses on volunteers failing to complete essential tasks. With regards to reward management, INGOs rely more heavily on intrinsic rewards to motivate their volunteers. This can involve recognizing volunteers for participating in a specific project or for carrying out their work to an exceptionally high standard. INGOs also benefit from emphasizing their mission in communication with their volunteers, as this increases volunteer commitment towards the organization and influences their retention and performance. Finally, induction programmes, training and ongoing support on task and emotional levels have a positive impact on volunteer attitudes and behaviours.

Conclusions

HRM in not for profit organizations is different from HRM in private organizations. As Vandenabeele *et al.* (2013) state:

> Public sector organizations operate under various constraints that are not imposed on the private sector (Ring and Perry 1985) and often have multiple goals that are frequently ambiguous or even opposites (Rainey 2009). A telling example is the list of goals the police are expected to serve, which includes keeping the peace, enforcing the law, controlling and preventing crime, assuring fairness and respect for citizen rights, and operating efficiently.

In terms of international HRM, the sectors are even more different. Fundamental to the public sector is the more salient role of stakeholders, a stronger political dimension both inside and outside the organization, more scrutiny and more complexity, for example, with regard to defining what is performance and what is good performance management. This implies the need for strong contextualization of HRM research in not for profit organizations, taking into account their unique administrative heritages, the external and internal institutional environment and the external market environment (Paauwe, 2004).

This is a much less researched sector. Specific themes that can be relevant for a future research agenda in IHRM in not for profit organizations are:

- The transfer of learning between the private and public sectors. Given the different contexts what can be transferred and what would be inappropriate?
- The transfer of learning between countries: what is relevant and what is not?
- Further understanding of the role of stakeholders in influencing HRM.
- The impact of the politicization of IHRM in NfP organizations.

There are also specific NfP research topics within IHRM, such as:

- Value-based recruitment (the right person–organization fit in combination with the right person–job fit) given the need to operate in countries with different values.
- The role and impact of training and development, given that spending tends to be lower.
- What learning might the private sector take from the significantly better outcomes of diversity management in the not for profit sector?
- Expatriate management in a highly competitive environment (talent management).
- The public service motivation of employees in not for profit organizations or motivation in these specific contexts (also related to affective commitment).
- Internal/external and horizontal/vertical staff mobility within and between the different parts of the NfP and between that and the private sector.
- Performance management in relationship to accountability and social legitimacy. Is there a danger that increased focus on manifest rewards will drive out intrinsic motivation?
- Employee engagement and employee health (job stress, safety and burnout risks).

Overall, there is considerable room for further research in NfP organizations, particularly in relation to international human resource management.

Key Learning Points

- The not for profit (NfP) sector comprises organizations that exist for purposes other than profit: these include the public sector, organizations directly working for, and at least part-funded by, the public sector and non-governmental organizations such as charities, religious organizations and sports and social clubs.
- In international HRM this will include the civil (diplomatic) and armed services operating outside the home country, intergovernmental organizations and international non-governmental organizations such as the Red Cross and FIFA.
- These organizations have more complex purposes and are run in a different way to private sector for-profit organizations. Each sector is different.
- Common to all are the importance of multiple stakeholders; politics and the political dimensions, and; performance and performance management. These have to be understood in order to understand HRM in the NfPs.

References

Alfes, K. (2016 forthcoming) 'People management in volunteer organizations and charities', in Brewster, C. and Cerdin, J.-L. (eds.) *Human Resource Management in Mission Driven Organizations*. New York: Pearson Education.

Antonsen, M. and Jorgensen, T. (1997) 'The "publicness" of public organizations', *Public Administration*, 75(2), 337–357.

Bach, S. and Bordogna, L. (2013) 'Reframing public service employment relations: the impact of the economic crisis and the new EU economic governance', *European Journal of Industrial Relations*, 19(4), 279–294.

Bach, S. and Kessler, I. (2007) 'HRM and the new public management', in Boxall, P., Purcell, J. and Wright, P. (eds) *The Oxford Handbook of Human Resource Management*. Oxford: Oxford University Press, pp. 469–488.

Beer, M., Boselie, P. and Brewster, C. (2015) 'Back to the future: implications for the field of HRM of the multi-stakeholder perspective proposed 30 years ago', *Human Resource Management*, 54(3), 427–438.

Boyne, G. (2002) 'Concepts and indicators of local authority performance: an evaluation of the statutory frameworks in England and Wales', *Public Money & Management,* 22(2), 17–24.

Boyne, G., Jenkins, G. and Poole, M. (1999) 'Human Resource management in the public and private sectors: an empirical comparison', *Public Administration*, 77(2), 407–420.

Boyne, G., Meier, K., O'Toole, L. and Walker, R. (eds.) (2006) *Public Service Performance: Perspectives on Measurement and Management*. Cambridge: Cambridge University Press.

Brewer, G. and Selden, S. (2000) 'Why elephants gallop: assessing and predicting organizational performance in federal agencies', *Journal of Public Administration Research and Theory*, 10(2), 685–711.

Brewster, C. and Lee, S. (2006) 'HRM in not-for-profit international organizations: different, but also alike', in Larsen, H.H. and Mayrhofer, W. (eds) *European Human Resource Management*. London: Routledge, pp. 131–148.

Brewster, C., Boselie, P. and Vos, E. (2013) *The Human Resource Management Impact of the Financial Crisis on International Organizations*. Geneva: AHRMIO.

Croucher, R., Tyson, S. and Brewster, C. (2004) *Human Resource Management Policies and Practices in International Organisations*. Geneva: AHRMIO.

Dahl, R. and Lindblom, C. (1953) *Politics, Economics and Welfare*. New York: Harper.

Department for International Development, Great Britain (2011) *Multilateral Aid Review, Taking Forward the Findings of the UK Multilateral Aid Review*. Available at: https://www.gov.uk/government/uploads/system/uploads/attachment_data/file/224993/MAR-taking-forward.pdf (accessed 3 November 2015).

Dunleavy, P., Margetts, H., Bastow, S. and Tinkler, J. (2006) 'New public management is dead – long live digital-era governance', *Journal of Public Administration Research and Theory*, 16(3), 467–494.

Farnham, D. and Horton, S. (1996) *Managing the New Public Services*. Basingstoke: Macmillan.

Goldfinch, S. and Wallis, J. (eds) (2009) *International Handbook of Public Management Reform*. Cheltenham, UK/Northampton, MA, USA: Edward Elgar.

Gould-Williams, J. (2003) 'The importance of HR practices and workplace trust in achieving superior performance: a study of public sector organizations', *International Journal of Human Resource Management,* 14(1), 28–54.

Grant, R. (2002) *Contemporary Strategy Analysis: Concepts, Techniques, Applications.* Oxford: Blackwell.

Hood, C. (1991) 'A public management for all seasons?', *Public Administration,* 69(1), 3–19.

Independent Sector (2014) *Independent Sector's Value of Volunteer Time.* Available at: https://www.independentsector.org/volunteer_time (accessed 3 November 2015).

Jacobs, R. and Johnson, J. (2013) 'Nonprofit leadership and governance', in Olson-Buchanan, J., Koppes Bryan, L. and Foster Thompson, L. (eds) *Using Industrial-Organizational Psychology for the Greater Good: Helping Those Who Help Others.* New York: Routledge, pp. 290–324.

Keegan, A. and Boselie, P. (2006) 'The lack of impact of dissensus inspired analysis on developments in the field of human resource management', *Journal of Management Studies,* 43(7), 1491–1511.

Kim, S. (2005) 'Individual-level factors and organizational performance in government organizations', *Journal of Public Administration Research and Theory,* 15(2), 245–261.

Leisink, P. and Bach, S. (2014) 'Economic crisis and municipal public service employment: comparing developments in seven EU Member States', *Transfer: European Review of Labour and Research,* 20(3), 327–342.

Leisink, P. and Steijn, B. (2009) 'Public service motivation and job performance of public sector employees in the Netherlands', *International Review of Administrative Sciences,* 75(1), 35–52.

Leisink, P., Boselie, P., van Bottenburg, M. and Hosking, D.M. (2013) *Managing Social Issues: A Public Values Perspective.* Cheltenham: Edward Elgar.

Liao-Troth, M.A. (2001) 'Attitude differences between paid workers and volunteers', *Nonprofit Management and Leadership,* 11(4), 423–442.

Lodge, M. and Hood, C. (2012) 'Into an age of multiple austerities? Public management and public service bargains across OECD countries', *Governance,* 25(1), 79–101.

Martinez Lucio, M. (2007) 'Trade unions and employment relations in the context of public sector change: the public sector, "old welfare states" and the politics of managerialism', *International Journal of Public Sector Management,* 20(1), 5–15.

Moore, M.H. (1995) *Creating Public Value: Strategic Management in Government,* Cambridge, MA: Harvard University Press.

Moore, M.H. (2000) 'Managing for value: organization strategy on for-profit, non-profit, and governmental organizations', *Nonprofit and Voluntary Sector Quarterly,* 29(1), 183–208.

Müller, A. and Schmidt, W. (2013) 'Performance-related pay and labour relations in German municipalities', *Paper presented at the 10th European Conference of the International Labour and Employment relations Association.* Amsterdam, 20–22 June 2013.

Osborne, S. (2008). *The Third Sector in Europe: Prospects and Challenges.* London: Routledge.

Paarlberg, L., Perry, J. and Hondeghem, A. (2008) 'From theory to practice: strategies for applying public service motivation', in Perry, J.L. and Hondeghem, A. (eds) *Motivation in Public Management: The Call of Public Service.* Oxford: Oxford University Press, pp. 268–293.

Paauwe, J. (2004) *HRM and Performance: Achieving Long-Term Viability*. Oxford, Oxford University Press.

Perry, J. and Wise, L. (1990) 'The motivational bases of public service', *Public Administration Review*, 50(3), 367–373.

Pestoff, V. and Brandsen, T. (2008) *Co-production, the Third Sector and the Delivery of Public Services*. London: Routledge.

Pollitt, C. and Bouckaert, G. (2004) *Public Management Reform*, Oxford: Oxford University Press.

Rainey, H.G. (2009) *Understanding and Managing Public Organizations*. 4th edn. San Francisco: Jossey-Bass.

Sawhill, J.C. and Williamson, D. (2001) 'Mission impossible?: Measuring success in nonprofit organizations', *Nonprofit Management and Leadership*, 11(3), 371–386.

Schillemans, T. (2011) 'Does horizontal accountability work?', *Administration & Society*, 43(4), 387–416.

Schillemans, T. (2012) *Mediatization of Public Services: How Public Organizations Adapt to New Media*. Frankfurt: Peter Lang.

Schmidtke, J.M. and Cummings, A. (2013) 'Salient challenges of staffing and managing employees in the nonprofit sector', in Olson-Buchanan, J., Koppes Bryan, L. and Foster Thomspon, L. (eds) *Using Industrial-Organizational Psychology for the Greater Good: Helping Those Who Help Others*. New York: Routledge, pp. 265–289.

Steijn, B. and Leisink, P. (2007) 'Public management reforms and public sector employment relations in the Netherlands', *International Journal of Public Sector Management*, 20(1), 34–47.

Steijn, B., van der Parre, P. and Leisink, P. (2006) ' "Forse" ambtenaren? De effecten van HRM bij de rijksoverheid', *Bestuurskunde*, 15(3), 38–44.

Truss, C. (2008) 'Continuity and change: the role of the HR function in the modern public sector', *Public Administration*, 86(4), 1071–1088.

United Nations Volunteers (2011) *State of the World's Volunteerism Report 2011*. Available at: http://www.unv.org/fileadmin/docdb/pdf/2011/SWVR/English/SWVR2011_full.pdf (accessed 3 November 2015).

Van Loon, N., Leisink, P. and Vandenabeele, W. (2013) 'Talking the talk of public service motivation: how public organization logics matter for employees' expressions of PSM', *International Journal of Public Administration*, 36(14), 1007–1019.

Vandenabeele, W. (2009) 'The mediating effect of job satisfaction and organizational commitment on self-reported performance: more robust evidence of the PSM-performance relationship', *International Review of Administrative Sciences*, 75(1), 11–34

Vandenabeele, W. (2014) 'Explaining public service motivation: the role of leadership and basic needs satisfaction', *Review of Public Personnel Administration*, 34(2), 153–173.

Vandenabeele, W., Leisink, P. and Knies, E. (2013) 'Public value creation and strategic human resource management: public service motivation as a linking mechanism', in Leisink, P., Boselie, P., van Bottenburg, M. and Hosking, D. (eds) *Managing Social Issues: A Public Values Perspective*. Cheltenham, UK/Northampton, MA, USA: Edward Elgar, pp. 37–54.

Vaughan-Whitehead, D. (2013) *Public Sector Shock: The Impact of Policy Retrenchment in Europe*. Cheltenham, UK/Northampton, MA, USA: Edward Elgar.

Wilson, J. (2000) 'Volunteering', in *Annual Review of Sociology*, 26(1), 215–240.

Wright, B., Moynihan, D. and Sanjay, S. (2012) 'Pulling the levers: transformational leadership, public service motivation and mission valence', *Public Administration Review*, 72(2), 206–215.

10 The HRM of Foreign MNCs Operating in Europe

CHUL CHUNG AND MASAYUKI FURUSAWA

Introduction

Europe has been a major destination for foreign direct investment (FDI) as one of the triad economies with the USA and Japan (UNCTAD, 2014). US MNCs and, later, Japanese MNCs, invested significantly in European countries in order to develop markets and expand their operations in the region. More recently, emerging MNCs from countries other than the triad economies have come to Europe and set up their operations. These various MNCs have brought not just financial resources but also human resources – expatriates – and in many cases, particular ways of managing workforces from their home base. Transferring HRM practices could be highly complex and challenging, as human resources are the most country-bounded resources (Rosenzweig and Nohria, 1994). Foreign MNCs operating in Europe face cross-national challenges stemming from the process of transfer and adaptation of HRM practices, due to the uniqueness of European traditions as well as the national diversity within Europe in relation to employment relations (Scullion and Brewster, 2002). This chapter examines how MNCs from three different countries – the USA, Japan (the two other triad economies) and South Korea (a home base of emerging MNCs) – have dealt with the challenges in managing human resources in their European operations within the given institutional contexts.

Managing Human Resources in MNCS

One of the key issues in managing human resources in MNCs is how to adapt their headquarters-based or global ways of managing human resources to the different national contexts in the host countries on the one hand, whilst on the other hand how to utilize their dispersed workforces and coordinate overseas HRM operations to exploit the benefits of scale and scope fully as multinational organizations (Evans *et al.*, 2011; Rosenzweig, 2006). Two aspects in managing human resources in MNCs have been highlighted in the international HRM literature: (1) the degree of global standardization versus localization of subsidiary HRM practices and (2) the utilization of parent country nationals (PCNs) versus host country nationals (HCNs) in subsidiary staffing of MNCs.

Researchers have identified a number of factors which shape subsidiary HRM practices by examining various institutional influences on such practices as shown in Figure 10.1. These include the home country influences on corporate level IHRM strategy and subsequently on the subsidiary ('country of origin effect'); the host country influences ('local effect'); and the transnational influences ('dominance effect') (Pudelko and Harzing, 2007). For example, it was claimed that as HRM practices of MNCs are subject to strong pressures to adapt to local ways of practicing HRM, they tend to adopt local practices (Rosenzweig and Nohria, 1994). Another variant of the research suggests that MNCs are deeply embedded in the national institutional arrangements of their country of origin and accordingly their HRM practices in foreign operations are strongly influenced by their home practices (Ferner, 1997). It was found that MNCs may adopt HRM practices from a dominant nation (e.g. the USA) that are perceived as advanced practices (Pudelko and Harzing, 2007). In short, subsidiary HRM practices are shaped by various institutional influences and the degree of the relative influences of the three forces on subsidiary practices may be different

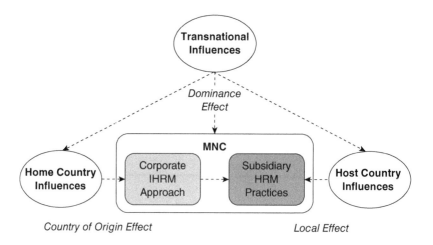

Figure 10.1 The influences on subsidiary HRM practices of MNCs

depending on a particular context. It should be noted that there is still room for manoeuvre by corporate or subsidiary actors who are involved in the design and implementation of subsidiary HRM practices in a given institutional context (Geppert and Williams, 2006).

In a similar vein, studies of subsidiary staffing have focused on whether and when MNCs utilize PCNs (or HCNs) for positions in subsidiaries (Gong, 2003). One of the key findings in the studies is the strong effect of country of origin on the tendency of utilizing PCNs in subsidiary key positions, as Japanese MNCs utilize PCNs more for subsidiary managerial positions than US or European MNCs (Harzing, 2001; Kopp, 1994). The contextual factors such as cultural distance (Gong, 2003) and institutional distance (Gaur *et al.*, 2007) between a home and a host country have been identified to explain when the use of PCNs (or HCNs) would be more beneficial for subsidiary performance. In short, a particular context of a home and a host country matters as a major factor that shapes the patterns of subsidiary staffing as well as subsidiary HRM practices.

The HRM of US MNCs

HRM in the US Context

The USA has been considered as a major source of contemporary HRM ideas and practices since the field of 'human resource management' was developed in the USA in the mid-1980s (Parry *et al.*, 2008). Though introduced and used widely across the world, HRM could be considered as a product that has evolved from particular social and institutional contexts in the USA (Guest, 1987). HRM in the US context has often been characterized by the high degree of freedom that companies enjoy in deciding how to manage their employees (Brewster, 1995). As a 'liberal market economy' (Hall and Soskice, 2001), the American business system imposes fewer restrictions on organizations' HRM practices, allowing US firms to experiment and develop distinctive HRM practices which might be geared toward pursuing shareholders' interests rather than wider societal values (Guest, 1990). HRM practices that are intended to enhance workforce flexibility and performance, such as contingent employment and pay systems, have been largely utilized by American firms (Brewster *et al.*, 2011). It was noted that employment practices in the USA, particularly their 'proactive' stance (Ferner *et al.*, 2011; Lawrence, 1996), contrast those in European countries where national governments and other social institutions play a significant role in shaping practices with regard to employment relations and employee welfare (Brewster, 1995).

Another notable aspect of US HRM is the high degree of formalization and standardization in its practices (Edwards *et al.*, 2010). Ferner and his colleagues (2004) pointed out that this distinctive feature has been shaped by a number of historical factors in the USA. First, the growth of large firms, which were increasingly dispersed across a wide range of geographical locations domestically and later internationally, promoted the development of bureaucratic control mechanisms in general and in personnel management systems in particular. In addition, the adoption of scientific management promoted the codification of job requirements and job descriptions (Baron *et al.*, 1986). The growth of white-collar occupational groups further facilitated the introduction of highly specified and formalized job structures and performance evaluation methods (Edwards, 1979). Second, in the two world wars, US firms were required by the government to control the number of hired employees and provide detailed information on their workforce in order to contribute to nation-wide manpower planning for the war economy (Jacoby, 1985). In response, firms developed a systematic classification structure to document employees' jobs by skill and wage categories. To create more efficient management of workforces, sophisticated techniques such as selection testing, job evaluation and internal career ladders were developed (Jacoby, 1985). Third, the use of systematic and formalized HRM practices for the fair and consistent treatment of employees was further promoted by the legislation of Equal Employment Opportunity (EEO) as well as the development of the company-level collective bargaining model in the post-war period to manage tensions arising from concerns for job security in the difficult economic condition (Jacoby, 1985). Although the American context of HRM can be characterized by relatively deregulated labour markets, legislation does exist in relation to equality and diversity issues in workplaces. US firms are liable for considerable penalties if they fail to proactively prevent incidents that can be associated with any form of discrimination under the EEO Act, which enforces affirmative actions against discriminations based on an individual's race, national origin, religion, sex, age, disability and sexual orientation (Ferner *et al.*, 2005).

HRM of US MNCs Operating in Europe

Influenced by these historical and institutional developments in the home country, the approach to international HRM of US MNCs is distinctive in two respects. One is the relatively strong tendency towards global standardization in HRM practices across different subsidiaries and the other is the more limited utilization of expatriates and the greater use of local employees in key positions in subsidiaries. These patterns in HRM of US MNCs were found in their European operations too.

Global Standardization of Subsidiary HRM Practices

Studies of HRM practices in the European subsidiaries of US MNCs have shown evidence of global standardization of subsidiary practices following the practices of US parent firms (see, for example, Collings *et al.*, 2008; Harzing, 1999). US MNCs tend to exert central control over their European subsidiaries by attempting to transfer their home practices to the European operations. In practice, though, they also adapt to local contexts to some degree (Collings *et al.*, 2008; Ferner *et al.*, 2004). Almond and his colleagues' (2005) intensive case study on the HRM policies of a large US IT company's operations in four European countries – Germany, Ireland, Spain and the United Kingdom – shows the typical approach of US MNCs. The orientation in international management of the American firm in Europe has evolved from a strongly ethnocentric approach, which lasted until the 1980s, to a decentralized approach giving greater autonomy to national subsidiaries during the late 1980s and then to a regionalization approach which allowed the European headquarters to exert more influence over subsidiaries in the region since the 1990s. Though the case study demonstrates a dynamic interplay of local effects and country of origin effects in subsidiary HRM practices, the strong tendency of global uniformity towards the US parent company's HRM model is clearly evident. In a large-scale survey research project on MNCs from the United States, Japan and Germany, across subsidiaries in the three countries, Pudelko and Harzing (2007) also found that subsidiaries of US MNCs tend to transfer their US parent practices more than their counterparts of German and Japanese MNCs.

These findings reflect the particular characteristics of US HRM practices developed in the home institutional context (Ferner *et al.*, 2011). As US firms developed early the formalized and standardized practices in managing geographically dispersed organizations in their home country, it tended to be taken for granted that they continued their particular way of managing dispersed units even when they expanded their business operations abroad (Ferner *et al.*, 2011). The high degree of codification of HRM practices in US firms would, it was assumed, make it straightforward to transfer the practices across the borders and, furthermore, the US dominance in the world economy during the last decades might lead US managers as well as subsidiary managers to consider US home practices as advanced ones (Ferner *et al.*, 2011).

However, it was also found that the transfer of the US home practices to subsidiaries in Europe is not entirely straightforward due to significant differences between the US and European contexts. One of the noticeable examples is the case of 'diversity management' practices. A case study on the UK operations of six US MNCs

(Ferner *et al.*, 2005) shows that the implementation of the transferred diversity management policies was, at best, incomplete and subject to considerable local adaptations, even when the associated practices were highly comprehensive and concrete, including global corporate value programmes; global organizational structures designed to support diversity initiatives; global target setting and monitoring; and international diversity training. Subsidiary managers claimed that the key features of the transferred policies were derived from 'pressures and opportunities specific to the American business system' (Ferner *et al.*, 2005: 315) and rejected aspects of the diversity policies on the basis of UK and EU legislation, which, for instance, prohibit positive discrimination such as target setting to increase the percentage of women managers, or the distinctive composition of local labour markets.

Another area of marked differences between the US and European contexts is the practice of employee voice and involvement. While collective communication channels such as statutory works councils and collective bargaining practices have been widely institutionalized across European countries, practices utilizing direct communication channels with employees are more prevalent in the USA due to the lack of legislation concerning employee involvement in the management decision making processes (Brewster *et al.*, 2011). However, there is evidence of wide variations among European subsidiaries of US MNCs in their adoption and implementation of European practices or US home practices depending on sector or firm-specific factors (Marginson *et al.*, 2004; Tempel *et al.*, 2006).

Localization in Subsidiary Staffing

In contrast to the ethnocentric tendency of US MNCs in managing their subsidiary HRM practices, it has been reported that, in terms of staffing, US MNCs utilize local employees for subsidiary key positions to a higher degree than MNCs from other countries. For example, Harzing (2001) found that 79.5 per cent of subsidiary managing directors of US MNCs were host country nationals, whilst it was 40.7 per cent and 37.5 per cent for German and Japanese MNCs respectively. The finding is largely consistent with previous studies: for instance, in Kopp's study (1994) the percentage of local nationals in overseas top manager positions, managerial and non-managerial positions of US MNCs was 49 per cent, 88 per cent, 98 per cent and respectively, in contrast to 26 per cent, 48 per cent, 81 per cent in the case of Japanese MNCs. The lower utilization of PCNs in subsidiary key positions in US firms can be partly explained by the type of control mechanism that US firms have developed and relied on. It could be argued that the highly codified and formalized nature of US management practices lessens the necessity of relying on direct and personal control mechanisms such as expatriation.

The HRM of Japanese MNCs

Stereotype of IHRM Issues in Japanese MNCs

Studies of international human resource management have pointed to the slow progress of localization of top management positions at overseas subsidiaries of Japanese MNCs (Furusawa, 2008; Harzing, 2001; Kopp, 1994, 1999). It is believed that localization will contribute to the acquisition and retention of capable human resources as well as reducing personnel expenses (Evans *et al.*, 2010; Tian *et al.*, 2014). Nonetheless, in the case of Japanese MNCs, the existence of a persistent glass ceiling has been giving them trouble in attracting and retaining the most talented local individuals for their overseas operations (Keeley, 2001; Kopp, 1994). This, in turn, has reinforced the Japanese companies' inclination to keep sending Japanese expatriates to top management positions in their overseas subsidiaries and so a vicious circle has been created. The ethnocentric international HRM practices in Japanese MNCs have been seen as their 'Achilles heel' (Bartlett and Yoshihara, 1988).

Earlier research discussed some structural problems behind the glass ceiling. For example, Yasumuro (1982) ascribed the issue to management style influenced by the high-context culture of Japan. As Hall (1976) mentioned, Japan is a typical high-context culture country where communication tends to be indirect and implicit. This leads to a management style in which the scope of responsibilities and authority of each employee is unclear or vague. Figure 10.2 compares J-style (Japanese style) organization and F-style (Foreign style) organization (Ishida, 1999). The white parts in the figure represent the jobs which are clearly allocated to individual employees. F-style organization exclusively consists of white parts, which means the responsibilities and authorities are explicitly defined. However, in J-style organizations, there are spaces (the black parts) as there are tasks that need to be done, but they are not distinctly allocated to any particular employee. Hayashi (1994) named the spaces 'green areas', where strategic decisions are made through information-sharing and cooperation among the members. Local employees in Japanese overseas subsidiaries (host country nationals) who are not familiar with such a system find it difficult to be able to work effectively that way. For them, these look like 'grey areas', which are difficult to understand (Hayashi, 1994).

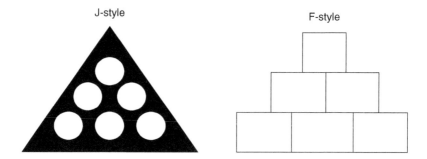

Figure 10.2 J-style organization and F-style organization

Yoshihara (1989, 2008) dealt with the issue from the viewpoint of the slow progress of 'internal internationalization'. Internal internationalization refers to the degree of internationalization at the headquarters in Japan. In general, the career path of top executives in Japanese MNCs has been domestic-centred. An assignment to an overseas country was often negatively received by Japanese employees for the following reasons (Yoshihara, 2008: 9): first, overseas operations were considered to be less important than the main domestic ones. Second, it was not unusual for repatriating employees to find that no appropriate jobs were available on return to their parent company in Japan. Third, expatriates at the foreign subsidiaries were afraid of being excluded from key networks in the Japanese headquarters or of the danger of obsolescence of their knowledge and expertise. These situations have brought about management teams with little overseas experience and limited foreign language capability. If the Japanese headquarters appointed local employees to top management positions at the overseas subsidiaries under these circumstances, they would find it hard to communicate with the subsidiaries in foreign languages, namely in English.

Some research has related the slow progress of localization to the peculiarity of social structures in Japan. Yoshino (1976) pointed out cultural homogeneity and group orientation as the characteristics of Japanese society. Such traits are likely to make an 'exclusive social nexus' where they build up interdependence within the group. He insisted that it was in this environment that the closed and exclusive managerial system of Japanese companies evolved. Hence, Yoshino was sceptical about the possibility that Japanese MNCs could adapt themselves to accommodate heterogeneous elements or promote localization of management and still function effectively in the international marketplace. Fernandez and Barr (1993) also explored the issue from the standpoint of Japanese social structure. According to them, the isolation policy in Japan from the mid-seventeenth to the mid-nineteenth century cultivated a very strong 'us-versus-them' mentality among Japanese people. Consequently, the Japanese view the homogeneity of their society as a key for success and regard any threat to it as being negative. Fernandez and Barr (1993) suggested that this attitude might lead to the ethnocentric management style that discriminates against non-Japanese employees in Japanese overseas subsidiaries.

HRM of Japanese MNCs Operating in Europe

Europe as an Investment Destination for Japanese MNCs

The Japanese MNCs' investment boom in Europe occurred in the period from the mid-1980s to the early 1990s. The main purpose was to avoid the anti-dumping taxes by the European Commission and, later, to become an insider in the unified European market. The number of production sites of Japanese MNCs in Europe doubled between 1985 and 1990 (JETRO, 2003). In addition, a lot of Japanese MNCs set up their regional headquarters in Europe. At first, the investment was concentrated in Western European countries and the most popular location for both manufacturing factories and their regional headquarters was the UK. As of 2001, the UK accounted for 46.6 per cent of the accumulated amount of direct investment from Japan to Europe (JETRO, 2004). There were three reasons why Japanese MNCs chose to establish their regional headquarters in the UK (JETRO, 2004: 11–12): the first was because of the official language in the UK. Doing business in English is much easier for Japanese expatriates compared to the other European languages. The second reason was that the UK had a rich pool of business people with international experience. Third, Japanese MNCs expected to operate their European business efficiently by concentrating their investment in the UK. However, since the mid-1990s, many Japanese MNCs have begun to move their production sites from Western Europe to Central and Eastern Europe (CEE) in response to the eastward enlargement of the European Union (EU) and relatively cheap labour costs in CEE countries. The total number of production sites in Poland, the Czech Republic, Slovakia, Hungary and Romania grew from two in 1990 to 110 in 2002 (JETRO, 2003).

Now the investment in Europe has entered a mature stage. As reported in a survey of Japanese multinationals by the Japan Overseas Enterprises Association (2012), the ratio of companies which have a plan to expand business activities in Europe[1] during the next three years is relatively low

(46 per cent) compared to other areas: other Asia[2] (89 per cent), China (78 per cent), Central and South America (56 per cent), and North America (48 per cent). The same is true in terms of plans to increase local employees at their overseas subsidiaries. The ratio in Europe is 32 per cent (other Asia = 84 per cent; China = 71 per cent; Central and South America = 49 per cent; North America = 39 per cent).

Recent Staffing Pattern of Japanese Overseas Subsidiaries

There are recent studies which show that the staffing pattern of Japanese overseas subsidiaries has been gradually changing. For instance, the survey of Japanese MNCs by the Japan Overseas Enterprises Association (2012) indicated that the ratio of non-Japanese CEOs in overseas subsidiaries of Japanese MNCs rose from 16 per cent in 2008 to 24 per cent in 2010 and 29 per cent in 2012. It also shows the differences by business sectors of parent companies and locations of subsidiaries. The ratio is higher in manufacturing businesses (31 per cent) than non-manufacturing (12 per cent). Concerning location, the ratio in Europe is the highest (51 per cent), followed by Oceania (46 per cent), North America (42 per cent), the Middle East and Africa (32 per cent), Central and South America (29 per cent), Asia (17 per cent), and China (13 per cent). The result seems to prove that localization is more advanced in developed countries, where the supply of well-educated and capable human resources is relatively abundant.

When we examined the staffing pattern of Japanese subsidiaries in the UK, where the Japanese MNCs have the largest number of subsidiaries in Europe, based on the data from *Kaigai Shinshutsu Kigyo Soran 2013* (Directory of Japanese Companies Abroad, 2013) compiled by Toyo Keizai Shinposha, it was found that non-Japanese personnel account for 38.3 per cent of CEOs in UK-based subsidiaries, in contrast to 26.2 per cent in overseas operations of Japanese MNCs in Kopp's (1994) study. The ratio is higher in manufacturing companies (45.7 per cent) than non-manufacturing (26.6 per cent) and companies with a relatively longer history of operations have a higher ratio of non-Japanese CEOs.

Three reasons can be offered to explain the progress of localization in overseas subsidiaries of Japanese MNCs. The first is the impact of globalization. In terms of sales, production and employees, overseas operations have already exceeded domestic operations at many Japanese MNCs (Yoshihara, 2008). Owing to its decreasing birth rate and ageing population, the Japanese domestic market has matured. It is now anticipated that future growth will largely take place overseas. The management of fast-growing overseas business requires an ample supply of human resources who can operate their subsidiaries effectively. Although Japanese MNCs used to send Japanese employees as expatriates to foreign countries for this purpose, they are not now able to respond to the requirement because of the shortage of qualified Japanese employees to fill the increasing management positions in their overseas subsidiaries scattered around the globe (Yoshihara, 2008).

The second reason is the progress of 'internal internationalization'. As a result of the long history and high growth rate of overseas operations, Japanese executives and managers with international experience were accumulated within the headquarters. Moreover, in accordance with the growing importance of overseas business, assignments for overseas subsidiaries have gradually become more attractive. Nowadays, there are many Japanese companies where overseas experience is a pre-requisite for promotion to senior management positions (Yoshihara, 2008). According to an interview-based study of Panasonic by one of the authors (Furusawa) in 2014, more than half of management executives on their board of directors and in corporate officer positions have overseas experience as expatriates. Such a qualitative change in top management will provide a foundation to promote the localization of top management positions at the overseas subsidiaries of Japanese MNCs.

The third reason concerns the reform of international HRM in Japanese MNCs. For many Japanese MNCs, international human resource management used to be almost synonymous with the management of Japanese expatriates. Japanese MNCs did not pay much attention to the management of local employees at their foreign subsidiaries (Furusawa, 2008, 2014). However, with growing global competition and the shortage of Japanese candidates for top management positions at their overseas subsidiaries, Japanese headquarters are beginning to take initiatives to recruit, develop and retain the best local talent in order to maintain global competitiveness.

Case study 10.1 Reform of International HRM in Panasonic[3]

Panasonic launched the 'Action Programme for Localization' in 2000. At that time, 85 per cent of CEO positions in their overseas subsidiaries were occupied by Japanese expatriates. Panasonic faced difficulties in attracting, motivating and retaining capable local human resources around the world. The target of the programme was to raise the ratio of non-Japanese CEOs to 25 per cent by 2007.

The execution of the programme consisted of five steps. The first was to scrutinize each CEO position in the overseas subsidiaries and decide whether it should be localized or not in the light

(continued)

(continued)

of their global strategy. If the position was to be localized, the second step was to set a target time period to realize localization. The third was clarifying whether there was a candidate for the position. If there was, a concrete promotion plan was developed. If there was not, the headquarters considered whether to promote from within or recruit from outside in order to fill the position as the fourth step. In the case of promotion from within, the fifth step proceeded to connect with the succession planning programme of Panasonic.

Their succession planning programme is a part of global talent management. The purpose of global talent management is to identify and develop high-potential staff for their 'Corporate Executive Posts', which are of great importance to Panasonic's global strategy. High-potential individuals are nominated based on performance appraisal and assessment of 'Panasonic Leadership Competency' which is rooted in the company's corporate philosophy. High-potential staff are grouped into three categories: HP1s, HP2s and HP3s. HP1s are people who are likely to be promoted to the Corporate Executive Posts within three years. HP2s are to be promoted within five years, while HP3s are future candidates for the posts. The total number of high potentials is approximately 1,000 worldwide and about 20 per cent of them are now non-Japanese. Individual high-potentials are reviewed for replacement every year by a committee in the headquarters.

The high-potentials are developed through both off-the-job training (Off-JT) and on-the-job training (OJT). For the Off-JT, Panasonic has a training programme called the 'Panasonic Executive Development Programme'. This annual programme, of six months duration, has approximately 50 manager participants from all over the world. The training content encompasses leadership development, decision management, business simulation, action learning and so on. As for the OJT, diverse tasks are prepared following the principle of '2 × 2 × 2': the high-potentials are required to have work experience as head of two business units, in two countries and two functions before they can be promoted to Corporate Executive Posts. Today, there are about 20 inpatriates working at the headquarters and trans-regional or trans-functional assignments are becoming common as well. A manager in charge of global talent management in Panasonic proudly remarked, 'such a globally-integrated HRM system has contributed to the improvement in attraction, motivation and retention of capable non-Japanese human resources.'

As a result of global talent management, the target of the 'Action Programme for Localization' has been achieved. Based on our analysis of 281 overseas subsidiaries of Panasonic in the *Kaigai Shinshutsu Kigyo Soran 2013*, we found that the ratio of non-Japanese CEOs in their overseas subsidiaries is 31.0 per cent. Remarkably enough, the number in Europe reaches 66.0 per cent and more than half of the CEOs in North America are non-Japanese, though ratios in areas of developing countries are still low. Additionally, Panasonic has three non-Japanese management executives in corporate officer positions today.

The HRM of South Korean MNCs

HRM in the South Korea Context

It is generally agreed that the rapid institutional change in employment relations during the last decades might be a major characteristic of the HRM context of South Korea (Debroux *et al.*, 2012). Bae (2012: 579) argued that the evolution of Korean HRM practices can be viewed as an example of a 'self-fulfilling process at a global level' – a process of collective attempts to fulfil certain expectations with regard to effective HRM, shaped by various local and global influences such as democratization in 1987 and the Asian financial crisis in 1997.

Before 1987, the paternalistic HRM model was largely prevalent among Korean firms (Bae and Rowley, 2003). Heavily influenced by Japanese HRM practices and Confucian tradition, internal-labour-market orientation, long-term employment and a seniority-based approach were the foundation of HRM practices to promote such values as harmony and loyalty in employment relations (Bae and Rowley, 2003). Mass recruitment targeting entry-level college graduates was the norm and employees were expected to work for a long time in a company (Debroux *et al.*, 2012). In determining pay and promotion, seniority was a major consideration (Bae and Rowley, 2003). These practices seemed to work well in the fast-growing economy based on cost-based competition until the mid-1980s.

After the Democracy Declaration in 1987, labour costs of Korean firms have risen sharply mainly due to the strong labour movement triggered by political democratization in Korea (Bae, 2012). Traditional HRM practices began to be questioned by Korean firms as they were perceived as too rigid and inefficient to cope with the changing employment environment. Some Korean firms tried to adopt new HRM practices that emphasized individual performance and competency development (Bae, 1997). However, due to the influences of traditional values, which still remained, and the emergence of strongly organized labour unions, the adoption of the new practices seemed to be partial at best. According to a survey conducted in 1995, only 20 per cent of sample firms introduced the new HRM practices (cited in Ahn, 1996).

The Asian financial crisis in 1997 could be considered as a major trigger for the dramatic changes in HRM practices of Korean firms (Debroux *et al.*, 2012). After 1997, traditional practices were blamed for causing the loss of competitiveness of Korean firms and the collapse of the national economy (Bae and Rowley, 2001). American firms' HRM practices, which are individual performance-based and more flexible to the changing conditions of labour markets, were introduced as 'global standards' and many Korean firms were pressured to adopt the new practices through normative, coercive and mimetic isomorphic mechanisms (DiMaggio and Powell, 1983; Kim and Bae, 2004). Mass redundancies, which had been illegal previously, were allowed, and Korean firms sacked a huge number of employees during the economic crisis (Debroux *et al.*, 2012). After 1997, more than 45 per cent of Korean firms were reported to be implementing performance-based pay systems (cited in Chang, 2006). It should be noted that despite the seemingly huge changes in HRM practices in Korea since the Asian financial crisis, the actual degrees of implementation of the newly introduced practices varied considerably across companies and the changes are still in progress and are contested (Bae and Rowley, 2003).

HRM of Korean MNCs Operating in Europe

Korean firms joined the third wave of MNC investment in European countries in the late 1980s, after the first and the second wave by US and Japanese firms respectively (Glover and Wilkinson, 2007). However, they began to get actively involved in the internationalization of their subsidiary HRM function from mid-2000, following the rapid increase of their overseas sales and workforce (Chung *et al.*, 2012).

Hybridization of Global Standardization and Localization

A case study of major Korean MNCs reported that their approach to subsidiary HRM practices could be characterized as hybridization, a blending of so-called 'global HRM standards' and local practices

(Chung *et al.*, 2014). Instead of imposing current parent practices to subsidiaries, Korean MNCs tried to select the components of practices for global standardization carefully based on relevant logics of action (e.g. sharing global corporate values, facilitating international transfer of employees, etc.) and utilized so-called 'global HRM best practices', largely informed by major US firms, as a template for global standardization of the selected components in subsidiary HRM practices. The use of benchmarking activities and multinational consultancies was the typical way of accessing 'global HRM best practices' (Chung *et al.*, 2014). On a surface level, these firms seem to pursue a more 'idealistic' version of globalization than their counterpart US and Japanese firms, which tend to show rather ethnocentric approaches in subsidiary HRM practices (e.g. the transfer of parent practices in US MNCs) or subsidiary staffing (e.g. the heavy utilization of expatriates for subsidiary key positions in Japanese MNCs).

Arguably, this more noticeable 'dominance effect' on subsidiary HRM practices of Korean MNCs could be explained by three factors (Chung *et al.*, 2014). First, Korean firms may find it difficult to utilize parent practices for the management of their subsidiary workforces as there is a lack of mature home practices due to the rapidly changing and contested institutional environment in relation to HRM in Korea. Second, it was found that Korean managers in corporate headquarters perceived weak legitimacy in their managerial authority as their firms are based in a non-dominant economy. Due to the perceived 'liability of origin' (Ramachandran and Pant, 2010) they might be reluctant to transfer their home practices to subsidiaries. Third, as a latecomer in the process of globalization, they are able to access information with regard to the HRM practices of MNCs which experienced the globalization of their HRM functions earlier through various available channels such as the media, benchmarking activities and the use of international consultancies.

Tensions between Espoused Practices and Informal Ones

One of the notable observations regarding the implementation of the 'best practices-based' hybrid model (Chung *et al.*, 2012) in Europe-based subsidiaries is the tension stemming from the gap between espoused HRM practices and informal ones (Glover and Wilkinson, 2007; Yang, 2015). While Korean MNCs' explicit HRM practices follow key features of 'global best practices', implicit practices which are rooted in their home country still remain (Yang, 2015). Some aspects of implicit and informal practices (e.g. top-down–oriented target setting, limited horizontal communication, hierarchical management styles) from Korea generate conflicts with local practices in subsidiaries in Europe (Glover and Wilkinson, 2007). In the home country, these potentially problematic practices are compensated by a paternalistic management style based on personal care, informal ties and communication amongst managers and employees (Yang, 2015). These moderating mechanisms, particularly between Korean expatriates (and managers in corporate headquarters) and local employees, might be lacking in subsidiaries in Europe. Thus local employees tended to be frustrated with inconsistent and mixed messages due to the discrepancy between formal and informal practices and the lack of moderating mechanisms (Glover and Wilkinson, 2007). In this regard, the actual implementation of the seemingly 'idealistic' globalization of HRM in Korean MNCs could be restrained and compromised. Arguably, MNCs from emerging economies might experience similar challenges in the process of globalizing their HRM practices.

Conclusion

MNCs try to manage the balance between global integration and local responsiveness in various ways through their policies and practices in managing international workforces. A combination of multiple institutional influences such as country of origin, locality and dominance effects the pattern of IHRM approaches adopted by an MNC. Intra-organizational factors, including HRM-related actors' capabilities, relationships amongst them and the arrangement of their involvement, also play a crucial role in the actual design and implementation of policies and practices in a given context (Chung et al., 2012).

As one of 'the Triad' in the world economy, Europe has attracted a significant flow of FDI investments. When MNCs come to Europe they show distinctive approaches to subsidiary HRM, largely originated from their home country, and more or less different challenges emerge as shown in the cases of US, Japanese and Korean MNCs. The challenges include adaptation to European institutional arrangements with regard to employment relations and employee involvement, localization in staffing of subsidiary key positions and the management of tensions stemming from the gap between espoused formal practices and informal practices embedded in a home country. Given the understanding of the challenges MNCs face and their responses, comprehensive and systematic examinations of the broader impact of foreign MNCs' HRM approaches on employment practices and outcomes in Europe will be crucial for future research.

Key Learning Points

- MNCs try to manage pressures for global integration and local responsiveness in HRM when they expand their businesses abroad.
- The employment-related institutional contexts in a home and a host country, as well as dominance effects from leading economies, are the major external factors which shape subsidiary HRM practices and staffing approaches of MNCs.
- US MNCs tend to adopt a global standardization approach to subsidiary HRM practices, but utilize local human resources for subsidiary key positions.
- Japanese MNCs rely upon extensive expatriate networks for control and coordinate dispersed subsidiary operations, but they have recently focused on developing local talents and replacing expatriates with them.
- Korean MNCs opt to pursue the hybridization of 'global HRM standards' and local practices, but they experience tensions stemming from the gap between the espoused practices and the informal practices rooted in the home country.

Notes

1 Europe includes Russia in the survey.
2 Other Asia in the data refers to the Asian countries or areas other than China (Mainland China). Hong Kong, Macao and Taiwan are categorized as other Asia in the survey.
3 This case study is based on a longitudinal interview survey of Panasonic by one of the authors (Furusawa). Interviews were conducted nine times from 2004 to 2014. The interviewees were general managers or managers in charge of the global talent management of Panasonic at the global headquarters in Japan and the European headquarters in the UK.

References

Ahn, H.-T. (1996) *The Current Situations and Future Directions of New Personnel Management Systems in Korean Firms*. Seoul: Korea Employers' Federation (in Korean).

Almond, P., Edwards, T., Colling, T., Ferner, A., Gunnigle, P., Müller-Camen, M., Quintanilla, J. and Wächter, H. (2005) 'Unraveling home and host country effects: An investigation of the HR policies of an American multinational in four European countries', *Industrial Relations: A Journal of Economy and Society*, 44(2), 276–306.

Bae, J. (1997) 'Beyond seniority-based systems: A paradigm shift in Korean HRM?', *Asia Pacific Business Review*, 3(4), 82–110.

Bae, J. (2012) 'Self-fulfilling processes at a global level: The evolution of human resource management practices in Korea, 1987–2007', *Management Learning*, 43(5), 579–607.

Bae, J. and Rowley, C. (2001) 'The impact of globalization on HRM: The case of South Korea', *Journal of World Business*, 36(4), 402–428.

Bae, J. and Rowley, C. (2003) 'Changes and continuities in South Korean HRM', *Asia Pacific Business Review*, 9(4), 76–105.

Baron, J.N., Dobbin, F.R. and Jennings, P.D. (1986) 'War and peace: The evolution of modern personnel administration in US industry', *American Journal of Sociology*, 92(2), 350-383.

Bartlett, C.A. and Yoshihara, H. (1988) 'New challenges for Japanese multinationals: Is organization adaptation their Achilles heel?', *Human Resource Management*, 27(1), 19–43.

Brewster, C. (1995) 'Towards a "European" model of human resource management', *Journal of International Business Studies*, 26(1), 1–21.

Brewster, C., Sparrow, P.R., Vernon, C. and Houldsworth, L. (2011) *International Human Resource Management, 3rd edn.* London: Chartered Institute of Personnel and Development.

Chang, E. (2006) 'Individual pay for performance and commitment HR practices in South Korea', *Journal of World Business*, 41(4), 368–381.

Chung, C., Bozkurt, O. and Sparrow, P. (2012) 'Managing the duality of IHRM: Unravelling the strategy and perceptions of key actors in South Korean MNCs', *The International Journal of Human Resource Management*, 23(11), 2333–2353.

Chung, C., Sparrow, P. and Bozkurt, O. (2014) 'South Korean MNEs' international HRM approach: Hybridization of global standards and local practices', *Journal of World Business*, 49(4), 549–559.

Collings, D., Morley, M. and Gunnigle, P. (2008) 'Composing the top management team in the international subsidiary: Qualitative evidence on international staffing in US MNCs in the Republic of Ireland', *Journal of World Business*, 43(2), 197–212.

Debroux, P., Harry, W., Hayashi, S., Jason, H.H., Jackson, K. and Kiyomiya, T. (2012) 'Japan, Korea and Taiwan: Issues and trends in human resource management', in Brewster, C. and Mayrhofer, W. (eds) *Handbook of Research on Comparative Human Resource Management*. Cheltenham: Edward Elgar, 620–664.

DiMaggio, P.J. and Powell, W.W. (1983) 'The iron cage revisited: Institutional isomorphism and collective rationality in organizational fields', *American Sociological Review*, 48(2), 147–160.

Edwards, R. (1979) *Contested Terrain: The Transformation of the Workplace in the Twentieth Century*. London: Heinemann.

Edwards, T., Edwards, P., Ferner, A., Marginson, P. and Tregaskis, O. (2010) 'Multinational companies and the diffusion of employment practices from outside the country of origin', *Management International Review*, 50(5), 613–634.

Evans, P., Pucik, V. and Björkman, I. (2011) *The Global Challenge: International Human Resource Management, 2nd edn.* New York: McGraw Hill-Irwin.

Fernandez, J.P. and Barr, M. (1993) *The Diversity Advantage: How American Business Can Out-Perform Japanese and European Companies in the Global Marketplace*. New York: Lexington Books.

Ferner, A. (1997) 'Country of origin effects and HRM in multinational companies', *Human Resource Management Journal*, 7(1), 19–37.

Ferner, A., Almond, P. and Colling, T. (2005) 'Institutional theory and the cross-national transfer of employment policy: The case of "workforce diversity" in US multinationals', *Journal of International Business Studies*, 36(3), 304–321.

Ferner, A., Almond, P., Clark, I., Colling, T., Edwards, T., Holden, L. and Muller-Camen, M. (2004) 'Dynamics of central control and subsidiary autonomy in the management of human resources: Case-study evidence from US MNCs in the UK', *Organization Studies*, 25(3), 363–391.

Ferner, A., Tregaskis, O., Edwards, P., Edwards, T., Marginson, P., Adam, D. and Meyer, M. (2011) 'HRM structures and subsidiary discretion in foreign multinationals in the UK', *The International Journal of Human Resource Management*, 22(3), 483–509.

Furusawa, M. (2008) *Global Jinteikishigen Kanriron (The Theory of Global Human Resource Management)*. Tokyo: Hakutou Shobou (in Japanese).

Furusawa, M. (2014) 'Global talent management in Japanese multinational companies: The case of Nissan Motor Company', in Al Ariss, A. (ed.) *Global Talent Management: Challenges, Strategies, and Opportunities*. Heidelberg: Springer, 159–170.

Gaur, A.S., Delios, A. and Singh, K. (2007) 'Institutional environments, staffing strategies, and subsidiary performance', *Journal of Management*, 33(4), 611–636.

Geppert, M. and Williams, K. (2006) 'Global, national and local practices in multinational corporations: Towards a sociopolitical framework', *The International Journal of Human Resource Management*, 17(1), 49–69.

Glover, L. and Wilkinson, A. (2007) 'Worlds colliding: The translation of modern management practices within a UK based subsidiary of a Korean-owned MNC', *The International Journal of Human Resource Management*, 18(8), 1437–1455.

Gong, Y. (2003) 'Subsidiary staffing in multinational enterprises: Agency, resources, and performance', *Academy of Management Journal*, 46(6), 728–739.

Guest, D.E. (1987) 'Human resource management and industrial relations', *Journal of Management Studies*, 24(5), 503–521.

Guest, D.E. (1990) 'Human resource management and the American dream', *Journal of Management Studies*, 27(4), 377–397.

Hall, E.T. (1976) *Beyond Culture*. Garden City, New York: Doubleday and Company.

Hall, P.A. and Soskice, D. (2001) *Varieties of Capitalism: The Institutional Foundations of Comparative Advantage*. Oxford: Oxford University Press.

Harzing, A.W. (1999) *Managing the Multinationals: An International Study of Control Mechanisms*. Cheltenham: Edward Elgar.

Harzing, A.W. (2001) 'Who's in charge? An empirical study of executive staffing practices in foreign subsidiaries', *Human Resource Management*, 40(2), 139–158.

Hayashi, K. (1994) *Ibunka Interface Keiei (Cross Cultural Interface Corporate Management)*. Tokyo: Nihonkeizaishinbun Shuppansha (in Japanese).

Ishida, H. (1999) *Kokusai Keiei to White-Collar (International Management and White-Collar Employees)*. Tokyo: Chuuou Keizaisha (in Japanese).

Jacoby, S.M. (1985) *Employing Bureaucracy: Managers, Unions, and the Transformation of Work in American Industry, 1900–1945*. New York: Columbia University Press.

Japan Overseas Enterprises Association (2012) *Kaigaigenchihoujin No Keiei No Global-Ka Ni Kansuru Ankeitochousa Kekka Houkoku Ni Tsuite (The Report of Questionnaire Survey of Globalization of Management in Overseas Subsidiaries)*. Tokyo: Japan Overseas Enterprises Association (in Japanese).

JETRO (2003) *Zai-Oushuu·Toruko Nikkeiseizougyou No Keieijittai: 2002-nendo Chousa (2002 Survey of Management in Japanese-Affiliated Manufacturing Companies in Europe and Turkey*. Tokyo: JETRO (in Japanese).

JETRO (2004) *Oushuu Ni Okeru Nikkeikigyou No Soshiki, Location Senryaku No Hensen To Mitooshi (Transition and Prospect of Organisation and Location Strategy in Japanese-Affiliated Companies in Europe)*. Tokyo: JETRO (in Japanese).

Keeley, T.D. (2001) *International Human Resource Management in Japanese Firms: Their Greatest Challenge*. New York: Palgrave Macmillan.

Kim, D. and Bae, J. (2004) *Employment Relations and HRM in South Korea*. Farnham: Ashgate.

Kopp, R. (1994) 'International human resource policies and practices in Japanese, European, and United States multinationals', *Human Resource Management*, 33(4), 581–599.

Kopp, R. (1999) 'The rice-paper ceiling in Japanese companies: Why it exists and persists', in Beechler, S. L. and Bird, A. (eds) *Japanese Multinationals Abroad: Individual and Organizational Learning*. New York: Oxford University Press, 107–128.

Lawrence, P. (1996) *Management in the USA*. London: Sage.

Marginson, P., Hall, M., Hoffmann, A. and Müller, T. (2004) 'The impact of European works councils on management decision-making in UK and US-based multinationals: A case study comparison', *British Journal of Industrial Relations*, 42(2), 209–233.

Parry, E., Dickmann, M. and Morley, M. (2008) 'North American MNCs and their HR policies in liberal and coordinated market economies', *The International Journal of Human Resource Management*, 19(11), 2024–2040.

Pudelko, M. and Harzing, A.W. (2007) 'Country-of-origin, localization, or dominance effect? An empirical investigation of HRM practices in foreign subsidiaries', *Human Resource Management*, 46(4), 535–559.

Ramachandran, J. and Pant, A. (2010) 'The liabilities of origin: An emerging economy perspective on the costs of doing business abroad', in Timothy, D., Torben, P. and Laszlo, T. (eds) *The Past, Present and Future of International Business & Management, Advances in International Management, Vol. 23*. Bingley: Emerald Group Publishing, 231–265.

Rosenzweig, P.M. (2006) 'The dual logics behind international human resource management: Pressures for global integration and local responsiveness', in Stahl, G.K. and Björkman, I. (eds) *Handbook of Research in International Human Resource Management*. Cheltenham: Edward Elgar, 36–48.

Rosenzweig, P.M. and Nohria, N. (1994) 'Influences on human resource management practices in multinational corporations', *Journal of International Business Studies*, 25(2), 229–251.

Scullion, H. and Brewster, C. (2002) 'The management of expatriates: Messages from Europe?', *Journal of World Business*, 36(4), 346–365.

Tempel, A., Edwards, T., Ferner, A., Muller-Camen, M. and Wächter, H. (2006) 'Subsidiary responses to institutional duality: Collective representation practices of US multinationals in Britain and Germany', *Human Relations*, 59(11), 1543–1570.

Tian, X., Harvey, M. and Slocum, J.W. (2014) 'The retention of Chinese managers: The Chinese puzzle box', *Organizational Dynamics*, 43(1), 44–52.

Toyo Keizai Shinposha (2013) *Kaigai Shinshutsu Kigyo Soran 2013 (Directory of Japanese Companies Abroad, 2013)*. Tokyo: Toyo Keizai Shinposha (in Japanese).

UNCTAD (2014) *World Investment Report 2014: Investing in the SDGS – an Action Plan*. New York and Geneva: United Nations Publication.

Yang, I. (2015) 'Cross-cultural perceptions of clan control in Korean multinational companies: A conceptual investigation of employees' fairness monitoring based on cultural values', *The International Journal of Human Resource Management*, 26(8), 1076–1097.

Yasumuro, K. (1982) *Kokusai Keiei Koudouron (The Theory of International Management Behavior)*. Tokyo: Moriyama Shoten (in Japanese).

Yoshihara, H. (1989) *Genchijinshachou To Uchinaru Kokusaika (Host Country National Presidents and Internal Internationalization)*. Tokyo: Toyo Keizai Shinposha (in Japanese).

Yoshihara, H. (2008) 'Belated change in international management of Japanese multinationals', *Rikkyo Business Review*, 1, 4–15.

Yoshino, M.Y. (1976) *Japan's Multinational Enterprises*. Cambridge, MA: Harvard University Press.

11 Human Resources and Corporate Responsibility

TODD CARDARELLI, DAVID GRAYSON AND MICHAEL DICKMANN

Introduction

Rapid advances in technology, markets, demographics and development, and values have intensified debates about the role and purpose of business and what responsibility business should take for its impacts (Grayson and Hodges, 2001). There has been a proliferation of institutions, initiatives and agreements in the public and private sectors to address some of the world's largest, most complex societal issues such as climate change, bio-diversity loss, shortages of raw materials and socio-economic inequality (Grayson and Nelson, 2013). Private sector efforts to address 'corporate responsibility' (CR) have become increasingly sophisticated over the decades, implying a recognition that business can be a catalyst for positive societal change (Grayson and Nelson, 2013).

Some readers may be tempted to skip this chapter, perhaps based on a limited interpretation of CR as a few charitable donations, some employee-volunteering programmes and some 'green initiatives'. That would be a mistake – the role of business in society, as we will show, is a priority concern for many of the world's largest companies. Many of the Fortune 500, FTSE 100 and other leading companies are redefining how they respond to societal expectations and environmental challenges to be more socially and environmentally responsible and to have a net positive impact (Forum for the Future, 2015).

> **Box 11.1 Broadening and Focusing Corporate Social Responsibility**
>
> In this chapter we consistently use corporate responsibility (CR) as a broader concept than corporate social responsibility (CSR). While recognizing that many people and many companies use terms such as 'corporate (social) responsibility', 'C(S)R', 'corporate citizenship', 'corporate sustainability' plus other terms, and sometimes interchangeably, it would clearly be better if they would not do so. It causes confusion and can slow progress in creating broader understanding (Smith, 2007). The President of one of the largest and arguably most influential CR coalitions, Peter Bakker of the World Business Council for Sustainable Development (WBCSD), recently argued that the term 'CSR is dead.' WBCSD represents 200 of the largest corporations in the world and Bakker's key argument is that leading companies are already going way beyond CSR in a series of stand-alone initiatives by integrating sustainability into everything they do. In this chapter, we follow the lead of Bakker and other leaders in eschewing corporate social responsibility (CSR). The EU Commission defines CR as the responsibility a business takes for social, economic and environmental impacts. Thus, CR is about mindset and behaviour: what responsibility is taken for all company actions – not just for some initiatives that a company may choose to label as 'CR' or 'CSR'.

This chapter explores the evolution in thinking and practice in CR and argues that human resource management (HRM) staff could play a much more active role in helping companies to embed CR. The purpose of this chapter is to show why and how HRM professionals could play this enhanced role. Then, we use a European perspective on CR and illustrate this with the example of the Dutch-headquartered company Desso. The chapter concludes with suggestions for further research and key take-aways.

Corporate Responsibility: A Journey

In 1953, Howard Bowen published his book, *Social Responsibilities of the Businessman*, and is largely credited with coining the phrase 'corporate social responsibility.' Bowen asked: 'what responsibilities to society can business people be reasonably expected to assume?' Bowen also provided an early definition: 'the obligations of businessmen to pursue those policies, to make those decisions, or to follow those lines of action which are desirable in terms of the objectives and values of our society'. Since then, many different definitions have been advanced. One recent academic study identified approximately 37 different definitions for CR (Dahlsrud, 2008).

Over time, a myriad of non-profit organizations, think-tanks and consultancies have arisen to encourage, coach and enable companies to design, implement and monitor CR initiatives. National governments have established CR ministers; supranational institutions (e.g. the United Nations) have adopted CR strategies and initiatives (e.g. the UN Global Compact); universities have established CR centres that work closely with businesses (e.g. Boston College Center for Corporate Citizenship and The First Bank Sustainability Centre of Lagos Business School); various CR think-tanks, consultancies and CR coalitions have emerged (e.g. Business in the Community (BitC), Business for Social Responsibility (BSR)) and global forums have arisen linking non-governmental organizations (NGOs) with businesses to establish multi-sector alliances focused on CR issues (e.g. the Clinton Global Initiative), (Grayson and Nelson, 2013). Several of the larger CR coalitions such as BSR, BitC and CSR Europe have work programmes and membership engagement on the employment dimensions of CR.

The Business Case for Corporate Responsibility

While more limited interpretations of CR as specific initiatives may still prevail in some companies, business leaders are increasingly recognizing that CR is not an optional extra, a bolt-on to business operations, but is about core business, how business behaves in all it does and, therefore, built-in to business purpose and strategy (Porter and Kramer, 2006). It is widely recognized in CR literature that the most effective approach to CR is a strategic approach, one that leverages the core competencies of the organization for the benefit of society as well as for the business itself (Cramer, 2005). Heslin and Ochoa argue that 'effective CR initiatives are those that derived from careful analysis of each organization's culture, competencies and strategic opportunities' (2008: 125). They recognize that strategic CR leverages the core competencies of the organization for the benefit of society and for the business itself.

Increasingly, multinational enterprises (MNEs) are under pressure to demonstrate socially responsible behaviour. Responding to greater societal pressure to be more socially responsible and enhance human resource outcomes represents an opportunity for MNEs to help differentiate themselves from their competitors and contribute to establishing a sustainable competitive advantage (Branco and Rodrigues, 2006; Heslin and Ochoa, 2008). The business case argument suggests that organizations engage in CR activities because they will be rewarded in economic and financial terms (Carroll and Shabana, 2010). Articulating the business case for CR is a widely researched area in the literature (Carroll and Shabana 2010; Vogel, 2005).

Caroll and Shabana (2010: 92) suggest that,

> The focus of CR theories has shifted away from an ethics orientation to a performance orientation. In addition, the level of analysis has moved away from a macro-social level to an organizational level, where the effects of CR on firm financial performance are closely examined.

This suggests that the business case argument for CR is highly relevant to organizations and merits further study.

Kurucz *et al.* (2008) organize the CR business case literature into four categories which summarize why organizations engage with CR: cost and risk reduction; competitive advantage; reputation and legitimacy; and synergistic value creation. Zadek (2004) suggests that companies pursue CR strategies to (1) defend their reputations, (2) justify benefits over costs, (3) integrate with their broader strategies and (4) learn, innovate and manage risk.

Although there is some critique in the literature of the business case for CR, namely that businesses will ultimately only adopt practices which are profitable (Surroca *et al.*, 2010), there is a converging body of research suggesting that CR has a positive impact on financial performance (Schreck, 2011; van Beurden and Gossling, 2008; Waddock and Graves, 1997) and other aspects of organizational performance.

In addition, businesses are realizing that engaging in CR can positively impact a firm's performance and help to create a sustainable competitive advantage (Bhattacharya *et al.*, 2008; Porter and Kramer, 2006; Smith, 2007). Competitive advantage is often described as an advantage that derives when an organization controls strategic assets that are valuable, rare and unique (Barney, 1991; Smith, 2007). Smith (2007) argues that competitive advantage through CR is created by strengthening the intangible assets of a firm, such as employee skills, employee engagement, community goodwill and perception of trustworthiness, all of which are difficult for competitors to emulate.

Specific areas of organizational performance where CR is thought to have a positive impact include operational efficiency (Branco and Rodrigues, 2006), customer reputation (Bhattacharya *et al.*, 2011), innovation (Preuss, 2011), access to capital markets (Smith, 2003), license to operate (Heslin and Ochoa, 2008), employee attraction (Bhattacharya *et al.*, 2008; Turban and Greening, 1997), employee professional development/skill acquisition (Tuffrey, 2003), job satisfaction and retention (Pettijohn *et al.*, 2008) and organizational commitment (Brammer *et al.*, 2007; Peterson, 2004; Turker, 2009).

CR on the Agenda of Global Companies

Given the strong business and moral arguments for CR, it is no wonder that CEOs have started to pay close attention to improving their organization's approaches. CEOs increasingly assert that CR is important to them and their business (PwC, 2014):

- Most CEOs surveyed agree that business has social as well as financial responsibilities.
- 80 per cent say it is important for their business to measure and reduce its environment footprint.
- Over three-quarters think that satisfying wider societal needs and protecting the interests of future generations is important to their business.
- 74 per cent agree that measuring and reporting non-financial impacts contributes to their business long-term success.
- 69 per cent say that the purpose of business is to balance the interests of all stakeholders.

A number of companies have made CR integral to their business purpose and strategy, in some cases radically changing their business models, for example, General Electric's *Ecomagination* and Unilever's *Sustainable Living Plan*. However, even CEOs of companies publicly committed to CR admit that there is a performance gap between what the CEOs believe businesses should do and what their own companies are doing.

One manifestation of this performance gap is that frequently, even amongst committed companies with specialist CR functions, there is patchy collaboration between the CR specialists and other parts of the business.

This appears to be particularly the case with CR specialists and the HR function. Yet the HR function is a source of specialist expertise and typically has a formal or supporting responsibility for various company performances and polices which can be re-focused or stretched to help embed CR. Traditionally CR sits with either the top leadership of the firm or within a public policy or corporate citizenship/responsibility

AND IT IS NOT JUST ABOUT VALUE, CEOs SEE MORE GAPS
BETWEEN AMBITION AND EXECUTION . . .

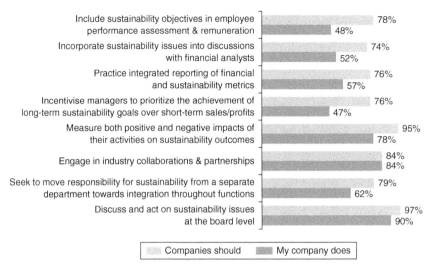

Figure 11.1 UNGC/Accenture CEOs' Sustainability Survey 2013
Source: UNGC, Accenture, The UN Global Compact-Accenture CEO Study on
Sustainability 2013, September 2013 http://www.accenture.com/SiteCollectionDocuments/
PDF/Accenture-UN-Global-Compact-Acn-CEO-Study-Sustainability-2013.PDF

function. In many cases, CR is driven by the firm's highest levels of
leadership. For example, in a study of CR ownership conducted by
the United Nations Global Compact and the Wharton School of the
University of Pennsylvania, 71 per cent of the 400 companies surveyed
indicated that their CR policies and practices were developed/managed
at the CEO level, 57 per cent at the board of directors level and 56 per
cent at the senior management level (Bhattacharya *et al.*, 2008). We
now address the HRM dimensions of CR.

Role of the HRM Function in Supporting CR Efforts

The above shows that there is vast agreement on the value of strategic
CR. However, there is little agreement on who should drive the
organizational change towards a more strategic approach to CR,
other than that it should be sponsored by the top leadership of the
organization. The literature suggests that a partnership between the
C-suite and HRM could be an effective arrangement combining
the influence, business understanding and strategic oversight of top
leadership with the ability of the HRM function to effectively manage
the required culture change associated with strategy implementation.

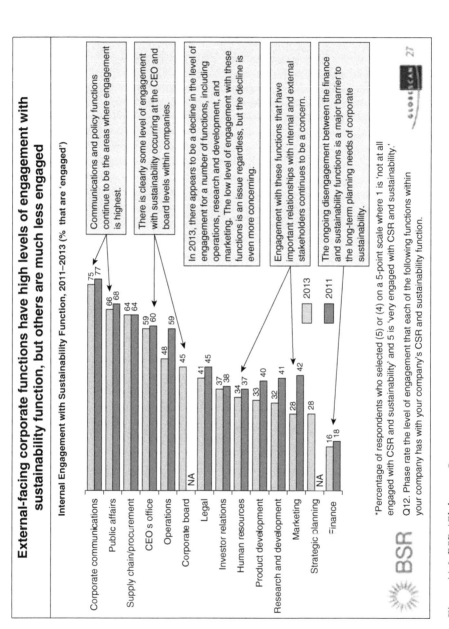

External-facing corporate functions have high levels of engagement with sustainability function, but others are much less engaged

Internal Engagement with Sustainability Function, 2011–2013 (% that are 'engaged')

Function	2013	2011
Corporate communications	75	77
Public affairs	66	68
Supply chain/procurement	64	64
CEO's office	59	60
Operations	48	59
Corporate board	NA	45
Legal	41	45
Investor relations	37	38
Human resources	34	37
Product development	33	40
Research and development	32	41
Marketing	28	42
Strategic planning	NA	28
Finance	16	18

Communications and policy functions continue to be the areas where engagement is highest.

There is clearly some level of engagement with sustainability occurring at the CEO and board levels within companies.

In 2013, there appears to be a decline in the level of engagement for a number of functions, including operations, research and development, and marketing. The low level of engagement with these functions is an issue regardless, but the decline is even more concerning.

Engagement with these functions that have important relationships with internal and external stakeholders continues to be a concern.

The ongoing disengagement between the finance and sustainability functions is a major barrier to the long-term planning needs of corporate sustainability.

*Percentage of respondents who selected (5) or (4) on a 5-point scale where 1 is 'not at all engaged with CSR and sustainability' and 5 is 'very engaged with CSR and sustainability.'

Q12. Phase rate the level of engagement that each of the following functions within your company has with your company's CSR and sustainability function.

Figure 11.2 BSR/Globescan Survey

Source: BSR and Globescan, State of Sustainable Business Survey 2014, October 2014 http://www.bsr.org/reports/BSR_GlobeScan_Survey_2014.pdf

CR is important for HRM professionals for three main reasons. First, many aspects of CR are concerned with how a business behaves towards its employees and the workplace impacts it has. Second, HRM professionals can play a crucial role in helping the rest of the business embed responsible business practices. Third, CR can help HRM professionals fulfil traditional objectives of creating an employer brand of choice with engaged and motivated employees.

Given the overlap between HRM and CR practices and the focus of CR initiatives to enhance HRM outcomes, one might expect HRM practitioners to play a significant role in the design and implementation of CR initiatives. HRM competence in the areas of training and development, performance management, change management and other disciplines relevant to the design and implementation of CR would suggest that HRM professionals should be key players in the development and implementation of CR. The literature claims that HRM professionals are well positioned to play an integral role in designing, implementing and embedding CR in organizations (Colbert and Kurucz, 2007; Gond *et al.*, 2011; Zappala, 2004).

In organizations characterized by a highly skilled workforce in which employees are a key driver of organizational performance, HRM is often a highly visible component of the overall business strategy (Alvesson and Kärreman, 2007; Maister, 1993). To the extent that these organizations have an explicit CR strategy, one might expect that a significant component of the CR strategy would be comprised of HRM practices which aim to develop critical skills and increase employee engagement, retention and organizational commitment.

Responsible business practices (or their opposite) may be of particular concern to HRM professionals. They are likely to include diversity and human rights; health and well-being; creating a learning organization with advancement based on merit; treating employees fairly and with respect; ensuring employees know what is expected of them and that they are empowered to do their jobs; establishing a culture of transparency and mutual accountability; and that there are robust procedures and protection for whistle-blowers.

Despite the apparent linkage between HRM and CR, it is clear from the literature that the HRM function is often absent from the design and implementation of CR strategy (Fenwick and Bierema, 2008; Parkes and Borland, 2012; Zappala, 2004).

Embedding Strategic CR: The Role of the HRM Professional

Impact of CR

There is an extensive amount of professional and academic literature on the relationship between HRM and organizational performance (Holbeche and Matthews, 2012; Huselid, 1995; Pfeffer, 1994). It is generally accepted as recommended business practice that the implementation of certain HRM policies and practices can enhance HRM outcomes (e.g. recruitment, skill development, employee engagement, organizational commitment and retention) and serve as a potential source of competitive advantage. This is thought to be especially true when these HRM policies and practices are aligned with the organization's strategy (Schuler and Jackson, 2007). However, the ubiquitous nature of these HRM practices among MNEs (Maister, 1993) makes differentiation through HRM difficult.

Strategic CR, in contrast, is a less-practiced field and has the potential to generate positive HRM outcomes which can serve to differentiate an organization. There is an emerging body of research which suggests that a strategic approach to CR can have a positive influence on HRM outcomes and contribute to creating a sustainable competitive advantage (Heslin and Ochoa, 2008, Porter and Kramer, 2006, 2011).

HRM can partner with those responsible for CR to ensure that the proposed and realized benefits of CR are aligned and support the organization's business goals and purpose and, importantly, the needs and expectations of employees. HRM should be equipped to understand the expectations of employees, given their experience in recruiting, expertise in the drivers of employee engagement, as well as access to exit interview data. Based on this understanding, HRM could help draft CR goals and objectives into the 'language' of various stakeholders, including leadership and employees. HRM can also play a key role in engendering the culture change that is often required in significant business change, such as the decision to embrace strategic CR.

Based on Grayson and Hodges's Seven Steps (2004), Table 11.1 is a brief illustration of how HRM professionals can support various stages of CR strategy development and implementation in an organization.

As Cramer (2005) suggests, embedding CR as a more central part of an organization will have an impact on a firm's corporate culture, because it may require an organization to review its values, norms and attitudes. It is likely that, through successive iterations, CR becomes more institutionalized, with changes anchored into organizational systems as well as corporate culture and values.

Table 11.1 Seven steps for CR implementation

Step	Characteristics of CR Implementation	Implications/Potential Roles for HRM
Step 1: • Triggering change: raise CR awareness inside the organization	• Top down or bottom up • Often triggered by a change in the way management perceives its business and societal environment	• Embed CR themes and messages in existing training events, or develop new sessions that explore the relationship between business and society • Position CR as an enabler to build professional skills • Develop training programmes to build awareness of CR issues • Facilitate focus groups, interviews or other processes to understand current state of CR awareness
Step 2: • Assessing most material impacts: corporate purpose in its societal context • Uncovering organizational systems, corporate norms and values • Identify key stakeholders and understand their issues	• CR focus aligned with the values, norms and mission of the organization • CR goals and decision-making process aligned with overall organizational goals and strategies • Culture evolves from a target-driven to a value-driven culture • Organizational culture is evolving to one that is receptive to change and can sustain a CR strategy over the long run • Benchmarking competitors' practices and CR norms and standards – gap analysis	• Facilitate the development of organizational values and policies linking CR to the business • Develop recognition and reward policies and practices to promote the firm's values and orientation towards CR • Review existing competency frameworks (if applicable) and embed CR language/themes as appropriate

(continued)

Table 11.1 (continued)

Step	Characteristics of CR Implementation	Implications/Potential Roles for HRM
Step 3: • Making the business case: establishing a vision and a working definition for CR	• Develop a common meaning for CR • A socially responsible shared vision that includes stakeholders' expectations and is compatible with the organization's long-term strategic goals • A vision is formulated and declared by top management and then formalized and communicated through official documents	• Facilitate discussions with firm leadership around CR to clarify the linkage to the firm's business objectives • Help to cascade the vision across the organization, through communications, training, presentations
Step 4: • Committing to action • Auditing current CR norms, standards and practices	• Review of existing mission statements, policies, codes of conduct, principles and other operating documents • Consultation with key managers who represent key business functions inside the organization and with CR and industry experts for further insight	• Undertake review of existing policies and practices to understand extent of CR-related activity • Lead discussions with external CR experts, especially in CR issues that involve employees (e.g. skill-based volunteering, community engagement) • Assemble results of internal review, develop findings and recommendations • Board and senior management team leadership and structure of board oversight agreed

Step 5: • Developing a CR–integrated strategic plan • Embedding CR in organizational strategy and practice	• Translating values, visions or policy statements into commitments, expectations and guiding principles • Development of targets and performance measures • Development of an integrated CR–enabling structure, such as designating a senior official or a committee responsible for overall CR implementation	• Advise on the change management implications involved in achieving the required behaviour change • Help develop appropriate KPIs and embed into existing performance management systems • Implement various initiatives to help strengthen the cohesiveness of the team dedicated to CR
Step 6: • Implementing the CR–integrated strategic plan • Implementing organizational initiatives and strategies linked to CR	• Top management determines the CR direction and strategy; middle management and employees implement • Communicate and enforce the top–down vision and CR implementation • Engage employees in implementation to ensure a sense of ownership of and pride in their organization's CR activities. Focus on awareness and ensuring that employees understand the context and background of the organization's CR approach, including the motivation, reasons for adopting a specific approach, relevance to the organization, how it fits with existing organizational objectives, any changes to current approaches and other implications	• Partner with the CR function to help manage the change, i.e. messaging, training, recognizing performance • Facilitate focus groups and types of sessions with employees to build awareness of CR strategy and how they can get involved. • Ensure their feedback feeds to CR leadership to help influence nature of CR strategy • Embed CR messages and themes within the HR agenda (e.g. use CR as a tool for leadership development) • Amend HR processes to include CR dimension (e.g. including a CR component to performance management)

(continued)

Table 11.1 (continued)

Step	Characteristics of CR Implementation	Implications/Potential Roles for HRM
Step 7: • Measuring and reporting	• Continuous internal communication about CR – internal communication plan • Anchor the CR vision in the day-to-day activities of the organization • External communication on achievements and plans • Formal evaluations and reviews to determine what works well, why, and how to ensure it will continue • Involving external auditors or publishing the performance results compared with the target standards • Stakeholders verification of results	• Ensure relevancy of CR messaging, based on organizational values and the needs, interests and perspective of employees • Review impact of CR activity on standard HR measures, e.g. recruitment, retention, motivation, performance

Source: Grayson and Hodges (2004) and Cardarilli (2015)

BSR and Executiva's (2012) report concluded that this changed context requires a wide range of integrated leadership competencies.

HRM areas of expertise include defining competencies for different jobs; ensuring job applicants' values are congruent with corporate values; incorporating the organization's commitment to CR in induction and continuous professional development; helping line-managers to define and set relevant CR key performance indicators; training line-managers to incorporate CR meaningfully into the appraisal process, and; working with compensation specialists to develop compensation schemes to reward managers and staff for both *what* they have achieved and *how* they have achieved it (Lawler and Mohrman, 2014).

An academic literature review, complemented by an examination of practices in several international companies, suggests a number of dimensions of an enabling environment for CR (Grayson *et al.*, 2013).

Achieving HRM Outcomes through Strategic CR: Creating a Sustainability Culture

A genuine commitment to CR can provide the narrative and impetus for an organization 'built to last', which can endure into the indefinite future. Creating a CR culture which is both the *desired* and the *actual* culture of the organization creates an alignment between the goals and actions of individual employees and that of the company as a whole. Both academic research and feedback from companies suggest that CR can help attract, develop and retain more engaged and committed employees. Furthermore, CR can improve operational effectiveness and stimulate innovation – including employee-inspired innovation such as social intrapreneurism: being entrepreneurial inside large companies to create value both for the business and for society (Doughty Centre for Corporate Responsibility and Business in the Community 2011).

HRM outcomes that have been explored include the influence of CR in attracting and retaining employees, organizational commitment, skill development and employee engagement (Bhattacharya *et al.*, 2008; Greening and Turban, 2000; Tuffrey, 2003; Zappala, 2004).

In one of the earliest studies of the relationship between CR and employer attractiveness, Turban and Greening (1997) found that the reputational benefits that arise from an organization's CR policies and programmes impact the level of employer attractiveness among potential applicants. CR has also been linked to positively influencing employee engagement and organizational commitment (Peterson, 2004; Smith and Langford, 2011; Turker, 2009).

CR/HRM Initiative in Focus: International Corporate Volunteering

Two seemingly independent global phenomena facing today's MNEs are accelerating in their pace and need for action. The first is an increasing pressure on MNEs to engage in socially responsible behaviour and to be seen by stakeholders as good corporate citizens. The other is a growing demand among MNEs for an increasingly global workforce to keep pace with accelerating international activity – i.e. to have professionals with the knowledge, skills and abilities (KSAs) to work effectively with others around the world (Caligiuri and Di Santo, 2001).

Until recently, MNEs would often aim to achieve these objectives with separate, distinct initiatives. For example, most MNEs have implemented CR initiatives to address stakeholder pressures. Some MNEs have gone beyond a 'defensive' (Zadek, 2004) approach to CR and have adopted a more strategic approach to achieve positive CR outcomes and enhance business performance (Porter and Kramer, 2006, 2011). To develop employees and managers with the KSAs to work effectively across borders, MNEs have implemented a number of global management development programmes, including sending high-potential managers on developmental international assignments (Caligiuri, 2006; Dickmann and Doherty, 2010).

A few of the world's largest MNEs, however, are beginning to combine a strategic approach to CR (strategic skill-based volunteering) with global management development. The approach is known as global corporate volunteering (global CV) (Morales and Loro, 2012). In such programmes individuals or teams travel to an international destination, often a developing country, usually for between three to six months to work on community projects – often in collaboration with a development agency or international NGO. Global CV is an increasingly visible component of CR among the world's largest organizations. Some of the world's largest MNEs have global CV programmes that are often portrayed as leading examples of global corporate citizenship behaviour (Morales and Loro, 2012). In one study of a global CV programme in a global professional services firm, Pless, Maak and Stahl (2012: 890) conclude that 'International service learning programmes [i.e. global CV] can play a crucial role in developing responsible business leaders and thereby support a company's CSR and sustainability efforts.'

A strategic approach to skill-based volunteering is often highlighted as a CR initiative that can help create positive HRM outcomes (Boccalandro, 2012). Employer-sponsored community volunteering is one of the most common and publicly visible CR initiatives used by organizations (Peterson, 2004; Zappala and McLaren, 2004). A recent survey of Fortune 500 firms indicated that 92 per cent of the firms have a formal corporate sponsored employee volunteering programme in place (Boccalandro, 2009).

Research suggests that corporate volunteering initiatives have a positive impact on the development of job-related skills (Peterson, 2004) including communication skills, coaching and mentoring, influencing, negotiation and conflict resolution, teaming, project management, leadership and flexibility to work with people in a variety of settings and from different backgrounds (Guarnieri and Kao, 2007; Tuffrey, 2003). De Gilder *et al.* (2005) explored the impact of participation in an employee volunteering programme and found that the programme had a positive impact on employee attitudes and behaviours, including organizational commitment of the participants. Similarly, Vian *et al.* (2007) reviewed a corporate volunteering programme from Pfizer (i.e. 'Pfizer Global Health Fellows') and found that the programme had positive effects on recipient organizations and improved the personal and professional skills of participating employees.

Research conducted by Hewitt Associates (Guarnieri and Kao, 2007) to explore the views of executives in MNEs on employee volunteering programmes found that 90 per cent of organizations it identified as 'Top Companies for Leaders' use community involvement as a way to enhance their company's reputation for leadership. Similarly, they found that 50 per cent of these companies highlighted CR as a 'significant to very significant' component of their leadership development strategy.

Maak and Pless (2006) describe how a few pioneering MNEs use skill-based employee community volunteering as part of their global leadership development programmes. One example is PwC, a global professional services firm. PwC has integrated corporate volunteering into a leadership development programme for new partners. Partners spend eight weeks working in a developing country together with international assistance organizations (for example, the United Nations Development Programme) on community development projects. The PwC programme is often highlighted in the literature as an example of skill-based volunteering that delivers positive societal change and benefits for participants and the organization, including enhancing global mindset, cross-cultural communication and flexibility to work with multinational teams, and motivation (Hirsch and Horowitz, 2006).

Employee volunteering programmes have also been linked to improving individual work attitudes. Research suggests that such programmes help build greater company loyalty among employees and can enhance job satisfaction and organizational commitment (de Gilder et al., 2005; Peterson, 2004).

Literature suggests that volunteering opportunities that align with the business strategy and focus of the organization, make use of employee technical and professional skills and adopt a long-term partnership focus with NGOs, can help achieve a sustainable competitive advantage (Porter and Kramer, 2002, 2006). They are likely to have the following characteristics:

- they use the professional and technical skills of the employees
- they are of a higher duration and require significant investment – e.g. sometimes involving months of preparation and international travel
- the organization sponsors the programme and partners with an NGO to facilitate project selection, employee training, management of employees on assignment and evaluation.

These types of volunteering initiatives provide global companies with a potentially effective way to help MNEs differentiate themselves and achieve positive HRM outcomes. They may also help to address the needs of MNEs in order to develop leaders who are aware of global societal issues and who can work effectively with people from many different countries and backgrounds. Global corporate volunteering is in its infancy (Morales and Loro, 2012) but is an accelerating trend among MNEs (Morales and Loro, 2012). Examples include Accenture Development Partnerships, EY's Enterprise Growth Services, GSK's PULSE and IBM Corporate Service Corps.

Some organizations like Barclays and Vodafone are using talent development-related corporate volunteering as one element in creating an enabling environment for social intrapreneurism (Grayson et al., 2014).

The European Perspective

There is a body of research on comparative CR, in particular focusing on European and Anglo-American approaches (Jackson and Apostolakou, 2010; Matten and Moon, 2008). The literature suggests that institutional factors, such as components of national business systems and national culture, will influence how CR is perceived and implemented at the local level (Jackson and Apostolakou, 2010; Matten and Moon, 2008). While it is beyond the scope of this chapter to focus on this field of research, it might be helpful to the reader to highlight a few propositions about why there may be differences in approaches to CR.

Matten and Moon (2008) suggest that differences in national institutional frameworks (i.e. national business systems) cause differences in CR practices between firms in the US and Europe. These differences influence how companies engage with their stakeholders (e.g. labour unions, employees, suppliers and government) (Jackson and Apostolakou, 2010). Companies respond to the different institutional frameworks through a mix of what Matten and Moon (2008) describe as 'implicit' and 'explicit' CR. Explicit CR refers to 'corporate policies that assume and articulate responsibility for some societal interests' (Matten and Moon, 2008: 409). Commitment to water or carbon neutrality is an example of explicit CR. Explicit CR is 'the result of a deliberate, voluntary, and often strategic decision of a corporation' (Matten and Moon, 2008: 410).

Implicit CR describes actions taken by organizations that comply with institutional expectations and 'consists of values, norms, and rules that result in (mandatory and customary) requirements for corporations to address stakeholder issues and that define proper obligations of corporate actors' (Matten and Moon, 2008: 409). Organizations do not usually communicate their implicit CR actions, as these are seen as part of normal business activity. Examples of implicit CR include collaborative relations with labour unions or progressive employee benefit systems. Matten and Moon (2008) argue that explicit CR may act as a substitute for weaker institutions in liberal countries such as the US or the UK, while remaining embedded within formal institutions in the more coordinated economies of Europe, such as Germany. Similarly, Doh and Guay (2006) suggest that differences in government policy, corporate strategy and NGO activism between the USA and Europe also help to shape different approaches to CR. They explore how these differences manifest in the conflicting views between the USA and Europe on approaches to the trade and regulation of genetically modified organisms, international environmental agreements and regulation in the pharmaceutical industry.

Overall, the CR discussion has been intensive in the last two decades and, uniquely, the European Union (EU) has developed cross-border guidance and regulations. In particular, there have been significant interventions at the EU and national government level to promote CR. This has included EU-funded information campaigns and awards; a series of EU Commission *Communications* on CR since the Millennium; an EU Multi-Stakeholder Forum; and in 2014 the adoption by the EU of reporting requirements requiring large companies to report on their social and environmental impacts. The EU Commission has also published a formal *Communication* outlining a framework for moving towards a Circular Economy.

HRM and CR in Europe: The Desso Example

The Dutch-headquartered company Desso is a good example of what CR can mean for companies. The firm makes carpeting for businesses, government offices, residential homes, airplanes and even athletic fields. It operates in an industry currently dominated by linear thinking – in 2010 alone, 600,000 tons of floor covering materials were thrown away and only 1 per cent was recycled.

In 2008, a new management team and new owners committed the company to Cradle to Cradle® (C2C) or Circular Economy. By 2020, the company hopes to use 100 per cent renewable energy in its production and corporate facilities. It also aims to have 100 per cent of its carpet tiles Cradle to Cradle® certified. The plan is to address carpet tile material first and then move into sport systems and wool carpets as Cradle to Cradle® success gains momentum. Ultimately, Desso intends to transition to a service-based model in which it leases out its carpets and later takes back the old tiles in order to recycle and reuse the underlying materials.

In 2008, Desso initiated its Take Back Programme (subsequently Desso Refinity Programme), which takes old carpet backing material and separates yarn and fibres for reuse. The used depolarized yarn is then returned to material manufactures to create new durable yarn in any colour. The used yarn can also be upcycled to produce expensive, durable plastic.

Further, since 2010, Desso has partnered with Aquafil, a yarn supplier, to embrace the initiative 'Healthy Seas, a Journey from Waste to Wear'. As a result of this collaboration, Desso now uses ECONYL yarn made of material from ocean waste like fishnets. ECONYL is 100 per cent recyclable and maintains durability even when repeatedly reused.

Desso's EcoBase carpet tiles have been awarded the Cradle to Cradle® Silver Certificate for eliminating 97 per cent of toxic materials. The company also reduced CO_2 emissions by 50 per cent between 2007 and 2011. Perhaps most notably, over 90 per cent of its commercial carpet tile is now Cradle to Cradle® certified and bottom-line performance has improved markedly.

The human resources team has been an important part of the corporate efforts to achieve this business transformation. As Cathy Ockers (Desso HR Manager) states:

> If you want to really carry forward the C2C philosophy, you also need to do something about all your employees and make them aware of what we are doing and also try to implement C2C in your internal organization.

Cathy Ockers and her small team have been tasked with executing their leadership's ambition to embed a C2C mindset across the wider organization. She describes how initially it was challenging to connect people with the C2C philosophy in ways that were relevant to them:

Initially, we found that it's difficult for individuals to make C2C something of their own. Environment/sustainability examples are easier to grasp, and people can act on this for themselves potentially more than C2C.

Another challenge in the organization during the initial rollout of C2C was a degree of scepticism (in particular among production employees) – a type of 'wait and see' attitude among staff, to understand whether C2C was just another management fad. Employees wanted to see how serious management was about C2C, what C2C would mean in practice to them and how it would impact their way of working. Given this scepticism, it was critical for Cathy and her team to create the 'what's in it for me' (WIIFM) messaging for employees. Cathy explains the challenge:

How do you take the C2C concept, which is very relevant for manufacturing teams and easy for the marketing and sales teams to talk about how it applies to DESSO, and get the company to apply C2C internally, especially in parts of the business where the link to C2C is not intuitive (e.g. customer service, finance)?

Motivated by these challenges, management decided to use C2C as a springboard to embed environmental sustainability across the organization – to address the question, 'How can we make Desso a more sustainable company?' The HRM team seized on this opportunity to develop and lead campaigns to build awareness of C2C and promote environmental sustainability across Desso. Awareness building of C2C and promoting environmental sustainability became a key component of HRM's focus during the early days of C2C implementation and continues to this day.

One of the first actions led by the HRM team was to form a cross-disciplinary group (with representatives from marketing, finance, production) to identify ways of raising awareness of C2C and sustainability across the organization. Examples of initiatives that the group developed include:

- developing posters that explain C2C in simple, engaging ways and placing them across production facilities and offices (see Figure 11.3 for an example);
- creating a C2C 'idea tree' – a place for employees to share their ideas on actions to make the company more environmentally sustainable. Many examples of the company's sustainability efforts were drawn from suggestions by employees from the 'idea tree' (e.g. plastic coffee mugs were changed to more environmentally friendly C2C-certified paper cups);

- nominating 'C2C ambassadors' – representatives from across various functional departments whose role is to raise awareness of C2C across the business. The ambassadors are educated in the more complex C2C issues/cases so they are also the 'go to people' when employees have questions on C2C;
- posting of large stickers on light switches to encourage people to turn lights off;
- creating a waste separation process in the company canteen;
- including hybrid and low emission cars in the menu of leased car options for employees.

Another way that the HRM team helped to build awareness of C2C, both internally and externally, was by publishing *C2C Time*, a company-wide magazine. The quarterly magazine describes how C2C is being implemented throughout Desso and includes articles on C2C developments outside the organization. Although the publication was initially targeted at Desso employees, demand from clients and other companies has led management to broaden circulation to companies that are interested in applying C2C to their operations.

In an attempt to embed C2C into behaviours, the HRM team has worked with senior managers to include C2C in their performance management system. Management encourages professionals to include KPIs that reflect C2C behaviours, as suggested below:

> Cradle to Cradle is a very large part of the management team's KPIs. And then they cascade down into the organization in every department from design to development from marketing to sales, they have KPIs.

Beyond C2C: Enabling Culture Change

Apart from the emphasis on building awareness and engagement around C2C and environmental sustainability, management also implemented various initiatives to help create a more engaged, enabled workforce and to help drive a more results-oriented culture. One of the key elements in this change was to implement a more rigorous, transparent, performance management system with role-specific KPIs. In designing the new process, the company first had to develop role profiles and competencies for each role. Roles were designed with the question, 'What does excellent look like?', e.g. 'What does an excellent salesperson do?' 'What do you actually see him/her do (in behaviour) which makes him/her excellent?' Employees were closely involved in developing role descriptions/expectations. Teams from each of the departments and each function designed the competencies and expectations and 'star qualities' of employees in their departments.

Another initiative designed to engage employees was the introduction of an employee survey to provide management with an understanding of how engaged, enabled, motivated and connected employees feel, as well as understanding their level of awareness of C2C. This was the first time since the launch of C2C, that Desso had taken action to formally measure levels of awareness and employee perceptions of C2C.

Using C2C as a springboard, the HRM team is now also taking steps to enhance employer branding. One of the ways management will demonstrate the refreshed brand will be through a revamp of its corporate internet site. The site will provide readers with a more transparent, engaging experience of Desso culture through interviews with staff and leadership.

Another HRM-led initiative is to ensure that the working environments (e.g. corporate and sales offices) are designed in a way that fosters creativity and flexibility and which are C2C compliant with respect to the furniture and office equipment.

How Has C2C Impacted the Culture of Desso?

Management believes that the reputation that Desso has developed in the market as a champion of C2C has resonated well with younger job seekers. Management believes that C2C has enabled Desso to attract higher quality, more educated professionals. Desso executives comment that they are seeing a different type of person applying to Desso – people generally of a higher education background, who share Desso's concern for the environment and want to make a difference in society. The company is also receiving more applications for open positions than ever before.

Management has also commented that they have noticed a significant increase in employee engagement and pride since the launch of C2C. One executive commented, 'Employees are proud to know that other companies want to emulate Desso.' The initial scepticism among staff has abated – in part perhaps because staff have realized that leadership really believes in C2C beyond what it can do for the bottom line. As one executive describes it:

> You definitely see the move upwards when it comes to quality of people or the quality they show. Yes, you definitely see change. That [change] comes because you have a focus on results and you have a focus on behaviour and before we did not have a focus on results. It was flying around, yes, whatever, flying around the company all the time and not knowing what was going on and no real strategy.

It is unclear exactly how C2C has specifically impacted the culture, but it is apparent to leadership that the culture has evolved dramatically over the last few years. When asked, 'In your view, would those changes achieve the same results if C2C was not part of the whole equation?', one executive remarked:

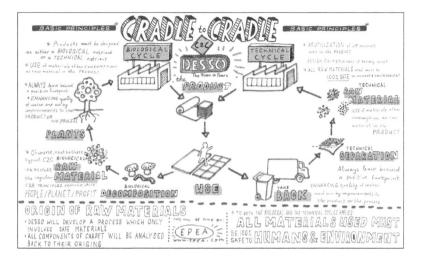

Figure 11.3 From Cradle to Cradle: The Desso approach

No, I don't think we would have achieved the same then, because C2C is also a way of thinking and it's a way of doing business and it's a way of innovation which, probably if our leaders had never mentioned Cradle to Cradle and we were still doing things the old way, it would be a totally different company.

The small HRM team has played a significant role in helping to raise awareness of C2C, champion efforts to promote a more environmentally and socially responsible organization and lead efforts to create a more empowered and engaged organizational culture.

Opportunities for Further Research

The link between the HRM function and corporate responsibility remains an under-researched area. We believe there are many opportunities for further research on the role of HRM in helping to embed CR. This includes how organizations link rewards and recognition to individual, team and corporate performance on CR and realignment of rewards, especially in financial services. Other topics include: how CR is incorporated in job competencies, induction and continuous professional development; how companies create an enabling environment for corporate social innovation including social intrapreneurism; and does more engagement of employees lead to more successful embedding of CR? Other areas might focus on how CR initiatives are being used for HRM-related objectives, for example, how are companies using CR in their leadership development initiatives? Another area of research could explore how regional, industry-related or other institutional factors influence the role of HRM in embedding strategic CR in an organization.

With respect to the European CR context, research on the impact of the EU initiatives on firms, their strategies, policies and practices would be fascinating. Understanding CR in different industries and countries will aid theoretical and practical insights. In addition, exploring the engagement and motivation levels of staff – including distinguishing variables such as age, gender, educational backgrounds, career motivations, etc., could generate insights into some of the HR outcomes of CR activities.

Interestingly, some authors move beyond the concept of CR. Ainsbury and Grayson (2014) argue that Corporate Sustainability (CS) is a higher stage of CR and offer a refined and expanded version to the PricewaterhouseCoopers (PwC)/SAM Yearbook definition of CR. Their additional words are in italics: 'Corporate Sustainability is *a business commitment to sustainable development*, and an approach that creates long-term shareholder *and societal* value by embracing the opportunities and managing the risks associated with social, environmental and economic developments.' This is somewhat similar to the concept of 'shared value' of CR, which companies like Nestle and various Asian firms have adopted, where organizations redesign themselves, develop new lines of business and/or change the way they operate to be more socially responsible and profitable (Porter and Kramer, 2011). The links between CR and CS are deep and may be more explicitly explored in future research.

Conclusions

Long-term megatrends suggest that CR is likely to become ever more central to business. These megatrends include planetary boundaries (such as climate change, bio-diversity loss, shortages of raw materials, the Food-Water-Energy Security Nexus) and a growing middle class with global connectivity through the Internet, social media, etc., who have higher expectations of how businesses should behave. It thus becomes ever more important for human resource management professionals to understand CR and, crucially, what it might mean for the human resources function.

The EU is on the forefront of thinking and acting on CR. The highest number of organizations with excellent CR is headquartered in Western Europe. Companies like Desso have demonstrated that embedding sustainability as a way to do business can create competitive advantage and achieve societal benefit. The case also demonstrates the role that HR can play to embed a culture of sustainability.

Embedding CR into the strategy of the organization is critical for sustainable change. One-off CR initiatives or those that are not aligned to the business objectives of the organization will not generate sustainable change in the organization. Initiatives such as strategic global corporate volunteering have the potential to make a sustainable change to an organization's workforce and help to embed a culture of CR in an organization.

Human resource professionals have an opportunity to play a major role in the design and implementation of a strategic approach to CR and to embed an appropriate culture. To date this is an opportunity that has not been fully realized. The aim of this chapter was to provide guidance on how to increase HR's contribution in this area.

Key Learning Points

- Business leaders increasingly recognize that CR is not an optional extra, a bolt-on to business operations but is about core business, how business behaves in all it does and, therefore, built-in to business purpose and strategy (Grayson *et al.*, 2014).
- European MNEs are at the forefront of CR and have developed a range of interesting approaches to strategic CR and sustainability. The EU has been actively formulating Europe-wide regulations related to CR and has worked towards creating interest and insights into this important area.
- CR is important for HRM professionals for three main reasons. First, many aspects of CR concern how a business behaves towards its employees and the workplace impacts it has. Second, HRM professionals can play a crucial role in helping the rest of the business embed responsible business practices. Third, CR can help HRM professionals fulfil traditional objectives of creating an employer brand of choice with engaged and motivated employees.
- The HRM function can play an important role in helping an organization embed CR and sustainability in its culture – by refocusing HRM core activities (e.g. talent development) around a sustainability agenda. This requires CR (including sustainability ideas) to become embedded within the core purpose and strategy of the business and then HRM strategy, policies and practices to be aligned to and support overall corporate mission and strategy. The Desso case study illustrates HRM's role in supporting this transformation. As a company's engagement around CR matures, the HRM function can support this evolution through a wide variety of practical and strategic initiatives.
- One approach that companies are increasingly adopting to help embed a sustainability culture is skill-based volunteering or global corporate volunteering. Apart from helping to achieve various

talent-related benefits, including increased retention, motivation, organization commitment and skill development, the use of such initiatives can help drive wider organizational change around sustainability.

References

Ainsbury, R. and Grayson, D. (2014) 'Business Critical: Understanding a Company's Current and Desired Stages of Corporate Maturity', Doughty Centre for Corporate Responsibility, Cranfield University School of Management.

Alvesson, M. and Kärreman, D. (2007) 'Unraveling HRM: Identity, Ceremony, and Control in a Management Consulting Firm', *Organization Science*, 18(4): 711–723.

Barney, J. (1991) 'Firm Resources and Sustained Competitive Advantage', *Journal of Management*, 17: 99–120.

Bhattacharya, C.B., Sen, S. and Korschun, D. (2011) *Leveraging Corporate Responsibility: The Stakeholder Route to Maximizing Business and Social Value*. Cambridge: Cambridge University Press.

Bhattacharya, C.B., Sen, S. and Korschun, D. (2008) 'Using Corporate Social Responsibility to Win the War for Talent', *MIT Sloan Review*, 49(2): 37–42.

Boccalandro, B. (2009) *Mapping Success in Employee Volunteering: The Drivers of Effectiveness for Employee Volunteering and Giving Programs and Fortune 500 Performance*, The Boston College Center for Corporate Citizenship, USA.

Boccalandro, B. (2012) 'A Productive End to Employee Volunteering: The Tantalizing Potential of Corporate Employee Service to Societal Causes'. In M. Morales and S. Loro (eds) *Handbook and Business Cases Global Corporate Volunteering: A Strategic Tool to Involve Companies and Employees in the Fight Against Poverty*. Madrid: Codespa, pp. 327–334.

Bowen, H. (1953) *Social Responsibilities of the Businessman*. Reprint edition 2013. Iowa: University of Iowa Press.

Brammer, S., Millington, A. and Rayton, B. (2007) 'The Contribution of Corporate Social Responsibility to Organizational Commitment', *International Journal of Human Resource Management*, 18(10): 1701–1719.

Branco, M. C. and Rodrigues, L.L. (2006) 'Corporate Social Responsibility and Resource-Based Perspectives', *Journal of Business Ethics*, 69: 111–132.

BSR and Executiva (2012) *Sustainability and Leadership Competencies for Business Leaders*, BSR. Available at: http://www.bsr.org/en/our-insights/report-view/sustainability-and-leadership-competencies-for-business-leaders (accessed 3 November 2015).

Caligiuri, P. (2006) 'Developing Global Leaders', *Human Resource Management Review*, 16(2): 219–228.

Caligiuri, P. and Di Santo, V. (2001) 'Global Competence: What Is It, and Can It Be Developed Through Global Assignments?', *Human Resource Planning*, 24(3): 27–35.

Cardarilli, T. (2015) unpublished, manuscript Doctoral Thesis, Cranfield University, School of Management.

Carroll, A.B. and Shabana, K.M. (2010) 'The Business Case for Corporate Social Responsibility: A Review of Concepts, Research and Practice', *International Journal of Management Reviews*, 12(1): 85–105.

Colbert, B.A. and Kurucz, E.C. (2007) 'Three Conceptions of Triple Bottom Line Business Sustainability and the Role for HRM', *Human Resource Planning*, 30(1): 21–30.

Cramer. J. (2005) 'Company Learning about Corporate Social Responsibility', *Business Strategy and the Environment*, 14: 255–266.

Dahlsrud, A. (2008) 'How Corporate Social Responsibility Is Defined: An Analysis of 37 Definitions', *Corporate Social Responsibility and Environmental Management*, 15: 1–13.

de Gilder, D., Schuyt, T. and Breedijk, M. (2005) 'Effects of an Employee Volunteering, Program on the Work Force: The ABN-AMRO Case', *Journal of Business Ethics*, 61: 143–152.

Dickmann, M. and Doherty, N. (2010) 'Exploring Organizational and Individual Career Goals, Interactions, and Outcomes of Developmental International Assignments', *Thunderbird International Business Review*, 52: 313–324.

Doh, J.P. and Guay, T.R. (2006) 'Corporate Social Responsibility, Public Policy, and NGO Activism in Europe and the United States: An Institutional-Stakeholder Perspective', *Journal of Management Studies*, 43(1): 47–73.

Doughty Centre for Corporate Responsibility (2011) *The Business Case for Responsible Business*. Available at: http://www.som.cranfield.ac.uk/som/p17139/Think-Cranfield/2011/December-2011/Responsible-business-the-business-case (accessed 3 November 2015).

Fenwick, T. and Bierema, L. (2008) 'Corporate Social Responsibility: Issues for Human Resource Development Professionals', *International Journal of Training and Development*, 12(1): 24–34.

Forum for the Future (2015), information accessed in April 2015, from https://www.forumforthefuture.org/project/net-positive-group/overview.

Gond, J.P., Igalens, J., Swaen, V. and El Akremi, A. (2011) 'The Human Resources Contribution to Responsible Leadership: An Exploration of the CSR–HR Interface', *Journal of Business Ethics*, 98: 115–132.

Grayson, D. and Hodges, A. (2001) *Everybody's Business: Managing Risks and Opportunities in Today's Global Society*. Dorling Kindersley and *The Financial Times*.

Grayson, D. and Hodges, A. (2004) *Corporate Social Opportunity!* Sheffield: Greenleaf Publishing Limited.

Grayson, D., McLaren, M. and Spitzeck, H. (2014) *Social Intrapreneurism and all that Jazz*. Sheffield: Greenleaf Publishing Limited.

Grayson, D. and Nelson, J. (2013) *Corporate Responsibility Coalitions: The Past, Present and Future of Alliances for Sustainable Capitalism*. Stanford, CA: Stanford University Press and Sheffield: Greenleaf Publishing.

Grayson, D., Spitzeck, H., Alt, E. and McLaren, M. (2013) *Creating Sustainable Businesses Through Social Intrapreneurism*, A Doughty Centre for Corporate Responsibility Occasional Paper (2013). Available at: http://www.networkedcranfield.com/doughty/Document%20Library/Occasional%20papers/OP_Creating%20Sustainable%20Business%20Through%20Social%20Intrapreneurism_March%2013.pdf (accessed 3 November 2015).

Greening, D.W. and Turban, D.B. (2000) 'Corporate Social Performance as a Competitive Advantage in Attracting a Quality Workforce', *Business and Society*, 39: 254–280.

Guarnieri, R. and Kao, T. (2007) 'Leadership and CSR – a Perfect Match: How Top Companies for Leaders Utilize CSR as a Competitive Advantage', *People & Strategy*, 31(3): 34–41.

Heslin, P. and Ochoa, J. (2008) 'Understanding and Developing Strategic Corporate Social Responsibility', *Organizational Dynamics*, 37(2): 125–144.

Hirsch, P. and Horowitz, P. (2006) 'The Global Employee Volunteer: A Corporate Program for Giving Back', *Journal of Business Strategy*, 27(3): 50–55.

Holbeche, L. and Matthews, G. (2012) *Engaged: Unleashing Your Organization's Potential Through Employee Engagement*. Bognor Regis: John Wiley & Sons.

Huselid, M.A. (1995) 'The Impact of Human Resource Management Practices on Turnover, Productivity, and Corporate Financial Performance', *Academy of Management Journal*, 38: 635–672.

Jackson, G. and Apostolakou, A. (2010). 'Corporate Social Responsibility in Western Europe: An Institutional Mirror or Substitute?', *Journal of Business Ethics*, 94(3): 371–394.

Kurucz, E., Colbert, B. and Wheeler, D. (2008) 'The Business Case for Corporate Social Responsibility'. In A. Crane, A. McWilliams, D. Matten, J. Moon and D. Siegel (eds), *The Oxford Handbook of Corporate Social Responsibility*. Oxford: Oxford University Press, pp. 83–112.

Lawler, E.E. III and Mohrman, S. (2014) 'The Crucial – and Underappreciated – Role of HR in Sustainability', *MIT Sloan Management Review Sustainability Blog* (accessed 5 November 2014).

Maak, T. and Pless, N.M. (2006) 'Responsible Leadership in a Stakeholder Society: A Relational Perspective', *Journal of Business Ethics*, 66: 99–115.

Matten, D. and Moon, J. (2008). '"Implicit" and "Explicit" CSR: A Conceptual Framework for a Comparative Understanding of Corporate Social Responsibility', *Academy of Management Review*, 33(2): 404–424.

Maister, D.H. (1993) *Managing the Professional Service Firm*, New York: Free Press.

Morales, M. and Loro, S. (eds.) (2012) *Handbook and Business Cases Global Corporate Volunteering: A Strategic Tool to Involve Companies and Employees in the Fight against Poverty*. Madrid: Codespa, pp. 327–334.

Parkes, C. and Borland, H. (2012) 'Strategic HRM: Transforming Its Responsibilities Toward Ecological Sustainability - The Greatest Global Challenge Facing Organizations', *Thunderbird International Business Review*, 54(6): 811–824.

Peterson, D.K. (2004) 'Recruitment Strategies for Encouraging Participation in Corporate Volunteer Programmes', *Journal of Business Ethics*, 49: 371–386.

Pettijohn, C., Pettijohn, L. and Taylor, A.J. (2008) 'Salesperson Perceptions of Ethical Behaviors: Their Influence on Job Satisfaction and Turnover Intentions', *Journal of Business Ethics*, 78(4): 547–557.

Pfeffer, J. (1994) 'Competitive Advantage through People', *California Management Review*, 36(2): 9-28.

Pless, N., Maak, T. and Stahl, G.K. (2012) 'Promoting Corporate Social Responsibility and Sustainable Development through Management Development: What Can Be Learned from International Service Learning Programs?', *Human Resource Management*, 51(6): 873–903.

Porter, M.E. and Kramer, M.R. (2002) 'The Competitive Advantage of Corporate Philanthropy', *Harvard Business Review*, 80(12): 56–68.

Porter, M.E. and Kramer, M.R. (2006) 'Strategy and Society: The Link between Competitive Advantage and Corporate Social Responsibility', *Harvard Business Review*, 84(12): 78–92.

Porter, M.E. and Kramer, M.R. (2011) 'Creating Shared Value', *Harvard Business Review*, 89(1/2): 62–77.

Preuss, L. (2011) 'Innovative CSR: A Framework for Anchoring Corporate Social Responsibility in the Innovation Literature', *The Journal of Corporate Citizenship*, 42: 17–33.

PwC (2014) 'Global CEO Survey: Fit for the future – Capitalising on Global Trends', London: PricewaterhouseCoopers. Available at: http://www.pwc.com/gx/en/ceo-survey/ (accessed 3 November 2015).

Schreck, P. (2011) 'Reviewing the Business Case for Corporate Social Responsibility: New Evidence and Analysis', *Journal of Business Ethics*, 103: 167–188.

Schuler, R.S. and Jackson, S.E. (2007) *Strategic Human Resource Management*, 2nd edn. Singapore: Blackwell Publishing.

Smith, A. (2007) 'Making the Case for the Competitive Advantage of Corporate Social Responsibility', *Strategic HR Review*, 8(3): 186–195.

Smith, N.C. (2003) 'Corporate Social Responsibility: Whether or How?', *California Management Review*, 45(4): 1–25.

Smith, R. (2007) *Defining Corporate Social Responsibility: A Systems Approach for Socially Responsible Capitalism*, Pennsylvania: University of Pennsylvania Scholarly Commons.

Smith, V. and Langford, P. (2011) 'Responsible or Redundant? Engaging the Workforce through Corporate Social Responsibility', *Australian Journal of Management*, 36(3): 425–447.

Surroca, J., Tribo, J. and Waddock, S. (2010) 'Corporate Responsibility and Financial Performance: The Role of Intangible Resources', *Strategic Management Journal*, 31: 463–490.

Tuffrey, M. (2003) *Good Companies, Better Employees: How Community Involvement and Good Corporate Citizenship Can Enhance Employee Morale, Motivation, Commitment and Performance.* London: The Corporate Citizenship Company.

Turban, D.B. and Greening, D.W. (1997) 'Corporate Social Performance and Organizational Attractiveness to Prospective Employees', *Academy of Management Journal*, 40(3): 658–672.

Turker, D. (2009) 'How Corporate Social Responsibility Influences Organizational Commitment', *Journal of Business Ethics*, 89: 189–204.

van Beurden, P. and Gossling, T. (2008) 'The Worth of Values: A Literature Review on the Relation between Corporate Social and Financial Performance', *Journal of Business Ethics*, 82(2): 407–424.

Vian T., McCoy, K., Richards, S., Connelly, P. and Feeley, F. (2007) 'Corporate Social Responsibility in Global Health: The Pfizer Global Health Fellows International Volunteering Program', *Human Resource Planning*, 30(1): 30–35.

Vogel, D. (2005) 'Is There a Market for Virtue: The Business Case for Corporate Social Responsibility?', *California Management Review*, 474: 19–45.

Waddock, S.A. and Graves, S.B. (1997) 'The Corporate Social Performance–Financial Performance Link', *Strategic Management Journal*, 18(4): 303–319.

Zadek, S. (2004) 'The Path to Corporate Responsibility', *Harvard Business Review*, 82(12): 125–132.

Zappala, G. (2004) 'Corporate Citizenship and Human Resource Management: A New Tool or a Missed Opportunity?', *Asia Pacific Journal of Human Resources*, 42(2): 185–201.

Zappala, G. and McLaren, J. (2004) 'A Functional Approach to Employee Volunteering: An Exploratory Study', *Australian Journal of Volunteering*, 9(1): 41–54.

12 Age and Diversity in Europe

EMMA PARRY, HEIKE SCHRÖDER, MATT FLYNN AND DEIRDRE ANDERSON

Introduction

This chapter focuses on the reactions of European policy makers and employers to the ageing workforce and increased age diversity. Most HRM specialists are aware that the population in Europe and in most of the world is ageing, and with it the labour market is becoming more diverse. For instance, the development of the European Union (EU) has brought with it increased ethnic and cultural diversity as EU citizens move between nations. In fact, Becker (2004: 133) described the EU as 'an ongoing project in diversity management'. Many EU employers have benefited from the ability to recruit from EU member states, while individuals move easily across EU boundaries to find work. In the United Kingdom (UK) alone, net migration in the 12 months up to September 2014 was 298,000 (ONS, 2015). The numbers don't add up – clearly the most common are intra-EU movements. The number of EU citizens moving to the UK increased from 158,000 in the time period October 2011 to September 2012 to 251,000 in the time period October 2013 to September 2014 (ONS, 2015). The resulting multi-cultural society means that employers must learn to account for ethnic, cultural and religious differences and can no longer count on shared values in the organization, unless they create them for themselves (Parry and Tyson, 2014). Aside from ethnic diversity, gender diversity in the workforce is also increasing. The Labour Force Participation (LFP) rate of women aged 15 to 64 in EU15 countries has increased significantly from 60.2 per cent to 67.8 per cent between 2000 and 2013. This is even though the female LFP rate remains well below that of men (78.7 per cent in 2000 compared with 79.5 per cent in 2013) (OECD, 2015).

One area of diversity that has received significant attention in recent years and the main focus of this chapter is age diversity. This chapter examines:

1 the nature and implications of ageing workforce demographics across Europe;
2 national level reactions to these trends; and
3 organizational responses to the ageing workforce, before presenting conclusions and learning points.

The European population is ageing due to increased life expectancy and lower birth rates. The average life expectancy at birth for EU members born in 2008–10 is now 75.3 years for men and 81.7 years for women, a rise of 2.7 and 2.3 years respectively since 1998–2000 (OECD, 2012). Despite variations in life expectancy between EU member states, the result of this ageing population coupled with lower birth rates is that there will be a higher proportion of older individuals and fewer younger individuals in the workforce. In the UK alone, it is projected that by 2050 there will be 19 million people over 65 years of age – around a quarter of the population – and 8 million of these will be over 80. While this trend is one that is beginning to affect most of the Western world, it is particularly significant in Europe.

The changing age demographics are of particular importance for governments and institutions because of their potential implications for the sustainability of social security and health systems. They also have implications for employers. We will discuss each of these in turn. The increasing proportion of older individuals is likely to lead to a need for increased spending on health (United Nations, 2002) and pensions. The fact that a relatively low proportion of the over 65-year-old population is economically active also means that (unless it can be increased) the proportion of over 65-year-olds in employment is likely to fall, meaning that the ratio between those who are economically active and those who require social security support will also decrease. In the UK, the ratio of people of working age to every pensioner is projected to fall from 3.20 to 2.74 by 2037 (ONS, 2008). This situation has been called the 'time bomb' threatening European pensions (Cowell, 2004) – several commentators have highlighted the potentially negative impact on nations through increased public debt resulting from public health and social security expenditure (Grant *et al.*, 2004), as well as on individuals who will be required to work longer, pay higher taxes and save more in order to be financially secure in retirement (Turner, 2004).

For organizations and employers, the ageing workforce could have a significant impact on the availability of the labour and skills that they need. Indeed, concerns have been raised about the potential impact of population ageing in relation to a loss of human capital and talent shortages (Rappaport et al., 2003) and the loss of essential organizational knowledge (DeLong, 2004) as it becomes more difficult to replace the skills and experience lost through retirement (Parry and Harris, 2011). Generally, this trend means that the workforce contributions of the over 50-year-old group are becoming more important (Parry and Harris, 2011). Indeed, this has long been known in the UK at least, with Taylor (2002) highlighting the significance of workers over 50 in the development of the UK labour market.

The above issues for societies and organizations emphasize the need for both governments and employers to identify ways of encouraging older workers to be economically active and remain in the workforce for longer. It is worth noting that the attention of both policy makers and employers has recently moved slightly away from the older end of the workforce. The global economic downturn has resulted in high youth unemployment in several European countries. For example, in the UK, 740,000 people aged 16 to 24 years were unemployed between February and April 2015, an unemployment rate of 16.1 per cent (Dar, 2015). In other areas of Europe the situation for young people is much more serious, with over 50 per cent of young people aged 18 to 24-years-old unemployed in Greece and Spain. This could potentially lead to a degree of tension between the need to deal with the issues presented by an ageing workforce and also to address high youth unemployment. It is therefore important to consider both 'ends' of the workforce when examining and developing national and organizational policies on age and age diversity. In the remainder of this chapter we will focus on both national and organizational reactions to population ageing, specifically focusing on the case studies of the UK and Germany.

National Reactions to Demographic Change and Old Age Employment: The Examples of the UK and Germany

From the 1970s to the late 1990s, most industrialized countries pursued a strategy that fostered labour market exit prior to national retirement and/or pension age. This strategy was a reaction to economic pressures caused by adverse effects of globalization, and consequential high and persistent unemployment (Buchholz et al., 2006). Externalizing older workers aimed to create employment opportunities for younger individuals (Gruber et al., 2009) and was supported, or at least accepted, by trade unions in what Ebbinghaus (2001: 38) calls a 'collusion for early retirement' in order to sustain peaceful labour relations (Flynn et al., 2013).

While an early retirement paradigm could be observed in most industrialized societies, approaches taken by nations differed along the traditional Varieties of Capitalism (VoC) divide (Schils, 2008). In liberal market economies (LMEs), such as the UK, the state maintained a 'light touch' approach towards workplace regulations (Flynn *et al.*, 2014). It thereby enabled organizations to 'push' or entice older workers out of employment via performance-based dismissals and firm restructuring in order to address productivity and competitive pressures. The British labour market was therefore rather flexible, providing firms with the autonomy to adapt their workforce to changes in market demands. While the UK government abolished state-financed early retirement pathways in 1989 (though with exceptions), it did not buffer the potentially negative (financial) effects of redundancy–induced early retirement, for example, through social provisions and state pensions, but left it to the individual to obtain sufficient pension funds through occupational and private pension schemes (Hofäcker *et al.*, 2016). Further, the government as an employer is continuing to use early retirement via public sector pension schemes as a tool for managing job attrition. The National Audit Office (2012) estimates the number of civil servants accepting early retirement or redundancy between 2010 and 2012 to be 17,800, while in Scotland the figure is estimated to be 14,000 (Audit Scotland, 2013).

Contrary to this, the state played a more proactive role with regard to early retirement in most coordinated market economies (CMEs), including Germany. Here, the state actively fostered early retirement through institutionalized and state-financed pathways out of work. Older (male) German workers were incentivized to retire early and were therefore 'pulled out' of the labour market (Buchholz, 2006) through financially generous state pension systems and other social transfer schemes, including unemployment and disability insurances (Börsch-Supan *et al.*, 2004) that guaranteed a sufficient standard of living throughout (early) retirement. Similar pension schemes and approaches existed, for example, in the Netherlands (van Oorschot and Jensen, 2009) and in France (Gendron, 2011). In addition to the pension system that actively fostered early retirement, the German employment context was shaped by strong internal labour markets, a focus on the acquisition of formal education at the beginning of the life course, as well as the strong involvement of social partners. These factors resulted in an insider-outsider labour market structure in which unemployed (older) workers experienced difficulties finding re-employment (Buchholz, 2006), particularly those with low qualifications. It was therefore especially these older low qualified individuals who were both 'pushed' and 'pulled' into early retirement through a lack of re-employment opportunities on the one hand and financially attractive, state-financed pathways out of work on the other (Hofäcker *et al.*, 2016). As a consequence of early retirement trends, labour force participation rates of men aged 55 to 64 in OECD countries decreased significantly between 1960 and 1995 from 84.7 per cent to 62.3 per cent (OECD, 2015), though with profound differences between countries (Conde-Ruiz and Galasso, 2004).

Due to population ageing as well as projected labour and skill shortages, early retirement as a direct or indirect labour market instrument was increasingly regarded as unsuitable, as it negatively influenced economic growth (Bloom *et al.*, 2010) as well as threatened the sustainability of national social security systems (Blossfeld *et al.*, 2011). Based on these macroeconomic challenges as well as the existence of persistent ageism (McVittie, McKinlay and Widdicombe, 2003) and age discrimination in employment (Wood *et al.*, 2008) as well as in other spheres of (public) life (Fealy *et al.*, 2012), in 2000 and 2001 the European Commission (EC) passed two directives. These obliged member states to increase the employment participation rate of those aged over 55 as well as to foster age equality in employment (EC, 2000, 2001). As a consequence of both pre-existing national pressures and legal EU pressures, national policy makers started to promote longer working lives and to discourage early retirement already in the mid-1990s (Muller-Camen *et al.*, 2011). These measures include changes to early retirement pathways and pension systems as well as instruments to increase older workers' employability and hence their 'attractiveness' for employers. However, the scope and effect of these national policies, or 'stay factors' (Ebbinghaus and Hofäcker, 2013), again diverge from one another, as can be seen in the example of Germany and the UK.

The UK government's approach towards increasing its old age employment rate is mainly based on two state policies:

- the abolition of the default retirement age (DRA) as part of a broader measure to make workplace age discrimination unlawful; and
- the increase of the state pension age (SPA).

In 2006, the government set the DRA to age 65 when employees could be lawfully dismissed based on their age, though it ruled that employees had a 'right to request' to work past the DRA; a request which at least had to be considered by employers (Flynn, 2010). In its draft of the Employment Equality (Age) Regulations 2006 (DTI, 2006), the government acknowledged that the DRA regulation might have to be reviewed and hence decided in October 2011 to abolish the DRA altogether. Dismissal because of age has since only been lawful in occupations in which this step is objectively justified due to job demands (Flynn *et al.*, 2013) although a recent Supreme Court ruling has given employers some scope to reintroduce a DRA for workforce planning reasons, such as avoiding career blockage for younger workers (Flynn, 2014). As a consequence, most workers beyond the age of 65 can remain employed, with organizations only being able to dismiss them due to performance reasons.

A second policy approach focuses on the harmonization of the SPA to age 65 for both genders and then to achieve a step-wise increase of the SPA to age 68 by 2029. Workers are therefore eligible to access their state pension later. Hence, the British Labour Force Survey data suggests that the labour market participation of those aged 65 to 69 has slightly increased between 2011 and 2012, at least for men (Banks *et al.*, 2014).

Besides implementing these two policy changes, the British government has done little to actively help older individuals back into work or to extend their employment careers, for example, through active labour market interventions. The government therefore maintains its liberal 'light touch' approach and shifts the responsibility for later life employment and extended working life to organizations and individuals.

While organizations have to find ways to maintain older workers' productivity or else to externalize (unproductive) older workers, given the abolition of the DRA (Barnard, 2011), individuals have to navigate the financial necessity of remaining employed due to the later availability of the state pension. This especially affects low-qualified workers who might not have access to occupational and private pension schemes, as the state pension accounts for 42 per cent of all pension expenditure only (OECD, 2011). In the absence of active labour market policies that help enable older workers to stay employable, especially those with low initial qualifications and/or (occupational) health problems, 'new' socio-economic problem groups might arise that on the one hand have to remain employed for financial reasons, but on the other hand often do not have the option to do so (Hofäcker *et al.*, 2016).

Contrary to that of Britain, the German government long favoured early retirement to actively manage the labour market. However, as this paradigm became financially unsustainable in the 1990s, the government started to implement measures to reform the pension and welfare state systems, thereby closing off state-financed early retirement pathways and making them less attractive financially (Muller-Camen *et al.*, 2011). Furthermore, similar to Britain, the German government decided in 2007 to raise the SPA for both genders step-wise from age 65 to age 67 by 2029. Moreover, active labour market policies played a greater role in Germany than in Britain, with the German government implementing training measures for the over 50 age group that aimed at increasing older workers' employability (Sproß, 2010). In addition, the government made available subsidies to both employers who hired individuals aged over 50 as well as to older workers themselves. In the first case, employers are given subsidies to compensate them financially for the potentially lower productivity of the newly hired older worker ('integration subsidy') (Stephan, 2009). In the second case, older workers are financially compensated by the state for accepting potentially lower wage levels if re-entering the labour market after spells of unemployment ('integration vouchers'), though, up until 2011, this instrument was only moderately successful in re-integrating older workers in the workforce (Dietz et al., 2011). Nevertheless, employment rates of workers aged over 50 in Germany have started to increase since the late 1990s (Dietz and Walwei, 2011), reversing the previously dominant early retirement trend (Ebbinghaus and Hofäcker, 2013). Therefore, while the British government mainly set the policy scene for the increasing labour market participation of older workers by abolishing the upper age limit for employment as well as by possibly forcing individuals to stay employed out of financial reasons, the German government actively worked on enabling older workers to remain employed by offering at least some qualification measures and by providing financial incentives.

This relatively proactive German model, however, has recently taken 'a step backwards', as the current Grand Coalition decided in 2014 to re-introduce early retirement opportunities for those who have collected at least 45 contribution years (i.e. those who have worked and paid into the social security system for 45 years). This pension reform allows individuals from the age of 63 (and in some cases from the age of 61) to draw their old age pension without actuarial deductions (Spiegel, 2014). The reform has triggered mixed reactions. It receives support in large parts of the population. Especially, the government is praised for the opportunity for long-term employed individuals to enjoy their well-deserved retirement, particularly those in strenuous occupations (BMAS, 2014). Other commentators criticize that the pension reform leads to more inequalities, especially for younger generations who will have to finance the reform (FAZ, 2014a) and that it might be unconstitutional, as suggested in a report by the academic service of the German national parliament (Süddeutsche, 2014). Furthermore, it was suggested that the reform runs counter to government efforts that aim to encourage people to stay in work longer and hence motivate firms to implement age-neutral HRM measures in support of this group of workers. Instead, with the 2014 pension reform, employers might use this state-financed early exit option (again) as a means for socially acceptable job attrition (Welt, 2014), though some employers, for example, in the chemical industry, are also critical of the reform and consider it counter-productive to their own efforts to manage skill shortages (FAZ, 2014b).

Managing an Ageing Workforce: The Case of Employers

This section will talk about employer practices across Europe and their HRM approaches towards their ageing workforces, before providing a brief comparison of the situation in the UK and Germany.

Based on national and EU-wide policies, employers have been encouraged to adopt human resource management (HRM) policies that are aimed at encouraging older workers to delay retirement. While the focus here has been very much on the retention of older workers, more recent dialogue has also highlighted the need to create consistent and fair policies across age groups in order to avoid issues around inter-generational fairness (CIPD, 2013). HRM policies and practices to support age diversity can be broadly categorized into the following areas, according to EUROFOUND (Naegele and Walker, 2006), the International Labour Organization (ILO) (2009), the United Nations (2004) as well as according to age diversity good practice guides which have been distributed by governments (DWP, 2013) and stakeholder organizations such as employer groups, trade unions and age advocacy groups (Flynn and McNair, 2011):

- *Flexible working hours*: the opportunity to adjust working hours in order to improve work/life balance; accommodate caring responsibilities or participate in voluntary work or other retirement activities.
- *Lifelong learning*: the opportunity to improve one's skills through training, especially employer sponsored workplace training.
- *Job rotation*: the opportunity to adjust job content through promotion, lateral transfer or winding down towards retirement. This can also include measures such as experienced workers engaging in skills transfer, for example, by mentoring younger workers.
- *Healthy working*: interventions to improve health and well-being and to address physical and mental health risks associated with work.
- *Age inclusivity*: the promotion of age inclusive work environments through formal age equality and diversity policies; age mixed work teams and age management training for managers.
- *Pre-retirement planning* so that employees can make informed choices about when they retire and how they can afford to retire comfortably.
- *Career planning and appraisals* so that employees, especially older ones, have the opportunity to discuss with their managers their work and retirement plans, as well as what support they need to make the best use of their skills, experience and abilities.

Nevertheless, even though these basic recommendations are similar across countries, it has to be kept in mind that any implementation thereof will depend on and will be mediated by national institutions, such as, for example, legal requirements regarding contractual working hours (Boehm *et al.*, 2013).

Flexible working

Of these interventions, flexible working appears to be the most popular amongst older workers and the type of support that employers are most likely to provide (Stewart and Rowlatt, 2011). The most common form of this is part-time working, although some employers, especially in the public sector, are implementing a more formalized approach to flexible working that provides employees with a broad range of choices on how they can adjust their working hours, such as flexi-working (whereby the employee can adjust his or her working hours around a mandatory 'core' working time); job-sharing (which as the name suggests involves two or more employees sharing responsibility for a post) and occasional or on-call work. Most employers say that they offer at least one form of flexible working for staff and those which already employ staff on a flexible basis report that it is easy to extend such provision to others (McNair and Flynn, 2012).

Flexible working has proven critical for older workers with caring responsibility (especially those who care for both elderly and younger relatives: the so-called sandwich generation), although they are still less likely to have access to such arrangements than parents of young children (Age UK, 2012). Older carers, particularly women, without access to some form of flexibility are at risk of early exit, as the stress of managing both full-time work and family responsibilities mounts (Mooney and Stratham, 2002).

Tri-partite agreements in Belgium, Denmark, the Netherlands, Finland and Germany have all included some scope for older employees to request flexible working (EUROFOUND, 2013). In the UK, employees have, by statute, the right to request flexible working. The right was originally limited to workers with childcare responsibilities, but was subsequently extended to those caring for elderly relatives. From 2014, the right has been extended to all workers. Although it is hard to say now to what extent the new law will enable older workers to work flexibly, previous studies by the UK Department for Work and Pensions indicate that over 90 per cent of requests from carers to work flexibly have been granted, although only a minority of employees were aware that they had the right to request (Elsmore, 2009).

Many employers are now taking advantage of using flexible working for older employees in order to manage labour costs. BAE Systems, for example, reached a collective agreement with unions to offer phased retirement to employees, gradually tapering work as employees start drawing their pensions. The scheme enabled the manufacturer to manage head count as demand peaked and troughed (Flynn *et al.*, 2013).

Training and Career Development

While flexible working is growing in popularity amongst older workers, job change in late career is seldom requested, in large part because of workers' concerns about the impact that a change of position, particularly self-demotion, could have on their occupational pensions (Maitland, 2010). Nevertheless, many older workers say that they would like to spend at least some of their time mentoring and taking part in other forms of knowledge sharing. Likewise, although there is a small but significant cohort of older 'lifelong learners', most older workers feel that their skills are either about right or exceed the requirements for their jobs (McNair, 2010). Although this may appear to show a general disinterest amongst older workers in training and development, it has also been noted that older workers would have more interest if training was shorter and built on their existing skills and knowledge (McNair, 2011). There is also evidence that older workers are reluctant to ask for training for fear of 'signalling' a lack of job competence.

In order to overcome barriers older workers might face with career transitions and skills development, governments in Norway, Finland, the Netherlands and France have begun to fund career advice services across the life course (EUROFOUND, 2013). Also, the UK Business, Innovation and Skills Department is piloting a programme of universal career guidance for people at or around the age of 50 in order to help them manage their late careers as well as retirement (DWP, 2014).

Health and Workplace Design

Employers are also investing in workplace redesign to support workers young and old with long-term health conditions (LHC). Many older workers have a LHC (in the UK, 41 per cent do so according to the British Labour Force Survey) but most are able to continue to work with moderate support from their employers. Most employer interventions are individualized forms of support for employees with LHC's, such as adjustments to their workstations or new chairs to help manage back or limb problems. They do not necessarily involve the purchase of new equipment; for example, an employer may change the working hours of an employee who needs support in managing stress so that he can avoid travelling during rush hour (McNair and Flynn, 2012).

Some organizations have invested in corporate level programmes in order to manage health across the workplace. One of the best known interventions is that of the car manufacturer BMW, which retooled its production line to fit the expected age profile of the company by 2017. One of the major lessons learned from the programme was that interventions which support older workers in maintaining employability can also help younger workers avoid injuries that could otherwise lead to early retirement on health grounds (Loch *et al.*, 2010).

Such an approach to healthy working across the life course is one of the central aims of the Finnish Workability Index, which assesses the relationship between an individual worker's physical and mental capacity and the work (s)he carries out. The aim is to identify likely problems in the employee's workplace or role which could lead to future health problems and, in so doing, enable the employer to take remedial measures to avoid health injury (Ilmarinen, 1999).

Finally, it should be noted that, while ageing workforces may seem to be a problem for employers, many are taking advantage of changing work processes in order to make best use of older workers' skills, knowledge and experience. Manufacturers in particular are moving towards the 'servitization' of marketing and are redeploying their older employees from the factory line to customer service work so as to enable their older workers to rely on skills and experience rather than physical capacity (McNair *et al.*, 2013). While such redeployments might enable an individual worker to remain employed, such strategies might also make business sense (Kunze *et al.*, 2011). Nevertheless, positive process and performance outcomes of age-heterogeneous teams depend on the effective management of such teams by employing an age-inclusive leadership style, by creating a positive diversity climate and by implementing age-neutral HRM practices (Boehm and Dwertmann, 2015).

A Comparison of the UK and Germany

While many employers across Europe have taken on the 'demographic challenge' one way or the other, a systematic qualitative review of motivations, policies and practices across matched pairs of German and British case study organizations found that the national institutional policy context tends to shape organizations' HRM strategies with regard to older workers. While the lack of continued early retirement options and pressures from social partners in Germany towards age-neutral HRM forced the two German manufacturing firms in that study to pursue extensive age-neutral HRM, their two UK counterparts had more scope to design their HRM strategies due to the British free market context (Schröder *et al.*, 2010). Furthermore, an analysis of quantitative firm-level survey data in these two countries confirms the overall path-dependent orientation of old age-related HRM (Schröder *et al.*, 2009). However, employers are not necessarily actors who are 'slavishly devoted to the reproduction of habits' (Battilana *et al.*, 2009: 67) deriving from the national institutional context. The cases of the two matched German and British retail firms in the qualitative study above show that actors (i.e. employers) have space to design the kind of HRM that follows a business rationale and makes most economic sense in their specific sector, in spite of otherwise existing institutional pressures (Schröder *et al.*, 2014).

Summary

The above discussion makes it clear that the pressures resulting from ageing workforce demographics have led both governments and employers to react by introducing policies and initiatives to extend working life. Potential difficulties in relation to social security and skills availability have led policy makers to make attempts to reverse the former emphasis on early retirement by increasing the state pension age and encouraging later retirement. These approaches differ according the national context, with a relatively hands-off approach from the UK government, compared to a more proactive approach in Germany.

Employers have introduced a range of initiatives to attract and retain older workers, including: flexible working, lifelong learning, job rotation, healthy working, age inclusive work environments, pre-retirement planning and career planning. Flexible working in particular seems to have been promoted as a means of engaging older workers, particularly those with caring responsibilities. The Finnish approach of workability has also provided a useful framework in which to assess and manage older workers abilities.

Despite the myriad of initiatives at both a national and organizational level that have been introduced within the past 15 years, the recent recession and increasing youth unemployment have removed the emphasis from older workers back onto the younger end of the workforce. This means that the drive towards extending working life has stalled, with resources being taken up by initiatives to improve youth skills and employment (e.g. through funding for apprenticeship schemes in the UK). Despite this, the pressing problem of workforce ageing has not gone away and the potential implications of this trend do not seem to have yet been alleviated by government or employer action. Governments and employers have yet to develop HRM systems that aim to attract, motivate and retain employees across the life-span – instead they tend to focus on particular age groups (older or younger). While this age-based approach might lead to conflict and to incoherence among policies, it might not capture the full potential of older workers, who, as a group, become more heterogeneous as they age and who therefore require divergent and individually negotiated sets of policies to foster their motivation, employability and retention (Bal *et al.*, 2012).

Key Learning Points

- Workforce ageing is likely to lead to problems for both governments (in relation to dependency ratios) and employers (as skills shortages). Despite the recent emphasis on youth skills and employment, this trend continues and needs to be addressed via effective initiatives to extend working life, while not disadvantaging younger workers.
- Government reactions to population ageing have been driven not only by the nature of the population but by the institutional environment in that country, with CMEs likely to take a more proactive and involved path compared to the hands-off approach of LMEs.
- Skills shortages are significant drivers which are leading employers to develop new ways to manage older workers. The 'competition for talent' means businesses will be looking for ways to retain skilled employees. Nevertheless, there remain significant barriers faced by the older unemployed (both skilled and unskilled) to find work.
- Flexible working arrangements, lifelong learning and career development and initiatives around health and workplace design are practices most commonly adopted by employers to extend working life. However, the effectiveness of these initiatives is not clear, despite slight increases in the workforce participation of older workers.
- Managing older workers is not terribly different from managing younger ones. Many of the HRM tools which employers use to attract and retain young talent can be applied to the older workforce. This will increasingly be the case as ageing demographics result in changing career, learning and family patterns.

References

Age UK (2012) *A Means to an End*. London: Age UK.
Audit Scotland (2013) *Managing Early Departures from the Scottish Public Sector*. Edinburgh: Audit Scotland.

Bal, P.M., De Jong, S.B., Jansen, P.G.W. and Bakker, A.B. (2012) 'Motivating employees to work beyond retirement: a multi-level study of the role of i-deals and unit climate', *Journal of Management Studies*, 49(2), 306–331.

Banks, J., Emmerson, C. and Tetlow, G.C. (2014) 'Effect of pensions and disability benefits on retirement in the UK', *National Bureau of Economic Research Working Paper Series*, No. 19907, 1–54.

Barnard, C. (2011) 'Retiring gracefully', *The Cambridge Law Journal*, 70(2), 304–306.

Battilana, J., Leca, B. and Boxenbaum, E. (2009) 'How actors change institutions: towards a theory of institutional entrepreneurship', *The Academy of Management Annals*, 3, 65–107.

Becker, M.A. (2004) 'Managing diversity in the European Union: inclusive European Citizenship and Third-Country Nationals', *Yale Human Rights and Development L.J.*, 7, 132–183.

Bloom, D.E., Canning, D. and Fink, G. (2010) 'Implications of population ageing for economic growth', *Oxford Review of Economic Policy*, 26(4), 583–612.

Blossfeld, H.-P., Buchholz, S. and Kurz, K. (eds) (2011) *Aging Populations, Globalization and the Labor Market: Comparing Late Working Life and Retirement in Modern Societies.* Cheltenham: Edgar Elger.

BMAS (2014) *Das Rentenpaket ist da!*, Bundesministerium für Arbeit und Soziales, Berlin.

Boehm, S. and Dwertmann, D.J.G. (2015) 'Forging a single-edged sword: facilitating positive age and disability diversity effects in the workplace through leadership, positive climates, and HR practices', *Work, Aging and Retirement*, 1(1), 41–63.

Boehm, S., Schröder, H. and Kunze, F. (2013) 'Comparative age management: theoretical perspectives and practical implications', in Field, J., Burke, R.J. and Cooper, C.L. (eds) *The SAGE Handbook of Aging, Work and Society.* London: Sage, 211–238.

Börsch-Supan, A., Schnabel, R., Kohnz, S. and Mastrobuoni, G. (2004) 'Micro-modeling of retirement decisions in Germany', in Gruber, J. and Wise, D. (eds) *Social Security Programs and Retirement around the World: Micro-estimation.* Chicago, IL: University of Chicago Press, 285–344.

Buchholz, S. (2006) 'Men's late careers and career exits in West Germany', in Blossfeld, H.-P., Buchholz, S. and Hofäcker, D. (eds) *Globalization, Uncertainty and Late Careers in Society.* London: Routledge, 55–78.

Buchholz, S., Hofäcker, D. and Blossfeld, H.-P. (2006) 'Globalization, accelerating economic change and late careers: a theoretical framework', in Blossfeld, H.-P., Buchholz, S. and Hofäcker, D. (eds) *Globalization, Uncertainty and Late Careers in Society.* London: Routledge.

Chartered Institute of Personnel and Development (2013) *The Changing Contours of Fairness.* London: CIPD.

Conde-Ruiz, J.I. and Galasso, V. (2004) 'The macroeconomics of early retirement', *Journal of Public Economics*, 88(9–10), 1849–1869.

Cowell, A. (2004) 'Demographic time bomb threatens pensions in Europe', *New York Times*, 26 November.

Dar, A. (2015) 'Youth Unemployment Statistics', *House of Commons Briefing Paper*, No. 05871, 17 June 2015. London: House of Commons Library. Available at: http://researchbriefings.parliament.uk/ResearchBriefing/Summary/SN05871 (accessed 7 July 2015).

DeLong, D. (2004) *Lost Knowledge: Confronting the Threat of an Ageing Workforce.* Oxford: Oxford University Press.

Dietz, M., Koch, S., Krug, G. and Stephan, G. (2011) 'Die Entgeltsicherung für Ältere: ein Auslaufmodell?', *WSI-Mitteilungen*, 5, 226–233.

Dietz, M. and Walwei, U. (2011) 'Germany: no country for old workers?', *Zeitschrift für ArbeitsmarktForschung*, 44(4), 363–376.

DTI UK (2006) *Equality and Diversity: Coming of Age.* Report on consultation on the draft Employment Equality (Age) Regulations 2006. London: Department of Trade and Industry.

DWP UK (2013) *Employing Older Workers: An Employer's Guide to Today's Multi-Generational Workforce.* London: Department for Work and Pensions.

DWP UK (2014) *Fuller Working Lives: A Framework for Action.* London: Department for Work and Pensions.

Ebbinghaus, B. (2001) 'When labour and capital collude: the political economy of early retirement in Europe, Japan and the USA', in Ebbinghaus, B. and Manow, P. (eds) *Comparing Welfare Capitalism: Social Policy and Political Economy in Europe, Japan and the USA.* New York: Routledge.

Ebbinghaus, B. and Hofäcker, D. (2013) 'Reversing early retirement in advanced welfare economies: a paradigm shift to overcome push and pull factors', *Comparative Population Studies*, 38(4), 807–840.

EC (2000) *Lisbon European Council 23 and 24 March 2000: Presidency Conclusions.* Brussels: EC. Available at: http://www.europarl.europa.eu/summits/lis1_en.htm (accessed 7 July 2015).

EC (2001) *Stockholm European Council 23 and 24 March 2001: Presidency Conclusions.* Brussels: EC. Available at: http://www.consilium.europa.eu/ueDocs/cms_Data/docs/pressData/en/ec/00100-r1.%20ann-r1.en1.html (accessed 7 July 2015).

Elsmore, K. (2009), *Caring and Flexible Working.* London: Department for Work and Pensions.

EUROFOUND (2013) *Role of Governments and Social Partners in Keeping Older Workers in the Labour Market.* Available at: http://www.eurofound.europa.eu/publications/report/2013/working-conditions-labour-market-social-policies/role-of-governments-and-social-partners-in-keeping-older-workers-in-the-labour-market (accessed 7 July 2015).

FAZ (2014a) 'Isabel Schnabel - Künftige Wirtschaftsweise: rente mit 63, nicht gerecht', *Frankfurter Allgemeine Zeitung*, 7. Frankfurt: FAZ.

FAZ (2014b) 'Chemiebranche in Rhein-Main: die Rente mit 63 ist die falsche Botschaft', *Frankfurter Allgemeine Zeitung*, 18, Frankfurt: FAZ.

Fealy, G., McNamara, M., Treacy, M.P. and Lyons, I. (2012) 'Constructing ageing and age identities: a case study of newspaper discourses', *Ageing & Society*, 32(1), 85–102.

Flynn, M. (2010) 'The United Kingdom government's "business case" approach to the regulation of retirement', *Ageing & Society*, 30(3), 421–443.

Flynn, M. (2014) *Representing an Ageing Workforce: Challenges and Opportunities for Britain's Unions.* London: TUC.

Flynn, M. and McNair, S. (2011) *Managing Age: A Guide to Good Employment Practice.* 2nd edn. London: CIPD.

Flynn, M., Schröder, H., Higo, M. and Yamada, A. (2014) 'Government as institutional entrepreneur: extending working life in the UK and Japan', *Journal of Social Policy*, 43(3), 535–553.

Flynn, M., Upchurch, M., Muller-Camen, M. and Schröder, H. (2013) 'Trade union responses to ageing workforces in the UK and Germany', *Human Relations*, 66(1), 45–64.

Gendron, B. (2011) 'Older workers and active ageing in France: the changing early retirement and company approach', *The International Journal of Human Resource Management*, 22(6), 1221–1231.

Grant, J., Hoorens, S., Sivadasan, S., van het Loo, M., DaVanzo, J., Hale, L., Gibson, S. and Butz, W. (2004) *Low Fertility and Population Ageing: Causes, Consequences and Policy Options*. Santa Monica: RAND Corporation.

Gruber, J., Milligan, K. and Wise, D.A. (2009) *Social Security Programs and Retirement around the World: The Relationship to Youth Employment, Introduction and Summary*. Cambridge: National Bureau of Economic Research.

Hofäcker, D., Schröder, H., Li, Y. and Flynn, M. (2016) 'Trends and determinants of work-retirement transitions under changing institutional conditions: Germany, England and Japan compared', *Journal of Social Policy*, 45(1), 39–64.

Ilmarinen, J. (1999) *Ageing Workers in the European Union: Status and Promotion of Work-ability, Employability and Employment*. Helsinki: FIOH.

ILO (2009) *International Symposium to Discuss Responses to the Demographic Challenges in the Workplace*. Geneva: ILO. Available at: http://www.ilo.org/public/english/dialogue/actemp/whatwedo/events/2009/symposium.htm (accessed 7 July 2015).

Kunze, F., Boehm, S.A. and Bruch, H. (2011) 'Age diversity, age discrimination climate and performance consequences: a cross organizational study', *Journal of Organizational Behavior*, 32(2): 264–290.

Loch, C., Sting, F., Bauer, N. and Mauermann, H. (2010) 'How BMW is defusing the demographic time bomb', *Harvard Business Review*, March, 1–6.

McNair, S. (2010) *Learning and Work in Later Life*. London: Nuffield Foundation.

McNair, S. (2011) *Older People and Skills in a Changing Economy*. Leicester: NIACE.

McNair, S. and Flynn, M. (2012) *Managing a Healthy Ageing Workforce: A Business Imperative*. London: CIPD.

McNair, S., Myerson, J., Gheerawo, R. and Ramster, G. (2013) *Foresight: Implications of an Ageing Society for Manufacturing*. London: Foresight Future.

McVittie, C., McKinlay, A. and Widdicombe, S. (2003) 'Committed to (un)equal opportunities?: "New ageism" and the older worker', *British Journal of Social Psychology*, 42(4), 595–612.

Maitland, A. (2010) *Working Better: The Over 50s, the New Work Generation*. London: EHRC.

Mooney, A. and Stratham, S. (2002) *The Pivot Generation: Informal Care and Work after 50 Fifty*. Bristol: The Policy Press.

Muller-Camen, M., Croucher, R., Flynn, M. and Schröder, H. (2011) 'National institutions and employers' age management practices in Britain and Germany: "path dependence" and option exploration', *Human Relations*, 64(4), 507–530.

Naegele, G. and Walker, A. (2006) *A Guide to Good Practice in Age Management*. Dublin: European Foundation for the Improvement of Working and Living Conditions.

National Audit Office UK (2012) *Managing Early Departures in Central Government*. London: NAO.

OECD (2011) *Pensions at a Glance 2011*. Paris: OECD.

OECD (2012) *Life Expectancy and Healthy Life Expectancy at Birth*. Paris: OECD. Available at: http://www.oecd-ilibrary.org/social-issues-migration-health/health-at-a-glance-europe-2012/life-expectancy-and-healthy-life-expectancy-at-birth_9789264183896-4-en (accessed 24 July 2014).

OECD (2015) *Labour Force Statistics (LFS) by Sex and Age (Indicators)*. OECDStatExtracts (ed.). Paris: Retrieved from stats.OECD.org. Available at: http://www.oecd-ilibrary.org/employment/data/labour-market-statistics/labour-force-statistics-by-sex-and-age-indicators_data-00310-en (accessed 7 July 2015).

ONS UK (2008) *National Population Projections*. Available at: www.ons.gov.uk (accessed 1 March 2013).

ONS UK (2015) *Migration Statistics Quarterly Report, February 2015*. Available at: http://www.ons.gov.uk/ons/rel/migration1/migration-statistics-quarterly-report/february-2015/index.html (accessed 23 April 2015).

Parry, E. and Harris, L. (2011) *The Employment Challenges of an Ageing Workforce*. ACAS Future of Workplace Relations Discussion Paper. London: ACAS. Available at: http://www.acas.org.uk/media/pdf/e/p/The_Employment_Relations_Challenges_of_an_Ageing_Workforce.pdf (accessed 7 July 2015).

Parry, E. and Tyson, S. (2014) *Managing People in a Contemporary Context*. London: Routledge.

Rappaport, A., Bancroft, E. and Okum, L. (2003) 'The aging workforce raises new talent management issues for employers', *Journal of Organizational Excellence*, 23(1), 55–66.

Schils, T. (2008) 'Early retirement in Germany, the Netherlands, and the United Kingdom: a longitudinal analysis of individual factors and institutional regimes', *European Sociological Review*, 24(3), 315–329.

Schröder, H., Flynn, M. and Muller-Camen, M. (2010) 'Rationale for and implementation of age-neutral HRM in divergent institutional contexts: examples from Britain and Germany', in Kunisch, S., Boehm, S.A. and Boppel, M. (eds) *From Grey to Silver: Managing Demographic Change Successfully*. Heidelberg: Springer, 101–116.

Schröder, H., Hofäcker, D. and Muller-Camen, M. (2009) 'HRM and the employment of older workers: Germany and Britain compared', *International Journal of Human Resources Development and Management*, 9(2–3), 162–179.

Schröder, H., Muller-Camen, M. and Flynn, M. (2014) 'The management of an ageing workforce: organisational policies in Germany and Britain', *Human Resource Management Journal*, 24(4), 394–409.

Spiegel DE (2014) 'Rentenreform: Gesetzeslücke erlaubt Berufsausstieg mit 61', *Der Spiegel-Online*, 27, June. Hamburg: Spiegel-Verlag. Available at: http://www.spiegel.de/wirtschaft/soziales/rente-gesetzesluecke-erlaubt-berufsausstieg-mit-61-a-977787.html (accessed 7 July 2015).

Sproß, C. (2010) *Germany: Public Policy, Global Policy Brief*. Boston, MA: The Sloan Centre on Aging and Work at Boston College.

Stephan, G. (2009) 'Employer wage subsidies and wages in Germany: some evidence from individual data', *IAB Discussion Paper 9/2009*. Available at: http://doku.iab.de/discussionpapers/2009/dp0909.pdf (accessed 7 July 2015).

Stewart, E. and Rowlatt, A. (2011) 'Flexible working: working for families, working for business: a report by the Family Friendly Working Hours Taskforce', *Ageing and Society*, 24(2), 147–165.

Süddeutsche DE (2014) 'Rente mit 63 möglicherweise verfassungswidrig', *Süddeutsche Zeitung*, 9, July, München.

Taylor, P. (2002) *New Policies for Older Workers*. Bristol: The Policy Press.

Turner, A. (2004) *Turner Commission Report: Pensions, Challenges and Choices*. London: Independent Pensions Commission.

United Nations (2002) *World Population Ageing: 1950–2050*. New York: UN Population Division.

United Nations (2004) *The Madrid International Plan of Action on Ageing: From Conception to Implementation*. New York: UN.

van Oorschot, W. and Jensen, P.H. (2009) 'Early retirement differences between Denmark and the Netherlands: a cross-national comparison of push and pull factors in two small European welfare states', *Journal of Aging Studies*, 23(4), 267–278.

Welt DE (2014) 'Regierung hilft beim fröhlichen Personalabbau', *Die Welt*, 27 January.

Wood, G., Wilkinson, A. and Harcourt, M. (2008) 'Age discrimination and working life: perspectives and contestations – A review of the contemporary literature', *International Journal of Management Reviews*, 10(4), 425–442.

13 International Migration and International Human Resource Management

AKRAM AL ARISS, JEAN-LUC CERDIN AND
CHRIS BREWSTER

Understanding the Importance of Migration

In 2013 it was estimated that there are 232 million migrant workers around the world, as indicated in Table 13.1 (United Nations, 2013). Although the facts are not as clear as we might like, it seems that migration is increasing substantially. War, income inequality, climate change, shifts in demography and globalization are among the many factors that influence more and more workers and their families to leave their countries in search of work and security.

Given its previous rise and expectations of a continuing rise in the future, migration has become a key topic in many political agendas around the globe. The issue has evoked a sense of urgency in many societies, particularly those in the Western developed world and in areas such as the Arab Gulf countries. Decision-makers are grappling with controversial, often virulently controversial, aspects of migration. It is clear that it is for many societies a 'two-edged sword'. One edge of the sword relates to the benefits of migration. There seems to be a consistent link between immigration and the growth and development of societies. Migrant CEOs/entrepreneurs contribute to the success of the economies of their host countries and migrant workers make substantial contributions to those countries' growth and development. At the same time, their countries of origin benefit significantly from their remittances whilst abroad and can, if they return, benefit from the skills they acquired during the period of their stay outside the home country. The other edge of the sword relates to the pressure that migrants put onto local communities, their housing

Table 13.1 International migrant populations by major area of origin and destination, 2013 (millions)

| 2013 | Origin | | | | | | | | |
		Africa	Asia	Europe	LAC	NAM	Oceania	Various	Total	Retention by Destination %
Destination	Africa	15.3	1.1	0.8	0.0	0.1	0.0	1.4	18.6	82
	Asia	4.6	53.8	7.6	0.7	0.6	0.1	3.4	70.8	76
	Europe	8.9	18.6	37.8	4.5	0.9	0.3	1.3	72.4	52
	LAC	0.0	0.3	1.2	5.4	1.3	0.0	0.2	8.5	64
	NAM	2.0	15.7	7.9	25.9	1.2	0.3	0.0	53.1	2
	Oceania	0.5	2.9	3.1	0.1	0.2	1.1	0.1	7.9	14
	Total	31.3	92.5	58.4	36.7	4.3	1.9	6.4	231.5	
	Retention by origin %	49	58	65	15	28	58			

Source: United Nations (2013) *Population Facts.* Department of Economic and Social Affairs, Population Division September (2013/3). New York: United Nations.

Note: 'LAC' stands for 'Latin America and the Caribbean' and 'NAM' for 'Northern America'. Retention by destination is calculated as the number of persons residing in a destination (major area) who were also born in the same major area. Retention by origin is calculated as the number of persons from an origin (major area) who were also residing in the same major area.

and employment, their education, social services and health systems. Further, migration is often linked with a dramatic under-utilization of skills and, at the bottom end of the employment market, is all too often linked to unacceptable labour practices, with abdication of responsibility in sanctioning them (Rodriguez and Mearns, 2012). For example, Sparrow's (2008) review for the UK's government's Sector Skills Development Agency, drawing on Dench et al. (2006) discussed the risk that organizations exploit incoming migrants, whilst undercutting the local workforce compared to the potential benefits of closing skills gaps and increasing productivity. He questioned the capacity of migration systems to strategically support the skills needs of employers.

There is a unique issue in the European Union, where citizens from any member country are free to move to, to work in, to buy property in and to enjoy the social benefits and healthcare system of every other country in the EU. This lawfully allowed mobility puts Europe in a different position in terms of migration than any other region of the world. Europe as a whole still, of course, has significant migration in from non-European countries, of the kind that would be recognized in any part of the globe. The intra-EU mobility adds an extra dimension.

There are rich pickings here for political controversy and populist pressure groups and parties. There are complex challenges inherent in the migration process that are related to governance, workers' rights and security and the linkages between migration and development and international co-operation. In this chapter, our primary focus is on the under-recognized and hence under-researched connection between migration and international human resource management.

Defining Who Is a Migrant

International organizations such as the United Nations (UN) (1998), the International Labour Organization (ILO) (2014) and the Organization for Economic Co-operation and Development (OECD) (2003) generally define a long-term migrant as a person who moves to a country other than that of his or her usual residence for a period of at least a year (12 months), whereby the country of destination becomes his or her new country of normal residence. The person will be a long-term emigrant from the perspective of the country of departure, and a long-term immigrant from that of the country of arrival.

A short-term migrant is a person who moves to a country other than that of his or her usual residence for a period of at least three months but less than 12 months except in cases where the movement to that country is for purposes of recreation, holiday, visits to friends or relatives, business, medical treatment or religious pilgrimage (United Nations, 1998).

These definitions have not been widely adopted by academic scholars and have proved difficult to apply. For example, and relevantly to our case here, in business and management there is no clear distinction between an expatriate (particularly the now widely-used self-initiated expatriate – Andresen *et al.*, 2012; Cerdin and Selmer, 2014; Suutari and Brewster, 2000) and short-term migrants, and many of the issues and consequences seem to be very similar (Al Ariss, 2010). A short-term migrant may well expect to work in the host country and go back to their own country within a limited timescale – but so do short-term expatriates (or, in the UN definition, migrants on business). Furthermore, the categories may not be consistent over time: a migrant may have every intention and expectation of staying in the host (their new home) country and the self-initiated expatriate may have every intention and expectation of going home within a short period – but in many cases the former will go home within a few months or years and in other cases the latter may stay on for the rest of their lives.

The difficulty of defining the concept of migration rests partly on the fact that migration is a multi-disciplinary topic (covered by, for example, economists, applied geographers, anthropologists and IHRM academics). Academics generally tend to consider migration within the wider process of international 'movement', covering all forms of human mobility. It has generally been neglected by management scholars and even by IHRM scholars. Addressing the topic from an IHRM perspective adds value as it allows consideration of the mobilization and utilization of another element in the international talent pool. Thus it can help an organization to attain its strategic business purposes while better recognizing the work-life experiences and needs of migrants. International human resource management offers avenues to studying the choices organizations make about resourcing strategies of international migrants, new forms of international working and knowledge transfer that might offer flexible employment forms.

The difficulties of establishing consistent and coherent categories aside, however, the UN's terminology provides a useful benchmark for statistical compilation and analyses, even as efforts are still being made for better harmonization and application of them.

Key Figures and Facts about Migration

For analysis purposes the UN divides the world into the poor and economically struggling countries of the South and the rich, developed countries of the North (even though some of the former are geographically much further north than some of the latter). According to UN estimates, South–South migration is as common as South–North migration (United Nations, 2013). In 2013, approximately 82.3 million international migrants who were born in the South were residing in other Southern countries. This is roughly the same number of international migrants who have left the South and are now living in the North (81.9 million). Figures for international migrants from the North and residing in the North were estimated at 53.7 million, whereas a much smaller number of 13.7 million international migrants from the Northern countries lived in the South (see Figure 13.1).

Countries vary markedly in the numbers of migrants and levels of foreigners. The exact definition of these terms is crucial in making international comparisons. The most commonly applied criteria used in defining a 'migrant' are nationality and place of birth. Any person who has ever migrated from his/her country of birth to his/her current country of residence falls within the category of 'migrant' or 'foreign-born population'. So the migrant category includes persons who still have the nationality of their country of origin but may also include persons born in the host country. The foreign-born population includes persons born abroad and will include in that nationals of their current country of residence (Thite *et al.*, 2009).

The definitions vary by country. Differing legislation governing the acquisition of nationality in each country has an influence on the size of the foreign-born population and the foreign population. In some countries, children automatically acquire citizenship if born there (*jus soli*, the right of soil), whereas in others they keep the nationality of their parents at birth (*jus sanguinis*, the right of blood). Some countries allow them to keep the nationality of their parents at birth and still grant citizenship of the host country when they reach their majority. To illustrate this, residency requirements vary from as few as three years in Canada to as many as ten in other countries. In Australia, Canada and New Zealand rates of naturalization are high, as they are also in some European countries such as Belgium, Sweden and the Netherlands.

Reasons for these figures vary and are usually linked to a complex of different explanations (Castles *et al.*, 2014). Obviously, the size and wealth of a country are great attractors, as are the perceived safety and security of the country and the perceived welfare support. The (mainly European) countries that have a history of international expansion and empire tend to have larger numbers of migrants. The foreign-born population data shown in Table 13.3 include persons born abroad as nationals of their current country of residence. The prevalence of such persons among the foreign born can be significant in some countries, especially those such as France and Portugal, who received large inflows of home-country repatriates from former colonies.

The intrinsic meaning of migration will be different in different contexts: in a large country like Japan, with a homogeneous population, migrants may be seen as exotic and strange. And this may also apply to emigrants – for such a large country, Japan has a very limited diaspora. By contrast, in Australia, another Pacific rim country, almost all the population consists of migrants or the family of relatively recent migrants. In the United Arab Emirates the overwhelming majority of the population (more than eight out of every ten people) consists of migrants or expatriates (Mohyeldin and Suliman, 2006). Some local citizens in some European countries may not look upon immigrants favourably (Reichel *et al.*, 2013), but others will.

It is important to make the point that wherever there is immigration there is almost certainly always illegal immigration – migrants who are not known to the authorities in that country or who have entered the country without a legal permit but are known to the authorities and have not been forcibly repatriated by them. Almost by definition, we have much less information on this group, but they will often be working in the host society and are a largely un-researched aspect of the labour market (though see, e.g. Bloch *et al.*, 2011).

Despite the extensive work carried out by the ILO and other international bodies, there remains a real need to take stock of what has been achieved so far with a view to identifying clearly what remains to be done to address the multiple aspects of the issues of migration and emigration from an HRM perspective (International Labour Organization, 2014).

Typology of Migration and Its Consequences in Terms of IHRM

So migrants are by no means a coherent group. In fact there are a great many types of migrants and the overall category can be analysed in a variety of ways. There is for example growing interest in the movement of high-skilled migrants and knowledge workers; the development of more globalized labour markets for craft-skilled employees – for example, the influx of Polish immigrants into the UK as self-employed businesses; the growth of 'global care chains', where the lifestyle of relatively wealthy individuals and households in developed countries is made possible by people from the second or third world, and involves the transfer of services associated with childcare, homecare and personal care such as nannies and maids; and the gravitation of productivity towards, and hence development of, global cities, such as London.

With our focus here on the connection of such migrants to international HRM, we apply an analytical frame that examines migrants in terms of their employment options, looking at their individual characteristics and their organizational relevance. In this section, we adopt a multilevel perspective in order to better understand migration (Al Ariss and Crowley-Henry, 2013; Al Ariss and Syed, 2011).

Our argument is that in order to have a nuanced understanding of migration, it is important to recognize individual, organizational and macro-social factors which are all of influence. For example, at the individual level, factors that matter include: the type of migration

Table 13.2 A typology of migration

Broad Levels	Specific Themes
Individual level	Agency of migrants, qualifications of migrants, work-life experiences of migrants, strategies of leaving a country for another one, strategies to overcome structural barriers in the destination country, experiences of migrants in terms of their ethnicity/religion/sex/age/physical abilities among other characteristics
Organizational level	Human resource management strategies for migrants, discrimination practices against migrants, diversity strategies/practices for accommodating migrants, underemployment of migrants in organizations, link between experiences in organizations in the home/destination countries, human resource development strategies
Macro-context	Regional and national legislation/policies/guidelines on the employment and work of migrants, country(ies) of origin/destination(s), discriminatory and anti-discriminatory policies, diversity policies, unemployment settings, formal policies of recognition of education and skills of migrants

Source: Adapted from Al Ariss and Crowley-Henry (2013)

(high-skilled/low-skilled migrants; legal/illegal migration); the country of origin/ethnicity/gender of migrants, and languages/skills/other forms of capital that migrants have. At the organizational level, issues that matter include: the role of national origin/sector/size of the company which might influence who and how they recruit migrants; and the history and experience of the company in terms of recruiting migrants. Finally, at the macro-social level, issues such as legislation and the role and attitudes of professional bodies as well as the country's history of migrant communities (positive or negative) and changes over time all influence migration. These three levels should be seen as interacting with each other rather than being separate. Given space limitations, our discussion below does not aim to be exhaustive, but rather attempts to tackle some key relevant topics on migration of relevance to HRM at each of the three levels mentioned.

Understanding the Micro-Individual Level of Migration

A major distinction between migrants lies in their level of skills. Highly qualified migrants (QIs) have recently been studied in the management literature. These are migrants who hold at least a bachelor degree when they migrate (Zikic *et al.*, 2010). The management literature has generally not studied low-skilled migrants, although they have been examined by disciplines such as economics, sociology, economic geography or political science and in journals dedicated to migration issues. Qualified migrants are more easily related to the issue of talent management, as they bring their qualifications to their employers (Cerdin *et al.*, 2014). Mulholland and Ryan (2014), studying intra-EU migration, see high-skilled migration as a key issue for the global talent pool of the host economy.

High-skilled and low-skilled migrants confront different challenges in their host country. High-skilled migrants are concerned with employment difficulties, earnings below their level of qualifications and skill under-utilization (Almeida *et al.*, 2012). Low-skilled migrants may also get low earnings, not because of the non-recognition of their general skills, but because of their inability to speak the local language. As a result, they may live in a 'language minority enclave', with few opportunities for training and employment (Chiswick, 1991). Illegal immigration is much more likely to be low-skilled rather than qualified immigrants.

High-Skilled Migrants: Qualified Immigrants

The lack of qualification recognition by employers during the hiring process may be due to a lack of knowledge of the immigrant's overseas-based work experience (Almeida *et al.*, 2012). In addition to this lack of knowledge, discrimination and prejudice often play a role in this skill under-utilization (e.g. Almeida *et al.*, 2012; Evans and Kelley, 1991).

Qualified immigrants do not constitute a homogenous group. On the contrary, they present considerable diversity in many aspects such as their motivation to migrate, their career orientations and their integration in the host country. For instance, Zikic *et al.* (2010: 667) find three career orientations amongst QIs from France, Spain and Canada, namely 'embracing, adaptive and resisting orientations – with each portraying distinct patterns of motivation, identity and coping'. The embracing career orientation corresponds to migrants who are highly motivated to overcome barriers they perceive as natural. They are ready to acquire the skills to face their new reality as migrants. Migrants with the adaptive career orientation are motivated by the prospect of success, with a particular focus on family success. Survival jobs may be part of their strategy to adjust to their host country. They are quite positive, even though less so than those with an embracing career orientation, despite career difficulties and obstacles they must overcome when they arrive in the host country. Finally, the resisting career orientation describes migrants stuck with the former professional identity they had before migrating. As they cannot find new motivations to cope with their new situation, they become discouraged by all barriers, both personal and professional. As a result, they see their migration as a career failure.

Cerdin *et al.* (2014) focus on motivations and identify four orientations, with some similarities to the Zikic *et al.* (2010) categories: Dream, Felicitous, Chance and Desperate migrants. Dream migrants are those who have long wanted to settle in their host country, attracted by

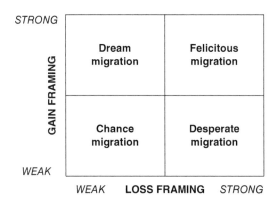

Figure 13.1 Typology of QIs mobility according to their motivation to migrate
Source: Cerdin *et al.* (2014): 156

stories about it; Felicitous migrants were pushed from their home country, but were also attracted to their new host country; Chance migrants were also forced out of their home country but in this case 'found themselves' in the host country without having had any real previous attraction to it; and Desperate migrants were the ones pushed from their home country and actively not wanting to be in their new one. Organizations need to take into account these different types of migrants in order to put in place adequate support policies. For instance, selecting migrants would require assessing and acknowledging 'the unique combination of risks, gains and losses that varies for each QI' (Cerdin *et al.*, 2014: 165). Motivation to migrate has an impact on a migrant's integration in the host country. Understanding the stories behind QIs' migration matters for the organization, since future job performance is at stake. Organizational integration policies such as support from the HRM department with residency and work permits or language training can have a positive impact on immigrants' motivation and integration. However, the efficacy of integration policies depends on the type of Qualified Immigrant. These policies have a greater impact on Felicitous and Desperate migrants than on Dream and Chance migrants (Cerdin *et al.*, 2014).

Low-Skilled Migrants

Low-skilled migrants may face specific obstacles in the process of integration. One of the major obstacles they face is the lack of 'language capital', i.e. speaking, reading and writing skills in the host language (see, for example, Chiswick, 1991). Natives generally have less favourable attitudes towards low-skilled migrants in comparison with qualified migrants, not for material self-interest reasons, but rather as a result of cultural and ideological factors (Hainmueller and Hiscox, 2010). Low-skilled migrants may face these negative attitudes toward them in their work environment. As a result, their integration, both inside and outside the organization may be more difficult than the integration of Qualified Immigrants. The level of skills may determine what integration policies could be implemented to help migrants to perform well in the organization.

Understanding the Meso-Organizational Level of Migration

Organizations play an important role in managing and benefiting from the talents of their migrant workforce. Foley and Kerr (2013) examined the impact of ethnic origin of scientists and engineering innovators on the international activity of the US companies that employ them.

Their work addressed three particular questions: (1) how far do such innovators enable multinational expansion into countries associated with their own ethnicity? (2) In what way do these innovators affect how the multinational's research and development (R&D) and patenting activities are distributed throughout the world? (3) Do multinationals that employ ethnic innovators have less need for joint venture partners in developing affiliates in countries associated with the ethnicity of these employees? Analyses were made of official data on innovators in conjunction with that on the operations of international affiliates of US multinationals. For the former, extensive data were consulted from the US Patent and Trademark Office on all patents granted in the period from 1975 to 2008, inferring the ethnicity of the innovators on the basis of their names by means of commercial databases of ethnic name origins. For the latter, data were drawn from the US Direct Investment Abroad surveys conducted by the Bureau of Economic Analysis (BEA) for the years 1982, 1989, 1994, 1999 and 2004, which cover details such as the measures of assets, sales, employment, and employment compensation, as well as where R&D takes place and structures of ownership for the affiliate in question. Results show that the percentage of US domestic patents awarded to Anglo-Saxon ethnic innovators in public companies significantly decreased, while the shares of Indian and Chinese ethnicities, for example, doubled and tripled, respectively. From the analyses, it is apparent that there is indeed a link between greater percentages of innovation on the part of company employees of a given ethnicity and greater activity on the part of their employer company in affiliates in countries related to that same ethnicity. This is naturally more so among multinationals that are initiating activities abroad and therefore have reason to value the knowledge and connections of ethnic innovators. The findings also indicate that these ethnic innovators are enabling a change in how and where innovation takes place, facilitating the conducting of R&D as well as the generation of patents in foreign countries, and allowing multinationals greater ownership of foreign affiliates thanks to the insights provided into foreign markets. US multinational firms are also, as suggested by the results, less and less dependent on the local joint venture partners for their affiliates abroad.

The 'reverse' phenomenon, the impact of the organization on migrants, is often negative. For example, Rodriguez and Mearns (2012) discuss issues, at the meso-organizational level, that influence migrants' employment. Such issues include: restrictions on migrants' physical mobility, poor work conditions and abuse by employers, and culture-related stereotypes leading sometimes to discrimination. The case of migrant nurses in the health sector is of interest here for its explanatory power. Newton *et al.* (2012) reviewed recent literature covering migration and experiences of transition of internationally educated nurses (IENs). The authors conducted a database search of CINAHL, Medline, Scopus and Web of Science, followed by a hand-search of certain prominent nursing journals, resulting in 21 articles – quantitative and qualitative sources. The searches admitted only articles published in English between January 2004 and June 2009. Findings showed that while a principal reason for migration is the expectation of improved income and/or career advancement, it seems such hopes are generally disappointed when it comes to the nurses' employment experiences. Some of the challenges which emerged include: (1) long, expensive and complex processes of migration, with little help provided by employers; (2) barriers of language and communication, both personal and professional, feeling an outsider, dissimilarity of nursing education and practice; (3) obtaining recognition of credentials such as licences and registration from the home country was difficult and it was hard to achieve them in the destination country; and (4) experience of discrimination, stereotyping, marginalization, limited support from peers or managers, skills and qualification unacknowledged/ rejected by patients and colleagues, unfair treatment – migrant nurses given most difficult assignments, unpleasant shifts; overlooked for promotion opportunities.

In sum, companies such as multinationals can play a key role in mobilizing their migrants' human resources to meet their business strategies and knowledge diffusion. Skilled migrants are a significant part of the global talent pool. They could be of huge value in operating abroad and they have the potential to improve a multinational's competitive advantage in foreign locations.

Understanding the Macro-Social Level of Migration

While individual migrants might be seen now to have greater agency in choosing where in the world to work, in reality, borders and restrictions on migration control international mobility, making it accessible to some individuals and not to others (Rodriguez and Mearns, 2012). One of the most important determinants of who/ when/how a migrant enters a country are migration policies. Migration policies are constituted by legislation and administrative rules that determine the way labour immigrants enter the country as well as their access to employment. These also regulate diversity actions practised in the organizations and sanctions against discrimination. Migration policies result from the interaction of political, management, financial, and administrative mechanisms that guide a host country (or a group of countries in the case of the European Union) government's actions in reaching goals that may be in the public interest or for other interests such as the government's welfare (Windsor, 2002).

The case of the European Union (EU) is useful to illustrate the complexity of migration at the macro-social level. The free movement of labour between member states is a fundamental feature of the EU. The immigration of non-EU nationals is by intergovernmental agreements in the hands of nation-states, with EU policies accepted only when these are compatible with national interests (Lettner, 1997). Therefore, the immigration flow within the EU cannot be readily constrained by nation-states, though they can use administrative devices to limit it somewhat, but they continue to have a legitimate choice in relation to extra-EU immigration. The nation-states often have contrasting visions of the utility of an international workforce, especially as unemployment rates of nationals in the EU vary greatly from one country to another.

Lettner (1997) explains that immigration policies that are developed by EU countries have two important dimensions. These are: first, geographic admission determining access to residence and work within the national territory, governed by asylum and policies of labour immigration; and, second, granting access to citizenship rights: civil, political, and social rights, governed by naturalization policies. Civil rights include freedom of movement and work, political rights include such matters as voting, and social rights refer here to eligibility for welfare state programmes such as public education, healthcare and family allowances, as well as unemployment and retirement benefits. The policies of naturalization in European countries restrict access to citizenship by imposing a list of conditions before a foreigner can become naturalized. Such a model of migration, based on the two dimensions discussed above, is expected to serve mostly the national interests of EU countries such as the economic well-being of existing citizens and the preservation of a national culture and identity (Bauböck and Faist, 2010).

Al Ariss (2009) explains that in the latter part of the 1980s, with the rise of anti-foreigner, right-wing extremism in Western European countries, most national governments tightened their migration policies for non-EU nationals. Thus, increased migration pressures from outside EU territory generated increased activity to coordinate their migration policies. This was facilitated by a compromise, namely that none of the EU member countries would be declared migration states. The decision-making power with respect to immigration matters remains imbalanced between the EU institutions and the governments of the EU countries. For example, historically, the European Parliament has been in favour of the eventual granting of equal rights for legally resident non-EU nationals, such as in terms of their movement and work in member states. However, the decision-making process remains primarily in the hands of public officials of member states, most of whom prefer migration policies that are restrictive. By analysing the making of migration policies in the

EU, Guiraudon (2003) concludes that the failure of EU countries to coordinate their policies of immigration and integration is expected to reinforce the emergence in the future of policies that are anti-immigrant and anti-EU unification. The declaration by the British Prime Minister in November 2014 that he would push the EU to restrict the entitlement to UK benefits of EU citizens from outside the UK may be seen as evidence of the accuracy of Guiraudon's analysis.

Differences in the rights accorded to legally resident non-EU nationals compared to EU nationals are manifest in EU immigration policies. For example, citizens of member states automatically become EU citizens as a sort of secondary citizenship. EU citizens also have the right to travel and live freely in the member states, as well as the right to vote and to become candidates in municipal and European Parliament elections in their country of residence. Such rights do not apply to non-EU citizens.

Relevance of This Typology to HRM Policies/Practices

A failure of much of the literature on international HRM has been that it has paid real attention to only a limited part of an MNE's human resources, sometimes just the assigned expatriates, sometimes both expatriates and local employees. A comprehensive definition of IHRM though would cover all the human resources of the organization around the world, though of course with special attention to expatriates. The attraction of this approach is that it is clear that organizational values are best spread through expatriation (Mäkelä and Brewster, 2009) and that expatriation also brings the organization benefits of developing a global mindset (Levy et al., 2007) amongst its employees. But the people on a company's expatriate roster are not the only people they have with international experience. Self-initiated expatriates (SIEs) are much cheaper for the organization and share many of the benefits of assigned expatriates for the organization (Andresen et al., 2012; Suutari and Brewster, 2000). So are bi-cultural employees (Furusawa and Brewster, 2015). And so are migrants.

To get best value out of the migrants though, an organization needs to know what kind of migrants they are dealing with, in what situation, and how best to manage them. The theoretical typology given here (Figure 13.2) indicates the type of migrants that will participate in the labour force. Clearly, managing 'Dream' migrants, who will generally be positive about their location and their employment, but may be less willing to share their understanding of their previous country, for example, will be different from managing Chance migrants, who may be ready to leave or Desperate migrants, who have limited commitment to the organization and the country. Different strategies will be appropriate for each.

In broad terms organizations that operate internationally would gain from utilizing all the internationally experienced employees within their staff. That includes not just expatriates but also others with knowledge of different environments, cultures and languages. To do that, organizations first need to monitor the international nature of their whole workforce and ensure that records are kept of international experience, language skills and cultural knowledge. Organizations should create an environment that welcomes diversity; should enable and encourage professional mentorships of migrants; should prepare co-workers and managers to positively receive and integrate them; should ensure that managers understand the recruitment and integration of those with international experience and knowledge; and should perceive and monitor the payback of assigning migrants to relevant positions within their area of expertise.

Specific HRM Practices for Migrants

Even though migrants may require specific HRM policies, those policies need to be fully integrated in the global HRM of the organizations. These HRM policies aim to help migrants overcome the barriers they face. As there is diversity among migrants, the first step for an organization would be to identify those barriers according to the type of expatriates in order to implement relevant HRM policies. These HRM policies aim at increasing efforts to adjust and finally to integrate in terms of life satisfaction, job satisfaction and career success (Cerdin *et al.*, 2014). In the end, the organizations have to make sure the migrants, like all employees, perform well.

As the theory of motivation to integrate (Cerdin *et al.*, 2014) suggests, the decision to migrate itself can be the source of some barriers. Thus, organizations should understand the motivations to migrate when managing migrants. The motivation to migrate is especially complex for skilled migrants. The impact of integration policies varies according to the type of skilled migrants (Cerdin *et al.*, 2014) and, therefore, these policies need to be appropriately tailored. For instance, support from the organization in the form of mentoring would work better for Dream and Felicitous immigrants while the impact would be smaller for Chance and Desperate immigrants (Cerdin *et al.*, 2014). In terms of career orientations, the adaptive and the resisting QIs would need more support for their career than the embracing Qis, for whom crafting a new career path may be easier (Zikic *et al.*, 2010).

Taking into account this diversity, the first step in designing an HRM policy for migrants is to clearly identify the type of migrants the organization is dealing with. This is not an easy task, as migrants could be reluctant to share their story with HRM staff and their manager. External consulting may facilitate this.

Organizations may want to assess the cultural intelligence of their managers who are dealing with migrants to help them develop their management skills towards individuals coming not only from a different culture but also from a different background. The story behind a migration might be distressing. Dealing with these stories, such as fleeing a war, could require specific skills from the management team.

Management training could be necessary for organizations recruiting migrants. Organizations that regularly recruit migrants may have a strong interest in investing in this type of training for their managers and HRM staff. This would facilitate migrants' recruitment and integration. Regarding their integration, migrants would also benefit from specific coaching and counselling, depending on their story related to their migration and the efforts they are ready to make once in their host country.

Management could be a challenge, particularly when migrants do not master the local language. Mastering the local language may be more challenging for unskilled migrants than skilled ones. Therefore, organizations should pay particular attention to this question so that they can alleviate the difficulties faced by migrants who do not master the host language, not only within the frontiers of the organization, but also in their daily life outside its walls. Technical skills may also be an issue. For skilled migrants, establishing the equivalence of academic degrees may be tricky, in particular in some strictly regulated professions such as law or medicine. Unskilled migrants by definition lack certain technical skills, which are not always easy to acquire, particularly when the mastering of the host language is an issue. This is why little training can be performed before the issue of language is resolved. Training could be done in the migrants' native language when resources are available or in the language of the host country when migrants have some command of the language, or an intermediate language (migrants may for example, be able to learn in English, even though they have not moved to the UK. The options of doing the training in their native language may be much more restricted).

Low-skilled migrants may be more sensitive than the skilled ones to the issues of compensation. Not all European countries have the same level of national minimum wage, if any is specified at all. In some countries, migrants may be attractive to employers, since they might be prepared to work for lower pay. In some cases, they may accept work doing jobs locals would turn down. Career issues would also be very different between skilled and unskilled migrants. Organizations could help skilled migrants to re-establish themselves in their earlier careers before migrating, or grow into a new career path in the host countries. For unskilled migrants, career management may not be a priority.

Clearly, HRM policies address migrants who enter the host country legally. When organizations recruit migrants before they migrate, they need to ensure the legality of the migration. Thus, managing migrants requires some administrative expertise. The level of administrative complexity depends on the countries involved in the migration process. The experience of the host country, specifically of the host organizations, will play an important role.

The administrative aspect of the migration may be complicated by a lack of stability in the migration policies of a country. For instance, in France the *circulaire Géant* in 2011 tightened the criteria for the issuance of residence permits to non-EU graduates. Some organizations, for instance in the IT sector, were unable to recruit skilled migrants to cope with labour shortage. Organizations may be constrained to recruit migrants from specific locations, narrowing their talent pool.

Conclusion

Bringing together two usually distinct scholarly fields, migration and international human resource management (IHRM), requires overcoming two main challenges. The first challenge concerns distinguishing the population that migration encompasses from other forms of international mobility. The distinction between assigned expatriates, self-initiated expatriates and migrants remains blurry. Individuals can move from one category to another one. Within the category of migrants, there is also a great diversity. This second challenge related to the diversity of migrants leads to implementation specific HRM policies in order to tailor the particular characteristics of each category. Even within one category such as skilled migrants, HRM policies also need to take into account a diverse population (see Table 13.5). Low-skilled migrants pose a significant challenge as they have been quite ignored in the management literature and could not be the priority of HRM policies. Yet, training could be a way to enhance these migrants' performance. Human resource management policies are crucial to make all types of migrants contribute to organizational performance.

Table 13.3 Type of migrants and HRM policies

Type of Migrants	HRM Policies
Migrants	Career management and (depending on the type of migrants):
• Dream	Training (culture and language) and administrative support (paper work) – moderate efficacy
• Chance	Training (culture and language), administrative support (paper work) – moderate efficacy – and retention policies
• Felicitous	Training (culture and language) and administrative support (paper work) – strong efficacy
• Desperate	Training (culture and language) and administrative support (paper work) – strong efficacy
Plus, for low-skilled migrants	Local language training focused on speaking, reading and writing skills Evaluation of the level of skills to define the most appropriate integration policies Career management not really an issue

Source: Cerdin *et al.* (2014)

Key Learning Points

- The academic distinctions between assigned expatriates, self-initiated expatriates and migrants are in reality blurry-edged and fluid. People move from one category to another.
- Migrants are a significant element of the international workforce with knowledge and skills that can aid the internationalization of the organization. Monitoring and record-keeping beyond the standard expatriate/local distinction would pay dividends. Migrants can be a cost-effective option for internationalization.
- Different kinds of migrants will have different motivations and will need different forms of management to be of most value to the organization. The four types of qualified migrants, Felicitous, Dream, Chance and Desperate migrants, with their particularities, need to be addressed by the HRM policies. In all cases, integration policies help migrants to integrate. However, in general, integration policies have a greater impact on Felicitous and Desperate migrants than on Dream and Chance migrants.

References

Al Ariss, A. (2009) *Careers of Skilled Immigrants: A Study of the Capital Accumulation and Deployment Experiences of the Lebanese in France*. PhD thesis.

Al Ariss, A. (2010) 'Modes of engagement: migration, self-initiated expatriation, and career development', *Career Development International*, 15(4), 338–358.

Al Ariss, A. and Crowley-Henry, M. (2013) 'Self-initiated expatriation and migration in the management literature: present theorizations and future research directions', *Career Development International*, 18(1), 78–96.

Al Ariss, A. and Syed, J. (2011) 'Capital mobilization of skilled migrants: a relational perspective', *British Journal of Management*, 22(2), 286–304.

Almeida, S., Fernando, M. and Sheridan, A. (2012) 'Revealing the screening: organisational factors influencing the recruitment of immigrant professionals', *The International Journal of Human Resource Management*, 23(9), 1950–1965.

Andresen, M., Al Ariss, A. and Walther, M. (2012) *Self-Initiated Expatriation: Mastering the Dynamics*. New York: Routledge.

Bauböck, R. and Faist, T. (2010) *Diaspora and Transnationalism: Concepts, Theories and Methods*. Amsterdam: Amsterdam University Press.

Bloch, A., Sigona, N. and Zetter, R. (2011) 'Migration routes and strategies of young undocumented migrants in England: a qualitative perspective', *Ethnic and Racial Studies*, 34(8), 1286–1302.

Castles, S., de Haas, H. and Miller, M.J. (2014) *The Age of Migration: International Population Movements in the Modern World*. Basingstoke: Palgrave Macmillan.

Cerdin, J.-L. and Selmer, J. (2014) 'Who is a self-initiated expatriate? Towards conceptual clarity of a common notion', *The International Journal of Human Resource Management*, 25(9), 1281–1301.

Cerdin, J.-L., Abdeljalil Diné, M. and Brewster, C. (2014) 'Qualified immigrants' success: exploring the motivation to migrate and to integrate', *Journal of International Business Studies*, 45(2), 151–168.

Chiswick, B.R. (1991) 'Speaking, reading, and earnings among low-skilled immigrants', *Journal of Labor Economics*, 9(2), 149–170.

Dench, S., Hurstfield, J., Hill, D. and Akroyd, K. (2006) *Employers Use of Migrant Labour: Main Report 04/06*. London.

Evans, M.D.R. and Kelley, J. (1991) 'Prejudice, discrimination, and the labor market: attainments of immigrants in Australia', *American Journal of Sociology*, 97, 721–759.

Foley, F. and Kerr, W.R. (2013) 'Ethnic innovation and US multinational firm activity', *Management Science*, 59(7), 1529–1544.

Furusawa, M. and Brewster, C. (2015) 'The bi-cultural option for international human resource management: the Japanese/Brazilian *Nikkeijin* example', *Journal of World Business*, 50(1), 133–143.

Guiraudon, V. (2003) 'The constitution of a European immigration policy domain: a political sociological approach', *Journal of European Public Policy*, 10(2), 263–282.

Hainmueller, J. and Hiscox, M.J. (2010) 'Attitudes toward highly skilled and low-skilled immigration: evidence from a survey experiment', *American Political Science Review*, 104(01), 61–84.

International Labour Organization (ILO) (2014) *Fair Migration: Setting an ILO Agenda. Report of the ILO Director General to the International Labour Conference*. Geneva, International Labour Office.

Lettner, H. (1997) 'Reconfiguring the spatiality of power: the construction of a supranational migration framework for the European Union', *Political Geography*, 16(2), 123–143.

Levy, O., Beechler, S., Taylor, S. and Boyacigiller, N.A. (2007) 'What we talk about when we talk about "global mindset": managerial cognition in multinational corporations', *Journal of International Business Studies*, 38, 231–258.

Mäkelä, K. and Brewster, C. (2009) 'Inter-unit interaction contexts, interpersonal social capital and the differing levels of knowledge sharing', *Human Resource Management*, 48(4), 591–613.

Mohyeldin, A. and Suliman, T. (2006) 'Human resource management in the United Arab Emirates', in P. Budhwar and K. Mellahi, *Managing Human Resources in the Middle East*. London: Routledge.

Mulholland, J. and Ryan, L. (2014) 'Doing the business: variegation, opportunity and intercultural experience among intra-EU highly-skilled migrants', *International Migration*, 52(3), 55–68.

Newton, S., Pillay, J. and Higginbottom, G. (2012) 'The migration and transitioning experiences of internationally educated nurses: a global perspective', *Journal of Nursing Management*, 20, 534–550.

Organization for Economic Co-operation and Development (OECD) (2003) *Glossary of Statistical Terms*. Available at: http://stats.oecd.org/glossary/detail. asp?ID=1284 (accessed 3 November 2015).

Organization for Economic Co-operation and Development (OECD) (2013) *OECD Factbook 2013. Economic, Environmental and Social Statistics*. Paris: OECD Publications.

Reichel, A., Erlen-Buch, C., Chudzikowski, K. and Mayrhofer, W. (2013) 'In and from the heart of Europe: global careers and Austria', in C. Reis and Y. Baruch (eds) *Careers Without Borders: Critical Perspectives*. New York: Routledge, pp. 55–77.

Rodriguez, J.K. and Mearns, L. (2012) 'Problematising the interplay between employment relations, migration and mobility', *Employee Relations*, 34(6), 580–593.

Sparrow, P.R. (2008) *International Recruitment, Skills Supply and Migration*. Sector Skills Development Agency (SSDA) Catalyst Report, Issue No. 4, 1–20.

Suutari, V. and Brewster, C. (2000) 'Making their own way: international experience through self-initiated assignments', *Journal of World Business*, 35(4), 417–436.

Thite, M., Srinivasan, V., Harvey, M. and Valk, R. (2009) 'Expatriates of host-country origin: "coming home to test the waters"', *International Journal of Human Resource Management*, 20(2), 269–285.

United Nations (1998) *Recommendations on Statistics of International Migration. Revision 1*. Statistical Papers. Series M, No. 58, Glossary. New York: United Nations.

United Nations (2013) *Population Facts*. Department of Economic and Social Affairs, Population Division September (2013/3). New York: United Nations.

Windsor, D. (2002) 'Public affairs, issues management, and political strategy: opportunities, obstacles, and caveats', *Journal of Public Affairs*, 1(4), 382–415.

Zikic, J., Bonache, J. and Cerdin, J.-L. (2010) 'Crossing national boundaries: a typology of qualified immigrants' career orientations', *Journal of Organizational Behavior*, 31(5), 667–686.

Part III

Micro-Views: Organizational Approaches and Individual (Re-)Actions in Europe

14 Micro-Views: Organizational Approaches and Individual (Re)Actions in Europe – Overview of Part III

CHRIS BREWSTER, MICHAEL DICKMANN AND
PAUL SPARROW

Having considered some of the latest thinking on micro- and mezzo-level issues in HRM in Europe, Part III of the book identifies and examines some of the HRM issues at organizational level that make Europe unique. There are, of course, a large number of other areas in which recent developments in research, since the first edition of this book, have considerably advanced the academic understanding of HRM. But we cannot cover all topics in HRM: our focus here is on issues that have some distinctly European focus, not only in practice, because arguably that would cover all aspects of HRM, but also in terms of the way that the topic is understood and judged. We have selected issues on which we think there is a European angle on what might be thought of as good HRM.

The easiest issue to choose was *employment relations*. Europe is the continent with, by a long way, the largest proportions of members in free trade unions in the world. For many people in Europe the right of people to choose freely to belong to trade unions and to enjoy the benefits of trade union activities is a key touchstone of democracy. In this widespread view, countries that refuse people the right to be trade union members, or put unreasonable barriers in their way when they want to join them and equally, countries where people have to be members of trade unions to benefit from certain rights, cannot meet the tests for being truly democratic. Hence the relevance of the careful examination of developments since 1995 offered by Richard Croucher in Chapter 15 to HRM in Europe. Noting the wide range of systems of employment relations and significant differences in union membership and paying particular attention to the way that the Central and Eastern European (CEE) countries have adapted their employment relations to the different options offered in Western Europe, he shows that whilst there has been a reduction in collective employee representation in Europe that has been adopted enthusiastically by employers in some of the CEE states, it remains a significant feature of the HRM landscape in Europe.

It is not so obvious that *recruitment and selection* in Europe differs from that elsewhere, but there are some distinguishing features, as indicated in Chapter 16 by Geoff Wood and Leslie Szamosi. They note in particular the costs of making wrong decisions (it is expensive to get the wrong employee out of the organization), the influences of the differing comparative capitalisms at play in Europe and the fact that small companies source their employees differently from medium-sized and large ones. They also point to the effects of the economic crisis that began in 2008 (see Chapters 1 and 7) and the substantial increase in zero-hours contracts, unpaid and lowly paid internships – employment that is 'only just' employment – and argue that the 'costs' of making wrong decisions may be reducing to a less developed country average.

The field of IHRM has developed enormously in recent years and the topic of *global careers* is now important for many employers in this continent. Europe is distinguished from other continents in that the members of 28 sovereign states have the unqualified right to live and work in all the other states and the EU offers programmes to encourage its citizens to move to another country. In Chapter 17, Michael Dickmann, Wolfgang Mayrhofer and Jean-Luc Cerdin define global careers as involving a move to another country for work and summarize the field, focusing on the issues and benefits from the perspective of both the careerists themselves and their employers.

The connected topic of *talent management in European MNCs* is taken up by Agnieszka Skuza, Hugh Scullion and David Collings in Chapter 18. The authors offer a general overview of the topic and then examine the European context for talent management. They note that Europe is, on many measures, the most internationalized continent and that it has numbers of characteristics that mark it out as different from other regions. On that basis they examine the empirical research that has been conducted on talent management in Europe. The key features are a growing use of psychological contracts as an analytical lens, the attention to context, including different cultural approaches and the effects of different strategies on different outcomes. They argue that the European research has brought the context and the individual into sharper focus in talent management research.

Our Chapter 19, on *pay for performance in Europe*, by Ihar Sahakiants, Marion Festing and Stephen Perkins, takes a wide view of the topic as encompassing almost all contingent pay systems. They argue that the banking crisis that began in 2008 has raised the profile of the topic to the point where the EU is creating Directives limiting bankers' bonuses. They show the extensive use of such schemes in the CEE countries. They draw upon Mayrhofer *et al.* (2011), to argue that this may be one area where there are signs of convergence of practice and agree with Vaiman and Brewster (2014), that we should be wary of assigning these variations to cultural differences and explore the institutional differences between European countries. They conclude that the difference in practice between European states is likely to diminish, but slowly.

Financial participation in Europe is an associated theme, explored by three of the world's leading experts: Erik Poutsma, Eric Kaarsemaker and Paul Ligthart in Chapter 20. They note that financial participation is a controversial topic, with different parties in different locations, but also point to its spread throughout the developed world. They discuss both employee share option schemes and profit sharing, examining the rationales for their adoption and their impact. They examine the role of MNCs in the spread of schemes and provide evidence of the incidence of such schemes in both their narrow-based (managerial only) and broader-based (all employees) manifestations. Noting the importance of national context, they provide pen-pictures of the state of pay in a number of key countries and draw conclusions for HRM.

Finally, we examine a topic that has been gathering a lot of attention recently: *flexible working in Europe*. Europe has arguably been one of the regions of the world that has developed the most constraints on managerial autonomy and has thus worked the hardest to find new ways of being flexible. In Chapter 21, Clare Kelliher reviews the different types of flexible working that are available. Clare points to the different reasons for flexible working, including industry differences and the different implications it has for both employers and employees. She notes the spread of flexible working and the different forms adopted for preference in the different countries and in this instance, the fact that the CEE countries seem to prefer more traditional ways of working.

References

Mayrhofer, W., Brewster, C., Morley, M. and Ledolter, J. (2011) 'Hearing a different drummer? Evidence of convergence in European HRM', *Human Resource Management Review*, 21(1), 50–67.

Vaiman, V. and Brewster, C. (2014) 'How far do cultural differences explain the differences between nations? Implications for HRM', *International Journal of Human Resource Management*, 26(2), 151–164.

15 Employment Relations in Europe

RICHARD CROUCHER

Introduction

In this chapter, we take as our starting point Chris Brewster's argument, first made in 1995, that Europe presented a very different institutional environment for HRM from the USA and ask how far it holds good two decades later. Brewster's argument was that HRM would necessarily take a different form in Europe because the institutional environment was very different from that in the USA, where the HRM approach originated. Managers were not as free to develop and apply HRM in Europe because they had less space to do so. Norms, laws and institutions of collective employee voice (mainly trade unions and works councils) meshed together to constrain managers, but also provided them with distinctive opportunities to shape relations with employees.

We conceptualize collective 'employment relations' in a way that is compatible with his argument. The term implies above all a (power) relationship and we define it here as the joint regulation of employment between management and employee representative bodies. Even the strongest jointly regulated national systems of employment relations in Europe are best seen as a set of options for managers and employees to negotiate the employment relationship's terms. These options are taken in webs of interlocking legal, institutional and normative circumstances. Managers may prefer options that allow them more freedom to take decisions and they and their companies have sought greater autonomy, but choosing these can also incur costs arising from employee opposition or de-motivation if the latter find them unacceptable. If the costs appear to be too high, managers are likely to avoid them.

'Employee representative bodies' essentially means trade unions (one term for a very wide range of representative bodies) representing their members and works councils who represent all employees (again, in very different ways in different workplaces). Throughout, we are concerned with the question of how far managerial prerogative, that is the capacity of managers to decide matters unilaterally and without any element of joint regulation, has increased since 1995. The extent of joint regulation in Europe appeared rather surprising to some American commentators in the 1990s. In 1990, German co-determination seemed to a US-based researcher to be a 'highly-evolved instrument of industrial democracy' (Havlovic, 1990), an assessment that might have seemed rather over-optimistic to some of those directly involved in it even at the time and probably more so today.

When Brewster referred to 'Europe', he meant the European Union, which then essentially comprised the countries of Western and Northern Europe. In 1995, the 'post-Soviet' countries had only just begun their economic 'transition'. Moreover, trade links between Western and East European countries were much less well developed than they are today (Russian Federal Statistics Service, 2013). Despite recent assertions that a 'new Cold War' has begun, and without denying the great importance of recent developments in the Ukraine, these economic links are now much more developed than in 1995. For instance, in 1995 it was hard to imagine the domination of the Russian food and drinks market by foreign companies (Russian Federal Statistics Service, 2013).

We define Europe geographically and we therefore pay some attention to employment relations in three types of country. The first is those countries in the 'old' (pre-1995) European Union: the industrialized countries of Western Europe. The second is the new EU accession countries that joined the EU after 1995. The third is often excluded from discussion of 'Europe': the huge area between the edge of the EU and the Urals: Belarus, Russia, Ukraine and Moldova, which we designate the BRUM countries. These are important for understanding employment relations throughout Europe west of the Urals. They developed links with Western industry even in Soviet times and in recent years West European investments in Russia have grown still further (Russian Federation Statistical Service, 2013). There are many industrial links spanning a wide range of industries and countries. Western car companies use Russian manufacturing facilities and the food industry in Russia is dominated by Western MNCs (Mihalev, 2012; Nestlé, 2014). The cases of Ukraine and Moldova are rather different; in clothing (Moldova) and manufacturing (Ukraine), local companies supply finished and part-finished goods to Italian and German firms respectively, while several other local industries also have strong links to the West

(Ukrstat, 2014; Ursu, 2013). In the ex-Soviet manufacturing heartland of Belarus, Austrian companies have also made direct investments but here too the Netherlands, the UK and Germany are significant direct investors (Belstat, 2013; Manenok, 2014). Thus, this huge area is directly linked to the EU's industrial centres both through considerable foreign direct investment (FDI) and by organic manufacturing ties. It provides the institutionally distinctive and much less employee-friendly model of employment relations that has become well known to many West European companies since 1990. Productivity in these countries is similar to that in Eastern Europe, but earnings are far lower (Piketty, 2014). Many millions of migrants from BRUM countries work in the West and carry with them distinctive norms concerning the employment relationship, heightening Westerners' awareness of huge disparities in earnings and employment norms.

The chapter is structured as follows. We begin with a sketch of the situation in 1995, and proceed by examining the evolution of national-level institutions across subsequent decades. Next, we examine collective bargaining and social pacts at national level, following this with an assessment of the evolution of European-level institutions. Finally, we briefly make a broad estimate of what all of this means for employment relations and especially management prerogative at workplace level.

European Employment Relations in 1995

In 1995, systems of collective employee representation were legally embedded at international (EU), national, regional and company levels. The main institutions were trade unions which in many West European countries were and are involved in multi-employer negotiations about pay and terms and conditions more widely. These often worked in tandem with works councils: workplace-based bodies with rights to receive information, consult with management and 'co-determine' certain issues (meaning that management must have works councillors' agreement before making changes). These organizations continue to operate, but generally speaking not in quite the same ways as in 1995 (Arrowsmith and Pulignano, 2013).

In its 'ideal type', European employment relations took the following form. At the EU level, trade unions (or 'social partners') played a role in the European Union's structures, where they could at least theoretically exert some political influence. At national level, similar arrangements also existed and these extended to some important areas of joint regulation such as training in Germany. Collective bargaining on pay and conditions was conducted in large companies and the public sector at either industry or company level. Within companies, employee representatives were elected to supervisory boards and works councils exercising their co-determination rights.

However, in Europe as defined geographically, this was only one of two systems. In 'post-Socialist' Europe, in the countries soon to join the European Union as 'accession countries' and also in the BRUM nations, very different systems existed. In all of these countries, the employment relations situation was strongly marked by the Communist legacy. The legal frameworks remained essentially those of Soviet times, with strong labour codes which were only weakly observed, while trade union structures and practices remained essentially unchanged. Privatization had made limited progress, works councils did not exist and the majority 'official' (government-approved) unions were enterprise-level bodies with welfare and workforce-disciplining rather than bargaining functions. A small group of 'independent' unions had begun to emerge in some countries, but these remained an embattled minority restricted to a few industries and with limited influence throughout our period. Through their national-level federations the official unions were involved in tripartite arrangements dubbed in Russia 'social partnership'. These arrangements were typical of Eastern Europe, where elites used tripartism to ease the transition. It was a form according to David Ost (2000) of 'illusory corporatism' which integrated labour in the seismic changes then occurring in industry and society without giving any substantial benefits to labour. 'Illusory corporatism' was marked by token negotiation, non-binding agreements and exclusion of the private sector.

Under Post- 'Socialist' regimes, managerial prerogative, subject not only to state but also to considerable informal worker challenge in large workplaces, was beginning to increase as systemic change and massive industrial disruption destroyed the bases of worker power (Morrison *et al.*, 2012). In the countries of Eastern Europe that were soon to join the EU, links developed with the EU unions through intensive training programmes, which meant that although still marked by their history they gradually became broadly similar to their EU counterparts (Croucher and Rizov, 2012). This was far from the case in the BRUM countries, where unions remained locked into their previous ossified structures and modes of operation.

Thus, throughout the countries of Eastern Europe, a very different version of the 'European model' existed in 1995; the unions' institutional form was broadly similar to that in Western Europe but the content of their activities and the consequences of these for managers were quite different. In Eastern countries, unions were structurally unable to exercise any significant representative function. Limited and fragmented but disruptive industrial actions from below occurred outside of the official union structures. Since that point, the 'accession' countries have entered the EU but the BRUM countries have not, while Russian foreign policy has become increasingly antagonistic towards it.

Even in Western Europe, employee representative bodies have become weaker since 1995, reflecting many employees' position in relation to employers caused by extensive industrial re-structuring, changing legal frameworks, increasingly 'flexible' labour markets, seismic shifts in the nature of employment itself and the financial crisis (Arrowsmith and Pulignano, 2013).

National Laws and Institutions

National law, together with the norms and values that it embodies and reflects, continues to constitute the main framework governing collective relations between employers and employees throughout Europe. An international index of the strength of nations' employment laws and employees' normative protection shows that European countries continued to vary greatly in the degree to which they restrict managerial prerogative ten years after Brewster published his argument. Botero *et al.* (2004) also showed that European countries then had relatively high legal employee protection scores in world terms. Botero *et al.*'s index, derived from a large sample of countries worldwide, ranked employee protection from 0 (non-existent) to 1 (extremely high). The global median is 0.4613. Most European countries score above that. For example: Germany = 0.6071; Spain = 0.5863; Poland = 0.5655; Ukraine = 0.5774; and Norway = 0.6488. The high degree of de-regulation in the UK since the 1980s is shown by a rating of 0.1875, which is lower than the USA at 0.2589. Despite an extension of trade union recognition rights in 1999, the general trend in the UK was towards a 'bonfire' of liberties, including collective labour rights under New Labour (Ewing, 2010). With this exception, Europe's countries, geographically defined, did indeed have stronger collective employment laws than most other nations in 2003. Changes to these laws and their observation have only proceeded slowly in most countries. How they are observed is, of course, a separate issue.

In the BRUM countries, rhetorical commitment to 'social partnership' by the political and industrial elites sits uneasily with the harsh reality of employment relations, part of a picture causing many Moldovan and Ukrainian workers to migrate not only to the EU but also to

Russia (Morrison, Sacchetto and Cretu, 2013). Labour law in all these countries has been significantly revised since 1995 in ways that erode employee rights; the revised Russian Labour Code, which came into force in 2002, is typical of the BRUM countries. The revised code essentially shifts employment law on to an individual basis and greatly reduces all collective organizations' legal functions (Rymkevitch, 2003). One expert in the area describes Russian employment law as 'totally disregarded' in practice (Rymkevitch, 2003).

Unions themselves have been shown to play a significant role in ensuring that employment law is enforced (Harcourt *et al.*, 2004). Union density is also related to union influence on management defined more widely than simply enforcing employment law (Vernon, 2006). European legal frameworks continue to support quite high density figures for many European countries when compared to the USA, where density is around 8 per cent. Union density figures vary greatly, from 74 per cent of employees in Finland, 70 per cent in Sweden and 67 per cent in Denmark, to 10 per cent in Estonia and Lithuania. The average level of union membership across the entire European Union, weighted by the numbers employed in the different member states, is 23 per cent. The average is reduced by relatively low levels of membership in some larger EU countries: Spain at 19 per cent, Germany at 18 per cent, Poland with 12 per cent and France with 9 per cent. Membership in most countries is particularly strong in the public sector. In the private sector, membership is highest in larger companies. However, union membership is not the only relevant indicator of strength, and French unions often show their ability to mobilize workers in large-scale strikes and demonstrations.

If levels of union membership are generally high in global terms but also very varied within Europe, the direction in which they have moved since the mid-1990s is relatively uniform. Only six states – Belgium, Cyprus, Italy, Luxembourg, Malta and Norway – have experienced gains in employed union membership in recent years. However, in most states, with the apparent exception of Italy, the increases have not kept pace with the overall growth in employment, meaning that even in these countries union density has drifted downwards. Membership losses have been most marked in the states of Central and Eastern Europe, where industrial restructuring and a fundamental change in unions' roles have had major impacts. However, there are also signs of membership stabilizing in some of the countries as unions have responded by organizing drives (all statistics from European Foundation for the Improvement of Living and Working Conditions, 2013). Simultaneously, by 1999, coverage of collectively bargained agreements had sunk to just 15 per cent of enterprises, even if these were by far the largest and most economically significant enterprises.

The result of this latter trend, which accelerated after the Hartz labour market reforms, was that Germany moved from having one of the smallest wage dispersions in Europe in the mid-1990s to having one of the largest a decade later (Antonczyk *et al.*, 2010).

Co-determination systems, within which employee representatives have the legal right to receive information, be consulted and 'co-determine' (or jointly regulate) certain issues with management, have also become rather weaker since 1995. In Germany, the heartland of co-determination, the system has become focused on larger companies. Works councils must be requested by five or more employees, and employees in smaller companies have become increasingly reluctant to make requests. A large 'co-determination free zone' has therefore emerged, centred on smaller companies and those based in the East. Hence, since union membership fell simultaneously, the two main pillars of the German system (trade unionism outside of the workplace and co-determination within it) were being eroded (Hassel, 1999). These developments were typical of the situation in Western Europe more broadly (Arrowsmith and Pulignano, 2013).

Across Europe, trade unions made differential attempts to develop their internal organization, increase their membership and improve their members' living standards across the period, but these efforts have been very variable and strongly marked by their history (Gumbrell-McCormick and Hyman, 2013). In some cases, West European unions simply relied on the institutional framework and took relatively passive approaches to declining membership. Others worked hard to recruit new groups of workers, such as those in precarious employment. The wider difficulties of adapting union organizations with strong cultures became evident across the two decades. German unions, for example, were slow to adopt an 'organizing' approach. The historically powerful German engineering union IG Metall took some time to overcome their earlier stance that they would not give 'legitimacy' to certain types of worker by trying to recruit them (Gumbrell-McCormick and Hyman, 2013). These difficulties of organizational adaptation led to the emergence of alternative institutions such as unofficial 'grassroots' representative employee networks to defend interests even in unionized German firms such as Siemens (Croucher, Martens and Singe, 2007). In short, European unions – and especially those supported by relatively strong legal and institutional frameworks – are organizations whose structures, orientations and cultures have frequently proved difficult to shift in response to external conditions.

It is not only trade unions that have had to change to adapt to new environments, including employers' demands for increased autonomy. So, too, have employers' associations, but Traxler (1995) argued that they have made more consistent efforts to adapt to external conditions. Employers' associations are an integral part of systems that impose certain disciplines on firms by, for example, being responsible together with unions for upholding collective agreements where wage bargaining occurs across industries. They often, therefore, appear to employers to be part of a union support ecosystem. Nevertheless, employers' associations offer important advantages to some companies in ensuring strong employer–employer links, the capacity to pressure government, training and advice services and so on. One important cause of the decline in industry-wide collective bargaining coverage in Germany has therefore been the growth of employer association membership 'ohne Tarif', in other words, without the need to adhere to the industry-wide bargain. In this way, employers' associations have been able to stabilize their membership levels, while re-shaping collective bargaining as a more single-company based activity (Helfen, 2011).

The extension of industry-wide bargaining has long been a demand of unions in the accession countries, but this has made little or no progress and this is one reason why Employer's Associations remain weak in that part of Europe. Employers' associations in BRUM countries have always been weak, reflecting their minimal employment relations roles. All of the 'post-Socialist' countries lack solid legal bases for such associations and, where they exist, they lack the capacity to engage in sectoral dialogue (Muller, 2005).

Overall, we can conclude that trade unions, works councils and employers' associations have all had either diminished or at least different roles since 1995. The interlocking institutional systems that historically constrained managers in 1995 have become somewhat looser, especially in the case of smaller companies (Silvia and Schroeder, 2007). Larger companies remain relatively well-integrated into these arrangements although the systems themselves have also become more flexible, adaptable to individual company circumstances and susceptible to modification in the direction of managerial prerogative.

National-Level Collective Bargaining and Social Pacts

Both national legal provisions on the status of collective agreements and the institutions of collective employee voice may act to limit managerial prerogative in the key area of employee reward. Countries fall into two main categories in this respect. The first is those where industrial-level bargaining on wages and benefits is the norm; this important group includes Germany, the Netherlands, Belgium, Ireland, Slovakia and Slovenia. The second smaller group includes the UK, France,

Poland, the Czech Republic and Romania. Here, wage bargaining is predominantly decentralized to company level. In the EU accession countries of Eastern Europe and the BRUM nations, company-level bargaining predominates. Thus, bargaining and, arguably, trade unionism in Western Europe are both moving broadly in the BRUM direction. The general trend, even where industry-level bargaining is widespread, has been towards allowing flexibility to companies within the industrial bargain, for example through 'opening clauses' in industry agreements which allow works councils to modify them. Since the financial crisis, there has also been a marked trend towards diminishing legal support for industry bargaining, especially in the states of Southern Europe (Clauwaert and Schömann, 2012).

Social pacts and tripartite structures have played a considerable role in national employment policy and wage setting in several EU countries since the mid-1990s, outside of the liberal market economy of Britain where tripartism no longer exists. In Germany, corporatist relations between trade unions and employers' associations at national level have played a major role in two respects since the mid-1990s. First, the Hartz labour market reforms pushed through under Schröder stimulated the creation of a large number of 'mini-jobs' with reduced hours and often low pay; the growth of such jobs has recently led to the decision to create a national minimum wage, previously thought unnecessary because of the strength of industry bargaining. Second, in the sizeable (in employment terms) part of the economy by employment where collective bargaining remains important and large exporting companies operate, wages have been kept under firm control through tripartite integration of the unions into governmental perspectives. This has ensured that German products remain competitive on cost as well as quality grounds. Broadly similar pacts operated in several other European countries including Ireland, contributing to the success of the Irish economy prior to the financial crisis. In both Germany and Ireland, albeit for very different reasons, real earnings have diminished in recent years, generating a sentiment that collective bargaining has been ineffective in defending workers. In Southern Europe, a similar trend accelerated dramatically with the financial crisis. In these countries, the state has played an increasingly interventionist role in employment relations. This has tended to undermine and even usurp trade unions' independent roles as bargaining agents and, consequently, remove their capacity to defend living standards from serious damage. This has hit union membership (Molina, 2014).

In Russia, tripartite 'social partnership' arrangements have existed since early in the economic and political 'transition' and constitute a coercive form of corporatism which has served to marginalize unions' bargaining roles since unions survive as government- and company-sponsored institutions and state sponsorship may be a condition for their survival. 'Social partnership' has buttressed the position of the largely Soviet-style trade unionism of the 'official' trade unions in the main union federation, the FNPR, at the expense of the 'independent' unions at enterprise as well as at national level. The Global Union Federations devoted considerable resources between 1995 and 2005 to attempting to reform the official unions in the BRUM countries, trying to transform them into genuine bargaining organizations. Although they had some limited success (Croucher, 2004) these unions currently remain largely locked into 'social partnership' mode. The influence of unions on management in the Eastern European EU accession countries has been shown to be real if small (Croucher and Rizov, 2012); that in the BRUM countries is, overall, still smaller although not entirely absent (Croucher and Rizov, 2011; Morrison et al., 2012). Limited unofficial conflict has emerged through strikes and employee networks in the West European car companies located in St Petersburg, but generally Western managements have been able to use plants located in BRUM countries as part of a 'coercive comparison' strategy with which to control their Western unions (Bernaciak, 2010). The more optimistic accounts of East European unions' relations within European MNEs focus on accession countries where EU membership encourages unions to see themselves as part of an EU-wide union movement (Lee and Trappmann, 2014).

The European Level: Institutionalizing 'Social Dialogue'?

Although the content of trade unionism in the EU is more positive for workers than in the BRUM countries, the results of 'social dialogue' within the EU are only slightly more tangible than those of its equivalent in Russia. The EU is a distinctive regional organization. In contrast to the North American Free Trade Area (NAFTA), it embodies an aspiration towards political union and a distinctive vision of good quality employment and 'social dialogue' (on NAFTA's labour clause and its consequences, drawing a comparison with Europe see Ozarow, 2013). The EU has itself been concerned to develop European-level institutions involving the 'social partners' as one way of developing a transnational European identity; in this section we examine the very restricted effects of these efforts on managerial prerogative since 1995.

Importantly, the EU has in practice no capacity to legislate on fundamental trade union rights, which is a matter for the national level. Its employment initiatives have sought to develop the internal market and to ensure its efficiency. The EU has issued numerous directives relevant to employment relations since the Maastricht Treaty, which introduced the European Monetary Union. These directives, which were linked to the accession of the states of Central and Eastern Europe who were felt to lack many aspects of the West European model, occurred between 1993 and 2004 and there have been relatively few such measures since their accession. The directives covered working time (1993 and 2003), European works councils (1994), European companies (2001), non-discrimination (2001), national-level information and consultation of employee representatives (2002), European co-operatives (2002), gender equality (2004) and the movement of workers (2004). All of these measures were then transposed into national law. The transposition process was very uneven between countries and the original directives were applied in very different ways. This gave rise to what Falkner and Treib (2008) called a 'world of dead letters', characterized by comparatively poor transposition processes. That 'world' included the new member states of Central and Eastern Europe, but also encompassed at least two countries from among some more established EU members, viz Ireland and Italy. Thus, pseudo-compliance was modelled by the new entrant states but some other countries acted in similar ways (Falkner and Treib, 2008). The resultant national legislation impacted the institutional framework and even changed and informed management practice, but only to a very limited extent. To take just one important area: the impact of the information and consultation directive requiring companies to have mechanisms for informing and consulting employees: the main British authority on the law estimated that it had only marginal results at company level (Hall *et al.*, 2013).

Perhaps the most important EU initiative in an institutional sense was the European Works Councils (EWC) Directive. This encouraged sizeable companies employing workers in different European countries to establish information and consultation bodies for elected employee representatives (Hall *et al.*, 2013). In effect it attempted to transpose a weak (because it contained no element of joint regulation or 'co-determination') form of German consultation law to the European level. Thus, the German unions emphasized that it gave employee representatives no legal powers to put pressure on management. A considerable group of companies based in the UK and the USA have not established EWCs at all, but where they have there is evidence that under certain circumstances, including pre-existing solid industrial relations and cohesive worker representation, they have had some impact on management decision-making (Marginson *et al.*, 2004). However, while a minority of EWCs work well, experts estimate that a majority are less effective (Hall *et al.*, 2013). One reason for this has been the relatively weak integration of employee representatives from

Eastern Europe and especially of those from outside the EU (Stirling and Tully, 2004). Meardi (2004) argues that employee representatives from the accession countries tend to 'short circuit' the EWC's co-ordinating function by using the opportunity to access Western headquarters management directly.

EU action in employment relations also encouraged dialogue between the 'social partners' (trade unions and employers associations) to conduct 'sectoral social dialogue'. Léonard (2008) correctly points out that this is a top-down institution where institutionalization has preceded action. Consequently, it has only limited scope to impact employment relations at workplace level. She argues that it calls the EU's capacity to assist in the creation of a viable EU system of employment relations into question. Prosser (2006) further shows that uneven and limited implementation of 'sectoral dialogue' decisions mean that despite attempts to intensify it, the effects on managerial prerogative have been negligble since the dialogue creates consensus decisions that may be effectively ignored by managers. Rather, strong national unions remain the drivers of international union co-ordination (Schroeder and Weinert, 2004).

According to one influential account, unions are helping to develop a European industrial/political space and to address the EU's democratic deficit by influencing industrial policy (Erne, 2008). This 'Euro-democratization' thesis rests however on an analysis of one case – Alsthom – albeit one of considerable European significance. It appears to show that there is some scope within the EU for unions, where they are exceptionally well co-ordinated, to influence industrial policy at European level. In the case of Alsthom, this had considerable impact on management industrial strategy through intervention at European level.

There has also been the gradual and uneven creation of an area that was relatively weakly developed when Brewster wrote in the mid-1990s. Developments in co-ordinated collective bargaining in historically well-organized industries such as metalworking, and in consultation through European works councils between unions and employers' associations has been an element in developing (West) European employment relations since 1995 (Arrowsmith and Marginson, 2006; Edwards *et al.*, 2006; Léonard, 2008). Overall, while there have been significant developments at this level, they are fragmented and partial, heavily impacted by the financial crisis and have had little effect on managerial prerogative even in Western Europe (Glassner and Pusch, 2013).

In the BRUM countries, tensions have played out between EU and post-Soviet norms of trade unionism and labour management. Up until the Global Union Federations' abandonment of their attempts to reform unions in Belarus following Lukashenko's election as

President, prospects for a more representative and bargaining-oriented trade unionism throughout the region appeared reasonably good (Croucher, 2004). From that point onwards, they diminished almost to vanishing point. Belarus looked increasingly to Russian and Chinese investment and political models, while Putin tightened his political grip in Russia via a xenophobic nationalism that alienated many migrant workers from Moldova and Central Asia (Morrison *et al.*, 2013). In 2014, Russia extended its influence into Ukraine's East, the home of its heavy industry and much of its trade unionism. In Belarus, trade unions became a constraint on managements because they adopted a surveillance role for the state and not because they represented workers (Danilovich and Croucher, 2011). Thus, the prospects of union reform in the region diminished dramatically. So, too, did the political possibilities of EU-based unions making positive links to their colleagues in the BRUM countries with a view to making collective cause in relation to multi-national enterprises (MNEs).

Employment Relations at Workplace Level

We now attempt a necessarily very broad and brief estimate of continuity and change in European employment relations in workplaces and how they have affected managerial prerogative since 1995. At a very general level, employment relations remain distinctive in comparison with those in the USA (see Appendix 15.1). HR managers in large companies in continental Western Europe still deal with employee representatives from day-to-day, settling a wide range of relatively small-scale issues which works councillors are legally entitled to raise. Managers in these countries also continue to make pragmatic use of trade unions and works councils as communications channels to workforces, since unionized workforces tend to remain more sceptical of management information than their non-unionized equivalents. At the same time, and especially in the UK and Ireland, there has also been growth in employer-driven 'employee voice' mechanisms, such as 'company councils', as managers attempt to get the benefits of employee voice without allowing the reduction of their prerogative (Gollan and Perkins, 2009). In the EU 'accession countries', union representatives have some influence on managers, especially in older, state-controlled industrial companies where workers feel relatively secure (Croucher and Rizov, 2012). In the BRUM countries, managers continue to enjoy much greater and almost unrestricted power in relation both to employees and trade unions. This is reflected in the formal legally mandated collective agreements that specify employees' terms and conditions; few are genuinely negotiated. This level of managerial power also probably underlies the declining willingness of Russian employees to make extra discretionary effort since the mid-1990s (Croucher and Rizov, 2011). Managers in the Ukraine tend to make exclusive use of the Soviet legacy and legally-recognized general meeting of employees ('the assembly of the working collective') for communicating with workers, in preference to using often ossified union structures (Croucher, 2010). Throughout Europe, the consequences of the ongoing financial crisis have clearly been very material, especially in workplaces in the Mediterranean countries most severely affected, but as yet very little systematic research has appeared on that subject (for a partial exception see Molina, 2014).

Changes at workplace level have generally been gradual, but in some cases they have been dramatic and have increased managerial prerogative. If we briefly examine the situation at Chemnitz Union's machine tool factory in Eastern Germany, we may effectively illustrate our point. The factory, Germany's oldest machine tool manufacturer, currently employs several hundred skilled engineering workers and sells its products in Russia, Germany and the developing world; under Communism it employed thousands. Since then, the workforce experienced closure threats, mass job losses and five changes of ownership. At one time –brought back from the threat of total closure by formation of a workers' co-operative at a manager's initiative – it was recently taken over by the German company Herkules, whose chief executive points to low labour costs as a source of competitive advantage (Wagstyl, 2014). Although many of the skilled workers remain union members, the workplace has been through huge change that has disrupted work groups, union organization and the works council. Workers compare their situation not only with their Western counterparts but also with that of their many ex-colleagues and with the workers in Russia and Eastern Europe with whom they are often in contact through their work (Wagstyl, 2014).

Conclusion

The gradual erosion of the collective institutions that shaped managerial choices in the second half of the twentieth century has widened managerial prerogative at workplace level since 1995, albeit in uneven ways. Nevertheless, the content and processes of employment relations in many large West European companies in 2015 would be broadly recognizable to the practitioners of two decades previously.

Indeed, it was already being argued in 1995 that a process of 'organized decentralization', whereby states ensured that decentralized company-level bargaining proceeded in an orchestrated fashion, was underway. This increased managements' scope for action, while leaving systemic features otherwise intact (Traxler, 1995). One recent analysis of collective bargaining in densely unionized Denmark provides a good example of this in practice. Ilsøe (2012) found that bargaining at enterprise level was indeed essentially intact. She also speculated that the future might bring change because of the difficulties posed in smaller companies where managers and employees alike had less involvement than in their larger counterparts. However, others have offered quite different and in a sense contrary prognoses. Haipeter (2011) argues that the changes in the German system are not simply signs of erosion but on closer examination actually offer new bargaining possibilities for both unions and employers associations, albeit in novel directions. The contrast between the two viewpoints illustrates both the unevenness of the current situation and the acute difficulty involved in forecasting future developments.

The pressures are evident, but we have drawn attention to one that is often ignored. We have argued that there is not one model of employment relations in Europe but at least two; the BRUM countries represent a completely different and much less employee-friendly model on the EU's borders. The BRUM model is well known to many West European companies, especially those in industries such as clothing, the automotive industries and food, where much manufacturing is conducted in BRUM countries. This constitutes an additional pressure on the (EU) 'European' model.

Nevertheless, the demise of the European system analysed by Brewster in 1995 has not occurred despite real pressures upon it and the minimal efforts made by the EU to defend it. There is a considerable degree of national 'path dependence' in institutional employment relations in the countries of Europe. Perhaps the last word should be given to the American researchers Crossland and Hambrick (2011), who recently argued that managers of US-based firms still have more latitude than their counterparts in many European countries (see Appendix 15.1 for a summary of the continued differences between the USA and those of continental Europe).

Key Learning Points

- Brewster's argument in 1995 that Europe requires a different approach to HRM from the approaches used in the USA continues to have force because the institutional framework in Europe remains distinctive twenty years later.

- The power of union and works council representatives to influence management decisions affecting employees has nevertheless diminished since 1995. Managers in large companies make pragmatic use of employee representation for communications purposes.
- The coverage of collective bargaining and co-determination within the EU has diminished.
- The effects of EU law-making have played a real but minor role in maintaining the strength of European worker representation; strong national unions have led European inter-union co-ordination.
- There is not one 'European model' but at least two. An Eastern model based in the countries of Belarus, Russia, Ukraine and Moldova has only changed in minor ways since 1995. Only some of the unions in these countries have moved significantly towards representation and bargaining. Employment relations in these countries constitute an alternative, less employee-friendly model that is well known to some Western companies.
- The financial crisis is clearly affecting employee representation negatively, but it is hard to specify the effects in detail yet.

References

Antonczyk, D., De Leire, T. and Fitzenberger, B. (2010) *Polarization and rising wage inequality: comparing the US and Germany*. ZEW Berlin Discussion Paper 10-015.

Arrowsmith, J. and Marginson, P. (2006) 'The European cross-border dimension to collective bargaining in multi-national companies', *European Journal of Industrial Relations*, 12(3), 245–266.

Arrowsmith, J. and Pulignano, V. (2013) *The transformation of employment relations in Europe*. London: Routledge.

Belstat (2013) *Investments and construction: a statistical yearbook*. Minsk: Belarusian State Statistical Committee (pdf). Available at: http://belstat.gov.by/homep/ru/publications/archive/2013.php (accessed 31 March 2014).

Bernaciak, M. (2010) 'Cross-border cooperation and trade union responses in the enlarged EU: evidence from the auto industry in Germany and Poland', *European Journal of Industrial Relations*, 16(2), 119–136.

Botero, J.C., Djankov, S., La Porta, R., Lopez-de-Sillanes, F. and Shleifer, A. (2004) 'The regulation of labour', *Quarterly Journal of Economics*, 119(4), 1339–1382.

Brewster, C. (1995) 'Towards a "European" model of Human Resource Management', *Journal of International Business Studies*, 26(1), 1–21.

Clauwaert, S. and Schömann, I. (2012) *The crisis and national labour law reforms: a mapping exercise*. Brussels: European Trade Union Institute.

Crossland, C. and Hambrick, D.C. (2011) 'Differences in managerial discretion across countries: how national-level institutions affect the degree to which CEOs matter', *Strategic Management Journal*, 32(8), 797–819.

Croucher, R. (2004) 'The impact of trade union education: experience from three countries in Eastern Europe', *European Journal of Industrial Relations*, 10(1), 90–109.

Croucher, R. (2010) 'Employee involvement in Ukraine Companies', *International Journal of Human Resource Management*, 21(14), 2659–2676.

Croucher, R. and Rizov, M. (2011) 'Employees' entrepreneurial contributions to firms in Russia, 1995–2004', *Human Resource Management Journal*, 21(4), 415–431.

Croucher, R. and Rizov, M. (2012) 'Union influence in post-socialist Europe', *Industrial and Labor Relations Review*, 65(3), 630–650.

Croucher, R., Martens, H. and Singe, I. (2007) 'A German employee network and union renewal: the Siemenskonflikt', *Relations Industrielles/Industrial Relations*, 62(1), 143–169.

Danilovich, H. and Croucher, R. (2011) 'Labour management in Belarus: transcendent retrogression', *Journal of Communist Studies and Transition Politics*, 27(2), 241–262.

Edwards, T., Coller, X., Ortiz, L., Rees, C. and Wortmann, M. (2006) 'National industrial relations sytems and cross-border re-structuring: evidence from a merger in the pharmaceuticals sector', *European Journal of Industrial Relations*, 12(1), 69–88.

Erne, R. (2008) *European Unions: labor's quest for a transnational democracy*. Ithaca, NY: ILRR Press.

European Foundation for the Improvement of Living and Working Conditions (2013) *Industrial relations and working conditions developments in Europe 2012*. Dublin: European Foundation.

Ewing, K.D. (2010) *Bonfire of the liberties: New Labour, human rights and the rule of law*. Oxford: Oxford University Press.

Falkner, G. and Treib, O. (2008) 'Three worlds of compliance or four? The EU 15 compared to new member states', *Journal of Common Market Studies*, 46(2), 293–313.

Glassner, V. and Pusch, T. (2013) 'Towards a Europeanization of wage bargaining? Evidence from the metal sector', *European Journal of Industrial Relations*, 19(2), 145–160.

Gollan, P.J. and Perkins, S.J. (2009) 'Voice and value: Pandora's ICE box and big ideas around employer branding', *Human Resource Management Journal*, 19(2), 211–215.

Gumbrell-McCormick, R. and Hyman, R. (2013) *Trade unions in Western Europe: hard times, hard choices*. Oxford: Oxford University Press.

Haipeter, T. (2011) '"Unbound" employers' associations and derogations: erosion and renewal of collective bargaining in the German metalworking industry', *Industrial Relations Journal*, 42(2), 174–194.

Hall, M., Hutchinson, S., Purcell, J., Terry, M. and Parker, J. (2013) 'Promoting effective consultation? Assessing the impact of the ICE regulations', *British Journal of Industrial Relations*, 51(2), 355–381.

Harcourt, M., Wood, G. and Harcourt, S. (2004) 'Do unions affect employer compliance with the law? New Zealand evidence on age discrimination', *British Journal of Industrial Relations*, 42(3), 527–541.

Hassel, A. (1999) 'The erosion of the German system of industrial relations', *British Journal of Industrial Relations*, 37(3), 483–505.

Havlovic, S.J. (1990) 'German works' councils: a highly evolved institution of industrial democracy', *Labor Studies Journal*, 15(2), 62–73.

Helfen, M. (2011) 'Institutional continuity in German collective bargaining: do employer associations contribute to stability?', *Economic and Industrial Democracy*, 33(3), 485–503.

Ilsøe, A. (2012) 'The flip side of organised decentralisation: company-level bargaining in Denmark', *British Journal of Industrial Relations*, 50(4), 760–781.

Lee, A.S. and Trappmann, V. (2014) 'Overcoming post-communist labour weakness: attritional and enabling effects of multinationals in Central and Eastern Europe', *European Journal of Industrial Relations*. Available at: http://ejd.sagepub.com/content/early/2014/02/20/0959680114524204.abstract (accessed 10 May 2014).

Léonard, E. (2008) 'European sectoral social dialogue: an analytical framework', *European Journal of Industrial Relations*, 14(4), 401–420.

Manenok, T. (2014) 'Investors were sent to the open field', *Belorusy i rynok*. Available at: http://www.belmarket.by/ru/259/200/20622/%D0%98%D0%BD%D0%B2%D0%B5%D1%81%D1%82%D0%BE%D1%80%D0%BE%D0%B2-%D0%BE%D1%82%D0%BF%D1%80%D0%B0%D0%B2%D0%B8%D0%BB%D0%B8-%D0%B2-%D1%87%D0%B8%D1%81%D1%82%D0%BE%D0%B5-%D0%BF%D0%BE%D0%BB%D0%B5.htm (accessed 31 March 2014).

Marginson, P., Hall, M., Hoffmann, A. and Müller, T. (2004) 'The impact of European Works Councils on management decision-making in UK- and US-based multinationals: a case-study comparison', *British Journal of Industrial Relations*, 42(2), 209–233.

Meardi, G. (2004) 'Short circuits in multi-national companies: the extension of European Works Councils to Poland', *European Journal of Industrial Relations*, 10(2), 161–178.

Mihalev, A. (2012) 'Made in Russia: AutoVAZ competitors will increase the production of vehicles in Russia', *Lenta.ru*. Available at: http://lenta.ru/articles/2012/08/30/russiancars/ (accessed 30 March 2014).

Molina, O. (2014) 'Self-regulation and the state in industrial relations in Southern Europe: back to the future?', *European Journal of Industrial Relations*, 20(3), 21–36.

Morrison, C., Croucher, R. and Cretu, O. (2012) 'Legacies, conflict and "path dependence" in the Former Soviet Union', *British Journal of Industrial Relations*, 50(2), 329–351.

Morrison, C., Sacchetto, D. and Cretu, O. (2013) 'International migration and labour turnover: workers' agency in the construction sector of Russia and Italy', *Studies of Transition States and Societies*, 5(2), 7–20.

Muller, A. (2005) *Legal frameworks for employers' organizations in Eastern European and Central Asian Countries*. Working Paper Number 45, Geneva: International Labour Office. Available at: http://www.ilo.org/public/english/dialogue/actemp/downloads/projects/legalframeworks_en.pdf (accessed 10 May 2014).

Nestlé (2014) *Investments in production*. Available at: http://www.nestle.ru/aboutus/russuiannestle/investments (accessed 30 March 2014).

Ost, D. (2000) 'Illusory corporatism in Eastern Europe: neo-liberal tripartism and post-communist class identities', *Politics and Society*, 28(4), 503–530.

Ozarow, D. (2013) 'Pitching for each other's team: the North American Free Trade Agreement and labor transnationalism', *Labor History*, 54(5), 512–526.

Piketty, T. (2014) *Capital in the Twenty-First Century*. Cambridge: Belknapp Press.

Prosser, T. (2006) 'Is the "new phase" of the European Social Dialogue the development of an autonomous and effective form of social dialogue?', *Warwick Papers in Industrial Relations*, No. 82, September.

Russian Federal Statistical Services (2013) *Russia in figures – 2013*. Available at: http://www.gks.ru/bgd/regl/b13_12/IssWWW.exe/stg/d02/24-11.htm (accessed 31 March 2014).

Rymkevitch, O. (2003) *The codification of Russian labour law: issues and perspectives*. Available at: http://www.bollettinoadapt.it/old/files/document/1969WP_02_8.pdf (accessed 10 May 2014).

Schroeder, W. and Weinert, R. (2004) 'Designing institutions in European industrial relations: a strong Commission versus weak trade unions?' *European Journal of Industrial Relations*, 10(2), 199–217.

Silvia, S.J. and Schroeder, W. (2007) 'Why are German employers' associations declining? Arguments and evidence', *Comparative Political Studies*, 40(12), 1433–1459.

Stirling, J. and Tully, B. (2004) 'Power, process and practice: communications in European Works Councils', *European Journal of Industrial Relations*, 10(1), 73–89.

Traxler, F. (1995) 'Farewell to labour market associations? Organized versus disorganized decentralisation as a map for industrial relations', in Crouch, C. and Traxler, F. (eds) *Organised industrial relations in Europe: what future? (Perspectives on Europe)*. Aldershot: Avebury, pp. 3–20.

Ukrstat (2014) *Investments of foreign economic activity in Ukraine – 2013*. Statistical bulletin. Available at http://ukrstat.org/druk/publicat/kat_r/publ6_r.htm (accessed on 31 March 2014).

Ursu, V. (2013) 'Where do investments to Moldova come from?', *Capital Market*. Available at: http://capital.market.md/ru/content/%D0%BE%D1%82%D0%BA%D1%83%D0%B4%D0%B0-%D0%B8%D0%B4%D1%83%D1%82-%D0%B2-%D0%BC%D0%BE%D0%BB%D0%B4%D0%BE%D0%B2%D1%83%83-%D0%B8%D0%BD%D0%B2%D0%B5%D1%81%D1%82%D0%B8%D1%86%D0%B8%D0%B8 (accessed on 31 March 2014).

Vernon, G. (2006) 'Does density matter? The significance of comparative historical variation in unionization', *European Journal of Industrial Relations*, 12(2), 189–209.

Wagstyl, S. (2014) 'Chemnitz's journey back from the brink', *Financial Times*, 7 November.

Appendix 15.1 Continued key differences in employment relations. Western Continental Europe and USA compared

USA	Western Continental Europe	Comments
High level of managerial prerogative in workplaces; low level of joint regulation with employee representatives	Moderate level of managerial prerogative in workplaces; moderate level of joint regulation in most workplaces through works councils	Small and medium-sized enterprises have low levels of joint regulation in USA and Continental Europe
Low–very low trade union density especially outside public sector and major manufacturing industry;	Moderate trade union density in public sector and larger industrial units in most countries;	
moderate–low levels of regulation of employment relationship	moderate–high levels of regulation of employment relationship	According to Botero *et al.* (2004), US levels of regulation of employment are higher than UK levels
Employers' organizations act as lobbying bodies	Employers' organizations exist as lobbying and collective bargaining/concertation bodies, interacting with governments and unions in weak tripartite senses such as national wage pacts	
Collective bargaining conducted at company level	Collective bargaining conducted at industry and company levels	

16 Recruitment and Selection: Debates, Controversies and Variations in Europe

GEOFFREY WOOD AND LESLIE T. SZAMOSI

As Brewster (1995) notes, organizational level HR practices are intimately bound up with context. Hence Sparrow and Hiltrop (1997) and Ignjatović and Svetlik (2003) suggest that the distinctiveness of Human Resource Management (HRM) in Europe reflects institutional factors including legislation, informal regulation and the nature of state intervention, as well as associated cultural dynamics.

This chapter seeks to analyse and review the nature of recruitment and selection (R&S) within the context of Europe, taking account of commonalities and differences. It draws on a cross-section of existing knowledge and empirical data and focuses particular attention on varieties of practice including liberal market economies, the Nordic band of countries, continental Europe, the Central and Eastern European transitional economies and the Mediterranean countries in the EU.

The Foundations of Recruitment and Selection (R&S)

R&S is routinely put forward as one of the most important process functions in HRM (Costen, 2012; Nikandrou and Panayotopoulou, 2012). It is an area where relative fairness and equity become particularly visible (Noon et al., 2013). Moreover, even in lightly regulated contexts where firms can easily reverse mistakes, forced exit imposes costs not only on the employer but also the organization, which may leave both sides worse off.

Although many times lumped together into a single definition, it is important to note that recruitment and selection are defined separately and distinctly and are more commonly referred to today as 'employee resourcing' (Price, 2011). Recruitment is viewed as a series of activities undertaken by an organization to attract the most appropriate applicants for positions currently available or anticipated in the near future (see, for example, Wood *et al.*, 2014). For Brewster *et al.* (2015) the purposes of recruitment are:

- to determine present and future staffing needs in conjunction with job analysis and human resource planning;
- to increase the pool of applicants at minimum cost;
- to increase the success rate of the (subsequent) selection process: fewer will turn out to be over- or under-qualified;
- to increase the probability of subsequent retention;
- to encourage self-selection by means of a realistic job preview;
- to meet responsibilities, and legal and social obligations;
- to increase organizational and individual effectiveness;
- to evaluate the effectiveness of different labour pools.

In contrast, selection is viewed not necessarily as a process, but as the 'act' of determining, based on the recruitment undertaken, who, if any, is the most appropriate match to what is required by the organization (e.g. Heraty and Morley, 1998). For Brewster *et al.* (2015) the purposes of recruitment are to:

- obtain appropriate information about jobs, individuals and organizations in order to enable high-quality decisions;
- transform information into a prediction about future behaviour;
- contribute to the bottom line through the most efficient and effective way to produce service/production;
- ensure cost-benefit for the financial investment made in an employee;
- evaluate, hire and place job applicants in the best interests of organization and individual.

Therefore the entire R&S activity should be one that aims to have in place the most appropriate candidate, given the set of characteristics, talents and capabilities the organization is seeking and willing to pay for (Favell, 2008).

Bryson *et al.* (2012) suggest a clear demarcation between the practices of R&S predicated on a textbook versus disciplinary focused approach; while the latter focuses on the mechanisms as to 'how' this is done, the former brings together the contexts of work psychology, labour economics and HRM. R&S marks the initiation of any new or advanced association inside an organization and sets the foundation within which the formal and informal rules, and expectations of a job are inherently set and put into motion regardless of the position or level (Gold, 2003).

An effective overall process, whether generated from the inside or outside (i.e. internal versus external R&S), is linked to the development of a careful person–job 'fit' in line with the demands of the role in question or job as it is to 'crafted' by the individual, or person–organization fit in line with the organizational culture, needs and values (Boon *et al.*, 2011). This linkage has a 'knock-on' effect to other areas of HRM including overall skill levels, training and development needs, employee retention, trade union membership and employee relations, diversity management and pay and benefits, among others (Searle, 2009). Consequently, R&S plays a pivotal role in terms of a 'first contact' element in establishing the future relationship between the organization and its potential employees (Baron and Kreps, 1999).

Heraty and Morley (1998) suggest that, in practice, few organizations link R&S directly to the inherent organizational strategy. Founded in a comprehensive overview of the literature, Wood *et al.* (2014: 26) posit the stages of the recruitment and selection process as shown in Figure 16.1. They suggest, however, that few organizations follow the process in a formalistic and sequential manner; this view, therefore, suggests what might be considered an ideal case, although not perhaps in reality, 'best practice'. Most firms recruit via personal contacts and

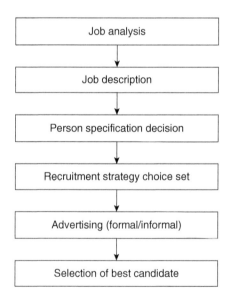

Figure 16.1 Recruitment process

word of mouth. Moreover, small and medium enterprises (SMEs) are particularly likely to make usage of informal techniques (Behrends, 2007; Szamosi, 2006).

Recruitment

The recruitment process is commonly viewed as being initiated through a process of job analysis; this is generally viewed as an initiation stage to understanding what particular jobs involve (Morgeson et al., 2014). In turn, this leads to the job description or what a prospective candidate should be able to do, or achieve, in the position, and then the development of the person specification or the characteristics sought from the 'ideal' candidate (Favell, 2008). Job analysis has traditionally been viewed as key to issues such as training, performance evaluation and compensation systems (Brannick et al., 2007). More recently there has been a suggestion that both job analysis and job description are being slowly fertilized by competency modelling as a more robust strategic tool that helps link more effectively to organizational culture and socialization criteria (Sanchez and Levine, 2009).

In practice, however, it could be argued that this process tends not to be a very scientific one, based on previous experience and subjective interpretations thereof, as well as the likely and desired pool of applicants, organizations come up with a view as to who they want and then formalize this, making adjustments where needed in light of legal pressures and informal norms and conventions and trade-off analysis.

SMEs tend to be more practically than strategically oriented and Cassell et al. (2002) suggest that organizations and managers tend to view the formal process of job analysis and description sceptically. More optimistic accounts suggests that job analysis can play a pivotal role in the development of new types of work, thus trying to ensure that a new generation of candidates may be attracted into 'modern organizations' (Sanchez and Levine, 2012). Here, a word of caution is in order. It could be argued that, implicit in such accounts, is a whiff of ageism; words like 'modern' or 'forward-thinking organizations' and 'new generation' might suggest that older job applicants are unwelcome or undesirable. Moreover, the usage of such terms in formal job descriptions or advertisements may, through accident or design, inherently deter older applicants (Harcourt et al., 2010). No job description is neutral, as some applicants or incumbents will always be favoured over others; by the same measure, more developed or sophisticated systems of job analysis or descriptions may be utilized as a tool to evade equity legislation. Recruitment strategy varies from the internal to external sourcing of candidates and the use of formal and informal networks. Each combination is associated with both pros and cons and organizations are most likely to develop an appropriate compromise based on the type of position being recruited for.

Testing in the UK has shown that internal promotion versus external recruitment at lower levels has been shown to increase overall profitability (e.g. DeVaro and Morita, 2013). Moreover, internal recruitment may help organizations meet equity targets in contexts where key groupings in society have been historically disadvantaged. Morris *et al.* (2004) suggested that in the case of Malaysia, equity legislation led to a small grouping of privileged individuals from such groupings being able to bid up job offers and readily job hop; firms that concentrated on developing their own talent from within were very much better equipped to meet equity targets and to optimize retention. Similar findings have been made in the case of the Gulf States (Morris *et al.*, 2004).

What about external recruitment? Here there is some evidence of common trends within elite categories of labour. For example, at the European level, Beaverstock *et al.* (2012) identify the dramatic growth and proliferation of executive recruitment and search throughout the Union; this would suggest a form of 'harmonization' of elite R&S as such firms begin to adopt similar policies in line with their clients' needs throughout the Union. This, however, is only likely to apply to a small grouping of individuals.

As suggested by Brock and Buckley (2013) there is little doubt about the use of social and electronic media in the recruitment process going today and going forward; as an advertising resource tool, information technology oriented applications provide wide scope and lower costs to reach potential employees as well as to specifically target current ones. Having said this, one cannot underplay the persistent importance of the direct contact of friends and/or family in the advertising realm for positions, as both formal and informal referrals generally are found to generate more effective longer-term job matches (Dustmann *et al.*, 2011) and are generally less costly. The downside of this is the attraction of similar types of people, akin to internal promotion, which may inhibit innovatively oriented thinking and development (Russo *et al.*, 1995). It may also entrench existing inequalities within the workplace, as insider groupings are likely to favour greater recruitment from amongst their own.

Selection

Selection is seen as the 'conclusion' of the R&S process, as suggested in Figure 16.1, but it is also seen as distinct from recruitment itself in the literature. A critical assumption in selection is that those in charge of selection understand the job and what it entails, which is not often clearly the case (Heraty and Morley, 1998). Many times, decision-makers do not have position-specific experience, are not the ones who will have to work with the candidate, and lack the overall understanding and background of how to effectively choose a candidate (Horverak *et al.*, 2013). Moreover, there is a tension between tools and techniques that have been developed to make the process of selection as objective as possible and the fact that a great deal of selections are made on the back of prior knowledge of the candidate and subjective 'gut' feelings.

Two notions are fundamentally linked to selection: organizational and individual; the first relates to fit between the person and the organization, while the second links to individual capacity to accomplish the tasks sets out for the particular position (Russo *et al.*, 1995). Farr and Tippins (2013) outline the variety of instruments available in selecting the most appropriate candidates, but default on the variety of psychometric instruments available. The use of assessment centres, interviews and third-party opinions round out the most commonly utilized selection methods.

Noe *et al.* (2011) suggest that generic 'standards' need to be met in the selection process including: legality, generalizability, validity, reliability and utility. Selection is clearly not a science that drives towards the 'right and wrong' decision, but a series of activities designed to amplify the chances of success while striving towards reliability. In reviewing a wide cross section of selection data, Smith and Smith (2007) found that only structured interviews and tests of mental agility proved valid and that when a test was administered in a more 'incremental' manner (i.e. staged), it was found to provide more accurate results than those deemed as 'one-offs'. The literature, however, also suggests that, despite interviews being more 'valid' than other techniques, they have tended to be poor in terms of predicting future performance (Gold, 2003; Smith and Smith, 2007). The track record of psychometric tests is arguably even weaker however.

The usage of so-called 'scientific approaches' to selection (e.g. assessment centres, psychometric testing) has gone through 'phases' in terms of organizational and academic interest with the notion being that testing is becoming more rigorous and 'accurate' in terms of identifying the correct personal attributes (McCormack and Scholarios, 2009); however, scientifically, their accuracy still shows mixed results (Searle, 2009). Indeed, they could be categorized as a 'pseudo-science' in that they make very ambitious claims of scientific rigour which are not always borne out by objective evidence. Rynes, Giluk and Brown (2007) outline the widening gap that exists between the formalized research evidence and HR practice regarding selection tools, suggesting that practitioners are unaware of such findings or merely ignore them. Indeed, there is some evidence that even SMEs are making greater usage of psychometric tests in a more formalized way in the selection process (Wapshott, Mallett and Spicert, 2014). Why might they do so? Psychometric tests can absolve the individual of difficult decisions and be a way in which those entrusted with selection may absolve themselves of later responsibility from failings in selection. A real danger with psychometric tests is a recent trend for confidential psychometric test sheets and associated manuals to be leaked on the internet; this allows unscrupulous job seekers to identify the most appropriate answers for a given job and vary their responses accordingly. The persistent popularity of psychometric tests would suggest that many engaging in selection have chosen to ignore this development, demonstrating how indispensable the comforts of pseudo-science can become.

European Context and R&S

The literature on comparative capitalism may provide some insights into how dominant R&S practices may vary according to national setting. Liberal market economies (LMEs) rely on competitive market forces, while the coordinated market economies (CMEs) rely on a strategic coordination (Hall and Soskice, 2001). Later developments and extensions of the literature on comparative capitalism identify further national archetypes. For example, Amable (2003) suggests that Europe may not only be divided between LMEs (UK and Ireland) and continental European capitalism (e.g. Germany, Benelux and Austria), but also other archetypes: Social Democratic Economies (e.g. Finland, Sweden, Denmark, Norway), and Mediterranean Economies (e.g. Portugal, Greece, Spain). Again, Hancke *et al.* (2007) categorize the Mediterranean world as Mixed Market Economies (MMEs) on account of the fact that they incorporate both features of liberal and coordinated ones. Finally, they add a category of Emerging Market Economies (EMEs) to capture the long transitional economies of Central and Eastern Europe (ibid.).

European LMEs have been characterized by reductions in the role and presence of unions and limited state intervention; in CMEs, conversely, the presence of unions is much more visible and strong and there is much greater state intervention in business (Hancke *et al.* 2007). In MMEs, economies are divided between large SME and informal sectors and their larger somewhat heavily regulated (and unionized) counterparts. EMEs incorporate elements of the past order and both LMEs and CMEs. Finally, in the Scandinavian social democracies, unions – and countervailing stakeholder power more generally – can be seen to be even stronger than CMEs (ibid.).

The original Hall and Soskice (2001) account was somewhat amoral in its assumption that both LMEs and CMEs were equally viable, with the perceived negative consequences of one system being mitigated by complementarities elsewhere. Later work adopted a more sophisticated understanding of complementarity that saw the potentially negative consequences of one set of complementarities being offset by another. For example, Crouch (2005) argued that the vocational skill afforded to workers in Germany enhanced an employee's overall marketability and job mobility potential within a specific sector. In turn, the negative consequences of higher job protection (necessary to encourage long-term investments in organization specific human capital) – potential numerical inflexibility – are offset by the relative ability to access similar jobs within a specific sector.

Unlike the literature centred on national labour movements, VOC (Varieties of Capitalism) contends that firms represent the fulcrum of the economic activity of a nation (Hall and Gingerich, 2009). Since firms mirror the wider social context in which they are located, they feature a particular VOC that reveals their specific way of interacting with other market participants encompassing suppliers, employees, stakeholders, trade unions, clients and business associations (Hall and Thelen, 2009). Furthermore, these particular relationships depend, in turn, on the institutional support offered to them by the political economy system which varies from country to country (Farndale *et al.*, 2008).

As Wood, Dibben and Ogden (2014) note, despite being ostensibly firm-centred approaches, the literature on comparative capitalism has tended to be rather thin on detail when it comes to in-firm practices towards employees and potential employees; however, there are a number of key issues that bear consideration. First, as the Regulation Theorists remind us, national institutional configurations are associated with both formal and informal norms and rules. On the one hand, governance and regulatory responsibility for either recruitment or selection, both at the national and European level, is limited and tends to centre on fairness and equity legislation. No employment contract yet exists, however, placing potential job seekers at a disadvantage when seeking redress for unfair decisions. It is up to the individual job candidate to prove unfair treatment, which is likely to be a high risk process. They will generally lack recourse to a union (as unions represent those in jobs) and will risk being shunned (even at the short-listing phase) by future employers if they are seen as litigious. Unsuccessful job seekers have only their personal resources to bring to bear against the full capabilities of the organization. Moreover, unfair treatment may be difficult to prove. As noted above, organizations may make usage of subtle hints in advertisements to deter candidates from undesired backgrounds.

The regulation of recruitment does not only concern formal rules and norms, but also informal rules and understandings, which are likely to vary not only according to setting, but also time. For example, the casual racial discrimination practised by many UK organizations in the 1950s and 1960s would be untenable today. At the same time, the higher unemployment rates for Muslims in contemporary Britain, even when variations in skills profiles are accounted for, would suggest the persistence, or even rise of, religious discrimination following the onset of the interminable 'wars against terrorism'. Again, the clustering of female workers in 'women's jobs' – secretarial and basic office administrative work and in the care professions – would reflect not only the socialization process, but also variations in how firms practice recruitment.

But, how is recruitment and selection likely to vary according to national setting? As security of tenure in LMEs is relatively weak, it is easier for organizations to reverse mistakes in recruitment and selection. Thus, in turn, it would seem that firms in LMEs may devote fewer resources to this process. This, of course, is not without costs as a higher staff turnover rate will necessitate a greater spend on basic induction training. Higher staff turnover will also mean that recruitment and selection will occur more often: in other words, whilst perhaps a less skilled or rigorous process, it will have to be repeated more often than in more regulated contexts. As external labour market conditions are subject to constant change in line with shifts in the business cycle, this may necessitate firms constantly adjusting their recruitment techniques to find suitable candidates. Indeed, Wood *et al.* (2014) suggest a greater range of recruitment techniques in LMEs than in other national settings.

Any longer-term costs associated with this 'high churn model' may be discounted owing to cost short-term savings in wage costs, attractive in national models where shareholder value is primary. For example, implicit in most employment contracts is a tacit agreement that a low initial level of pay will be offset by higher later career earnings as the individual advances up the salary scale and job ladder. If security of tenure is weak, it is relatively easy for firms to renege on this implicit agreement, replacing staff due for promotion and/or a pay increase with new entrants. The costs of losing accumulated wisdom and experience may be higher than any immediate saving in pay, but these will only become visible in many years time. Again, it allows firms to rapidly downsize in hard times, gaining immediate cost advantages, even if a fresh round of recruitment will be due once the economy 'turns around'.

It is likely that this model of high volume and low rigour recruitment will be replicated – or even accentuated – in any context where security of tenure is weak. Within the large informal and SME sectors in MMEs, there may be an important variation. In the type of authoritarian patriarchal HRM practiced in such systems (Psychogios and Wood, 2010), weak employee voice and rights are offset by informal ties and implicit understandings. Typically, the latter may include a strong emphasis on the usage of informal personal networks for recruitment, and the implicit understanding that family of existing staff will be prioritized (Psychogios and Wood, 2010). In other words, in MME's a more paternalistic form of management style makes personal relationships more important in the R&S process (Molina and Rhodes, 2007). In contrast, within larger firms in such settings, it is likely that entrenched formal bureaucratic processes will persist, but mitigated by uneven regulatory enforcement and innovations driven (where applicable) by new foreign owners.

Authors such as Babos (2010) and Brewster and Viegas Bennett (2010) suggest that in EMEs, countries are currently carving out their own trajectories and R&S is less easily categorized and compartmentalized. Whilst Slovenia (and some aspects of the Slovakian system) has become more akin to a CME, Estonia, for example, has become more LME-like; however, weaker regulation in the latter may be offset by country of origin effects on HR practice within the many Scandinavian MNEs operating in it.

In continental European CMEs, it is likely that more intense labour market regulation will discourage firms from readily shedding staff; this vests the recruitment and selection process with a great deal of importance. At the same time, whilst imposing demands on the firm, any costs will be offset by stronger organizational commitment and lower induction training costs. A key difference between most continental European CMEs (with the notable exception of the Netherlands) and Scandinavian social democracies such as Norway and Denmark is that in such flexicurity economies, security of tenure is weaker, compensated for by superior access to additional further skills and training, ensuring that employees are suitably qualified at all stages of their careers. As such, they have a degree of security in employment, if not in a single employer. As noted above, however, it is not just the law, but also norms, informal rules and conventions that count. Trade unions enjoy higher levels of support and social benefits which are engrained in the national fabric, the pool of labour is more limited given lower levels of unemployment and organizations are more likely to provide for employees; consequently, organizations are likely to be more dynamic and proactive in R&S (Harcourt and Wood, 2003). The extent to which many Scandinavian organizations take recruitment seriously would suggest is it not an exercise simply around cost cutting; moreover, there is much evidence that temporary work is used as a filtering device, making sure that those who receive permanent posts are the best possible candidates (Eriksen, 2011). In contrast, in LMEs, temporary work is often a long-term feature of many careers. Again, this would underscore the extent to which similar practices may take on different meanings in different settings, in the same manner as a high spend on training may simply reflect necessary induction training when security of tenure is low.

Conclusions

Going forward, authors such as Doherty and Norton (2013) stress the importance of re-understanding how companies practice the fundamentals of HRM, including R&S; as with all firm level practices, ways of recruiting and selecting may become entrenched, but this does not mean that they are immune to change. Hence, R&S is likely to change in Europe due to the 2008 economic crisis and its impact on the various national systems and infrastructures. As well, given the higher levels of unemployment throughout the Union it is highly probable that organizational tactics in the selection process which 'skirt' the law are less likely to be reported for fear of future reprisals. It is very likely, given the legislation changes occurring throughout Europe, that reductions in restrictions related to firing and employee dismissal may downplay the R&S process; the hypothesis to be further researched suggests that organizations will have 'less to lose' with a hiring decision. Moreover, the movement towards temporary work and zero-hours contracts further supports this notion. At the same time, weak regulation and persistent crisis is likely to be associated with greater informalization of the economy; in turn, this will mean that a greater number of jobs will be precarious and filled through personal networks rather than formal procedures. Such trends are likely to be most pronounced in MMEs and parts of Central and Eastern Europe (Psychogios et al., 2010). It is too soon, however, to suggest a general degradation of work and employment and associated HR practices. Many firms in CMEs have remained wedded to the traditional features of their national recipes and retain a longer-term approach to staffing, with a commensurate emphasis on rigour in R&S.

Key Learning Points

- Recruitment. This is initially the process of attracting suitable applicants to a job. Firms may make usage of external or internal recruitment. Although there has been a move to make greater usage of electronic media, in practice, much recruitment continues to take place via informal personal networks and word of mouth.
- Selection. A key tension here is between the desire to make the process as objective as possible and the complex needs and social dynamics of organizations. And, whilst scientific approaches to selection come in and out of fashion, the evidence as to their effectiveness is mixed.
- Context. In contexts where job security is stronger, firms have to take recruitment and probationary periods more seriously, as it is harder to rectify mistakes later. At the same time, it can be argued that this makes for a better fit between individuals and jobs and reduces longer term turnover, saving on induction training costs. Coordinated market economies (e.g. Germany, Scandinavia, Japan) are associated with stronger job protection and liberal market economies (e.g. the US, the UK) with weaker job protection.

References

Amable, B. (2003) *The Diversity of Modern Capitalism*. Oxford: Oxford University Press.

Babos, P. (2010) 'Varieties of capitalism in central and eastern Europe: Measuring the co-ordination index of a national economy', *SEER Journal for Labour and Social Affairs in Eastern Europe*, 13(4), 439–458.

Baron, J.N. and Kreps, D.M. (1999) *Strategic Human Resources: Frameworks for General Managers*. New York: Wiley.

Beaverstock, J.V., Faulconbridge, J.R. and Hall, S.J. (2012) 'Executive search', in Ritzer, G. (ed.), *The Wiley-Blackwell Encyclopedia of Globalization*. Chichester: John Wiley and Sons Ltd, pp. 615–621.

Behrends, T. (2007) 'Recruitment practices in small and medium size enterprises: An empirical study among knowledge-intensive professional service firms', *Management Review*, 18(1), 55–74.

Boon, C., Den Hartog, D.N., Boselie, P. and Paauwe, J. (2011) 'The relationship between perceptions of HR practices and employee outcomes: Examining the role of person–organisation and person–job fit', *The International Journal of Human Resource Management*, 22(1), 138–162.

Brannick, M.T., Levine, E.L. and Morgeson, F.P. (2007) *Job Analysis: Methods, Research, and Applications for Human Resource Management*. 2nd edn. Thousand Oaks, CA: Sage.

Brewster, C. (1995) 'Towards a "European" model of human resource management', *Journal of International Business Studies*, 26(1), 1–21.

Brewster, C. and Viegas Bennett, C. (2010) 'Perceptions of business cultures in Eastern Europe and their implications for international HRM', *Human Resource Management Journal*, 21(4), 2568–2587.

Brewster, C., Sparrow, P.R., Vernon, C. and Houldsworth, L. (2015) *International Human Resource Management*. 4th edn. London: Chartered Institute of Personnel and Development.

Brock, M.E. and Buckley, M.R. (2013) 'Human resource functioning in an information society practical suggestions and future implications', *Public Personnel Management*, 42(2), 272–280.

Bryson, J., James, S. and Keep, E. (2012) 'Recruitment and selection', in Bach, S. and Edwards, M. (eds), *Managing Human Resources: Human Resource Management in Transition*. Chichester: John Wiley & Sons, pp. 125–149.

Cassell, C., Nadin, S., Gary, M. and Clegg, C. (2002) 'Exploring human resource management practices in small and medium sized enterprises', *Personnel Review*, 31(6), 671–692.

Costen, W.M. (2012) 'Recruitment and selection', in Rothwell, W.J. and Prescott, R.K. (eds), *The Encyclopaedia of Human Resource Management: Short Entries*. San Francisco, CA: Pfeiffer, pp. 379–387.

Crouch, C. (2005) 'Three meanings of complementarity', *Socio-Economic Review*, 3(2), 359–363.

DeVaro, J. and Morita, H. (2013) 'Internal promotion and external recruitment: A theoretical and empirical analysis', *Journal of Labor Economics*, 31(2), 227–269.

Doherty, L. and Norton, A. (2013) 'Making and measuring good HR practice in an SME: The case of a Yorkshire bakery', *Employee Relations*, 36(2), 128–147.

Dustmann, C., Glitz, A. and Schönberg, U. (2011) *Referral-Based Job Search Networks* (No. 5777). Discussion paper series/Forschungsinstitut zur Zukunft der Arbeit.

Eriksen, T.A. (2011) 'Applicant reactions to selection procedures: Method validity, cost, and utility', *Scandinavian Journal of Organizational Psychology*, 3(2), 45–67.

Farndale, E., Brewster, C. and Poutsma, E. (2008) 'Coordinated vs. liberal market HRM: The impact of institutionalization on multinational firms', *International Journal of Human Resource Management*, 19(11), 2004–2023.

Farr, J.L. and Tippins, N.T. (eds) (2013) *Handbook of Employee Selection*. New York: Routledge.

Favell, I. (2008) 'Recruitment', in Muller-Carmen, M., Croucher, R. and Leigh, S., *Human Resource Management: A Case Study Approach*. London: CIPD.

Gold, J. (2003) 'Recruitment and selection', in Bratton, J. and Gold, J., *Human Resource Management: Theory and Practice*. London: Palgrave.

Hall, P.A. and Gingerich, D.W. (2009) 'Varieties of capitalism and institutional complementarities in the political economy: An empirical analysis', *British Journal of Political Science*, 39(03), 449–482.

Hall, P.A. and Soskice, D. (2001) 'Introducing varieties of capitalism', in Hall, P.A. and Soskice, D., *Varieties of Capitalism*. Oxford: Oxford University Press.

Hall, P.A. and Thelen, K. (2009) 'Institutional change in varieties of capitalism', *Socio-Economic Review*, 7(1), 7–34.

Hancke, B., Rhodes, M. and Thatcher, M. (2007) 'Introduction', in Hancke, B., Rhodes, M. and Thatcher, M. (eds) *Beyond Varieties of Capitalism: Conflict, Contradiction, and Complementarities in the European Economy*. Oxford: Oxford University Press.

Harcourt, M. and Wood, G. (2003) 'Under what circumstances do social accords work?', *Journal of Economic Issues*, 37(3), 747–767.

Harcourt, M., Wilkinson, A. and Wood, G. (2010) 'The effects of anti-age discrimination legislation: A comparative analysis', *International Journal of Comparative Labour Law and Industrial Relations*, 26(4), 447–466.

Heraty, N. and Morley, M. (1998) 'In search of good fit: Policy and practice in recruitment and selection in Ireland', *Journal of Management Development*, 17(9), 662–685.

Horverak, J.G., Sandal, G.M., Bye, H.H. and Pallesen, S. (2013) 'Managers' selection preferences: The role of prejudice and multicultural personality traits in the assessment of native and immigrant job candidates', *Revue Européenne de Psychologie Appliquée/European Review of Applied Psychology*, 63(5), 267–275.

Ignjatović, M. and Svetlik, I. (2003) 'European HRM clusters', *EBS Review*, 17(Fall), 25–39.

McCormack, A. and Scholarios, D. (2009) 'Recruitment', in Redman, T. and Wilkinson, A. (eds), *Contemporary Human Resource Management*. London: FT/Prentice Hall, pp. 64–88.

Molina, O. and Rhodes, M. (2007) 'The political economy of adjustment in mixed market economies: A study of Spain and Italy', in Hancké, B., Rhodes, M. and Thatcher, M. (eds), *Beyond Varieties of Capitalism: Conflict, Contradictions and Complementarities in the European Economy*. Oxford: Oxford University Press, pp. 223–252.

Morgeson, F.P., Spitzmuller, M., Garza, A.S. and Campion, M.A. (2014) 'Pay attention! The liabilities of respondent experience and carelessness when making job analysis judgments', *Journal of Management*, 40, 1075–1097.

Morris, D., Wood, G. and Yaacob, A. (2004) 'Attitudes towards pay and promotion in the Malaysian higher educational sector', *Employee Relations*, 26(2), 137–151.

Nikandrou, I. and Panayotopoulou, L. (2012) 'Recruitment and selection in context', in Brewster, C. and Mayrhofer, W. (eds), *Handbook of Research on Comparative Human Resource Management*. Cheltenham: Edward Elgar Publishing, pp. 121–138.

Noe, R.E., Hollenbeck, J.R., Gerhart, B. and Wright, P.M. (2011) *Human Resource Management*. 4th edn. Boston, MA: McGraw-Hill Irwin.

Noon, M., Healy, G., Forson, C. and Oikelome, F. (2013) 'The equality effects of the "hyper-formalization" of selection', *British Journal of Management*, 24(3), 333–346.

Price, A. (2011) *Human Resource Management*. 4th edn. Boston, MA: Cengage.

Psychogios, A. and Wood, G. (2010) 'Human resource management in Greece in comparative perspective: Alternative institutionalist perspectives and empirical realities', *International Journal of Human Resource Management*, 21(14), 2614–2630.

Psychogios, A.G., Szamosi, L.T. and Wood, G. (2010) 'Introducing employment relations in South Eastern Europe', *Employee Relations*, 32(3), 205–211.

Russo, G., Rietveld, P., Nijkamp, C. and Gorter, C. (1995) 'Issues in recruitment strategies: An economic perspective', *The International Journal of Career Management*, 7(3), 3–13.

Rynes, S.L., Giluk, T.L. and Brown, K.G. (2007) 'The very separate worlds of academic and practitioner periodicals in human resource management:

Implications for evidence-based management', *Academy of Management Journal*, 50(5), 987–1008.

Sanchez, J.I. and Levine, E.L. (2009) 'What is (or should be) the difference between competency modeling and traditional job analysis?', *Human Resource Management Review*, 19(2), 53–63.

Sanchez, J.I. and Levine, E.L. (2012) 'The rise and fall of job analysis and the future of work analysis', *Annual Review of Psychology*, 63, 397–425.

Searle, R. (2009) 'Recruitment and selection', in Collings, D. and Wood, G. (eds), *Human Resource Management: A Critical Approach*. London: Routledge, pp. 151–168.

Smith, M.J. and Smith, P. (2007) *Testing People at Work: Competencies in Psychometric Testing*. Oxford: British Psychological Society/Blackwell.

Sparrow, P.R. and Hiltrop, J.M. (1997) 'Redefining the field of European human resource management: A battle between national mindsets and forces of business transition?', *Human Resource Management*, 36(2), 201–219.

Szamosi, L.T. (2006) 'Just what are tomorrow's SME employees looking for?', *Education+ Training*, 48(8/9), 654–665.

Wapshott, R., Mallett, O. and Spicer, D. (2014) 'Exploring change in small firms' HRM practices', in Machado, C. and Davim, J.P. (eds), *Work Organization and Human Resource Management*. Cham: Springer International Publishing, pp. 73–92.

Wood, G., Dibben, P. and Ogden, S. (2014) 'Comparative capitalism without capitalism, and production without workers: The limits and possibilities of contemporary institutional analysis', *International Journal of Management Reviews* DOI: 10.1111/ijmr.12025, early online available at: http://onlinelibrary.wiley. com/doi/10.1111/ijmr.12025/abstract (accessed 3 November 2015).

Wood, G., Brewster, C., Demirbag, M. and Brookes, M. (2014) 'Understanding contextual differences in employee resourcing', in Wood, G., Brewster, C. and Brookes, M. (eds), *Human Resource Management and the Institutional Perspective*. New York/Abingdon: Routledge, pp. 25–38.

17 Global Careers in European MNEs: Different Career Patterns in Europe?

MICHAEL DICKMANN, JEAN-LUC CERDIN AND
WOLFGANG MAYRHOFER

Global Careers: An Exploration

Christopher Columbus (or Cristóbal Colón) did not really know
what he saw when he discovered the 'West Indies' in the morning
of 12 October, 1492. Rarely have errors, like this wish to reach
India sailing from Europe to the West, had such an impact on world
history. Columbus was pursuing a global career and thanks to his
voyages he became 'Viceroy and Governor of the Indies' and would
never in his life admit that he did discover a continent previously
unknown in Spain.

International working started much earlier. Some 3,500 years before
the discovery of America, trading organizations run by Assyrians
had active strategies to pursue geographical expansion across several
regions. They had foreign workers and their subsidiaries in these
distinct regions had expatriate managers (Moore and Lewis, 1999).
All subsequent empires not only had soldiers but also non-military
organizations within their expanse which would use expatriate labour.
Global careers within companies such as the Royal African Company,
the Hudson's Bay Company, the Muscovy Company or the Dutch
and English East India companies have always existed (Carlos and
Nicolas, 1988). However, in the last 50 years the popularity of
working abroad – be it company-sponsored or self-initiated – has

dramatically increased (Al Ariss, 2014; Andresen *et al.*, 2013; Scullion and Collings, 2011).

Peiperl and Jonsen (2007: 351) have observed that a 'global career is a career that takes place in more than one region of the world, either sequentially or concurrently' and Dickmann and Baruch (2011: 7) have expanded Arthur *et al.*'s (1989) definition to define global careers as 'an evolving sequence of a person's work experience over time when part of the sequence takes place in more than one country'. All expatriates are migrants according to legal definitions. To distinguish expatriates from (mere) migrants the former have to be lawfully employed (Andresen *et al.*, 2014).

There are many forms of international work and global careers. Baruch *et al.* (2013) distinguish 20 distinct types of international work. They argue that global careerists experience differences in their time exposure to foreign environment(s); the intensity of cross-national contacts; the breadth of interaction; the legal context; the driver of the international sojourn; the cultural gap and the needs of the role/job. The most popular global career patterns include self-initiated expatriation (Andresen *et al.*, 2013); traditional long-term expatriation; short-term expatriation and frequent business travel (Brookfield Global Relocation Services, 2014). Inpatriation, defined as 'the practice of developing host country or third country managers via a transfer to the corporate headquarters' (Cerdin and Sharma, 2014: 79), could also be included in global careers and is particularly relevant in Europe where many multinational enterprise (MNE) headquarters are located. Inpatriates come from other European countries and also from other continents where the MNEs have subsidiaries.

The above makes it clear how important and varied global careers are. This chapter describes the particularity of global careers in the European context, characterized by a unique configuration of historical, political, economic and demographic factors. Both the organizational and individual perspectives of global careers are examined. From the organizational perspective, this chapter investigates the main challenges faced by MNEs who manage global careerists, such as successfully managing repatriation. From the individual perspective, this chapter examines different kinds of considerations that come into play when individuals embark on a global career. Then, the main global career management policies are examined for multinational companies. We conclude the chapter by discussing global careers and global career management in the European context.

Europe: Its Quest for Higher Integration and International Mobility

While there is some uncertainty about the exact number and delineation, there are 47 countries that are internationally recognized as independent states and that have their entire area lying in the geographical region of Europe. Only Africa has more states. Europe has the biggest percentage of intra-regional merchandise trade from any continent, amounting to about US$5 trillion; approximately two-thirds of all international trade of a European country will be conducted with another European state (WTO, 2012). Given the strong trading and other business links, international work may be deemed as having a relatively high likelihood in Europe.

In addition, 28 member states (as of 2015) with more than 500 million citizens have strong political and economic links through the European Union (EU). The single market allows the free circulation of goods, services, capital and people across EU member state borders. Through this, some substantial barriers to mobility – such as the need to gain visa/residency rights and working permits – have been minimized or abolished for EU citizens. These legal rights for all EU citizens support mobility across borders, which should be a factor in increasing cross-national flows.

The EU encourages its citizens to live and work abroad. Ackers (2005) shows how the EU facilitates cross-border moves through the harmonization of training and the internationalization of higher education. The Leonardo Programme aimed to increase vocational cross-border mobility and has supported more than 84,000 individuals (Doherty et al., 2010). Overall, the Lifelong Learning Programme (LLP) – which included the long-standing Erasmus Programme (*European Community Action Scheme for the Mobility of University Students*, since 1987) – intended to enable EU citizens to take part in learning and training across Europe. It had a budget of €7 billion and is continued through the current Erasmus+ Programme, which runs until 2020.

Beyond such common denominators, Europe, covering roughly the same geographical area as the USA, constitutes a unique context for organizational decision-makers because of substantial heterogeneity in various dimensions. A few examples may suffice. In terms of language, the European Union alone has 24 official languages and in excess of 60 indigenous regional or minority language communities.[1] Historically, an often belligerent centuries-old relationship between European countries has established a tradition of tension and rivalry. This is true for large European states like the UK, France, Spain, Germany and Italy, as well as smaller states or ethnic groups, e.g. conflicts in Northern Ireland, Bosnia and the Basque Country and Hungarian minorities in Slovakia and Romania. Culturally, notable differences exist not only between culture clusters – for example, a Nordic, an Anglo-Saxon, a Romanic and a Germanic cluster – (see Hofstede, 1980; Trompenaars and Hampden-Turner, 1997), but also between closely related countries such as, for example, Germany and Austria (Brück, 2002), indicating deep-rooted cultural specifics at the level of values/norms and basic assumptions. Economically, countries with a comparatively high GDP per person employed, such as France (41,420) or the UK (39,336), are in stark contrast to countries of comparable size such as Turkey (10,945) or Poland (13,431), not to mention countries like Romania (9,499) or the Ukraine (3,900) (source: World Bank Data, all figures shown are for 2013[2] in US dollars). Institutionally, great heterogeneity applies to labour law, especially in the area of protection of employees, as well as to different basic systems of law and jurisdiction, e.g. common law in the UK and Ireland versus civil law in the rest of Europe.

From this it follows that 'European' in this chapter does not implicate a monolithic European context. Both commonalities and differences exist. Depending on the level of 'zooming in' (for this telescopic metaphor see Brewster, 1995), even more detail within the big picture emerges. Vice versa, 'zooming out' provides a broad overall picture. While none of the chosen levels of detail are in themselves wrong or inaccurate, some are more useful for some purposes than for others.

MNEs and Global Careers: 'Organizational Perspective'

The United Nations measurement of the transnationality of MNEs incorporates the stock of foreign investment, sales turnover and employees outside the country-of-origin of a company. The transnationality index, therefore, is a good indicator of the importance of global careers within MNEs. In 2012, the European Union (EU) had 51 of the top 100 non-financial MNEs),[3] with broader Europe adding another six (Switzerland 5 and Norway one). In contrast, the USA sported 16 and Canada had one MNE in the top 100. No country in Africa had a MNE represented amongst the most transnational firms, while Asia had 13. In addition, the average degree of transnationality within these firms was substantially higher in Europe. It might be argued that global careers in Europe are particularly important – at least in many large MNEs.

What is the effect of these activities on the numbers of global careerists in the EU? In 2012, 34.3 million foreign citizens lived in the EU; 17.2 million of these had been born in a different EU state, which represented more than 3 per cent of the whole EU population (Eurostat, 2014). Amongst these were 571 thousand students in 2010 (Eurostat, 2014). These large numbers raise the question of why people choose to live and work abroad in general and whether there are European specifics.

The Motivations of Global Careerists and Some European Specifics

There are many reasons why individuals decide to work abroad – be they company-sponsored assigned expatriates (AEs) or self-initiated expatriates (SIEs) who move abroad under their own planning and initiative. Andresen *et al.* (2014) provide an extensive classification of the different forms of living abroad. The multitude of expatriation drivers can be categorized into individual factors, including personal interests, motivations and experiences, career and development drivers, partner and family considerations, national and specific location factors and organizational considerations (see also Cerdin, 2013; Dickmann, Doherty, Mills and Brewster, 2008).

Individual Factors

The decision to become a global careerist is partly determined by a person's own values (Schein, 1990). Indeed, for SIEs personal agency as well as self-efficacy impacts on an individual's receptivity to global careers (Tharenou, 2003). Amongst the expatriation drivers are the desire for travel, adventure and life change as well as personal challenge and a feeling that one can cope abroad (Doherty *et al.*, 2011). Overall, global careerists tend to pursue personal interests through their foreign sojourns (Tung, 1998). One way to capture personal interests is through career anchors, 'that one element in a person's self-concept, which he or she will not give up, even in the face of difficult choices' (Schein, 1990:18). The internationalism career anchor (Cerdin, 2007; Lazarova *et al.*, 2014; Suutari and Taka, 2004) is particularly relevant for global careerists, as they will make career choices based on the opportunity to work in an international environment.

Partner and Family Considerations

A range of authors suggest that partner and family-related considerations are, on average, only moderately important when deciding to embark on a global career (Cerdin, 2013; Doherty *et al.*, 2011). However, it is obviously the case that considerations of dual careers, family education or being united with one's partner can be paramount for individuals (Richardson, 2006).

Career and Development Drivers

One of the key drivers for working abroad is the nature of the job, professional development, and career progression for AEs and, to some extent, for SIEs (Cerdin, 2013). Global careerists often want to gain unusual skills and look for enriching, foreign experiences (Hippler, 2009). The effects of their overseas work experiences – especially in relation to the next job down the line – are paramount for AEs (Dickmann et al., 2008) and important (but somewhat less so) for SIEs (Richardson and Mallon, 2005). This leads us to consider broader organizational factors that may be motivators for global careerists.

Organizational Considerations

Financial considerations have long been recognized as being important for global careerists in their decision to work abroad – especially to AEs (Doherty et al., 2011). However, there may be some differences as to the country of origin of the global careerists with respect to how important the 'expatriation package' is (see p. 316f).

National and Specific Location Factors

There has been much research on cultural distance (Shenkar, 2001) and adjustment to a host country environment (Haslberger, Brewster and Hippler, 2014). Beyond that, security considerations, the individual's assessment of national economic prosperity, the host culture alongside general climate and language differences, can be important in a global careerist's career choice (Dickmann, 2013; Tharenou, 2003; Yurkiewicz and Rosen, 1995).

Some European Specifics

Beyond the general findings outlined above, some European specifics exist. Fourage and Ester (2007) found that within the European Union the intentions to move to another country are stronger if the perceived social and employment effects are not negative. Compared to their older counterparts, younger EU citizens have a stronger intention to live abroad – after all, they can use the skills, knowledge and networks acquired through their foreign stay for a longer period (see also Doherty et al., 2010; Dries et al., 2008). These young workers had a strong persuasion that they are competent to succeed abroad and that they are likely to benefit from a foreign sojourn in terms of improved educational and economic opportunities. Personal relationships and having a family were substantial barriers to cross-national moves – even if the expectation of benefits of working abroad was high.

With regards to incentives for going abroad, Stahl et al. (2002) point out that German managers appear to be putting lower importance on the monetary package vis-à-vis other American data (Yurkiewicz and Rosen, 1995). Other research (Dickmann et al., 2008; Doherty et al., 2011) on predominantly European AEs and SIEs also indicates that financial considerations are less important than many other factors, especially those related to development and career (AEs) and individual drivers (SIEs).

MNEs and Global Career Management

There is a strong mutual dependency between organizations and their global careerists. Edström and Galbraith (1977) list predominant reasons why organizations encourage global careers through international assignments. They include leadership development, skills/experience shortages in the host country, corporate control and organizational coordination drivers. More recently, other motivations such as knowledge transfer and innovation have been added (Bonache and Dickmann, 2008; Edwards et al., 2005).

Dickmann and Baruch (2011: 112–114) build on the expatriate cycle (Harris et al., 2003) to distinguish strategic factors as well as considerations related to before, during and after global assignments using a mutual dependency approach. We analyse these three stages in turn. To focus the discussion and allow a quicker overview we outline three tables that chart the key factors before, during and after a global career sojourn and give policy recommendations. While the tables concentrate mostly on considerations that are important for company-assigned expatriates, we will also discuss implications for self-initiated expatriates and frequent business travellers.

Pre-assignment Considerations

Strategic Global Career Management

Based on Porter's ideas of competitive advantage (Porter, 1980), Bartlett and Ghoshal (1989) have developed a typology of organizational configurations that indicate how much a company strives to standardize its operations in search of efficiency, how many degrees of freedom it wants to allow its foreign subsidiaries in order to create local responsiveness and how it shapes its cross-border communication in order to strive for innovation. Dickmann and Müller-Camen (2006) have explored these issues of global standardization and knowledge networking to outline four international HRM (IHRM) configurations – the less highly standardized, more locally responsive multidomestic firm having a tendency to need fewer global careerists. Arguably, focused global career management will need a thorough understanding of the company's configuration and its way to compete. This will allow a company to design career management approaches that support the competitive strength of the organization. For instance, a global, highly standardized enterprise will strive for common policies and practices and is likely to have many global assignments driven by control and coordination purposes. The difference between the multidomestic and global organization is not simply the number (and likely driver) of cross-border assignments; other forms of mobility are also affected with global (as well as international and transnational) enterprises having a greater need for several forms of international work, including intensive cross-country business travelling.

In addition, internal and external communication and the kudos of working abroad will depend on the chosen configuration. Organizations strive to communicate a distinct, positive and clear image to the outside world and to potential applicants (Edwards, 2009). Developing a comprehensive employer brand requires knowing what attracts potential candidates in terms of their career in different international contexts. Career anchors can help to determine what factors exert the desired 'pull' effect and which ones lead the recruit to be 'pushed' away because of a perceived distance between his or her career orientation and the employer brand (Martin and Cerdin, 2014). Thus, corporate branding is of particular concern for SIEs who might like to apply to work for an organization because of the prospect of a global career. Overall, well-thought out, coherent and integrated global career strategies, policies and practices would be beneficial for many large MNEs. Table 17.1 addresses key issues in the pre-assignment stage. We explain them in more detail below.

Job Factors

Several job factors which are listed in Table 17.1 impact the adjustment process and time. In essence, for global career management and the leadership pipeline in an organization, it is important that both global careerists and organizational stakeholders understand the required talent

Table 17.1 Global career management: strategic and operational pre-assignment considerations

Area	Organizational Action	Comments
Strategic Global Career Management	Design and Implement adequate IHRM configuration.	*Strategy and policy considerations*
		Understand the broader organizational context and corporate competitive advantage.
	Define and execute corporate branding strategy that covers global careers.	Corporate branding will be most important for SIEs, internal kudos of international work for AEs and business travellers.
	Clarify diverse purposes of global careers within organization and specify those in relation to career opportunities/international moves.	Select the primary purpose of global career steps – development, control and coordination, skills-filling, knowledge transfer, etc.
	Attractive degree of existing internationalization (for individuals).	
	Create coherent global career approaches – they may be simply thinking in terms of careers rather than international mobility.	*Choose most suitable overall IHRM configuration – transnational, global, multidomestic or cognofederate/international.*
Job Factors	Give discretion in the job.	*Job considerations*
	Clarify job expectations and responsibilities.	Choose a job that the candidate will find only a slight stretch.
	Gain agreement as to job objectives between individual, home and host country.	Adjustment to a new team and new culture is already a challenge.
	Provide overlap with incumbent to facilitate 'hitting the ground running'.	Create challenges for top leadership candidates – the stretch might be larger. This might include changing divisions, functions or more radical job content alterations.
	Align any other conflicting expectations regarding performance standards, job, working environment, etc.	*Understand talent management and global leadership challenges to find the 'right' candidate in relation to position.*

(continued)

Table 17.1 (continued)

Area	Organizational Action	Comments
Selection, Negotiation and Rewards	Sophisticated selection factoring in personality factors, soft competencies, performance and potential.	*Some key individual characteristics*
		Self-confidence and optimism.
		Willingness to learn about different cultures and business environments.
	Involve partner in selection and consider extended family responsibilities.	Inter-personal orientation.
		Good communication skills.
	Use psychometric and other instruments and give feedback to candidate and partner regarding cross-cultural strengths and weaknesses (also link to adjustment and reverse adjustment).	Cultural sensitivity and willingness to critically review own values and norms
		openness
	Match candidate's profile to inter-cultural job demands.	global mindset
		behavioural flexibility
	Provide realistic job, local team and country previews (and also 'look-see visits').	inquisitiveness
		ability to successfully manage uncertainty
	In negotiation: understand individual motivations.	resilience.
	In negotiation: understand the implications of diverse primary goals on individual and organizational benefits.	*Design packages that take account of diverse interests and organizational pay-offs.*

Training and Development	Provide rigorous training for increased job demands; ideally linked to organizational configuration. Provide inter-cultural training (pre-departure and post-arrival) and language classes. Include partner in the training. Enable interaction with repatriates from assignment region/area.	*T&D considerations* Distinguish between local position requirements, global or international control, coordination and innovation responsibilities. Aim for the capabilities that make individuals successful when working abroad (see Selection). Provide support through corporate sponsor, mentors and coaches. Encourage global careerist to join expatriate networks. *Explore the whole learning environment for global careerists' immediate and future performance and motivation.*
Administrative and Logistical Compliance and Support	Provide effective administrative support in relation to the international mobility framework, compensation and benefit questions. Provide good logistical support and high quality in terms of moving abroad, accommodation (abroad and at home), health insurance, banking, schooling, return visits, etc. Monitor own and service provider pre-assignment activities and gain expatriate feedback for improvements.	*Administrative issues* Set an end-of-assignment date in order to avoid assignments that 'drag on'. Brief and update global careerists regarding organizational structures, strategies, policies and practices. *Deliver strong logistical support and communicate in order to manage expectations.*

Note: Tables 17.1–17.3 based on Dickmann (2015) with own further developments. The ideas by authors such as Andresen *et al.* (2013), Black *et al.* (1991), Harris *et al.* (2003), Haslberger *et al.* (2013), Lazarova and Caligiuri (2001), McNulty *et al.* (2013) and Tharenou and Caulfield (2010) are acknowledged.

management challenges and that they create a fit with the key purpose of the assignment. These considerations are valid for several types of global careerists, including AEs, SIEs and frequent business travellers.

Selection and Negotiation

Much has been written about formal/informal and open/closed selection systems for global assignments, with the frequent call to increase the quality of decisions and incorporate more information regarding key competencies (Scullion and Collings, 2011). The suggested qualities include a strong interpersonal orientation, excellent communication skills, a desire to learn from other cultures and the willingness to critically assess one's own cultural persuasions (Osland *et al.*, 2006).

When a potential global careerist is identified, a period of negotiation with the individual often follows. Ideally, the employer would understand the motivations of the person but it has been shown, in a predominantly European sample, that the organization often overestimates the importance of financial incentives and underestimates expatriates' interests in career and development (Dickmann *et al.*, 2008). In addition, the diverse primary goals of expatriation have different impacts on the development and learning of expatriates. Overall, MNEs would benefit from designing expatriation packages that take the various assignment patterns, the diverse interests of their employees and the individual and organizational pay-offs into account (Dickmann and Baruch, 2011).

Training and Development

Because of the demands of an international position in a different country many authors have suggested that expatriates should receive extensive pre-departure training (Puck *et al.*, 2008). However, the reality is that many companies leave little time between the selection of expatriates and their departure and spend little on training activities (Doherty and Dickmann, 2012). In Table 17.1 we outline a range of learning, training and development activities (including coaching and networking) geared to the particular position, country and individual in question. It is important to realize that while these activities may take place before departure, they aim to create both immediate and long-term effects. Ideally, companies would explore the whole learning environment as well as individual and organizational needs in order to create a positive impact on performance and motivation. It is highly important for global career management to communicate with the assignees and their families, with a view to creating realistic expectations of expatriates for their work abroad and for longer-term career progression.

Administrative and Logistical Support

Much effort has been concentrated on providing administrative and logistical support to expatriates and their families (for a highly detailed list see The RES-Forum, 2014). In general, most MNEs offer (often outsourced) services to obtain visa and work permits, to enable the physical move to the host country, to support the family in finding accommodation, open bank accounts, find doctors and schools. Many global mobility departments and their external service providers are highly competent with regards to tax, social security and administrative effectiveness of any foreign secondment (Dickmann and Debner, 2011).

During an Assignment

Individual adjustment is very important for the performance of global careerists. It is seen as an important contributor to success in a global career (Cerdin and Bird, 2008), measured not only in terms of job performance but also in terms of job satisfaction and career satisfaction. Overall, there are many initiatives in the areas of administrative and logistical support, social context, training and development, performance, career and reward management that MNEs can implement in order to aid the short- and long-term success of global work. Some key activities are outlined below and summarized in Table 17.2.

Global Career Management

While mutual dependency of individuals and their employers exists when an individual moves from the Czech Republic to France, the dependency is even higher if this individual moves to highly insecure and culturally distant countries such as Afghanistan or Syria. The investment in a global careerist is also particularly high (Doherty and Dickmann, 2012) so that long-term career planning by the organization – in close liaison with the expatriate – is important.

Some modern career approaches regard global assignees as masters of their own careers (for a critical view see, Inkson et al., 2012). Protean as well as boundaryless career approaches are often used to analyse global sojourns. The protean career (Hall, 1996) emphasizes an individual's own values and conscious self-management. The boundaryless career framework, where traditional boundaries are seen as having diminished or fallen away (Arthur and Rousseau, 1996), is highly suitable for global career studies (Shaffer et al., 2012).

Table 17.2 Global career management during international work

Area	Organizational Action	Some Characteristics That Would Help
Global Career Management	Link selection to individual's long-term career plan and organizational career management (avoid 'out of sight, out of mind' syndrome). Foster the acquisition of knowing how, knowing why and knowing whom capital. Design support mechanisms such as business sponsors, formal and informal networks, shadow career planning.	*Career Planning* Consider NOT to promote on the way out – instead, actively consider to promote upon repatriation. Consider expatriation to centres of excellence and ways how to apply insights and use social capital in the job upon return. Conduct long-term career planning in order to aid career management, retention and commitment. *The mutual dependency of individuals and organization is especially strong during an IA. There is a case for more long-term career planning which may take career capital considerations into account.*
Administrative and Logistical Compliance and Support	Provide good support for yearly taxation and other local/cross-border administrative issues. Guarantee security as much as possible and provide protection in high risk areas. Monitor own and service provider activities and gain expatriate feedback during the assignment.	*Administrative Issues* Consider periodically whether the assignment objectives have been fulfilled and, therefore, keep the option of early return open. Provide support through corporate sponsor, mentors and coaches who proactively approach the assignees in regular intervals during the work abroad. *Support the global careerist in many activities that need local regulatory knowledge; set up support mechanisms to counter the 'out of sight, out of mind' phenomenon.*

		Social Facilitation
Social Context and Family	Encourage local national employees to provide support to new assignees and families.	Consider setting up local 'buddies' for self-initiated, assigned expats and other international workers and their partners.
	Collect and provide information regarding social, religious, sport, cultural organizations and enable expatriates and their families to join these.	Support partners in carving out meaningful roles for themselves.
	Develop social support networks.	Design organizational approaches that encourage host country nationals to view expatriates as 'ingroup' rather than 'outgroup'.
	Provide an Employee Assistance Programme (EAP) for people experiencing culture shock and train local manages to recognize symptoms.	Brief and prepare locals with liaison roles.
		Work towards a host environment which is welcoming and supporting.

		T&D Considerations
Training and Development	Give post-arrival cultural training and briefings – consider including partner in these.	Distinguish between general communication skills and development of personality of individual.
	Provide host country coach/mentor.	Distinguish between work and social environment and include family where appropriate.
	Provide team-building initiatives together with new team.	*Encourage cultural and operational learning, work towards the diffusion of ideas from expatriate to host country team and reverse.*
	Provide (where useful) extensive briefings to local employees regarding role and function of assignee.	
	Enable interaction with other expatriates in assignment region/area (also from other companies).	
	Provide rigorous training for increased job demands.	
	Give networking skills training.	

(continued)

Table 17.2 (continued)

Area	Organizational Action	Some Characteristics That Would Help
Performance Management	Use globally integrated performance management system to encourage comparability. Find a balance between local and global objectives. Assignment-specific objectives should be meaningful and attractive to local operating units and appraisers. The primary purpose of the assignment (developmental, control, coordination, skills-filling) should be reflected in the performance management and appraisal. Link performance management to development, career and succession planning.	*Performance Management* Implement a PM philosophy that is acceptable in all regions and countries that the organization operates in. Encourage local–global cooperation rather than competition for resources or preservation of balance sheet orientation. Be conscious of timing, tasks and roles. *Design a PM system that is flexible in so far as local and higher level (European/global) criteria can be used.*

Reward Management: Principles and Design	Perceived reward equity. Create salary transparency and avoid large pay differentials between locals and expatriates as well as within the expatriate population. Minimize insecurity and tax exposure to both individuals and organizations. Understand the diverse social security and taxation systems and find a solution that balances organizational and individual needs. Keep administrative complexity low. Consider rewards for the development of a global perspective – including global skills, abilities, knowledge and networks. Consider to design tie–over pay approaches for repatriates.	*Reward Design Considerations* Balance the need for attracting highly capable individuals with cost saving pressures. Reward global capability acquisition (especially on developmental assignments). Investigate individual drivers in order to link compensation and incentives to these. Understand the implicit rules of career management – informal systems will reward social capital acquisition more highly. *Understand individual motivations and organizational rationale in the design of reward approaches.*

Note: Tables 17.1–17.3 based on Dickmann (2015) with own further developments. The ideas by authors such as Andresen *et al.* (2013), Black *et al.* (1991), Harris *et al.* (2003), Haslberger *et al.* (2013), Lazarova and Caligiuri (2001), McNulty *et al.* (2013) and Tharenou and Caulfield (2010) are acknowledged.

The intelligent careers (IC) framework (Parker *et al.*, 2009) has strong links to both career approaches. It consists of three forms of career capital: 'knowing why', 'knowing whom' and 'knowing how', which are interlinked and mutually reinforcing. 'Knowing why' is highly linked to protean career drivers and gives individuals a sense of purpose for their careers. This is likely to energize and motivate global careerists. 'Knowing whom' is highly linked to social capital, manifested in intra- and extra-organizational networks, mutual obligations towards contacts and results in individual reputation and information access. Lastly, 'knowing how' career capital consists of insights and competencies that are useful to pursue one's career.

Table 17.2 uses the intelligent career concept from the unusual perspective of the organization to recommend managerial action. It suggests designing support mechanisms for global careerists and recommends concentrating on activities that allow individuals to build their global career capital. For instance, going to a centre of excellence is likely to be beneficial for 'knowing how' accumulation. Not promoting on the way abroad may result in a job that is relatively more similar to the 'old position'. This may facilitate adjustment as expatriates can devote more of their energies and attention to the cultural differences. In turn, promoting on the way 'back' can work against reverse culture shock and therefore may help the motivation levels of repatriates (Dickmann and Baruch, 2011). As we will see later, a crucial condition would be that the acquired career capital is useful in the current job and can be transferred to a new location and new job.

Administrative and Logistical Support

Many organizations seem to focus their logistical efforts on making the physical move to a different country happen and to cover the immediate time after arrival. Many of these activities are outsourced to service providers and it is seen as important to ascertain the global careerists' feedback as to the quality of provision. At least the global mobility departments seem to be generally content with service levels, especially in terms of reliability (The RES-Forum, 2014).

Expatriation often involves substantial extra costs for an organization (Doherty and Dickmann, 2012). A periodic assessment on whether the MNE would continue to need an expatriate, whether this person has fulfilled the assignment objectives or whether it is possible to localize the position, can be important for the effectiveness and efficiency of an organization (Dickmann and Baruch, 2011).

The location context is crucial – not just for the administrative support. In fragile and dangerous environments it is important to provide additional security measures such as bodyguards or geotracking. Crisis scenarios often consist of evacuation plans which, interestingly, show a large amount of variety in terms of whether to treat global careerists, their families and domestic employees similarly or not (The RES-Forum, 2014).

Social Context

A welcoming and supportive social context at work (and outside) is likely to aid the global careerist in understanding the norms, values and behaviours of the host culture (Huang, Chi and Lawler, 2005). Local colleagues can help an expatriate's socialization and facilitate information exchange and idea diffusion (Toh and DeNisi, 2007). A reward system that is relatively equal across borders would work against an 'envy factor' and can encourage a supportive atmosphere between global careerists and host teams (Leung et al., 2009). However, helping foreign colleagues is normally voluntary and down to individual norms and values, as it is rarely part of a formal performance management system (Templer, 2010) and is unlikely to be connected to monetary rewards. In addition, Dowling et al. (2013) suggest that Employee Assistance Programmes can support global careerists in their adjustment and host country managers should be sensitized to pick up the signals when assignees (and their families) find the host culture difficult to adjust to. It might be argued that these issues are less severe for frequent travellers (Welch and Worm, 2006) than individuals who live long-term in one country.

Training and Development

The literature on international mobility, talent management and global leadership overlaps and all strands have a range of recommendations for activities to strengthen the learning of global careerists. Training and development as well as coaching and mentoring, that is geared to the specific foreign challenges that expatriates face, their current job demands and likely future organizational developments, can help individuals to increase their effectiveness and motivation in the present and the future (Scullion and Collings, 2011). Team-building initiatives can help expatriates to understand their context in more depth and can also help host country nationals to develop more tolerance of their foreign colleagues (Toh and DeNisi, 2007). Overall, these could lead to less culture shock and fewer frictions between locals and global careerists. In addition, the expatriation literature suggests post-arrival culture and language training (Harris et al., 2003) for global careerists. Encouraging cultural learning, operational excellence and mutual understanding in cross-cultural teams can lead to a better diffusion of ideas to the host environment and a reverse diffusion of ideas towards the sending unit (Edwards et al., 2005).

Performance Management

One of the key challenges for performance management is to find the 'right' balance between the central goals that the global careerist is meant to pursue and local interests (Evans et al., 2011). The importance of operational effectiveness for the organization depends on the primary expatriation rationale (Edström and Galbraith, 1977) and can cover diverse time horizons from immediate (in the case of fire-fighting or skills filling) to very long-term (in the case of coordination, control and, especially, developmental objectives). Thus, performance management of global careerists does not exist independent of the context and strategic objectives of the organization. In addition, performance management is only one part of people management, with learning, retention, reward and succession considerations intimately connected. We have seen in the earlier part of this chapter that European global careerists value developmental and career considerations more highly than performance and reward implications at the point of the decision to work abroad.

Reward Management: Principles and Design

The RES-Forum Report (2014) shows that global mobility experts predominantly design reward packages for global careerists in order to save costs, to keep administrative complexity low, to ensure compliance to local laws and to manage compliance with local and international tax and social benefit regulations. Very often, MNEs resort to specialized service providers in order to keep their own exposure limited and gain expert insights as the regulatory context is highly complex, divergent and dynamic. Key approaches to the actual reward package design for global assignees are home-country based (with a cost of living adjustment factored in to take account of differences in living costs) or host-country based (either local salaries or approaches such as 'local plus', that start from comparable local salaries and add certain benefits such as private schooling or travel allowances). Companies would be well advised to seek perceived reward equity, to minimize expatriate uncertainty and tax exposure and to understand diverse social security systems (Dickmann and Debner, 2011). Designing reward packages for non-traditional global careerists such as frequent business travellers has unique challenges (how do you/how can you compensate increased travel times, isolation and work/non-work balance issues?).

However, companies seem to consider some 'softer' elements in the reward package design far less, despite the repeated calls from some authors to do so (Andresen *et al.*, 2013; Dickmann and Baruch, 2011). For instance, it might be useful to consider rewarding global careerists for the acquisition of international business knowledge, skills and insights or the construction of wider, global networks that may have business benefits. In addition, understanding individuals' motivations to work abroad could also be factored into the reward package design (Dickmann *et al.*, 2008).

Global Career Management during the Transition Phase to the Next Position

For most expatriates, moving into a new role after their assignment (be it either in their country of origin or elsewhere) will become a reality. The repatriation of SIEs is less explored (for an exception see Andresen *et al.*, 2013) and this chapter is predominantly concentrating on a traditional expatriate's return home. Table 17.3 outlines major issues in more detail which we briefly address below.

Strategic Global Career Management

Individuals thinking about their own global career are likely to consider scenarios that stretch beyond the immediate role abroad. There has been a call to incorporate a long-term perspective into organizational global career management, for instance, as outlined by the expatriate cycle (Harris *et al.*, 2003). Of course, if an individual returnee leaves the organization, then the career management efforts of the employer have often (but not always) become meaningless for the organization. Therefore, return on investment considerations linked to the retention of repatriates, their career progression and performance become highly relevant (Doherty and Dickmann, 2012).

We know from earlier research that the financial, career and development effects of international assignments are important for individuals when they embark on a global career (Doherty *et al.*, 2011). Therefore, MNEs should strive for the creation of a global career proposition that is seen as attractive in these terms. This also needs to ensure that international work continues to carry kudos both during and after an assignment (Doherty and Dickmann, 2009). To facilitate such an effect it would be important for the communication of global mobility policies and reality to be closely aligned.

Table 17.3 Global career management at the point of the next move

Area		Organizational Action	Some Characteristics That Would Help
Strategic Global Career Management		Conduct long-range planning for repatriation. Ensure that international work continues to have high kudos. Communicate so that there is little or no significant gap between statements of top management and implementation with regards to repatriation and career opportunities.	*Organizational Choices* Ensure that the globalization strategy continues to be clear and to be seen as attractive. Execute global career policies and practices in a coherent and consistent manner. Work towards a perception that international staffing policies are fair or advantageous for global careerists. *Create a global career proposition to staff that is seen as financially, developmentally and career-wise attractive even after the sojourn.*
Global Career Management Practice		Prepare the global careerist for the next position in advance of return. Brief and update regarding organizational structure, goals, politics and changes in the new locations. Pre-return and after return dialogues to manage expectations/build realistic pre-return expectations. Encourage networking with colleagues in destination location. Continue to operate a mentor/global business sponsor system until repatriate is 'settled'.	*IM Choices* Conduct an open and honest assessment of the global careerist's situation in relation to the organization. Explore long-term career opportunities. Encourage the global careerist to continuously communicate with home during work abroad. *Work openly and honestly with the returnee to explore mutually beneficial career opportunities. Manage expectations.*

Social Context and Family	Give ongoing support for a time after return. Help for partner to find meaningful activity such as job and career re-entry. Help for family to (re-)settle.	*Family Choices* Organizational – family boundaries need to be evaluated with a view to social obligation and individual expectation. *Understand that after a long absence the re-entry of global careerists and their families may be complicated and may be supported by the organization.*
Job Factors	Ensure that the new job is challenging. Design the responsibilities so that global careerists can use their new capabilities and networks.	*Job Design Choices* Work towards a high level of responsibility (ideally not reduced when compared with earlier position). Preserve as much autonomy at work as is reasonable. *Design challenging jobs.*
Training and Development	Offer repatriation seminars on the emotional response. Continue to invest in repatriates so that they can systematically develop: professional skills personal skills leadership skills. Provide financial and tax counselling, advice and help for time after return/next move.	*T&D Choices* Use of professional skills in next position. Use of personal skills in next position. Use of leadership skills in next position. *Encourage the returnees to use the competencies, insights and networks that they have acquired abroad.*

(continued)

Table 17.3 (continued)

Area	Organizational Action	Some Characteristics That Would Help
Rewards: Principles and Design	Consider rewards for having developed and being able to use: an international perspective a worldwide network global skills and culturally sensitive abilities. Offer tie-over pay for repatriates.	*Reward Choices* Use both extrinsic and intrinsic reward approaches. Value international experience, learning and networks in the long-term (also symbolically). *Structure rewards to motivate repatriates, encourage capability transfer and increase retention chances.*
Exit Management	Create a fair process and a fair deal if competitive pressures or unforeseen circumstances (reorganizations, disinvestments) pressurize the organization to make repatriates redundant. Reduce risks with respect to negative comments within (internet-based) social networks. Retain contact if people may return to the organization or may become ambassadors for it.	*Exit Management* Be conscious of the symbolic message the organization sends with respect to global careers – if many people leave the organization upon return it sends a sign to potential expatriates that there are high risks involved in international mobility. *Manage the communication and psychological contract aspects when international workers leave.*

Note: Tables 17.1–17.3 based on Dickmann (2015) with own further developments. The ideas by authors such as Andresen *et al.* (2013), Black *et al.* (1991), Harris *et al.* (2003), Haslberger *et al.* (2013), Lazarova and Caligiuri (2001), McNulty *et al.* (2013) and Tharenou and Caulfield (2010) are acknowledged.

Global Career Management Practice

It has long been well known that expatriates want to know about their next move well in advance (Lazarova and Cerdin, 2007) and strive for career progression (Harris *et al.*, 2003). There are a range of activities that organizations can undertake in order to manage the expectations of their returnees. While the encouragement of networking, the provision of mentors or sponsors with power in the business are amongst those activities, openness and honesty are also virtues highly valued by global careerists (Lazarova and Caligiuri, 2001).

SIEs and AEs perceive positive outcomes for all three areas of career capital from their foreign sojourns (Jokinen *et al.*, 2008). While it is not clear whether global careerists can use their acquired career capital immediately in their next job after return (Dickmann and Baruch, 2011), over time the effect on all areas of the intelligent career is positive. Eight years after an initial study, global workers valued their cross-cultural competencies, international networks and deep insights even more highly than at the time of their foreign work (Dickmann *et al.*, 2012).

Social Context and Family

A pre-return conversation between the organization and its global careerists is useful for expectation management. If this conversation does occur, it is likely not to be restricted simply to work-related matters but has a high probability of also covering the social and family concerns of a move back. Ongoing logistical and (extra) financial support for a set period of time during and after the return of the global careerists and their families is often provided (The RES-Forum, 2014). It may be speculated that an understanding of the difficulties associated with resettlement after a long absence and the offer of further help would be appreciated by repatriates and their families (Dickmann and Baruch, 2011). This may smooth re-entry and help with reverse culture shock.

Job Factors

Repatriates often complain about the lack of career planning that has resulted in a job they do not perceive as challenging or short-term project work that is regarded as insecure (Richardson and Mallon, 2005). It would be better for global careerists if their 'new' job would allow them high levels of responsibility, autonomy and career progression. It is clear, however, that guaranteeing these attributes is nearly impossible and often impractical for organizations, so that managers tend to promise a 'best endeavour'. This is why promotion upon return might alleviate some of the returnees' concerns (Dickmann and Baruch, 2011).

Training and Development

Global careerists usually wish to acquire a range of professional and personal skills, so continuing to invest in these repatriates is likely to increase their work performance and motivation (Scullion and Collings, 2011). Hence, global careerists may benefit from repatriation seminars to increase their insights, sensitivities and capabilities in order to deal with the emotional, behavioural and cognitive challenges of returning home after a long time abroad. Overall, companies would be well advised to prepare repatriates before their move back and to encourage them to use their competencies, insights and the networks they have developed abroad for the benefit of the organization. Adopting a talent management perspective of expatriation by considering expatriation as a career issue would result in a decrease in repatriation failure (Cerdin and Brewster, 2014).

Rewards: Principles and Design

Tie-over pay to repatriates can help to overcome some degree of financial adjustment that individuals might go through – from 'highly' paid global worker to more 'normally' paid domestic worker. Doherty and Dickmann (2012) have outlined that in their sample, expatriates had a substantial mark-up to their non-expatriated peers. The reward design may factor in that returnees are likely to have more in-depth understanding of international business, superior skills and a higher cultural sensitivity. However, this is likely to be an indirect consideration and may only be captured through actual performance or promotion. Overall, Dickmann and Baruch (2011) suggest structuring rewards so as to motivate repatriates, encourage capability transfer and increase retention chances.

Exit Management

Amongst the darker aspects of global careers belongs a scenario in which an MNE goes through a restructuring or the sending unit experiences financial difficulties. Equally, the specific capability pattern of the returning global careerist is deemed to be not in demand or bad/non-existing career planning has meant that there is no job for the repatriate to go to (Dickmann and Doherty, 2010). This has the potential to lead to the individual being made redundant. In order to minimize negative effects of redundancy, it is suggested that MNEs manage their communication with the repatriate and the wider workforce. Additionally, the recommendations from the psychological contract literature (Conway and Briner, 2005) suggest that consistent processes and fair deals are used. Obviously, there are also communication implications if expatriates themselves decide to leave.

Global Careers in European MNEs

In the sections above, we have outlined global career patterns using both individual and organizational career management perspectives. In various places throughout the chapter we have indicated that in the unique European context, organizations have a multitude of strategic and operational options to shape, influence and utilize the effects of global careers. The antecedents and motivations of individual global careerists, their profiles and work patterns are also highly diverse. It is the mutual dependency of organizations and international workers and the wide array of possible actions that make the field of global careers such an interesting research focus.

We have also seen that global careers in European organizations unfold differently. The EU encourages international mobility actively. MNEs are more highly transnational and they face lower regulatory barriers to move EU nationals across borders in Europe. In addition, the motivations of global careerists in Europe are distinct – they tend to be more job content, development and career driven and less financially inspired. This calls for a more detailed analysis of individual expatriation drivers and a more flexible, yet sophisticated design of strategic and operational global career management, including associated policies in the areas of selection, training and development, rewards, performance and exit management.

Key Learning Points

- Europe has many MNEs that are highly transnational, which increases the need for global mobility.
- The European Union pursues an active policy to encourage global careers.
- The motivation for working abroad varies widely between assigned expatriates and self-initiated global workers. European global careerists rate developmental, job content and career aspects more highly and financial package drivers less highly than expatriates on other continents.

- Younger EU workers have a stronger interest to live abroad in comparison to their older peers (see Chapter 12 in this book) – a phenomenon that has strong implications for countries more affected by the financial crisis (see Chapter 7 in this book).
- Attracting and managing global careerists is highly important for companies – it is surprising that many MNEs (especially the largest companies in Germany and France) neglect to communicate international mobility opportunities for graduates on their websites.
- There are many global career strategies, policies and practices that European (and other) MNEs can design and implement to benefit individuals, the organization and society. A large range is outlined in the tables.

Notes

1 http://ec.europa.eu/languages/policy/language-policy/official_languages_en. htm (accessed: 30 Oct 2014).
2 http://data.worldbank.org/indicator/NY.GDP.PCAP.CD (accessed: 30 Oct 2014).
3 www.UNCTAD.org (accessed: 23 Feb 2014).

References

Ackers, L. (2005) 'Moving people and knowledge: Scientific mobility in the European Union', *International Migration*, 43(5): 99–131.

Al Ariss, A. (Ed.) (2014) *Global Talent Management: Challenges, Strategies, and Opportunities*. Cham: Springer.

Andresen, M., Al Ariss, A. and Walther, M. (eds) (2013) *Self-Initiated Expatriation. Individual, Organizational, and National Perspectives*. London, New York: Routledge.

Andresen, M., Bergdolt, F., Margenfeld, J. and Dickmann, M. (2014) 'Addressing international mobility confusion: Developing definitions and differentiations for self-initiated and assigned expatriates as well as migrants', *International Journal of Human Resource Management*, 25(16): 2295–2318.

Arthur, M.B. and Rousseau, D.B. (eds) (1996) *The Boundaryless Career. A New Employment Principle for a New Organizational Era*. New York, Oxford: Oxford University Press.

Arthur, M.B., Hall, D.T. and Lawrence, B.S. (1989) 'Generating new directions in career theory: The case for a transdisciplinary approach'. In: M.B. Arthur, D.T. Hall and B.S. Lawrence (eds), *Handbook of Career Theory*. Cambridge: Cambridge University Press, pp. 7–25.

Bartlett, C. and Ghoshal, S. (1989) *Managing Across Borders*. Boston, MA: Hutchinson.

Baruch, Y., Dickmann, M., Altman, Y. and Bournois, F. (2013) 'Exploring international work: Types and dimensions of global careers', *International Journal of Human Resource Management, Special Issue: 11th International HRM Conference*, 24(12): 2369–2393.

Black, J.S., Mendenhall, M. and Oddou, G. (1991) 'Toward a comprehensive model of international adjustment: An integration of multiple theoretical perspectives', *Academy of Management Review*, 16(2): 291–317.

Bonache, J. and Dickmann, M. (2008) 'The transfer of strategic HR know-how in MNCs: Mechanisms, barriers and initiatives'. In: M. Dickmann, C. Brewster and P. Sparrow (eds), *International Human Resource Management: The European Perspective*. London: Routledge, pp. 67–84.

Brewster, C. (1995) 'Towards a "European" model of human resource management', *Journal of International Business Studies*, 26(1): 1–21.

Brookfield Global Relocation Services (2014) '2014 global mobility trends survey'. http://www.brookfieldgrs.com.

Brück, F. (2002) *Interkulturelles Management. Kulturvergleich Österreich-Deutschland-Schweiz*. Frankfurt a. M., London: IKO – Verlag für Interkulturelle Kommunikation.

Carlos, A. and Nicolas, S. (1988) 'Giants of an earlier capitalism: The chartered trading companies as modern multinationals' *Business History Review*, 62(3): 398–419.

Cerdin, J.-L. (2007) *S'expatrier en toute connaissance de cause*. Paris: Eyrolles.

Cerdin, J.-L. (2013) 'Motivation of self-initiated expatriates'. In: M. Andresen, A. Al Ariss and M. Walther (eds), *Self-Initiated Expatriation: Individual, Organizational and National Perspectives*. London: Routledge, pp. 59–74.

Cerdin, J.-L. and Bird, A. (2008) 'Careers in a global context'. In: M. Harris (ed.), *Handbook of Research in International Human Resource Management*. New York: Lawrence Erlbaum Associates, pp. 207–227.

Cerdin, J.-L. and Brewster, C. (2014) 'Talent management and expatriation: Bridging two streams of research and practice'. *Journal of World Business*, 49(2): 245–252.

Cerdin, J.-L. and Sharma, K. (2014) 'Inpatriation as a key component of Global Talent Management'. In: A. Al Ariss (ed.), *Global Talent Management: Challenges, Strategies, and Opportunities*. Heidelberg: Springer, pp. 79–92.

Conway, N. and Briner, R. (2005) *Understanding Psychological Contracts at Work*. Oxford: Oxford University Press.

Dickmann, M. (2013) 'Why do they come to London? Exploring the motivations of expatriates to work in the British capital', *Journal of Management Development*, 31(8): 783–800.

Dickmann, M. (2015) 'International HRM's role in managing global careers'. In: D. Collings, G. Wood and P. Caligiuri (eds), *The Routledge Companion to International Human Resource Management*. London: Routledge, pp. 511–531.

Dickmann, M. and Baruch, Y. (2011) *Global Careers*. New York, Milton Park: Routledge.

Dickmann, M. and Debner, C. (2011) 'International mobility at work: Companies' structural, remuneration and risk considerations'. In: M. Dickmann and Y. Baruch (eds), *Global Careers*. London: Routledge, pp. 268–293.

Dickmann, M. and Doherty, N. (2010) 'Exploring organisational and individual career goals, interactions and outcomes of developmental international assignments', *Thunderbird International Business Review*, 52(4): 313–324.

Dickmann, M. and Müller-Camen, M. (2006) 'A typology of international human resource management strategies and processes', *International Human Resource Management Journal*, 17(4): 580–601.

Dickmann, M., Doherty, N., Mills, T. and Brewster, C. (2008) 'Why do they go? Individual and corporate perspectives on the factors influencing the decision to accept an international assignment', *The International Journal of Human Resource Management*, 19(4): 731–751.

Dickmann, M., Suutari, V., Brewster, C., Tanskanen, J., Tornikoski, C. and Mäkelä, L. (2012) 'Career capital development of assigned and self-initiated expatriates: Long-term perceptions'. *EAISM Workshop on New Analyses of Expatriation*. 13–14 December 2012, Paris, France.

Doherty, N. and Dickmann, M. (2009) 'Exploring the symbolic capital of international assignments', *The International Journal of Human Resource Management*, 20(2): 301–320.

Doherty, N. and Dickmann, M. (2012) 'Measuring the return on investment in international assignments: An action research approach', *International Journal of Human Resource Management*, 23(16): 3434–3454.

Doherty, N., Dickmann, M. and Mills, T. (2010) 'Mobility attitudes and behaviours among young Europeans', *Career Development International*, 15(4): 378–400.

Doherty, N., Dickmann, M. and Mills, T. (2011) 'Exploring the motives of company-backed and self-initiated expatriates', *International Journal of Human Resource Management*, 22(3): 595–611.

Dowling, P.J., Festing, M. and Engle Sr., A.D. (2013) *International Human Resource Management* (6th edn). London: Cengage Learning EMEA.

Dries, N., Pepermans, R. and De Kerpel, E. (2008) 'Exploring four generations' beliefs about career: Is "satisfied" the new "successful"?', *Journal of Managerial Psychology*, 23(8): 907–928.

Edström, A. and Galbraith, J.R. (1977) 'Transfer of managers as a coordination and control strategy in multinational organizations', *Administrative Science Quarterly*, 22(2): 248–263.

Edwards, M.R. (2009) 'An integrative review of employer branding and OB theory', *Personnel Review*, 39(1): 5–23.

Edwards, T., Almond, P., Clark, I., Colling, T. and Ferner, A. (2005) 'Reverse diffusion in US multinationals: Barriers from the American business system', *Journal of Management Studies*, 42(6): 1261–1286.

Eurostat (2014) *EU Citizenship-Statistics on Cross-Border Activities*. Brussels: European Union.

Evans, P., Pucik, V. and Björkman, I. (2011) *The Global Challenge: International Human Resource Management* (2nd edn). New York: McGraw-Hill.

Fourage, D. and Ester, P. (2007) 'Factors determining international and regional migrations in Europe'. *Dublin, European Foundation for the Improvement of Living and Working Conditions*.

Hall, D.T. (1996) 'Protean careers of the 21st century', *Academy of Management Executive*, 10(4): 8–16.

Harris, H., Brewster, C. and Sparrow, P. (2003) *International Human Resource Management*. London: CIPD.

Haslberger, A., Brewster, C. and Hippler, T. (2013) 'The dimensions of expatriate adjustment', *Human Resource Management*, 52(3): 333–351.

Haslberger, A., Brewster, C. and Hippler, T. (2014) *Managing Performance Abroad: A New Model for Understanding Expatriate Adjustment*. New York, London: Routledge.

Hippler, T. (2009) 'Why do they go? Empirical evidence of employees' motives for seeking or accepting relocation', *The International Journal of Human Resource Management*, 20(6): 1381–1401.

Hofstede, G. (1980) *Culture's Consequences: International Differences in Work-Related Values*. Newbury Park: Sage Publications.

Huang, T.-J., Chi, S.-H. and Lawler, J.J. (2005) 'The relationship between expatriates' personality traits and their adjustment to international assignments', *International Journal of Human Resource Management*, 16(9): 1656–1670.

Inkson, K., Gunz, H., Ganesh, S. and Roper, J. (2012) 'Boundaryless careers: Bringing back boundaries', *Organisation Studies*, 33(3): 323–340.

Jokinen, T., Brewster, C. and Suutari, V. (2008) 'Career capital during international work experiences: Contrasting self-initiated expatriate experiences and assigned expatriation', *International Journal of Human Resource Management*, 19(6): 979–998.

Lazarova, M. and Caligiuri, P. (2001) 'Retaining repatriates: The role of organization support practices', *Journal of World Business*, 36(4): 389–401.

Lazarova, M.B. and Cerdin, J.-L. (2007) 'Revisiting repatriation concerns: Organizational support versus career and contextual influences', *Journal of International Business Studies*, 38(3): 404–429.

Lazarova, M., Cerdin, J.-L. and Liao, Y. (2014) 'The internationalism career anchor: A validation study', *International Studies of Management & Organization*, 44(2): 9–33.

Leung, K., Zhu, Y.X. and Ge, C.G. (2009) 'Compensation disparity between locals and expatriates: Moderating the effects of perceived injustice in foreign multinationals in China', *Journal of World Business*, 44(1): 85–93.

McNulty, Y., De Cieri, H. and Hutchings, K. (2013) 'Expatriate return on investment in the Asia Pacific: An empirical study of individual ROI versus corporate ROI', *Journal of World Business*, 48(2): 209–221.

Martin, G. and Cerdin, J.-L. (2014) 'Employer branding and career theory: New directions for research'. In: P. Sparrow, H. Scullion and I. Tarique (eds), *Strategic Talent Management: Contemporary Issues in International Context*. Cambridge: Cambridge University Press, pp. 151–176.

Moore, K. and Lewis, D. (1999) *Birth of the Multinational*. Copenhagen: Copenhagen Business Press.

Osland, J., Bird, A., Mendenhall, M. and Osland, A. (2006) 'Developing global leadership capabilities and global mindset: a review'. In: G. Stahl and I. Bjorkman (eds), *Handbook of Research in International Human Resource Management*. Cheltenham: Edward Elgar, pp. 197–222.

Parker, P., Khapova, S.N. and Arthur, M.B. (2009) 'The intelligent career framework as a basis for interdisciplinary inquiry', *Journal of Vocational Behavior*, 75(3): 291–302.

Peiperl, M. and Jonsen, K. (2007) 'Global Careers'. In: H. Gunz and M. Peiperl (eds), *Handbook of Career Studies*. Thousand Oaks, CA: Sage Publications, pp. 350–372.

Porter, M.E. (1980) *Competitive Strategy: Techniques for Analyzing Industries and Competitors*. New York: Free Press, pp. 20–35.

Puck, J. F., Kittler, M.G. and Wright, C. (2008) 'Does it really work? Re-assessing the impact of pre-departure cross-cultural training on expatriate adjustment', *International Journal of Human Resource Management*, 19(12): 2182–2197.

Richardson, J. (2006) 'Self-directed expatriation: Family matters', *Personnel Review*, 35(4): 469–486.

Richardson, J. and Mallon, M. (2005) 'Careers interrupted? The case of the self-directed expatriate', *Journal of World Business*, 40(4): 409–420.

Schein, E.G. (1990) *Career Anchors: Discovering Your Real Values*. San Diego, CA: Pfeiffer & Company.

Scullion, H. and Collings, D. (eds.) (2011) *Global Talent Management*. London: Routledge.

Shaffer, M.A., Kraimer, M.L., Chen, Y.-P. and Bolino, M.C. (2012) 'Choices, challenges, and career consequences of global work experiences: A review and future agenda', *Journal of Management*, 38(4): 1282–1327.

Shenkar, O. (2001) 'Cultural distance revisited: Towards a more rigorous conceptualization and measurement of cultural differences', *Journal of International Business Studies*, 32: 519–535.

Stahl, G.K., Miller, E.L. and Tung, R.L. (2002) 'Toward the boundaryless career: A closer look at the expatriate career concept and the perceived implications of an international assignment', *Journal of World Business*, 37(3): 216–227.

Suutari, V. and Taka, M. (2004) 'Career anchors of managers with global careers', *Journal of Management Development*, 23(9): 833–847.

Templer, K.J. (2010) 'Personal attributes of expatriate managers, subordinate ethnocentrism, and expatriate success: A host-country perspective', *International Journal of Human Resource Management*, 21(10): 1754–1768.

Tharenou, P. (2003) 'The initial development of receptivity to working abroad: Self-initiated international work opportunities in young graduate employees', *Journal of Occupational and Organizational Psychology*, 76(4): 489–515.

Tharenou, P. and Caulfield, N. (2010) 'Will I stay or will I go? Explaining repatriation by self-initiated expatriates', *Academy of Management Journal*, 53(5): 1009–1028.

The RES-Forum (2014) *Key Trends in Global Mobility*, written by M. Dickmann. 102 pages. London: The RES Forum, UniGroup Relocation Network and Equus Software.

Toh, S.M. and DeNisi, A.S. (2007) 'Host country nationals as socializing agents: A social identity approach', *Journal of Organizational Behavior*, 28(3): 281–301.

Trompenaars, F. and Hampden-Turner, C. (1997) *Riding the Waves of Culture: Understanding Cultural Diversity in Business* (2nd edn). London: Nicholas Brealey.

Tung, R.L. (1998) 'American expatriates abroad: From neophytes to cosmopolitans', *Journal of World Business*, 33(2): 125–144.

UNCTAD (2007) The universe of the world's largest transnational organizations. UN Conference on Trade and Development.

Welch, D.E. and Worm, V. (2006) 'International business travellers: A challenge for IHRM'. In: G. Stahl and I. Björkman (eds), *Handbook of Research In International Human Resource Management*. Cheltenham: Edward Elgar Publishing, pp. 283–301.

WTO (2012) *World Trade Organization World Trade Developments*, 'Table I.4 intra- and inter-regional merchandise trade 2011'. Geneva: World Trade Organization, p. 23.

Yurkiewicz, J. and Rosen, B. (1995) 'Increasing receptivity to expatriate assignments'. In: J. Selmer (ed.), *Expatriate Management: New Ideas for International Business*. Westport: Quorum Books, pp. 37–56.

18 Talent Management in Europe

AGNIESZKA SKUZA, HUGH SCULLION AND
DAVID G. COLLINGS

Introduction

Although access to talented employees has always been important for
organizational success, recent demographic trends, the rapid process
of globalization and competitive pressures have highlighted talent
shortages and resulted in increasing interest in talent management
practices (Sparrow *et al.*, 2014; Sonnenberg *et al.*, 2014 Farndale *et al.*,
2014). Indeed, recent practitioner reports indicate that talent
management has emerged as a high priority for the majority of
multinational corporations (MNCs) and will continue to be a key
challenge that companies will face in the near future (CIPD, 2012;
Ernst and Young, 2010; PricewaterhouseCooper, 2012; Strack *et al.*,
2013). Consequently, from the perspective of practice, the challenge is
not whether or not to invest time and resources in talent management,
but how to identify talent, which talent management practices provide
the greatest returns and 'how to drive greater consistency, integration,
and alignment of talent practices with the business strategy' which,
according to 40 per cent of the surveyed companies in a recent study,
is far from sufficient (Human Capital Institute, 2008: p. 6). Those
challenges are particularly significant given the absence of established
theoretical foundations combined with concerns over the definition,
scope and overall goals of talent management to guide practice. It is
interesting that, despite the increased attention given to the topic,
the academic community has been relatively slow to embrace the
study of talent management in a rigorous and critical way. Some
see talent management as a fad or fashion created by consultants and
management gurus and characterized by a lack of conceptual and

intellectual foundations (Dries, 2013; Iles *et al.*, 2010). However, for the last decade or so there has been an upsurge of research activity in talent management reflected in an increasing number of theoretical and empirical academic contributions and the development of stronger theoretical base to study this emerging field (Lewis and Heckman, 2006; Boudreau and Ramstad, 2007; Cappelli, 2008; Collings, 2015; Collings and Mellahi, 2009; Scullion *et al.*, 2010; Bjorkman *et al.*, 2013; Dries, 2013; Garavan *et al.*, 2012; Gallardo-Gallardo *et al.*, 2015; Gelens *et al.*, 2013; Sparrow and Harkam, 2015).

The dominant influence of North American scholars and scholarship, which reflects the specific challenges that US organizations face, on the early theoretical and empirical development of talent management, has also been recognized (Collings *et al.*, 2011). While those US-based contributions have advanced our understanding of talent management significantly, more recently there has been an upsurge of theoretical and empirical insights from European scholars (Gallardo-Gallardo *et al.*, 2015). This has helped to develop our understanding of talent management by drawing on insights and learning from the different cultural and institutional contexts which are found in Europe and beyond. In this chapter we introduce both the European context of talent management and consider some evidence of the nature of talent management in European MNCs. We begin by introducing the concept of talent management and presenting the key debates that emerged around this topic.

Talent Management: Overview

Ever since the publication of the report *The War for Talent* by a group of McKinsey consultants in the late 1990s (Michaels *et al.*, 2001), the topic of talent management became increasingly important. The 'war for talent' emerged as a response to the notion that human capital had become the most important source of competitive advantage, whilst at the same time tightening labour market conditions made attracting and retaining talented employees more and more difficult. The idea of paying special attention to talented employees quickly spread among practitioners and academics. Recent reviews (Dries, 2013; Gallardo-Gallardo *et al.*, 2015; Thunnissen *et al.*, 2013) show a significant increase in the number of publications on talent management during the last 10 years. However, from over 7,000 articles that appeared in the period up to the end of 2013, only around 100 were published in academic journals (Dries, 2013), which shows a serious imbalance between practitioner and academic contributions to the literature on talent management. This may be attributed to scepticism within the academic community owing to the ambiguity of the theoretical and intellectual foundations of talent management and the lack of clarity of definitions both with regard to what talent is and how to effectively manage those designated as talent (Festing *et al.*, 2013; Scullion and Collings, 2011; Lewis and Heckman, 2006). The need to understand the conceptual boundaries of the topic and to establish a working definition of talent management resulted in academic publications of a mainly conceptual nature, although more recently we can also observe an upsurge of research activity around this topic with important contributions from European scholars (Dries and Pepermans, 2008; Boussebaa and Morgan, 2008; Sheehan, 2012; Hoglund, 2012; Gallardo-Gallardo *et al.*, 2013; Bjorkman *et al.*, 2013; Festing *et al.*, 2013; Skuza *et al.*, 2013; Tansley and Tietze, 2013; Valverde *et al.*, 2013; Farndale *et al.*, 2014; Sonnenberg *et al.*, 2014).

Following Thunnissen *et al.*'s (2013) recent review of the field, below we present three key streams of focus with regard to talent management: (1) the conceptualization of talent and talent management; (2) the intended outcomes and effects of talent management; and (3) talent management activities and practices.

The Conceptualization of Talent and Talent Management

The first key body of literature places a significant emphasis on the definition of talent in organizations. The major premise of these studies is an assumption that advancing the field is not possible without establishing a working definition of talent. The first key debate in the literature questions whether approaches to talent should be exclusive or inclusive. Some authors advocate an exclusive approach directed at a small, elitist group of talented employees who are strategically important for the organization (Morton, 2005; Collings and Mellahi, 2009; Silzer and Church, 2010; Gelens *et al.*, 2013), while others favour an inclusive approach that is built on the premise that all people are talented to some degree and can contribute to competitive advantage, though in different ways, and it is suggested that organizations should help all employees to develop their talent (Yost and Chang, 2009; Guthridge *et al.*, 2008). Although critics of exclusive approaches claim that it may damage the morale of the rest of the organization (Guthridge *et al.*, 2008), the exclusive approach seems to be more and more common in the literature and in practice (CIPD, 2012). In the exclusive approach, investment in specific groups of employees is shown to be more cost-effective and efficient (Collings and Mellahi, 2009) and has a greater impact on sustainable organizational performance (Sonnenberg *et al.*, 2014; Boudreau and Ramstad, 2007; Collings, 2014). However, there are a number of critiques of the exclusive approach based on the lack of objectivity of both evaluations of performance and potential (Gallardo-Gallardo *et al.*, 2013; Sparrow *et al.*, 2014).

The second theme in this stream focused upon the degree to which talent can be acquired (Meyers *et al.*, 2013; Gallardo-Gallardo *et al.*, 2013). Innate perspectives imply that talent is a mix of inborn cognitive abilities and personality which are stable and rather hard to develop (Davies and Davies, 2010; Buckingham and Vosburgh, 2001). In contrast, acquired perspectives advocate that talent is a mix of knowledge, skills and abilities that are capable of being developed and implies a focus on deliberate practice, education and learning. Authors in this stream state that although not all people have equal potential, talent emerges mainly through effort and experience (Ericsson *et al.*, 2007; Pfeffer and Scutton, 2006; Tsay and Banaji, 2011). The belief that talent is fixed (entity theory) or malleable (incremental theory: Dweck, 1999) influences talent management practices in the way that the former places much greater emphasis on talent identification and selection, the latter implies much more focus on talent development.

The third theme focuses on the degree to which talent should be operationalized through high performance (manifested in the past and present results and behaviour) or high potential (ability to perform effectively in the future). High performance is measured through realized outputs such as achievements, results and performance, which are easier to measure. However, identifying talent on the premise that past performance predicts future performance has been subjected to criticism by many authors (Martin and Schmidt, 2010; Silzer and Church, 2009). High potential on the other hand, is defined through input factors and implies that 'an individual has the qualities (e.g., characteristics, motivation, skills, abilities, and experiences) to effectively perform and contribute in broader or different roles in the organization at some point in the future' (Silzer and Church, 2009: p. 380). Despite its popularity among practitioners, the concrete meaning and definition of high potential is not clear, as potential itself 'exists in possibility' (Silzer and Church, 2009: p. 381) and measuring potential requires a clear understanding of what kind of individual abilities and skills the organization will need in the future to be able to perform effectively.

As discussed above, different philosophies around the nature of talent have a strong impact on talent management practices and implicit beliefs of the decision makers with regard to who they perceive as talent. Recent academic studies call for more empirical research that would help to test different talent operationalization and its consequences for talent management effectiveness.

The Intended Outcomes and Effects of Talent Management

The second key stream of talent management literature covers the issue of intended outcomes and effects of talent management. Most of those outcomes and effects are discussed at the organizational level and concern the potential of talent management to contribute to three areas: first, the narrowing of the talent supply–demand gap (Michaels et al., 2001; Beechler and Woodward, 2009); second, overall firm performance, strategic goals and organizational capabilities (Cappelli, 2008; Tansley et al., 2007; Morton, 2005; Heinen and O'Neill, 2004; Sparrow and Hakram, 2015); and third, filling strategic positions or key roles (Collings and Mellahi, 2009; Becker et al., 2009; Becker and Huselid, 2006). The outcomes are also analysed at an individual level and involve employee satisfaction, engagement, commitment, turnover intentions and motivation (Meyers and van Woerkom, 2014; Lepak and Snell, 1999). Those outcomes are also considered mediators between talent management and organizational outcomes (Collings and Mellahi, 2009). However, as highlighted by Bjorkman et al. (2013), still there is a lack of empirical research that examines the effects of talent management on individuals, notably when it comes to potentially conflicting goals of different internal stakeholders (e.g. higher motivation of those included in the talent pool versus lower motivation of those not included; different career expectations of different generational cohorts, etc.) or to understanding how employees interpret and react to talent management practices. These highly neglected aspects only recently started to be uncovered with regard to talent management by studies which use psychological contract perspective based on social exchange theory (Festing and Schafer, 2014; Bjorkman et al., 2013; Sonnenberg et al., 2014; Hoglund, 2012) or the theory of perceived organizational justice (Gelens et al., 2013; Dries, 2013; Jerusalim and Hausdorf, 2007).

Talent Management Process

The third stream of research focuses on talent management practices and tools that help to effectively manage talent in organizations. These studies are significant as there is little evidence that organizations manage talent effectively (Strack et al., 2013; Cohn et al., 2005). Indeed, a CIPD study (2012) showed that only 6 per cent of organizations rated their talent management activities as very effective, while a report by the Boston Consulting Group found that although talent management was a key priority for European organizations, it was the HRM issue they felt least prepared to deal with (Strack et al., 2013). Companies typically integrate their talent management process around attracting, selecting, developing and retaining their best employees

(Scullion *et al.*, 2010; Stahl *et al.*, 2007). The simple rebranding of HRM as talent management has led to a degree of critique as to the extent to which talent management represents anything more than a new term for existing practice (Lewis and Heckman, 2006; Iles *et al.*, 2010). However, recent studies appear to point to important distinctions between talent management and HRM. Key examples of differentiation in this regard include the practice of workforce differentiation (Iles *et al.*, 2010; Collings and Mellahi, 2009; Chuai *et al.*, 2008). Debate around talent management practices involves the tensions between identification of talented individuals versus identification of key positions or strategic roles as a point of departure for talent management strategies (Boudreau and Ramstad, 2007; Becker and Huselid, 2006; Collings and Mellahi, 2009), the balance between organizational and individual focus of talent development strategies (Pruis, 2011; Bjorkman *et al.*, 2013) and the tension between developing talent internally (making talent) or buying talent from the external market, which can differ considerably in different industries and different companies (Groysberg, 2010; Scullion and Collings, 2011; Gallardo-Gallardo *et al.*, 2013; Collings, 2013; Meyers and van Woerkom, 2014). Increasingly scholars also stress the importance of differentiated talent development architecture reflective of different development needs, different developmental pathways and differentiated HRM architecture to support talent management (Gandz, 2006; McDonnell and Collings, 2011). However, as yet we have an incomplete understanding of how those development pathways are designed for different categories of talent (Garavan *et al.*, 2012).

The notion of a differentiated architecture is central to one of the more influential definitions of talent management developed by Collings and Mellahi (2009: p. 305):

> the systematic identification of key positions which differentially contribute to the organisation's sustainable competitive advantage, the development of a talent pool of high potential and high performing incumbents to fill these roles, and the development of a differentiated human resource architecture to facilitate filling these positions with competent incumbents and to ensure their continued commitment to the organisation.

European research arguably reflects differing scientific and epistemological traditions in the European context (Collings *et al.*, 2011). Arguably, a key consideration in the European context is the importance of context and the challenge to universalistic models of management practice (Brewster, 1995). The debates evident in talent management literature resonate with earlier debates around HRM more generally in the European context. The European model of management has been characterized as *inter alia*, tied to the idea of European integration; reflective of values such as pluralism and tolerance, while not being necessarily developed from them; and more associated with a balanced stakeholder philosophy, recognizing the role of social partners (Thurley and Wirdenius, 1991). Having considered the broad debates around the nature of talent management, we now move to explaining talent management in the European context, followed by the presentation of some evidence on the nature of talent management in the European MNCs.

The European Context of Talent Management

Europe is a significant player in the global economy (see Chapter 1 of the current volume). The 27-member European Union alone contributes around 20 per cent of the world's total gross domestic product (International Monetary Fund, 2013). The EU is recognized as the world's largest trading block and accounts for 15 per cent of global trade in goods and 22.5 per cent of global trade in services (European Union, 2014). Europe is also recognized as one of the triad of regions (apart from NAFTA and Asia) where the concentration of sales and activities of MNCs is the highest (Rugman and Verbeke, 2004). According to UNCTAD (2010) over 60 out of 100 largest non-financial MNCs are headquartered in Europe and the recent Global 500 ranking published by *Fortune* magazine (*Fortune*, 2013) ranks 38 European MNCs on the list of 100 world's largest corporations. Acknowledging the importance of Europe in international trade and the increasing role of MNCs in shaping local human resources practices, we will present below the distinctive forces in Europe that impact talent management programmes in European MNCs.

First, due to the relatively small size of their domestic market, European MNCs emerged as earlier internationalizers. They tend to earn a higher percentage of revenues from their foreign operations and they also have a longer history of moving their talents across borders than US MNCs, which are more focused on their huge domestic market (Scullion and Brewster, 2001). Internationalization of European companies can be seen when the index of transnationality is calculated (which is an arithmetic mean of the following three ratios: average of ratio of foreign assets to total assets, ratio of foreign sales to total sales and ratio of foreign employment to total employment). According to UNCTAD (2012) in 2011 the European Union (EU) had the highest average index of transnationality and out of the 20 world's top MNCs ranked by transnationality, 16 were headquartered in Europe (all of the top 10 firms were European). This internationalization is also supported by the development of the European Union, which decreased the barriers to the movement of goods, services, capital and labour between member states, increasing cross-border trade and strengthening the growth in movement of talent across borders. What sets the EU apart from other free-trade areas globally is the lack of legal and administrative barriers in transferring foreign workers between EU countries. Moreover, the geographic proximity of the member countries (most European locations are within one to three hours flying time) gives more options with regard to alternative forms of international assignments, which have become particularly popular in the European context. Indeed, the growth of short-time and commuter assignments reflects the ability of European MNCs to develop more flexible staffing policies in response to the more turbulent international environment (Collings *et al.*, 2007; Forster, 2000). Therefore, with the growing recognition of the critical role played by international talent management for the success of MNCs, Europe seems to have particularly favourable conditions in facilitating the development of talent across borders.

One of the major constraints to this assumption is, however, a high degree of autonomy that European MNCs typically allow their subsidiaries which, regardless of high levels of internationalization, might restrict the development of effective talent pipelines at the regional or global level and the implementation of globally integrated talent strategies (Collings *et al.*, 2011). For example, a study by Scullion and Starkey (2000) of 45 European MNCs highlighted the emergence of different approaches to the management and mobility of senior managers in highly coordinated versus highly decentralized MNCs. In the former there was a much higher degree of corporate control over the management of the mobility and careers of the key talents. In the latter, effective co-ordination was more difficult due to more tensions between HQ and divisions and the emergence of silo mentalities at divisional or subsidiary level, where barriers emerged to the free flow of talent across the global network (Scullion and Starkey, 2000).

Second, increasing economic and social integration across the European Union has resulted in a more unified context for organizations to operate in (Brewster, 1995; Mayrhofer and Larsen, 2006) and may suggest the emergence of a European model of HRM. Indeed, as Scullion and Brewster (2001) pointed out, giving Ford Europe as an example, many MNCs increasingly treat the European market as a single entity and seek to integrate human resource strategies on the European regional level. However, while market forces and diverse institutional regulations within the EU increase the convergence of HRM practices, deep-seated national differences both on institutional and cultural levels still play an important role for local talent management systems.

Third, the context in which talent management takes place in Europe differs significantly from the US context, where most of the early theory on talent management has emerged (Brewster, 1995; Brewster, Mayrhofer and Morley, 2000). On the legislative level, there are differences in the degree of employment protection (greater regulations in the process of dismissals, collective wage agreements), legislative requirements on pay and hours of work (e.g. in France limited by law to 35 hours per week) and legislation on the forms of employment contract (Brewster, 2004). European-level legislation and national-level requirements in Europe are much more extensive than US legislation and influence the way people are recruited, how much they should be paid, the number of days holiday, the range of management decisions that must be consulted with employees, trade union bargaining power level, etc. A further key factor in the context of talent management is the significant role of the state in the development of employee skills and competencies, for example, as observed in Germany or Switzerland (dual education systems with professional education on the job and parallel education at a vocational school). Next, significant differences emerge in how firms are financed in Europe. In many Southern European countries, ownership of even large companies is controlled by single families; in Germany, a small number of substantial banks own a substantial proportion of companies (Brewster, 2004); in Sweden shareholders are obligated to be involved in big strategic decisions (Swedish model of active ownership of companies). Such patterns of ownership promote a longer-term approach to firm-financing and close involvement of shareholders in management decisions, which is in contrast to the dominant short-term approach in the USA. Considering the above, we suggest that in the context of talent management in Europe, MNCs must pay much more attention to exogenous factors that play a significant role in management behaviour and decisions.

Finally, research (Paauwe, 2004; Sparrow and Hiltrop, 1997; Thurley and Wirdenius, 1991) has demonstrated that within the European Union some characteristics of HRM are quite distinct from US patterns. The differences include organization structure and management control systems and processes, with European MNCs putting stronger emphasis on socialization and American MNCs concentrating more on formalization and centralization (Edwards and Ferner, 2002; Scullion and Brewster, 2001), which requires different approaches to talent management. Nikandrou *et al.* (2006) also stress the importance of the contextual paradigm in European research, which emphasizes the need to focus on understanding and explaining differences in HRM systems in different contexts (cultural values, norms, societal structure, language, etc.) in contrast to the American universalist approach. In summary, talent management systems in Europe need to adopt a multilevel approach that would consider national culture and the above-mentioned European and national legislation differences, state involvement and the effect of European-level and national-level institutionalism (educational, financial, industrial relations systems) on MNC business patterns.

Talent Management in Europe[1]

In spite of the increasing popularity of talent management, the research base on talent management in European MNCs is rather limited, reflecting the general lack of empirical studies in this field. In this section we consider some of the important empirical studies on talent management in the European context. Reviewing empirical research in the European context we distinguish among several dominant themes of research. First, we observe that authors increasingly use a psychological contract perspective as a lens through which to explore the dynamics between talent management and individual-level responses. Second, authors analyse talent management processes and provide insights into how organizations deploy talent management systems in Europe and what challenges they face in different institutional and cultural contexts. Third, European authors also investigate careers of high potentials examining cultural differences in the nature of the expatriate career concept and yield some insights into the boundaryless career concept in Europe. Finally, they examine the effect of different types of talent management strategies on individual and organizational-level outcomes.

A Psychological Contract Perspective on Talent Management

A key theme in recent European studies has been advancing our understanding of the dynamics between talent management and individuals, particularly drawing on the psychological contract perspective based on social exchange theory. For example, in their recent study of 11 Nordic MNCs, Bjorkman *et al.* (2013) used a psychological contract lens to test a number of hypotheses with regard to the association between talent identification and a variety of employee attitudes. They demonstrated that informing talented individuals of their status has a motivational effect on those individuals, supporting the general logic of talent management. Those who perceived that they were identified as talent were more likely to display positive attitudes (including commitment to increased performance, to build valuable competencies, to actively support organization strategic priorities, identification with the focal unit, or lower turnover intent) than those who were not identified as talents. Therefore, informing an individual acts as a signal that individual contribution is valued and that the employer has fulfilled its contract, which in turn influences the talents' intention to remain a member of such organizations. Bjorkman *et al.* (2013) also found that informing individuals that they are not talents has little negative effect which, they speculate using cognitive dissonance theory, may result from downplaying the importance of being a member of a talent pool.

The importance of making talent management practices explicit was also reinforced by Sonnenberg *et al.* (2014) in their recent study of 21 European MNCs. They found that a better understanding of who is designated as talent by organizations leads to a higher psychological contract fulfilment and that talent management practices will not automatically profit from the increased psychological contract fulfilment unless they ensure that those practices are perceived appropriately and utilized by the targeted employees. Sonnenberg *et al.* (2014) also found that although many organizations favour an inclusive approach to talent identification, in practice all make distinctions between employees, although often they do not communicate those distinctions to employees. However, they pointed out that the existence of talent management practices without clear and uniform communication leaves much more space for misinterpretation of who is seen as talent, which may create false expectations and result in a number of negative consequences such as higher turnover, lower commitment, etc. They also suggest that organizations should employ an exclusive differentiation strategy rather than an inclusive strategy in attempting to minimize talents' perceptions of incongruence and to achieve higher effectiveness of talent management efforts. Well-targeted talent management investments and making an effort to ensure that talents perceive talent management practices as intended, has a significant positive effect on psychological contract fulfilment, which has been shown to be a good predictor of important talent management outcomes.

The psychological contract perspective on talent management was also adopted by Hoglund (2012) in his study of 17 Finnish, Swedish and Norwegian multinationals, followed by a study among 126 respondents from various organizations in Finland. Hoglund (2012) examined both the direct and indirect effect of HRM practices on human capital from a talent management perspective, adding talent inducement as a mediating variable. He applied the psychological contract perspective to assess employee perceptions on the extent to which organizations induce talent (mainly with regard to career and promotion opportunities) and the effect of such perceptions on the obligation to develop skills. The results of Hoglund's study confirmed that 'differential treatment of employees based on criteria constituting talent can have positive effects on employee motivation and felt obligations to develop skills and apply these in service of the organization' (Hoglund, 2012: p. 136). While the direct effect of skill-enhancing HRM practices on human capital turned out to be insignificant, the total indirect effect of skill-enhancing HRM practices on human capital through talent inducements turned out to be significant, which shows the positive consequences that talent management may have on employees' attitudes and psychological contract obligations.

Talent Management Process in Different Institutional and Cultural Contexts

A second key stream of research on talent management in Europe focuses on the talent management process. Tansley and Tietze (2013), drawing on the work of Van Gennep (1960), illustrate how talent progression through successive levels of talent management process can be explained through a series of rites of passage (such as involvement in stretch projects, passing professional exams, meeting with top management, etc.) and they highlight how talent advancement is contingent on the development of appropriate identities. Their study tracks the experiences of individual talent in three different talent pools; Rising Talent, Emerging Leaders and Next Generation Leader, in a consulting organization. Their findings suggest that talent advancement is based on the development of technical expertise and the emergence of particular dispositions and work orientations in this context. The study presents an interesting perspective on the dynamism of work identities, which requires a constant readjustment whilst an individual is going through different rites of passage and their different stages (separation, liminality and incorporation). The role of regulated behaviour and self-discipline that talent has to develop to be able to quickly connect and disconnect from locations, relationships and work groups to be able to progress through the talent pools, also emerges as key. This paradoxical aspect of the talent progression process along with the sense of liminality that should be accepted by talents as the perpetual way of living and working requires talent management programmes to support talents in their critical self-reflection and the ability to challenge the values and norms of corporate engagement.

The process perspective also provides insights into how organizations deploy talent management systems in Europe. Taking an institutionalist approach to explain the deployment of common talent management systems across borders, Boussebaa and Morgan (2008) explore how differences between the British and French institutional contexts manifest themselves in different approaches to talent management and different talent management practices. Their findings point to the tensions which emerge in the utilization of a framework of talent management developed in the UK and France, which resulted in the complete failure of implementation of a common talent management system. Those incompatibilities concerned both high potential identification and development processes. The British logic underscoring the talent management framework assumed equality of opportunity for all managers and was based on meritocracy, meaning that talent identification and career progress depended on proven performance within the roles and managerial potential, which should be measured by internally administered tests and developed by coaching, mentoring or training. In France, however, talent was not assessed internally, but through the *grandes écoles* system that is the top tier of the higher education system. Graduates of these universities become *cadres* that constitute an elite that run French organizations and it is extremely rare for *non-cadres* to advance to the highest organizational levels. Therefore potential in France is identified at the point of entry, where the diploma from *grandes écoles* already proves their potential. Career progress is then subsequently based on seniority, international mobility and political tasks of activating the networks from the *grandes écoles*. Boussebaa and Morgan (2008) also showed deep divergence in talent development practice. The British preference for pragmatism and practical skills and the French inclination towards intellectualism and abstract thinking created various conflicts and misunderstandings between the two managerial groups. Overall, they emphasize that the failure of a common talent management programme was the result of the lack of understanding of the institutional context that varied in both countries and which had to be considered when different management practices are implemented in MNCs across varied locations.

The importance of the institutional context for deployment of talent management practices is also highlighted in the context of German small and medium-size enterprises (SMEs) (Festing *et al.*, 2013). This study identified how talent management may vary significantly between different types of companies and national contexts. For example, they demonstrated that German SMEs, which they define as those firms employing up to 2,000 employees, prefer a more inclusive approach to talent management, targeting all or the majority of employees, in contrast to a more exclusive approach which appears to be favoured in larger MNCs (Stahl *et al.*, 2012). The German national education system (promoting equality) and the long-term approach typical of the German national business system orientation are identified as key explanatory factors in this regard. The study also provides interesting insights on the process of talent management, which appear highly dependent on the CEO/owner in terms of talent recruitment and development and which focus heavily on retaining talents through training and development activities accessible to a majority of employees. Further, larger SMEs placed much more emphasis on talent management than smaller SMEs and had more developed external collaborative networks (universities, other companies) in their talent management activities. Building networks and cooperation were identified as an innovative responses to the talent shortages faced and the German SMEs effectively combined resources and knowledge to develop a more professional HRM function.

Similarly, in the Spanish context, Valverde *et al.* (2013) demonstrated that even whilst there is little awareness of the term and discourse of talent management in the SME sector in Spain, talent management practices were seen to exist and operate effectively. Indeed their research highlighted a paradox: the companies involved in the study were generally successful in managing their talent, yet the managers did not relate to the concept of talent management. There was a tendency to distance themselves from the formalization of the talent management concept, seeing it as a management fad, while at the same time they appeared to have implemented what could be considered key talent management practices. This reflected the business traditions of Latin Europe, with a high degree of informality of HRM practices in SMEs (Dundon and Wilkinson, 2009). Valverde *et al.* (2013) also highlighted that talents in Spanish medium sized organizations tended to be seen primarily as loyal, committed, trustworthy and consistent, which conflicts with the talent management literature which focuses on high potential. The study stresses the importance of the country-specific context of talent management and calls for comparative empirical studies of talent management in European countries, which would take into account the specific institutional, historical and cultural factors. Their study also highlighted the importance of informal talent management practices in the attraction, motivation, development and retention of key staff. Specifically, the issue of succession planning was identified as a problematic area. Overall, this study provides a welcome and fresh perspective to the study of talent management in Europe and constitutes an important contribution to previous research on talent management that focuses mainly on large MNEs with Anglo-Saxon traditions.

Turning to Central and Eastern Europe (CEE), Skuza, Scullion and McDonnell (2013) made an important contribution to our understanding of talent management through their study of multinationals in Poland. Empirical research on talent management in this region is practically non-existent (Vaiman and Holden, 2011), in spite of the increasing significance of the region in the European economy. Skuza *et al.* (2013) identified several key challenges to talent management deployment particular to the CEE region in three key areas: talent identification, development and evaluation. For example, in the CEE countries there remains a tendency to appoint to talent pools based on individual technical abilities rather than leadership or personal skills, the latter not being considered important for managerial effectiveness. Further, typical to the region was a lack of recognition of individual successes, which often resulted in discouragement to undertake a talent role and the creation of a negative atmosphere around talent management. Reliance on personal relations and private networks in management decisions emerged as another barrier to effective talent management and high potentials were often seen as a threat to the position of established senior managers. In addition, cultural factors led to an unwillingness to include employees in the decision-making process, a low level of innovativeness and willingness to learn, short-termism and a lack of transparency in the evaluation process. The issues of talent management in CEE countries are only now starting to be of interest to both practitioners and scholars, as even the strategic approach to HRM is still in its infancy in the CEE region. Lack of knowledge and experience about talent management in those countries, as well as cultural complexities and historical experiences of the region make it difficult to adapt Western talent management practices directly and the study of Skuza *et al.* (2013) highlights the need for organizations to understand the institutional and cultural context in which they operate and also the need to develop an appropriate domestic talent strategy that would link talent management with the overall global strategy and the corporate culture (Vaiman and Holden, 2011).

Careers of High Potentials and Boundaryless Career Concept in Europe

A third key stream of research on talent management in Europe focuses on the careers of high potentials. For example, Dries and Pepermans (2008) highlighted the career issues both from the perspective of high potentials and their organizations in the Belgian context. Their study provides some important insights on the applicability of boundaryless career theories (in which employees often change employers as they aspire to freedom and flexibility) and employability in the European context. While many point to a shift from traditional to more boundaryless careers as inevitable, the authors found that this assumption is somewhat out of kilter in the expectations of high potentials, who continue to expect more traditional career options demonstrated in high upward mobility and low inter-organizational mobility. This is also in line with organizational efforts to promote talent from within and to invest time and resources to develop those that demonstrate above-average abilities and the drive to progress within the organization. As investments in those talents are high, more efforts are made to retain those people in the organization. Therefore, Dries and Pepermans question the universality of the boundaryless career concept and highlight that while such career imperatives might be salient for some segments of the workforce, they may not for others (i.e. high potentials). Another key finding of the study is the universalism of employability. The study suggests that high potentials 'are still getting the "old deal" as they are promised long-term career perspectives and upward advancement' (Dries and Pepermans, 2008: p. 102). They also hypothesize that non-core employees learn more through lateral moves than high potentials, acquiring the employability needed to be attractive for other organizations, while allowing high potentials to move up in the organization. This study advances our understanding of how workforce segmentation might affect organizational career structures – from the boundaryless orientation of non-core employees whose employability is a key to progress with inter-organizational career paths, to non-boundaryless career opportunities for high potentials and experts (difficult to replace and possessing organization-specific professional knowledge and skills) who move within the organization. Establishing stimulating career tracks for key experts is a key challenge facing organizations. Self-direction and initiative taking are key characteristics of high potentials careers, yet while talents like to manage their own careers, at the same time, they expect some guidance from their organizations. Finally, while the study suggested that organizations should deliver well-organized succession planning and be transparent about career opportunities, it also suggested that high potentials should be realistic and patient about their careers, as higher positions may not be available as fast as they would wish.

Career management issues in the European context were also studied by Stahl and Cerdin (2004) in a sample of French and German expatriates. Their study explored whether there are cultural differences in the nature of the expatriate career concept and yielded some insights into the boundaryless career concept in countries other than the USA. The study showed that while intrinsic motives, such as personal challenge and professional development, were the most important reasons to accept an international assignment both for French and German talents, monetary incentives, family consideration and encouragement from spouse/partner were more important for French talents, while personal challenge, career advancement opportunities and anticipated job success were more important for German talents. Their study also confirmed that a majority of expatriate talents from both countries were frustrated with how their companies managed their repatriation plans. However, while the French were concerned with their career development in their companies upon return to their home country, German talents were much more optimistic as they perceived their international assignment as a competitive asset that made them more valuable to the external labour market. Half of the German respondents were willing to leave the company upon return when compared to one-third of the French. Finally Stahl and Cerdin (2004) made an important observation that while international assignments may be beneficial for talents in European organizations, they may be risky for organizations if they do not integrate international assignments into succession and career plans. Indeed, the integration of global mobility and global talent management has been proposed as a key research agenda in global talent management (Cerdin and Brewster, 2014; Collings, 2014; Farndale *et al.*, 2014).

Organizational and Individual-Level Outcomes of Talent Management

More recently European researchers have also developed empirical studies which focus specifically on talent management outcomes. For example, a recent study by Sheehan (2012) conducted in 143 UK-owned MNCs with subsidiaries located in Czech Republic, Hungary and Poland, examined the association between talent management (specifically management development) and perceived subsidiary performance and also examined whether national context mediates this relationship. The findings of this study confirm that investing in managerial talent will have a positive influence on perceived subsidiary performance, although the national context influences the associated returns. Specifically, the author highlighted that economic environment and the national quality of human capital is significant. The study thus argues that investing in managerial development may yield positive returns even in uncertain and volatile economic environments.

Taking a broader approach to talent management outcomes in the European context, Bethke-Langenegger *et al.* (2011) examined the effect of different types of talent management strategies on organizational and individual-level outcomes among Swiss corporations. They analysed four strategies: talent management focused on corporate strategy and corporate goals; talent management focused on succession planning; talent management focused on attracting and retaining talents; and talent management focused on developing talents. A major finding was that talent management practices with a strong focus on corporate strategies and the alignment to overall corporate goals have an important impact on organizational outcomes such as company profit, company attractiveness, the achievement of business goals, customer satisfaction, as well as on individual outcome of performance motivation. A second key finding was that talent management focused on succession planning also impacted corporate profit and some individual outcomes – performance motivation, work quality and trust in leaders, which can be the result of perceived expectations about possible career advancement and more open communication with leaders about career opportunities. A third finding was that talent management strategy, based on attracting new talented employees, identifying talents within the organization and offering incentives to retain them, was correlated to customer satisfaction and all individual outcomes – performance motivation, commitment, work quality and trust in leaders. Surprisingly, there was no significant effect on company profit, which, as the authors hypothesize, is associated with the perception of high investments on retaining talents that may exceed the benefits from this strategy. Fourth, strategy focused on talent development showed positive correlations with all organizational and individual outcomes, which reveals the significance of focusing on employee development needs and expectations. The authors conclude that while all strategies influence various organizational and individual outcomes, demonstrating the important role of talent management strategy, based on succession planning, overall has the weakest impact on non-financial outcomes both on an organizational (i.e. customer satisfaction) and individual level.

The above review highlights the diversity of approaches to talent management in the European context. Arguably the focus on psychological contract, process issues in talent management and talent management in context reflect the greater consideration of context, and a greater awareness of pluralism and tolerance based on a more balanced stakeholder approach in European management scholarship (Brewster, 1995; Thurley and Wirdenius, 1991). It is clear European scholars have recently made an important contribution to the development of theoretical foundations of talent management and the growing number of recent empirical research studies on talent management in Europe shows an increasing academic interest in this field, which helps to develop our understanding of talent management processes, their impact on individuals and their careers and their influence on corporate performance.

Conclusion

There is little doubt that the topic of talent management has entered the mainstream for European scholars and practitioners alike. Indeed, recent advances in theorizing and empirical evidence are beginning to delineate the particular European context of talent management. Indeed, while acknowledging great variety within the region, the context in which people management takes place in Europe is significantly different to the US context, where much of the theory around talent management has emerged (Brewster, 1995; Brewster *et al.*, 2000; Holt Larsen and Mayrhofer, 2006). For example, the relative emphasis on legislative frameworks (both national and supranational in the context of the EU) on the management of employees, reflected in greater regulation of recruitment and dismissal, the relative power of trade unions and collective approaches toward employee management in a number of key countries, institutional arrangements around communicating with employees, works councils and the like is striking in Europe (Brewster, 1995; Brewster *et al.*, 2000; Pieper, 1990). Further, owing to the role that the state plays in the development of employee skills and competencies in countries such as Germany (Thelen, 2001) governments often have a greater controlling influence on behaviour (through legislation) and a greater supportive role (through financing) than in the US, resulting in comparatively less autonomy for employers in managing employees in the European context (Brewster, 1995). Further, the nature of the financing of firms in the European context (although this is not universal, with the UK model much closer to the US model) differs greatly to other countries such as the US. In contrast to the short-termist shareholder approach which dominates the US model, more coordinated market economies in the European context (Hall and Soskice, 2001) are characterized by a more patient, stakeholder approach. Corporate funders such as banks generally adopt a more patient approach to firm financing, meaning that firms can adopt a longer-term approach to employee relations. This has the potential to drive more sustainable talent management strategies in European countries (Collings, 2014).

As our review of research in the European context has demonstrated, there is an emerging body of empirical work which helps us to understand the concept of talent management in Europe better and more broadly from a theoretical perspective. We have argued that European scholarship has brought the individual back into the discussion on talent management to a greater degree, for example, through work that explores the interaction of talent practices and the psychological contracts of talents and 'non' talents in organizations (Bjorkman *et al.*, 2013; Hoglund, 2012). Further, European research on talent management has developed our understanding from process and institutionalist perspectives (Boussebaa and Morgan, 2008; Festing *et al.*, 2013; Tansley and Tietze, 2013). This is arguably illustrative of differing philosophical and theoretical preferences in the European context vis-à-vis the US context, where much of the earlier scholarship emerged. European research has also expanded our understanding of talent management in organizations beyond the major MNCs that have dominated much of the early work in the field (Festing *et al.*, 2013; Valverde *et al.*, 2013). Given the sheer volume of SMEs and the numbers employed by these firms, research in such firms is a particularly important avenue of study. Finally, there is an emerging body of work which provides comparative insights on talent management in different European countries. Clearly such studies are important in helping us to understand the extent to which globally standardized approaches to talent management are emerging versus more distinctive national models. While, as yet, we do not have the evidence base to reach a conclusion on the extent to which talent management practices are converging globally, based on what we do know we can conclude that; within multinational organizations (and particularly large ones) there is the emergence of some consistent set of global best practices (Stahl *et al.*, 2012); however, in smaller organizations it appears that there is more diversity with perhaps a sense that national cultural and institutional traditions are significant in influencing talent management practice.

Key Learning Points

Having read this chapter, readers should now understand the:

• different definitions and approaches to talent management;
• general features and specificities of talent management in the European context;
• key empirical research streams in talent management in Europe;
• potential for more sustainable talent management strategies in the European context.

Note

1 Owing to space restrictions this review is illustrative rather than exhaustive.

References

Becker, B.E. and Huselid, M.A. (2006) 'Strategic human resources management: Where do we go from here?', *Journal of Management*, 32(6), 898–925.
Becker, B.E., Huselid, M.A. and Beatty, R.W. (2009) *The differentiated workforce: Transforming talent into strategic impact*. Boston, MA: Harvard Business Press.
Beechler, S. and Woodward, I.C. (2009) 'The global war for talent', *Journal of International Management*, 15(3), 273–285.
Bethke-Langenegger, P., Mahler, P. and Staffelbach, B. (2011) 'Effectiveness of talent management strategies', *European Journal of International Management*, 5(5), 524–539.

Bjorkman, I., Ehrnrooth, M., Mäkelä, K., Smale, A. and Sumelius, J. (2013) 'Talent or not? Employee reactions to talent identification', *Human Resource Management*, 52(2), 195–214.

Boudreau, J.W. and Ramstad, P.M. (2007) *Beyond HR: The new science of human capital*. Boston, MA: Harvard Business School Press.

Boussebaa, M. and Morgan, G. (2008) 'Managing talent across national borders: The challenges faced by an international retail group', *Critical Perspectives on International Business*, 4(1), 25–41. doi:10.1108/17422040810849749.

Brewster, C. (1995) 'Towards a "European" model of human resource management', *Journal of International Business Studies*, 26(1), 1–21.

Brewster, C. (2004) 'European perspectives on human resource management', *Human Resource Management Review*, 14(4), 365–382.

Brewster, C., Mayrhofer, W. and Morley, M. (2000) *New challenges for European human resource management*. Basingstoke: Macmillan.

Buckingham, M. and Vosburgh, R.M. (2001) 'The 21st century human resources function: It's the talent, stupid!', *Human Resource Planning*, 24(4), 17–23.

Cappelli, P. (2008) *Talent on demand: Managing talent in an age of uncertainty*. Boston, MA: Harvard Business Press.

Cerdin, J.-L. and Brewster, C. (2014) 'Talent management and expatriation: Bridging two streams of research and practice', *Journal of World Business*, 49(2), 245–252.

Chartered Institute of Personnel Development (2012) *Learning and talent development 2012*. London: CIPD.

Chuai, X., Preece, D. and Iles, P. (2008) 'Is talent management just "old wine in new bottles"? The case of multinational companies in Beijing', *Management Research News*, 31(12), 901–911.

Cohn, J.M., Khurana, R. and Reeves, L. (2005) 'Growing talent as if your business depended on it', *Harvard Business Review*, 83(10), 62–71.

Collings, D.G. (2013) 'Integrating global mobility and global talent management: Exploring the challenges and strategic opportunities', *Journal of World Business*, 49(2), 253–261.

Collings, D.G. (2014) 'Towards mature talent management: Beyond shareholder value', *Human Resource Development Quarterly*, 25(3), 301–319.

Collings D.G. (2015) 'The contribution of talent management to organizational success', in Passmore, J., Kraiger, K. and Santos, N. (eds) *The Wiley Blackwell handbook of psychology of training, development and feedback*. London: Wiley Blackwell.

Collings, D.G. and Mellahi, K. (2009) 'Strategic talent management: A review and research agenda', *Human Resource Management Review*, 19(4), 304–313.

Collings, D.G., Scullion, H. and Morley, M.J. (2007) 'Changing patterns of global staffing in the multinational enterprise: Challenges to the conventional expatriate assignment and emerging alternatives', *Journal of World Business*, 42(2), 198–213.

Collings, D.G., Scullion, H. and Vaiman, V. (2011) 'European perspectives on talent management', *European Journal of International Management*, 5(5), 453–462.

Davies, B. and Davies, B.J. (2010) 'Talent management in academies', *International Journal of Educational Management*, 24(5), 418–426.

Dries, N. (2013) 'The psychology of talent management: A review and research agenda', *Human Resource Management Review*, 23(4), 272–285.

Dries, N. and Pepermans, R. (2008) '"Real" high potential careers: An empirical study into the perspectives of organizations and high potentials', *Personnel Review*, 37(1), 85–108.

Dundon, T. and Wilkinson, A. (2009) 'Human resource management in small and medium sized enterprises', in Wood, G. and Collings, D. (eds), *Human resource management: A critical introduction*. London: Routledge.

Dweck, C.S. (1999) *Self-theories: Their role in motivation, personality, development*. Philadelphia, PA: Psychology Press, pp. 39 and 84.

Edwards, T. and Ferner, A. (2002) 'The renewed "American Challenge": A review of employment practice in US multinationals', *Industrial Relations Journal*, 33(2), 94–111.

Ericsson, K.A., Prietula, M.J. and Cokely, E.T. (2007) 'The making of an expert', *Harvard Business Review*, 85(7/8), 115–121.

Ernst and Young (2010) *Managing today's global workforce: Evaluating talent management to improve business*. London: Ernst and Young.

European Union (2014) *European trade and investment report*. Luxembourg: Publications Office of the European Union.

Farndale, E., Pai, A., Sparrow, P. and Scullion, H. (2014) 'Balancing individual and organizational goals in global talent management: A mutual-benefits perspective', *Journal of World Business*, 49(2), 204–214.

Festing, M. and Schäfer, L. (2014) 'Generational challenges to talent management: A framework for talent retention based on the psychological-contract perspective', *Journal of World Business*, 49(2), 262–271.

Festing, M., Schäfer, L. and Scullion, H. (2013) 'Talent management in medium-sized German companies: An explorative study and agenda for future research', *International Journal of Human Resource Management*, 24(9), 1872–1893.

Forster, N. (2000) 'The myth of the international manager', *International Journal of Human Resource Management*, 11(1), 126–142.

Fortune (2013) Fortune Global 500. Available at: http://money.cnn.com/magazines/fortune/global500/2012/europe/ (accessed: 12 July 2015).

Gallardo-Gallardo, E., Dries, N. and González-Cruz, T.F. (2013) 'What is the meaning of "talent" in the world of work?', *Human Resource Management Review*, 23(4), 290–300.

Gallardo-Gallardo, E., Nijs, S., Dries, N. and Gallo, P. (2015) 'Towards an understanding of talent management as a phenomenon-driven field using bibliometric and content analysis', *Human Resource Management Review*, 25(3), 264–279.

Gandz, J. (2006) 'Talent development: The architecture of a talent pipeline that works', *Ivey Business Journal*, 1, 1–4.

Garavan, T.N., Carbery, R. and Rock, A. (2012) 'Mapping talent development: Definition, scope and architecture', *European Journal of Training and Development*, 36(1), 5–24.

Gelens, J., Dries, N., Hofmans, J. and Pepermans, R. (2013) 'The role of perceived organizational justice in shaping the outcomes of talent management: A research agenda', *Human Resource Management Review*, 23(4), 341–353.

Groysberg, B. (2010) *Chasing stars: The myth of talent and the portability of performance*. Princeton, NJ: Princeton University Press.

Groysberg, B., Lee, L. and Abrahams, R. (2010) 'What it takes to make "star" hires pay off', *MIT Sloan Management Review*, 51(2), 57–61.

Guthridge, M., McPherson, J.R. and Wolf, W.J. (2008) 'Upgrading talent', *The McKinsey Quarterly*, (December), 1–8.

Hall, P.A. and Soskice, D. (eds) (2001) *Varieties of capitalism: The institutional foundations of comparative advantage*. Oxford: Oxford University Press.

Heinen, J.S. and O'Neill, C. (2004) 'Managing talent to maximize performance', *Employment Relations Today*, 31(2), 67–82.

Hoglund, M. (2012) 'Quid pro quo? Examining talent management through the lens of psychological contracts', *Personnel Review*, 41(2), 126–142.

Holt Larsen, H. and Mayrhofer, M. (2006) (eds) *Managing human resources in Europe*. London: Routledge.

Human Capital Institute (2008) *Talent management strategy: A profit & loss perspective for real-world business impact*. Vermont: Human Capital Institute Analyst.

Iles, P., Preece, D. and Chuai, X. (2010) 'Is talent management a management fashion in HRD? Towards a research agenda', *Human Resource Development International*, 13(2), 125–145.

International Monetary Fund (2013) http://www.imf.org/external/pubs/ft/weo/2013/02/weodata/weoselagr.aspx (accessed: 15 April 2014).

Jerusalim, R.S. and Hausdorf, P.A. (2007) 'Managers' justice perceptions of high potential identification practices', *Journal of Management Development*, 26(10), 933–950.

Lepak, D.P. and Snell, S.A. (1999) 'The human resource architecture: Toward a theory of human capital allocation and development', *Academy of Management Review*, 24, 31–48.

Lewis, R.E. and Heckman, R.J. (2006) 'Talent management: A critical review', *Human Resource Management Review*, 16(2), 139–154.

McDonnell, A. and Collings, D.G. (2011) 'The identification and evaluation of talent in MNEs', in Scullion, H. and Collings, D.G. (eds) *Global talent management*. London and New York: Routledge, pp. 56–73.

Martin, J. and Schmidt, C. (2010) 'How to keep your top talent', *Harvard Business Review*, 88(5), 54–61.

Mayrhofer, W. and Larsen, H. (2006) 'European HRM: A distinct field of research and practice', in Larsen, H. and Mayrhofer, W. (eds), *Managing human resources in Europe*. London: Routledge.

Meyers, M.C. and van Woerkom, M. (2014) 'The influence of underlying philosophies on talent management: Theory, implications for practice, and research agenda', *Journal of World Business*, 49(2), 192–203.

Meyers, M.C., van Woerkom, M. and Dries, N. (2013) 'Talent: Innate or acquired? Theoretical considerations and their implications for talent management', *Human Resource Management Review*, 23(4), 305–321.

Michaels, E., Handfield-Jones, H. and Axelrod, B. (2001) *The war for talent*. Boston, MA: Harvard Business School Press.

Morton, L. (2005) *Talent management value imperatives: Strategies for execution*. New York: The Conference Board.

Nikandrou, I., Campos, E., Cunha, R. and Papalexandris, N. (2006) 'HRM and organizational performance: Universal and contextual evidence', in Larsen, H. and Mayrhofer, W. (eds) *Managing human resources in Europe*. London: Routledge, pp. 177–196.

Paauwe, J. (2004) *HRM and performance: Achieving long-term viability*. New York: Oxford University Press Inc.

Pfeffer, J., and Sutton, R.I. (2006) *Hard facts, dangerous half-truths, and total nonsense: Profiting from evidence-based management.* Boston, MA: Harvard Business School Press.

Pieper, R. (ed.) (1990) *Human resource management: An international comparison.* Berlin: Walter de Gruyter.

PricewaterhouseCoopers (2012) *15th annual global CEO survey.* London: PWC.

Pruis, E. (2011) 'The five key principles for talent development', *Industrial and Commercial Training*, 43(4), 206–216.

Rugman, A.M. and Verbeke, A. (2004) A perspective on regional and global strategies of multinational enterprises, *Journal of International Business Studies*, 35(1), 3–18.

Scullion, H. and Brewster, C. (2001) 'The managing expatriates: Messages from Europe', *Journal of World Business*, 36(4), 346–365.

Scullion, H. and Collings, D.G. (2011) *Global talent management.* London: Routledge.

Scullion, H., Collings, D.G. and Caligiuri, P. (2010) 'Global talent management', *Journal of World Business*, 45(2), 105–108.

Scullion, H. and Starkey, K. (2000) 'In search of the changing role of the corporate human resource function in the international firm', *International Journal of Human Resource Management*, 11(6), 1061–1081.

Sheehan, M. (2012) 'Developing managerial talent: Exploring the link between management talent and perceived performance in multinational corporations (MNCs)', *European Journal of Training and Development*, 36(1), 66–85.

Silzer, R. and Church, A.H. (2009) 'The pearls and perils of identifying potential', *Industrial and Organizational Psychology*, 2(4), 377–412.

Silzer, R.F. and Church, A.H. (2010) 'Identifying and assessing high-potential talent: Current organizational practices', in Silzer, R.F. and Dowell, D.E. (eds), *Strategy-driven talent management: A leadership imperative.* San Francisco, CA: Jossey Bass, pp. 213–279.

Skuza, A., Scullion, H. and McDonnell, A. (2013) 'An analysis of the talent management challenges in a post-communist country: The case of Poland', *The International Journal of Human Resource Management*, 24(3), 453–470.

Sonnenberg, M., van Zijderveld, V. and Brinks, M. (2014) 'The role of talent-perception incongruence in effective talent management', *Journal of World Business*, 49(2), 272–280.

Sparrow, P. and Hiltrop, J.M. (1997) 'Redefining the field of European human resource management: A battle between national mindsets and forces of business transition', *Human Resource Management*, 36(2), 201–219.

Sparrow, P. and Makram, H. (2015) 'What is the value of talent management? Building value-driven processes within a talent management architecture', *Human Resource Management Review*, 25(3), 249–263.

Sparrow, P., Scullion, H. and Tarique, I. (2014) *Strategic talent management: Contemporary issues in international context.* Cambridge: Cambridge University Press.

Stahl, G., Bjorkman, I., Farndale, E., Morris, S., Paauwe, J., Stiles, P., Trevor, J. and Wright, P. (2012) 'Six principles of effective global talent management', *MIT Sloan Management Review*, 53(2), 25–32.

Stahl, G.K., Björkman, I., Farndale, E., Morris, S.S., Paauwe, J., Stiles, P., Trevor, J. and Wright, P.M. (2007) *Global talent management: How leading multinational build and sustain their talent pipeline.* Faculty and Research Working Papers, 2007/24/OB, 2007. France: INSEAD.

Stahl, G.K. and Cerdin, J.-L. (2004) 'Global careers in French and German multinational corporations', *Journal of Management Development*, 23(9), 885–902.

Strack, R., Caye, J.M, von der Linden, C., Haen, P. and Abramo, F. (2013) *Creating people advantage 2013: Lifting HR practices to the next level*. London: BCG. Available at: https://www.bcgperspectives.com/content/articles/human_resources_organization_design_creating_people_advantage_2013/#chapter1 (accessed: 9 July 2014).

Tansley, C. and Tietze, S. (2013) 'Rites of passage through talent management progression stages: An identity work perspective', *The International Journal of Human Resource Management*, 24(9), 1799–1815.

Tansley, C., Turner, P.A., Foster, C., Harris, L.M., Stewart, J., Sempik, A. (2007) *Talent: Strategy, management, measurement*. Plymouth: Chartered Institute of Personnel and Development.

Thelen, K. (2001) 'Varieties of labour politics in the developed democracies', in Hall, P.A. and Soskice, D. (eds), *Varieties of capitalism: The institutional foundations of comparative advantage*. Oxford: Oxford University Press.

Thunnissen, M., Boselie, P. and Fruytier, B. (2013) 'Talent management and the relevance of context: Towards a pluralistic approach', *Human Resource Management Review*, 23(4), 326–336.

Thurley, K. and Wirdenius, H. (1991) 'Will management become "European"? Strategic choice for organizations', *European Management Journal*, 9(2), 127–134.

Tsay, C. and Banaji, M.R. (2011) 'Naturals and strivers: Preferences and beliefs about sources of achievement', *Journal of Experimental Social Psychology*, 47(2), 460–465.

UNCTAD (2010) *World Investment Report 2010*. Geneva: UNCTAD.

UNCTAD (2012) *World Investment Report 2012*. Geneva: UNCTAD.

Vaiman, V. and Holden, N. (2011) 'Talent management's perplexing landscape in Central and Eastern Europe', in Scullion, H. and Collings, D. (eds), *Global talent management*. Abingdon: Routledge, pp. 178–193.

Valverde, M., Scullion, H. and Ryan, G. (2013) 'Talent management in Spanish medium-sized organizations', *International Journal of Human Resource Management*, 24(9), 1832–1852.

Van Gennep, A. (1960) *The rites of passage*. London: Routledge Kegan Paul.

Yost, P.R. and Chang, G. (2009) 'Everyone is equal, but some are more equal than others', *Industrial and Organizational Psychology*, 2(4), 442–445.

19 Pay-for-Performance in Europe

IHAR SAHAKIANTS, MARION FESTING AND
STEPHEN PERKINS

Introduction

Pay-for-performance has become one of the most frequently
implemented compensation practices and dates back to the earliest
recorded history (Peach and Wren, 1991). Indeed, this link to
performance is inherent in the essence of the notions of compensation
or pay for labour provided.

In the latest edition of the volume *Compensation*, by Milkovich *et al.*
(2014, p. 686), pay-for-performance plans are defined as 'pay that
varies with some measure of individual or organizational performance,
such as merit pay, lump-sum bonus plans, skill-based pay, incentive
plans, variable pay plans, risk sharing, and success sharing'. This
definition underscores a number of important aspects of pay-for-
performance, such as (1) its variable character, (2) the need for relevant
and measurable performance indicators[1] and (3) the multiplicity of
pay-for-performance plans and instruments used, including cash-
based and equity-based compensation. Compared to the notion
'variable pay', which denotes a varying compensation component
linked to achievements and provided additionally to base pay, 'pay-
for-performance' has a more general meaning that also includes
performance-related base pay rises, for instance merit increase
programmes, or even seniority increases which have 'rudiments of
paying for performance' (Milkovich *et al.*, 2014, p. 690).[2]

Recently, discussions in the mass media as well as in the practitioner
and academic literature have centred on the issue of executive pay and
compensation in the banking industry, a subject fuelled by corporate
governance problems revealed during the last financial crisis (for

instance, Bebchuk and Fried, 2010). One of the most prominent responses of political powers to this discussion is the so-called banker bonus cap, a directive made by the European Parliament and the Council of the European Union limiting variable pay in this industry (Baetz, 2013). However, executive and banker compensation represents a rather narrow field, though it does enjoy wide public attention. Even more challenging in practice is the use of pay-for-performance compensation schemes for the remaining employee groups, especially given the number of employees affected and the multiplicity and national specificities of the pay approaches used.

On the topic of pay-for-performance in Europe, it is necessary to take into consideration the diversity of traditional compensation approaches, which have been determined by historical and current institutional contexts (Perkins and Vartiainen, 2010) such as cultural attitudes, the importance and impact of national institutions such as laws, trade unions and collective bargaining and the historical past, as in the case of post-state socialist European countries.

In the following sections we concentrate on the issue of the national distinctiveness of pay-for-performance systems from the cultural perspective, before focusing on the institutional contexts of rewards and then finally building on path dependence theory. Next, we discuss the cross-national transfer of the respective pay schemes, by building on the neo-institutional theoretical perspective. A section dedicated to the specific issues of pay-for-performance schemes in multinational enterprises in Europe precedes the conclusions of this chapter.

National Pay Distinctiveness

Practitioner-oriented and academic research alike have underscored the country-specific differences related to typical pay-for-performance schemes implemented across the world (Festing et al., 2012). Such differences between European countries are well illustrated by the results of the latest (third) European Company Survey (ECS), which was conducted in 2013 in 28 EU member states and Iceland, the Republic of Macedonia, Montenegro and Turkey (Eurofound, 2014c). The survey was based on 30,113 interviews with managers and 9,094 interviews with official employee representatives in companies located in the above-mentioned nations. The largest number of interviews with management employees in one single state was 1,673 (in Germany), while the lowest was 300 in Montenegro (Eurofound, 2014a). The survey covered companies with at least 10 employees in all industries except for agriculture, forestry and fishing, as well as activities of households as employers and those of extraterritorial organizations and bodies (Eurofound, 2014b).

In the following, we present the results of the survey examining the use of pay-for-performance schemes in the investigated countries. Although these data state the percentage of companies implementing the respective pay schemes, they do not provide any information about the number or the hierarchical level of the employees concerned, or the exact design of the pay-for-performance implemented; however, they

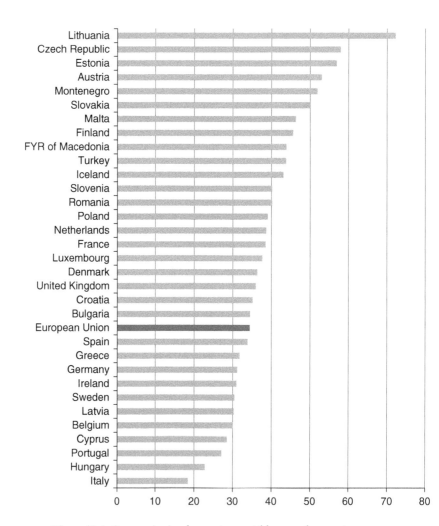

Figure 19.1 Companies implementing variable pay schemes, in percentage terms

Source: Eurofound (2014)

do serve as a good illustration of the differences in the use of variable compensation schemes among European states.

Interestingly, variable pay is used most frequently by companies operating in Lithuania, the Czech Republic and Estonia – all of them European transformation countries whose economies were organized during the state-socialist period in accordance with a centrally planned system. In line with this finding, Figure 19.2 shows that team-based variable pay is offered most frequently in Eastern and South-eastern

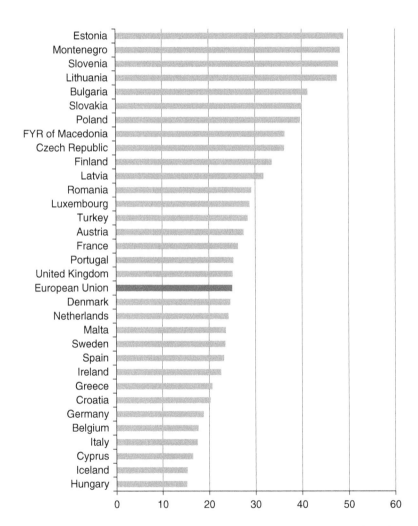

Figure 19.2 European companies implementing variable pay schemes based on team performance, in percentage terms

Source: Eurofound (2014)

Central European economies – in Estonian, Montenegrin, Slovenian, Lithuanian, Bulgarian, Slovak, Polish, Macedonian and Czech companies.

The Czech Republic, Slovenia, Montenegro and Lithuania, again all of which are European transition states, are the three leading countries in which the surveyed companies implement pay-for-performance schemes based on individual results.

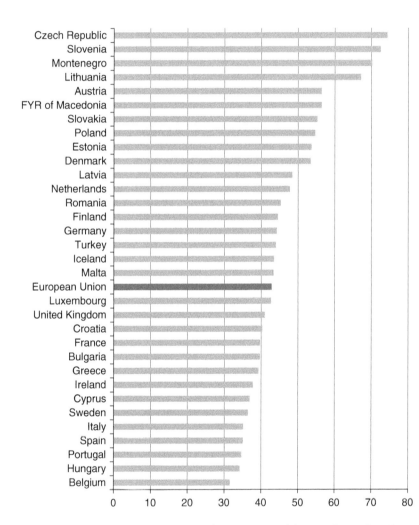

Figure 19.3 European companies implementing variable pay schemes based on individual performance, in percentage terms

Source: Eurofound (2014)

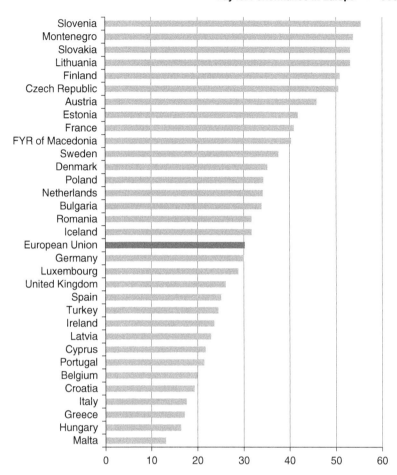

Figure 19.4 European companies implementing profit-sharing schemes, in
percentage terms
Source: Eurofound (2014)

Figure 19.4 presents survey results related to the incidence of profit-sharing schemes. Again, such pay models are offered most frequently by companies situated in European transition states, namely Slovenia, Montenegro, Slovakia and Lithuania in this instance.

While the above results cannot be used to draw any conclusions on the particularities of pay-for-performance plans in the single European countries surveyed, or with respect to the specific compensation schemes provided to employees of a particular group (by occupation, position, hierarchical level, etc.), these data nevertheless show us that in some countries or regions variable pay schemes are much more commonly used by companies than in other nations. Moreover, this information shows that even at this more general level of analysis, there is little commonality with respect to the provision of variable pay in Europe.

Academic research in the field of compensation management has concentrated on a number of theoretical approaches to explain country-specific idiosyncrasies with respect to pay-for-performance, summarized under the notions of cultural and institutional perspectives presented below.

Cultural Perspective

According to cultural explanations, reward systems, including pay-for-performance, are determined by the specifics of the national culture, which is defined as 'the values, beliefs and assumptions learned in early childhood that distinguish one group of people from another' (Newman and Nollen, 1996, p. 754). For instance, a number of studies (Schuler and Rogovsky, 1998; Tosi and Greckhamer, 2004) have investigated the link between country-specific compensation practices and the dimensions of the national culture suggested by Hofstede (1980) and based on the international employee surveys results carried out by IBM in the late 1960s and early 1970s: power distance, individualism, uncertainty avoidance and masculinity/femininity. According to Hofstede (1980), *power distance* denotes the extent of accepted inequality in a given culture, *individualism* is a dimension indicating the level of emotional independence from other society members, *uncertainty avoidance* stands for the degree to which the representatives of a given society tend to minimize uncertainty or avoid ambiguous situations and *masculinity/femininity* signifies the extent to which masculine values such as assertiveness and materialism, as opposed to feminine values such as quality of life and personal relationships, prevail. Table 19.1 presents values for some of the countries scoring high on these cultural dimensions.

An example of the arguments based on Hofstede's cultural dimensions is the statement by Rogovsky *et al.* (2000, p. 36) on the link between national culture and compensation:

> The role of national culture seems to be crucial in explaining cross-national HR practice differences because it is the most stable component of a business environment and affects all other factors . . . , whether directly or indirectly. [. . .] North American compensation practices encourage individualism and high performance; continental European programs emphasize social responsibility.

As shown in Table 19.2, many of the hypotheses and propositions tested in academic studies and based on the cultural dimensions proposed by Hofstede (1980) have been fully or partly confirmed. From the findings of the research presented in the table, the most

Table 19.1 Index values for cultural dimensions

Country	Power Distance	Individualism	Masculinity/ Femininity	Uncertainty Avoidance
Australia	36	90	61	51
Austria	11	55	79	70
Belgium	65	75	54	94
Canada	39	80	52	48
Great Britain	35	89	66	35
Greece	60	35	57	112
Italy	50	76	70	75
Japan	54	46	95	92
Netherlands	38	80	14	53
Portugal	63	27	31	104
Switzerland	34	68	70	58
United States	40	91	62	46

Source: Hofstede and Bond (1988, pp. 12–13)

robust results relate to the use of variable schemes which seem to be implemented more frequently in countries with high individualism values, such as the United States, the United Kingdom or Australia.

Although the above studies offer an interesting explanation of the national distinctiveness of rewards, it is necessary nonetheless to consider several important caveats. For instance, Gomez-Mejia and Welbourne wrote: '"National culture" is an abstract, general concept. In practice, intra-cultural differences may be huge, particularly in large heterogeneous countries' (1991, p. 39). Milkovich and Bloom (1998, p. 18) argue in a similar manner, by pointing out that '[it] has long been recognized that compensation and reward systems, because of their social as well as economic significance, exemplify and reinforce cultural norms', stating furthermore that 'this does not mean that social and cultural norms necessarily coincide with national boundaries'. Especially challenging in this respect is the issue of European transition states. The transformation process in these countries not only included the restructuring of previously state-socialist economies, but it was also accompanied by changes in national borders. For instance, none of the countries of the former Soviet bloc was included in the original survey analysed by Hofstede, as Yugoslavia was the only European state-socialist economy studied (Hofstede and Bond, 1988). However, even in the case of the latter state, there is evidence of significant differences in cultural values in the former republics of Yugoslavia, especially if compared to the scores for Yugoslavia resulting from Hofstede's

Table 19.2 Proposed link between national cultural dimensions and pay-for-performance

Cultural Dimension	Propositions/Hypotheses	Empirical Support
Power distance	'The proportion of variable pay to total compensation (VC/TC) is negatively related to power distance' (Tosi and Greckhamer, 2004, p. 661).	No (for CEOs)
	'Employee share options/ stock ownership plans will be less prevalent in countries with higher levels of Power Distance' (Schuler and Rogovsky, 1998, p. 166).	Yes (except for managers)
Individualism-collectivism	'The proportion of variable compensation to total CEO compensation (VC/TC) is positively related to individualism' (Tosi and Greckhamer, 2004, p. 661).	Yes (for CEOs)
	'Pay-for-performance compensation practices will be used more widely in countries with higher levels of Individualism' (Schuler and Rogovsky, 1998, p. 165).	Yes
	'Employee share options/stock ownership plans will be more prevalent in countries with higher levels of Individualism' (Schuler and Rogovsky, 1998, p. 167).	Yes
Uncertainty avoidance	'The proportion of variable compensation to total compensation (VC/TC) is negatively related to uncertainty avoidance' (Tosi and Greckhamer, 2004, p. 661).	Yes (for CEOs)
	'Pay-for-performance is likely to be less prevalent in countries with higher levels of Uncertainty Avoidance' (Schuler and Rogovsky, 1998, p. 166).	No
	'Employee share options/stock ownership plans will be more prevalent in countries with lower levels of Uncertainty Avoidance' (Schuler and Rogovsky, 1998, p. 167).	Yes
Masculinity-femininity	'Individuals in masculine countries should elicit a stronger preference for financial rewards and individual-based performance reward systems than those in feminine cultures' (Chiang, 2005, p. 1549).	No

Sources: Chiang (2005, p. 1549), Schuler and Rogovsky (1998, pp. 165–167), Tosi and Greckhamer (2004, p. 661)

original study (Milkovich and Bloom, 1998). Consequently, the proposed cultural dimensions cannot be used as a potential explanation for a rather high incidence of variable pay in European transition states, as shown by the results of the recent European Company Survey presented in Figures 19.1 to 19.4.

The above arguments would not only be true with respect to Hofstede's original dimensions but would equally apply to the further dimensions proposed by Hofstede, such as *Confucian dynamism* (Hofstede and Bond, 1988), or more differentiated studies such as the Global Leadership and Organizational Effectiveness (GLOBE) project (House, Hanges, Javidan, Dorfman, and Gupta, 2004), which was also criticized for promoting 'cultural stereotypes' (Graen, 2006).

Institutional Contexts of Rewards

Recently, there has been growing academic interest in the analysis of compensation practices based on theoretical perspectives emphasizing the impact of institutions. *Institutions* are defined by Scott (2001, p. 49) as 'multifaceted, durable social structures, made up of symbolic elements, social activities, and material resources' that build on three major pillars: regulatory, normative and cultural-cognitive elements. While the cultural perspective discussed in the previous section fits in general into the cultural-cognitive strand, regulatory forces in the form of rules, laws and sanctions, as well as 'normative rules that introduce a prescriptive, evaluative, and obligatory dimension into social life' (Scott, 2001, p. 54), represent additionally important aspects in relation to institutional foundations.

To date, varieties of capitalism (Hall and Soskice, 2001) and national business systems (Whitley, 1992, 1999) perspectives, representing two major approaches offering comprehensive frameworks for the analysis of institutional contexts across countries, have been used increasingly in academic research in the field of human resource management (Edwards *et al.*, 2013; Tempel and Walgenbach, 2007).

The *business systems* approach rests on three fundamental questions related to the coordination and control of 'economic activities and resources', the organization of 'market connections between authoritatively coordinated economic activities in firms', and the organization and direction 'through authority relations' of 'activities and skills within firms' (Whitley, 1992, p. 6). According to Whitley (1999), ownership coordination, non-ownership coordination and employment relations are the major aspects characterizing business systems which are structured depending on the major features and the role of the state, the financial system, skills development and control systems, as well as trust and authority relations.

The *varieties of capitalism* perspective is an actor-centred approach to the analysis of institutional contexts, focusing on five major spheres: industrial relations, vocational training and education, corporate governance, inter-firm relations and 'coordination problems vis-à-vis their own employees' (Hall and Soskice, 2001, p. 7). Depending on the ways used by economic actors to coordinate their activities in all five spheres mentioned above, two groups of economies are differentiated: *liberal market economies* (LME) and *coordinated market economies* (CME). Herein, the USA is presented as a typical LME, while Germany is argued to be a classical example of a CME.

Although these two approaches differ with respect to the primary focus and analytical levels of the underlying models, both perspectives show similarities in pointing out major relevant elements of the national institutional contexts. Both of them underscore the importance of industrial and employment relations in institutional analysis, which is useful in an analysis of country-specific forms and the incidence of pay-for-performance.

For instance, in their analysis of the German HRM model based on the business system perspective, Giardini et al. (2005) show that traditional compensation approaches in the country are determined by the specifics of industrial relations. While there is a growing acceptance of pay-for-performance schemes for non-exempt employees on the part of trade unions, variable compensation models are still widely opposed by employee representatives, in particular work councils. Moreover, based on their analysis of pay-for-performance in Austria, Norway, Spain and the UK, Traxler et al. (2008) underscored the link between the regulatory contexts, bargaining systems and variable pay models used by firms.

Similar to the above approach to the analysis of institutional contexts, the varieties of capitalism perspective concentrates on the investigation of *institutional complementarities*, which suggests that 'nations with a particular type of coordination in one sphere of the economy should tend to develop complementary practices in other spheres as well' (Hall and Soskice, 2001, p. 18). For instance, in their description of the German case of CMEs, Hall and Soskice (2001, p. 23) argue that

> by equalizing wages at equivalent skill levels across an industry, this system [of industry-wide collective agreements between trade unions and employers' associations] makes it difficult for firms to poach workers and assures the latter that they are receiving the highest feasible rates of pay in return for the deep commitments they are making to firms.

Related to pay-for-performance, one could develop the argument of the varieties of capitalism theorists, in that the increased flexibility and individualization of compensation systems, by using variable components, could contradict the nature of CMEs and would rather fit the logic of LMEs, in which employment relations match 'highly fluid labor markets' (Hall and Soskice, 2001, p. 30).

Path Dependence

One of the most distinctive properties of institutions is their resistance to change (Scott, 2001), which is often referred to in the academic literature as *path dependence*. For instance, employment systems and HR practices in European transition states have been denoted as path-dependent (Aguilera and Dabu, 2005; Whitley and Czaban, 1998), i.e. embedded in the pre-transformation practices of the state-socialist period. However, the path analysis goes beyond the 'vague notion that "history matters" or that "the past influences the future"' (Mahoney, 2000, p. 508) and concentrates on historical events and institutional self-reinforcing mechanisms that lead to path formation and to the situation of lock-in or ultimate resistance to change. Organizational path dependence is defined by Sydow *et al.* as 'a rigidified, potentially inefficient action pattern built up by the unintended consequences of former decisions and positive feedback processes' (2009, p. 696).

Festing and Sahakiants (2013) used this theoretical perspective to analyse and explain the continuity of compensation practices in three Eastern Central European subsidiaries of a North American multinational enterprise (MNE). The findings of the study have not only important implications with respect to organizational practices in MNEs operating in this region, but they also offer an explanation for the high incidence of pay-for-performance schemes in European transition states. In particular, during the state-socialist period, variable pay schemes were seen primarily as a means of increasing centrally planned base pay and achieving the flexibility necessary to attract and retain skilled labour. In many cases, bonuses had a guaranteed character and by far exceeded monthly base pay. As in cases of widespread piece-rate schemes, where the distribution of 'well-paying jobs' among workers often depended on personal relationships or political privilege, the allocation of monetary bonuses, which were formally linked to the fulfilment of specific objectives such as production plans, generally lacked transparency and procedural clarity. Although the designs of pay-for-performance schemes have been changed to a great extent since the fall of state-socialist regimes, variable pay is still widely perceived as an attractive and important part of the reward system. However, there is, in many cases, still a 'taken-for-granted attitude' towards pay-for-performance. Moreover, in the European transition countries studied, there is in general no a priori negative attitude towards pay-for-performance schemes on the part of trade unions – as has been the case traditionally in CMEs.

Diffusion of Pay-for-Performance in Europe

While we have pointed out important differences with respect to pay-for-performance in Europe, determined by institutional contexts and historical developments, we also observe some convergence of typical national performance-linked compensation models on the continent. Based on the results of the longitudinal analysis of the survey data collected in 13 European countries from 1992 to 2004 within the CRANET project, Mayrhofer *et al.* stated that there is at least 'considerable evidence of directional similarity - practices increasing or decreasing in the same way across the countries' (2011, p. 50), pay-for-performance being one of the few practices showing strong convergence of this kind. Specifically, the authors found a trend towards more use of variable compensation schemes throughout the sample. However, according to the above authors, there is no evidence of the 'final convergence – countries becoming more alike in the way they manage people' (Mayrhofer *et al.*, 2011, p. 50).

The neo-institutionalist perspective, in particular the theory of institutional isomorphism coined by DiMaggio and Powell (1983), offers an explanation for such confirmed or suggested convergence. Similar to the theory of path dependence, the theory of institutional isomorphism represents a dynamic perspective. However, contrary to the path dependence theory, which explains resistance to change, this approach illuminates the mechanisms of institutional change leading to the isomorphism or homogenization of organizations within their institutional fields, i.e. 'those organizations that, in the aggregate, constitute a recognized area of institutional life: key suppliers, resource and product consumers, regulatory agencies, and other organizations that produce similar services or products' (DiMaggio and Powell, 1983, p. 148). Consequently, coercive, normative and mimetic mechanisms are the main antecedents of institutional isomorphism.

Examples of *coercive mechanisms* are direct regulation of pay, as in the example of salary caps for executives in Polish state-owned enterprises (Festing and Sahakiants, 2011), or industry-wide collective agreements (Festing and Sahakiants, 2010), which represent a characteristic feature of many CMEs. Companies operating in a specific country and industry are often forced to implement very similar pay schemes. In Europe, the main sources of coercive isomorphism are national and EU laws. A recent example of EU legislation affecting pay systems is Directive 2013/36/EU of the European Parliament and of the Council of 26 June 2013, which in accordance with Article 94(1)(g) limits the proportion of variable pay for employees in the banking sector to 100 per cent of their fixed remuneration or 200 per cent of the fixed part of total pay under condition of approval by the shareholders or owners of the respective institution. According to the Directive, lower maximum percentages of variable pay components in relation to total remuneration may be set by EU member states. This piece of EU legislation, which has already been criticized, mainly in the UK (Baetz, 2013), will potentially lead to some homogenization of variable pay structures in the banking industry across Europe. One example of a recently adopted piece of national legislation is the Swiss law implementing the requirements of the *Minder Initiative*, by proposing a ban on so-called 'golden parachutes' and 'golden hellos' and strengthening the say-on-pay rights of shareholders, including the involvement of pension funds in affirming executive pay (Sahakiants and Festing, 2014). There is at least anecdotal evidence that the respective ordinance of the Swiss Federal Council has resulted in the increased interest of Swiss companies in reviewing the executive pay-for-performance schemes implemented in their organizations.

DiMaggio and Powell (1983) state that the main source of *normative isomorphism* is the process of professionalization. As applied to pay-for-performance schemes, this could be the professionalization of HR professionals and managers responsible for compensation and benefits, who promote state-of-the-art, sophisticated variable compensation models (Festing and Sahakiants, 2010, 2013). This professionalization is sustained by professional organizations and educational institutions offering specialized programmes for professionals and managers in the field of compensation and benefits. The Certified Compensation Professional® (CCP®), by WorldatWork, or the Global Reward Management Programme offered by Vlerick Business School (Belgium) and ESCP Europe (Germany and France) can also be viewed as sources of normative isomorphism promoted by formal education.

Mimetic isomorphism relates to the introduction of organizational practices by copying them from successful companies as a response to uncertainty. Pudelko and Harzing (2007) state that this mechanism is responsible for the adoption of best practices. With respect to rewards, mimetic isomorphism seems to play an important role in promoting similarities between specific compensation practices, for instance in the field of executive rewards or broader pay-for-performance schemes based on direct comparisons or compensation benchmark information provided by management consultancies. For instance, Festing and Sahakiants (2010) argued that mimetic considerations have been strong drivers of the use of 'Western-type' rewards, including pay-for-performance schemes, in European transition states during the transformation period, while Bender (2004) found that mimetic mechanisms play an important role in designing variable executive pay.

However, in practice, it is often impossible to identify a specific isomorphic mechanism affecting compensation practice. For instance, in their analysis of executive share-based pay schemes in Poland, Festing and Sahakiants (2012) showed that although the rare use of such compensation forms in Polish state-owned enterprises (SOEs) was related to the direct regulation of pay in the country, this fact could be attributed instead to normative or mimetic factors: even companies not falling under the respective law seem to use other large SOEs as their points of reference, or they can involve structures and decision-making processes linked to the period prior to their privatization. It could also be argued in a similar vein that national legislation implementing European regulations (coercive factors) such as the Recommendation of the European Commission 2004/913/EC of 14 December 2004, 'fostering an appropriate regime for the remuneration of directors of listed companies' (Festing and Sahakiants, 2011) which promotes the detailed disclosure of executive compensation, could additionally trigger mimetic mechanisms, whereby companies might lean toward using information disclosed by other companies to design similar pay schemes.

The Case of Pay-for-Performance in MNEs

The discussion on pay-for-performance in multinational corporations typically relates to the assumptions of country-of-origin effects and the related discussion on the localization and standardization of pay practices.

Pudelko and Harzing (2007, p. 538) describe the country-of-origin effect as a situation when 'HRM practices at the subsidiary level . . . resemble practices in the home country more so than practices of local firms.' Wächter *et al.* (2003) showed that US-American MNEs in Germany tend to avoid collective bargaining constraints typical of the German business system, which also confirms the findings of Muller (1998). The analysed subsidiaries implemented pay-for-performance schemes for all their employees. A strong 'nationality effect' on the implementation of pay-for-performance schemes was also found by Björkman and Furu (2000) in Finnish MNEs' foreign subsidiaries. In this respect, in addition to the importance of the local isomorphic pressures presented by Rosenzweig and Nohria (1994) and discussed in the previous section, Ferner and Quintanilla (1998) point out the importance of *cross-national isomorphism* whereby 'the behaviour of the subsidiary is (in specific respects) similar (isomorphic) to the behaviour of the parent' (Ferner, 2000, p. 30).

Bloom *et al.* (2003) suggest that in pursuit of their global strategies companies implement three international compensation models:

(1) *adapters* seek to localize their pay systems in response to local contextual pressures, (2) *exporters* follow the standardization strategy by implementing home-country practices and (3) *globalizers* design their worldwide pay systems by 'gather[ing] the best practices that can be used consistently across subsidiaries and local host contexts' (Bloom *et al.*, 2003, p. 1356). In practice, however, the compensation strategies of MNEs predominantly represent a mix of localized and globally standardized practices (Festing *et al.*, 2007; Festing and Sahakiants, 2013). For instance, in their analysis of the use of employee share-based pay in Europe, Poutsma (2005) found that US-American MNEs promote the use of executive (narrow-based) schemes, while respective pay practices for the remaining employee groups (broad-based schemes) are largely influenced by local institutional constraints. Thus, apart from executive rewards, which are typically standardized to a great extent, MNEs might implement in their subsidiaries pay-for-performance schemes based on local market benchmarks with respect to the proportion between the fixed and variable parts of a pay deal. At the same time, multinationals might use globally standardized procedures to determine pay such as common key performance indicators (KPIs) or the use of standard market benchmarks (average, median, seventy-fifth percentile, etc.).

An interesting perspective on the success or limits of transferring organizational practices, including pay-for-performance schemes, offers the concept of institutional distance (Kostova, 1999; Kostova and Roth, 2002), which denotes 'differences between the institutional profiles [consisting of regulatory, cognitive and normative characteristics] of the two countries – the home country of the practice and the country of the recipient organizational unit' (Kostova, 1999, p. 316). According to this perspective, specific pay systems can be transferred more easily to subsidiaries located in less institutionally distant countries, such as the case of a transfer from US-based MNEs to Australian subsidiaries, than in locations featuring high institutional distance away from the home country of the MNE, such as German subsidiaries of US-American corporations. Indeed, the concept of the institutional distance seems to become even more relevant with the rise of emerging markets, for instance Chinese or Indian MNEs which may be seeking to export further nuanced approaches to employee rewards as they expand operations into Europe and elsewhere. Although there are reports that emerging country multinationals, in particular the Chinese ones, tend to implement pay practices typically used by Western MNEs (Warner and Nankervis, 2012), the respective compensation systems might still reflect the traditional reward preference in China-based companies, including inclination toward team rather than individual incentive plans and seniority-related pay (Cai *et al.*, 2011).

Conclusion

Despite the increased political and economic unification of Europe, compensation systems in single European states, including pay-for-performance, are still dominated mainly by their specific institutional (including cultural) contexts, which is an indicator of a lack of convergence of reward practices in the European region and elsewhere (Festing and Sahakiants, 2012). The lack of evidence to suggest 'final convergence' in the adoption of variable pay among European employers may be underscored further by recent geo-political developments following the European–US economic crisis that started in 2008, with economic commentators such as Martin Wolf (2014) pointing out the destabilizing effect of global imbalances.

However, we expect that growing globalization and cooperation, in the first instance, between EU member states, will lead to more similarity of organizational practices than has been found up to this point in the academic literature (for instance, Mayrhofer *et al.*, 2011). We suggest that large MNEs will play an important role in this context, mainly stemming from developed industrialized countries. For instance, Ferner and Edwards (1995, p. 229) stated that '[through] their role in transmitting industrial relations practices across borders, multinational enterprises . . . may be considered one of the principal agents of the observed convergence of aspects such as payment systems, work flexibility, training and equal opportunities arrangements'. As an example, Kurdelbusch links the increased use of variable pay schemes in German companies to the internationalization processes, whereby 'the trend towards decentralization and flexibility of remuneration schemes indicates a change toward a more Anglo-American business system' (2002, p. 325). Overall, however, there is not sufficient evidence to suggest a universal European preponderance to setting pay by reference to employee performance (variable or at risk pay) – despite actions by (US) MNEs seeking to export country-of-origin approaches.

Key Learning Points

- Comparative data analysis indicates that variable pay seems especially prevalent in transforming European economies, as well as those associated more traditionally with it in so-called liberal market economies. However, the forms and characters of pay-for-performance in these countries are historically determined and in many cases differ from the prevalent respective compensation schemes in developed European economies.
- Setting pay contingent on performance is most prevalent among individuals in executive management roles. While this may reflect

mimetic drivers, justified by reference to 'market forces', it has become increasingly subject to regulatory pressures to contain levels, to determine and expose specific financial returns to employers and corporate investors.

- Explanations for pay variations across European countries can be found, to some extent, in cross-cultural theorizing and more persuasively from the institutional and path dependence perspectives. Since the latest financial crisis, EU regulatory moves have offered evidence of coercive isomorphic explanations, at least among senior level employees and those in the banking and financial services, leading to controversy and efforts to counteract the alleged consequences in terms of retaining and motivating individuals whose skills are deemed to be in demand.
- While, as noted, some indicators of transnational 'directional convergence' may be attributable to MNC strategies, successful implementation is affected by proximity to the parent company or home country's socio-economic or business systems context.
- Lessons learned from evaluating pay-for-performance in Europe thus suggest plenty of scope for debate and further analysis on the part of students, policymakers and their regulatory institutions, as well as employers of all forms.

Notes

1 In this respect, it is necessary to broaden the above mentioned definition of pay-for-performance plans to include team – along with individual and organizational – performance measures.
2 An interesting perspective on pay-for-performance, following evidence of its detrimental effect, was offered in the late 1990s by Brown and Armstrong (1999), who advocated the 'pay for contribution' notion, combining the ability to perform, working in the overall interests of the organization and output-oriented performance.

References

Aguilera, R.V. and Dabu, A. (2005) 'Transformation of Employment Relations Systems in Central and Eastern Europe', *Journal of Industrial Relations*, 47(1), 16–42.

Baetz, J. (2013) *EU Lawmakers Vote for Banker Bonus Cap*. Available at: http://www.businessweek.com/ap/2013-04-16/eu-lawmakers-vote-for-banker-bonus-cap (accessed 18 April 2013).

Bebchuk, L.A. and Fried, J.M. (2010) 'Paying For Long-Term Performance', *University of Pennsylvania Law Review*, 158(7), 1915–1959.

Bender, R. (2004) 'Why Do Companies Use Performance-Related Pay for Their Executive Directors?', *Corporate Governance: An International Review*, 12(4), 521–533.

Björkman, I. and Furu, P. (2000) 'Determinants of Variable Pay for Top Managers of Foreign Subsidiaries in Finland', *International Journal of Human Resource Management*, 11(4), 698–713.

Bloom, M., Milkovich, G.T. and Mitra, A. (2003) 'International Compensation: Learning from How Managers Respond to Variations in Local Host Contexts', *International Journal of Human Resource Management*, 14(8), 1350–1367.

Brown, D. and Armstrong, M. (1999) *Paying for Contribution: Real Performance-Related Pay Strategies*. London: Kogan Page.

Cai, Z., Morris, J.L. and Chen, J. (2011) 'Explaining the Human Resource Management Preferences of Employees: A Study of Chinese Workers', *International Journal of Human Resource Management*, 22(16), 3245–3269.

DiMaggio, P.J. and Powell, W.W. (1983) 'The Iron Cage Revisited: Institutional Isomorphism and Collective Rationality in Organizational Fields', *American Sociological Review*, 48(2), 147–160.

Edwards, P.K., Sánchez-Mangas, R., Tregaskis, O., Levesque, C., McDonnell, A. and Quintanilla, J. (2013) 'Human Resource Management Practices in the Multinational Company: A Test of System, Societal, and Dominance Effects', *Industrial and Labor Relations Review*, 66(3), 588–617.

Eurofound (2014a) *3rd European Company Survey: Technical Report*. Available at: http://www.eurofound.europa.eu/surveys/ecs/2013/documents/ecs2013docs/3rdECS2013TechnicalReport.pdf (accessed 11 September 2014).

Eurofound (2014b) *ECS 2013: Methodology*. Available at: http://www.eurofound.europa.eu/surveys/ecs/2013/ecsmethodology/index.htm (accessed 23 June 2014).

Eurofound (2014c) *European Company Survey 2013*. Available at: http://www.eurofound.europa.eu/surveys/ecs/2013/ (accessed 23 June 2014).

Ferner, A. (2000) *The Embeddedness of US Multinational Companies in the US Business System: Implications for HR/IR*. De Montfort University, Leicester. Occasional Paper 61.

Ferner, A. and Edwards, P. (1995) 'Power and the Diffusion of Organizational Change within Multinational Enterprises', *European Journal of Industrial Relations*, 1(2), 229–257.

Ferner, A. and Quintanilla, J. (1998) 'Multinationals, National Business Systems and HRM: The Enduring Influence of National Identity or a Process of "Anglo-Saxonization"', *The International Journal of Human Resource Management*, 9(4), 710–731.

Festing, M. and Sahakiants, I. (2010) 'Compensation Practices in Central and Eastern European EU Member States: An Analytical Framework Based on Institutional Perspectives, Path Dependencies, and Efficiency Considerations', *Thunderbird International Business Review*, 52(3), 203–216.

Festing, M. and Sahakiants, I. (2011) 'Determinants of Share-Based Compensation Plans in Central and Eastern European Public Companies: An Institutional Analysis', *Journal for East European Management Studies*, 16(4), 338–357.

Festing, M. and Sahakiants, I. (2012) 'The Use of Executive Share-Based Compensation: Empirical Evidence from Poland', paper presented at the *IFSAM 2012 World Congress*, Limerick, Ireland, 26–29 June 2012.

Festing, M. and Sahakiants, I. (2013) 'Path-Dependent Evolution of Compensation Systems in Central and Eastern Europe: A Case Study of Multinational Corporation Subsidiaries in the Czech Republic, Poland and Hungary', *European Management Journal*, 31(4), 373–389.

Festing, M., Eidems, J. and Royer, S. (2007) 'Strategic Issues and Local Constraints in Transnational Compensation Strategies: An Analysis of Cultural, Institutional and Political Influences', *European Management Journal*, 25(2), 118–131.

Festing, M., Engle, A.D., Dowling, P.J. and Sahakiants, I. (2012) 'HRM Activities: Pay and Rewards', in Brewster, C. and Mayrhofer, W. (eds), *Handbook of Research in Comparative Human Resource Management*. Cheltenham: Edward Elgar Publishing, 139–163.

Giardini, A., Kabst, R. and Müller-Camen, M. (2005) 'HRM in the German Business System: A Review', *Management Revue*, 16(1), 63–80.

Gomez-Mejia, L.R. and Welbourne, T. (1991) 'Compensation Strategies in a Global Context', *Human Resource Planning*, 14(1), 29–41.

Graen, G.B. (2006) 'In the Eye of the Beholder: Cross-cultural Lesson in Leadership from Project GLOBE: A Response Viewed from the Third Culture Bonding (TCB) Model of Cross-Cultural Leadership', *Academy of Management Perspectives*, 20(4), 95–101.

Hall, P.A. and Soskice, D. (eds) (2001) *Varieties of Capitalism: The Institutional Foundations of Comparative Advantage*. Oxford: Oxford University Press.

Hofstede, G. (1980) *Culture's Consequences: International Differences in Work-Related Values*. Beverly Hills, London: Sage Publications.

Hofstede, G. and Bond, M.H. (1988) 'The Confucius Connection: From Cultural Roots to Economic Growth', *Organizational Dynamics*, 16(4), 5–21.

Kostova, T. (1999) 'Transnational Transfer of Strategic Organizational Practices: A Contextual Perspective', *Academy of Management Review*, 24(2), 308–324.

Kostova, T. and Roth, K. (2002) 'Adoption of an Organizational Practice by Subsidiaries of Multinational Corporations: Institutional and Relational Effects', *Academy of Management Journal*, 45(1), 215–233.

Kurdelbusch, A. (2002) 'Multinationals and the Rise of Variable Pay in Germany', *European Journal of Industrial Relations*, 8(3), 325–349.

Mahoney, J. (2000) 'Path Dependence in Historical Sociology', *Theory and Society*, 29(4), 507–548.

Mayrhofer, W., Brewster, C., Morley, M.J. and Ledolter, J. (2011) 'Hearing a Different Drummer? Convergence of Human Resource Management in Europe – A Longitudinal Analysis', *Human Resource Management Review*, 21(1), 50–67.

Milkovich, G.T. and Bloom, M. (1998) 'Rethinking International Compensation', *Compensation and Benefits Review*, 30(1), 15–23.

Milkovich, G.T., Newman, J.M. and Gerhart, B. (2014) *Compensation*. New York: McGraw-Hill.

Muller, M. (1998) 'Human Resource and Industrial Relations Practices of UK and US Multinationals in Germany', *International Journal of Human Resource Management*, 9(4), 732–749.

Newman, K.L. and Nollen, S.D. (1996) 'Culture and Congruence: The Fit between Management Practices and National Culture', *Journal of International Business Studies*, 27(4), 753–779.

Perkins, S.J. and Vartiainen, M.A. (2010) 'European Reward Management? Introducing the Special Issue', *Thunderbird International Business Review*, 52(3), 175–187.

Poutsma, E., Ligthart, P.E.M. and Schouteten, R. (2005) 'Employee Share Schemes in Europe: The Influence of US Multinationals', *Management Revue*, 16(1), 99–122.

Pudelko, M. and Harzing, A.-W. (2007) 'Country-of-Origin, Localization, or Dominance Effect? An Empirical Investigation of HRM Practices in Foreign Subsidiaries', *Human Resource Management*, 46(4), 535–559.

Rogovsky, N., Schuler, R.S. and Reynolds, C. (2000) 'How Can National Culture Affect Compensation Practices of MNCs?', *Global Focus*, 12(4), 35–42.

Rosenzweig, P.M. and Nohria, N. (1994) 'Influences on Human Resource Management Practices in Multinational Corporations', *Journal of International Business Studies*, 25(2), 229–251.

Sahakiants, I. and Festing, M. (2014) *The Minder Initiative and Executive Pay Narratives in Germany and Russia: Cases of Path Dependence?* ESCP Europe Working paper No. 64. Berlin: ESCP Europe.

Schuler, R.S. and Rogovsky, N. (1998) 'Understanding Compensation Practice Variations Across Firms: The Impact of National Culture', *Journal of International Business Studies*, 29(1), 159–177.

Scott, W.R. (2001), *Institutions and Organizations*. Thousand Oaks, London, New Delhi: Sage Publications.

Sydow, J., Schreyögg, G. and Koch, J. (2009) 'Organizational Path Dependence: Opening the Black Box', *Academy of Management Review*, 34(4), 689–709.

Tempel, A. and Walgenbach, P. (2007) 'Global Standardization of Organizational Forms and Management Practices? What New Institutionalism and the Business-Systems Approach Can Learn from Each Other', *Journal of Management Studies*, 44(1), 1–24.

Tosi, H.L. and Greckhamer, T. (2004) 'Culture and CEO Compensation', *Organization Science*, 15(6), 657–670.

Traxler, F., Arrowsmith, J., Nergaard, K. and López-Rodó, J.M.M. (2008) 'Variable Pay and Collective Bargaining: A Cross-National Comparison of the Banking Sector', *Economic and Industrial Democracy*, 29(3), 406–431.

Wächter, H., Peters, R., Tempel, A. and Müller-Camen, M. (2003) *The 'Country-of-Origin Effect' in the Cross-National Management of Human Resources*. Munich and Mering: Rainer Hampp Verlag.

Warner, M. and Nankervis, A. (2012) 'HRM Practices in Chinese MNCs: Rhetoric and Reality', *Journal of General Management*, 37(3), 61–80.

Whitley, R. (1992) 'Societies, Firms and Markets: The Social Structuring of Business Systems', in Whitley, R. (ed.), *European Business Systems: Firms and Markets in Their National Contexts*. London, Newbury Park, New Dehli: Sage Publications.

Whitley, R. (1999) *Divergent Capitalisms. The Social Structuring and Change of Business Systems*. New York: Oxford University Press.

Whitley, R. and Czaban, L. (1998) 'Institutional Transformation and Enterprise Change in an Emergent Capitalist Economy: The Case of Hungary', *Organization Studies*, 19(2), 259–280.

Wolf, M. (2014), *The Shifts and the Shocks: What We've Learned – and Have Still to Learn – from the Financial Crisis*. London: Allen Lane (Penguin).

20 Employee Financial Participation

ERIK POUTSMA, ERIC KAARSEMAKER AND
PAUL LIGTHART

Learning Objectives

- insight into the global phenomenon of employee financial participation;
- insight into why companies adopt employee financial participation;
- insight into the role of multinational companies in the spread and use of employee financial participation;
- insight into the diversity in adoption and use of employee financial participation across the globe.

Introduction

In recent decades many countries have witnessed an increase in the use of all-employee financial participation, also called broad-based financial participation, where all employees are eligible to join the plan. At the end of the last century the phenomenon of employee financial participation gradually emerged as a 'normal' attribute of the employment relationship in important corners of the world and of the workforce. Covering such systems as profit sharing, employee share ownership and personnel stock option plans, employee financial participation is becoming part of the employment relationship of an increasing number of employees, especially in the industrialized world (Poutsma and de Nijs, 2003).

Employee financial participation in individual enterprises generally has two principal objectives: to stimulate worker effort and improve labour–management co-operation. It is therefore a basic feature of the problem of management control, that is, safeguarding that employees do their jobs efficiently and in alignment with the company's strategic objectives. There are several other objectives derived from the principal ones, like satisfaction and commitment effects and building an ownership culture (Kaarsemaker and Poutsma, 2006). In modern HRM literature the use of employee financial participation is considered as part of the high-performance workplace and is recommended as one of the best practices of HRM. Having a relational perspective on the phenomenon, employee financial participation alters the employment relationship from a transactional and adversarial one to one that emphasizes mutual commitments (Hansmann, 1996, 1999; Rousseau and Shperling, 2003). Other protagonists may have more macro-oriented reasons for the existence of employee financial participation: harmony between labour and capital, better economic performance of sectors of the economy, wage flexibility and wage moderation, and, for some others having a transactional perspective on employee financial participation, a 'tax efficient measure to prevent unionization'.

In research, the phenomenon of employee financial participation can be divided into three main approaches. The first approach is strictly economic and seeks to model enterprises with (substantive) employee financial participation. The second approach takes an economic organization perspective, uses mainly agency thinking and tries to develop expectations of employee behaviour and outputs. The third approach takes a human resource-based perspective and tries to explain the phenomenon using organizational behaviour and human capital thinking. HRM theories based on the theoretical framework of the so-called 'resource-based view of the firm' focus on the relation between HRM strategies and performance outcomes. Within this paradigm, financial participation is viewed as a particular HRM practice aiming at the realization of competitive advantage of the organization. In this chapter, we will emphasize this perspective.

There is diversity between societies in the definition and design of employee financial participation. Varied strategic choices set within heterogeneous cultures and ideologies, political and economic conditions, industrial relations institutions and power distributions have influenced the use, the types and the forms of employee financial participation arrangements. Important actors such as governments, employers, trade unions, fiscal and financial services companies and several non-governmental organizations (NGOs) try to influence employee financial participation on a more or less ideological basis.

However, the variety of motives and objectives of financial participation and the many forms have also led to polemic views at various levels in society, in which the contradictions cut across parties. There are governments that actively support the phenomenon, such as in the UK and France, while others oppose it (the Swedish government, for example). Also, there are big differences between trade unions: parts of the Irish trade unions are in favour, while parts of the German, French and Spanish trade unions are among the main opponents. Even amongst employers there are polemical views about the phenomenon (for reviews see Poutsma, 2001; Pendleton and Poutsma, 2004). The European Commission is a cautious advocate and has developed guidelines (CEC, 2002). It published the so-called PEPPER reports in 1991 (see Uvalic, 1991) and 1997 and in 2006 (Hashi et al., 2006). PEPPER stands for Promotion of Employee Participation in Profit and Enterprise Results (including equity). Its position is that financial participation is an important tool for effective and sustainable relationships that can do justice to a better distribution of the appreciation on the company level and at the level of society.

Multinationals face an important difficulty in developing global equity plans given the differences in treatment of these plans in different nations. They face the dilemma of standardization or localization. Multinationals of US origin play a central role in the transfer of employee financial participation practices, especially for share schemes and stock option plans. This dominance effect is found in Europe.

What Is Employee Financial Participation?

Employee financial participation is a term used to describe mechanisms through which employees can gain some form of financial or equity share in their companies, through three broad categories of schemes: profit sharing, employee share ownership or stock options.

Profit sharing is the sharing of profits by giving employees, usually in addition to a fixed wage, a variable income component linked directly to profits or some other measure of enterprise outcomes. Profit sharing is a collective scheme applied to all or to a large group of employees, thus distinguishing it from individual bonuses. Related to the profit sharing schemes are so-called 'gain-sharing' arrangements. Such schemes are not dependent on the financial performance of a company, but other criteria, such as cost savings or certain quality objectives.

In practice, profit sharing can take various forms. It can be paid in cash, enterprise shares or other securities; or it can be allocated to specific funds invested for the benefit of employees; it can provide employees with immediate or deferred benefits. Deferred profit sharing is a form of compensation where the benefit is not immediately available to the employee. The allocated profit share is held by the employer, in trust, or under specific administered accounts, usually for a period of three to four years. A scheme might allocate a percentage of profits to enterprise funds, which are then invested (either in the company, other companies or other investment vehicles) in the name of the employee. Where tax concessions to employer or employees are involved, countries regulate plan features, such as eligibility, contribution rates, vesting, investments and distribution.

There can be a close relationship between profit sharing and share accumulations or savings plans. The employee's profit shares may be paid into an enterprise-based savings plan for the employee. In some instances, employee contributions into these plans from profit sharing are matched by further employer contributions. In some countries, governments give bonuses on employee contributions. There has been increasing attention to using these schemes as a vehicle to contribute to personal pension plans.

Employee share ownership provides for employee participation in enterprise results either by receiving dividends or by the appreciation of employee-owned capital, or a combination of both. There are several types of employee share ownership plan: allocation of free shares to employees and plans that provide for purchase of shares, possibly on favourable terms. Employers may match the purchases made by employees. And there may be a link with pensions in that the share purchases may be part of larger and wider portfolios of investments made by the employee in conjunction with their employer (as in 401 k plans in the United States of America). The deferred form of share ownership plans allocates the shares in a trust. This is typically of ESOPs (Employee Share Ownership Plans) in the USA. ESOPs have grown in the United States tremendously over the last 30 years, largely as a result of favourable tax treatment.

By and large, employee share ownership plans should be differentiated from workers' co-operatives and worker-managed firms. Co-operatives are usually required to abide by a set of principles including 100 per cent worker ownership and equal distribution of ownership by employee-owners, though it is not necessarily the case that all those employed by co-operatives are owners. Co-operatives are often small in size and are often concentrated in certain areas of economic activity, such as those that are labour-intensive, although there are some well known large ones, such as the multinational Mondragon group from Spain, and an example of a large majority owned company is the John Lewis Partnership from the UK.

In *stock options plans* employees are granted the right to acquire shares at some point in time, typically after three or four years. Although this does not necessarily lead to ownership, because the employee may simultaneously exercise the option and sell the shares, in most all-employee plans of this sort some employees will exercise and hold. There is another potential link with savings plans in that there may be arrangements for employees to save from their salary so as to accumulate the capital necessary to exercise the option.

There is a wide diversity of taxation arrangements for profit sharing, employee share ownership and stock option plans depending on the kind of gains that employees make from them. Tax advantageous schemes may waive income tax liability (and associated social insurance charges) on the benefits for employees. The growth in value of shares may be taxed at more advantageous capital gains tax rates rather than income tax rates. There is wide diversity between countries on the point at which tax becomes liable in plans, especially those based on granting of options. Some tax at grant, some at exercise, some at sale of the shares and some on a combination of these.

There are a number of dimensions of variance of employee financial participation plans that are important to note. The first is the substance of 'control' and 'return' rights (Ben-Ner and Jones, 1995). It ranges from full control of the affairs by direct voice and the right to full returns, as found for example in co-operatives, to limited or hardly any form of control (i.e. non-voting shares), and low participation in results (i.e. small profit share in the form of secured savings). Profit sharing can be part of income but in practice in most cases it is an arrangement on top of salary. Co-operatives and labour-managed firms suggest majority-owned firms where employees own more than 50 per cent, but in most cases the 'mainstream' employee ownership covers less than 5 per cent of capital (Kaarsemaker *et al.*, 2010). Another important dimension is coverage; broad-based schemes, where all or most employees are eligible to join, and narrow-based schemes, usually targeted to top and senior management and/or core professional groups.

heoretical Approaches

The explanation of the adoption of employee financial participation is frequently based on the principal-agent theory, where the managers or employees are seen as opportunistic agents who should be monitored by the shareholding owners of the firm. The research on adoption and outcomes of financial participation is divided into a branch focusing on schemes for executives and a branch focusing on so-called broad-based schemes, eligible for all employees. Similar theoretical arguments are used for the impact of narrow and of broad-based schemes, such as the above-mentioned agency and incentives approach, but there are also important differences. In this chapter we focus on theoretical arguments for broad-based schemes, more specifically on the attitudinal and behavioural effects of employee financial participation.

Klein (1987) argues that there are three main theoretical models for the impact of financial participation schemes on the attitudes and behaviour of employees.

1 The intrinsic motivating effect, also called the ownership impact model. The argument is that by receiving a share of the firm employees develop the feeling of co-ownership and act accordingly. The argument is that ownership changes the mindset in such a way that psychological ownership (Pierce *et al.*, 1991; Pierce *et al.*, 2003) is developed, which causes changes in attitudes and behaviour. The behavioural outcome is extra effort to sustain the firm and protect it from external threats. It generates ownership behaviours that support organizational performance.

2 The extrinsic motivation effect, also called the incentive model, where employees are expected to deliver extra effort because they expect to receive an extra reward in the end. Although this relates to the agency theory, much of the broad-based literature refers also to the expectancy-valence theory of Vroom (1964). The expectancy-valence theory argues that employees should value the reward (profit share, share ownership or stock option) that is gained in the end before any changes in attitude and behaviour will occur. This expectancy-valence may differ between employees. The incentive model argues that employee financial participation will lead to extra effort.

3 The commitment impact, also called the instrumental involvement model, where, through financial participation and alignment of interests, both employees and employer act upon the common interest. A psychological contract is developed where employer and employees commit to each other in exchange and sharing (Rousseau and Shperling, 2003). This is expressed by a focus of employee attitudes and behaviour on a willingness to participate in strategic decision-making, a focus on profit and profitability of the firm, and on cost effective working.

The models received empirical support from several studies (Kaarsemaker, 2006; Pendleton, 2001; Pendleton *et al.*, 1998; Wagner *et al.*, 2003).

It is important to note that different schemes may relate differently to the theoretical models. There are important differences between the schemes in their nature and in their effects, especially between shares-related schemes and profit sharing arrangements. Profit sharing is typically directed to the short-term and is also easier to allocate in cash, which makes the extrinsic motivation impact more direct and stronger than in case of share ownership. Compared with profit sharing plans, share plans are better able to create feelings of ownership and involvement.

The objectives of stock option plans are consistent with Klein's extrinsic motivation and commitment effect. Compared with share plans, option plans are less inclined to generate feelings of ownership. Ownership might occur at the point of exercise but in practice in most cases the shares are sold immediately (Heath *et al.*, 1999; Weeden *et al.*, 2001). However, a study showed that those who are motivated to participate in option plans according to the instrumental involvement model keep the shares, whereas those who participate for extrinsic reasons immediately sell the shares (Pendleton, 2005).

In addition to above models, other explanations, such as retention devices and protection of firm specific skills, are all business case arguments that favour the adoption and implementation of these plans. In addition, the determinants literature suggests that the adoption of employee financial participation is likely to vary depending on a number of contextual factors, such as firm age (younger) and size (larger), technology and capital intensity (more capital intensive; high tech industry), trade union influence (in general less in unionized work places), industry (high tech and financial sector), structure of ownership (more in public listed companies), international character of the company (more in MNCs) and the geographical location of the company (diversity between countries) (see for an overview Pendleton *et al.*, 2003).

Outcomes

Since the 1970s, a large number of studies investigated the claimed effects of employee financial participation plans on the attitudes and behaviour of employees as well as on organizational performance. A number of studies provide an overview of the research results of the impact of employee financial participation (Poutsma and Braam, 2012; Doucouliagos, 1995, Kaarsemaker, 2006; Kruse and Blasi, 1997; Pérotin and Robinson, 2003). These reviews show that most studies found favourable effects of share plans on identification, satisfaction, commitment and turnover. Looking at organizational performance, most studies found a small but positive effect, in particular on productivity. This relationship is stronger when there is a more widespread distribution, i.e. a majority of the employees have a stake in the company. Profit sharing plans have a slightly positive significant effect on productivity. Most research on the effects of stock options is about options for executives. This research provides a mixed picture of the impact of options on performance, both negative and positive effects, where in general, the positive effects are limited (Bryson and Freeman, 2010; Sesil and Lin, 2011).

Latest discussion in the literature is that there may be important synergy effects on outcomes and performance if companies combine plans. Research shows that workers assess differently to what extent different financial participation plans motivate them to work harder for or to be involved more in the firm (Blasi *et al.*, 2010). This can be related to risk aversion and other worker characteristics, such as position and level of pay. Companies may look for different plans that fit differences in preferences. Bryson and Freeman (2010) found that companies typically combine plans and also switch between plans for optimal outcomes. Looking at retention in stock option plans, Pendleton's study (2005) shows that portfolio diversification is an important determinant of retaining shares by employees. Those who keep the shares also have more alternative, share-based investments than those who sell shares after exercise of the options. The shared capitalism project, reported in Kruse *et al.* (2010), collected several studies with different data and research design with positive outcomes for companies and employees. One of the studies looked at a combination of plans, using what they called the shared capitalism index, and report positive outcomes of combination of plans (Blasi *et al.*, 2010).

Recent literature emphasizes the need for the embeddedness of employee financial participation in high performance work systems. The use of financial participation schemes may form a key part of a wider human resource management (HRM) strategy in creating a competitive advantage for the company (Kaarsemaker and Poutsma, 2006). It is therefore suggested to consider financial participation as a tool alongside other HRM instruments. Several HRM practices have been included in the research, with differing results. This mostly relates to forms of participation in decision-making, but also to information sharing, and training for business literacy, and profit sharing. The literature suggests that in order to be effective, an HRM system with employee ownership as a central element and core HRM practice should also include the following HRM practices: participation in decision-making, profit sharing, information sharing, training for business literacy and mediation (Kaarsemaker and Poutsma, 2006: 678).

Critics

There are arguments against the adoption of employee financial participation. We focus on three theoretical arguments: the free rider effect, the risks perspective and the attitude of management towards sharing.

The free rider problem argues that no extra effort is developed from collective incentive plans such as employee financial participation, and no subsequent higher organizational performance because of the possibility of free riding of colleagues (i.e. only some work extra hard but all get the resulting benefit). Especially in larger companies this might block the alleged benefits of such plans. However, the theoretical models of ownership and involvement particularly argue that workers may resist shirking colleagues. Freeman *et al.* (2010) find that workers are most likely to take action against shirkers in workplaces where employees participate in profit sharing, gain sharing, stock options or other forms of ownership. They show also that workers in workplaces where there is more anti-shirking behavior report that co-workers work harder and encourage other workers more, and that their workplace is more effective in several dimensions related to productivity and profits.

Clearly there are risks involved when total remuneration is affected by future performance. Thus, it is expected that workers will be risk averse in mixing their own capital with that of the firm, putting effort and capital investment in one basket. The objective risks could be mitigated by setting limits to amounts and proportion relative to total wage and creating a portfolio of different financial participation plans. The study by Blasi *et al.* (2010) suggests that workers' lack of influence in their workplace and poor relations with management combined with their objective personal economic risk makes the workplace a risky place to be (ibid.: 120). The findings suggest that a good corporate culture – the respective expectations and norms to have a say at work and be treated fairly in employment relations – play an important role in mitigating the risks issue and producing the desired effects.

As with all human resource management practices, management commitment to the policy and practice is key for effective implementation and use. Employee financial participation may not be in the interest of some managers, especially when it relates to wider participation in decision-making. The recent literature suggests that employee financial participation works best when it is combined with other partnership arrangements (for an overview, see Kalmi *et al.* 2005). However, these participative requirements, essential for a scheme's success, are a high price to pay for those managers or employers who want to adhere to traditional prerogatives (D'Art, 1992: 6). This reluctance may be found in several schemes and may question the effectiveness of these schemes to stimulate motivation and co-operation. It is suggested that investing in not only the scheme but also in a cooperative culture pays off.

Employee Financial Participation in an International Context

A key question for this chapter concerns the incidence of financial participation schemes in different countries and the reasons for this. It has been widely observed that government legislation on financial participation, and the availability of tax concessions, are key determinants of national differences in the incidence of schemes (Pendleton and Poutsma, 2012; Poutsma, 2001; Poutsma *et al.*, 2003; Uvalic, 1991). Poole (1989) proposed that 'favourable conjunctures' could explain the popularity or growth of financial participation in given countries. This might be a conjuncture of economic and political circumstances. For instance, the UK position can partly be explained by a shift of economic power from workers to firms and 'a political emphasis on undermining trade unionism and promoting employer–employee co-operation in the early 1980s; these formed a backdrop to legislation to promote employee share ownership' (Pendleton and Poutsma, 2012: 345).

Highly relevant for the diversity in adoption of these schemes, are explanations that take a neo-institutional approach, where the decision to adopt and implement employee financial participation is affected by key aspects of the institutional environment in which organizations operate. The main question in this approach is to what extent institutional factors lead to institutional isomorphism (homogenization) in the use of employee financial participation. Organizations may mimic their competitors in the use of practices, they may react to coercive institutional pressures to conform to legislation and informal rules, or they may follow certain normative practices and professionalization in the sector (Oliver, 1997).

More recently, notions of 'national business systems' and 'varieties of capitalism' (Amable, 2003; Hall and Soskice, 2001; Whitley, 1999) provide a more comprehensive way of investigating diversity in the use of financial participation. They may help to explain why various forms of financial participation are more appealing in some national contexts than others (Croucher *et al.*, 2010). Share ownership plans receive most support from governments in those countries that are viewed as 'liberal market economies'. In these countries it is said that exchanges between employees and employer are predominantly transactional in character, whereas in 'coordinated market economies' there is greater emphasis on relationships. Thus, in the latter, employee commitment might be secured through well-developed systems for employee involvement and representation whereas in LMEs there is a greater reliance on market-based rewards such as company stock plans (Gospel and Pendleton, 2003). In addition, in economies where there are well-developed and liquid stock markets and dispersed ownership, such as liberal market economies, stock-based instruments are more likely viewed as a viable form of employee reward. Black *et al.* (2007) find that the prevalence of share ownership plans in countries is associated with the extent of ownership dispersion in the listed company sector.

The extent of both institutional and competitive isomorphic pressures in any national context will depend on the characteristics of that country. These characteristics can be described in terms of the power of the various stakeholders in the employment relationship, the extent of government intervention in labour issues, and how developed a market is relative to international competition (Djelic *et al.*, 2003). According to this approach dominant actors may influence the isomorphic pressures in terms of enforcement and shaping. For employee financial participation the dominant actors are governments, trade unions and employer organizations as well as any representative bodies in and around the firm. These organizations influence the use and features of financial participation at company level. In other words, the institutional environment in which firms operate is likely to structure and influence the decisions on adoption and use. It is particularly important to take account of these views as we explore cross-national diffusion of employee financial participation and the role of multinational companies. Over the last decade or so there have been major changes in institutions, especially in systems of collective bargaining and other elements of employment relations that open up the possibility of employee financial participation. In many of the more centralized national systems of collective bargaining, like Germany and the Scandinavian countries, there has been substantial decentralization of collective bargaining. Alongside these changes, pay systems themselves have become more individualistic (Traxler *et al.*, 2008). Financial participation is often seen as being a key component of these trends (Kaarsemaker and Poutsma, 2006; Poutsma and de Nijs, 2003). This suggests a gradual growth of the phenomenon in the near future.

MNCs and Employee Financial Participation

Globalization and the increasing importance of the multinational corporation (MNC) have boosted research on the transfer of organizational practices (Harzing and Sorge, 2003). MNCs can potentially significantly affect employment practices in host countries (Edwards and Walsh, 2009; Kostova *et al.*, 2008). MNCs may encourage convergence of HRM practices, as they aim to achieve consistency among their subsidiaries abroad. They may also act as strategic role models for local companies. Gooderham *et al.* (1999) suggest that US MNCs operate as important role models in Europe.

Country-of-origin literature focuses on transfer of practices across borders, paying special attention to the role of US MNCs. In this context, the so-called dominance effect is cited as an important additional factor (Smith and Meiksins, 1995). This effect occurs when practices are shaped according to the country that sets the standards for 'what are perceived as global best practices' (Pudelko and Harzing, 2007: 536). In this way, MNCs of different national origin may be more likely to converge on a 'global best practice' model of employee financial participation. Given the dominance of the US business system in the world economy, this global best practice model of employee financial participation is likely to tend towards US practice (Ferner and Almond, 2013).

At the same time, the subsidiary confronts pressures to adapt to the institutional environment of the host country. As a result, foreign subsidiaries are confronted with two distinct sets of isomorphic pressures. Kostova and Roth (2002) refer to this situation as *institutional duality*. The amount of discretion that management has in a specific country in order to adopt and implement practices is therefore a key issue. According to Whitley (1999), the business system of the host country may differ in terms of the openness and receptiveness of dominant practices. In a permissive environment the transfer of practices is easier than in a more constraining host country environment (cf. Whitley and Czaban, 1998). This allows incoming MNCs choice as to whether to transfer parent country practices, adopt local practices or follow a dominant best practice model.

A large number of empirical studies have concentrated on the role of MNCs in promoting convergence of HRM practices across national borders (for an overview, Harzing and Sorge, 2003). Fenton-O'Creevy *et al.* (2008) found that MNEs based in the USA in particular have greater centralized control over HRM. They also found that this centralized control is more developed in subsidiaries where pressure by active institutional constituents such as labour unions is low. For financial participation it is argued that MNEs will resist host country pressures except when forced to comply with the prevailing values and regulations in host country industrial relations systems. In case of transfer of employee financial participation, several studies show the significant effect of MNCs on adoption but at the same time the adaptation to local environments. In Ireland, foreign-owned companies, particularly from the USA and the UK, are much more likely to have financial participation schemes (Geary and Roche, 2001; Morley *et al.*, 1999). Poutsma *et al.* (2005) found that being a subsidiary of a foreign MNC is a strong determinant for the existence of employee financial participation in European countries. Poutsma *et al.* (2006) found that MNCs adoption varies with the local adoption, i.e. there is lower uptake by MNCs in environments where there is also lower adoption by local companies.

Incidence

There are not many comparative data sources that have information on the incidence and development of financial participation across nations. The only comprehensive sources of comparative data are the CRANET HRM Surveys, with organization level data covering most of the European countries; the European Company Survey, also with organizational level data; and the European Working Conditions Surveys, with employee level data. The CRANET survey is carried out on a global scale in over 40 countries. The data are collected using a survey of senior HRM Directors from organizations in all sectors of the economy with more than 100 employees. The survey is conducted periodically and therefore also provides longitudinal information about human resource management policies and practices, including employee financial participation.

Figures 20.1 to 20.3 provide overviews of the use of different categories of employee financial participation schemes in countries, based on the CRANET network data of 2009/2010. These are data of private sector organizations with more than 100 employees. Since the incidence rates are significantly related to firm size, the figures present higher levels than for the population of firms as a whole. The incidence rates in smaller firms are much lower. The figures present a coverage dimension, i.e. narrow-based plans, only for management, and broad-based plans, where also other occupational groups (professionals, clerks and/or operational/manual personnel) are eligible to participate. The figures show the incidence of schemes as the proportion of companies with the particular scheme per country, and do not capture exactly the proportion of employees under the schemes. 'Broad-based' does not necessarily mean a high participation rate. The data do not provide this information, but we know from other sources that participation rates in share schemes are typically lower (usually around 30 per cent) than in profit sharing schemes (usually between 70 per cent and 80 per cent).

Figure 20.1 presents the incidence of narrow-based and broad-based employee share ownership schemes. In general, the proportion of companies with schemes is low; on average 20 per cent for broad-based schemes and 9 per cent for narrow-based schemes. High levels are found in Japan and Taiwan. This reflects a long tradition in both countries. In particular, the highly entrepreneurial culture in Taiwan has led to a more rapid embrace and expansion of broad-based stock

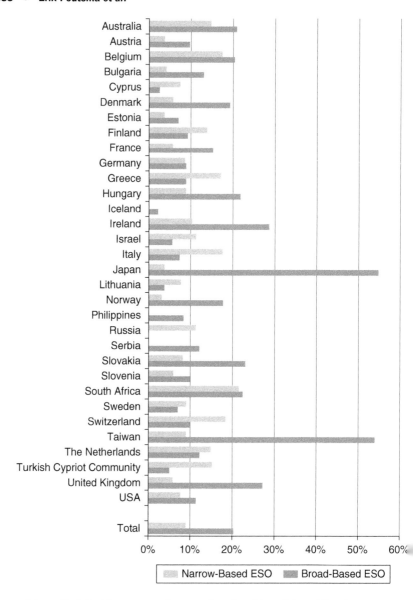

Figure 20.1 Incidence rate of narrow-based and broad-based Employee
Share Ownership (ESO) per country (proportion of companies;
companies with >100 employees)
Source: CRANET, own calculations; year: 2009/2010, total N = 3315

option plans and combination plans featuring both profit sharing and
employee ownership (Cin *et al.*, 2003). Similar arguments account for
the development in Japan (Kato, 2006), where ESOPs are the main

vehicle for employee share ownership. Typically, top management is excluded from these plans.

In Europe, broad-based share ownership plans are most common in Ireland and the UK, followed by Slovakia, Hungary and Belgium. Mediterranean countries, such as Italy, Cyprus and Greece, and some other European countries, such as Estonia and Finland, have the lowest incidence. Although some former communist countries in Eastern Europe promoted employee share ownership as part of the privatization process at transition, employee share ownership has declined in most of these countries since (Hashi *et al.*, 2006). Note that the data show an unexpected average rate for the USA of 11 per cent. However, this may have to do with the CRANET survey that only covers larger firms. The ESOP arrangements in the USA are typically also directed towards smaller firms. By comparison, 8 per cent of firms with less than 100 employees have share schemes (Blasi *et al.*, 2013) whereas this percentage is much lower in Europe.

The table also shows that the differences between countries are more pronounced for broad-based schemes than for narrow-based schemes. This is very similar to the analysis of previous CRANET surveys (see Pendleton *et al.*, 2003), where it was found that narrow-based schemes are less determined by country and institutional differences than broad-based schemes. This suggests that country characteristics have a profound influence on the existence of broad-based schemes.

The incidence rates of profit sharing are generally higher than for share schemes, 26 per cent for broad-based and 10 per cent for narrow-based schemes (see Figure 20.2). As can be seen, France and Finland have substantially more broad-based profit sharing than any other country. This is because profit sharing is mandatory for larger organizations in France, and in Finland a long tradition of Personnel Funds determined the development. A second set of European countries with relatively high incidence of broad-based profit sharing comprises Germany, Austria, Netherlands and Switzerland. Narrow-based profit sharing is more evenly distributed among countries, suggesting again that certain arrangements in specific countries may influence the existence of broad-based schemes.

Figure 20.3 presents the incidence rate for stock option plans. On average only a minority of companies offer these plans; 9 per cent broad-based and almost 15 per cent narrow-based plans. Different from share schemes and profit sharing schemes, the incidence rate of narrow-based schemes is higher than broad-based schemes in most countries (with exceptions for Taiwan, the United States of America, the UK, Bulgaria, Serbia and Greece). Stock options are most probably a more developed element of reward policy for management

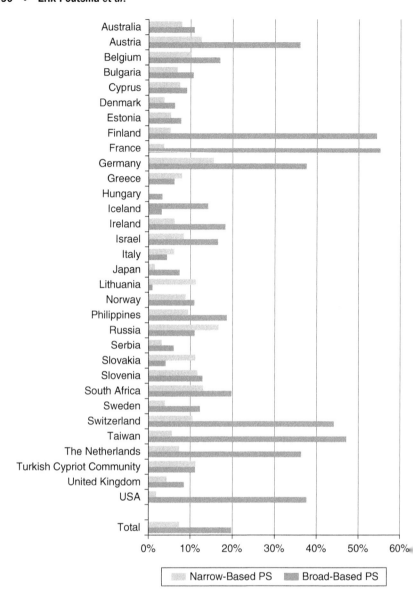

Figure 20.2 Incidence rate of narrow-based and broad-based Profit Sharing
Schemes (PS) per country (proportion of companies; companies
with >100 employees)

Source: CRANET, own calculations; year: 2009/2010, total N = 3315

than for all employees. Again, large differences in incidence rates
between countries suggest country-specific determinants of the
existence of schemes.

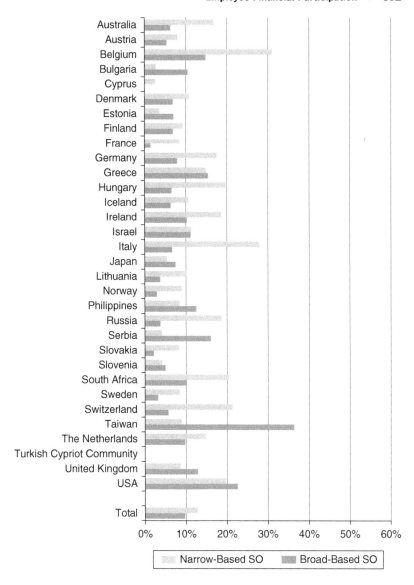

Figure 20.3 Incidence rate of narrow-based and broad-based Stock Options
(SO) per country (proportion of companies; companies with >100
employees)

Source: CRANET, own calculations; year: 2009/2010, total N = 3315

The CRANET data provide organization level data. Welz and
Fernández–Macías (2008) used employee level data from the European
Working Conditions Survey (EWCS) to discover the spread of financial
participation in Europe. This employee level survey is conducted
periodically in all EU and other European countries by the European

Foundation for the Improvement of Living and Working Conditions. The survey is primarily concerned with working and employment conditions rather than reward, but delivers some indicators for examining financial participation. This survey gives a rather different picture to that provided by CRANET, which covers only larger organizations. It is well known that employee financial participation is significantly related to the size of the organization. The EWCS shows that the use of employee financial participation is very low in most countries, lower than estimated by CRANET in larger organizations: only around 12 per cent of European employees receive income from some form of profit sharing scheme, and only 2.3 per cent from shares in the companies they work for, compared with the situation in the USA, 40 per cent receive income from profit share and 21 per cent from shares (Blasi *et al.*, 2013). In six countries (Slovakia, Slovenia, Sweden, the Netherlands, Finland and France) more than one-fifth of employees receive profit shares, and in only four (Ireland, France, Luxembourg and Belgium) more than 5 per cent receive income from shares.

Comparing data from the surveys in 2000/2001 and 2005 Welz and Fernández-Macías (2008) conclude that in almost all cases there is an increase in the proportion of employees receiving income from profit sharing and shares. There have not been increases in most Central and Eastern European countries. Analysis of developments among European countries using CRANET data revealed similar conclusions regarding the increase of schemes. Despite the major economic crisis in the period of investigation, employee financial participation experienced increase or stability in development during the last 20 years (Pendleton *et al.*, 2013).

It must be noted that financial participation is very unevenly distributed among different jobs and individuals. The EWCS data show that managers are more than four times as likely to participate in these schemes than manual workers, even after controlling for variables such as sector, establishment size or education. Also, men have a higher chance of receiving income from financial participation than women; and, permanent workers have a higher chance than temporary workers. The findings suggest that financial participation schemes may reinforce pre-existing inequalities in pay (Welz and Fernández-Macías, 2008: 495).

Country Profiles

The above account of incidence and development is based on abstract indicators of the existence of schemes. However, schemes under the same label can have substantial differences in aims, characteristics and design in different countries. National histories, regulations (tax, securities, and income and labour laws) and culture influence the form that schemes take. There are country-specific employee financial participation profiles, following country-specific institutional profiles.

Some countries explicitly promote collective incentive schemes while others do not. For instance, in the UK there is a long tradition of governmental promotion of share option schemes focusing on promotion of an enterprise culture. The framework consists mainly of deferred share-based profit sharing via option schemes and receives tax concessions. There are two main broad-based plans: the Save As You Earn (SAYE) share options savings plan, introduced in 1984 and the Share Incentive Plan (SIP) introduced in 2000. In SAYE employees can take out options to be exercised in three, five, or seven years time, at up to 20 per cent discount on market value at the time of grant. There is no income tax payable but a lower level of capital gains tax on the sale of shares. The Share Incentive Plan provides for grants of free shares, for share purchases by employees, and for awards of matching shares. There are additional share schemes arrangements focusing more on share plans for managers, especially in non-listed smaller companies. The position of unions in the UK can best be described as engaged scepticism. Financial participation in many UK companies is kept separate from collective bargaining over pay and the terms and conditions of employment. Both employers and trade unions tend to accept that the legal regulations governing financial participation may limit the scope for negotiation on the content of profit sharing and share ownership schemes.

In contrast to the UK, profit sharing is deeply entrenched in France. France has a framework of extensive, state-regulated (partly mandatory), broad-based, deferred profit sharing with the aims of promoting employee savings, the broader distribution of wealth, and wage flexibility. Introduced by General de Gaulle in the 1960s with the aim of bridging capital and labour, the system in France has evolved into a system where employee savings are invested in funds, which in turn either invest in a diversified fund or in the shares of the employer. The profit share is paid into a fund attracting tax advantages when held in the fund for at least three years. Over the years the system has expanded with more voluntary arrangements (*Interessement*), where profit shares are paid into a company savings scheme (*PEE*), where these contributions can be complemented by bonus payments or voluntary savings. Most of the savings are invested in *Fonds Communs de Placement d'Entreprise* (*FCPE*), which in turn either invest in a diversified fund or in the shares of the employer. In other words, French companies are responsive to employee share schemes, provided they fit the legal framework. Moreover they have to be agreed by the employees or their representatives, including the unions.

In Germany the development of financial participation is relatively modest. Several laws regulate the possibility of using employee savings (matched with a premium from the state) to invest in the employing firm, to acquire shares, to make a loan to the employer, or to enter into a silent partnership with the employer. In the latter, employees do not acquire control rights as full shareholders normally have. The eligibility is restricted to lower-income groups and the tax concessions are rather modest.

The Finnish financial participation system is dominated by the typical Finnish Personnel Fund (PF). The Personnel Funds law was enacted in the beginning of the 1990s inspired by US employee stock ownership plans (ESOPs) and Swedish wage-earner funds. A PF typically distributes its shareholdings quite widely and invests also in other securities, whereas employee share ownership plans invest only in their own firm. In practice, many of the personnel funds invest part of the assets in their own company and the rest in other assets. PFs are company level agreements, established by a collective decision of the employees in the company, but in Finland both share schemes and profit sharing schemes are largely developed outside the domain of collective bargaining on higher levels. The PF is owned by the employees and administers the assets it receives from the company.

In a number of European countries there are other arrangements, such as in Austria and Belgium, but in most countries there are no institutional arrangements to promote financial participation.

Consequences for IHRM

In summary, the above account of cross-national diversity of employee financial participation poses challenges for international human resource management in international companies. Clearly, the description of diversity between nations means that these global equity plans have to cope with national differences. These imply that plans are adjusted to:

- securities law
- withholding and reporting
- plan document requirements
- taxation
- social insurance
- data privacy laws
- restrictions on payroll deductions
- exchange control requirements
- labour issues.

Despite the diversity, MNCs do develop global equity plans in order to strive for consistency. They may do so on an an abstract level to make sure that missions, objectives and treatment in terms of fairness and equality are the same everywhere. In practice the type of employee financial participation that is covered by the global equity plans is stock options. Partly this is due to the experience that stock options are well known and understood globally and increasingly are treated similarly. Global equity plans are in most cases less broad-based although there are examples that try to enroll the plan to all, such as the multinational company Arcadis.

Key Learning Points

- There are important favourable effects of share plans on identification, satisfaction, commitment and turnover and productivity. These effects are stronger when there is a more widespread distribution, i.e. a majority of the employees have a stake in the company. Profit sharing plans have a slightly positive significant effect on productivity. For stock options the effects are more mixed.
- There is a need for the embeddedness of employee financial participation in high performance work systems. The use of financial participation schemes may form a key part of a wider human resource management (HRM) strategy in creating a competitive advantage for the company.
- There is diversity between societies in the definition and design of employee financial participation. Varied strategic choices set within heterogeneous cultures and ideologies, political and economic conditions, industrial relations institutions and power distributions have influenced the use, the types and the forms of employee financial participation arrangements. There are country-specific employee financial participation profiles, following country specific institutional profiles.
- Multinationals face an important problem in developing global equity plans given the differences in treatment of these plans in different nations. They face the dilemma of standardization or localization.
- Multinationals of US origin play a central role in the transfer of employee financial participation practices, especially for share schemes and stock option plans. This dominance effect is found in Europe.
- Financial participation is important for HR professionals for three main reasons. First, financial participation is relevant to consider since it has been diffused in companies worldwide and has important

impacts on the individual and the organization. Second, HR professionals can play a crucial role in helping the business to embed financial participation in a high performance work system strategy. Third, HR professionals can help to adjust the financial participation schemes to local needs.

References

Amable, B. (2003) *The Diversity of Modern Capitalism*. Oxford: Oxford University Press.

Ben-Ner, A. and Jones, D.C. (1995) 'Employee Participation, Ownership and Productivity: A Theoretical Framework', *Industrial Relations*, 34, 532–555.

Black, B., Gospel, H. and Pendleton, A. (2007) 'Finance, Corporate Governance, and the Employment Relationship', *Industrial Relations*, 46(3), 643–650.

Blasi, J.R., Freeman, R.B. and Kruse, D.L. (2013) *The Citizen's Share*. New Haven CT: Yale University Press.

Blasi, J.R., Kruse, D.L. and Markowitz, H.M. (2010) 'Risk and Lack of Diversification under Employee Ownership and Shared Capitalism', in Kruse, D.L., Freeman, R.B. and Blasi, J.R. (eds), *Shared Capitalism at Work: Employee Ownership, Profit and Gain Sharing, and Broad-based Stock Options*. Chicago, IL: University of Chicago Press, pp. 105–136.

Blasi, J.R., Freeman, R.B., Mackin, C. and Kruse, D.L. (2010) 'Creating a Bigger Pie? The Effects of Employee Ownership, Profit Sharing and Stock Options on Workplace Performance', in Kruse, D.L., Freeman, R.B. and Blasi, J.R. (eds), *Shared Capitalism at Work: Employee Ownership, Profit and Gain Sharing, and Broad-based Stock Options*. Chicago, IL: University of Chicago Press, pp. 139–166.

Bryson, A. and Freeman, R.B. (2010) 'How Does Shared Capitalism Affect Economic Performance in the United Kingdom?', in Kruse, D.L., Freeman, R.B. and Blasi, J.R. (eds), *Shared Capitalism at Work: Employee Ownership, Profit and Gain Sharing, and Broad-based Stock Options*. Chicago, IL: University of Chicago Press, pp. 201–224.

Cin, B., Han, T.S. and Smith, S.C. (2003) 'A Tale of Two Tigers: Employee Financial Participation in Korea and Taiwan', *International Journal of Human Resource Management*, 14(6), 920–941.

Commission of the European Communities (CEC) (2002) Communication from the Commission to the Council, the European Parliament, the Economic and Social Committee and the Committee of the Regions: On a Framework for the Promotion of Employee Financial participation. C. o. t. E. Communities, COM (2002) 364 final. Brussels.

Croucher, R., Brookes, M., Wood, G. and Brewster, C. (2010) 'Context, Strategy and Financial Participation: A Comparative Analysis', *Human Relations*, 63(6), 835–855.

D'Art, D. (1992) *Economic Democracy and Financial Participation*. London. Routledge.

Djelic, M.-L., Nooteboom, B. and Whitley, R. (2003) 'Organization Studies: Special Issue on Institutions, Markets and Organizations', *Organization Studies*, 24, 1579–1580.

Doucouliagos, C. (1995) 'Worker Participation and Productivity in Labor-Managed and Participatory Capitalist Firms: A Meta-Analysis', *Industrial and Labor Relations Review*, 49(1), 58–78.

Edwards, T. and Walsh, J. (2009) 'Foreign Ownership and Industrial Relations', in Brown, W., Bryson, A., Forth, J. and Whitfield, K. (eds), *The Evolution of Modern Workplace*. Cambridge: Cambridge University Press, pp. 285–306.

Fenton-O'Creevy, M., Gooderham, P. and Nordhaug, O. (2008) 'HRM in US Subsidiaries in Europe and Australia: Centralisation or Autonomy?', *Journal of International Business Studies*, 39(1), 151–166.

Ferner, A. and Almond, P. (2013) 'Performance and Reward Practices in Foreign Multinationals in the UK', *Human Resource Management Journal*, 23(3), 241–261.

Freeman, R.B., Kruse, D.J. and Blasi, J.R. (2010) 'Worker Responses to Shirking under Shared Capitalism', in Kruse, D.L., Freeman, R.B. and Blasi, J.R. (eds), *Shared Capitalism at Work: Employee Ownership, Profit and Gain Sharing, and Broad-based Stock Options*. Chicago, IL: University of Chicago Press, pp. 77–103.

Geary, J. and Roche, W. (2001), 'Multinationals and Human Resource Practices in Ireland: A Rejection of the "New Conformance Thesis"', *International Journal of Human Resource Management*, 12, 109–127.

Gooderham, P.N., Nordhaug, O. and Ringdal, K. (1999) 'Institutional and Rational Determinants of Organizational Practices: Human Resource Management in European Firms', *Administrative Science Quarterly*, 44(3), 507–531.

Gospel, H. and Pendleton, A. (2003) 'Finance, Corporate Governance, and the Management of Labour: A Conceptual and Comparative Analysis', *British Journal of Industrial Relations*, 41(3), 557–582.

Hall, P.A. and Soskice, D. (2001) *Varieties of Capitalism: The Institutional Foundations of Comparative Advantage*. Oxford: Oxford University Press.

Hansmann, H. (1996) *The Ownership of Enterprise*. Boston, MA: Harvard University Press.

Hansmann, H. (1999) 'Employee Ownership and Unions: Lessons from the Airline Industry', in Estreicher, S. (ed.), *Employee Representation in the Emerging Workplace: Alternatives/Supplements to Collective Bargaining*. Kluwer Law International, pp. 573–580.

Harzing, A.W. and Sorge, A.M. (2003) 'The Relative Impact of Country-of-Origin and Universal Contingencies on Internationalization Strategies and Corporate Control in Multinational Enterprises: World-Wide and European Perspectives', *Organisation Studies*, 24(2), 187–214.

Hashi, I., Lowitzsch, J., Uvalic, M. and Vaughan-Whitehead, D. (2006) 'PEPPER III: An Overview of Employee Financial Participation', in Lowitzsch, J. (ed.), *The PEPPER II Report: Promotion of Employee Participation in Profits and Enterprise Results in the new Member and Candidate Countries of the European Union*. Berlin: Free University, Inter-University Centre at the Institute for Eastern European Studies.

Heath, C., Huddart, S. and Lang, M. (1999) 'Psychological Factors and Stock Option Exercise', *Quarterly Journal of Economics*, 114, 601–627.

Kaarsemaker, E. (2006) *Employee Ownership and Human Resource Management. A Theoretical and Empirical Treatise with a Digression on the Dutch Context*. Doctoral Dissertation, Radboud University: Nijmegen.

Kaarsemaker, E. and Poutsma, E. (2006) 'The Fit of Employee Ownership with Other Human Resource Management Practices: Theoretical and Empirical

Suggestions Regarding the Existence of an Ownership High-Performance Work System, or Theory O', *Economic & Industrial Democracy*, 27(2), 669–685.

Kaarsemaker, E., Pendleton, A. and Poutsma, E. (2010) 'Employee Share Ownership', in Wilkinson, A., Gollan, P.J., Marchington, M. and Lewin, D. (eds), *The Oxford Handbook of Participation in Organizations*. Oxford: Oxford University Press, pp. 315–337.

Kalmi, P., Pendleton, A.D. and Poutsma, E. (2005) 'Financial Participation and Performance: New Survey Evidence from Europe', *Human Resource Management Journal*, 15(2), 54–67.

Kato, T. (2006) 'Determinants of the Extent of Participatory Employment Practices: Evidence from Japan', *Industrial Relations: A Journal of Economy and Society*, 45(4), 579–605.

Klein, K.J. (1987) 'Employee Stock Ownership and Employee Attitudes: A Test of Three Models', *Journal of Applied Psychology*, 72(2), 319–332.

Kostova, T. and Roth, K. (2002) 'Adoption of an Organizational Practice by Subsidiaries of Multinational Corporations: Institutional and Relational Effects', *Academy of Management Journal*, 45(1), 215–233.

Kostova, T., Roth, K. and Dacin, M. (2008) 'Institutional Theory in the Study of MNCs: A Critique and New Directions', *Academy of Management Review*, 33(4), 994–1007.

Kruse, D.L. and Blasi, J. (1997) 'Employee Ownership, Employee Attitudes, and Firm Performance: A Review of the Evidence', in Lewin, D., Mitchell, D.J.B. and Zaidi, M.A. (eds), *The Human Resource Management Handbook, Part 1*. Greenwich: JAI Press.

Kruse, D.L., Freeman, R.B. and Blasi, J.R. (eds) (2010) *Shared Capitalism at Work: Employee Ownership, Profit and Gain Sharing, and Broad-based Stock Options*. Chicago, IL: University of Chicago Press.

Morley, M.J., Gunnigle, P. and Heraty, N. (1999) 'Constructing the Reward Package: The Extent and Composition of Change in Wage and Non Wage Increases in Ireland', *International Journal of Employment Studies*, 7, 121–150.

Oliver, C. (1997) 'Sustainable Competitive Advantage Combining Institutional and Resource-Based Views', *Strategic Management Journal*, 18, 697–713.

Pendleton, A. (2001) *Employee Ownership, Participation and Governance: A Study of ESOPs in the UK*. London and New York: Routledge.

Pendleton, A. (2005) 'Sellers or Keepers? Stock Retentions in Stock Option Plans', *Human Resource Management*, 44(3), 319–336.

Pendleton, A. and Poutsma, E. (2004) *The Policies and Views of Peak Organisations towards Financial Participation*. Luxembourg: Office for Official Publications of the European Communities.

Pendleton, A. and Poutsma, E. (2012) 'Financial Participation', in Brewster, C. and Mayrhofer, W. (eds), *Handbook of Research in Comparative Human Resource Management*. Cheltenham: Edward Elgar Publishing, pp. 345–368.

Pendleton, A., Wilson, N. and Wright, M. (1998) 'The Perception and Effects of Share Ownership: Empirical Evidence from Employee Buy-Outs', *British Journal of Industrial Relations*, 36(1), 99–123.

Pendleton, A., Poutsma, E., Ligthart, P. and Brewster, C. (2013) 'The Development of Employee Financial Participation in Europe', in Parry, E., Stavrou, E. and Lazarova, M. (eds), *Global Trends in Human Resource Management*. Basingstoke: Palgrave Macmillan.

Pendleton, A., Poutsma, E., Van Ommeren, J. and Brewster, C. (2003) 'The Incidence and Determinants of Employee Share Ownership and Profit Sharing in Europe', in Kato, T. and Pliskin, J. (eds), *The Determinants of the Incidence and the Effects of Participatory Organizations*. Amsterdam: JAI Press.

Pérotin, V. and Robinson, A. (2003) *Employee Participation in Profit and Ownership: A Review of the Issues and Evidence*. Luxembourg: European Parliament.

Pierce, J.L., Kostova, T. and Dirks, K.T. (2003) 'The State of Psychological Ownership: Integrating and Extending a Century of Research', *Review of General Psychology*, 7, 84–107.

Pierce, J.L., Rubenfeld, S.A. and Morgan, S. (1991) 'Employee Ownership: A Conceptual Model of Process and Effects', *Academy of Management Review*, 16, 121–144.

Poole, M. (1989) *The Origins of Economic Democracy: Profit-Sharing and Employee-Shareholding Schemes*. London: Routledge.

Poutsma, E. (2001) *Recent Trends in Employee Financial Participation in the European Union*. Luxembourg: Office for Official Publications of the European Communities.

Poutsma, E. and Braam, G. (2012) 'Financial Participation Plans and Firm Financial Performance: Evidence from a Dutch Longitudinal Panel', in Bryson, A. (ed.), *Advances in the Economic Analysis of Participatory and Labor-Managed Firms*. Emerald Group, pp. 13, 141–185.

Poutsma, E., Ligthart, P. and Schouten, R. (2005) 'Employee Share Ownership in Europe: The Influence of US Multinationals', *Management Revue*, 16(1), 99–122.

Poutsma, E., Ligthart, P.E.M. and Veersma, U. (2006) 'The Diffusion of Calculative and Participative HRM Practices in European Firms', *Industrial Relations*, 45(2), 513–546.

Poutsma, F. and de Nijs, W.F. (2003) 'Broad-Based Employee Financial Participation in the European Union', *International Journal of Human Resource Management*, 14(6), 863–893.

Poutsma, F., Hendrickx, J.A.M. and Huijgen, F. (2003) 'Employee Participation in Europe: In Search of the Participative Workplace', *Economic and Industrial Democracy*, 24(1), 45–76.

Pudelko, M. and Harzing, A.-W. (2007) 'HRM Practices in Subsidiaries of US, Japanese and German MNCs: Country-of-Origin, Localization or Dominance Effect?', *Human Resource Management*, 46(4), 535–559.

Rousseau, D. and Shperling, Z. (2003) 'Pieces of the Action: Ownership and the Changing Employment Relationship', *Academy of Management Review*, 28(4), 553–570.

Sesil, J.C. and Lin, Y.P. (2011) 'The Impact of Employee Stock Option Adoption and Incidence on Productivity: Evidence from US Panel Data', *Industrial Relations*, 50(3), 514–535.

Smith, C. and Meiksins, P. (1995) 'System, Society and Dominance Effects in Cross-National Organisational Analysis', *Work, Employment and Society*, 9, 241–267.

Traxler, F., Brandl, B. and Glassner, V. (2008), 'Pattern Bargaining: An Investigation into Its Agency, Context and Evidence', *British Journal of Industrial Relations*, 46(1), 33.

Uvalic, M. (1991) The Promotion of Employee Participation in Profits and Enterprise Results. C. o. t. E. Communities. Social Europe, Supplement 3/91. Luxembourg: Office for Official Publications of the European Communities.

Wagner, S., Parker, C. and Christiansen, N. (2003) 'Employees that Think and Act Like Owners: Effects of Ownership Beliefs and Behaviors on Organizational Effectiveness', *Personnel Psychology*, 56(4), 847–871.

Weeden, R., Rosen, C., Carberry, E. and Rodrick, S. (2001) *Current Practices in Stock Option Plan Design*. 2nd edn. Oakland, CA: National Center for Employee Ownership.

Welz, C. and Fernández-Macías, E. (2008) 'Financial Participation of Employees in the European Union: Much Ado About Nothing?', *European Journal of Industrial Relations*, 14(4), 479–496.

Whitley, R. (1999) *Divergent Capitalisms: The Social Structuring and Change of Business Systems*. Oxford: Oxford University Press.

Whitley, R. and Czaban, L. (1998) 'Institutional Transformation and Enterprise Change in an Emergent Capitalist Economy: The Case of Hungary', *Organization Studies*, 19(2), 259–280.

21 Flexible Working in Europe

CLARE KELLIHER

Introduction

This book deals with contemporary HRM issues in Europe. Flexible working has been a central concern for employers, employees and for policy makers in many European countries in the past few decades. Over this time the European Union has developed a series of policies on workplace flexibility, designed to both assist organizations in member states to achieve greater flexibility and to help individuals balance the work and non-work aspects of their lives more effectively. This chapter aims to examine flexibility across Europe, including both that which is designed to assist organizations and that which supports employees. The objectives of this chapter are to:

- provide an introduction to the different forms of flexible working practices and the reasons for their use;
- provide an overview of the context in which flexible working has increased in recent years;
- examine the different approaches to flexible working used across European countries;
- propose areas for future investigation.

The chapter commences by defining flexibility, examining the different forms it may take and why it might be used. An overview of recent developments in the world of work will then be presented, in order to provide a context in which the recent growing interest in flexibility has taken place. This will involve exploring changes in both business and social environments, which have shaped the way in which organizations operate and the way in which individuals interact with work. Next, the chapter will go on to examine the ways in which the various forms of flexibility are utilized across different countries in Europe. The chapter will also examine Europe-wide policy and the role of governments in fostering and regulating the different forms of flexibility. Finally some overall observations will be made about the likely future of flexibility in Europe.

Defining Flexibility, Why and When Is It Used?

The different approaches to flexibility have traditionally been examined along the lines of 'employer-' or 'employee-driven' flexibility (Henly *et al.*, 2006), or flexibility *of* and *for* employees (Alis *et al.*, 2006). The essential distinction here is based on who is seeking flexibility in the employment relationship. Employer or organizationally driven flexibility is where employers seek to use labour in non-traditional ways in order to deploy it in a way that matches their business needs more closely. This typically includes variations in the amount of work undertaken, the timing and location of work, the duration of the employment relationship and the work undertaken by employees.

Employer-driven flexibility is frequently classified on four dimensions:

- Numerical flexibility involves changes to the numbers of employees and/or the hours worked. For example, employers may use part-time workers where their need for labour does not arise in units of full-time hours. Retail employers might use part-time staff to enable them to have additional staff available at peak times of operation, but not have to bear the cost of full-time employees. An extended degree of flexibility over hours worked, which has attracted considerable attention in recent times is the use of zero-hours contracts. With a zero-hours contract, the amount of work offered to the employee varies in line with the employers' needs and without a commitment to a minimum amount of work. Employers may choose to offer temporary and/or fixed-term contracts, where they experience seasonality, or are uncertain of their future pattern of business activity. This may involve either direct employment of temporary staff, or procuring them through a temporary employment agency.
- The use of functional flexibility is where employees are deployed across different tasks, sometimes at short notice, according to the demand for different types of work.
- Temporal flexibility is where the employer varies the time at which work is carried out. This may involve shift work where employees work at non-standard times, or there may be shorter-term variations subject to demand levels.

- Spatial flexibility is concerned with where work is done and allows employers to relocate staff to different workplaces. More recently, for office workers in particular, some employers have reduced designated workspaces for employees, requiring them to 'hot desk' at the workplace and/or work remotely.

These types of arrangements, whilst being designed to suit the needs of employers, are often seen as detrimental to employees and are sometimes referred to as 'contingent work', since employees may experience job insecurity and/or uncertainty over their work schedule. The use of functional flexibility however can enable employers to offer full-time and permanent employment, since multi-skilled staff can be used in different ways. Some research, though, suggests that irregular and short-term redeployment may be stressful for employees and result in work intensification (Kelliher and Gore, 2006).

In contrast, employee-driven flexibility practices are designed to allow employees some control over their working arrangements, in order to help them achieve a better relationship between their work and non-work lives. This approach tends to include flexibility over where, when and how much employees work (Putnam et al., 2014) and typically might include reduced hours working, some form of schedule flexibility, such as flexitime and remote working, where employees do some or all of their work away from a designated workplace. The distinguishing factor here is that it is the employee who is able to exercise the flexibility. Employees may look for flexibility in their working arrangements for a number of reasons.

For example, employees who have childcare responsibilities may wish to reduce their working hours, or work at different times in order to fit with their caring commitments. In those European countries, such as the UK and the Netherlands, where legislation exists to enable flexible working, this has tended to be geared to those with childcare responsibilities. Increased life expectancy in many countries also means that a growing number of employees have elder care responsibilities (Eurofound, 2014a), which may mean that they wish to make changes to their working arrangements in order to accommodate these responsibilities. Employee health may be a reason for seeking flexibility. Similarly, employees with disabilities or undergoing treatment may wish to alter their working arrangements, perhaps by reducing the hours they work, or by working from home when convalescing.

Older workers have been found to favour flexible working arrangements (Loretto et al., 2005; Vickerstaff et al., 2004). The availability of alternative work arrangements may mean that employees who would otherwise not participate in the labour force may be persuaded to remain in employment. The extension of working lives is a particular concern in those countries with an ageing population. Older workers may prefer to work part-time, or to work from home and/or at different times, perhaps to avoid stressful commutes to work. Changing attitudes to work and increased concern for work–life balance also mean that employees may seek changes to their working arrangements to pursue other activities which they value, such as education, leisure, community involvement and participation in religious or volunteering activity (Casper *et al.*, 2007; Ozbilgin *et al.*, 2011).

Although these types of arrangements are essentially designed to accommodate employees' needs, there is also evidence that they can have beneficial outcomes for employers. First, allowing employees discretion over their working arrangement has been shown to engender positive sentiments in the form of increased job satisfaction (Cotti *et al.*, 2014; Kelliher and Anderson, 2008) and organizational commitment (Glass and Finlay, 2002; Kelliher and Anderson, 2010). Studies have also linked flexible working arrangements to employee performance (Eaton, 2003; Gajendran and Harrison, 2007) and reduced levels of absenteeism (Kauffeld *et al.*, 2004). However, other research shows little impact on these outcomes and some even suggests that there are costs associated with implementation (for an overview of the relevant research see de Menezes and Kelliher, 2011). In addition, increasing interest in work–life issues means that offering flexible working can act as a means of attracting and retaining high calibre staff (Foster Thompson and Aspinwall, 2009; Stavrou, 2005).

It should be noted that although the above practices are implemented for different reasons, in practice they may look similar which suggests the possibility of matching the flexibility both employers and employees seek. This issue will be returned to later in the chapter.

Changes in the Environment Resulting in Increased Need for Flexibility

A number of economic and social changes have taken place in Europe in recent years, which have stimulated greater interest in flexibility, both on the part of the employer and the employee. These have included (Gratton, 2011; Kelliher and Richardson, 2012):

- the growing competitive pressure experienced by many European companies;
- increased global integration;
- advances in information and communication technologies (ICT);
- changing demographics and attitudes to work.

Increased competitive pressures, particularly from lower wage economies in Asia, have meant that European companies have had to look for ways to reduce costs and to increase efficiency. Matching the way in which labour is employed more closely with their needs is one means of achieving this, particularly for those organizations where labour represents a significant proportion of total costs. Employers may use numerical, temporal and functional flexibility to help them do this and also to allow them to respond more rapidly to changes in their business environment. The economic crisis experienced in Europe in recent years has served to increase these pressures. Greater global integration has been an important stimulus for flexibility.

Not only does it change the competitive environment, but it also has an influence on the way in which organizations operate. For example, working with customer or suppliers in different time zones may mean that organizations need employees to be available for work at different times, in order to facilitate real-time communication with those elsewhere in the world. Furthermore, global restructuring in international organizations may mean that work teams are distributed across distant locations and time zones, requiring more flexible approaches to work (Collins and Kolb, 2012).

Developments in ICT mean that employees can often access work systems from any location and at any time. This can allow employees greater choice over where and when they work, rather than being tied to the workplace, although some research shows that this can lead to an 'always on' environment, which may have negative implication for employee well-being (Besseyre des Horts *et al.*, 2012). If work can be done from almost anywhere, this may raise the question for employers about the need for workspace and in response to this some employers have reduced the availability of workplace accommodation accordingly. It does, however, need to be recognized that there may be some costs associated with this approach, since some tasks may be best completed through face-to-face interaction.

Finally, changing demographics and attitudes to work have also been important stimuli to greater flexible working. In many countries across Europe there has been growing concern amongst employees for a better balance between work and non-work activities and this has been supported by the policies of the European Union, seeking to create not only more, but also better jobs throughout Europe. For employers, responding to employee preferences for a better work–life balance by offering flexible work arrangements may be an important way of recruiting and retaining high calibre staff in a competitive labour market. An ageing population in much of Europe means that governments are keen to promote extending working lives and opportunities for more flexible working can be a way of attracting older workers to remain in some form of employment.

A number of more general trends in the labour market that represent a move away from the archetypal mode of regular, full-time employment are also important here, such as the growth of non-employment contract work and co-employment (Cappelli and Keller, 2013). In these contexts organizations have fewer responsibilities towards those who carry out work for them, but also have less control and ability to direct what workers do and how work is carried out. In a similar vein an important development is the growth in numbers of self-employed workers (Eurofound, 2012a). Self-employed professionals in particular may work in this way as a lifestyle choice, allowing them greater control over their working lives.

In addition to the above trends the individual country context is likely to be important in shaping the way in which different forms of flexibility develop across Europe. The type of business system in which they operate (Whitley, 1999) is likely to be influential, including the role played by national governments and the degree of existing regulation of work and work relationships, either through legislation or collective agreements.

In the next section we turn to examine some of the different patterns of employer- and employee-driven flexibility across Europe.

Employer-Driven Flexibility across Europe

Workplace flexibility occupies a central position on the EU agenda, however member states have responded in different ways to the implementation of greater flexibility. These differences can be explained, at least in part, by institutional and cultural differences (Fey et al., 2009) and the degree of regulation in the labour market, either through legislative provisions or the degree of collective organization. For example, employer action is typically more highly regulated in the Scandinavian countries, than in those with a more liberal regime such as the UK and Ireland. However, more recent developments as described above, have resulted in shifts taking place which may challenge traditional clusters and make them less useful as a means of predicting the situation in a particular country. In this section we examine some of these patterns across Europe.

Overall, the use of fixed-term contracts in Europe is relatively low, with approximately 80 per cent of workers having a traditional, permanent contract of employment. However, as shown in Figure 21.1 usage varies quite considerably across Europe. In 2014 in Spain, Portugal, Poland and the Netherlands more than 20 per cent of employees had a contract of limited duration, whereas in Estonia, Latvia, Lithuania and Romania this was the case for less than 4 per cent of employees. Although overall figures are relatively low, in some countries many employers employ some of their workforce in this way. For example, in the Netherlands and in Poland 70 per cent of employers use some fixed-term contracts. In contrast, in countries such as Cyprus, Austria and Malta this is a less common approach, with fewer than 20 per cent of employers using fixed-term contracts (Eurofound, 2011). However, even where usage is high amongst employers, in most cases fixed-term contracts only represent a relatively small proportion (less than 20 per cent) of the workforce. Only a small minority of companies (8 per cent) across Europe use fixed-term contracts for a high proportion of their workforce. These are concentrated in certain countries (e.g. the UK, Turkey) and certain industries (e.g. hospitality, construction).

There are also significant variations across Europe in the use of fixed-term contracts between sectors. Typically sectors such as industrial cleaning, computer programming and administrative and support services are higher users of fixed-term contracts than utilities supply or the insurance sector (Eurofound, 2014b). Research shows that the climate of retrenchment in the public sector in recent years has, in some countries (e.g. France, Germany, Sweden), encouraged the increased use of temporary labour (Vaughan-Whitehead, 2012). By their very nature, fixed-term contracts represent insecure employment, although it is noteworthy that a further offer of employment with the same company is common throughout Europe (Eurofound, 2011).

The use of temporary agency workers by employers, again whilst not representing a large percentage of employment, has grown in Europe in recent years and is used most commonly by employers in Belgium (almost 60 per cent), Denmark (50 per cent), France and the UK, but least commonly in Poland, Turkey and Croatia, where less than 5 per cent of employers do so (Eurofound, 2011).

Overall, less than a quarter of European employees work part-time, although as with the above forms, use varies between member states as indicated in Figure 21.2. The Netherlands is distinguished by high levels of part-time employment (51 per cent), but countries such as Austria, Germany, Switzerland, the UK and the Scandinavian countries also have comparatively high levels of part-time employment. By contrast, part-time employment is much less common in the emerging economies of Bulgaria, Croatia and Slovakia.

Whilst the use of part-time work is often used as an indicator of employer-driven flexibility, it is hard to make general observations, since this can also be an indicator of employee-driven flexibility. For

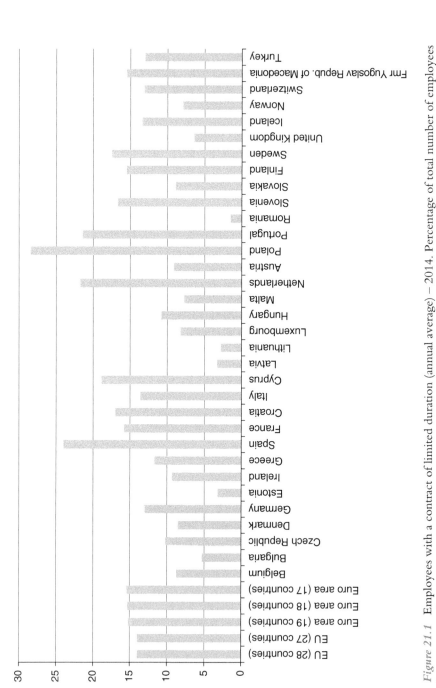

Figure 21.1 Employees with a contract of limited duration (annual average) – 2014. Percentage of total number of employees
Source: Eurostat © European Union, 1995–2015. Available at: http://ec.europa.eu/eurostat/tgm/table.do?tab=table&init=1&plugin=1&language=en&pcode=tps00159 (accessed 3 November 2015)

example in the Netherlands and the Scandinavian countries, these figures are likely to also include employees negotiating part-time employment to meet their needs.

Data from the Fifth European Working Conditions Survey show that functional flexibility, or some form of task rotation was reported by 47 per cent of workers across Europe, with significant variations by sector. Food and beverage services, retail, health and care activities all exhibit relatively high levels (Eurofound, 2014b).

Overall, it is worth noting that with the exception of Luxemburg, there has been a reduction in working hours across Europe in recent years. Across Europe in 2010 the average working time was 37.5 hours a week. In Germany, for example, there has been a reduction of 2.7 per cent since 2007 and Belgium, Italy, France and the UK have seen similar reductions (Eurofound, 2012a; European Commission, 2012). This overall decrease may be explained by a number of factors including, increased part-time work, fewer people working very long hours, short-time working in response to economic circumstances and reductions in working hours through collective agreements.

In line with a move to an increasingly 24/7 society, there have been some shifts away from a standard 9–5 working day over the typical Monday–Friday working week, which can at least in part be explained by longer operating hours in many services and increased global integration. Nevertheless, most workers still work standard working hours and a standard week and experience a high degree of regularity in their employment. Seventy-seven per cent of European workers work the same number of days each week, 67 per cent work the same number of hours each week and 58 per cent the same hours each day (Eurofound, 2012a). However, some weekend working is common for just over half the workforce and in the region of one-fifth do some work during night-time hours (10 p.m. to 5 a.m.).

Support from the European Commission for greater labour market flexibility has been based on the principle of 'flexicurity', which aims to combine the benefits of flexibility and security. Flexicurity is premised on the recognition that technological developments and competitive pressures will impact industries differently and that both employers and employees need to be more adaptable in response to these changes. Flexicurity policies are designed to allow employers greater flexibility in hiring and firing, or reducing the amount of time worked and at the same time to provide employees with greater security through high levels of benefit, when unemployed, and enhanced employability. The approach to flexicurity is based on four interconnected elements. These involve: (1) contractual arrangements that are flexible and reliable, based in labour law and collective agreements; (2) comprehensive life-long

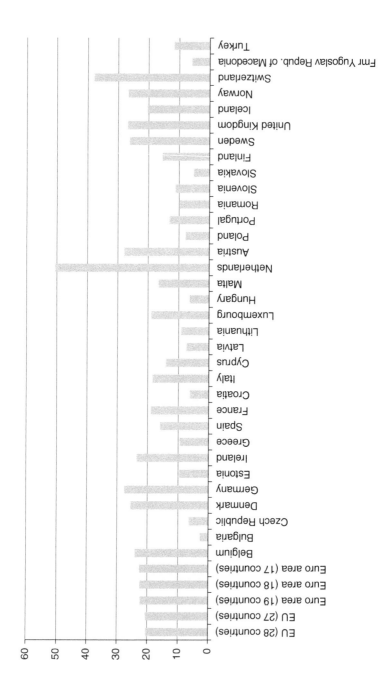

Figure 21.2 Persons employed part-time – total – 2014. Percentage of total employment

Source: Eurostat © European Union, 1995–2015. Available at: http://ec.europa.eu/eurostat/tgm/table.do?tab=table&init=1&plugin=1&language=em&pcode=tps00159 (accessed 3 November 2015

learning strategies, allowing the workforce to maintain and upgrade their skills to ensure adaptability and employability; (3) labour market policies that help people cope with change, make transitions between jobs and reduce the duration of unemployment; and (4) social security systems that provide adequate income protection and encourage employment and mobility. Flexicurity, based on social dialogue between employers and employees, is seen as a means of achieving an optimal balance between labour market flexibility and security for employees and moves away from protecting jobs, to protecting the employability of the workforce (Eurofound, 2011).

Short-time working, where the amount of hours the employee works is reduced, has been used as a means to reduce costs in the private sector in response to the economic downturn in Europe, brought about by the Global Financial Crisis (European Commission, 2011). In some countries governments have supported short-time working by using public funding to protect the income of employees whose working hours have been reduced. This is seen as a means to preserve employment and minimize job loss in the face of reduced demand (Eurofound, 2012b). Short-time working is seen to offer a number of advantages as a strategy in response to economic downturn. Jobs are protected, as are the skilled workers in them. Employers are then able to respond to an upturn in demand when it arrives, instead of having to create new jobs and hire new workers. It also means that employers avoid the costs associated with redundancy. For governments, this is likely to be less expensive than providing unemployment benefits, since the employer still pays for some of the employee's time and, in order to promote employability, in some cases employee benefits have been tied to participation in training. Short-time working has been largely used in the private sector. In the public sector concern has not been so much with reduced demand, but with budget restrictions and reductions. In some cases this has actually resulted in public sector workers working longer hours (e.g. Spain and Ireland).

Employee-Driven Flexibility across Europe

The European Union has committed to improving job quality through its 'More and Better Jobs' programme. Whilst there is some debate about exactly what job quality entails (Clark, 2005), many definitions include having some flexibility over working arrangements and being able to balance work and non-work life as core dimensions and this has been central to the consideration of job quality in recent policy discussion (UNECE, 2010; Walqing European Policy Brief, 2010). The UNECE (2010) identifies seven dimensions of job quality which include 'working hours and balancing work and non-working life', along with safety and ethics; income and benefits; security of employment and social protection; social dialogue; skills development and training; workplace relationships and work motivation. Specifically, being able to reconcile work and private life is seen as key to the quality of work and employment in Europe and is identified in the Europe 2020 Strategy (European Commission, 2010). The implementation of policies designed to facilitate achieving a satisfactory work–life balance is also seen as an important element in gender equality and a means to increase the participation of women in work.

A survey of employers in France, Germany, Italy, Poland, Sweden and the UK (together these countries account for 63 per cent of the EU27 population) in relation to the use of family friendly policies shows that the overwhelming majority of employers recognize family friendly working as 'important', or 'fairly important' for their organization. In the UK and Sweden, this was reported to be the case by more than 85 per cent of managers. Polish managers, however, rated family friendly working as less important for their organizations than managers from other countries in the study. Similarly, a large majority of managers recognized the importance of these policies for employees. Perhaps not surprisingly, a similar pattern is evident, with UK and Swedish managers attributing high average importance and Polish managers attributing less importance to family friendly working for employees. Only just over 4 per cent of UK managers did not recognize these practices as either important or fairly important, which is likely to be a reflection of the introduction of the 'right to request' flexible working legislation first introduced in the UK in 2003. In most cases employers across the countries in the study offered a range of policies and arrangements for flexibility over working time (e.g. variations to daily or weekly hours, individually agreed hours and part-time working), although these were less prevalent amongst employers in Italy and Poland. The most common reason given by employers for offering family friendly policies was, with the exception of Germany, to comply with legislation, or with collectively agreed arrangements. However, employers in these countries also recognized other benefits, such as increased job satisfaction, increased productivity and as a means to assist with the recruitment and retention of qualified staff. The survey also asked about the obstacles they saw to the implementation of these policies. The existence of statutory provisions or collective agreements was in some cases seen as sufficient and in Poland in particular, an unfavourable business climate was cited by 76 per cent of respondents. However, overall, the effects of the economic crisis were not reported to have influenced the provision of these policies to any noticeable degree, with the exception of Italy, where 40 per cent reported that they had either been withdrawn, or their introduction postponed (Eurofound, 2013).

Across the EU, 18 per cent of employees report that they have a poor work–life balance (Eurofound, 2014b). The sectors where this is most commonly experienced (a quarter to a third of employees) are transport and storage, accommodation, and food and beverage services. It is noteworthy that these are also sectors where atypical and irregular hours are worked. By contrast, work–life balance is only seen as poor by a comparatively small number of employees (less than 15 per cent) in furniture, computer programming and education. Men are shown to be more likely to experience problems with work–life balance than women. Having children in the household and the division of home-based work both have implications for being able to achieve a satisfactory work–life balance (Eurofound, 2012a). The findings of the Fifth European Working Conditions survey show that the amount of time worked affects the ability to achieve a satisfactory work–life balance. Less than 10 per cent of part-time workers (working 34 hours per week or less) experienced problems with work–life balance, but 38 per cent of those working more than 48 hours per week reported problems balancing their work and non-work activities. Regularity of working hours and having autonomy over working hours and being able to take time off in emergencies were other factors found to have a positive effect on achieving a satisfactory work–life balance.

In spite of standard working hours remaining the dominant model of employment across much of Europe, there have been some developments in various forms of flexible working. The European Company Survey 2009 found a growing number of employers offering employees a variety of opportunities to exercise flexibility over working time. Arrangements for flexibility over working time can take a number of forms, including formal or informal flexitime schemes, to the use of working time accounts, allowing employees to 'bank' time worked above their normal commitments to be taken off at some point in the future. Arrangements for increasing 'time sovereignty' can assist employees in achieving a better work–life balance (Eurofound, 2011). Fifty seven per cent of employers allow some variation to start and finish times and about 40 per cent have some form of working time account where the employee can take off accumulated time, but the prevalence of arrangements that enable flexibility over working time differs across European countries (see Figure 21.3). Flexibility over working time is most common in Finland, Denmark, Sweden and the UK, but in Macedonia, Greece and Bulgaria, only in the region of a third of employers have such schemes in place. There are also some considerable differences between sectors.

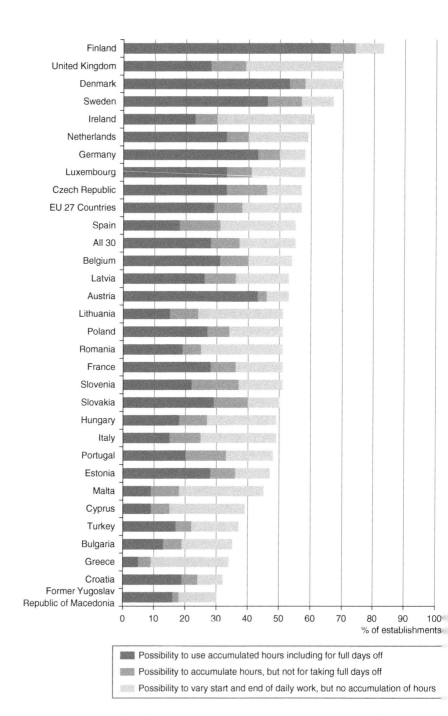

Figure 21.3 Flexible working time arrangements, by country and flexibility scope (%)

Source: ECS 2009

Part-time working is a widely used form of flexibility in Europe, but here also there are significant variations across countries. In the Netherlands, over 90 per cent of companies have some part-time workers. It is also common in Belgium, Germany, the UK and Sweden, however it much less common in the South-east European countries. Part-time work is more prevalent in the service sector and amongst women workers. Part-time work may be on the basis of set hours, but in lower paid part-time jobs in particular, hours may not be determined in advance (Eurofound, 2011).

The prevalence of flexibility over place of work can be hard to assess, because it can take many forms. For example, it may include teleworkers who are permanently based at a location remote from the employer's premises; those who work remotely for part of their working time, either on a scheduled, regular basis, or on an ad hoc basis influenced by patterns in their work and non-work activity; to those who are mobile workers who can work from any location including a workplace. These so called e-nomads make up in the region of a quarter of the EU workforce, although perhaps not surprisingly they are more strongly represented in some countries than in others. In emerging economies such as Bulgaria and Romania, they make up only about 5 per cent of the workforce, whereas in countries such as the Netherlands and the Scandinavian countries the incidence is 40–45 per cent (Eurofound, 2012a). Across Europe they tend to be most commonly represented in sectors such as financial services, education and public administration and particularly amongst those in managerial and professional roles.

It is noteworthy that some of the differences observed between countries in Europe can be attributed to different cultural traditions and in particular in relation to the role of family members acting as care givers, patterns of business activity and how the availability of flexible work options shapes the participation of men and women in paid employment. The social security system in different countries is also important. In many countries there has been some shift away from the traditional male breadwinner model. The most common arrangement in Europe is the so-called 'modified male breadwinner' model (where, in addition to a male breadwinner, the female partner participates in the labour market to some degree), followed by the dual earner couple model (Eurofound, 2012a).

Discussion

In this chapter we have examined the different forms of flexible working that can be designed to meet the needs of employers and of employees; the reasons behind their use and the context in which there has been growing interest in flexible working in recent decades. We have also examined the patterns of use across European countries. Drawing on data collected by the European Foundation for the Improvement of Living and Working, a number of distinct patterns can be observed. Flexible working practices designed to help employers become more competitive and responsive to their market conditions, such as the use of temporary contracts, have been used by countries such as Spain and Portugal as a response to the economic downturn and business uncertainty. However, in the emerging economies in Europe a more traditional model of employment persists. Similarly, part-time employment is uncommon in the emerging economies, but widespread in the Netherlands and to a lesser degree in Scandinavian countries and the UK. Support from the European Union for greater organizational flexibility is evident through the development of the flexicurity policy, designed to compensate employees who suffer job loss or reduced working and to assist them in maintaining their employability.

Flexible working practices aimed at helping employees obtain a better work–life balance also display different usage across Europe. These type of policy are not, in the main, widespread in the emerging economies, but are offered to large numbers of employees in for example the UK and the Scandinavian countries. The UK represents an example of where national level (albeit weak) legislation has acted as a stimulus for the introduction of flexible working policies by a number of employers The EU has also placed priority on jobs that allow employees' work and non-work lives to be balanced, through it's 'More and Better Jobs' strategy.

Given the nature of changes in the business and social environments described earlier and the support from the EU at policy level, it seems likely that the demand for these practices will continue to grow and may also become more common in the emerging economies as they develop and move away from more traditional models of employment. Although, the motivations for introducing employer- and employee-driven flexibility vary, it is noteworthy that in practice they may often take similar forms (e.g. part-time working, remote working, schedule flexibility). This at least suggests the possibility that there may be greater scope to match the interests of the two groups. Working time accounts are sometimes cited as an example of this, whereby employees who work additional time to suit the employer's needs can recoup these additional hours by taking time off at time that suits their own needs. However, if it is difficult for the employee to take the accumulated time off, or to take it off at times that are suited to their needs, due to business pressures, then the degree of real flexibility for them may be limited. The lack of attention given to trying to align the needs of employers and employees may be explained by their differing objectives. Employer-driven flexibility is about performance and is often managed by operations and/or line managers, whereas employee driven flexibility has its roots in diversity and more recently as a means to engender positive employee attitudes and assist recruitment and retention. Given that for some countries in Europe there is now considerable experience of implementing employer-and employee-driven flexibility practices, it is perhaps apposite for managers and researchers to pursue this further.

Key Learning Points

- The use of practices to increase flexibility in the employment relationship have expanded across Europe in recent years, fuelled by more intense competition, greater global integration, developments in ICT and changing workforce demographics, and perceptions of the work–life relationship.
- Flexibility designed to meet the needs of employers can be classified as numerical, functional, temporal and spatial, allowing employers to match the use of labour more closely to their business requirements.
- Flexibility designed to meet the needs of the employee and assist in the achievement of a better work–life balance (e.g. schedule flexibility, remote working, etc.) have also been shown to have positive organizational outcomes, such as increased job satisfaction and reduced absenteeism.
- The EU has supported both forms of flexibility through policies on flexicurity and job quality, however different patterns of use can be observed across member states. At a general level the developed economies in Europe have tended to make greater use of flexible working practices and the emerging economies have tended to display a more traditional approach to employment.
- The desire for greater flexibility in the workplace is likely to grow in the future and the potential scope for employer and employee needs to be matched more closely needs further exploration by managers and researchers.

References

Alis, D., Karsten, L. and Leopold, J. (2006) 'From gods to godesses', *Time and Society*, 15, 81–104.

Besseyre des Horts, C.H., Dery, K. and MacCormick, J. (2012) 'Paradoxical consequences of the use of Blackberrys? An application of the Job Demand-Control-Support Model', in Kelliher, C. and Richardson, J. (eds), *New ways of organizing work: Developments, perspectives and experiences*. New York: Routledge, pp. 16–29.

Cappelli, P. and Keller, J.R. (2013) 'Classifying work in the new economy', *Academy of Management Review*, 38, 575–596.

Casper, W.J., Eby, L.T., Bordeaux, C. and Lockwood, A. (2007) 'A review of methods in IO/OB work–family research', *Journal of Applied Psychology*, 92, 28–41.

Clark, A.E. (2005) 'Your money or your life: Changing job quality in OECD countries', *British Journal of Industrial Relations*, 43, 377–400.

Collins, P. and Kolb, D. (2012) 'Innovation in distributed teams: The duality of connectivity norms and human agency', in Kelliher, C. and Richardson, J. (eds), *New ways of organizing work: Developments, perspectives and experiences.* New York: Routledge, pp. 140–159.

Cotti, C.D., Haley, M.R. and Miller, L.A. (2014) 'Workplace flexibilities, job satisfaction and union membership in the US workforce', *British Journal of Industrial Relations*, 52, 403–425.

de Menezes, L. and Kelliher, C. (2011) "Flexible working and performance: A systematic review of the evidence for a business case', *International Journal of Management Reviews*, 13, 452–474.

Eaton, S. (2003) 'If you can use them: Flexibility policies, organizational commitment and perceived performance', *Industrial Relations*, 42, 145–167.

Eurofound (2011) *Eurofound yearbook 2010: Living and working in Europe.* Luxembourg: Publications Office of the European Union.

Eurofound (2012a) *Fifth european working conditions survey.* Luxembourg: Publications Office of the European Union.

Eurofound (2012b) *Eurofound yearbook 2011: Living and working in Europe.* Luxembourg: Office for Official Publications of the European Communities.

Eurofound (2013) *EU employers take family-friendly working seriously.* http://www.eurofound.europa.eu/ewco/surveyreports/EU1302011D/EU1302011D.htm (accessed 31 October 2015).

Eurofound (2014a) *Third European quality of life survey - quality of life in Europe: Families in economic crisis.* Luxembourg: Publications Office of the European Union.

Eurofound (2014b) *Working conditions and job quality: Comparing sectors in Europe. overview report.* Dublin.

European Commission (2010) *Europe 2000: a strategy for smart, sustainable and inclusive growth.* COM(2010)2020. Brussels.

European Commission (2011) *Industrial relations in Europe 2010.* Luxembourg: Publications Office of the European Union.

European Commission (2012) *News skills and jobs in Europe: Pathways towards full employment.* Luxembourg: Publications Office of the European Union.

Fey, C.F., Morgulis-Yakushev, S., Park, H.J. and Bjorkman, I. (2009) 'Opening the black box of the relationships between HRM practices and firm performance: A comparison of MNE subsidiaries in the USA, Finland, and Russia', *Journal of International Business Studies*, 40, 690–712.

Foster Thompson, L. and Aspinwall, K.R. (2009) 'The recruitment value of work/life benefits', *Personnel Review*, 38, 195–210.

Gajendran, R.S. and Harrison, D.A. (2007) 'The good, the bad, and the unknown about telecommuting: Meta-analysis of psychological mediators and individual consequences', *Journal of Applied Psychology*, 92, 1524–1541.

Glass, J. and Finley, A. (2002) 'Coverage and effectiveness of family-responsive workplace policies', *Human Resource Management Review*, 12, 313–337.

Gratton, L. (2011) 'Workplace 2025 – what will it look like?', *Organizational Dynamics*, 40, 246–254.

Henly, J.R., Shaefer, H.L. and Waxman, E. (2006) 'Nonstandard work schedules: Employer and employee-driven flexibility in retail jobs', *Social Service Review*, 80, 609–634.

Kauffeld, S., Jonas, E. and Frey, D. (2004) 'Effects of a flexible work-time design on employee and company related aims', *European Journal of Work and Organizational Psychology*, 13, 79–100.

Kelliher, C. and Anderson, D. (2008) 'For better or for worse? An analysis of how flexible working practices influence employees' perceptions of job quality', *International Journal of Human Resource Management*, 19, 421–433.

Kelliher, C. and Anderson, D. (2010) 'Doing more with less? Flexible working practices and the intensification of work', *Human Relations*, 63, 83–106.

Kelliher, C. and Gore, J. (2006) 'Functional flexibilty and the intensification of work: Transformation within service industries', in Askenazy, P., Cartron, D., de Connick, F. and Gollac, M. (eds), *Organisation et Intensite du Travail*. Toulouse: Octares, pp. 93–102.

Kelliher, C. and Richardson, J. (2012) 'Recent developments in new ways of working', in Kelliher, C. and Richardson, J. (eds) *New ways of organizing work: Developments, perspectives and experiences*. New York: Routledge, pp. 1–15.

Loretto, W., Vickerstaff, S. and White, P. (2005) *Older workers and options for flexible work*. Working Paper Series No. 31. Manchester: Equal Opportunities Commission.

Ozbilgin, M.F., Beauregard, T.A., Tatli, A. and Bell, M.P. (2011) 'Work-life, diversity and intersectionality: A critical review and research agenda', *International Journal of Management Review*, 13, 177–198.

Putnam, L.L., Myers, K.K. and Gailliard, B.M. (2014) 'Examining the tensions in workplace flexibility and exploring options for new directions', *Human Relations*, 67, 413–440.

Stavrou, E.T. (2005) 'Flexible work bundles and organizational competitiveness: A cross-national study of the European work context', *Journal of Organizational Behaviour*, 26, 932–947.

United Nations Economic Commission for Europe (UNECE) (2010) *Measuring quality of employment – country pilot reports*. Geneva: United Nations Publications.

Vaughan-Whitehead, D. (2012) 'Public sector shock in Europe: Between structural reforms and quantitative adjustments', in Vaughan-Whitehead, D. (ed.), *The public sector in shock*. Geneva: International Labour Office, pp. 1–42.

Vickerstaff, S., Baldock, J., Cox, J. and Keen, L. (2004) *Happy retirement? The impact of employers' policies and practices on the process of retirement*. Bristol: Joseph Rowntree Foundation/Policy Press.

Walqing European Policy Brief (2010) *Work and life quality in new and growing jobs*. November, pp. 4–5.

Whitley, R. (1999) *Divergent capitalism: The social structuring and change of business systems*. Oxford: Oxford University Press.

22 Conclusions: The Evolving HRM Landscape in Europe

PAUL SPARROW, CHRIS BREWSTER AND
MICHAEL DICKMANN

Introduction

In the previous two editions of this book we reviewed the
contemporary issues in IHRM in Europe (Brewster and Harris, 1999;
Dickmann *et al.*, 2008). The series falls within a long tradition of
writing through which we, with various colleagues, have addressed the
specific question of the existence of a 'European model' of HRM. Not
long after the creation of the Single European Market back in 1992,
there was a debate about the level of transition that might be expected
within HRM across Europe. Throughout the 1990s, a series of
contributions laid out the contours of a European perspective (Brewster
et al., 1992; Brewster and Larsen, 1992; Brewster, 1993, 1995; Sparrow
and Hiltrop, 1994, 1997; Brewster and Hegewisch, 1994).

For Sparrow and Hiltrop (1994, 1997), the starting point was the
range of factors that resulted in distinctive national patterns of HRM.
There have been many models that have laid out the most important
comparative factors (Dickmann, 2003), but they captured these under
four significant influences: the business system, structure and labour
markets; institutional influences on the employment relationship; the
influence of national culture; and the role and competence of the
HRM function. Together, these were seen to create a distinctive
European model. The European context was characterized as being one
in which there were more restricted levels of organization autonomy
in HRM decisions such as recruitment, dismissal and training; a
history which had produced a lower exposure of organizations to
market processes; a greater emphasis on the role of the group over
the individual; an increased role of social partners (trade unions and

employee representatives) in the employment relationship; and higher levels of government intervention in direct employment and indirectly in the management of other businesses and the people within them.

However, things change over time and we need a dynamic and not just comparative perspective. So we follow Sparrow and Hiltrop (1994, 1997) in using a force field framework, through which we can deepen our understanding of comparative factors by examining in parallel the competing 'reinforcing' and 'uncoupling' factors – or pressure points in the business environment – that have the potential to recast or remix HRM by changing either the context or content of practice.

It was also clear that there were then, as there are now, strategic pressures and initiatives at the level of the firm that, if not capable of totally transforming national patterns of HRM, could clearly make these national and regional models more receptive to change. The factors that were signalled then (Sparrow and Hiltrop, 1997) as being potentially disruptive, sound very familiar to us today:

- changing professional frames of reference;
- increased competitiveness versus social protection and welfare;
- state subsidies versus the rising cost of unemployment;
- higher flexibility and productivity versus commitment; and
- the aging population.

The debate then was whether or not there was a set of external influences, changes of emphasis in leadership within European organizations and pressures on the credibility of HRM functions that would be capable of shifting the frames of reference and mindsets of European HRM managers and chief executives. Already in the 1990s it had become clear that age dependency ratios were substantially rising and that welfare systems within Europe would come under increasing strain. Sparrow and Hiltrop (1997) identified a challenge for European organizations facing a multitude of conflicting pressures from young, highly educated workers striving for growth, self-determination and meaningful work and less-educated workers who might be less interested and committed to work overall while being exposed to work patterns that give more flexibility and power to organizations.

Generally, the sources of tension discussed in the early to mid-1990s were the international quality, efficiency and productivity pressures that were turning attention around the world to the social costs of employment as competition between business systems grew. In Europe, the question was whether there needed to be a trade-off between the need for increased competitiveness and the strong tradition of social protection and welfare provisions found in most European countries and particularly in the Northern ones.

In parallel to the question of transition, Sparrow and Hiltrop (1994, 1997) were also interested in the processes through which there might be integration within HRM. The task of integration drew attention to internal organization developments, which included adapted control systems and business processes; shifts in power and organizational culture that could result from firms bringing in changes to criteria for corporate performance; the geographical composition and scale of their European organizations; processes of rationalization of employment; and the impact of power imbalances, business networks and political legitimacy on HRM decision making. Mergers and acquisitions, more transnational coordination within industrial sectors and new cadres of international managers capable of executing complex international business strategies, were seen as the likely vehicles for strategic integration (and transition).

Yet, from the very first CRANET surveys to the more recent analyses (Brewster *et al.*, 2000; Tregaskis and Brewster, 2006; Mayrhofer *et al.*, 2011; Walker *et al.*, 2014; Brewster *et al.*, 2015), evidence has continued to demonstrate a nuanced picture but, overall, only limited degrees of convergence in HRM across Europe and a continued regional distinctiveness in comparison to other geographies around the world.

Reviewing HRM in Europe over the last decades raises a number of key questions. Is it that the institutional and cultural forces of distinctiveness trump the forces of transition and change towards the globalization of HRM? Or is change just slow and thus hardly perceptible? Is it that Europe failed to deliver on the change agenda that was anticipated but only managed to delay an inevitable reckoning? Is it that we did not have the cadres of managers capable of executing complex strategies, or the resolve for internal organizational developments that would change frames of reference? Perhaps Europeans did not recognize the legitimacy of the narrative of business change or globalization? Or is it that both Europe and other countries changed in a way that means Europe remained distinctive?

Macro-Level Trends

Many of the macro-level issues discussed in this book can be seen as today's collection of potential uncoupling or integrating forces. The book shows the importance of economic crises and reveals different responses made to it by clusters of countries wedded to different forms of capitalism and business systems. Our choice of topics in the opening section – pressures on employment relations systems and the HRM context in country clusters linked by Mediterranean, Western European, Central and Eastern European, and Nordic geography – allows us to place the analysis of country-level differences into a new social and political context. At the level of pan-national institutions, if not at the level of organizations and people, the sense of 'Europeanness' feels a little more abstract now compared to the time of the previous editions. There are apparent tensions within and across the European Union, reported in the media every day. Perhaps this is an inevitable consequence of disruptive change and debate around an all-too-near future. These futures are already presenting societies with difficult questions to resolve. They present us with dilemmas about the relative power and role of markets, nation states, organizations, cultures, individuals (and generations). In turn, all countries within Europe are necessarily debating the balance between the social versus economic considerations that these developments throw up. They are juxtaposing the desire or need to drive productivity, competitiveness and technological development, against what are different expectations, models or goals for the nature of flexibility, living standards, inequalities, skills and capabilities.

The chapters trace key macro developments in the labour markets in Europe. In so doing, some trends for the future of working and workers in different European regions become exposed. Youth unemployment in Southern Europe can be very high and will have massive effects on organizations – the lack of work experience and job-related skills as well as low career satisfaction will shape segments of the labour market in the future. In turn, it increases the impetus for careerists to leave their home countries in search for better opportunities abroad (often in the EU as there is a right to work and live in member countries). In turn, Nordic or Western European countries experience much lower (youth) unemployment figures. In some of the more coordinated market economies this coincides with a high degree of multi-skilling of workers. In the Anglo-Saxon liberal market economies the high level of employment also guarantees more work experiences, but may result in more skills-based fragmentation to which organizations may react in terms of more numerical and temporal flexibilization. In terms of the work-related dreams and aspirations of younger careerists in different parts of Europe, this raises various possibilities in relation to the future of work and working. We may even move from a notion of the 'future of work' to the emergence of a notion of 'future *or* work', where available job opportunities do not conform to individuals' visions of professional growth, identity and compensation.

All of these macro questions might potentially reframe our analysis of IHRM and certainly create a contemporary set of questions and problems that we must solve. By taking a macro-level perspective in the opening section of the book, the questions we believe IHRM researchers could usefully reflect upon are as follows:

- Will the responses to social change that we are seeing move us away from the cultural and institutional predictors with which IHRM researchers have long been comfortable, to ones that might have more to do with the differences across generations?
- Or should we adopt a lens based on the new political economy that is being shaped and driven by pan-national and global technological, business systems and social developments?
- Having long been debated, but never really yet reflected in the data on HRM practices, is there now an inescapable 'future of work' agenda to be faced?
- Will the changing agenda be met with more or less success across Europe?
- Is this future of work, embedded as it is in a world of global risks and solutions, revolutionary changes in core production and process and life technologies, digitalization and virtualization of work and business models, be akin to an industrial revolution that will level the playing field, or create new winners and losers?
- Or, are the changes that seem so threatening or exciting now, merely a blip, a by-product of turbulent times and economies, with a new restatement of 'Europeanness' soon to re-emerge?

The opening chapters reinforce the legitimacy of such questions. They reveal different sets of social and economic forces shaping contemporary IHRM in Europe and layer these issues into the traditional regional and country clusters, once assumed to characterize the nature of HRM in Europe. The chapters build a picture of complex patterns of continuity and change within the HRM of these sub-regions of Europe and not always in ways that might have been assumed. They show that questions must now be asked not just about the relative level of change across Europe, but also about the depth (or not) of resilience to what are increasingly stark and debatably, inescapable, demands for social change within country or regional systems.

In terms of cultures, there is anyway an implicit question underlying our opening macro analysis. It is this: are our ways of understanding sufficient to identify what is happening? Will these issues of continuity and change, resilience or collapse, lead us to think about there being new clusters of culture, or new definitions of 'Europeanness'? When you look at an object (such as the behaviour of institutions, organizations or of functions, such as HRM) through the lens of culture, then like a prism, culture bends and shapes the image that you see and the sense or not that you can then make of that image. Cultures are resilient and the cultural lens is often enduring, if always capable of being rewritten or reimagined by history.

In terms of institutions, it is clear that these are changing (if perhaps too slowly for some commentators' and practitioners' wishes) as our contributors note. They are changing at a European, national and organizational level. It has been argued that in terms of HRM, institutions have more impact than cultures (Vaiman and Brewster, 2015). But they do not (yet, perhaps?) seem to have produced change that is reflected in any major lessening of national and European distinctiveness. Where the post-2008 crises were most devastating in Europe, change may have been most significant. For instance, our contributors recommend a change in HRM approaches to bring Greece back more into line with Western European notions of strategic people and change management.

Mezzo-Level Trends

One of the ways that we attempt to address these issues is to examine a series of cross-national trends and developments that are nonetheless intimately linked to organizational-level responses. We do this in order to help identify the responses that are being seen and the extent to which there is a European theme in this response.

The chapters in the second section of the book show that several forces are now having an impact on the behaviour of MNCs, not for profit, international non-governmental organizations and inter-governmental organizations alike. Whatever the organizational form, they all face challenges of social legitimacy, relevance, efficiency and effectiveness. They are pursuing many common strategies, generally aimed at enabling more inter-dependence and collaboration, flexibility to demographic shifts and risk management.

The systemic analyses presented in Part II all recognize that it is difficult for IHRM researchers to divorce their analysis of the responses that organizations might make to specific challenges from the broader socio-economic backdrop. The chapters help to broaden out our frame of analysis in IHRM. For example, the discussion of migration suggests that freedoms around the movement of capital and labour act as a backdrop to the requisite roles, responsibilities and accountabilities of a wide range of actors. The generic pursuit of corporate responsibility strategies broadens our scope of analysis beyond the impact of international economic developments to include factors such as the effects of population ageing, environmental risks and the public management reform movement in Europe. The analysis of the not for profit sector points to common learning agendas across the different organizational forms and a greater acceptance that the

HRM strategies of firms are inevitably deeply embedded in national policy, demographic and institutional contexts. These developments are leading to more critical questions about the performance of MNCs, not for profit, international non-governmental organizations and inter-governmental organizations and a greater sensitivity to their relative achievement of outcomes. The analysis of the impact on HRM of overseas MNCs operating within Europe raises questions about the different trajectories or paths to globalization taken by MNCs, either from emerging economies or from less-dominant geographies. It shows the greater complexity that is faced as organizations pursue these different pathways, having to deal both with the traditional and stable points of European uniqueness and also with the moderating mechanisms that seem to be unique to each pathway to globalization.

Part II, then, suggests that many of the mezzo-level challenges can only be handled through more collaborative and innovative work practices. As each organization exerts a degree of agency and creates a more hybrid solution or strategy in response to the mezzo-level pressures we cover, this is doing six things:

- drawing our attention towards the importance of the intra-organizational factors within IHRM that enable new firm-level responses;
- reiterating the importance of inter-organizational collaboration;
- embedding our analysis of functional strategies (such as those originating within the HRM function, or in marketing, or in operations) into the broader cross-functional and strategic dialogue that is taking place within the organization;
- stressing the importance of corporate legitimacy and outside stakeholders for the operations, brand and survival of organizations;
- moving us away from overly-simplistic views about global integration and local responsiveness and shifting our level of analysis down towards a more micro-level understanding and, at the same time;
- helping us to understand that whilst we need to be more sensitive to the fine detail within the explicit strategies being pursued, the notion of implicit strategies, or organizational practice, remains very important.

These developments lead us towards a research agenda that allows for more nuanced views, but also one that allows us to link these micro-level elements to those actions that still comply with institutional expectations, or continue to align the actions within European organizations to the broader values, norms and rules. In short, we need to establish the relative weight of public expectations and implicit and institutional action within the process of transition and change.

Micro-Level Questions

We noted earlier that Part III of the book identifies and examines some of the HRM issues at the organizational level that make Europe unique. In some cases there are obvious reasons why it would be difficult to understand developments in Europe without a specific chapter on a particular topic whilst, in other cases, a European interest may not be so direct but may offer important insights for non-Europeans. In most cases what distinguishes Europe is greater attention to and a greater say for the interests of others than the owners of businesses (Beer, Boselie and Brewster, 2015).

Employee relations is clearly in the first category. The extensive 'unionization' of Europe means that, in this continent in particular, it is impossible to understand HRM without taking cognisance of employee relations. The interest of employees and their representative organizations are enforced by law in Europe. Even here, however, as is noted in the relevant chapters, the influence of collective employee representation in Europe has diminished. It remains a significant feature of the HRM landscape in Europe but one that is increasingly under challenge.

Global careers and talent management are also distinct in Europe in that all citizens of the EU have the right to take work in any of the other 27 states and, indeed in less definite ways, several other linked states too. The EU itself encourages movement and alongside other features of the European labour market this has created a much greater international awareness amongst Europeans – working in another country, either temporarily or permanently is not seen as something confined to an elite.

The interests of employees are reflected also in the widespread notion that employees have rights to their job. So we note the importance of making correct decisions in recruitment and selection, given the costs of correcting wrong ones. As with all of these issues, the overall picture is nuanced with significant differences between European states and between smaller and larger employers. The growth of 'only just' employment means that the 'costs' of getting the recruitment and selection decisions wrong is reducing.

On reward issues, Europe is perhaps less distinctive and there may be more signs of convergence. On financial participation, as one particular aspect of rewards, Europe is unique. France has compulsory profit-sharing and many countries encourage share options. This seems likely to continue to be a factor on the European scene for the future.

One effect of the greater attention to the interests of employees is that Europe has arguably been one of the regions of the world that has developed the most constraints on managerial autonomy in the organization of work. However, that also means that this is one of the areas that has, within that framework, done most to develop new ways of being flexible. This is another area where, arguably, Europe is converging towards accepting the interests of the owners of business as dominant but, interestingly, this is one topic on which the ex-communist countries appear more ready to accept the traditional European approaches.

Part III raises a number of key issues:

- Technical and societal change has meant that a variety of 'only just' employment has emerged with risks to the selection decisions becoming smaller. On the other side, the importance of high-skilled jobs is increasing. What is the impact in terms of the sophistication of the selection process, the investment in resourcing or the period of on-boarding? What are the implications of organizations using more social networking and cross-border searches for European work flows?
- Global careers and talent management are increasingly common and highly important for both organizations and individuals. What patterns will emerge to manage global workers? How will individual navigate within the EU where they have a right to work abroad? How will the crises and high unemployment levels in some states shape the willingness of people to work abroad and what will happen if/when they return to their country of origin? Or, more broadly, what will be the long-term impact of micro-level decisions on macro- and mezzo-level arrangements?
- The European Union has arguably more of a social market agenda which has many impacts on formal laws and regulations as well as informal influences on the shape of HRM in Europe. Therefore, it is no great surprise that it strives to enable stronger flexibility for employees and organizations as well as being mindful with respect to workers' security. What will the impact of flexicurity policy be over time and in different countries of the EU?
- Employment relations in many countries in Europe are increasingly under strain with trade union and workers' rights often being reduced. What are the longer-term implications for a myriad of stakeholders, such as, for the distribution of power and wealth, the work context, flexibility of work organization, security, etc?

Conclusions

Examining IHRM through a European lens means keeping the external context and the interests of different stakeholders much more clearly in mind. Practitioners do this intuitively and arguably studies of HRM that ignore these issues and concentrate on a direct link between HRM policies and organizational results fail to appreciate the complexity of HRM. In Europe, these issues are much more likely to be at the forefront of the minds of both practitioners and researchers. Thus, not only do studies that take a European perspective on IHRM help us identify factors that are specific to the continent and where general prescriptions do not apply, but even where there is nothing specifically 'European' in a practice they offer a richer understanding of IHRM.

We have seen that there remains a distinctive European pattern of HRM and this is evidenced still across business systems, labour markets, institutional influences on the employment relationship, national culture and the role and competence of the HRM function. But, we also continue to see developments that have the potential to change the frames of reference in European organizations. We have characterized these as potential uncoupling or integrating forces. Some reflect long-standing concerns – notably around international quality, efficiency, productivity, competitiveness, social protection, welfare, flexibility, commitment and changing demographics. But in addition we also see new pressures, largely resulting from the economic crisis. For example, the impact of youth unemployment is expected to have significant effects on the future labour market and levels of migration in ways that are negative for individuals and organizations alike. As once more we begin to ask questions about the fundamental connections between work and society, we argue that we shall not just debate the notion of the 'future of work', but potentially also the notion of 'future *or* work'. The European labour markets of the Anglo-Saxon liberal market economies and those of Southern Europe, seem destined to produce very different outcomes for individuals and organizations for at least a generation.

By adopting a multi-level perspective, covering macro-, mezzo- and micro-level issues, we hope that this book encourages IHRM researchers to adopt some new and interesting analytical frames. Our coverage of macro issues, for example, suggests that we could adopt lenses based on the new political economy that is being shaped and driven by pan-national, global, financial, technological, business system and social developments. We also have to accommodate changes in production, process and life science technologies, along with the digitalization and virtualization of work and business models, into our study of core IHRM topics. These developments will impact the nature of international work organization and from this the nature of international mobility, the shape of international assignments, the form of global knowledge transfers and the resilience and role of country and regional systems of management. All of this points to the need to consider IHRM in the context of new types of global risk, solution and opportunity. One final macro-level conclusion is that we need to impose a cross-generational lens to our analysis of and judgements about the success and utility of IHRM and the outcomes it creates. Questions about costs, benefits, outcomes and fairness now necessitate solutions that will work across time and thereby across generations in most of the areas that are of interest to IHRM researchers.

These cross-national trends and developments are being reflected in a number of responses at the level of organizations, again changing the type of outcomes by which we might judge the success or not of their IHRM. Whether organizations are MNCs, inter- or non-governmental, or indeed not for profit, they are judged more starkly than before in terms of social legitimacy, relevance, efficiency and effectiveness. Strategies are becoming more collaborative and inter-dependent both across organizations, but also between organizations, institutions and national policy makers. This means that there is an increasingly wide range of actors involved in any one IHRM policy or practice. For researchers, the task is one of incorporating the perspectives of multiple actors rather than just those at the organizational level, adopting more inter-disciplinary models and frameworks to capture strategy and taking a more nuanced and less prescriptive view on what is meant by global integration versus local responsiveness. For practitioners, the task is one of managing the requisite roles, responsibilities and accountabilities of different actors, but also being less prescriptive about the design of global HRM practices, allowing both for their refinement and more implicit use and positioning at local level.

Finally, the book shows that once we focus at a more micro-level on specific HRM policies and practices, the distinctive European desire at least (if not always reflected in the action of various actors) for there to be greater attention and voice given to the interests of others than just the owners of businesses, remains in place. This desire, however, continues to be challenged by practice, especially if we look at areas such as employee relations, financial participation, resourcing and selection, flexibility and the organization of work. Yet it remains strongly evidenced in some other areas, such as careers and talent management, where international mobility is no longer just restricted to elites. These contrasting trends will create new tensions and dilemmas, especially where micro-level decisions or behaviours create pressures on the macro- and mezzo-level arrangements.

In the final analysis and returning to the many findings in the book that demonstrate that solutions to the macro-, mezzo- and micro-issues covered must increasingly be co-designed between pan-national policy, national labour market, organizational, institutional and individual actors, the successful resolution of these issues will likely bring many of the contemporary European agendas to the attention of the broader IHRM community as they too witness many of these developments, whatever their home geography.

References

Beer, M. Boselie, P. and Brewster, C. (2015) 'Back to the future: Implications for the field of HRM of the multi-stakeholder perspective proposed 30 years ago', *Human Resource Management*, 54(3), 427–438.

Brewster, C. (1993) 'Developing a "European" model of human resource management', *International Journal of Human Resource Management*, 4(4), 765–784.

Brewster, C. (1995) 'Towards a "European" model of human resource management', *Journal of International Business Studies*, 26(1), 1–21.

Brewster, C. and Harris, H. (eds) (1999) *International Human Resource Management: Contemporary Issues in Europe*. London: Routledge.

Brewster, C. and Hegewisch, A. (eds) (1994) *Policy and Practice in European Human Resource Management: The Price Waterhouse Cranfield Survey*. London: Routledge.

Brewster, C. and Larsen, H.H. (1992) 'Human resource management in Europe: Evidence from ten countries', *International Journal of Human Resource Management*, 3(3), 409–434.

Brewster, C., Mayrhofer, W. and Morley, M. (eds) (2000) *New Challenges for European Human Resource Management*. London: Macmillan.

Brewster, C., Wood, G. and Goergen, M. (2015) 'Institutions, unionization and voice: The relative impact of context and actors on firm level practice', *Economic and Industrial Democracy*, 36(2), 195–214.

Brewster, C., Hegewisch, A., Holden, L. and Lockhart, T. (eds) (1992) *The European Human Resource Management Guide*. London: Academic Press.

Dickmann, M. (2003) 'Implementing German HRM abroad: Desired, feasible, successful?', *International Journal of Human Resource Management*, 14(2), 265–284.

Dickmann, M., Brewster, C. and Sparrow, P.R. (eds) (2008) *International Human Resource Management: Contemporary Issues in Europe*. London: Routledge.

Mayrhofer, W., Brewster, C., Morley, M. and Ledolter, J. (2011) 'Hearing a different drummer? Evidence of convergence in European HRM', *Human Resource Management Review*, 21(1), 50–67.

Sparrow, P.R. and Hiltrop, J. (1994) *European Human Resource Management in Transition*. London: Prentice-Hall.

Sparrow, P.R. and Hiltrop, J.M. (1997) 'Redefining the field of European human resource management: A battle between national mindsets and forces of business transition', *Human Resource Management*, 36(2), 201–219.

Tregaskis, O. and Brewster, C. (2006) 'Converging or diverging? A comparative analysis of trends in contingent employment practice in Europe over a decade', *Journal of International Business Studies*, 37(1), 111–126.

Vaiman, V. and Brewster, C. (2015) 'How far do cultural differences explain the differences between nations? Implications for HRM', *International Journal of Human Resource Management*, 26(2), 151164.

Walker, J.T., Brewster, C. and Wood, G. (2014) 'Diversity between and within varieties of capitalism: Transnational survey evidence', *Industrial and Corporate Change*, 23(2), 493–533.

Index

A10 countries 26, 46
accession countries 263, 265–6, 270, 274
acquisition of talent 332
active labour market policies 224–5
activity measurement 162
administrative support 307, 309, 310, 314–15
age and diversity issues 9–10, 143, 219–36, 421; flexible working 403–4, 405–6; managing an ageing workforce 226–30; Mediterranean countries 55–6; national reactions to demographic change and old age employment 221–5; public sector organizations 149–50
age inclusivity 226
agile organizations 124
Ainsbury, R. 213
Alsthom 273
ambassadors for C2C 210
Amnesty International 160, 161
appraisals 88–9, 226
Asian financial crisis 182
attitudes: employees' 338–9; to work 404, 405–6
austerity programmes 42, 119
Australia 242

BAE Systems 227–8
Bakker, P. 191
banker bonus cap 355
Barber case 32–3
Barr, M. 177
basic pay 91
Belarus 263–4, 273–4
Berlin Wall, fall of 73
'best places to work' organizations 124–5
best practices-based hybrid model 182–3
Bethke-Langenegger, P. 345–6
bilateral social dialogue 36
Bjorkman, I. 338–9
Blasi, J.R. 383
BMW 229
board, HR on the 86, 104
Botero, J.C. 266
boundaryless careers 309, 343–5
Boussebaa, M. 340–1
Bowen, H. 191–2
Brewster, C. 262, 283
broad-based employee financial participation schemes 387–92
BRUM countries 263–4, 265–6, 266–7, 270, 271, 273–4, 274–5, 276
BSR/Globescan State of Sustainable Business Survey 196

budgets 158–9
Bulgaria 78
business case for CR 192–4
business systems perspective 363–4

capacity measurement 162
career anchors 301, 304
career planning 226
career progression 228, 302
caring responsibilities 227, 403
Carlzon, J. 109
Carroll, A.B. 193
Central and Eastern Europe (CEE) 6,
18–19, 73–99, 118, 272; context
for developments in HRM
76–82; FDI in 23–4, 81–2, 83;
Japanese MNCs' investment
in 177; organization-level
developments in HRM 82–91;
pay-for-performance 361–3; talent
management 342–3; unionization
91–2; see also Eastern Europe
CEOs 194, 195
Cerdin, J.-L. 245–6, 344–5
chance migrants 245–6, 250, 254
Chemnitz Union 275
Circular Economy 207, 208–12
client participation 151–2
co-determination 106–7, 268
coercive isomorphism 366–7, 368
collective agreement systems 66
collective bargaining 36–7; national-
level 269–71
collectivism–individualism
dimension 360–1, 362
Collings, D.G. 334
Columbus, C. 297
combination of financial
participation plans 382
commitment 421
commitment impact 380–1
Communist Party 74–5
company-level collective bargaining
269–70
competencies 203
competition 421; competitive
pressures 404, 405
competitive advantage 193
compulsory redundancy 61–2, 87

contracts: fixed-term 60, 406–7,
408; non-renewal of 61–2, 87
control and return rights 379
co-operatives 378, 379
coordinated market economies
(CMEs) 222–3, 364–5;
recruitment and selection
288–9, 291–2
corporate goals 345–6
corporate responsibility (CR) 9,
141–3, 190–218, 425; business
case for 192–4; creating a
sustainability culture 203; Desso
208–12; embedding strategic CR
198–203; European perspective
206–7; global corporate
volunteering 204–6; on the
agenda of global companies
194–5; research opportunities
212–13; role of the HR function
195–7
corporate social responsibility (CSR)
125, 191
corporate strategy 86, 345–6
corporate sustainability (CS) 213
costs 146–7
country of origin effects 170, 368
co-workership 108–10, 110–11
Cradle to Cradle (C2C) 208–12
Cranet Surveys 82, 104–5, 387–91
crises: financial see financial crises;
HRM challenges 119–23;
HRM's role in dealing with
123–7; reactions and adjustment
to in Western Europe 6–7,
19–20, 115–34; three-fold
framework 125–6
culture 424; cultural context and
talent management 340–3;
cultural differences 77, 300;
culture change at Desso 210–12;
and pay-for-performance 360–3;
of sustainability 203, 208–12
customer services 229
Cyprus 51, 53–4, 55, 69–70
Czech Republic 75, 78

default retirement age (DRA) 223–4
Denmark 101–2, 103, 107, 111, 276

desperate migrants 245–6, 250–1, 254
Desso 208–12
differentiated talent management
architecture 334
DiMaggio, P.J. 366
Directives: on age and diversity 223;
employment relations 28–32,
271–2; EWC 30, 37–8, 272
diversity: age and diversity issues
see age and diversity issues;
management in US MNCs
operating in Europe 173–4
dominance effect 170, 183, 386
Draft Vedeling Directive 37
dream migrants 245–6, 250, 254
Dries, N. 343–4

early retirement 61–2, 87, 221–3,
224, 225
Eastern Europe 26–7; employment
relations 263, 265–6, 270, 274;
see also Central and Eastern
Europe (CEE)
ECONYL yarn 208
emerging market economies (EMEs)
288–9, 291
employability 344
employee-driven flexibility 402,
403–4, 411–15, 416–17
employee financial participation 12,
58–9, 261, 375–400, 427; CEE
countries 91; consequences for
HRM 394–5; country profiles
392–4; critics 382–3; employee
share ownership 58–9, 378,
381, 387–9; in an international
context 384–5; incidence
387–94; Mediterranean countries
58–9; MNCs and 385–7; nature
of 377–9; outcomes 381–2;
profit sharing 58–9, 359, 377–8,
379, 380–1, 389, 390, 393; stock
options plans 58–9, 379,
381–2, 389–91, 393; theoretical
approaches 379–83
employee protection index 266
employee share ownership
58–9, 378, 381; incidence
387–9

employees: attitudes 338–9;
communication with 174;
resilience 100–1; response in
crises 121; volunteering 204–6;
well-being 124
employeeship 108–10, 110–11
employer-driven flexibility 402–3,
406–11, 416–17
employers' associations 268–9;
European social dialogue 34–8
employment policy 38–41
employment relations 11, 259–60,
262–81, 427, 428; Directives
relating to 28–32, 271–2; EU
legal influences on 28–34,
271–2; EU market influences
21–2, 23–8, 44; European
employment relations in 1995
264–6; European level 271–4;
influence of European integration
5, 17–18, 21–48; Mediterranean
HRM 63–7; national laws and
institutions 266–9; national-level
collective bargaining and social
pacts 269–71; Nordic countries
105–10; workplace level 274–5
employment relations system 23–5
engrenage 39
environment: changes driving
flexible working 404–6; working
environement 124–5
environmental risks 149–50
environmental sustainability 208–10
Equal Employment Opportunity
(EEO) Act 172
Erasmus Programme 299
espoused practices 183–4
Estonia 78
ethnic innovators 247
ETUC 34
Eurodemocratization thesis 273
Europe 2020 41
European Court of Justice (ECJ)
32–4
European employment strategy
(EES) 39
European model of HRM 336–7,
420
European non-CEE countries 84–91

European perspective 1–4
European Semester 40–1
European social dialogue 34–8, 271–4
European Union (EU) 263; accession countries 263, 265–6, 270, 274; context of talent management 335–8; directives on age and diversity 223; eastern enlargement 23–5, 77; employment policy 38–41; employment relations 264–5; higher integration and international mobility 299–300; impact of European integration on employment relations 5, 17–18, 21–48; institutional influences 21–2, 28–34, 44; legislation affecting pay 366–7; legislation on employment relations 28–32, 271–2; macroeconomic influences 21–2, 34–44; market influences 21–2, 23–8, 44; migration policies 249–50; 'More and Better Jobs' programme 411; promotion of CR 207
European Working Conditions Survey (EWCS) 391–2
European Works Council Directive 30, 37–8, 272
European Works Councils (EWCs) 37–8, 272–3
Europeanization 77
Eurozone crisis 116
exclusive approaches to talent management 331–2, 339
exit management 320, 322–3
expatriates 240, 250, 298; see also global careers
explicit CR 207
external recruitment 286
extrinsic motivation effect 380–1
ex-Yugoslav tradition 77–80

F-style organizations 175, 176
family 50; care responsibilities 227, 403; and global careers 301–2, 311, 315, 319, 321
family friendly working policies 412–13

felicitous migrants 245–6, 254
femininity–masculinity dimension 360–1, 362
Fenton-O'Creevy, M. 386
Fernandez, J.P. 177
Fernández-Macías, E. 391–2
Festing, M. 91, 341–2, 365, 368
financial crises: Asian 182; global see global financial crisis
financial incentives 153–4, 303
financial participation see employee financial participation
Finland 102, 103, 111; employee financial participation 389, 394
Finnish Workability Index 229
fixed-term contracts 60, 406–7, 408
flat organization 109
flexible working 12–13, 261, 401–19, 428; ageing workforce 226, 227–8; defining flexibility 402–4; environmental changes driving 404–6; employee-driven flexibility 402, 403–4, 411–15, 416–17; employer-driven flexibility 402–3, 406–11, 416–17
flexisecurity 107, 291–2, 409–11
Foley, F. 246–7
force field framework 421–2
foreign direct investment 169; in CEE countries 23–4, 81–2, 83; Japanese MNCs' investment in Europe 177–8
foreign MNCs operating in Europe 8, 139–41, 169–89, 426; Japanese MNCs 8, 169, 177–81, 185; Korean MNCs 8, 140–1, 182–4, 185; managing human resources in MNCs 169–71; US MNCs 8, 140, 169, 172–5, 185
formal rules and norms 289–90
formalization 172
four freedoms 33–4
framework Directives 29–32
France 118, 253; employee financial participation 389, 393; talent management 340–1, 344–5
free rider problem 383
Freeman, R.B. 383
functional flexibility 402, 403, 409

gain-sharing arrangements 377
Garavan, T.N. 85–6
GDP: CEE countries 77, 78–9;
    impact of global financial crisis
    101–3, 116–17
gender diversity 219
Geneva Group nations 157–8
Germany 117–18; age and diversity
    issues 143, 222, 224–5, 229–30;
    employee financial participation
    394; employment relations
    23–5, 268, 270, 276; talent
    management 341–2, 344–5
glass ceiling 175
global career management 303;
    during an assignment 309–14;
    practice 318, 321; pre-assignment
    303–4, 305; transition phase 317,
    318
global careers 11–12, 260, 297–328,
    427, 428; during an assignment
    309–17; EU higher integration
    and international mobility
    299–300; motivations 301–3;
    organizational perspective 300–1;
    pre-assignment considerations
    303–9; transition phase to next
    position 317–23
global corporate volunteering
    204–6
global equity plans 394–5
global financial crisis 17, 149, 411;
    EU influence on employment
    relations 42–4; Mediterranean
    countries 51–2, 55; Nordic
    countries 101–4; reactions and
    adjustment in Western Europe
    6–7, 19–20, 115–34
global HRM best practices 182–3
Global Leadership and
    Organizational Effectiveness
    (GLOBE) project 363
global standardization 173–4, 182–3,
    303–4, 367–8
global talent management 180–1
globalization 178–9, 404, 405
grandes écoles system 341
Grayson, D. 198, 213
'Great Place to Work' 105

Greece 50–1, 52–3, 54, 60, 66, 68–
Gustavsen, B. 107

Hall, P.A. 364–5
Handelsbanken 109–10
health 226, 228–9
high churn recruitment model 290–
high-context culture 175
high potentials 332; careers of 343–
high-skilled migrants 244–6, 251–2,
    253, 254
Hiltrop, J. 421–2
Hodges, A. 198
Hofstede, G. 360–1, 363
Hoglund, M. 339–40
home country influences 170
host country influences 170
host country nationals (HCNs) 170,
    171, 174
HR function: embedding strategic
    CR 198–203; importance in
    CEE countries 85–6; role in
    supporting CR 195–7
HR strategy 86, 104
HRM policies for migrants 250–3,
    254
Hungary 75, 76, 78, 82, 83
hybridization 182–3

Iceland 102, 103–4, 111
idea tree 209
illegal immigration 242, 244
illusory corporatism 265
impact measurement 162
implicit CR 207
incentive model 380–1
inclusive approaches to talent
    management 331, 339
individualism–collectivism
    dimension 360–1, 362
individuals: individual level of
    migration 243–4, 244–6;
    outcomes of talent management
    345–6; pay-for-performance
    schemes 358; reasons for global
    careers 301–2
industrial-level collective bargaining
    269–70
inflation 78–9

informal practices 183–4
informal rules and norms 290
information and communication
   technologies (ICT) 404, 405
innateness of talent 332
innovators 246–7
inpatriation 298
institutional complementarities 364
institutional distance 368
institutional duality 386
institutional isomorphism 366–8,
   384–5
institutions 425; context for talent
   management 340–3; contexts of
   rewards 363–5; EU institutional
   influences on employment
   relations 21–2, 28–34, 44; HR
   institutions in Nordic countries
   104–5; Mediterranean HRM
   institutional challenges 49–56,
   67–70; national institutional
   frameworks and CR 206–7;
   national institutions and
   employment relations 266–9
instrumental involvement model
   380–1
integration: higher in the EU
   299–300; within HRM 422
intelligent careers (IC) framework
   310–13, 314
intergovernmental organizations
   (IGOs) 138, 147, 148, 154–9
internal internationalization 176, 179
internal market system 23–5
internal promotion/recruitment 286
internal transfer 61–2, 87
international non-governmental
   organizations (INGOs) 139,
   147–8, 159–63
international working *see* global careers
internationalization 335–6
internationally educated nurses 248
interviews 287
intrinsic motivation effect 380–1
Ireland 270
Italy 66

J-style organizations 175, 176
Japan 242, 387–9

Japanese MNCs 175–81; operating
   in Europe 8, 169, 177–81, 185
job analysis 284, 285
job description 284, 285
job factors, in global careers 304–8,
   319, 321–2
job quality 411–12
job rotation 226
jobs–skills matching 55
judicial activism 32–4

Kerr, W.R. 246–7
Klein, K.J. 380
Korean MNCs 181–4; operating in
   Europe 8, 140–1, 182–4, 185
Kurucz, E. 193

labour markets: CEE countries
   77–80; changes and the need
   for flexibility 406; impact of the
   global financial crisis 117–19;
   national 25–8
labour mobility 25–8
Laval case 43–4
leadership 86, 127
league tables 152–3
legislation and law: affecting pay
   366–7, 368; EU Directives
   relating to age and diversity
   223; EU legal influences on
   employment relations 28–34,
   271–2; national 266–9, 367,
   368; USA compared with
   Europe 337
legitimation, crisis of 125–6
Leonardo Programme 299
Levinson, C. 36–7
liberal market economies (LMEs)
   171, 222, 364–5, 384–5;
   recruitment and selection 288–9,
   290–1, 292
life expectancy 220
lifelong learning 226, 228
Lifelong Learning Programme (LLP)
   299
Lisbon strategy 39–40
Lithuania 78–9
local effect 170
local responsiveness 304

localization 174–5, 178–81, 182–3,
367–8
location factors 302
logistical support 307, 309, 310, 314–15
long-term health conditions (LHCs)
228
long-term migrants 239
low-skilled migrants 244, 246,
252–3, 254
low-wage labour markets 27–8

Maastricht criteria 149
Maastricht Treaty 35
macro-economic influences 21–2,
34–44
macro-level issues/trends 5–7,
17–20, 422–5, 429–30
macro-social level of migration
243–4, 248–50
management, crisis of 125, 126
management training 252
managers: attitudes towards
employee financial participation
383; HR managers' role in crises
126–7; reactions in crises 121–2
market influences 21–2, 23–8, 44
masculinity/femininity dimension
360–1, 362
Matten, D. 207
Mayrhofer, W. 366
McDonnell, A. 342–3
Mearns, L. 247
medarbetaskap (co-workership)
108–10, 110–11
Mediterranean countries 4, 5–6,
18, 49–72, 118; institutional
challenges 49–56; integration of
institutional and organizational
challenges 67–70; organizational
challenges 56–67
Mellahi, K. 334
mezzo-level issues/trends 7–10,
137–44, 425–6, 430
micro-level issues/trends 11–13,
259–61, 427–8, 430
migration 10, 143–4, 237–56, 425;
defining a migrant 239–40; facts
and figures 241–2; importance
237–9; labour mobility and

employment relations 25–8;
macro-social level 243–4,
248–50; Mediterranean countries
54; meso-organizational level
243–4, 246–8; micro-individual
level 243–4, 244–6; relevance
of the typology 250–1; specific
HRM practices for migrants
251–3; typology of 242–50
migration policies 248–50
Milkovich, G.T. 354
mimetic isomorphism 367–8
mission creep 158
mixed market economies (MMEs)
288–9, 291
mobility 299–300; of labour 25–8
moderate interventionist model 80
modified male breadwinner model
415
Moldova 263–4
Møller, C. 108–9
Moon, J. 207
morale 121
Morgan, G. 340–1
motivation 121; employee financial
participation 380–1; global
careers 301–3; to migrate 251
multinational companies (MNCs):
and employee financial
participation 385–7; foreign
MNCs operating in Europe
see foreign MNCs operating
in Europe; global careers see
global careers; influence in CEE
countries 81–2; Japanese MNCs
8, 169, 175–81, 185; Korean
MNCs 8, 140–1, 181–4, 185;
managing human resources in
169–71; pay-for-performance
368–9; talent management
see talent management;
transnationality 300; US MNCs 8,
140, 169, 171–5, 182, 185, 385–6
multiple stakeholders 146, 151–2,
156–7, 160

narrow-based employee financial
participation schemes 387–92
national action plans (NAPs) 39

national culture 360–3
national institutions 266–9
national labour markets 25–8
national legislation 266–9, 367, 368
national-level collective bargaining
    269–71
national pay distinctiveness 355–65
national reform programmes 40–1
naturalization 241, 249
negotiation 306, 308
neo-institutional approach 366–8,
    384
Netherlands, the 122
Newton, S. 247–8
non-European Anglo-Saxon
    countries 84–91
non-renewal of contracts 61–2, 87
Nordic countries 4, 6, 19, 100–14;
    economic development and crisis
    101–4; HR institutions 104–5;
    work relations 105–10
normative isomorphism 367–8
Norway 102, 103, 111–12, 118
not for profit (NfP) sector 7–8, 138–9,
    145–68, 425–6; importance 145–8;
    intergovernmental organizations
    138, 147, 148, 154–9; international
    NGOs 139, 147–8, 159–63; public
    sector organizations 138, 146, 147,
    148, 149–54, 155, 163
numerical flexibility 402
nurses 248

Ockers, C. 208–9
older workers see age and diversity
    issues
open method of coordination
    (OMC) 39, 40
operational crisis 125, 126
organizations: factors in global
    careers 302; organizational
    challenges for Mediterranean
    HRM 56–70; organization-level
    developments in CEE HRM
    82–91; organizational level
    of migration 243–4, 246–8;
    outcomes of talent management
    345–6; resilience 123–4; role of
    HRM in crises 123–4

organized decentralization 275–6
orthodox Soviet system 80
outcomes: employee financial
    participation 381–2; talent
    management 333, 345–6
outsourcing 61–2, 87
ownership impact model 380–1
ownership patterns 337

Panasonic 179–81
parent country nationals (PCNs)
    170, 171, 174
part-time working 31, 60, 407–9,
    410, 415
partner/family considerations 301–2
paternalism 181, 291
path dependence 365
pay: CEE countries 90–1;
    cuts in crises 118, 119–20;
    Mediterranean countries 56–7,
    58–9; reward management in
    global careers 306, 308, 313,
    316–17, 320, 322
pay-for-performance 12, 260–1,
    354–74; cultural perspective
    360–3; diffusion in Europe
    366–8; institutional contexts of
    rewards 363–5; Mediterranean
    countries 57, 58–9; MNCs
    368–9; national pay
    distinctiveness 355–65; path
    dependence 365; public sector
    organizations 153–4
pension reform 225
Pepermans, R. 343–4
PEPPER reports 377
performance: NfP sector 146,
    152–4, 158–9, 162–3; talent
    management 332
performance appraisals 88–9, 226
performance gap 194, 195
performance management: CEE
    countries 88–9; global careers
    312, 316; NfP sector 146, 152–4,
    158–9, 162–3
performance-related pay see
    pay-for-performance
permanent representatives 157
person–job fit 284, 287

person–organization fit 284, 287
personnel funds (PFs) 394
Pocztowski, A. 74, 93
Poland 75–6, 82, 83, 88
politics and political dimension 146,
    152, 157–8, 161–2
population ageing *see* age and
    diversity issues
Portugal 51, 66
Poutsma, E. 386–7
Powell, W.W. 366
power distance 360–1, 362
pre-retirement planning 226
principal–agent theory 379
process perspective on talent
    management 333–5, 340–3
productivity 421
professional development 302; *see
    also* training and development
professionalization 367
profit sharing 58–9, 359, 377–8, 379,
    380–1, 393; incidence 389, 390
protean careers 309
psychological contract perspective
    338–40
psychometric testing 287–8
public sector organizations 138, 146,
    147, 148, 149–54, 155, 163
public service motivation (PSM) 154
PwC 205

qualification mismatch 55
qualified immigrants (QIs) 244–6,
    251–2, 253, 254

Rainey, H.G. 150
recruitment freeze 61–2, 87
recruitment and selection (R&S) 11,
    260, 282–96, 427, 428; European
    context 288–92; foundations
    of 282–5; recruitment 285–6;
    selection 87, 286–8; stages of the
    process 284
redundancy: compulsory 61–2, 87;
    voluntary 61–2, 87
regulation of recruitment 289–90
remote working 415
resilience 100–1, 110–11;
    organizational 123–4
responsible business practices 197

retirement: delayed in
    Mediterranean countries 55–6;
    early 61–2, 87, 221–3, 224, 225
reward management 306, 308, 313,
    316–17, 320, 322; *see also* pay,
    pay-for-performance
right to strike 33–4
risks: employee financial participation
    383; environmental 149–50
rites of passage 340
Rodriguez, J.K. 247
Rogovsky, N. 360
role-specific KPIs 210
Russia 76, 79, 263–4, 270–1, 274

Sahakiants, I. 91, 365, 368
Save As You Earn (SAYE) share
    options savings plan 393
savings plans 378, 379
Sawhil, J.C. 162
schedule flexibility 413, 414
science and engineering innovators
    246–7
scientific approaches to selection
    287–8
Scott, W.R. 363
Scullion, H. 342–3
sectoral social dialogue 36, 273
security of tenure 290–2
selection 87, 286–8; global careers
    306, 308; *see also* recruitment and
    selection (R&S)
Serbia 79
Shabana, K.M. 193
Share Incentive Plan (SIP) 393
share ownership plans 58–9, 378,
    381, 387–9
shared value of CR 213
Sheehan, M. 345
short-term migrants 240
short-time working 117–18, 409,
    411
skill-based volunteering 204–6
skills-based fragmentation 423
skills–jobs matching 55
Skuza, A. 342–3
Slovakia 79, 81, 82, 83
Slovenia 76, 79
small and medium-size enterprises
    (SMEs) 341–2

Social Action Programme (1974)
28–9
social context 311, 315, 319, 321
social dialogue 34–8, 271–4
social dumping 33–4
social pacts 42, 269–71
social partnership 270–1
social protection and welfare 421
social structure 176–7
socialist regimes 74–5, 76, 265, 365
socially embedding flexibilization
strategies 25
socio-economic trends: CEE 76–7,
78–9; Nordic countries 101–4
Sonnenberg, M. 339
Soskice, D. 364–5
South-east Asian countries 84–91
South Korean MNCs *see* Korean
MNCs
Southern Europe 270; *see also*
Mediterranean countries
sovereign debt crises 43
Spain 51, 53, 66, 342
Sparrow, P.R. 421–2
spatial flexibility 403
stability programmes 40–1
staffing: CEE countries 87; foreign
subsidiaries 171, 174–5, 178–81;
Mediterranean countries 57–60,
61–2
Stahl, G.K. 344–5
stakeholders, multiple 146, 151–2,
156–7, 160
standardization 172; global 173–4,
182–3, 303–4, 367–8; pay
practices 367–8
state pension age 223, 224
state-socialist regimes 74–5, 76, 265,
365
stock options plans 58–9, 379,
381–2, 393; incidence 389–91
strategic CR 192–5; achieving
HR outcomes through 203;
embedding 198–203
strategic global career management
303–4, 305, 309–14, 317, 318
strategy: corporate 86, 345–6; HR
86, 104
strikes 66; right to strike 33–4
succession planning 345–6

sustainability 121; BSR/Globescan
State of Sustainable Business
Survey 196; corporate 213;
environmental 208–10; UNGC/
Accenture CEOs' sustainability
survey 195
sustainability culture 203, 208–12
Sweden 102, 103, 107, 108, 111
Switzerland 367

Taiwan 387–8
*Taking Forward the Findings of the UK
Multilateral Aid Review* 158
talent 331–2
talent attraction and retention 345–6
talent development 345–6
talent management 12, 260, 329–53,
427, 428; careers of high
potentials and boundaryless
careers 343–5; conceptualization
331–2; European context 335–8;
institutional and cultural contexts
340–3; intended outcomes
and effects 333; organizational
and individual-level outcomes
345–6; Panasonic 180–1;
process perspective 333–5,
340–3; psychological contract
perspective 338–40
Tansley, C. 340
taxation 379
team-based variable pay 357–8
technical skills 252
teleworkers 415
temporal flexibility 402, 409
temporary agency workers 31, 407
temporary employment contracts 60,
406–7, 408
Thelen, K. 25
Tietze, S. 340
trade unions 42, 43, 264–6, 377;
CEE countries 80, 91–2;
European social dialogue 34–8,
273; levels of membership 91–2,
267–8; Mediterranean countries
66–7; NfP sector 151; Nordic
countries 106
training and development: CEE
countries 89–90; global careers
307, 308, 311, 315–16, 319, 322;

managing the ageing workforce
226, 228; Mediterranean
countries 60–3, 64–5; migrants
252; at Panasonic 180
transition states *see* Central and Eastern
Europe (CEE), Eastern Europe
transnational influences 170
transnationality index 300
Troika, the 43, 51–2

Ukraine 263–4, 275
Ulrich role model 105
uncertainty avoidance 360–1, 362
unemployment 117; CEE countries
77, 78–9; Mediterranean countries
52–3; rise in Nordic countries
101–2, 103–4; youth 221, 423
UNESCO 157
unfair treatment 289–90
UNGC/Accenture CEOs'
Sustainability Survey 195
Union of Industrial and Employers'
Confederations of Europe
(UNICE) 34
unionization, levels of 91–2, 267–8
United Arab Emirates 242
United Kingdom (UK) 122; age
and diversity issues 143, 220,
222, 223–4, 227, 229–30;
employee financial participation
384, 393; Japanese MNCs in
177, 178; migration 219; talent
management 340–1
United Nations (UN) 157–8, 241
United States of America (USA)
262, 337–8; employment
relations compared with Western
Continental Europe 274, 281
United States MNCs 171–5, 182,
385 6; operating in Europe 8,
140, 169, 172–5, 185

Val Duchesse talks 35
Valverde, M. 342
Vandenabeele, W. 148, 163
variable pay 91, 354; *see also*
pay-for-performance

varieties of capitalism (VoC)
perspective 222, 289, 363–5
Viking case 33–4
voluntary redundancy 61–2, 87
volunteering 159–60; global
corporate volunteering 204–6;
performance management 162–3
Volvo cars 107–8, 109

Wallander, J. 109
'war for talent' 330
Welz, C. 391–2
Western Europe: employment
relations 263, 274, 281; reactions
and adjustment to crises 6–7,
19–20, 115–34; *see also under
individual countries*
whipsawing 24
Whitley, R. 363
Williamson, D. 162
work–life balance 53–4, 413
work relations *see* employment
relations
worker-managed firms 378, 379
workforce ageing *see* age and
diversity issues
workforce reduction 61–2, 87, 122
working conditions 120–1
working environment 124–5
working hours: flexible 226, 227–8,
413, 414; reductions 117–18,
409, 411
working time accounts 413, 416
workplace design 228–9
workplace-level employment
relations 274–5
works councils 264, 265, 268;
European 37–8, 272–3
World Business Council for
Sustainable Development
(WBCSD) 191

Yoshihara, H. 176
Yoshino, M.Y. 176
youth unemployment 221, 423

Zadek, S. 193